The Western Dream of Civilization:
The Modern World
Volume II

The Western Dream of Civilization:
The Modern World
Volume II

Doug Cantrell
David Bowden
Gary Stearns
Elizabethtown Community College
Elizabethtown, Kentucky

Barbara D. Ripel
Suffolk County Community College
Riverhead, New York

Timothy D. Holder
Morehead State University
Morehead, Kentucky

John Moretta
Houston Community College System
Houston, Texas

Louise A. Mayo
County College of Morris
Randolph, New Jersey

Carl Luna
San Diego Mesa College
San Diego, California

Amerjit K. Johl
Merced College
Merced, California

Abigail Press   **Wheaton, IL 60187**

Design and Production: Abigail Press
Typesetting: Abigail Press
Typeface: AGaramond
Cover Art and Maps: Sam Tolia

The Western Dream of Civilization: The Modern World
Volume II

First Edition, 2002
Printed in the United States of America
Translation rights reserved by the publisher
ISBN 1-890919-22-5

ABOUT THE AUTHORS

Doug Cantrell is an Associate Professor of History and head of the history program at Elizabethtown Community College in Elizabethtown, Kentucky where he has taught for 15 years. He holds a B.A. from Berea College, an M.A. from the University of Kentucky, and has completed 30 hours toward the Ph.D. He is co-author of *American Dreams & Reality: A Retelling of the American Story* and *Historical Perspectives: A Reader and Study Guide* published by Abigail Press. He also has written numerous journal and encyclopedia articles and contributed book reviews to academic journals. Professor Cantrell also teaches various history courses on the web, and serves as the social science discipline leader for the Kentucky Virtual University, He is listed in *Who's Who in America, Who's Who in the World,* and *Who's Who in the South and Southwest.* In addition, he is former editor of the Kentucky History Journal and past president of the Kentucky Association of Teachers of History.

David Bowden is an Associate Professor of History at Elizabethtown Community College in Kentucky, where he teaches European, United States, and World War II history. He earned a B.B.A. degree in Marketing and an M.A. degree in History from the University of Kentucky. He has taught full-time for Elizabethtown Community College for seven years and previously served as an adjunct faculty member for the University of Louisville and Elizabethtown Community College. David Bowden has published an article on Native American history in the *Chronicles of Oklahoma* and has presented a research paper at the Indiana State University's Conference on Baseball in Literature and Culture. He served as Secretary and then as Community College Representative for the Executive Committee of the Kentucky Association of Teachers of History for six years.

Gary Stearns received his B.A., M.A., and Ph. D. from the University of Kentucky, where he majored in Modern British and Modern European History. He has taught as a visiting Assistant Professor at the University of Cincinnati and at Casper College, Wyoming. He is presently an Associate Professor at Elizabethtown Community College, where he teaches European and British History and was for two years the Co-Director and Co-Instructor of ECC's Honors Program. A member of the North American Conference of British History, he has presented papers and published articles and numerous book reviews on topics in British and Commonwealth history. He has received two grants to do research in Britain, the latest being a grant to do post-doctoral research at Regents College, Oxford University.

Barbara D. Ripel is Professor of History at Suffolk County Community College, Riverhead, New York. Her B.A. and Ph.D are from SUNY Stony Brook, and her M.A. is from Rutgers University in New Jersey. The *West Georgia Quarterly* published her article on Harbottle Dorr, and *The William and Mary Quarterly* published her research on Early ProSlavery Petitions from the 1780s. Besides her background in American History, Professor Ripel has taught Western Civilization survey courses, Political Science, Anthropology, and Sociology. She recently directed the Honors Program on the Suffolk Campus. In 1998, she received the New York State Chancellor's Award for Excellence in Teaching. In 2002 she received a NEH (National Endowment for the Humanities) Summer Fellowship at Harvard University for an Integrated Study of Eurasia. Dr. Ripel serves as the campus advisor to Phi Theta Kappa, the International Honor Society for Two Year Colleges.

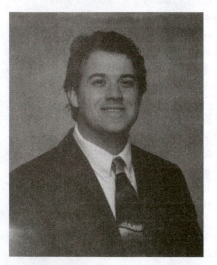

Tim Holder is a Visiting Assistant Professor at Morehead State University in Morehead, KY and an Adjunct Professor at Indiana University Southeast in New Albany, Indiana. He has been teaching for three years at the college level and for ten years overall. He has an M.A. and a Ph. D.from the University of Kentucky. He wrote his dissertation on kingship in medieval England. He has taught survey courses on American History, European History, Global Studies, and the World in the Twentieth Century. He has had numerous reviews published of books in the following genres: history, historical fiction, and culture.

John A. Moretta earned a B.A. in History and Spanish Foreign Language and Literature from Santa Clara University in CA, an M.A. in History from Portland State University in Oregon, and a Ph.D. in History from Rice University in Houston, TX. He is currently Professor of History and Chair of the History, Philosophy, and Geography Dept. of Central College, Houston Community College System in Houston, Texas. In his twenty years with Central College, Dr. Moretta has won several outstanding college teaching awards and has been nominated fifteen times for Who's Who Among American teachers. Dr. Moretta has also published a book on Texas history, *William Pitt Ballinger, Texas Lawyer Southern Statesman, 1825-1888*, which was runner-up for the best book in Texas history awarded by the Texas State Historical Association. Dr. Moretta's book did win the best research award given by that same organization for 2001.

Louise Mayo is the Chairperson of the Department of History/ Political Science at County College of Morris, Randolph, NJ, where she has been a professor for the past twenty-six years. She is the author of *The Ambivalent Image* (1988), *A House Divided: America in the Era of Civil War and Reconstruction*, and numerous articles and papers in the fields of Jewish and minority history. She has an M.A. from Cornell University in Modern European and Russian History and a Ph.D. from City University of New York in American History, specializing in immigration and minority history. She has taught courses in American History, including Twentieth Century America, and World History, including the Modern Middle East and History of Russia.

Dr. Luna is a professor of Political Science and chair of the Accelerated College Program at San Diego Mesa College and a lecturer on politics and international political economy at the University of San Diego. He received his Ph.D. from the American University, Washington D.C. and his B.A. in political science, history and philosophy from the University of San Diego. He is a reviewer for the library journal CHOICE and a revision author for the American government text *People and Politics*. Dr. Luna has been a recurrent guest on San Diego KPBS public radio and television's *"These Days"* since 1995. Dr. Luna received a 10-month Fulbright Scholars award to lecture on American politics and political economy at Nizhniy Novgorod State University, Russian Federation during the 1999/ 2000 academic year.

Amerjit Kaur Johl is Professor of History at Merced College in Merced, California, where she teaches courses in Modern European and United States History. She previously taught for five years as a lecturer in the Humanities for the School of Humanities and Fine Arts at California State University, Chico. She holds an M.A. degree in the field of Modern European History from the University of California, Los Angeles and has completed graduate studies towards the Ph.D. in the fields of Modern European History and Comparative Labor History at UCLA. Professor Johl is a nationally distinguished Andrew W. Mellon/Woodrow Wilson Foundation Fellow in Humanistic Studies.

Contents in Brief

Contents

CHAPTER FOURTEEN
A NEW KIND OF WORLD

CHAPTER FIFTEEN
THE FRENCH REVOLUTION AND NAPOLEON BONAPARTE, 1789-1815

CHAPTER SIXTEEN
THE INDUSTRIAL REVOLUTION 1760-1850

CHAPTER SEVENTEEN
REACTION, REFORM & REVOLUTION, 1815-1848

CHAPTER EIGHTEEN
NATIONALISM & REALPOLITIK 1848-1871

CHAPTER NINETEEN
LA BELLE EPOCH: EUROPE'S GOLDEN AGE 1871-1914

CHAPTER TWENTY-ONE
THE INTERWAR ERA 1920-1939

CHAPTER TWENTY-TWO
WORLD WAR II 1939-1945

CHAPTER TWENTY-THREE
THE POSTWAR ERA 1945-1968

CHAPTER TWENTY-FOUR
A NEW EUROPE & THE TWENTY-FIRST CENTURY

Chapter 12

THE REFORMATION

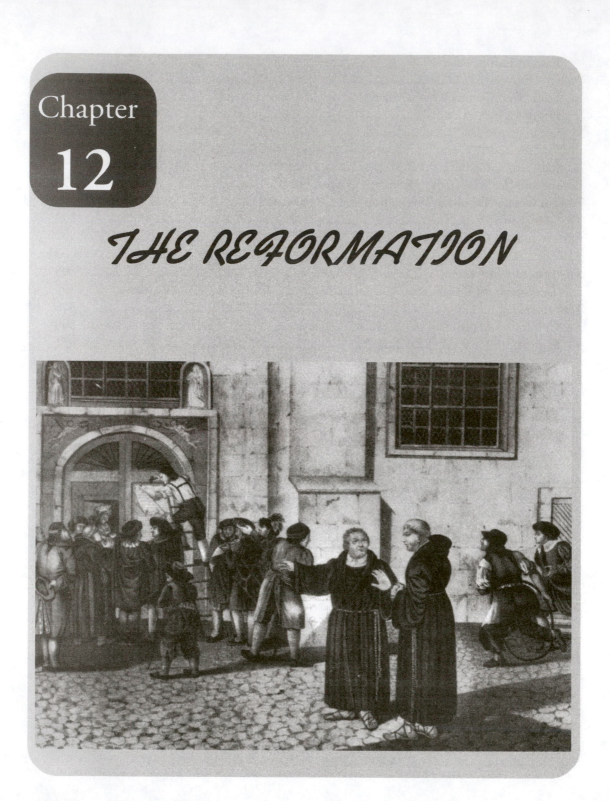

Martin Luther, the second son of a German copper miner who had become a mine owner, was alone and frightened while crossing a field during a severe thunderstorm. Without warning, a loud clap of thunder and a bolt of lightening knocked Luther, a man in his early twenties, to the ground. The experience terrified him. He began to see his short life passing in front of his eyes. Thinking that he was dying, Luther cried out to St. Anne, the mother of the Virgin Mary and the patron of travelers in distress, that he would enter a monastery if God allowed him to live. Miraculously, or so he thought, the storm abated. Luther arose, thanked God and St. Anne, and continued on his way. The thunderstorm experience changed Luther's life and the history of Western Christianity. Because Luther had promised St. Anne that he would enter a monastery and devote his life to God if he were spared, the young German faced a dilemma. His father, Hans, an omnipotent figure who dominated the Luther household, was determined that his second son would become a lawyer, a profession that would enable Luther to earn a handsome living and offer many opportunities for the family's upward social mobility. Hans had spent considerable money and endured personal deprivation to see that his son received a good education. Eventually, Luther earned a Masters' degree with distinction in 1505. At his parents' behest, Luther enrolled in law school but never studied law. Without consulting Hans, Luther entered the Order of the Hermits of St. Augustine on July 17, 1505, keeping his vow to St. Anne. Hans was furious. He ranted and raged, thinking that the money and personal sacrifice he had expended to make his son a lawyer had been wasted. Little did he know that Luther would begin a revolution twelve years later that would completely change western civilization.

Luther's decision to enter a monastery was actually an attempt to resolve a long-standing spiritual conflict within his mind. The young German was obsessed with his own sinfulness and tormented by guilt. He joined a monastery hoping that life as a hermit would enable him to be forgiven of his earthly sins and absolve him of guilt. Luther was a conscientious friar, pursuing every possible way of penitence, including lengthy fasts, prayers, self-denial, frequent confessions, and self-flagellation. None of these acts relieved the sense of guilt he felt at being a sinner until another extraordinary experience in a castle tower (restrooms were located in castle towers) at Wittenberg, where he served as a university lecturer on theology, alleviated his guilt. While in the tower, Luther received what he believed to be a visionary insight from God that brought peace to his troubled mind. Prior to the tower experience, he could not understand how a sinner could receive anything from God other than being cast in hell's fiery pits. In the tower vision, however, Luther understood that God was merciful and just. This insight enabled him to develop the principle of "justification by faith" upon which the Protestant Reformation was based. Luther now understood that God forgave sinners and made them righteous through the gift of grace, which was achieved by faith. Luther then began to question activities within the Catholic Church, such as the sale of indulgences, that violated this "truth" God had revealed in the Wittenberg castle tower. In 1517 Luther nailed his Ninety-five Theses to the church door in Wittenberg, beginning the Protestant Reformation that shattered the unity of Western Christendom. Had the young German become a lawyer, as his father wanted, the Protestant Reformation might not have occurred, and Luther most likely would not have had an influence upon the world a half millennium after his life ended.

Chronology

1483	Martin Luther born.
1484	Ulrich Zwingli born.
1509	John Calvin born.
1517	Ninety-Five Theses composed.
1519	Leipzig Debate with John Eck.
1520	Luther branded as a heretic by a Papal Bull.
1521	Luther's ideas published in three pamphlets.
1521	Diet of Worms.
1521-1555	Habsburg-Valois Wars
1524-25	The Peasant's War
1525	Luther marries a former nun.
1527	Henry VIII requests an annulment of his marriage to Catherine of Argon.
1529	Term Protestant first used after Diet of Speyer.
1529	Zwingli meets with Luther at Marburg
1533	Calvin converts to Protestantism.
1534	Calvin flees from France and goes to Geneva.
1534	Acts of Supremacy passed by English Parliament.
1535	Melchiorites gain control of Munster
1535	Order of Ursuline Nuns founded
1536	Calvin publishes *The Institutes of the Christian Religion*.
1541	Calvin establishes a theocracy in Geneva.
1545	Council of Trent convened.
1549	Book of Common Prayer Written.
1553-1558	Bloody Mary reigns in England.
1558	Elizabeth I becomes English Queen.
1560	John Knox creates Calvinist church in Scotland.
1563	Thirty-Nine Articles composed.
1564	Book of Common Order Published.
1572	St. Bartholomew's Day Massacre.
1585	War of the Three Henrys begins.
1588	Spanish Armada defeated.
1598	Edict of Nantes
1618	Thirty Years War begins.

BACKGROUND TO THE REFORMATION

For sixteenth-century Europeans, the most momentous event in their lives was not overseas exploration, nationalism, or the Renaissance but the Protestant Reformation, an event that shattered the unity of Western Europe under the Roman Catholic Church. Two sides within Christianity—the protestors, or Protestants, and Catholics—arose, and each believed that its views and doctrines were righteous while those of the other were heretical. This confrontation between Catholics and Protestants throughout Europe lasted for more than a century, produced countless wars, and killed thousands of people, leading one wit to comment, "more people have been killed in the name of God than for any other reason."

The Protestant Reformation occurred among such a wide complex of change that scholars often regard the sixteenth century as the transition from medieval Europe to the modern age. By 1500, the Renaissance, after a century and a half in Italy, blossomed on both sides of the Alps. In intellectual circles classical antiquity furnished the inspiration for arts and learning, and the courtier had replaced the monk as the "ideal" person. Commercial expansion and overseas exploration had broadened the horizons of Western Europe while secularism and humanism had created a strong interest in temporal things. The emphasis of the medieval manorial and guild economy on community welfare was being replaced by individualistic capitalism that emphasized profit making. Middle class people were challenging nobles and high-ranking church officials for power, privileges, and prestige. Peasants and artisans were becoming impatient with medieval obligations and restrictions. The increasing power of national monarchies, which upheld the principle of state sovereignty, reduced the power of the Catholic Church, its Pope, and the Holy Roman Empire, institutions that during the Middle Ages had largely controlled the Christian Commonwealth (*Corpus Christianum*). Amid all this change, the Protestant Reformation fragmented the ecclesiastical unity of Western Europe.

Despite the secular tendencies the Renaissance stimulated, the sixteenth century was still a religious age, and the Reformation was primarily a religious movement that involved most people in European societies. From one perspective, the Reformation was a religious revival whose main concern was salvation. Individuals took religion seriously, and it was a way of life. Sixteenth-century Europeans looked to both the church and state to foster religious life. Religious issues were closely tied to economic, political, and social issues. Demands for social justice usually were couched in religious language taken from the Bible. It is difficult to understand why people vexed by social, economic, and political changes they did not understand would also support religious reform.

The need for reform in the Church was a theme found within Christianity almost from the time of its inception. Early Christian monasticism, the Benedictine Rule, the Cluniac, Cistercian, and Franciscan movements were all motivated by a desire to bring Christian life into conformity with the highest Christian ideals. The medieval conflict between church and state began as an attempt to free the church from political control, which had subordinated Christian values to political expediency. Medieval reform, however, was not permanent. After a few years the Church, like the ancient Israelites, strayed from the "will of God" and needed to be taken back to its original commitment. In the century and a half before Luther began his reformation, most serious efforts within the Church had failed. The Englishman, John Wyclif, for example, had been declared a heretic. Jan Hus and Girolamo Savonarola had been burned at the stake. Desiderius Erasmus had been ordered to keep quite, and the Roman Church banned his books. Church councils, which had been called from time to time, accomplished little. Popes, bishops, abbots, and priests often behaved immorally. Monks were perceived as being fat and lazy. Not all Church officials fit these perceptions but enough did to give the Church a bad reputation. The behavior of Church officials, coupled with the corruption, was enough to undermine respect lay people had for the institution. When various individuals began criticizing the Catholic Church, common people, aware of problems within the Church, began to take allegations of the detractors seriously.

PROBLEMS IN THE CHURCH AND ORIGINS OF THE REFORMATION

Dissatisfaction within the Roman Catholic Church was apparent by the first decade of the sixteenth century. The authority of the Pope had been declining for over two centuries. Three events—conflict with German Emperor Frederick II in the thirteenth century, the Babylonian Captivity from 1309 to 1376 when Philip the Fair forced the Pope to live in Avignon, France so that he could control the Church, and the Great Schism from 1378 to 1418 when three individuals claimed to be the true Pope—weakened the Church. Even though the Council of Constance had ended the Great Schism by 1418, it encouraged the Concilian Movement, an attempt to give papal authority to Church councils and make the papacy a constitutional monarchy. The Concilian Movement failed largely because Wyclif and Hus convinced secular rulers to oppose it. Their action, which probably delayed the Reformation for a century, was an indication that Western Christendom faced serious trouble.

Further weakening the authority of the Church was secularization produced by the Renaissance. Popes, like many people in Europe, became increasingly concerned with worldly things. They behaved like kings, employing diplomacy and war to gain territory, surrounding themselves with an elaborate court, and patronizing artists and writers. From the perspective of many observers, the papal concern with temporal matters seemed more important than the Pope's religious duties. Various popes, including Alexander VI and Julius II, used their spiritual authority to raise money for non-religious activities, such as building palaces, funding private armies, etc. Although funds available to the Church increased as a result of these prac-

tices, corruption within the Church became widespread. Wealthy individuals and families could purchase high ecclesiastical offices. Usually nobles who bought Church offices did so not to further religion but because such offices could be used to attain wealth and power.

Abuses were also apparent at lower levels within the Catholic Church where the religious life of most Europeans took place. Priests at parishes in local villages, like most of the European population, were peasants who lived in abject poverty. To raise funds for themselves and the Church, parish priests sometimes granted forgiveness for sins in return for money. Lay people viewed such practices as an attempt to sell divine grace. Parish priests also vulgarized religion, sometimes combining religious and pagan symbols into daily life.

By the beginning of the sixteenth century, critics of the Catholic Church attacked it on three fronts: immorality within the Church, the lack of knowledge of parish priests, and clerical pluralism. These things made it seem that the Church was not fulfilling its religious mandate and meeting the spiritual needs of parishioners. These attacks occurred largely because over the centuries the Church had become more institutionalized, more formal, and its doctrines were supported by a detailed system of canon law, theology, pomp, and ritual. Increasingly, Church officials promoted as important the sacraments and the role of priests in performing them. Moreover, the doctrine that good works, fasting, self-denial, and charity must accompany faith was becoming more dominant within the Church.

Immorality was a big problem. It particularly manifested itself in the requirement that priests and Church officials remain celibate. This practice, which dates to the fourth century, was often violated. Parish priests, as well as higher-

Public burnings ensured that the crowds would witness the execution and hear the agonizing screams of the dying.

ranking Church officials, including Pope Alexander VI, commonly had sexual relations with females in their congregations. Sometimes these priests even lived with concubines, sired children, and raised families. Immorality was not confined solely to sexual transgressions. Clergy often appeared in public wearing fancy clothes, gambled, and drank alcoholic beverages to excess. Such conduct, which contradicted Church doctrine and teaching, caused lay people to view Church officials as hypocrites.

Clerical ignorance was another problem. Even though Church law required priests to be educated, bishops rarely enforced this regulation because it was difficult to find educated people who wanted to become priests. Consequently, priests were often poorly educated. Many could barely read and write. They understood the Bible

little better than the parishioners they ministered to. Church record books were usually not well maintained. Records of deaths, births, and marriages were sometimes inaccurately recorded, if they were recorded at all. Financial records were usually in disarray. Because of these problems, which could be solved by having an educated clergy, Christian humanists and other Renaissance intellectuals who valued learning criticized the poorly educated priests, mocking them as they recited Latin words in Mass that neither priest nor parishioner could understand.

Clerical pluralism also provided ammunition critics used to attack the Church. Many Church officials held several *benefices* or Church offices simultaneously. This meant that absenteeism was a problem. It was impossible for one official to regularly visit different offices they held in various countries and carry out the spiritual duty each office required. However, these officials collected revenue from all offices held. Priests were usually hired by absentee office holders to perform the spiritual duties each office entailed. These priests were paid a small fraction of the revenue the office holder collected. Thomas Wolsey, an advisor to England's Henry VIII, for example, held the position as Archbishop of York for a decade and a half before he visited the diocese he controlled. Antoine du Prat, the French diplomat under Louis XII, served as Archbishop of Sens without ever visiting a church in his diocese. The only time he was ever in a church in the diocese he controlled was for his own funeral. It was common for Italian church officials to hold high offices in foreign countries that they seldom, if ever, visited. Yet, these absentee foreign officials collected revenue from benefices in England, France, Spain, Germany, and other countries. Clerical pluralism and absenteeism created resentment within congregations and others at the local level, leading to harsh condemnation of the Catholic Church. Critics complained about the way money changed hands every time a new bishop was appointed.

A fundamental problem with the Roman Catholic Church by the sixteenth century was that it simply did not provide for the spiritual needs of local parishioners in an acceptable manner. Most laypersons wanted a more personal relationship with God than the elaborate pomp and ritual present in the Church enabled them to have. They found little comfort in formalized institutional rituals because such practices had little meaning unless the believer could find within them the presence of God. Part of the difficulty was due to the fact that the Catholic Mass was conducted in Latin, which most people did not understand.

Some individuals who wanted a closer personal relationship with God turned toward mysticism because its practitioners stressed religious freedom and individualized worship. Mystics rejected Scholastic theology that dominated the Catholic Church, denounced its authority, and turned to the ancient scriptures and writings of early figures within the Christian Church for guidance. St. Augustine's writings particularly influenced Mysticism. Mystic religious groups had arisen in European cities by the sixteenth century. Such groups were particularly numerous in Germany. By allowing individuals to engage in private devotions, they met the spiritual needs of Christians in ways the Catholic Church could not. One of the largest Mystic organizations in Germany was the Brotherhood of the Eleven Thousand Virgins. Its members met regularly to sing hymns and read psalms. By 1450 over one hundred Mystic societies existed in Hamburg, a city that contained only about eleven thousand people. Other cities in Germany, Italy, and other countries contained similar groups.

Officials within the Roman Catholic Church tried to suppress Mysticism and ordered Mystic societies to disband. These efforts at suppression met with little success. Itinerant preachers traveled throughout Europe spreading Mystic doctrines and beliefs. At every place they preached Mystic evangelists exhorted listeners to communicate directly with God. Mystic ministers told the large crowds they drew to rid themselves of corrupt priests, free themselves from the institutionalized doctrine and ritual of the Catholic Church, and seek a deeply personal relationship with God.

One of the most famous and popular Mystic preachers was Girolamo Savonarola, a Dominican friar who wanted to outlaw materialism and secularism present throughout the

Catholic Church. Everywhere this Italian friar preached hundreds, and perhaps thousands, of lay Christians flocked to receive his message. In 1496, for example, he preached in Florence, Italy and presided over a tremendous bonfire fueled by the burning of secular items that included "heathen literature," art, cosmetics, gambling devices, and other worldly items. The tremendous following Savonarola attracted, along with his condemnation of secularism within the Church, drew the attention of Catholic officials. Eventually the Pope issued a warrant for his arrest and had Savonarola executed for heresy.

Another Mystic group was the Brethren of the Common Life. This group was active in Holland. The lay people that organized it tried to imitate Christ in their daily lives. They lived simple lives and performed daily acts of charity, such as feeding the hungry, providing shelter for the homeless, and aid to the sick. The Brethren did these things because they believed Christ taught all Christians to do them. In addition, members of this Mystic society also taught in local schools. Through their teaching, the Brethren of the Common Life urged students, many of whom were training to be Catholic priests, to develop an inner, personal relationship with God and to provide opportunities for future parishioners to develop the same kind of relationship with their God. Thomas Kempis, a member of the Brethren of the Common Life, even wrote *The Imitation of Christ* that was widely read in Holland. In this book he exhorted Christians to view Christ as their role model and lead a simple, unadorned life similar to that the Savior had led. By the mid-fifteenth century the Brethren of the Common Life had spread beyond Holland into Germany. There they would influence many people, including Martin Luther.

LUTHER AND THE BIRTH OF PROTESTANTISM

The problems in the Catholic Church prior to and during the first two decades of the sixteenth century caused Martin Luther (1483-1546), a German Augustinian monk, to officially break with the Church and launch the Protestant Reformation. Even though he did not intend to break away from the Church, Luther was appalled at conditions within the institution. He believed the institution had strayed from practices, beliefs, and teachings of Christ, the Apostles, and first-century Christians.

Luther was particularly troubled by the Catholic practice of selling indulgences. An indulgence allowed sinners to be forgiven of their sins and repair the relationship with God the sin had broken. According to Catholic teaching, individuals who sin become estranged from God. Reconciliation can only occur if the sinner confesses the sin before a priest and is given penance to perform. Penance usually amounted to requiring sinners to reject the wrong and then reciting certain prayers or performing some kind of community service or good deed as atonement for the evil. However, the Pope insisted that because the Church was the embodiment of Christ upon earth it had the authority to grant sinners forgiveness for any sin they might have committed. The doctrine of indulgences was originally developed in the twelfth century so that the Pope and bishops could reward crusader knights for fighting to free the Holy Land from Muslim infidels. Individuals who received an indulgence from the Church, it was believed, would not face punishment for their sins while alive on earth or after entering purgatory. These individuals, at the moment of death, would be granted immediate entry into heaven. Luther was especially upset that people who bought in-

Martin Luther, German scholar, was one of the fathers of the Protestant movement.

cal pluralism), had received a special papal dispensation to simultaneously hold all three offices. He had borrowed money from the Fuggers, a wealthy Jewish banking family in Augsburg, to pay Leo X for the dispensation allowing him to hold all three offices. As part of the agreement, Leo X had authorized Albert to sell indulgences to raise money to repay the Fuggers and fund construction of St. Peter's Basilica. Albert hired John Tetzel, a Dominican friar, to sell the indulgences near Wittenberg where Luther was teaching in 1517. Tetzel was one of the first people to engage in modern advertising. To sell indulgences, he constructed a chart with different prices for different sins and composed a "cute" but disturbing slogan "As soon as coin in coffer rings, from purgatory the soul springs." Individuals could purchase indulgences not only for themselves but also for dead relatives.

Frederick of Saxony, one of the seven electors within the Holy Roman Empire, and the ruler of the German principality where Wittenberg was located, forbade Tetzel to sell indulgences in the Duchy of Saxony. Tetzel simply moved across the border to Jutenborg, Thuringia where he continued to preach and sell indulgences. Many Saxony residents, including some of Luther's students at the University of Wittenberg, crossed the border and purchased forgiveness for their sins. Luther, a Biblical scholar, had found no scriptural authority allowing the Church to grant indulgences. Furthermore, he believed that Tetzel was cheating German citizens out of their hard-earned money. He found it objectionable that the Catholic Church was making worthless promises to people that their sins would be forgiven when the Church did not have the authority to grant forgiveness. Luther's studies told him only Christ could forgive sin. Since the Church had no official doc-

dulgences believed they could commit any sin afterwards without having to confess the sin and do penance.

The event that disturbed Luther most was Pope Leo X's selling of indulgences to raise funds to construct St. Peter's Basilica. In 1517 Albert of Magdeburg, the Archbishop of Mainz, Halberstadt and Magdeburg (an example of cleri-

trine on the sale of indulgences, Luther believed the matter was open for academic discussion.

Luther wrote a letter to Archbishop Albert stating his objections to the sale of indulgences. This letter contained a document written in Latin called the "Ninety-five Theses on the Power of Indulgences." After Luther's death, Philip Melanchthon, one of his disciples, claimed that on All Hallow's Eve in 1517 Luther posted the Ninety-five Theses on the door of Wittenberg Castle Church. Whether Luther nailed this document to the church door is controversial. Some historians have concluded that the event never occurred. Nevertheless, Luther's argument in the Ninety-five Theses was that the sale of indulgences trivialized the penance sacrament, contradicted Biblical teaching, and caused Christians to forgo charitable penance. By the end of 1517 the Ninety-five Theses had been translated into German and were being read and discussed throughout the German principalities.

Luther's Ninety-five Theses was not intended to signal a break with Catholicism. The document stated what Luther believed to be the Biblical position on indulgences. Luther maintained that there was no Biblical basis for indulgences and rejected the notion that salvation could be purchased through an indulgence or achieved by performing good deeds. Instead, Luther maintained that salvation came only by the grace of God. There was nothing that an individual could do in the earthly life to obtain salvation. God granted salvation to individuals for reasons known only to the deity. Luther also maintained that the Pope could only remit temporal punishment imposed by the Church, that every Christian was saved so long as they accepted grace even if they did not purchase an indulgence and criticized papal wealth.

As word of Luther's attack on indulgences spread across Germany, the money Tetzel collected from their sale declined. This caused the Dominican Order to launch an attack on Luther, whom they perceived to be a presumptuous Augustinian. The Dominican attack was based in part on a longstanding rivalry with the Augustinian order. Augustinian beliefs were more liberal (more likely to question church practices) than those held by the Dominicans, who were defenders of Church orthodoxy and who would later play a prominent role in the Catholic Inquisition. In fact, Luther and other Augustinians often mockingly split the Dominican name into its two Latin parts *Domini canes*, which means dogs of the Lord. Initially, church officials, including Pope Leo X, took little interest in the controversy, regarding it as simply a dispute between friars. Eventually the controversy became so widespread that the Church could not ignore it. In 1519 Luther, in a public debate with John Eck, a prominent scholar, at Leipzig that attracted a large audience, challenged the authority of both the Pope and the Council of Constance, maintaining that both had been wrong when John Hus was convicted of heresy and burned at the stake.

In 1520 Luther wrote three brief essays outlining his views. The first, entitled *An Address to the Christian Nobility of the German Nation*, was an appeal to German nationalism. In this essay Luther urged his countrymen to reject the authority of a foreign pope. All Christians, said Luther, constitute the body of Christ (the Church) and have a responsibility to heal a defective institution and rid it of abuses such as indulgences. The second essay, *The Babylonian Captivity*, criticized the seven sacraments from which the Catholic Church derived much of its power. Luther argued that the Bible authorized only three sacraments—penance, baptism, and the Lords Supper (the Eucharist). The third letter, *Liberties of the Christian Man*, outlined

Luther's position on salvation, faith, good works, and grace.

Pope Leo X responded by condemning Luther's theology, ordering that his books be burned, and excommunicating him unless he publicly recanted within two months. Luther responded by burning Leo X's letter and calling the pontiff an Antichrist. Charles V, the Holy Roman Emperor, ordered Luther to defend his views before a diet (assembly) at Worms, a city on the Rhine, in 1521. When directed to disavow what he had previously said and written, Luther refused, stating that he could not go against his conscience or Biblical scripture. His refusal to recant prompted Charles to brand Luther an outlaw and issue an order for his arrest. Even though it was illegal to do so, Duke Frederick III of Saxony offered Luther protection against German and Church authorities, officials he viewed as foreign usurpers. Frederick had Luther taken to Wartburg Castle where the monk lived for a year. Ironically, Frederick never broke with the Catholic Church. His actions, however, enabled the Protestant Reformation to continue. Without his protection Charles V would probably have had Luther burned at the stake.

Luther's break with the Catholic Church was complete. From 1520 to 1530 he developed a theology different from Catholic orthodoxy. The theological principles Luther devised became the basic tenants all Protestant sects who were part of the Reformation followed. Lutheran theology was firmly rooted in Biblical scholarship.

Luther devised five primary doctrines that became the foundation for all Protestant theology. First was the principle of salvation. Traditional Catholic doctrine held that salvation resulted from faith and good works. Luther rejected the notion that good deeds played any role in salvation. Instead, he taught that the Bible clearly indicated salvation results solely from faith. There is nothing, Luther said, that humankind does to achieve salvation. Individuals are saved because God arbitrarily decides, for reasons known only to the deity, to grant certain people grace. Taking the sacraments, giving to charity, or doing good in everyday life would not save someone unless God granted that person grace. God, not people, Luther believed, initiated salvation.

Second, Luther rejected the Catholic notion that religious authority resides in two places—the Bible and traditional Church teachings. Rather, Luther stated that religious authority resides only in the Bible, which he believed was the word of God revealed to humans. Each person was free to interpret the Bible as his or her conscience dictated. For Luther, it was important that each individual read and study the Bible and then reflect on its teachings amid the presence of other Christians in a communal or church setting.

Third, Luther maintained that the church was the body of Christ and that all Christians, not just clergymen, were part of the institution. Catholics had previously taught that only priests were part of the Church, and, therefore, only priests were allowed to partake of wine during the Eucharist. Luther allowed the congregation to drink the wine, which lessened the authority of priests. Furthermore, Luther abolished much of the Catholic pomp in religious services, which simplified the liturgy and further decreased the power of priests.

Fourth, Luther developed the concept known as the *priesthood of the believer*. This is the idea that individuals can understand God's will as revealed in the Bible through prayer without the aid of priests. Nor, do people need a priest or church to attain salvation. God will grant grace outside church without the presence of a priest endowed with special powers. In other words, each believer can serve as his or her own priest and together all Christians share responsibilities Catholics reserved for priests. This idea was completely alien to Catholics whose theology made a clear distinction between clergy and laity. Since the doctrine of the priesthood of the believer meant that it must be possible for every person to read the Bible, Luther translated the Latin Bible into German, finishing the task in 1534.

Fifth was the doctrine of *consubstantiation*, which differed from the Catholic idea of *transubstantiation*. Catholics believed that during the Eucharist words uttered by the priest consecrated the wafer and wine, miraculously transforming them into the actual body and blood of Christ. Luther rejected this idea. His doctrine of consubstantiation held that after consecration the bread and wine changed spiritually so that the presence of Christ was found, but the wafer and wine were not really transformed into the body and blood.

Luther's basic principles were first codified in the Augsburg Confession of 1530. After his German Bible was published in 1534, Luther's new Christianity was doctrinally complete. Although Luther lived until 1546, he did little after 1534 to further spread his beliefs. Yet, the revolution he launched over the sale of indulgences would spread throughout Europe and around the world, producing wars and social change in its wake.

RELIGIOUS VIOLENCE AND THE PEASANT REBELLION

Luther's condemnation of the Catholic Church and its religious authority encouraged oppressed people across Germany to revolt. The first violence related to Luther's new theology occurred in the summer of 1522 between German princes and knights. Imperial knights, who usually owned only one castle and owed their allegiance to the Holy Roman Emperor, felt oppressed by the growing power of independent towns and the local princes who controlled vast territories in Germany. Since German princes usually held ecclesiastical offices, the imperial knights, who believed they represented the emperor, used Lutheranism to justify launching an attack on the Archbishop of Trier. This war, which lasted about a year before the knights were defeated, caused Luther's opponents to criticize Protestantism for inciting violence and undermining law, order, peace, and stability.

Lutheranism also was used to justify the peasant revolts that swept across sixteenth-century Germany. German peasants were particularly attracted to Luther's doctrines because he came from a peasant background. Peasants generally looked upon Luther as a hero because he had defied the authority of the Catholic Church, which was viewed by peasants as perhaps their greatest economic oppressor. German peasants took Luther literally when he proclaimed in *On Christian Liberty* in 1520 that Christianity makes humans "the most free lord of all and subject to none." Uneducated peasants who followed Luther's teachings understood the words to mean that Christ would liberate them from their earthly oppressors—the Church and government.

The peasant revolt began in Swabia in 1524 and within a few months spread throughout southern and central Germany. Citing Luther's beliefs, peasant representatives gathered at Memmingen in 1525 to compose a list of twelve grievances. The articles of grievance condemned ecclesiastical and temporal lords for practices that made peasant life difficult. Among the grievances, peasants wanted common land that nobles had seized returned to villages, freedom for serfs, an end to religious taxes or tithes, prohibitions on hunting and fishing lifted, excessive rents and fees for religious services lowered, unlawful punishments abolished, an end to death duties (the practice of peasant families being forced to give the church and nobles their best horses or cows when a death occurred in a peasant family), and the right to choose their own pastors. They also insisted that their revolt be judged by Biblical scripture rather than temporal law.

At first, Luther personally sympathized with the peasants' cause because he admired their unceasing toil and as a peasant child himself had experienced the drudgery of everyday life peasants endured. In 1525 Luther published *An Admonition to Peace*, which criticized German nobles and blamed them for causing the revolt: "We have no one…to thank for this…rebellion, except…lords and princes, especially…blind bishops, mad priests, and monks…. You do nothing but flay and rob your subjects…until the poor common folk can bear it no longer." However, when Luther realized that peasants were rebelling against all authority using his theology, he turned against the peasant rebellion, ignored the oppressive life they endured, and wrote *Against the Rapacious and Murdering Peasants*, a pamphlet that authorized German nobles to destroy rebellious peasants unmercifully until peace was restored. A few months later the Peasant Rebellion was crushed; its participants believed Luther had turned his back on a just cause, ignoring Biblical teachings that supported revolt. However, Luther did not see it this way. When he used the word "freedom," Luther meant freedom to obey the word of God without interference from the Roman Church. Freedom did not mean opposition to legally instituted governments. In fact, as Luther refined his theology, he increasingly demanded that

Christians support the state, that the church be subordinate to government, and condemned rebellion. Luther wrote "that nothing can be more poisonous, hurtful, or devilish than a rebel." Luther's critics maintained that he opposed the Peasant Revolt and supported the state because he realized that he and his faith needed the protection of German princes to oppose Roman Catholicism. Had Luther supported the Peasant Revolt, Germany's secular rulers likely would have denied him protection from Catholic authorities, condemning him and his movement to an early death. Regardless of why Luther opposed the Peasant Rebellion, historians estimate that German princes killed over seventy-five thousand peasants before crushing the revolt in 1525.

THE SPREAD OF PROTESTANTISM

Despite violence, such as the Peasant Rebellion that was associated with Lutheranism, the new faith spread across Germany and throughout Europe. Important to its spread was the printing press, which enabled publishers to rapidly reproduce Luther's writings and disseminate his ideas everywhere. Equally important was Luther's ability to turn a phrase. He was a gifted writer and speaker who expressed himself extremely well. Some scholars have maintained that only Shakespeare equals his use of language. Nevertheless, language was the sword that Luther, the peasant's son, used to seriously wound the Catholic Church.

Many people were attracted to Luther's ideas. Peasants, Renaissance humanists, nobles, merchants, and princes found desirable Luther's call for a simple religion based on personal faith and scripture and the abolition of elaborate ceremonies. Humanists across Renaissance Europe had advocated many of the same reforms. Ulrich von Hutten (1488-1523), for example, was a celebrated German humanist who joined Luther in advancing the Reformation. The conservatism within Lutheranism made it possible for anyone who accepted the idea of justification by faith and the authority of scripture to join the church. Converts could, with some modification, keep much from the Catholic faith they had grown up with, including the liturgy, music, and church organization.

One of the most important things that attracted rulers and nobles to Lutheranism was materialism. Since Lutheran theology did not permit the church to hold vast amounts of land or acquire substantial wealth, any prince who accepted the Protestant faith could confiscate the land and wealth controlled by Catholic monasteries, churches, and high officials in their kingdom. Although this strategy was risky because Emperor Charles V was a staunch supporter of the Catholic faith and could take away the title of prince from any German nobleman, if successful it could enrich the prince. Eventually, enough German princes risked alienating the Emperor by becoming Protestant that they developed enough strength to resist Charles. Protestant rulers convened at the Diet of Speyer in 1529 and produced a document protesting the Emperor's order that no new religious idea would be allowed in Germany. In fact, this is the origin of the word "Protestant." After Speyer, all non-Catholic Christians would be called Protestants. In 1530 the Lutheran princes further upset Charles V by voting to support the Confession of Augsburg, a document containing the basic principles of the Lutheran faith. Faced with this opposition, Charles threatened to use military force to crush Protestant princes. They responded by forming a military alliance against the Holy Roman Emperor at Schmalkalden, Saxony in 1531.

War did not occur between German Protestant princes and Charles V until 1546. From 1531 until 1546 German Protestants consolidated their power, enticed other princes to join their ranks, and negotiated with the Pope about returning to the Catholic fold. When the Roman Church was not willing to accept Protestant demands that Lutheran theology be made part of the Catholic faith, it became clear that war could not be averted. In 1546 German princes and Charles V fought a brief conflict. Charles easily defeated the weaker German princes, but his victory did not destroy Protestantism. Luther's theology had advanced too far by the time Charles acted. About half of the German population had become Protestant by 1546. There were so many Protestants in Germany, particularly in the northern and eastern principalities, that it was impossible for the Holy Roman Emperor to destroy Lutheranism. There were also pockets of Protestantism in southern cities like Nuremberg, which was the German center of Renaissance Humanism.

Catholic princes in Germany also made it difficult for Charles to destroy Protestantism. They feared the power the Holy Roman Emperor had amassed and were reluctant to help him assert control across Germany, refusing to provide German troops. Thus, Charles had to use Spanish troops to fight Protestant princes, which caused the German populace to resent this foreign intrusion. Historians believe that the use of Spanish troops caused even more Germans to become Protestant.

From 1546 to 1555 sporadic fighting occurred in Germany. Although Charles V was a staunch defender of the Catholic faith, his actions were partly responsible for the spread of Lutheranism. The Holy Roman Emperor did not understand or try to solve political, religious, social, and economic problems Germany faced in the sixteenth century. Rather than devoting attention to Germany, he was more concerned about Flemish, Spanish, and Italian territories he controlled. He also faced a threat from Turkish Muslims who besieged Vienna, ruled by Charles' brother, Ferdinand, in 1529 and went to war with the Valois kings of France five times between 1521 and 1555. Consequently, Catholic rulers of France supported German Protestant princes when they challenged Charles V's power. France wanted to keep Germany divided to weaken Charles. This struggle between Catholic France and Charles V, called the Habsburg-Valois Wars, fought over Habsburg lands due to the marriage of Maximilian and Mary of Burgundy, ironically promoted the spread of Protestantism.

As Protestant numbers increased, they became more formidable, and in 1555 a diet at Augsburg was held. This meeting produced a settlement between Catholics and Protestants in Germany. According to the agreement, known as the Peace of Augsburg, each German prince could determine what religion his kingdom would follow without interference from the Roman Pope or the Holy Roman Emperor. The Peace of Augsburg signaled that the unity of Western Christendom had ended and that Lutheranism would be safely entrenched in Germany. Other reformers, imitating Luther's example, also broke with the Catholic Church and carried Protestantism throughout Europe.

REFORMERS AND RADICALS

One of the most important reformers was the Swiss humanist Ulrich Zwingli (1484-1531). He introduced the Reformation into Switzerland. On January 1, 1519, less than two years after Luther composed his Ninety-five theses, Zwingli, a Catholic priest and disciple of Erasmus, informed his congregation that he would no longer preach sermons taken from official Catholic sources. Using the New Testament Erasmus had translated, he stated that he would cover the entire book from Matthew to Revelation. Like Luther, Zwingli believed a personal study of scripture was necessary to lead a Christian life. From 1519 to 1522 he developed a theology similar to Luther's. Zwingli's doctrine rejected priests serving as intermediaries between God and humankind, allowed ministers to marry, and disavowed the notion of purgatory.

Despite similarities, Zwingli's theology was vastly different from Luther's. Unlike Luther, Zwingli believed individuals were basically good and only needed discipline imposed by the church to lead Christian lives. To accomplish this, he created a magisterial tribunal comprised of ministers and lay people to enforce religious law. Whereas Luther made a distinction between religious and secular authority, Zwingli saw the two as being one and the same. Zwinglian tribunals were thus given authority to enforce all laws, secular and religious, excommunicate wayward Christians, rule on moral questions, require church attendance, and spy on parishioners using a network of informers. In short, Zwingli created a Protestant faith more dependent on the individual and less reliant on grace than Luther could accept. When Luther and Zwingli met in 1529 to work out differences in their theology, a disagreement over the importance of the sacraments prevented them from reaching an accord. Zwingli saw the sacraments as symbols of grace God previously bestowed on the individual whereas Luther believed God was actually present in the ceremony to bestow grace when the sacraments were administered. Under Zwingli's system, baptism and communion, for example, were not necessary; Luther saw them as central to the Christian faith.

The most important reformer other than Luther was John Calvin (1509-1564). Born in Noyon, France, Calvin studied law at the University of Paris before beginning a crusade to make the world Protestant. As a young man, Calvin underwent an experience that changed his life. He called this event his "sudden conversion" but refused to elaborate about it. Whatever the experience was, after its occurrence in 1533, Calvin converted to Protestantism, becoming its foremost sixteenth-century spokesperson. The theology he developed had a greater impact on subsequent generations than any other reformer, including Luther. Calvinistic doctrine greatly influenced the government, economy, society, attitudes, and character of Europeans and their settlers in various American colonies.

After his sudden conversion French authorities charged Calvin with heresy. Thereafter, he hid from authorities for more than a year until he moved to Basel, Switzerland. While living at Basel, Calvin wrote *Institutes of the Christian Religion* (1536) that discussed his religious doctrine. This essay contained the five principles central to Calvin's theology. First is the idea that humankind is totally depraved. Calvin theorized that humans, by nature, are evil and will almost always do wrong. Second is the concept of unmerited grace. Calvin maintained that all people who became sinners when Eve consumed the forbidden fruit in the Garden of Eden were damned to hell. However, for reasons known only to God, some sinners were given salvation. Yet, this grace was not earned. People who were saved could do nothing to earn or merit heaven. God arbitrarily chose the saints and condemned all others to spend eternity in hell. In other words, according to Calvin, God, not human beings, was sovereign. It did not matter how morally upright a life people lived on earth. They still could go to hell. Third is the notion of limited atonement. Calvin stressed that although God granted salvation to undeserving human sinners, the number of people who receive atonement for their sins was limited. God chose only a few people to enjoy heavenly bliss in the afterlife. Calvinists referred to the chosen ones as the Saints or the elect. The vast majority of people were condemned to eternal hell. Fourth was the idea of predestination. Calvin concluded that God had decided who was damned and who was saved before people were born. This decision, which was made before a child was even in his or her mother's womb, was completely independent of the earthly life an individual might lead. Fifth is the idea of irresistible grace. Calvin declared that God's will would be done regardless of what any human might do. Individuals granted grace had no choice but to accept salvation just as those sentenced to hell could not change their fate. God's grace was irresistible, and the deity's power was absolute. People were, Calvin said, "as meaningless to God as grains of sand upon the seashore."

Shortly after defining his basic theology in the *Institutes of the Christian Religion*, Calvin moved to Geneva, where he remained until his death. In 1541 he accepted an invitation from Geneva's citizens to establish the Protestant faith in the Swiss city after it deposed its prince who was also a Catholic bishop. Calvin established a theocracy to govern both Geneva and his church. A group of deacons and church elders controlled the theocracy. A body of lay elders, called the consistory, made decisions about both church and state in Geneva, enforced laws, excommunicated wayward Christians, and punished sinners. Strict discipline and a high degree of organization characterized Geneva and other communities controlled by Calvinists.

The Reformation produced individuals and religious sects even more radical than Luther,

Zwingli, and Calvin, who primarily represented moderate to conservative Protestantism. Left wing Protestant sects that embraced the Reformation were called Anabaptists. Controversy between mainstream and liberal Protestants erupted over the sacrament of baptism. Calvin, Luther, and most mainline reformers, wanting to preserve church authority, held that the individual became part of the body of Christ (the church) at the moment of baptism. This meant that infants who were baptized became Christians at the moment of immersion. Anabaptists, however, rejected infant baptism. They believed that only mature adults should undergo baptism. Radicals insisted that only mature adults, capable of exercising free will, could consciously accept grace and become Christian. Thus, Anabaptists insisted that all adults who had undergone infant baptism be re-baptized. (The term Anabaptist means to baptize again.) They maintained that there was no scriptural basis for infant baptism because immature children could not understand the concept of grace.

Generally, Anabaptist sects, each one unique, are characterized by several commonalities. All accepted the idea of religious diversity. They did not reorganize the church in an institutional form, did not allow priests, believed that personal communication between God and the individual was paramount, and valued religious tolerance. Anabaptists sought to recreate the Christian community they believed had existed during the first century after Christ's execution, a voluntary group of believers who had attained salvation. Anabaptist sects rarely numbered more than one hundred individuals. Many sects wanted to completely isolate themselves from the world, live a Christian life as they saw it, and set an example for worldly sinners to follow. Anabaptist sects were also generally eschatological, that is, they believed in the im-

minent coming of Christ. Some even went so far as to create "communistic" societies in which members held everything in common, including material possessions and husbands and wives. Mystical Anabaptist sects lived isolated, hermit-like lives completely apart from the world. They often experienced some sort of psychological trance, which they believed indicated direct contact with God. Each Anabaptist church and sect was completely independent of all other groups, chose its own ministers and officials, made its own laws, and devised its own theology. Some Anabaptist sects were the first Christian churches to accept women ministers while others allowed only males to preach. Most Anabaptists refused to hold civil offices and some were pacifists, refusing to serve in national militaries or fight for any reason.

Anabaptists also held that only a few "true believers" really achieved salvation and that church and state should be separated. Anabaptists believed that no government should promote any religious view. Nor did Anabaptists think individuals should proselytize, meaning Anabaptist sects did not force their religious views on others. Instead, Anabaptists allowed people to make up their own minds about religion.

Radical views meant that Anabaptists were destined to remain in the religious minority. Mostly, such sects attracted the poor, the dispossessed, the uneducated, and the downtrodden from Europe's urban areas. Also, because Anabaptist ideas threatened the church/state relationship during an age that made no distinction between the two institutions, these minority sects often faced persecution, religious hatred, and violence. Political and religious leaders in Protestant countries, including Luther, Calvin, and Zwingli, believed that separation of church and state would inevitably led to the creation of a completely secular society, which they opposed. Since Anabaptist ideas threatened existing governments, churches, and societies, members of radical sects often experienced brutality sanctioned by mainstream religious leaders. Some European towns drove Anabaptists out of the community while others maimed, tortured, and killed members of these radical groups. Many Anabaptists were burned at the stake for heresy, while others were brutally beaten to death, drowned, hanged, or drawn and quartered.

The assault on Anabaptist sects began in the mid-1520s in Germany and quickly spread throughout Europe. An imperial diet in 1529 condemned to death all Anabaptists. Consequently, most of their leaders were violently executed. One of the best examples of violence against an Anabaptist sect was suppression of the Melchiorites at Munster, Germany. The Melchiorites attracted a large number of industrial workers and craftspeople. In 1534 this Anabaptist sect gained political control of Munster and established a Christian community according to Melchiorite ideas. They instituted a legal code that, among other things, established the death penalty for wives who did not obey their husbands and forced women to marry or face banishment from the community. Women who refused to marry or leave the city were executed. Melchiorites rule also introduced into Munster polygamy, burned all books except the Bible, and preached an eschatological religion.

Religious and secular leaders perceived what the Melchiorites had done at Munster as threatening society. Catholic and Protestant rulers united, sent an army to attack Munster and rid the city of Melchiorite ideas. This assault was successful. Many Melchiorites were killed; a few escaped to Poland, England, and the Netherlands.

THE ENGLISH REFORMATION

Across the English Channel the Reformation took a different turn, having economic and political causes in addition to religious ones. The official split with the Catholic Church occurred when King Henry VIII, wanting a male heir in 1527, requested that Pope Clement VII grant an annulment to his marriage to Catherine of Argon. Previously, Pope Julius II had given Henry a special dispensation, which allowed him to wed Catherine who had been married to Henry's brother, Arthur. In asking for the annulment Henry stated that if Princess Mary, the child produced by his union with Catherine, inherited the English throne, anarchy would result. He also maintained a legal marriage to Catherine had never existed because of her prior marriage. Clement VII was a weak pontiff whose focus at the time was on Luther's Reformation in Germany and on the Habsburg-Valois War in Italy. Clement refused Henry's request for an annulment because he did not want to provide more ammunition to Protestant reformers who criticized the Church by saying that popes replaced God's law as revealed in scripture with their own rules. Henry's divorce petition claimed that Julius II erred because his special dispensation violated God's rule that a man could not marry his brother's widow. Had Clement recognized Henry's argument and granted the annulment, Lutherans would have used this to convince more people to join the Reformation. Compounding the situation was the sack of Rome in 1527 by Charles V, Catherine's nephew. Since Charles was in complete control of Rome, Pope Clement delayed action on Henry's request; he was afraid to annul the marriage of Charles V's aunt when the Holy Roman Emperor controlled Rome.

After Clement refused to grant the annulment, Henry joined the Reformation. He removed the English church from papal control and made himself head of the institution. In 1533, at Henry's request, Parliament passed the Act in Restraint of Appeals, which legalized the English Reformation by forbidding church officials to submit legal appeals to the Roman Pope. Instead, English churchmen were required to submit all religious disputes to the English monarch. Thus, Henry VIII became the highest religious authority in England. Later, Parliamentary laws more firmly codified the Reformation in Britain. The Act for the Submission of Clergy in 1534 required priests and all other church officials to obey the king's rules and forbade Christians from publishing theological principles without consent of the monarch. The Supremacy Act, also passed in 1534, made the English monarch the official head of the Anglican Church. Henry's opposition was unexpected because he had previously written an essay attacking Luther and the Reformation, for which the Pope had named him "Defender of the Faith" in England. While these acts made the break with Rome official, they caused controversy within England. A few Parliamentary representatives and other officials opposed passage of England's Reformation laws. Sir Thomas More, for example, resigned his chancellorship because he could not support leaving the Catholic fold and making the English monarch head of the Anglican Church. John Fisher, the Bishop of Rochester, also objected to the English Reformation, accusing the English clergy of cowardice when most did not protest when Henry removed the church from Rome's control. More, Fisher, and others who opposed the English Reformation were beheaded.

From 1535 to 1539 the English Reformation continued. Henry and Thomas Cromwell, his most influential advisor, abolished the monastery as an institution and confiscated its wealth. Monks, nuns, and abbots were driven from their homes. All monastic lands were taken; much of it was later sold to the upper and middle classes because the government needed money to finance various wars. The redistribution of lands also strengthened the rich and made them dependent upon the English king.

Because the English Reformation occurred more for secular than religious reasons, initially the Anglican Church kept many Catholic beliefs, doctrine, and practices, such as transubstantiation, celibacy for priests, and confession.

Edward VI wanted the country to be Protestant.

Anne Boleyn, mistress of Henry VIII, demanded that he annul his marriage to Catherine, causing an international controversy.

After Henry VIII's death, however, the English church became more Protestant. During the seven-year reign of Edward VI (1547-1553), Henry's son, Catholic practices and theology were replaced with Protestant ideas. Archbishop Thomas Cranmer ordered a simplification of the Anglican liturgy. The *Book of Common Prayer* was written in 1549. Protestant ministers began to roam the English countryside, spreading Calvinistic, Lutheran, and other religious doctrines.

After Edward's death, his half-sister, Mary Tudor, the daughter of Catherine of Argon, tried to undo the English Reformation. During her brief reign from 1553 to 1558 England faced religious instability. She rescinded most laws Henry VIII and Edward VI had enacted to further the Reformation. In their place, Mary passed legislation that completely returned England to the Catholic fold. Mary's religious changes, along with her marriage to the Spanish prince Phillip, son of Holy Roman Emperor Charles V, were not received well by her English subjects. When Mary began a campaign to persecute Protestants, many fled England, settling in countries where the Reformation was more firmly established. Under Queen Mary's rule, hundreds of Protestants, especially ministers and other leaders, were executed, earning her the name "Bloody Mary."

Mary's death brought her sister, Elizabeth I, to the throne. Under Elizabeth's reign from 1558 to 1603, religious stability came to England. Because Elizabeth was raised Protestant, she rescinded Mary's laws that had returned England to Catholicism. However, Elizabeth was not overly zealous initiating religious reforms. When she became queen, she faced pressure from Catholics who wanted England to remain part of the Roman Church and a group of Protestants called Puritans who wanted the Anglican Church to become Calvinistic. Puritans were especially vocal and political. They wanted Elizabeth to rid the English church of all vestiges of Catholicism. Elizabeth, who was perhaps the best monarch in English history, steered a middle course between Catholic and Protestant extremists. She gave England more religious freedom and toleration than it had ever had. Even though all English people were legally required to be Anglican, Elizabeth generally allowed her subjects to practice whatever religion they wanted so long as they did not try to force their beliefs on others. Nor was the Queen a strict doctrinalist. She demanded that peace and order be maintained throughout her realm and in religious services but did not precisely define how English services were to be conducted. Laws enacted by Parliament during her reign, called the Elizabethan

Settlement, were not unreasonable. They required that every English man and woman attend Anglican services; those that refused faced fines rather than execution or imprisonment. English bishops in 1563 drew up and approved the *Thirty-nine Articles* that briefly outlined Anglican beliefs. All Anglican services were required to be conducted in a uniform manner. The English language was used in services, Anglican priests were allowed to marry, and monasteries were prohibited from reopening. Still, these reforms were modest when considered in light of what Catholic and Protestant extremists wanted.

The Reformation in Scotland and Ireland was more radical than in England. John Knox, a staunch Calvinist, was the most important Reformation figure in Scotland. In 1560 he persuaded the Scottish legislature to pass legislation creating a Calvinistic Church. The Catholic Mass was forbidden. Any Scottish citizen who attended mass could be executed. Everyone was required to attend the Presbyterian Church, which was controlled by ministers called presbyters instead of bishops, which Knox founded. Calvinistic theology was introduced into Scotland. Knox, who previously had studied with Calvin in Geneva, attempted to create a theocracy in Scotland. The Presbyterian Church utilized a simple worship service dominated by hell fire and brimstone preachers. The *Book of Common Order* that Knox published in 1564 was adopted as the official liturgical tool in the Presbyterian Church.

Both James V and his daughter, Mary, Queen of Scots, opposed the Scottish Reformation. The Scottish monarchs were staunch Catholics who allied themselves with other Catholic monarchs in Europe. Because the Scottish monarchy was weak, James and Mary were powerless to stop the spread of Calvinism throughout their realm. Numerous Scottish nobles, who dominated Parliament, supported the Reformation. They saw religious change as a means whereby they could wrest more power from an already weak monarchy.

Ireland did not undergo a complete Reformation as Scotland did. In 1536 the English government ordered the Irish Parliament to pass legislation instituting the Reformation. These laws abolished the Catholic Church, made the English monarch head of the Irish church, outlawed monasteries, and created an Irish church similar to the English Church. The ruling class, which was primarily comprised of English nobles, quickly converted to Protestantism. However, the largest majority of the Irish population remained Catholic because they did not accept the political legitimacy of their English rulers and Parliament. Maintaining their Catholic faith was a way for the masses to defy their oppressive English rulers. The Catholic Church had to function as an underground institution. Its property was confiscated and sold. Profits went to England. Monasteries were destroyed. Despite these hardships, Catholicism survived in Ireland. Catholic priests and bishops became national leaders in the Irish resistance to English rule.

THE CATHOLIC REFORMATION
(Counter Reformation)

After Luther began the Reformation in 1517 it quickly spread across Europe. By 1547 all England and Scandinavia had become Protestant. Most of Germany and Scotland, as well as parts of France and Switzerland, were following the doctrines of Luther, Calvin, Zwingli, Knox, or some other reformer. The spread of Protestantism meant that the Catholic Church had lost its control over millions of Christians and had witnessed the confiscation of thousands of acres of real estate property and had lost millions of dollars in annual income. Faced with these problems, Catholics began to put the Church's affairs in order. Reforms within the Church were instituted as a result of the Protestant Reformation. Catholics refer to these reforms at the Catholic Revival while Protestants call it the Counter Reformation. Whatever its name, lasting changes in the Catholic Church resulted, and after 1540, with the exception of the Netherlands, no substantial number of people in a European geographic area would become Protestant.

Certainly, reform within the Catholic Church was needed. Protestantism had spread across Europe, taking several countries out of the Catholic fold. Even in countries that remained loyal to the faith, the Church had lost much of its influence. There also was no unified Catholic doctrine on justification, salvation, or the sacraments. This situation began to change in 1534 when Paul III was elected Pontiff. When his reign ended in 1549, the Catholic Revival was firmly established. Pope Paul III began to root out abuses within the Church. He tolerated little corruption from lay priests, high ranking bishops, or abbots and created the Roman Inquisition, which used violence to stifle dissent.

Paul's primary strategy to reform the Church was convening an ecumenical council that met at Trent, Italy in 1545. The Council of Trent, as it was known, met off and on for eighteen years until the work was finished in 1563. Delegates to the Council of Trent were instructed to reform the Catholic Church and induce reconciliation with wayward Protestants. Lutherans, Calvinists, and other Protestants were initially asked to participate. Those who attended insisted that the Bible was the sole authority of God, which made reconciliation difficult to achieve.

Throughout the Council's existence, national politics intruded on its religious mission. Representatives from Western European countries demanded that Rome share power while delegates from Italian states wanted the Church's power centralized under the Pope. Charles V refused to allow discussion on any topic he believed would upset Lutherans in his realm. If Lutherans were upset too much, Charles was likely to lose more land to Protestant German princes. Likewise, French representatives opposed reconciliation with Protestants because they wanted to keep Germany weak. So long as Lutheranism divided the German states, the less authority Charles V had. A religiously divided Germany meant that France, unified under Catholicism, would be stronger.

Despite the intrusion of national politics and the stubbornness of Protestants regarding the importance of Scripture, achievements of the Council of Trent were remarkable. Numerous decrees were issued at the meeting. The most important one rejected Protestant positions on Scripture, sacraments, and free will. The Bible was not, according to this decree, the sole authority on religious matters. Tradition, as well as rulings by the Pope and church officials, was also important. Moreover, the Council of Trent decided that all seven sacraments are valid representations of God's grace. Priests were the only people authorized to administer the sacraments. Delegates also reaffirmed the Catholic position that humans possess free will and that good works in conjunction with faith are necessary for salvation. The elaborate rites and ceremonies that had become part of Catholic worship remained part of the faith.

Numerous decisions of less importance were also handed down from Trent. Many abuses within the Church were corrected. Ecclesiastical discipline was strengthened; bishops were now required to live within the diocese they governed. The sale of indulgences was abolished, priests who lived with women were ordered to embrace celibacy, bishops were required to visit every church within their diocese at least once every two years, and every diocese was ordered to create a seminary to educate priests. St. Jerome's Latin translation of the Bible was made a holy book, and priests were required to preside over marriage ceremonies. The Council also established the Inquisition and the *Index of Forbidden Books* to root out dissent and inform Catholics about books the Church considered heretical.

Although the Council of Trent did not affect reconciliation with Protestants, it did create a renewed spirituality within the Church. Criticism of the Catholic Church abated after most abuses were abolished. Decisions made at Trent remained important to Catholics for centuries afterward.

The Catholic Reformation involved more than simply the Council of Trent. New Religious orders also came into existence. They developed primarily for two reasons—to improve morality within the Church and provide education for clergy and lay people. The two foremost orders were the Society of Jesus (Jesuits) and the Ursuline Nuns. Ignatius Loyola (1491-1556) founded the Jesuit Order in 1540. He believed the Protestant Reformation had occurred because of low spiritual moral within lay people. The antidote for the Reformation, he believed, was found in ministering to the spiritual needs of individual Catholics. Loyola molded the Jesuits into a highly centralized group whose members were willing to go to the far corners of the world in service to the Church. Individuals who wanted to become Jesuits had to undergo a novitiate (probationary period) of two years rather than the standard one-year period required of other religious orders. The Je-

suits became known for the schools they established. Jesuit monks educated children from both common and noble families. Over time, Jesuits exerted tremendous political influence, especially on the nobles and kings who had been educated in the order's schools.

The Ursuline Order of Nuns, founded by Angela Merici (1474-1540), focused on educating women. Originally established in 1535 to battle Protestant heresy by educating girls according to Catholic doctrine, the order eventually spread outside Italy, becoming known worldwide for its mission. The Ursuline goal was to make society more moral by teaching women who would become wives and mothers about Christian love. It was then hoped these Christian women could influence husbands and sons to exercise greater morality both inside and outside the home.

New religious orders were not the only institutions established as part of the Catholic Reformation. In 1542 Pope Paul III created the Inquisition to fight the spread of Protestantism within Catholic countries. The Roman Inquisition consisted of six cardinals who were given authority to act as a court to try individuals accused of heresy. This institution was given the power to issue warrants, arrest, try, imprison, and execute heretics. Trials run by the Inquisition were not fair to the accused. Judges accepted hearsay evidence. Accused heretics were not always informed of what they were charged with and torture was often applied to extract confessions. In countries controlled by Catholic monarchs Protestant heretics were effectively destroyed; in non-Catholic countries the Inquisition was not effective.

RELIGIOUS WARS

Wars plagued Europe for almost a century. From the 1560s to the 1650s countries fought over many issues, but religion was a common denominator in all the conflicts. Religion caused Catholics and Protestants to oppose each other. Both faiths saw the other as heretics and were convinced that God wanted all heretics destroyed. Catholics and Protestants developed a hatred for each other that bordered on fanaticism. This hatred caused members of both Christian sects to treat each other cruelly. Catholics executed Protestants by burning them at the stake; Protestants executed Catholics by drawing and quartering (ripping the body apart by hitching horses to all four limbs). Even corpses were not spared. Dead bodies were often mutilated as a warning to other heretics.

One of the most fervent anti-Protestant rulers was Philip II of Spain (1556-1598), the most powerful monarch in the world at the time. He ruled Spain, most of Italy, the Netherlands, most of South America, and parts of North America. Despite his vast possessions and wealth, Philip was not satisfied. He intensely disliked the Protestant Reformation and also hated Muslims who controlled parts of Africa and the Middle East. Philip believed that Islam and Protestantism were enemies of the Catholic Church; consequently, he wanted to destroy both. Philip waged a successful campaign in the Mediterranean against the Muslims. A naval victory at the Battle of Lepanto against Muslim forces curtailed Islamic power in the Mediterranean and made Philip a hero in the Catholic world. However, his successes against Islam did not translate into victory against Protestant forces.

One of the most serious setbacks for Philip was in the Netherlands, which he had inherited when his father Charles V abdicated in 1556, dividing his territories between Ferdinand (Charles's brother) and Philip. Problems arose because the Dutch considered Philip to be Spanish whereas Charles was one of their own, having been born in Ghent and raised in the Netherlands. Unlike Charles, who was Flemish in language and lifestyle, Philip spoke Spanish and the Dutch perceived him as a foreign ruler. In 1559 Philip named Margaret, his half sister, as ruler of the Netherlands and ordered her to destroy Protestantism in the kingdom. She quickly established the Inquisition to root out Protestantism. The problem in the Netherlands was not Lutheranism but Calvinism. Calvin's teachings had attracted a following among the Dutch middle and working classes. By the 1560s, Calvinist enclaves existed in most Dutch towns and the religion was well financed by bankers and merchants throughout the seventeen provinces that comprised the Netherlands. Margaret's immediate problem was raising capital to finance efforts to destroy Protestantism. Despite protests from the Dutch legislature that taxes were already too high, Margaret raised them. Her actions caused Dutch merchants, businessmen, and bankers who opposed the tax increase to unite with Calvinist leaders being persecuted by the Queen.

In 1566 working class Calvinists, faced with high food costs coupled with high taxes, revolted. Incited by Calvinist preachers, fanatical mobs attacked Catholic churches and their parishioners. The Catholic cathedral of Notre Dame at Antwerp, along with thirty other churches, was destroyed. Alters were smashed, windows broken, tombs opened, books were burned, and priests were killed. From Antwerp the violence spread across the Netherlands and throughout the Low Countries.

Philip II dispatched a Spanish army commanded by the Duke of Alva to crush the Dutch rebellion. In addition to using the Inquisition against Protestants, Alva established an institution called the Council of Blood. To finance the Spanish campaign, he increased taxes even more. On March 3, 1568, Alva's troops executed over fifteen hundred Protestant heretics. Protestants were publicly hanged, and rebel bands were ruthlessly slaughtered by Spanish forces as the troops sought to suppress treason and heresy. Often innocent people were killed. Two Dutch noblemen, for example, were executed because they demanded that Philip alter his repressive policy. The executions and tax increases, which produced economic hardship, caused Dutch Protestants to completely turn against their Spanish oppressors. Over the next ten years a civil war was fought between Protestants and Catholics in the Netherlands. Generally, Protestant forces won the war. In 1572 a group of Dutch sailors, whom the Spanish called "sea beggars," captured Brill, a North Sea fishing village. Their success prompted revolts in other Dutch towns. Spanish troops were dispatched to recapture Brill and other towns that had fallen to rebel forces but were defeated in 1574 when the dikes were opened, flooding Spanish troops who were only twenty-five miles from Amsterdam. In 1576 Protestants in all seventeen Dutch provinces united under the leadership of William of Orange.

Philip II sent his nephew, Alexander Farnese, the Duke of Parma, to crush the revolt. Farnese captured numerous towns in the southern provinces, including Ghent, Bruges, Maastricht, Tournai, and Antwerp. The fall of Antwerp was the last significant Spanish victory in the Netherlands. Farnese's success also meant that the Netherlands would be divided religiously. In the ten southern provinces Farnese conquered, Calvinism was stamped out. Protestants residing within them were either forced to become Catholic or migrate to a Protestant province. These ten provinces, called the Spanish Netherlands, remained under control of the Habsburg dynasty, eventually becoming the country of Belgium.

The seven northern provinces William of Orange controlled remained Protestant. In 1581, led by Holland, they signed the Treaty of Utrecht, declared their independence from Spain, and created the country of Holland.

Philip and Farnese refused to accept the political division of the Netherlands. They tried to subdue the northern provinces after 1581. Protestant Holland repeatedly asked Elizabeth I, the English monarch, for military assistance. England faced a serious dilemma. If Elizabeth helped the Dutch she would anger Philip II and likely produce war with Spain. But, if Spain conquered all the Netherlands provinces Philip would likely attack England to restore the Catholic religion in Albion. Compounding the problem, the Dutch revolt had harmed the English wool industry. The Netherlands was the largest market for English wool cloth. When it collapsed, Elizabeth's government lost tax revenue. The execution of William of Orange in July 1584 and the Spanish victory at Antwerp frightened Elizabeth. She believed that if Spain crushed the Dutch resistance Farnese would turn his army against England. Thus, Elizabeth I sent money and soldiers to help Dutch Protestants confront the Catholic armies of Spain in 1585.

Farnese insisted that before Spain could defeat the Dutch it must also defeat England and halt Elizabeth's support of the Protestant Netherlands. Philip agreed with Farnese because he had spent a fortune fighting the Dutch but had little to show for it. Upsetting Philip even more was the execution of Mary, Queen of Scots, Elizabeth I's cousin and heir to the English throne, on February 18, 1587. Mary, a staunch Catholic, had hatched a plot to assassinate Elizabeth and take the English throne for herself. Philip II, wanting to restore England to the Catholic fold, had provided Mary financial support. Had Mary's plot worked, English support of the

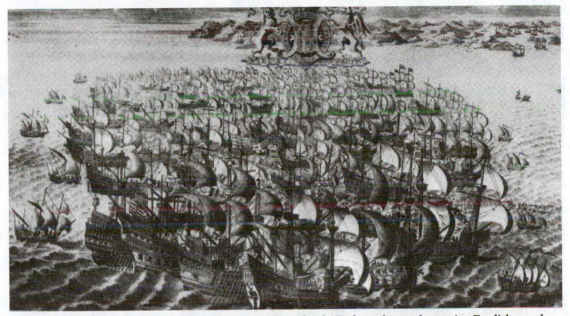

The powerful Spanish Armada set sail to attack England. Bad weather and superior English naval tactics, however, forced the crippled fleet to withdraw in defeat.

Dutch rebellion would have ended and Spain could have completed its Dutch conquest. After the plot failed, Elizabeth had Mary beheaded. Pope Sixtus V (1585-1590), after learning of Mary's death, was so upset that he offered Philip one million Italian gold ducats if Spain invaded England. Philip, after consultation with his military advisors, decided to assemble a large fleet to attack England.

On May 9, 1588, the Spanish Armada left Lisbon. This fleet, which consisted of about 130 ships, was one of the largest ever dispatched against an enemy. Unfortunately for Spain, England could assemble a larger fleet. About 150 English ships fought the Spanish Armada in the English Channel. The English ships, which were generally smaller, faster, more maneuverable, and had greater firepower than their Spanish counterparts, carried the day. Particularly damaging to Spain was England's use of fire ships that ignited and burned Spanish vessels. England de-

stroyed about a third of the Spanish fleet. On the return voyage to Spain several more ships sank in a storm off the Irish coast. Less than seventy Spanish ships survived to return home.

The defeat of the Spanish Armada did not immediately end the Netherlands war. Fighting continued between Protestants backed by England and Spain until 1609 when Philip III (1598-1621) signed a treaty in which Spain recognized the independence of the seven northern Dutch provinces. The English victory over the Spanish Armada meant that Philip II had failed to restore Catholicism to most parts of Europe. It also marked the ascension of England as the world's foremost naval power. Spain never again seriously threatened England.

France, like England, experienced war as a result of religious differences. Luther's writings had reached France by 1518 but attracted few converts. When Calvin's *Institutes of the Christian Religion* was published in 1536, large num-

The Spanish galleon was a mainstay of the powerful Spanish Armada.

bers of French Catholics adopted the Protestant faith. These converts were called Huguenots. Calvinism appealed to them in part because Calvin was French and wrote in the French language. Most French Huguenots lived in cities such as Paris, Lyons, Meaux, and Grenoble. Despite widespread persecution, which included burning at the stake, the numbers of French Calvinists grew, reaching about 9 percent of the population by 1560.

Civil war, rooted in religion, engulfed France in 1559 and lasted for thirty-six years. The weak French monarchs, all sons of Henry II, the last strong king France produced for a generation, were unable to maintain order. Francis II, who became king in 1159 after Henry II's death, died after ruling for only seventeen months. His successor, Charles II, who ruled from 1560 to 1574, was controlled by his Mother, Catherine de' Medici. Henry III, who succeeded to the throne in 1574 and ruled to 1589 experienced psychological problems due to guilt he experienced because he was homosexual in a society that did not tolerate gay people. It was not until Henry

The English ship was narrower, with gun ports along her side, which made her clearly superior to the Spanish galleon.

IV (ruled 1589-1610) became king that peace and stability came to France.

French nobles took advantage of royal weakness. Various nobles adopted Calvinism in an attempt to intimidate Lutheran princes in Germany and use religion to declare their independence from the king. In southern France Huguenot leaders, for a time, created a semi-autonomous state. Estimates indicate that perhaps half of all French nobles adopted Calvinism at some time. Clashes between Protestant and Catholic nobles were inevitable given the weakness of the monarchy. Among the nobility the real issue was power while among the working classes it was religion. Calvinists and Catholics viewed each other as heathens. Violence erupted throughout France. Not only did Catholic and Protestant armies led by various nobles clash, but violence often occurred at daily events, such as weddings, funerals, baptisms, and worship services. Catholics attacked Protestants and Protestants attacked Catholics. Huguenot ministers often exhorted their flocks to raid Catholic churches and destroy statues and art objects that Protestants viewed as idols. Likewise, Catholic priests urged parishioners to kill the Huguenot heretics.

The most notorious act of violence in France occurred on August 24, 1572. Called the Saint Bartholomew's Day Massacre, the event occurred when Huguenot nobles gathered for a wedding uniting Margaret of Valois, sister to the Catho-

Queen Elizabeth went to St. Paul's Cathedral for a service to celebrate the defeat of the Armada dressed in elaborate garb.

lic King Charles IX, to Henry of Navarre, the foremost Protestant leader. The marriage was intended to bring reconciliation to the warring Catholic and Protestant factions in France. Catherine de' Medici, who several times in the French civil war switched sides, felt that her Huguenot allies were becoming too strong and apparently ordered attacks on Protestant leaders gathered for the wedding. On the eve of the wedding Henry of Guise had Admiral Gaspard de Coligny, a Protestant leader who had replaced Catherine de Medici as primary advisor to King Charles, attacked. This event touched off rioting and violence in Paris that killed most of the Calvinist leadership. Only Henry of Navarre escaped. Within a short time, religious violence spread from Paris to the countryside. All French Provinces were engulfed in war. From the Saint Bartholomew's Day Massacre until early October Catholics slaughtered over ten thousand Huguenots throughout France.

This bloodshed produced the War of the Three Henry's. The conflict was a civil war between factions led by Henry of Guise, a Catholic nobleman, Protestant nobleman Henry of Navarre, and King Henry III who succeeded Charles IX in 1574. For fifteen years France experienced civil conflict. Even though Henry III was Catholic, he fought against Henry of Guise because the Catholic Guise faction had formed an alliance of Catholic nobles called the Holy League whose goals were to eradicate the Huguenots as well as overthrow the monarchy.

Several events brought the War of the Three Henry's to an end. One was the defeat of the Spanish Armada. When England defeated the

Armada, Henry of Guise lost his principal backer, Philip II of Spain. Henry III then had Henry of Guise assassinated. A few months later Henry III was also assassinated. The deaths of two of the three Henry's meant Henry of Navarre, the lone survivor, could take the French throne. He ruled as King Henry IV from 1589 to 1610. Even though he was Protestant, Henry IV realized that the majority of the French people were Catholic; therefore, he converted to Roman Catholicism in 1593 so that most French citizens would accept him as king. However, he issued the Edict of Nantes in 1598, which allowed Huguenots to legally hold worship services and exist as a religious minority throughout France.

THE THIRTY YEARS WAR

The Holy Roman Empire in Germany and central Europe were not immune from religious war. Conflict between Protestants and Catholics rocked the region, killing millions from 1618 until 1648. Known as the Thirty Years War, this conflict was the bloodiest of all wars that resulted from the Reformation. Central Europe was ravaged by this conflict, and every principal monarch in Europe eventually became involved.

Problems leading to the Thirty Years' War date to the Augsburg settlement in which each German prince acquired the right to determine whether his lands would be Catholic or Protestant. Catholics became alarmed when Protestants violated the Augsburg peace by expanding into German Catholic bishoprics. Catholics were particularly concerned about the aggressive spread of Calvinism. Since the Augsburg agreement was between Lutherans and Catholics, Calvinists ignored it, converting German princes at an alarming rate. Lutherans, like Catholics, also feared the spread of Calvinism into Germany. They believed that the Augsburg peace was in danger of collapse if the advances of both Calvinists and Catholics were not halted. Compounding the problem was that Jesuit missionaries had convinced several Lutheran princes to become Catholic. Lutheran principalities responded by forming the Lutheran League in 1608; Catholics in turn created the Catholic League in 1609. The primary goal of both alliances was to stop the other from enlarging its territory.

The war began after Ferdinand of Styria, a staunch Catholic, was elected king of Bohemia in 1617. He angered Bohemian Protestants in 1618 when he abolished laws enacted by the previous ruler, Emperor Rudolf II, that in 1609 had allowed Protestants to worship freely within Bohemia. Bohemians rebelled. Since the Bohemian king was elected, the electors declared that Ferdinand had been deposed. In his place they chose Fredrick II of Palatinate, the leader of Bohemian Calvinists. Violence erupted with the occurrence of the Defenestration of Prague. Protestants, upset with Ferdinand, threw two government officers from the window of a Prague castle on May 23, 1618. Both men miraculously survived after falling approximately seventy feet to the ground. Catholics maintained that angels caught the men, gently lowering them to the earth while Protestants claimed that a deep pile of horse manure softened the fall. Regardless of what happened, the Defenestration of Prague marked the onset of the Thirty Years' War.

The conflict escalated over time. From 1618 to 1625 it was primarily fought in Bohemia. This conflict was essentially a religious civil war between Ferdinand and his Catholic allies trying to reclaim the throne from Fredrick and his Calvinists allies. In 1620 Catholics won a major victory when they defeated Fredrick's army at the Battle of White Mountain. Ferdinand, who had also been named Holy Roman Emperor, took back the Bohemian crown. He unleashed persecution on Bohemian Protestants, forcing most to become Catholic and executing those who refused. By 1630 Protestantism no longer openly existed in Bohemia.

In 1625 the war escalated. King Christian IV of Denmark (ruled 1588-1648) intervened on the Protestant side. Largely ineffective as a military commander, Christian was unable to stop advances by Ferdinand's forces. Albert von Wallenstein, the commander of Catholic forces, won numerous victories over Protestant armies. By 1627 his army had began to attack Protestant strongholds in the northern regions of the Holy Roman Empire. Catholic forces took control of Silesia, Pomerania, Jutland, and Schlesuwig. Protestants had lost so much territory in Germany by 1629 that Ferdinand issued the Restitution Edict, which ordered all property taken from Catholics since 1552 returned. The Restoration Edict alarmed Lutheran princes throughout Germany. They feared that Ferdinand and the House of Habsburg he represented would eventually subdue all of Germany. Consequently, they united against Ferdinand, forcing the Holy Roman Emperor to fire Wallenstein at an electoral diet in 1630.

Protestant fortunes began to improve in 1630 when Swedish king Gustavus Adolphus (ruled 1594-1632) brought an army to support oppressed Lutherans. The French king, Louis XIII, wanting to weaken the Habsburgs in central Europe, provided financial support for Sweden. In 1631 Adolphus decisively defeated a Habsburg army at Breitenfeld. After Adolphus was killed in a victory over Catholic forces at Lutzen in 1632 and after a Swedish army was defeated at the Battle of Nordlingen in 1634, France entered the war. Even though France was a Catholic nation, its forces supported Protestants because the French monarch wanted to sty-

mie the advance of Habsburg power. The French intervention marked the beginning of the international phase of the Thirty Years' War. Over the next fourteen years French and Swedish armies ravaged Germany. More than a third of Germany's population was killed, agriculture was virtually destroyed, and economic devastation occurred when several German princes debased their currency. The war caused an economic depression that engulfed the entire European continent, causing deflation and falling commodity prices for the first time in over a century.

The Thirty Years' War lasted so long because no ruler had the ability and resources to win a complete victory. Fortunately, the primary conflict ended in October 1648 when the Peace of Westphalia was signed. Peace was achieved when two agreements, the Treaties of Munster and Osnabruck, were signed. France and the Habsburgs agreed that German princes would be sovereign and independent. Each prince could rule his territory as he saw fit, make any law he wanted, and determine what religion his subjects would follow. The Holy Roman Empire was effectively destroyed. Germany was now controlled by over three hundred princes, which meant that centralized authority represented by the Holy Roman Empire had ended. The position of France and Sweden in the European power structure improved. France received two new territories, the provinces of Alsace and Lorraine. Sweden received territory in Pomerania, Bremen, and Verden. In addition, the independence of Protestant Holland was recognized, and France got the right to intervene in German affairs. The issue between Catholics and Protestants was settled when the Westphalia Peace expanded the Augsburg agreement of 1555 to include Calvinists as well as Lutherans and Catholics. All three religions could legally exist in central Europe. This did not mean that religious toleration was accepted. German citizens usually followed the religion of their prince. In practice, principalities in northern Germany were Protestant while those in southern Germany remained Catholic.

WOMEN AND WITCHCRAFT

The Reformation introduced new ideas regarding women, marriage, and sexuality. Whereas Catholics saw marriage as a holy sacrament that could not be dissolved once the union was completed, Protestants viewed marriage as a legal contract between two individuals. Each partner under this contractual arrangement was legally required to fulfill various marital responsibilities. Wives were expected to maintain and manage the home, engage in charitable work, help husbands with farm or business work as the need arose, bear, rear, and tend children, and provide sex for husbands on demand. Women were generally discouraged from working outside the home because outside employment would interfere with homemaking duties. A husband's responsibilities, in contrast, included providing food, shelter, and clothing for his wife and children. Men generally worked on the farm or ran the business from which he earned the family's livelihood.

Although Protestant thought, as evidenced in literature about marriage, stressed that husbands, as head of the household, should rule their families fairly and justly, many husbands behaved like tyrants. Protestant writers justified the verbal and physical abuse women suffered as punishment for sins committed by the Biblical Eve. Men, they said, were also punished because God required them to work on a daily basis, earning their family's living "by the sweat of his brow."

Like Catholics, Protestants stressed sexual fidelity within marriage. Because marriage was perceived as a contract, Protestants permitted divorce for various reasons, including adultery. Protestants also allowed ministers to marry, which lessened the problem created by priests taking female lovers. Women who had been priests's concubines could legally become their lovers' wives.

Although civil governments in both Catholic and Protestant nations licensed prostitution houses, the world's most ancient profession was frowned upon. Legally licensed prostitution establishments catered only to single males. Some protestant countries paid government employees to live in the houses to ensure that married men did not partake of their sensual pleasures. Even though prostitution was legal throughout Europe, it reflected a double standard in sexual morality for men and women. Single males were free to satisfy their sexual cravings while women, with the exception of prostitutes, were expected to refrain from sexual intercourse outside marriage.

Even though Protestant women were expected to remain virginal until marriage, Luther, Calvin, Zwingli, and other Reformation leaders believed that celibacy was not necessary to lead a religious life. Luther maintained that God delighted in sexual activity so long as it occurred as part of marriage. Words Luther wrote a friend in a letter provide evidence of his views regarding sex: "Dear lad, be not ashamed that you desire a girl, nor you my maid, the boy. Just let it lead you into matrimony and not into promiscuity, and it is no more cause for shame than eating or drinking." Nuns in former Catholic countries were encouraged to marry after their convents were abolished. Marriage, Protestant reformers believed, provided women with economic, emotional, and cultural benefits while alleviating repression of sexual desires. Still, the emphasis was upon sex within marriage. Women who expressed their sensuality too openly or who behaved differently from the norm might be accused of practicing witchcraft.

The century of the Reformation witnessed the persecution of numerous women for practicing witchcraft. A belief in witchcraft was widespread throughout Europe. Educated and non-educated people alike believed that witches were real. Most people believed the earth was the battlefield between God and the Devil. Illness, injury, bankruptcy, deaths, or any misfortune were often blamed on witchcraft. Witches were generally thought to be older women who consorted with Satan and as a result possessed mysterious powers. Occasionally, younger women and children might be accused of witchcraft. Tradition held that witches rode broomsticks to *sabbats* (meetings with the Devil and other witches). At these sabbats witches supposedly engaged in wild sexual orgies with Satan and male witches called warlocks. These sexual escapades, which people believed included lesbian sex with other witches, supposedly lasted all night. Between bouts of sex, witches were believed to dine on the flesh of human babies.

Europeans generally believed that witches were married or widowed women who desired more sex than they were having. Women older than fifty were especially prone to accusations of witchcraft largely because they possessed some of the characteristics Europeans attributed to witches—aged, wrinkled skin, limbs crippled with arthritis or other diseases, deafness, poor eyesight, malnutrition, thinning hair, and various psychological disorders. Moreover, these women might practice midwifery and folk medicine, healing sick people with roots, herbs, and other folk cures. Moreover, most women accused of witchcraft did not follow the mild, meek roles assigned women in European society. Instead, they behaved aggressively, spoke their mind, and refused to be subservient to men.

The Protestant Reformation contributed to the witch hysteria that swept across the European continent from 1560 to 1660. Protestants, especially Calvinists, feared Satan's power and the religious wars wrecked havoc across Europe, creating much insecurity. Because reformers believed witches worshipped Satan, witchcraft was considered heresy. As a result, governments and religious reformers denounced witchcraft. Anyone suspected of witchcraft was subject to horrible prosecution. Thousands of women accused of witchcraft were executed across the European continent. Authorities in several southern German principalities burned over three thousand witches. Switzerland killed even more. Although the exact number of women tried for witchcraft will likely never be known, one estimate is that over nine million throughout the world stood accused over several centuries. Between 1450 and 1700 at least nine thousand people were tried for witchcraft on the European continent. Over half were found guilty and condemned to death. England, for example, executed about one thousand witches from 1560 to 1740.

Scholars differ about the cause of the European witch hysteria after the Reformation occurred. Most likely the fear of witches and the executions resulted from a variety of factors. First, most people believed in witchcraft. They tended to blame witches for life's misfortunes and feared the power of witches. Anything that could not be readily explained was usually blamed on witchcraft. Second, Protestant ministers preached strong sermons warning congregations about the Devil's power. These sermons created fear in the minds of ordinary people. Some began to look for signs of witchcraft in neighbors. Third, Christianity stressed a repression of sexual desire. All the sexual activities attributed to witches, some scholars believe, represented the repressed urges of sexually frustrated Christians. Fourth, witchcraft provided an easy means for tight knit, local communities that stressed social and cultural conformity to rid themselves of nonconformists. Anyone who did not behave like others in the community was likely to be accused of witchcraft. Fifth, the Christian belief that women were more susceptible to the Devil's intrigues likely played a role in the witch hysteria. European Christians believed that women inherited a tradition from Eve of being deceived by Satan. In light of this belief it is no wonder that women were accused of practicing witchcraft far more often than men. Whatever the reason for the witch persecutions, they took a tremendous toll on European women. Thousands were executed as witches at various times in European history.

CONCLUSION

When Luther nailed his Ninety-five Theses to the church door in Wittenberg, Western Christianity was forever changed. All of Western Europe would never again practice the same faith. Religious unity under the Catholic Church was forever broken. Other reformers, following Luther's example, disavowed Catholic doctrines and formed numerous Protestant denominations. John Calvin was the most strident of these reformers, creating a theocracy in Geneva. Calvinist ministers fanned out across Europe preaching the gospel as they saw it. Anabaptists, the most radical of Protestant groups, gained a foothold in parts of Europe. Henry VIII created a state controlled church in England as part of the Reformation.

Suggestions for Further Reading

Roland H. Bainton, *Here I Stand: A Life of Martin Luther* (1955).

William Bangert, *A History of the Society of Jesus* (1772).

William J. Bouwsma, *John Calvin: A Sixteenth Century Portrait* (1988)

John Calvin, *On God and Political Duty*. John T. McNeil, ed. (1950).

Owen Chadwick, *The Reformation* (1964).

Patrick Collinson, *The Religion of Protestants* (1982).

Jean Delumeau, *Catholicism Between Luther and Voltaire: A New View of the Counter-Reformation* (1977).

H. J. Hillerbrand, *The Reformation in its Own Words* (1964)

Anthony Kenny, *Thomas More* (1983).

James M. Kittelson, *Luther the Reformer: The Story of the Man and His Career* (1986).

Bernd Moeller, *Imperial Cities and the Reformation* (1972).

E. A. Payne, *The Free Church Tradition in the Life of England* (1952).

Bob Scribner and Benecke, Gerhard (eds.), *The German Peasant War of 1525: New Viewpoints* (1979).

W. A. Shaw, *A History of the English Church 1640-1660.*

Max Weber, *The Protestant Ethic and the Spirit of Capitalism* (1958).

EUROPE IN THE AGE OF ABSOLUTISM

Louis XIV's Palace of Versailles estate

The King had 56 Mistresses

Henry Bourbon, also known as Henry Navarre, was a French prince with a penchant for drama and contradiction. He became the "stuff" of legends. Switching political and religious sides, his friends and enemies, as well as Henry himself, made up fantastic stories about his life.

Born to a Protestant family in 1553, Henry was the leader of the Hueguenot faction vying for power in France. He married the Catholic king's sister, and three days later the infamous St. Bartholomew's Day Massacre saw the murder of thousands of Protestants. Henry renounced his Protestant ties and became a Roman Catholic. Within a few years, he escaped the pressure of the Church and restored his beliefs in the Protestant cause. With the death of the crown prince, Henry became the heir to the throne. To gain support he returned to the Catholic faith, making his famous quotation, "Paris is well worth a mass." In 1598 he issued the famous Edict of Nantes, extending religious freedom to Christian believers in France. He had a concern for the poor and proclaimed that under his administration there would be "a chicken in every peasant's pot." This gave Henry such popularity that he frightened his opponents into believing that if Henry survived, France would join the Protestant camps of Europe. He was assassinated in 1610.

All this political and religious activity was not the center of Henry's attention. He is rumored to have had fifty-six mistresses and many illegitimate children. Legend has it that one young mistresses drowned herself when he moved on to another woman.

The most famous of Henry's ladies was Gabrielle d'Estrees. Tall, slender with golden hair, Gabrielle d'Estrees met Henry Bourbon when she was a mere 20 years old. He was instantly attracted to her. Although Henry was King of France and married to Margery of Valois, he wanted the young beauty for his own. To keep her for himself, Henry commanded that she marry an old nobleman. She accepted the deal and moved to Henry's court.

Gabrielle served Henry well. She bore him three children, two boys and a girl, all of whom Henry legitimized and gave noble titles. Excelling at other "duties," she danced and sang for the king and he rewarded her. Her first title was Marchioness of Minceaux, but soon Gabrielle had to be addressed as the Dutchess of Beaufort. She was the ruler of twelve estates.

Gabrielle traveled with Henry, and he wrote her a series of passionate love letters. Thirty-five of these are still preserved, although many believe these to be forgeries. He claimed that he couldn't stand to be away from her and praised her beauty and flawless complexion. He commented on her intelligence and her grace. Sometimes he left battles just to spend time with her.

Gabrielle divorced her husband and set her sights on the throne. Henry planned to annul his marriage to Margery and the process was begun. It was completed in 1599, but in that year Gabrielle died at the age of 26. To be the king's favorite mistress was a powerful position in the late 1500s, and Gabrielle was a strong willed woman who made the best of her situation. Henry IV mourned her death but quickly moved on to marry again and continued his attraction to many mistresses.

Chronology

1500	Ferdinand of Aragon suppresses the Moorish revolt in Granada but Moors continue to fight for the next year
1504	Venice proposes to build a canal in Suez
1509	Henry VIII becomes King of England
1512	War between Russia and Poland
1515	Francis I crowned King of France; nationalized factories in France
1517	Portuguese reach China and open trade
1520	Royal Library founded in France
1523	Portuguese thrown out of China
1525	Peace between England and France
1529	Turks sack Austria
1535	Beginning of the London Exchange
1546	English navy founded
1547	Henry VIII dies; first predictions of Nostradamus
1559	Elizabeth of England crowned queen
1560	Charles IX of France crowned; Madrid becomes the capital of Spain
1572	Dutch war for independence begins; massacre of French Protestants during siege of St. Bartholomew's Day
1574	Henry III, King of Poland, crowned King of France
1581	Russia conquers Siberia
1582	Gregorian calendar introduced in Catholic countries of Europe
1587	Mary, Queen of Scots, executed by her cousin, Elizabeth I, for treason
1588	English navy defeats the Spanish Armada
1598-1714	Age of Absolutism in France
1594	Henry IV crowned King of France, first of the Bourbon kings
1598	Edict of Nantes in France offers freedom of worship to Protestants
1603	James VI of Scotland becomes James I of England, first of the Stuart Kings
1604	England and Spain declare peace
1610	Henry IV of France assassinated
1613	Turks invade Hungary
1618	Beginning of the Thirty Years War
1621	Phillip IV becomes King of Spain
1624	England declares war with Spain; England begins colonization of India
1629	Charles I dissolves the English Parliament; it does not meet again until 1640
1642-1649	English Civil War
1643	Louis XIV becomes king of France
1648	Treaty of Westphalia ends the Thirty Years War
1649	Charles Stuart, King of England beheaded after a trial for treason
1649-1652	The Fronde revolt in France
1653	Oliver Cromwell becomes Lord Protector of England
1660	Parliament invites Charles II to return to the English Throne
1714	Death of Louis XIV
1688-1689	The Glorious Revolution in England; William and Mary become the rulers

In the seventeenth and into the eighteenth century, change pervaded European society. The Reformation and the discovery of the American continents gave some Europeans the possibilities to make choices not available to them ever before. Some left for the New World. Millions stayed in the homelands, living through the turmoils. There continued to be conflicts between Catholics and Protestants and among various branches of Protestantism. There was economic upheaval due to the many wars that were fought. Countries across Europe examined the role of the monarchy. In some cases the power of the monarch became virtually absolute. In England, Parliament resisted absolute rulers and followed the path of constitutionalism. In France, Louis XIV made himself the Sun King. Boundaries were changed across the face of Europe as a result of wars, royal marriages, and political negotiations. In central Europe, the Holy Roman Empire remained only in name and was replaced by independent states coercing many potential ethnic groups into awkward political alliances under absolute rulers. New types of government and political thought were reframing Europe.

POLITICAL THOUGHT

Absolutism

Historians have viewed absolutism the same way they have viewed constitutionalism; both are seen as key ingredients in the transition between feudal government and modern government. Constitutionalism was adopted in England where greater rights were extended to commoners than existed during the feudal era. Absolutism saw monarchs drawing power to themselves that had previously been shared between the kings and their lords. The attitude that a king's wishes should be absolute was not just a manifestation of political ego on the part of the kings; it was also a result of the religious belief system of the kings of this era. They believed that events occurred because it was part of God's specific plan, therefore, they were kings by the grace of God. They believed that if God had chosen them specifically to be king, then people who objected to their decisions, or to them personally, were essentially arguing with God's will.

There were kings in France, England, and several other places who tried to rule as absolute monarchs, though this system did not prevail in England. In early seventeenth century England, James I and Charles I viewed their monarchies in absolutist terms, but Parliament resisted their efforts to rule as dictators. The tension between Charles and Parliament led to the English Civil War, which ended with Charles' death. Building on his father's efforts, Louis XIII tried to be an absolute ruler over France, but the aristocracy there resisted his efforts. It was under his son, Louis XIV, that absolute rule was most successful.

Traditionally, some historians believed that Louis XIV was able to circumvent problems with the aristocracy by skillful manipulation. Louis XIV invited leading members of the French aristocracy to Versailles where they were distracted and seduced with spectacles and parties and close association with the king. They were given prestige, but they lost power in the transaction. They were not physically close to their lands or to the people who answered to them. Louis XIV basically transferred their power to government workers of less noble birth. This group of people owed their success and future fortune to Louis, so understandably they tended to be completely loyal to him.

This picture of French absolutism is, however, simplistic. The lords that were so easily manipulated during the reign of Louis XIV were some of the same lords who were quite contentious before and after his reign. Some of the actions that Louis XIV's supporters admired, such as his rough treatment of the Huguenots and his arrogance in his dealings with the Pope, were criticized when Cardinal Richelieu engaged in them. Ultimately Louis XIV was successful because he did not completely undermine his lords; he worked in tandem with them, despite the perceptions of some historians. There was an increase in royal officials during the reign of Louis XIV, and they usurped some of the responsibilities of the aristocracy. But, aristocrats, especially beyond the sphere of Versailles, still retained quite a bit of power. Louis knew that if he undermined the authority of the other leaders in society, then he would ultimately be undermining a great deal of his own authority. He left them near the top of the societal structure, just beneath himself. Louis XIV also benefited from not being the first to implement absolute rule. By the time Louis XIV came to power, people had been exposed to the system for years. Louis XIV was not forcing a new type of rule on the people; he was inheriting an existing one. Louis also learned from the mistakes of his father and Richelieu. His improvements were pleasing to many. This is not to imply that everyone was happy with life in France in his reign; Louis simply did a more pleasing job than his predecessors in the opinion of many of the aristocrats of his age.

Constitutionalism

"Constitutionalism" was a belief system that evolved in England that espoused the rule of law as protection for the common people, as well as the aristocracy. In England, as in every other kingdom in Europe, the aristocracy controlled

HENRY VII

the government, so the laws of the land were accommodating for the aristocrats. As early as 1498, Henry VII expressed his desire "to keep his subjects low, because riches would only make them haughty." He was correct to a degree. England experienced economic growth as production, innovation, and trade increased mostly due to the efforts of the lower classes. As more people gained economic clout, they pushed for greater legal status. Many leaders of society in England—but not the English kings in the first part of the seventeenth century—came to believe that if they wanted to protect their prosperity and if they wanted their country to run smoothly, they needed to be sympathetic to these concerns. For example, agriculture was important to the economy of England so the interests of the farmers and landlords began to be taken into account when the government was making decisions. What was good for farmers was good for England. This did not mean that everybody was in agreement with every decision made by the government. Nor did it mean that the government was sympathetic to the concerns of every demographic group in society. What this did mean was that the government was more than just a tool that existed for the sole benefit of the monarchy, or the wealthy, or a combination of the two.

During the seventeenth century, Englishmen inside and outside the government began to feel that there was a connection between the greater protections the people enjoyed and the growing wealth and power of their kingdom. This perception fueled the desire to give evolving privileges and protections for commoners a legal status by having Parliament pass laws that made these new rights a part of the English constitution. This belief that the additions to the constitution made the lives of the English better and the Kingdom of England greater was the essence of constitutionalism.

The perception that greater legal status for more people in society led to greater prosperity certainly seems like a reasonable conclusion for the English to make. In other places in Europe— with the exception of the Netherlands, which followed the same model as the English—commoners were oppressed to a much greater degree. These commoners had little incentive to offer their best to their country. Given the harsh nature of their existence, it should come as little surprise that they were less productive than the English. The life for the average English was much more pleasant than it was for their counterparts throughout Europe. The English enjoyed greater personal freedom, greater religious toleration, protections against absolute monarchy, and relative legal equality between the social classes.

FRANCE: THE BOURBONS (HENRY IV – LOUIS XV)

The year 1589 marked one of many turning points in the history of France. The House of Valois gave up its hold on the throne with the death of Henry III. King Henry, like his two brothers before him, failed to produce an heir. Henry III was succeeded by yet another brother, but this brother died in 1584. Despite the change in dynasties, the given name of the king stayed the same. Henry IV did succeed Henry III, but the ruling house was no longer the Valois; it was the House of Bourbon.

During the 1460s to the 1470s a strong central government had been formed around Louis XI. After the religious wars of the sixteenth cen-

LOUIS XI

tury weakened the Valois monarchy, power filtered down to the aristocracy and the provinces. From the end of the sixteenth century to the middle of the seventeenth century, the Bourbon kings sought to re-establish their supremacy in France. France had severe political problems due to the slow demise of the House of Valois. Virtually all of the support for making Henry IV heir to the throne after 1584 came from his fellow French Protestants, the Huguenots. For a period of about ten years (1584-1594) France was divided over who its leader should be, and this division was quite violent. There were many who felt that the French king needed to be Catholic; anyone else would be a heretic. Even among Catholics there was division. Some leaders, like Henry of Guise, favored acceptance of Catholic Spain's offer of men and money to combat the Protestants, and others—led for a time by Henry III—wanted the Catholics in France to handle the Protestants themselves. In 1589 Henry III reversed his position and decided to accept Henry IV as his heir, but this did not bring peace to France. A Catholic friar named Jacques Clément murdered Henry III for siding with the Protestants. Ironically, the friar's actions handed the throne to the Protestants.

Henry IV became king, but for his first several years on the throne his authority was only recognized by his supporters. This changed in 1594 because of his success on the battlefield against some of his enemies and the fact that he became a Catholic. Henry IV was more interested in politics than religion. He had converted back and forth between Protestantism and Catholicism several times based on political expediency. When he became a Catholic in 1594, it was the fifth time he had done so. His famous quotation, "Paris is worth a Mass," shows his practical approach for combining religion and politics. Despite the fact that Henry IV was not

the most stalwart of Catholics, he had, at least, removed the biggest objection that Catholic forces had to him. Also, it was clear that he would not persecute either religious belief.

Once he became king, Henry IV began the process of implementing absolute rule in France. Henry took more power for himself than most previous French kings, but many in France were satisfied with this arrangement. By rising above the many factions that had been causing turmoil, Henry was able to impose unity on France. Henry quickly oversaw a return of peace and greater economic vitality to France. Henry's principal minister was Sully, the Grand Master of the Artillery. Sully was specifically in charge of the production of gunpowder, but his influence in France was much broader.

Under Henry's absolutist rule, he furthered the putting of industry under the control of the government. For example, the administration of mines in France was first overseen by the House of Valois, but Henry IV extended and strengthened royal control over this industry. Henry also placed the manufacture of gunpowder under royal auspices, thus providing Sully with his access to power. Private manufacturers were forbidden from producing it. Gunpowder was made in locations all over France, and they were authorized to make the ammunition only for the Crown. Not everyone in France followed this edict, but there was a strong effort made to enforce this law. It is understandable that Henry and his successors would want to control the production of gunpowder given the years of fighting that had taken place in France. Those who were caught making illicit ammunition faced punishment up to and including death. By overseeing industries, the Crown could gain revenue, as well as subjugate any rising merchant class into obedience to its demands.

Salt production was another government monopoly. The French had to buy their salt from the Crown. A problem arose when contraband salt became popular among the people, but the House of Bourbon dealt with this issue rather creatively. In many places in France, the people were required to buy more salt than they actually needed, therefore, no one had any incentive to buy salt from unauthorized dealers.

When Henry IV took the throne, he not only had to deal with a difficult political situation, he also faced serious economic and social problems. Inflation was high, and there was a drop in agricultural production and trade. Many peasants who were struggling with financial difficulties also had to deal with the devastating effects of disease. The resultant drop in population made problems with production even worse. Due to the horrible conditions they faced and the indifference of their leaders, peasants were driven to rebellion. These rebellions, called "jacqueries," because Jacque was a common peasant name, resulted in many deaths throughout France during the last decade of the sixteenth century.

Henry was interested in more than military and economic concerns. One of his priorities was making the monarchy the main artistic patron of France. By the beginning of the seventeenth century, Henry employed 480 master craftsmen, plus their assistants and their apprentices, to engage in royal projects. Painters, sculptors, and makers of clocks and tapestries were sent to work in the gallery of the Louvre. This patronage of the arts continued throughout the seventeenth century, but Henry did not live to enjoy it. He was assassinated by Catholic partisans in 1610.

The House of Bourbon was fortunate to have two talented government ministers to help direct their policies. Cardinal Richelieu, who is portrayed as a villain in *The Three Musketeers*, and Minister of Finance Jean Baptiste Colbert served Bourbon kings. By the efforts of these two men, great improvements occurred in the administrative, financial, legal, and military institutions of France.

Armand-Jean Du Plessis De Richelieu was an ambitious man who used a career in the Catholic Church to achieve political power. His family controlled the bishopric of Lucon, and Richelieu decided to fill the position himself after neither of his brothers took the job. He managed to have himself named as the chaplain of Anne of Austria, the young bride of Louis XIII. Anne's father was the King of Spain, Philip III, but given the tensions between France and Spain, she was always referred to as Anne of Austria after her mother's native country. With the queen's ear and his closeness to the throne, Richelieu became the second most powerful man in France; only Louis XIII was greater. The Cardinal had a profound affect on France's policies, which is impressive given his limitations. Illnesses ravaged Richelieu in a multiplicity of disorders including migraines, boils, bladder infections, and hemorrhoids. In addition to his physical problems, Richelieu had a personal one: most women disliked him. What he had in ambition, he lacked in social skills. He handled his apparent discomfort with small talk by simply talking very little. This silence made most people, especially the women, uncomfortable. A lack of any female allies might have been a fatal blow to some men at the French Court, where mistresses held "bedroom powers" over their men, but not Richelieu. He had an immense ego and was quite Machiavellian, meaning he would pursue his political agenda honestly if that was convenient but he could be dishonest and even ruthless if the situation required it. Louis XIII relied on Richelieu as a government minister because

Richelieu was good at his job. Louis was not a learned man, preferring carpentry and metal forging over reading, and he had little interest in the intricacies of political statesmanship. The king could indulge in his hobbies because he had full confidence in Cardinal Richelieu's ability to get things done, and he knew the Cardinal could do them better than he could himself. Richelieu's attempt to keep a tense peace in Europe by diplomatically playing the other nations against each other worked to France's advantage. Louis' considerable respect for Richelieu's abilities should not be construed as proof that the king actually liked him. A contemporary observer recorded that when Louis XIII saw that Richelieu was on his deathbed, the King walked away in an excellent mood. Cardinal Richelieu, the second most powerful man in France for decades and the architect of France's foreign policy designed to maintain the balance of power in Europe, died in 1642.

Though Louis XIII ruled France for over thirty years (1610-1643) and was known by historians as an absolute monarch, one institution he did not have absolute control over was the army, which was not a good thing given the frequency of war in this era. It would be misleading to describe the army in France as "Louis' army." Many of the forces who did the fighting were really under the control of various members of the aristocracy. By tradition the French king usually cast the deciding vote when it came to engaging in military action, but he did not have direct control over most of the troops. Perhaps this lack of absolute control over the French army is the reason that it resembled the worst of mercenary bands from the Middle Ages. The soldiers were capable of fighting hard but were poorly paid and poorly fed; often they lived off the land, taking what they needed when it was not supplied. Occasionally, harsh

discipline was imposed, and soldiers who were out of control were executed. But, for the most part soldiers did as they pleased between battles. Marauding bands of soldiers were as much a tradition on the French land as were the king's army. These groups were a menace to the local population and sometimes a threat to their own officers. When the army was called to duty, it was important to get them organized and moved out of the metropolitan area as quickly as possible, lest they begin to steal, rape, and brutalize their fellow citizens. For as much control as Louis XIII exerted on the civilian population during his reign, he was unable to deal successfully with the army. This situation remained an issue that was not handled until Louis XIV took power.

Louis XIV officially took the throne in 1643 at the age of four. The mother of Louis XIV, Anne of Austria, was the regent until 1661 when Louis took charge. From 1643 to 1661, the real power in France was held by the prime minister, Jules Mazarin. Louis XIV was not able to actually direct the affairs of France until Mazarin's death in 1661. When he took control, Louis was determined to rule alone. He demanded total obedience to his wishes and built a legend that called him the Sun King, where everything in court revolved around him. He moved the center of power from Paris to Versailles. The move was an emotional one for him, as he hated the Parisians. The city had turned on Louis, Anne and Mazarin when the citizens had revolted during the Fronde (which means "sling" and is associated with rioters throwing stones against Mazarin's windows). The three had to escape and went to an old hunting lodge that Louis now turned into an extravagant and beautiful palace.

Louis XIV recognized the problems that existed in his army, and he attempted to deal with them aggressively. One solution included

LOUIS XIV

genius, but in his arrogance he believed that he was. He believed he could direct France's campaigns but stay safely behind in the comfort of his palace at Versailles. Louis's ignorance was perpetuated by generals who did not want him on the front lines. They appealed to his vanity and praised his efforts, and he believed he was as brilliant at war strategy as they told him he was.

It was partially due to the character flaws of people like Louis XIV and Jean Baptiste Colbert that absolutism was a double-edged sword for France. The strength of the government allowed intelligent, industrious men like Louis XIV and Colbert to have the opportunity to lead France in a dynamic way. The downside was that there were no checks or balances in the system when Louis casually destroyed people's lives. Louis himself was the only check on Colbert's authority, so when the king was indifferent, Colbert was free to corrupt court cases that impacted him and to use his governmental powers to make himself rich. Another flaw of absolutism was that when Colbert died and when Louis's performance declined as the monarch aged, the kingdom's policies were left adrift.

Louis XIV died in 1714 at the age of 75, succeeded by his 5-year-old great grandson. No one in the court could offer strong leadership, and, for the most part, the aristocracy was effectively cut off. Also, the absolutist rule in France was so strong that individual initiative in the realm had been discouraged. For example, France was slower than England in allowing its citizens to own private property in the New World. English citizens flocked to the New World for a chance at a better life. Because the same opportunity was not available for the French, there was less interest in taking the dangerous journey. This put the French at a numerical disadvantage to the English when trouble between the two began in the New

keeping a cadre of officers in reserve between wars. These men were chosen based on merit and loyalty to the king. Also, an improved system for training young officers was put in place. Previously, men received what simply amounted to on the job training. As a result of Louis' changes, the army had a corps of officers who were more loyal to their king and more professional in their own behavior and in their oversight of troops. Under Louis XIV, France became the greatest military power Europe had ever known. This was because of Louis XIV and his efforts with the army. The seventeenth century is known to French historians as the *Grand Siécle* (Splendid Century). Despite the improvements made by Louis, the French army still had a major flaw. Louis XIV was no military

The Hall of Mirrors was a banquet and reception room in the Palace of Versailles. Floor-to-ceiling stacks of mirrors lined the hall's east side. Louis XIV busied the nobility with social activities to keep them under his control.

World. Thanks to the micromanagement of the Finance Ministry, an entrepreneurial spirit was lacking in France. No new enterprises could be started without royal permission and support. Creativity was stifled as a result. Another problem was that the most influential officials under the House of Bourbon, like Sully and Richelieu, were not interested in supporting labor saving or more fuel-efficient devices. These men were more interested in artistic quality than in functionality. Some historians have suggested that for these reasons the Industrial Revolution that took place in England a century later was not rivaled in France. When the Industrial Revolution spread to France, for the most part, the French were simply imitating what the English had initiated.

THE HABSBURGS

The House of Habsburg has worn the crowns of many kingdoms throughout Europe. A partial list of locations includes Austria, Bohemia (today known as the Czech Republic), Hungary, and other places that made up the Holy Roman Empire, the Netherlands and Spain. Members of the Habsburg family ruled over Spain from 1516 to 1700.

Spain

Past historians have referred to the Habsburg Philip II, who ruled Spain from 1556 to 1598, as an absolutist monarch, but this assessment is misleading. In Madrid, the capital of Spain since

The Palace of Versailles was a symbol of King Louis's status. It contained extravagant gardens, hunting grounds, and stables large enough to house two thousand horses.

1561, Philip had an impressive amount of control over the government. Philip's unbridled power, however, was more the exception than the rule. In many other places in the Habsburg Empire—Italy, the Netherlands, Portugal, and the part of Spain known as Aragon—there were laws that severely limited the power of the monarch.

Another misconception is that Spain was experiencing an unusually steep economic decline by the end of the sixteenth century. Evidence indicates that economic growth was taking place though some of the leading cities in the Spanish province of Castille—specifically Madrid and Seville—were in decline. The economic troubles Spain had at the end of the sixteenth and beginning of the seventeenth century were common throughout Europe.

Philip's foreign policy included interest in the religious and political chaos in France. Many in Spain hoped the demise of the Valois dynasty might bring France under Spanish control. Fighting took place between the two countries, but Spain's efforts lost momentum when Henry IV of France converted to Catholicism. Spain had lost a key issue in motivating its own people, as well as in dividing the French. The Treaty of Vervins officially ended the Franco-Spanish War in 1598, just a few months before the death of Philip II.

As was the case with Spain's relationship with France, the Dutch and the English were bigger problems than Philip II had anticipated. He decided to send a massive fleet of ships, known to posterity as the Spanish Armada, to deal with both problems in 1588. Philip thought that the Armada would hit England first and crush the English navy. Across England, Catholics would then rise up against their Protestant, female monarch, Elizabeth I, after this humiliating defeat. The Spanish Armada would then proceed to the Netherlands where it would destroy the Dutch navy and break Protestant control of that country. Philip's plan went awry when the smaller but more maneuverable English fleet defeated his Armada of 130 ships. Not only did Philip suffer the loss of men and ships, but the Protestants and the French were emboldened to challenge Spain's domination of the New World. Spain no longer looked invincible. When Philip III became the King of Spain in 1598, he continued his predecessor's foreign policy against the English and the Dutch into the new century. Unfortunately for Philip III, England and the Netherlands were rising powers, and Spain's wars were draining its treasury. For years, Spain had funded its treasury and its wars by resources bled from America. These resources were, at best, a mixed blessing for Spain. Gold and silver taken from America allowed Spain to prolong wars that it eventually lost, so essentially all that was gained was more dead Spaniards and greater acrimony from other countries. As the seventeenth century unfolded, the Spanish had to face the fact that the balance of power in the world was changing.

The reign of Philip III was overall an unsuccessful one. He did insure peace with France by marrying his daughter Anne to Louis XIII, and he also came to accept the fact that Castille was faced with severe economic problems. Philip tried to address the problems of an empty treasury, heavy taxes, and population shortages, but it was too late in his reign for him to make any headway. Philip III lacked both the intellect and the leadership to slow down the decline of his realm, much less reverse the trend. He died in 1621 and was succeeded by his son Philip IV.

Philip IV was smarter and more cultivated than his father but was not the most scrupulous ruler. Perhaps the new king's lack of character stemmed from the way royalty was treated in this era. For example, Philip's younger brother, Ferdinand, became a cardinal in the Catholic Church at the age of ten. Cardinals have the authority to cast a vote in choosing the Pope. Surely a 10-year-old boy would do as he was told. Given that conventional rules of wisdom and personal and social boundaries did not always apply to royalty, it should come as no surprise that they often behaved as self-absorbed individuals. They had been taught that they were above ordinary mortals and that conventional rules and restrictions did not apply to them.

Philip IV ruled until 1665. His administration, like that of his predecessors, was marked by wars with the French and the Dutch. One of the more significant events during his reign was Portugal's independence. Portugal had been taken over by Spain in 1580, but in 1640 Portugal successfully revolted against Spanish rule. Portugal had not been ruled by Spain long enough for the Portuguese to truly feel like they were a part of Spain, thus it was easy to rally the Portuguese around the idea of a rebellion. Portugal was also aided by French resources because France, looking toward being the major power on the continent, was interested in weakening its southern neighbor.

The Treaty of the Pyrenees in 1659 was another significant event. This treaty once again brought peace to France and Spain, but it also signified the last gasp of the Spanish dream of dominating Europe. Spain had made peace with the Dutch in 1648, and the Spanish Habsburgs had severed ties with the Austrian Habsburgs. Philip IV tried to draw some consolation from the wreckage of his foreign policy. He hoped that he could turn all of his resources against Portugal and regain control. Even this project was doomed to failure.

When Philip IV died in 1665, Charles II, the last of the Habsburgs to rule Spain, succeeded him and ruled until 1700. Spain's problems grew worse as 1700 approached. Charles had no children, and Louis XIV started a war to claim the throne for one of his heirs. Louis agreed to peace when it looked like diplomacy might bring him what he wanted, and his grandson took the throne of Spain as Philip V. Louis went to war again in 1702. England, the Holy Roman Empire, and other countries declared war on France and Spain. Fear of an eventual unification of the French and Spanish crowns would have hopelessly upset the balance of power in Europe. The war, known as the "War of the Spanish Succession" (except in England where it was called Queen Anne's War), dragged on until 1713 when Spain and France gave in to the demands of their enemies. In the Treaty of Utrecht, Philip V had to agree not to become King of France, and England was given Gibraltar, thus gaining control of the entrance to the Mediterranean Sea.

Austria

The Habsburg Rudolf II ruled the Holy Roman Empire from 1576 to 1612. Generally, the Habsburgs used Vienna, the modern day capital of Austria, as their imperial capital, but Rudulf was the exception to the rule. He moved the court temporarily to Prague in Bohemia. Like the rest of the Habsburg rulers, Rudolf was a committed Catholic. Unlike many leaders of the Catholic Church in this era, however, Rudolf was not antagonistic toward science. Rudolf patronized scientists like astronomer Johann Kepler.

Rudolf II had to struggle with the same problems that many other Austrian Habsburgs faced in the seventeenth century. France was hostile towards the Holy Roman Empire. The French feared the size and strength of the empire, so the French always sought to support and exploit any divisions that developed. The continued struggles over religion gave the French plenty of opportunities to cause the Habsburgs trouble. There were divisions between Christians that threatened stability in many places in Europe, but the Austrian Habsburgs' religious turmoil went beyond that. The Ottoman Turks were a major presence in the Balkans, and they also held territory in Hungary. It would be a difficult task for even a great leader to simultaneouly control the French to the west and the Turks to the east, and none of the Habsburgs were considered great leaders.

A series of inconsequential men ruled in the years after Rudolf, as the Holy Roman Empire experienced a series of events that led up to the Thirty Years' Wars. Setting aside the religious consequences of the war, the political ramifications for the Holy Roman Empire were staggering. The German states were essentially granted sovereignty by the Peace of Westphalia that ended the war in 1648. Even though the Holy Roman Empire was not officially destroyed until Napoleon's attacks in 1806, for all practical purposes it ceased to exist in 1648. What was left for the Habsburgs—Austria, Bohemia, Hungary, portions of Romania—would eventually become the Austrian Empire.

The Thirty Years' War, along with frequent wars with the Turks and an increase of trade between Western Europe, America, and Asia, impacted the economic and cultural development of Eastern Europe. In Western Europe the increase in trade and the growth of capitalism led to an increasingly strong merchant class. Peasants gained wealth, and wealth led to increased political power. This was more the case in England, but to a lesser degree these developments were mirrored elsewhere in Western Europe. Eastern Europe did not have such wide trade opportunities, so the peasant class did not gain the same kind of political power. Eastern Europe remained feudal to a greater degree and for a longer time than Western Europe.

The last Austrian Habsburg of the seventeenth century was Leopold I, who ruled from 1657 to 1705. Leopold was, like many of his contemporaries, an unpleasant ruler and a firm believer in absolute monarchy, harsh with his enemies and rather cold with his allies. Despite his unpleasantness Leopold was noteworthy for the length of time he held the throne and for his military success. Leopold did not conquer any new territory, but he saved the empire from a brush with catastrophe. In 1683, the Ottoman Turks fought their way to Vienna and laid siege to the capital. Leopold and his men held out against them until reinforcements arrived.

The seventeenth century saw the Habsburgs lose effective control over their German territories, but thanks to the efforts of people like Leopold, they maintained control over large areas in Eastern Europe. Through strong and intelligent rulers, they built a foundation for a monarchical structure that continued to maintain the family's control for another 300 years.

THE HOHENZOLLERN'S OF PRUSSIA

Prussia was a province of the Holy Roman Empire that evolved into an independent kingdom. Fact and legend have been used to relate different histories for the evolution of the kingdom, but the relevant story begins with Electoral Prince Johann Sigismund at the beginning of the seventeenth century. At this time, Prussia, led by Sigismund, began to expand to the east and the west, acquiring territories in both directions. In 1613 the House of Hohenzollern converted from Lutheranism to Calvinism, but most subjects remained loyal to Lutheranism. This tension led the Hohenzollerns to become absolute rulers, since they did not feel they could share power with men who opposed their religion. Though absolute rule is not generally associated with greater freedom for the

masses, that was precisely the case in Prussia where Christianity was concerned. The Hohenzollerns did not believe they could impose their minority religious views on their people, so they opted for greater religious tolerance than was the case in most other European kingdoms.

Frederick William inherited an impoverished Prussia from his father, George William, in 1640, but Frederick William was able to lead the province to prosperity. He was an attentive and morally courageous leader who maintained the fighting tradition of the soldiers of Brandenburg. Frederick William was not only interested in military prowess. For example, he once seized a rare opportunity to quickly increase the population and thus the profitability of his land. When Louis XIV revoked the Edict of Nantes in 1685, it meant that the religious freedom that had been promised to Protestants in France was lost. In response to this, Frederick William, known as the Great Elector, issued an edict of his own, the Edict of Potsdam. The Prussian edict invited French Protestants, known as Huguenots, to come to Prussia and worship freely. Prussia saw an influx of people from all walks of life: military officers, shop keepers, and farmers. The people benefited from the Prussian government's policy of religious tolerance, and the government benefited from the new settlers and the wealth they generated.

The Great Elector died in 1688, and was succeeded by his son, Frederick I. Frederick I pursued an active foreign policy unmatched by any other Prussian leader. He sent troops to help William of Orange's invasion of England that led to the Glorious Revolution. Frederick also got involved militarily in the War of the Spanish Succession, and he fought in Italy and against the Turks. Because of his many successes on the battlefield and his strong work ethic, Frederick, like his father before him, was one of the most popular rulers of Prussia. In 1701 Frederick successfully ended eight years of maneuvers aimed at gaining the consent of the Holy Roman Emperor to Frederick being crowned as King of Prussia. Prussia was at the height of its glory.

RUSSIA

When Ivan the Terrible's long reign ended in 1584, he was succeeded by his son Theodore, who ruled until 1598. It was a good transition for Russia. Ivan was an overbearing psychopath, whereas his son was a timid, pious man. Theodore was somewhat lacking both physically and mentally; he was content to follow whatever course of action his advisors thought most reasonable. Fortunately for Russia these advisors, particularly Boris Godunov, were generally competent. Godunov and the Patriarch of Constantinople orchestrated one of the most significant events of Theodore's reign. The Patriarch of Constantinople was the head of the Eastern Orthodox Church but not equivalent in power to the Pope. Originally there were five patriarchs in five leading cities who were virtually equal in authority, but the one in Constantinople was considered more significant to most Eastern Europeans because he was in the capital city of what was the Byzantine Empire. In 1589 the Patriarch of Constantinople agreed to elevate the head of the Russian branch of the Eastern Orthodox Church to the rank of patriarch. This was a proud moment for Orthodox believers in Russia, particularly the devout Czar Theodore. Also, it provided more leadership for Russia, which was needed in the "Time of Troubles," which was shortly ahead.

Difficulties were on the horizon in Czar Theodore's lifetime because of concerns over succession. In 1591, nine-year-old Dmitrii of Uglich, brother of the czar, was the only other male member of Russia's ruling family. Dmitrii was found with his throat slit, and the people of Uglich were so outraged they rioted. They believed that Dmitrii's guardians murdered the child because one of the guardians, Boris Godunov, wanted to be czar himself. Historians have generally agreed with this theory, despite the findings of the official investigation. Prince Basil Shuisky, who headed the investigation, concluded that Dmitrii had been playing with a knife and accidentally killed himself during an epileptic seizure.

Some evidence supports Shuisky's findings. First, Dmitrii's claim as heir to the Russian throne was dubious. Dmitrii was the son of Ivan the Terrible's seventh wife, but according to the Eastern Orthodox religion, only three wives are valid, so Dmitrii would not necessarily have been seen as a legitimate heir. Furthermore, Czar Theodore was still in his thirties, so he could have been expected to have sons of his own. Also, if Godunov had been behind the death, he was clever enough to have not aroused suspicion. Whatever the explanation, the death of Prince Dmitrii is "one of the most famous detective stories in Russian history," according to one Russian historian.

Whether Godunov was responsible for the death of Theodore's half-brother, he had worked aggressively for years to put himself in a position to take control of Russia after Theodore's death. Godunov's sister, Irene, was married to Theodore, and Godunov had acquired a great deal of power and wealth. He had obtained from the pliable Theodore the power to conduct foreign relations on behalf of Russia, and Godunov had set up his own court. Foreign officials were expected to present themselves to Godunov's court after presenting themselves to the czar. Godunov was virtually the *de facto* co-czar of Russia. Godunov became regent, much to the frustration of Prince Basil Shuisky and other rivals. Politics were such that Shuisky repudiated his own findings regarding Dmitrii's murder in an attack on Godunov's credibility. Godunov, however, was able to weather this storm from his opponents.

Entering the seventeenth century, Russia's leadership experienced unusual circumstances, which caused serious problems. As a result, the early years of the seventeenth century are known as the "Time of Troubles." Upon Theodore's death, official authority transferred briefly to Czarina Irene. But, even with Godunov as regent, Russians were not ready to follow a woman. Since no male was qualified by blood, Godunov was the logical choice. The aristocracy elected Godunov as czar, and Russia's future looked promising. Godunov tried to curb corruption in the judiciary and foster education—among other things he arranged for some young Russians to study in Western Europe. Despite his years of experience and talent, his problems began to mount. His health deteriorated, and he worried over the level of support he had from the people, given his lack of imperial blood, and the lingering questions about Dmitrii's death remained.

Exacerbating Godunov's concerns, Russian harvests from 1601 to 1603 were poor. Millions faced starvation. As the price of grain rose higher than people could pay, some were reduced to eating grass and bark. The imperial government decided to help the locals by passing out food in Moscow, but this made the problem even worse as thousands of people flocked to Moscow. In desperation, many serfs and slaves joined gangs of bandits who offered them an alternative to starving. They would prey upon anybody in better circumstances.

Godunov's problems with lawlessness escalated. More than one individual tried to provoke civil war. Two different men claimed to be Dmitrii, the murdered child prince. Both pretenders claimed that through a case of mistaken identity they had survived the assassination attempt. The pretenders relied heavily upon Polish military and financial assistance and the support of discontented Russians. The First False Dmitrii took over Russia in 1605, shortly after the death of Godunov. This Dmitrii was so unpopular with the people, aristocrats and serfs alike, that he was killed by an angry mob in 1606. After they beat him to death, his body was burned, and, then, his ashes were shot from a cannon. Next, there was a struggle for the throne between one of the instigators in the First False Dmitrii's death and others who wanted power, including the Second False Dmitrii.

This contest and the Time of Troubles ended when the first Romanov czar, Michael, took the throne in 1613 upon his election by the leaders of Russia, who had grown weary of the fighting. Michael ruled independently for six years before his father was freed from Polish captivity. His father, Philaret, was promptly made the Patriarch, the head of the Russian Orthodox Church. In reality, Philaret's personality was as strong as his son's was passive, and Philaret became the most powerful man in Russia until his death in 1633. Michael continued to rule until 1645, and when he was not following his father's lead, he was usually content to follow the suggestions of his imperial advisors as Theodore had been. Michael's son, Alexis, ruled from 1645 to 1676, and Alexis seemed to possess his grandfather's courage and decisiveness. These qualities were needed in a Russia wracked by warfare and internal instability. Six more years of inconsequential weak rulers were followed by a regent named Sophia, who ruled from 1682 to 1689. She provided Russia with strong rule and was well educated for a woman of her era. She was noteworthy for supporting the arts and instrumental in creating a treaty with the Polish-Lithuanian Commonwealth in 1686. One goal she failed to achieve was placing the imperial crown on her own head. Despite the fact that she is not well known today, Sophia is one of the two most significant female rulers Russia has ever had. (The other is Catherine the Great, who was crowned and took the throne after Peter I.)

Peter I, also referred to as Peter the Great, ruled as Czar of Russia from 1689 to 1725. For many reasons Peter deserves the title "Great." His foreign policy was bold, and he was courageous when threatened. He was also an imposing figure at almost seven feet tall. In an era when rulers rarely left home, he toured Western Europe because he wanted to learn from the West and modernize his country. He built up his army and navy and was humble enough to rely heavily upon Western European military officers for leadership. Peter founded an Academy of Sciences. Even though the academy did not open until after his death in 1725, and had to rely on the Holy Roman Empire for professors and students, it became a significant place of learning. Peter tried in vain to improve the bureaucracy in his country by changing the administrative infrastructure and increasing the education of the government officials.

Although Peter the Great was admirable in many ways, he was a flawed man, and Russia was the worse for his reign. His plans to modernize Russia, particularly his efforts to strengthen his military forces, led to heavy taxation of the people. Peter tried to take a census so he would know how much money to expect from a given region, but a combination of incompetence, corruption, and non-cooperation made the census unreliable. Without solid information, taxes were imposed arbitrarily.

Some regions simply did not have the assets that were demanded of them. In exasperation, Peter put units of the military in charge of collecting money that was supposed to go to the army. In an effort to collect their quota, the army mistreated the people they were supposed to protect.

Not only was the tax burden heavy, but Peter had to force men to support his policies in other ways. The czar conscripted men into the military. Peter wanted to enlarge his forces, and volunteerism was lacking. The military had a bad reputation in some places because of their methods of tax collection, and enlisted men received fewer benefits than the government promised them, so there was little enthusiasm for a career in the military. Peter also had to force young men to enter his schools. Young men were drafted for school the same way older men were drafted for the army and navy. Obviously, this was a less than ideal situation, but Peter was convinced that the majority of Russians were a lazy, backward people and the only way to lift Russia up to the level of the Western powers was to force his countrymen to act accordingly.

Peter had other flaws. He was not simply indifferent to the Russian Orthodox Church but hostile to it. Privately, he mocked its rituals; publicly, he made it subservient to his government. When the Patriarch died in 1700, Peter neglected to appoint a successor. He eventually set up a government agency, called the Holy Synod, to dominate the affairs of the Church. He limited the number of people who could enter religious orders (monasteries and convents) and mandated that those already there had to be given heavier responsibilities in caring for the general welfare. Where he felt that parishes had too many clergymen, Peter sent some of them off to the army. Internal security was another concern of Peter's. He laid the groundwork for Russia's secret police by creating a network of informants. Torture was used to extract confessions from enemies of the state, and sometimes Peter was personally involved. Perhaps the most shocking victim of this policy was his son, Alexis. The young man was charged with sedition and tortured so brutally he died. Some historians believe that Peter participated in at least a portion of the torture. Given these dark aspects of Peter's rule, one might be cautious in labeling his rule as "Great." Nevertheless, Russia was a stronger country in several ways and more open to change after his reign.

ENGLAND 1603-1715

The death of Queen Elizabeth I in 1603 marked a time of transition for England from the Tudor line of monarchs to the Stuart line. Because Elizabeth was unmarried, she had no legitimate heir to succeed her. The closest relation to the throne was the son of Mary, Queen of Scots. Mary was Elizabeth's cousin and the mother of King James of Scotland. He was the sixth Stuart to sit on the throne of Scotland, but he became England's first king named James. His ascendance to a second throne was somewhat unusual in European politics but it was not unheard of. In the previous century, Charles V was the King of Spain as well as the Holy Roman Emperor.

By controlling two separate thrones at the same time, James was doing something extremely difficult in an age of slow transportation and communication. In theory James had plenty of monarchical experience by the time he took the English throne in 1603. He had been crowned King of Scotland in 1567, but this was somewhat misleading since he was an infant at the time. He did not get out from under the control of various advisors until he was about eighteen.

One asset that James possessed was an outstanding education. As a child he was taught Greek, Latin, and French in addition to English, and he had a library of over 6000 books. No contemporary king was as well educated. Despite his education and experience, James struggled with the demands of being king. Once James took over in England, he never visited Scotland again. He stayed involved in Scottish affairs but not in a way that was pleasing to most Scots. He tried various ways of forcing the Presbyterian Church in Scotland to amend its practices and become more like the Church of England, and he tried to strengthen his control over the Highland Clans. James won few admirers over the years. The Scots felt alternately ignored and harassed.

There were some noteworthy events that occurred in the reign of James I. The publication of the King James Authorized Version of the Bible occurred after the king commissioned this vernacular translation early in his rule. Another significant event was the founding of the first successful English colony in the New World at Jamestown, Virginia in 1607.

Charles I, the second son of James I, succeeded his father to the thrones of England and Scotland after the death of James I in 1625. Charles had been overshadowed by his older brother, Henry, who was brilliant and charismatic and first in line for the throne. When Henry died from typhoid in 1612, Charles became the heir apparent. Unfortunately for England and Scotland, Charles did not possess the charisma of his older brother; Charles was cursed with the personality of his father. James and Charles both perceived themselves as absolute rulers. Like James, Charles believed that he had been placed on the throne by the grace of God, not the consent of men. It is

Elizabeth wrote to Mary, Queen of Scots, shortly before she signed her death warrant on February 1, 1587, "You have planned in divers ways and manners to take my life and to ruin my kingdom."

understandable that the Stuart kings had little interest in Parliament or consensus building when it came to the implementation of policies. James had gone so far as to write in his work, *Basilikon Doron,* that the king was very much like God when it came to ruling over the people. In 1629, Charles acted on his father's theory and suspended England's Parliament. He proceeded to rule without it for eleven years. He also dissolved Scotland's General Assembly.

Because Charles saw his political authority established by his religion, he felt that religious unity was paramount. Like his father he tried to force reforms on Scottish Presbyterians to bring them more in line with the Church of England. His desire for greater ceremony and formality was perceived erroneously by his subjects as a scheme to reintroduce Catholicism to Scotland. Regardless of the reforms themselves, his heavy-handed tactics likely would have bred resentment anyway.

Scotland became unified in its opposition to Charles' policies, though many of the most militant Scots did not blame Charles personally. They believed he was simply the victim of bad advice, which was ironic, given Charles' lack of interest in listening to others. Scotland fielded an army, Covenanters, to fight for their religious and political rights, so named because of a document, the National Covenant, asserting Scottish rights.

When Charles was unable to defeat the Covenanters with the meager army he was able to outfit, he was forced to reconvene Parliament to get additional revenues. After years of suffering under Charles' autocratic rule, Parliament was more concerned about dealing with him than they were the Scots. The term "Long Parliament" is applied to Parliament in this era because it stayed in session for eleven years. The Members of Parliament used the desperation of Charles I to wring concessions out of him that strengthened Parliament and placed limits on the king's power. Despite the changes, many members of Parliament still did not trust the king. They did not provide him with money for the large army he had been demanding, and they were uncomfortable with the forces he already had at his disposal.

Charles' need for a great army became even stronger when a rebellion took place in Ireland in 1641, but Parliament still refused to provide the troublesome Charles with money. Charles and his spokesmen urged Parliament to enable the king to help English settlers in Ireland, but the royal cause was hurt when one of the king's men suggested they could defuse the situation by granting Irish Catholics freedom of religion. This would have perhaps been a reasonable policy, but it once again made people wonder if Charles was secretly plotting to endorse Catholicism everywhere in his realm.

Parliament went so far as to ally itself with Scotland by promising to adopt Scottish religious practices in exchange for Scottish support against the king. Parliament did not follow through on its promise of religious change, but it did get the support it needed to start the English Civil War.

Forces loyal to Charles I in the English Civil War were labeled "Cavaliers" by their opponents. This was derived from the name for Spanish soldiers, "caballero." The Catholic caballeros were seen as the oppressors of Protestants in Spain. The Cavaliers called the forces of Parliament "Roundheads," as an insult directed at the shortly cut hair many of them favored. But these names were generalizations. Some of the members of Parliament dressed in a "cavalier" fashion, and other members of Parliament who were Puritans believed that wearing their hair long was a more appropriate look for a true servant of God.

The politics of the English Civil War included some surprising developments. Charles eventually lost, but lasted for several years because he enlisted the Irish to fight for his cause. The people that Charles wanted to suppress politically ended up coming to his assistance because they agreed with his Catholic religious ideals. Charles was even able to gain the support of some of the Scots, despite the treatment they had received from him and his father. The king's enemies were reluctant to pursue their course of action. During the six years of actual fighting, Parliament offered to compromise with Charles on nine separate occasions.

Charles I was tried by Parliament for treason. Actually, the king was not on trial, but rather the man, Charles Stuart. Tradition held that only God could judge the monarch, so the few remaining Parliamentarians who demanded that the ruler be held accountable retreated into a semantic loophole. Charles refused to testify, holding fast to the tradition that he was above human law. He was executed in 1649, and monarchs from around Europe were outraged at the audacity of the English. These monarchs felt that the English were rebelling against God's will and the natural order of things, though after

Charles I receives a comforting word from the clergy before his execution.

awhile these rulers established normal relations with the new leadership in England.

The *de facto* leader of England was Oliver Cromwell. Technically, Parliament ruled, but in reality Cromwell led the army, so Cromwell had as much control as he chose to exercise. Cromwell ordered that members of Parliament who did not share his outlook lose their seats. The remaining members formed what was known as the "Rump Parliament." The Rump Parliament dissolved the House of Lords, which was composed of members of the aristocracy. By taking power away from the monarchy and the aristocracy, the Rump Parliament and Cromwell turned England into a commonwealth.

Cromwell gave Parliament three assignments: overhaul the legal system, encourage godliness, and frame a new constitution. By 1653, Cromwell was convinced that the Rump Parliament was not equal to their tasks, so he told them God was done using them. He dissolved this body and called for an election of a new Parliament that would create a constitution, then abolish itself. This Parliament was unsuccessful and gave up. Cromwell and his advisors then created a new type of government with a smaller version of Parliament and a Council of State to advise the chief executive. Cromwell headed the new government, and his title was "Protector for life."

The Commonwealth officially became the Protectorate.

The Protectorate of England was unified with Scotland under Cromwell, who was a more fair-minded ruler than he had to be, given the fact that his authority was backed up by military strength and not the consent of the people. Scots were given seats in the English Parliament, and seven commissioners were selected to oversee legal affairs in Scotland. Four of the commissioners were English and three were Scottish. New sheriffs were appointed for every county in Scotland. The administration of Scotland was more fair and efficient than it had been in centuries, but the tax burden on the Scots was increased greatly. Cromwell allowed an early, limited form of freedom of religion in his realm. Local parishes were allowed to pick the type of minister they wanted. They did not have a government-appointed Anglican minister thrust upon them; there was, however, pressure to reform the Anglican Church toward more Calvinistic ideas.

Cromwell died in 1658 and was succeeded as Protector by his son, Richard, who was neither the political nor military leader his father had been. Some military officers were upset by the lack of piety among their comrades and pressured Richard Cromwell to appoint only godly men as officers. The army leaders also wanted more political power. Cromwell also faced one of the same problems that plagued James I and Charles I; England had serious financial difficulties. An expensive war with the Dutch created a particularly heavy monetary burden on the English. Richard Cromwell did not know how to solve England's problems, so he agreed to resign in 1659.

"The Restoration" occurred in 1660 when England returned to a monarchical system. The leaders of the Restoration were an English general

In 1653, Cromwell, backed by the army, expelled the rest of Parliament and ruled as a dictator with the title of Protector of the Commonwealth of England.

named George Monck, a key supporter of the Protectorate, and Sir Ewen of Lochiel, Scotland. They successfully installed Charles II, son of Charles I, on the thrones and reinstated a Parliament that included a House of Lords. Not all the forces behind the Restoration were pro-monarchy. Some wanted to put Charles II on the throne because they felt they could dominate him. They believed they would have more long-term control over a weak king than a dictator like the Cromwells had been.

Charles II tried to learn from his father's mistakes. He tried to be more engaging on an interpersonal level than his father and was more willing to compromise on political issues than his father had been. Despite the improved caliber of the man who wore the two crowns of England and Scotland, relations with the English Parliament were not appreciably better. Religion was a major area of contention. Charles I was insistent upon trying to force a more formalized and ritualistic type of Christianity on all people under his authority. Charles II demonstrated a different attitude. In 1672 he issued a Declaration of Indulgence, which suspended laws against a religious minority. Anglicans, Puritans, and Catholics were free to worship without fear of persecution. The Declaration did not allow total freedom of religion—Catholics could only worship in private homes. Charles II's public position was that he was simply exercising his duly established rights as head of the Church of England and was trying to treat his people in a benevolent manner. Politically, he hoped to prosper by gaining the support of all Christians in his realm, even those with minority views. Members of Parliament, however, saw something darker in his actions. They believed it was part of a larger plan to subjugate their country to the Catholic Church, and this was something they were adamantly against. Opposition to the expansion of Catholicism in their country was both religious and political. Staunch Protestants were united in their intense dislike of what they perceived as the corrupted religion of the Catholics. The political concern of many people was that the Catholic kings of France were absolute monarchs, and the Catholic kings of Spain tried to rule in the same way. A series of popes had approved of this type of leadership for the logical reason that a Catholic who ruled absolutely was better able to root out Protestantism in his kingdom and keep the peace. The result was that Parliament equated a Catholic monarch with absolute rule, and they wanted no part of it.

Charles' father and grandfather had both been accused of being Catholics because they preferred a more formal style of worship than the Church of England. Charles II was personally interested in Catholicism, plus he welcomed Catholics to his court and sought warm relations with the Catholic Louis XIV. Much to Charles' chagrin, Parliament passed a law that anyone wanting to serve in a public office or make use of the court system had to participate in Anglican religious practices and publicly repudiate Catholic doctrine. Charles tried to resist this legislation but was unsuccessful. Given the mood of Parliament, Charles was not able to show his true feelings until on his deathbed, where in the presence of a priest he converted to Catholicism in 1684.

Charles and his wife had no children so when Charles died, his brother, James II, inherited the throne. James was already Catholic, and even though he did not pursue a policy of forcing Catholicism on England, he tried to remove legal restrictions on Catholics. This disturbed members of Parliament. James' first wife, a Protestant, had borne James two daughters before her death in 1671. James' second wife was Catholic, and when she became pregnant, there was widespread concern that she might have a son. Since sons took precedence over daughters when it came to inheriting the throne, Parliament feared that England would be faced with multiple generations of Catholic rule.

Unexpected help came from Holland. William, Prince of Orange, nephew of Charles II, and husband of a Protestant daughter of James

William and Mary accepted the crown jointly, becoming the only husband and wife in the history of England to share the throne.

II, Mary, offered to come and take the crown. He suggested that he and his wife should rule jointly. William was motivated by more than just an interest in the English crown. Louis XIV was menacing Holland. William was afraid that his homeland would be defeated and Catholicism would be imposed. If England continued to move toward Catholicism, Louis might well have a powerful ally. If William and Mary became the monarchs of England, then Holland would have a powerful ally, and Louis could be kept in check.

Protestants in England were delighted with William's offer. Not only would William and Mary protect Protestantism, but the pair had close family ties to England, so they would not seem like foreigners.

James was beginning to aggravate Parliament not only due to his religion but because of his clumsy and hardheaded political maneuverings. He often turned completely against political allies if they differed with him even on any single issue.

William decided to invade England during the winter of 1688. At first winter winds prevented his fleet from leaving port. William persisted, and the winds changed direction, allowing William and his men to travel to England. Many of William's supporters attributed their successful arrival to divine intervention. James could not raise enough forces to oppose William. His navy was bottled up in the Thames River. James called for his troops to march into a position where they could attack the enemy, but many of them deserted *en route*. James was captured but allowed to escape; some say he boarded a ship dressed as a woman. William had what he wanted and holding on to

James would only complicate matters. William's ouster of James II and subsequent takeover of the throne was known as the "Glorious Revolution" for two reasons: Protestants felt that this event saved Protestantism in their country, and the revolution, as opposed to the Civil War, occurred with no bloodshed.

This was not the end of James II's quest. After building a private army, he tried to invade Ireland to establish a base of operations from which to attack William and Mary. James claimed that he was not so much fighting for himself as for the rightful inheritance of his young son. Regardless of his motives, William and Mary were too firmly entrenched in their positions. England supported their Protestant monarchs against their former king, and James' cause was lost. England's revolution was no longer bloodless, but James was not able to undo it. Despite the hopes of James II that his young Catholic son would one day rule England, it never came to pass, but both of James' daughters ended up presiding over the kingdom. Long after, the descendants of James continued the fight, finally losing in 1746 at the Battle of Culloden in Scotland.

William and Mary were crowned as monarchs of England in 1689, and they ruled jointly until the death of Mary in 1694. William ruled by himself before dying in 1702, where upon he was succeeded by his sister-in-law, Mary's sister, Anne. Anne was the first English queen to rule in her own right since Elizabeth I. Although the role of the English monarch had been diminished by Parliament over the course of the seventeenth century, Anne ably fulfilled the responsibilities of her office despite contemporary perceptions of women's inferiority.

Queen Anne's reign saw the final and complete unification between Scotland and England. After more than one hundred years of monarchs ruling over both kingdoms more or less separately, England's Parliament voted to formally join the two kingdoms. Scotland's legislative body, also a type of parliament, also voted in favor, and the Act of Union was ratified in 1707. Since England had more people and more economic strength, Scotland was dominated politically. The Scottish legislature knew this, but for some of them it did not matter. Many of the wealthiest politicians in Scotland held extensive lands in both Scotland and England. Enough other Scots were bribed into voting for unification that the Act of Union passed, despite a minority group of politicians led by Andrew Fletcher who strenuously objected. With the passage of the Act of Union, Great Britain, which consisted of England, Scotland, and Wales, was born. Their lives were simplified by having one political and legal system.

Upon Anne's death in 1714, Parliament decided to once again go outside of the kingdom for its monarch, chosing George I, a German from the House of Hanover and a distant relative of Anne. (During World War I, the House of Hanover changed its name to Windsor, the ruling family in England today.)

Significant changes took place in England between 1603 and 1714. A kingdom teetering on the brink of absolute rule embraced constitutionalism where the rule of law was determined not by a king's will but the will of elected legislators. They did not have democracy in the modern sense, but they were more democratic than contemporary alternatives in Europe. England turned away from politically enforced Catholicism once and for all, and there was more tolerance for various forms of Protestantism. Finally, due to the decline of France and Spain, England went from being a second class power to the leading power in the world.

Women As Monarchs

Luck, infertility, and strong personalities occasionally made women power holders and even queens in an age dominated by men. Women as leading monarchs started with Mary Tudor, who ruled England from 1553 to 1558; Elizabeth I, who ruled England from 1558 to 1603; and Mary Stuart, who ruled Scotland from 1561 to 1567. The arrangement of tolerating a woman ruler was continued in the British Isles during the seventeenth and early eighteenth centuries with William and Mary reigning jointly. Queen Anne succeeded the couple, ruling by herself over Great Britain; Anne's husband, Albert, bore the title Prince Consort. In mainland Europe the idea of a female monarch ruling over a kingdom was unacceptable. There were royal female figures who exercised a considerable amount of power, like Catherine de Medici in France. A woman might even technically be a regent, like Anne of Austria, who ruled during the minority of Louis XIV; and Sophie in Russia tried to convert her regency to czarina but failed. Mainland Europe was not ready for a woman to rule over the realm, believing their physical and mental powers were inferior to those of men.

QUEEN ANNE

CONCLUSION

Historian William Beik described the seventeenth century as an important link between the feudal era and the modern age.

During the feudal age there was no significant central authority in many places, particularly in what is now modern day France. The seventeenth century saw central authority become stronger than it had ever been in Europe in the form of absolute rule. Having a strong central government was a big step towards the creation of a modern state. England pursued a different path than France by rejecting absolute rule, but the result was the same. Increasingly, English citizens were governed by a growing number of national laws that protected their rights, not by local lords who were free to oppress those who lived on their lands. As Europe worked through various political and religious issues, dynasties were born and destroyed, and the map of Europe was redrawn in the process.

Suggestions for Further Reading

Jacques Barzun, *From Dawn to Decadence: 1500 to the Present* (2000).

William Beik, *Absolutism and Society in Seventeenth Century France: State Power and Provincial Aristocracy in Languedoc* (1997).

Jacques Boulenger, *The Seventeenth Century in France* (1963).

Thomas Brady Jr., Heiko A. Oberman and James D. Tracy. *Handbook of European History 1400-1600* (1996).

Manfred F. Bukofzer, *Music in the Baroque Era: From Monteverdi to Bach* (1947).

Norman F. Cantor and Michael S. Werthman, Editors. *The Fulfillment and Collapse of the Old Regime 1650-1815* (1967).

Stephen Coote, *Royal Survivor: The Life of Charles II* (2000).

Gerald R. Cragg, *The Church & the Age of Reason: 1648-1789* (1974).

J. H. Elliott, *Imperial Spain: 1469-1716* (1967).

Christopher Hill, *The Century of Revolution: 1603-1714* (1980).

Lionel Kochan and John Keep, *The Making of Modern Russia* (1997).

Rossiter Johnson, *The Great Events by Famous Historians* (1905).

W. H. Lewis, *The Splendid Century: Life in the France of Louis XIV* (1953).

Victor S. Mamatey, *Rise of the Habsburg Empire 1526-1815* (1971).

John U. Nef, *Industry and Government in France and England: 1540-1640* (1967).

Nicholas V. Riasanovsky, *A History of Russia* (1977).

J. M. Roberts, *A History of Europe* (1997).

Perry M. Rogers, *Aspects of Western Civilization: Problems and Sources in History* (199.

Kelley J. Sowards, *Makers of the Western Tradition: Portraits from History* (1997).

Tom Steel, *Scotland's Story* (1984).

Philip A. M. Taylor, Editor *The Origins of the English Civil War: Conspiracy, Crusade, or Class Conflict?* (1960).

Rudolf Von Thadden, *Prussia: The History of a Lost State* (1987).

A New Kind of World

Wisdom

The Scientific Revolution and the Enlightenment gave new definitions to the European worldview. The laws of nature and scientific discovery were described in complex mathematical formulas. Most of us would need years of training to perceive the intricacies of the calculations and diagrams of these great minds. Perhaps a more "enlightening" approach to the study of this period would be the biographies of a few men. Set into the historical period, little stories about their lives show a diversity of individuals who formed a coalition, although many never met, of the thinkers who laid the basis of the modern world. Along with their struggles to interpret concepts about the mind and the universe, many of these men had interesting personal stories.

One of the most temperamental men was Tycho Brahe (Tyge in his native Danish). Brahe was obsessed with numbers and created so many calculations about the planets that they formed extensive tables. He was so intense that after an argument with another mathematician with whom he disagreed, he fought his opponent in a sword fight, losing a large piece of his nose. For the rest of his life he had to keep his nose covered with a metal plate. Some accounts say he also contracted syphilis. He was a heavy drinker who loved to indulge. One night, at a party given by a prince, Brahe drank so much his bladder filled and he was in pain. It was rude, however, to leave the table before the host so Brahe had to wait until the prince left the meal. Meanwhile, his table mates encouraged him to continue drinking. Finally, his bladder burst and poisoned his body. Trying to cure himself, possibly with some mercury to cleanse his system, the toxins from the chemical increased his distress. He soon died from his politeness and from his extravagances.

An opposite type of personality and taste was exhibited by other man. John Locke did not even like poetry. He believed that such a form of literature was "fanciful" and detracted from the proper use of man's mind, reason. Locke never married and lived a celibate life; the only important woman in his life was his mother, and she died when he was very young. He spent his time working diligently on long, complicated manuscripts that, he boasted, kept him away from superfluous relationships with women. He usually kept to himself and when he did spend time with others, it was to exchange ideas and to fine tune his theories about government and the nature of humankind.

It is striking how many of the men of the era believed that marriage was not for them. Leibnitz, Pascal, Rousseau, and Voltaire, to name a few, were unmarried although the last two were hardly celibate.

Frederick I, King of Prussia, suffered from abuse from his fanatical father. The boy was so poorly treated that even though he was the crown prince, he opted to run away. His father sent the army after him. When they captured him, his father's punishment included Frederick watching his friend and accomplice beheaded. Another part of the punishment was to be forced to marry. As soon as he could, Frederick left his young wife and never again thought of any relationship with a woman. All through his life he was described as cold and distant. He would rather write and rule than be with friends.

William Pitt was Prime Minister of England from 1783 to 1802 and then 1804 to 1806. Pitt never married because duty to his country was his first and only dedication. He believed that a person might well be distracted by family and friends into frivolities that depleted one's valuable energies. His close circle of friends were those with whom he could discuss ideas. Pitt's concept of "noblesse oblige," or the obligations of the upper class to rule society, still simmered among his peers, a heritage from the Medieval times of chivalry. Thus, Pitt kept aloof and dedicated his time to his public tasks.

Perhaps it was Isaac Newton, the symbol of the Scientific Revolution, who cast the most rigid philosophy for individuals of science and who served in government. He had a strange and strained relation to his family as his father died before he was born and his mother left him in the care of first a wet nurse and then his grandmother. When she returned to his life, at age 11, his mother brought three noisy children whose disturbance was avoided only when he was sent away to school. Newton found books and calculations to be his only loyal friends and was devoted to his scientific investigations. He was known in the scientific and academic worlds as a cold, unsociable man who argued with almost everyone. He had little use for the "fairer sex" and claimed that throughout his life, he never lost a single drop of seminal fluid for such an action would definitely weaken his intellectual powers.

At another extreme, Voltaire and Rousseau were very involved with many women. Rousseau was notorious for his affairs, leaving one woman for another who could support his irresponsible ways (and at least 5 illegitimate children in orphanages). Voltaire, too, enjoyed the company and adulation of women. What is most unusual about Voltaire, however, occurred after his death. Since he had criticized the Roman Church, he was denied burial in any of the holy plots in Paris. He was finally buried in an abbey outside the city. Then his body was moved back to Paris in 1791. During a revolt of fanatics, he was removed from the magnificent sarcophagus that had honored him. His body was thrown into a garbage heap, never to be found again. During past "burials" his brain and heart had been surgically removed; his heart is in the Bibliotheque National, but his brain disappeared after "traveling" through many hands, sometimes auctioned off to the highest bidder.

This minimal survey of some of the great minds of the era proves little in the sense of brain power versus physical excess, but it certainly shows another side to the personalities of such famous people and their serious endeavors.

Chronology

1512	Copernicus states that the earth and planets revolve around the Sun
1522	Albrecht Durer designs a flying machine to be used in wars
1543	Copernicus published *De Revolutionibus Orium Coelestium*; Andreas Vesalius publishes *Concerning the Structure of the Human Body*
1596	Galileo Galilei invents the first thermometer
1600	Dutch opticians invent the first telescopes
1602	Galileo investigates the laws of gravitation and oscillation
1605	Francis Bacon publishes *Advancement of Learning*
1608	Galileo improves Dutch telescope and invents the astronomical telescope
1614	Development of the glass industry in England
1616	Galileo banned from scientific study by the Roman Catholic Church
1618	Kepler discovers the third law of planetary motion
1619	William Harvey discovers the process for circulation of the blood in human bodies
1624	Bernini begins statues of "Apollo and Daphne"
1627	Kepler places 1005 fixed stars
1632	Galileo publishes *Concerning the Two Chief World Systems*
1633	Galileo forced to renounce the Copernican theories of the universe
1634	Rembrant begins "Artemisia" painting
1637	Rene Descartes' *Discourse on Method*
1641	Descartes writes *Meditations*
1642	Galileo dies; Isaac Newton born
1651	Giovanni Riccioli makes map of the moon with names still used
1652	The minuet becomes fashionable in France; first opera house in Vienna
1665	Sir Isaac Newton experiments with gravity and invents calculus
1666	Antonio Stradivari builds his first violin
1668	Newton builds a refracting telescope
1669	John Locke writes a constitution for the colony of South Carolina
1685	Johannes Sebastian Bach born
1686	Edward Halley draws first meteorological map
1690	John Locke publishes his *Essay Concerning Human Understanding* and *Second Treatise on Government*
1704	Newton publishes *Optiks*
1748	Montesquieu publishes *Spirit of the Laws*
1751	First volume of Diderot's *Encyclopedia*
1759	Voltaire publishes *Candide*
1764	Rousseau's *Emile* & *The Social Contract*
1764	Cesare Beccaria publishes his *Essays on Crimes and Punishments*
1776	Adam Smith publishes *The Wealth of Nations*
1782	Immanuel Kant publishes *The Critique of Pure Reason*

The modern world and its point of view have long been associated with the beginnings of modern science, and there are links to the start of that view in the Renaissance. Of course, the word Renaissance means rebirth. Long before the Renaissance, the Greeks and Romans had toyed with the notion that humans could "know" their world. The Latin word "scio" became the basis for the ancient concept of "science." Until the 1600s, at least in Western Civilization, the word simply described what could be observed about the grand scheme created by some great force or forces that had set up and controlled the world. Whether that originator was Zeus, Jupiter, or the Judeo-Christian God, "scientists" could only peek into a pre-ordained system over which they had little control.

In Medieval times, humans were considered a unit in the Great Chain of Being, a design that "stuck" them between heaven and hell. If anything was to be investigated, it was to discover the part humans played in some divine plan, or at best how to "work the system" to find the pathway to a better world after this short and difficult life on earth. Most humans would fail in this effort until the Christian God offered a wider gate into His heaven. Then the task of finding the route became even more important since it was more possible, and Christianity took on the task of allowing its "intellectuals" to guide the masses to paradise. Membership and obedience to the Roman Catholic (and only) Christian church defined a person's earthly role and those who considered the theories of the universe's operation did so within the confines of Church doctrine.

The sixteenth and seventeenth centuries, however, were full of new definitions about the purpose of humans on earth. Drawing on the ideas of the Renaissance humanists and then those of the Reformation, leading theorists broke with the domination of the Church and began to see humans not simply as waiting for their fate in heaven or hell, but as actors in the scene of history. From Michelangelo's famous painting on the ceiling of the Sistine Chapel, where a man almost touched God, to the holy covenants of John Calvin who described his religious doctrine as a set of contracts between God and people, Western society began to see humans as responsible for their part in history.

The dawn of the sixteenth century saw a whole new concept of what the world looked like . . . there were two new continents added to the knowledge of Western Europe. The ideas about a "new" world added to the old provided possibilities about a person's actions and thoughts and these new notions began to swirl through society. People could not only hope, dream and pray, they could act, understand, and might even be able to change the world around them. The term "scio," simply to know, became "scio," to investigate, to explain. There was no moment in history when humans suddenly discovered their role to explore the universe, but rather it took many years to see that they could look into the secrets of the world around them. The pieces of the puzzle took centuries to find their places, and many remain missing.

As historians have tried to understand what has become known in modern history as the Scientific Revolution, care must be taken not to read the present into the past. People in the twenty-first century are so dependent on the "scientific attitude" that it is hard to think of cultures without such a perspective. Often people and civilizations who do not share this viewpoint are thought of as "primitives," lost in a world of mysticism and magic rather than guided by reason. The Western world, however, just after Michelangelo, Luther, Calvin,

Columbus, and Magellan, was far from primitive and so the whole structure of society must be examined.

THE NOTION OF SCIENCE

The framework of the past held on for a long time and no scientist, philosopher, or theologian in the sixteenth and seventeenth centuries consciously sought to throw away all the old notions and set up all new rules. In fact, the Scientific Revolution was firmly rooted in European history.

What made the notion of discovery of a new perspective possible? What made the idea that the secrets of the world could be investigated and explained? The connections to those possibilities went back as far as the concept of scio, back to Aristotle and the Greeks and probably farther. The fifteenth century rediscovery of Greek ideas about mathematics and the human power of reasoning were slowly reunited with Western European philosophy. There had been a few Greek theorists and mechanics who believed that the sun, not the earth, was the center of the universe. Some even believed that the earth moved but were ridiculed because if the earth moved, when you jumped up you should come down in a different place and no one could "prove" that you did.

The Greeks thought about the great scheme that defined the earth's place, as well as humanity's place, in a grand structure of the universe. Old Greek myths talked of the creation of people by the gods and how individuals had to relate and please those gods to survive. Those gods whimsically played with people like toys and a person's only hope of survival was to keep the gods happy. People had reason to observe their world and perhaps find a way not to disturb the super powers.

Some medieval theorists had used Aristotle's "empirical" approach to discover the secrets of the universe, meaning to watch for the connections between cause and effect. The Roman Church, however, felt that many of these attempts were attacks on the power of God to run His universe and so, since the Church controlled the universities of Europe, many professors were burned at the stake for blasphemy.

In the latter part of the thirteenth century a compromise between the Aristotelians and the Church was offered by Thomas Aquinas. The *Summa Theologica* of Aquinas stated that the Aristotelian method could be used to better understand the truth of God's world. Doctrine and empiricism were combined into Scholasticism in the hope humans could improve their chances of finding the route to heaven.

Of course there had always been "thinkers" who were more practical, in the sense of understanding the world around them. Humans had been using their environment to improve their survival on earth since the first pre-humans used sticks and stones as "tools." In pre-western society, the Egyptians and Mesopotamians had built massive pyramids and ziggurats to get closer to the spiritual rulers of earth, and all sorts of technologies had been honed out of the natural world to create "civilization." The Greeks used their talents to invent the ruler, the key and mathematical formulations that came close to measuring the correct distance between the earth and the sun. Thus, practical knowledge about the earth was not a total mystery. What the "Scientific Revolution" did was to re-orient Western people's idea about how they fit into the universe and what they could accomplish through investigating natural phenomena.

The Scientific Revolution of the sixteenth and seventeenth centuries was an epistemological transformation that had slowly changed the way people in Western Europe thought (and still think) about their world. (This is the meaning of epistemological.) Every aspect of Western culture was eventually affected by the change: government, politics, religion, art, architecture, and even the definition of individual personality. Investigation to understand, to affect, and to change slowly became the mantra of modern science.

RECONSTRUCTING THE DEFINITION OF "THE WORLD"

When Columbus' ships landed on the shores of a tiny island in the "West Indies," there was no inkling, even for him, of how the European notion of the world would be changed. He thought that he was either off the coast of China, or, more likely, of India (thus he called the natives Indians). The slow acceptance of the fact that land existed that had not been part of the European concept of the Island of the Earth (one large body of land surrounded by one large ocean) came only after many explorers' expeditions could not match the old notions to the new facts. Columbus himself stayed in an almost medieval frame of mind. On one of his last voyages, he reached the mouth of the Orinoco River (present day Venezuela), and viewing the tall mountain and the streams of the river's mouth, he believed he had found where the earth met heaven, perhaps the Garden of Eden.

If the true meaning of Columbus' "discovery" had been formed in 1492, or even over the next expeditions he led across the ocean, then the two huge continents would have been named after him and not some other explorer. Instead, in a small French town, St Die, a nameless printer edited an edition of the ancient writings of the Roman, Ptolemy, and included some letters by the explorer Amerigo Vespucci. As he added the new territory to the known world, the printer marked the land "America" and the title stuck.

At the same time that the external world was changing definition, the inner, or spiritual world, was also being redefined. The Protestant Reformation, again with roots as far back as religious aspirations, was beginning to formulate a more active role for individuals in their search for paradise. Martin Luther called all people to belong to a communion of saints and taught that each person was responsible for his or her soul. The church was a guide to heaven, not the only door as the Roman Church had preached. John Calvin taught that each Christian had a contract with God in which individuals worked hard at their callings and then God welcomed them into heaven's rewards.

As the Reformation, Renaissance and Age of Discovery became integrated into the European mind, "thinkers" and "scientists" became bolder in their presentations. Most were pious religious believers who were not seeking to unseat God's supremacy but rather to increase their understanding of the world He had given them.

THE EARLY MODERN SCIENTISTS

Historians argue about who were the first agents of the Scientific Revolution. Some say Copernicus, others say Leonardo da Vinci. Others credit the increasing contact and trade with the Arabic world and with the Muslim scientists who had preserved the writings of many of the ancient Greeks. Still others want to include Luther, Calvin and other religious reformers. There is no doubt that the roots and connections are wide spread and include many famous, as well as nameless, contributors.

Perhaps the Scientific Revolution began with the unnoticed combination of events that gave some individuals the inspiration or motivation to study the notion of cause and effect that Aristotle, Thomas Aquinas, and many others had quietly set into motion. The Renaissance "humanists" glorified humans as God's greatest creation. The Reformation theologians called each person to discover and act out his or her God given role on earth (the concept of the sainthood of ALL believers, not just of the priesthood). The Arabic connection had encouraged the investigation into the techniques of controlling this world: the words "chemistry," "alchemy," "alkali," "alembic," to name a few, are scientific <u>and</u> Arabic terms. These themes, combined with the discovery of the New World and the invention of the printing press (a device that made sharing information so much easier as well as beyond the control of the Church), presented the notion of possibility instead of a fixed world where people had no creative role. The possibilities gave rise to experimental science, the human quest to investigate and explain the world and all of its aspects and phenomena.

Perhaps the lives of two men who lived about 300 years apart, but who are "beginners" in the march toward the scientific attitude, might illustrate the slow progress of this notion. These men were Roger Bacon and Francis Bacon.

Roger Bacon was a contemporary of Thomas Aquinas although they probably never met. Bacon lived from about 1214 to 1294, an incredibly long life for the thirteenth century. Born in England, Bacon was educated at Oxford and the University of Paris where he learned to read Hebrew and Greek. About 1257, Bacon became a Franciscan friar. During the year 1267 to 1268, he worked for Pope Clement IV, preparing documents to reform education. His emphasis was that observation of the natural world was the surest way to understand God's plan for humans. He stressed mathematics and exact measurement. As his work was circulated, he was continually

Roger Bacon argued that logic must be supported with experimentation for a theory to be judged correct.

criticized by his Franciscan superiors and his writings suppressed. He probably spent some time in prison, and soon after his death, he was condemned as a sorcerer and a "wonder worker" instead of a faithful Christian. Later, members of the scientific community found his speculations about gunpowder, flying machines, telescopes, and mechanically drawn carriages as seeds to the technological future. But, in his own time, Roger Bacon was a man to be distrusted.

Francis Bacon was born in 1561, also in England. His father was a member of Queen Elizabeth's court, being Keeper of the Great Seal. Francis' father hoped his son would some day join the diplomatic service. His mother was an ardent Puritan who taught Francis that hard work and a studious mind were tremendous attributes.

Francis Bacon argued that Renaissance thinkers needed to shake off their reliance on the ancient Greeks and Romans.

For Francis, the road to recognition was not through the church but through the practice of law, and he studied at Trinity College, Cambridge. He became one of the leading lawyers of England and so earned the attention of Elizabeth's court and even of Elizabeth herself. In 1584, he gained a seat in the House of Commons. A rising star, he took a chance, criticized the royal taxation policy and lost the favor of the Queen. Realizing that he needed connections to win his way back, he made friends with the Earl of Essex and was appointed attorney general. Soon, however, both Essex and Bacon lost the favor of the Queen.

When Elizabeth died, the new king, James VI, was friendlier to Francis, and he rejoined the government but had an "up and down" career, not always holding to the royal political positions. He married well and rose through various posts and became Lord Chancellor in 1618. He became a baron in 1621; however, in the same year he admitted that he had taken bribes and was removed from his offices. Feeling disgraced, he retired from public life and devoted himself to study and literature.

Bacon is not remembered for his governmental service or even for the small crime that cost him his court association (that was later remitted). He is remembered for his insistence on the uses of induction to discover the rules of the universe, i.e., truth.

There are and can only be two ways of searching into and discovering truth. The one flies from the sense and particulars to the most general axioms: this way is now in fashion. The other derives axioms from the sense and particulars, rising by a gradual and unbroken ascent, so that it arrives at the most general axioms last of all. This is the true way, but as yet untried.

What an individual could know was what could be reasoned, not from religious doctrine but from what could be understood from the surrounding world. Such a process, later called the scientific method, became the basis for the discoveries that changed the world in the sixteenth and seventeenth centuries. Although the Bacons were not related genealogically, Francis "descended" from Roger in their ideas on how humans could reason and understand their world. It must also be noted that Roger existed within the confines of the Church, and his success as an individual was tied to this association. Francis's prominence and acceptance in society was directly associated with his political positions, even though they were not the final definition of his success.

A good analysis of the time is with the Renaissance. Although the names of Leonardo and Michelangelo are easily recognized, hundreds of others' works filled Europe with beauty and color. In the sixteenth and seventeenth centuries, many individuals tried to figure out the mechanics of the universe and of the physical world. Although their names are less famous, each contributed a tiny drop that would fill an ocean of new thought and then actual change in the configurations of society, as well as the conceptions of humans and their role on earth.

THE HEAVENS BECOME PART OF THE HUMAN UNIVERSE

The advance of European mathematics came with the introduction of Arabic numerals during the Middle Ages. These numbers made calculation and record keeping much simpler. Previously the Europeans used Roman numerals with their addition and subtraction of symbols to stand for numbers. (Try multiplying MCMCXLVII by CCCLXXII without converting them to Arabic numerals!) The Arabs used a place system; they began with 0 to 9, then placed a 1 in front of the 0, then 2, and so on. This allowed for rapid calculation. Mathematics took on a great fascination among Europeans, and they began to see it as a key to understanding and measuring their world.

Pythagoras and Plato, in ancient Greece, had developed mathematical formulas about the shapes and design of the world, but these too were credited to a super force whose knowledge was beyond most humans. Aristotle had developed mathematical notions, connecting cause and effect in his theory of the syllogism (if a is combined with b, then c will result). Reasoning went from the general to the specific; this was the system of deducing information.

Perhaps the most stirring quotation about how humans could study their world by building from the specific to the general (instead of the other way around) was made by Leonardo da Vinci.

Here, right here, in the eye, here forms, here colors, right here the character of every part and every thing of the universe, are concentrated into a single point. How marvelous that point is!...In that small space, the universe can be completely reproduced and rearranged in its entire vastness!"

For Leonardo, looking at the specific defined the road to the general. Here is the link between the two Bacons that spurred the thought that humans could know their world and that God would not be offended by their research. Of course, Leonardo did not seem to care whether God was offended, but most of the early scientists were still closely attached to the Church. Across Europe, the need to know was stirring a revolution in the way people thought.

Although it had been frequently questioned and to some degree altered, the major doctrine about the universe was that God had placed the Earth in the center and the planetary spheres, including the sun, circled the earth. Even the Arabic scientists had accepted this scheme. The only logical sense of this theory was that human life was so important that God had built the universe around it. This theory was devised by Ptolemy during the period of Greek history when the roots of Western Civilization were set, and it was later incorporated into the Roman Church's doctrine. To disagree with the theory was heresy.

Nicholas Copernicus was born in Krakow, Poland in 1453. His writings were the first of several propositions that finally changed the in-

Polish astronomer Nicolaus Copernicus believed
that the earth orbited the sun.

terpretation of where humans sat in the universe.
Copernicus was a religious man, trained by
church scholars and supported by his uncle who
was a bishop. He held positions within the
church hierarchy and had no intention of questioning official dogma. In fact, his famous book,
On the Revolutions of the Heavenly Spheres, was
not published until after his death. Fascinated
by mathematical calculations about the movement of the planets, Copernicus could not match
his investigations and observations with the official doctrine. Finally he came up with the
speculation, which he demonstrated with mathematical equations, that the sun, not the earth,
was the center of the universe, and the planets,
including the earth, circled the sun. In his quiet
life, far from Rome and in a small Polish city,
Copernicus could talk about his ideas with a
variety of interested people. He did not wish to
see the theory printed in a book, but his young
assistant found the means to have it published.

This was not the modern interpretation of the
system of the universe. It simply took the Ptolemaic system and switched the position of the
sun with the earth.

Copernicus' system was discussed behind
closed doors. It seemed to fit with Copernicus'
mathematical calculations, but it contradicted
the standard theory the Church had held for
many years. Since he was a religious man, with
Church orders protecting him and with powerful Church allies, Copernicus was allowed to
continue to work.

Another famous Danish mathematician,
Tycho Brahe, spent years calculating and considering the positions of the planets and stars
and concluded that Copernicus was wrong. He
proposed a "middle ground" between Ptolemy
and Copernicus. Brahe's "discovery" was that
the planets did circle the sun, all the planets except the earth, for the sun and the other planets
circled the earth! In his obsession to prove
Copernicus' theory inaccurate, he compiled a
huge listing of astronomical observations and
calculations. Even without a telescope, Brahe's
calculations were amazingly accurate. After his
death, these tables would be used to show
Copernicus, not Brahe, was correct.

Copernicus adhered to the Roman Church
while Brahe was a Lutheran. Since the sixteenth
century was also the century of the Protestant
Reformation, those "outside" the Church were
now freed to examine theories that were not part
of the official doctrine of the Roman Church.
Johannes Kepler, who was Brahe's assistant, came
from a German Lutheran family and was fascinated by Copernicus' work.

As opposed to the aristocratic life of his
mentor, Tycho Brahe, Kepler's family was not
distinguished. His father was a mercenary soldier and left home frequently, never returning
from a war in the Netherlands when Johannes

German astronomer Johannes Kepler demonstrated that the planets traced elliptical paths around the sun.

and was excommunicated by the Lutheran Church. He published a small book about his observations and sent a copy to Tycho Brahe, who by now was working at the court of the Holy Roman Emperor in Prague. Soon Kepler left his homeland and became Brahe's assistant.

Kepler did not have a simple life. His first wife and first son died in Prague, and then political troubles forced him to leave the country. Soon after he had to hurry home because his mother had been accused of witchcraft. In the midst of all this, he read a short essay, *The Harmony of the World*, written by the musician Vincenzo Galilei, Galileo Galilei's father.

Using the theme of harmony and Brahe's incredible tables of astronomical observations, Kepler discovered three laws of planetary motion. He calculated the most exact tables for proving the Copernican theory of a sun-centered universe. He converted Copernicus' "circles" to ellipses and solved many inconsistencies of the heliocentric theory. In other scientific disciplines, he worked in optics, discovered how to calculate the volume of solids, and applied mathematical formulas to many areas that needed to be defined. In many ways he succeeded in creating a sort of mathematical harmony for the world. He did, however, keep his notion of the universe as being the creation of the Christian God. He also spent years trying to mathematically prove Plato's concept of the Forms (where 5 solid shapes made up all the material designs of the universe), but he never found a workable solution.

was only five years old. His mother was the daughter of an innkeeper. The young boy served tables and helped with the inn but managed to impress the local school teacher with his abilities in mathematics. He earned himself a place in the University of Tubingen, then a stronghold of Lutheran reform. Kepler was a deeply religious man who spent his life dedicated to the notion that humans, made in the image of God, could understand the world around them.

There were, in Kepler's time, four divisions of the mathematical sciences: arithmetic, geometry, astronomy, and music. Kepler's instruction was primarily in astronomy. It was here that he learned of the new Copernican system. As he advanced in his thinking about the universe, Kepler also changed some of his religious views

HERESY AND DISCOVERY

Mathematical arguments continued, and their theoretical bases were defended by loyal advocates. The Church held fast to its position that the earth, not the sun, was the center of the uni-

Italian scholar Galileo Galilei concluded that the sun was the center of the universe. Because the Catholic Church decreed that the sun revolved around the earth, Galileo was forced to publicly recant his findings.

verse. Some clerics read the different authors with interest but rejected the new interpretations, saying that the numbers contradicted each other, i.e., there was no proof that the heliocentric (sun centered) proposition was accurate. This was challenged by a faithful Roman Catholic whose two daughters were nuns.

Galileo Galilei was born in Pisa, Tuscany in 1564. He was the son of a musician who challenged the formal foundations of Church music and incorporated Greek poetry and myths into a new style that eventually led to Italian opera. Since Galileo's father was not stopped by the notion of offending official authority, his son grew up with the idea he could change things and, if true, they would finally be accepted. He was ultimately right, but in his lifetime would

not get the recognition or the support he deserved.

Galileo first attended the University of Pisa to study medicine but quickly changed to the study of mathematics. He soon used his knowledge to determine why some objects floated and some did not. In a theory that would be revised in the modern world, he stated that objects heavier than water sink and those lighter (or less dense) than water float. Soon he was appointed Chair of Mathematics in Pisa, but, almost as soon, he was offered a position in Venice. Since it provided more prestige and money, he left his home city.

Venice was a new experience for Galileo, not only because of the change in geography (it is on the west coast of Italy, and Pisa is on the east) but in the openness of the society. A bustling city of merchants without the medieval customs of feudalism, Venetians drank some 40 million bottles of wine a year; courtesans seemed to be everywhere; and the money a person earned gained them recognition, not the family they came from. The young Pisan was impressed by his new city. He hobnobbed with rich young social leaders and had three children by a young woman he never married. Galileo weathered the years in which Venice was under interdict from the Church; the Jesuits were expelled from the city and more materialistic practices made it a lively place to live. His dedication to the Church made him serious, but his enjoyment of the freedom of Venice made him part of the less pious scene.

Galileo never lost his academic interests. At the age of 46, he was offered tenure at the University of Padua. Here he put to use his newly built device, a telescope, which could search the skies for information about the planets. Galileo did not invent the telescope; it was probably invented by Hans Lipershey, a spectacle maker in

Holland. He did, however, improve its quality and used it most effectively to study the stars and planets. His fame began to spread, and only a few months after coming to Padua, he left for an appointment as Mathematician and Philosopher to the Grand Duke of Tuscany.

The information that Galileo gained from his telescope increasingly confirmed the validity of the Copernican theories. He went to Rome to show the clergy who still opposed the sun-centered theory so that they could see the truth for themselves. The conservative churchmen felt tricked; Galileo left frustrated.

Galileo began publishing his findings, and the churchmen increased their pressure against him. Soon even those who supported him were backing away. In February 1616, the Copernican theory was officially condemned as heresy. The Church position was that the earth was the center of the universe and that although the planets and sun revolved around the earth, the earth itself did not move. All this they claimed was written in the Bible and could not be contradicted.

Friends warned Galileo he was on shaky ground with his work, but he continued, convincing himself that he could change the mind of the clerics. When an old friend, Maffeo Barberini, became Pope Urban VIII, Galileo thought he had a chance to right things. In 1632, he published *Dialogue Concerning the Two Chief Systems of the World—Ptolemaic and Copernican,* and in it he criticized those who did not accept the obvious: Copernicus was correct. His condemnation of "non-believers" spared no one— not even the Pope. Consequently Galileo was tried for blasphemy.

The stage was set. Either Galileo would give up his notion of a moving earth in a sun-centered universe or he would be condemned for heresy. He tried to plead that he did not wish to contradict the Church and that had he been warned to stop his investigations he would have done so. The prosecution was relentless. It claimed (and showed documents proving) that Galileo had been warned many times to stop and to cease publication. He confessed he had sinned against the Church and was sentenced to a life of imprisonment. Sympathetic friends got the sentence commuted to house arrest. He died in 1642. In 1984, 342 years later, a Papal commission declared an injustice had been done and cleared his name.

THE AGE OF NEWTON

Nature and Nature's law lay hid in night
God said, 'Let Newton be!' and all was light.
Epitaph intended for Sir Isaac Newton
The Poems of Alexander Pope

No one would separate the Scientific Revolution from the name of Isaac Newton. Born the year that Galileo died, this solitary genius blended the work of his predecessors into a grand scheme. He was not a friendly person and had to be encouraged to publish his work. He had few friends and quarreled with almost all the other leading intellectuals of his time. Yet, it is he that made the lasting impression.

Newton was born in England on Christmas Day. His father had died a few months before Newton's premature birth, and the baby was not expected to survive. When he was about three years old, his mother left the small farming village to marry a wealthy clergyman, and Newton stayed behind with his elderly grandmother. Eight years later, his mother, now a widow, returned with three noisy step-siblings. At 13, Newton was sent to boarding school where he stayed with the local druggist (in those days, called an apothecary); here he developed an in-

Sir Isaac Newton's scientific theories propelled the Enlightenment forward. Newton's laws dictated that the universe was an ordered place. People believed that the natural world worked on knowable principles.

terest in chemicals and the properties of different substances.

When Newton finished school, his family expected that he would return home and look after the family farm. However, the 17-year-old had no interest in farming. Fortunately his uncle liked Newton and encouraged his mother to send him to Cambridge University. He had to pay his way by waiting tables and cleaning the rooms of more wealthy students and perhaps their teasing accounted for his unsociable behavior later in his life. In the summer of 1665, the university closed because the plague made it too unsafe. Newton went home and spent two years concentrating on physic and mathematics. Here, all by himself, he later claimed he discovered the theory of gravity (the apple falling on his head); observed that light passing through a prism was broken up into colors; and he worked on math-

ematical formulas that became calculus and the notion of infinite series.

When Newton returned to Cambridge in 1667, his mentor, Isaac Barrow, convinced him to publish some of his work on infinite series. Respect for his intellectual abilities was so widespread that Barrow resigned from his Lucasian Professorship, and it was offered to Newton. The young man boldly challenged the university's demand that all professors belong to the Church of England, and King Charles issued a proclamation excusing Newton from the usual commitment. Newton served with no attachment to any formal church.

The question of how the planets revolved around the earth became increasingly the topic among scholars. Newton himself was fascinated and made both observations and calculations. He wondered why the planets stayed in their orbits and what controlled their paths. In an intense investigation, he combined many of the theories he had previously developed and gave the concept of nature organization as well as meaning. In 1687, the *Philosophiae Narualis Principia Mathematica* (The Mathematical Principles of Natural Philosophy*)* was published. Interestingly the "modern" ideas were presented in the last major work published in Latin, which Newton held to be the language of scholars.

Newton reasoned that the planetary paths were designed by the forces of gravity in the universe. He devised a mathematical system, calculus, to explain the laws of gravity and prove their relevance. The result was that by the eighteenth century, Western people believed they lived in a universe that was set up by rules of reason and mathematical surety, not simply the will (whim) of God. Humans could, by the use of this reason, understand and thus control their universe. If humans knew the rules, they could better play the "game" of life; they could design

Gottfried Leibnitz advocated that Germans stop taking Enlightenment ideas from foreign nations and begin to form their own ideas based on reason.

Isaac Newton, the scientist, had questioned the Grand Scheme, the Great Chain of Being, and found that people were not fixed simply between heaven and hell. Humans had been placed on earth with the mission to understand and to change, to improve their environment. The European world would never be the same after Newton. History, from now on, was a slow march toward "progress," and people, particularly Europeans, were the leaders in the search for a better world.

MACROCOSM AND MICROCOSM

When Newton finished his work, the earth sat among other planets and swirled around its sun. All moved in some mysterious motion that would eventually be called the "cosmic dance." Motion became the theme of the modern world. Objects all moved depending on their need and their newly discovered "possibilities." The Scientific Revolution became the term that illustrated this new perception. Science was for knowing how things worked. Revolution, the process of turning, symbolized the fluidity of the universe. The outer world, the macrocosm, was being redefined.

There was another world, one perhaps much more dangerous to explore. That world lay within individuals, and it was called the microcosm. The Church, however, had great control of the information about a person's spiritual character. For the Church, people's greatest asset was their soul and that mechanism must control the less holy nature, for sin and evil hid within the body. The chances for heaven came from the invisible soul that God had given each human being. To search for the invisible was probably blasphemy and surely meant the road to Hell.

For many years, the Church opposed human dissection. Leonardo and Michelangelo

society so that the best results would and could make the time spent on earth better. There were many possibilities simply by using God-given reasoning powers to understand the universe and improve it.

Newton was not without his critics and competitors. Gottfried Wilhelm von Leibnitz, from Leipzig, claimed that objects had their own qualities, which included movement; he wrote that there were no external sources such as Newton's notion of gravity. A mathematician, Leibnitz created a series of calculations that some claim are the basis of calculus although others believe Newton was the founder of this mathematical discipline. He shared another quality with the Englishman; he was not interested in relationships, neither marriage nor friendships, although he was more pleasant than the nasty Dr. Newton.

both had done dissections, but many of their contemporaries feared the vengeance of the Church and looked only "skin deep." Yet even cutting up the physical body held little promise for discovering the workings of the invisible side, the mind and the soul.

The Reformation had encouraged people to look into their spiritual nature and thus into their individual being. The first attempts to understand the human body and mind had to come from physical observations. What could be learned about how the body worked? The traditional interpretation about the body's functions came from Galen, an Asiatic Greek who lived in the second century. Galen was a physician to the Roman Emperor. He had collected and organized some of the ideas of the famous Hippocrates, the ancient Greek who was considered the father of medicine because he believed that disease was related to physical causes and was not a punishment of the gods. Dissection of humans was not practiced openly, and many later researchers claimed that Galen dissected animals and then made speculations about the human body. He did, however, describe the basic workings of the eye and ear and "invented" taking a pulse to see if a person were dead or alive. He also thought that there was a connection between the brain and the mind. By the sixteenth century, the Church had totally accepted Galen's hypotheses and claimed that no further research was necessary. The sixteenth century investigators began to resist this opinion.

Theophrastus Phillippus Aureolus Bombastus von Hohenheim, more popularly known as Paracelsus, was born in 1493 in Switzerland. He was a contemporary of Columbus, Copernicus, Luther, and Leonardo, and the other famous early sixteenth-century figures. His father was a physician who dabbled in the medi-

eval "science" of alchemy. This study was much more than the notion of changing lead to gold; it was the investigation into the properties of materials to see what affects they had in certain conditions. Paracelsus' father also visited mining camps, ministering to the wounded and sick, often commenting on the possible connections between their afflictions and their environment. The son learned some of his father's wisdom and then left the area to wander around Europe, learning the techniques of others.

Paracelsus never earned any formal degree and was frequently criticized by those who had formally studied. He was, however, often sought after to cure various ailments. His contribution was that disease could be cured by "medicines" made from "earthly" ingredients.

Born in Brussels in 1514, Andreas Versalius was descended from a long line of physicians who had been prominent in the court of the Holy Roman Emperors. Like many young men of the era, his basic schooling was done at a local grammar school, but then he was off to Louvain, then Paris, and as far away as Padua. His formal studies were in the Galenic tradition, but he wanted proof that the theories were actually the way the body worked. Slowly he acquired great skills in dissection. As he studied, he drew elaborate diagrams that became the basis for anatomical study across Europe. In an interesting interdisciplinary effort, the students of the famous painter, Titian, produced beautiful renditions of Versalius' anatomical findings. The charts became more and more detailed and began to prove that Galen had not really studied human anatomy but rather had used apes instead. Although there were similarities, there were striking differences.

Because he went against tradition, enemies began to call Versalius a madman and a heretic. One even labeled him the "Luther of the physicians," who should be condemned like the arrogant monk. He became so frustrated with the opposition he threw many of his books and writings into a great fire. This was the age of the Catholic Inquisition, and only the intervention of his friend, Philip II, saved him from a heretic's death. To prove his loyalty to the Church, Versalius set out on a pilgrimage to the Holy Land. He never returned to Europe, dying enroute. Versalius, however, set the stage for more investigation about the inner workings of the human body.

William Harvey also studied medicine in Italy but returned to his native England. Living during the Elizabethan years, he had the lucky chance to marry the daughter of Elizabeth's physician and so was immediately accepted at court. By 1616 he was lecturing at the College of Physicians on the nature of the circulation of the blood. His ideas were based on the dissection of other mammals, but they were easily applied to human beings. By 1628, Harvey's ideas had been published in Germany and quickly spread across Europe. The heart was the center of the system. It was a pump, and it pushed the blood through arteries and then slowly it was returned through veins.

Just as the invention of the telescope opened the outer world to humans, the invention of the microscope opened a tiny world that could not previously be seen by the naked eye. The Dutch had excellent abilities in optics, and in the mid-seventeenth century, Anton van Leeuwenhoek placed lenses together in such a way that the invisible universe became seeable.

Van Leeuwenhoek was the first to describe the cellular nature of living organisms and the first to see and describe bacteria and protozoa. A few years after Harvey died, Marcello Malpighi from Bologna used Van Leeuwenhoek's invention to watch the blood move from arteries to

Rene Descartes used the principles of mathematics to philosophize about human behavior. He used deductive reasoning to interpret ideas about God and morality.

veins through capillaries and another mystery was solved. Science was beginning to define the physical attributes of humans.

Humans, for all the period's investigators, were not simply a physical organism that functioned like a machine. A person had a soul, a mind, characteristics that did not have physical parts. Even the most human quality, reason, could not be physically observed. How could these parts be studied? Another set of physical philosophers began the quest to understand this puzzle.

In the beginning of the seventeenth century, a young French mathematician began making a contribution to the changing ideas about the world by applying the concepts of algebra to geometry. His name was Rene Descartes, and we call these rules Cartesian geometry.

Descartes was an unsettled man and worried that he did not know enough about anything. He left Paris for the University of Poitiers; then enlisted in the military school at Breda; went off to Holland, and finally decided to travel through Europe to see what else he could learn. Soon, he joined the Bavarian army. Finally he settled in Holland where he felt he could study and learn without the interference of the French aristocracy and the Roman Church. He composed a long treatise about thinking and researching called *Le Monde* (The World). Just as he was to present it, he heard of Galileo's trial and permanent house arrest. Descartes shelved his treatise, and it was published only after his death.

Descartes, however, did not stop writing. His now famous *Discors de la method* (Discourse on Method) describes what he believed to be the best way to obtain knowledge. He stated that only mathematics could prove the truth. Mathematics was not simply adding or subtracting, it was a way of reasoning. It was a process of observation and experimentation that showed the connections between cause and effect. Descartes' famous statement, "cogito ergo sum," (I think, therefore I am) is an example of the process he called mathematics. Through him, the notion of an individual being a thinker, an experimenter, an investigator, became the basis for the next stage of the new epistemology, the Enlightenment.

LOOKING FOR THE INVISIBLE

It took a long time to challenge and change the traditional views about the way the human mind functioned, i.e., those supported by the Church and accepted by society. Even the dedicated mathematician Descartes wrote about "animal spirits" entering the brain cavities to spread through the arteries and brain to form personalities. Robert Burton published *The Anatomy of Melancholy* in 1652, which was the first psychological text; he still talked about Galen's humors, spirit-like substances that created different types of behavior. He believed that these mysterious forces were beyond human understanding.

The new thought that the physical world was controlled by natural laws that showed the connection between cause and effect slowly attracted those who tried to define the conditions and results of human behavior. Johannes Kepler turned his attention from the skies to the mind, reasoning that similar rules must exist because there was harmony and consistency in the world's design. Galileo and Francis Bacon continued this notion and believed the world, as well as the behavior of humans, could be reduced to measurements and mechanical principles. If the workings of the mind could not be seen in the physical sense, then they could be determined by patterns that could be observed and connected to causes.

Descartes divided the body from the mind and described the mind as the power, or engine, that made the physical body perform. In some ways, this was a boon to physical investigators for it made dissection of the body less threatening as the essence of a person was invisible in nature and that would not be "disturbed" by a physical examination. The secret operation of the mind and its connection to the body would remain, and it seemed that only the Church could interpret the rules of a person's behavior.

The Scientific Revolution really involved only European intellectuals. Most of the population could not understand the detailed analyses that the scientists used to explain the universe. This, however, does not mean they were oblivious to the changing perceptions about the world. Average people thought about the New World, the Americas, and the Copernican heliocentric concept of the earth as part of the universe, not the center of it. For most people, however, it was more relevant to understand the environment and themselves.

The Reformation had emphasized education, at least through the basics of reading, and the growing business society (the rise of a middle class whose wealth was based on trade) gave the impetus for learning arithmetic and geography. Learning became necessary if ordinary people hoped to improve their lifestyles and choices. Thus, the ideas of the Scientific Revolution began to spread through society. Faith in the power of reason became a common topic. A new group of thinkers gained recognition, and the investigations turned to not only how the mind worked but how reason could be applied to make the world a better place to live.

RATIONAL AND IRRATIONAL

All through the sixteenth and seventeenth centuries, change and correction of old ideas did not come without a struggle. Witch hunts, religious wars, and an increase in the profitability and cruelty of the international slave trade certainly showed a different side to Western society than those involved in the Scientific Revolution. Censorship and despotism, the notion of the divine right of kings, and remnants of the Inquisition, as well as a growing rigidity in the new Protestant institutions, were counterpoint to the notion of reason and the hope of harmony within the universe.

Perhaps it takes the "underbelly," the less pretty part of an historical context, to move society to another place. The rising middle class (in French, the *bourgeoisie*) straddled the worlds of the powerful aristocracy and the lower classes. To some degree, although history and historical privilege divided the groups, the middle class was growing in wealth and power. Education became a key to opening doors that had been traditionally closed, and education meant information about new ideas. For the middle class, these new ideas began to demand new formulations about how society should be organized. They believed that society should be set on a foundation of reason, not particularly tradition. Conflict, not harmony, was about to begin.

THE ENLIGHTENMENT IN ENGLAND

In 1642, the English people (represented by a small number of Parliamentarians) executed their king. The public beheading of Charles I made it clear that history and tradition would now be replaced by a "rational" organization of government and thus society. The old view of a leadership group (the aristocracy, led by the king) that was sent by God to rule the masses faded as the Protectorship of the Puritans began the Commonwealth era. Even the term "commonwealth" depicted a new interpretation of how a society should be organized: it meant that the government should look to the needs of the whole of the community, that success (wealth) was based on a government that aimed at the common good. These new terms were defined by the Puritan majority and did not meet the theoretical goal (government for the people). The "experiment" failed with royalty returning in 1660.

In 1660, Thomas Hobbes published his discourse on government, *The Leviathan*. Hobbes had written a variety of tracts about humans and their progress in society, but the authoritarian notion of human's basic evil nature caused Hobbes to write a long study of how the state of nature was a time of crisis and conflict. The

John Locke believed that people were born with the ability to reason. He believed that a government should take its powers from the people.

transition about government's role was seen in the transition of the intellectual scene of England from the writings of Hobbes to those of John Locke. For Hobbes, life on earth was "nasty, brutish, and short," with the emphasis on the notion that humans were "brutish," unreasoning, and even "evil." By the time John Locke wrote his *Essay on Human Understanding* and *Treatises Concerning Government*, in the 1680s and 1690, the notion was that humans were reasonable and could discover the needs of their community and build a government that suited them. The English Civil War was much more than a political battle, it was an impetus to a new way of looking at people and their government.

One of the biggest changes concerned the role God played in setting up human institutions. The old notion of divine right, where God chose the rulers and the rest had to obey, was fading in England. Charles I was tried and con-victed of treason in an English court. The king was tried as a citizen (Charles Stuart), not as a representative of God (a royal person). Charles, in his traditional role, claimed the court had no jurisdiction over him as he answered only to God, but the court beheaded him anyway. The entire structure of the English government was destroyed since there was no king to head the organization. A new one had to be composed, and it had to be made by people.

John Locke wrote his famous books during this period of reorganization and correction (the return of the monarchy). He too came from a non-traditional background, not being a member of the ruling aristocracy. Locke attended Oxford University where he was not particularly distinguished. He first gained recognition in medicine. During an outbreak of smallpox, Lord Shaftesbury became worried about his family and invited Locke, whom he had met at Oxford, to vaccinate his wife and children. Vaccination was a new idea that was quite risky. People were given a small dose of a disease and monitored so that the ill affects did not kill them. Many died in the effort to save themselves, but Shaftesbury's family was successfully protected. Locke was immediately admitted to the Shaftesbury family circle.

This was more than an economic improvement in Locke's life. Shaftesbury was a powerful man in England. Through the Civil War years, Anthony Ashely Cooper (his family name) adroitly managed to be on the right side of a shifting political scene. He grew in power, was named one of the proprietors for the Carolina colony in North America, and became the first Earl of Shaftesbury. In 1672, he became lord chancellor and Locke was appointed as one of his secretaries. From a struggling clerk at Oxford, Locke quickly began to associate with men of political power.

Shaftesbury was a skillful politician and had many ideas about reforming society. (It has been supposed that he, not Locke, wrote the famous Essays and Treatises but allowed them to be published under someone else's name to avoid public criticism and perhaps condemnation.) He formed a group of intellectuals who met frequently and discussed these ideas. Locke was present for many of these meetings. The group laid the foundation for the eighteenth century political association called Whigs (as opposed to the Tories, or King's men). The politics of seventeenth century England were precarious, and both Shaftesbury and Locke found themselves out of favor in the 1680s so they went to Holland where political innovation was not so easily stifled. Shaftesbury died in Holland, but Locke returned to England in 1689.

Locke's name is associated with many ideas that became the hallmark concepts of the Enlightenment. In his famous *Essay on Human Understanding*, he connected the notion that a person is born into this world a "blank slate (*tabula rasa*) and that experience taught the human mind everything it could know. This theory, called empiricism, is still the basis of much of Western science.

Using the design that people learn only through experience, Locke developed theories about how people should and could live in their environment. In his *Two Treatises of Government*, Locke determined that people began their existence on earth in a "state of nature" in which there was no formal government or social institutions. A person was basically a good, happy, reasonable creature, not like Hobbes' brute.

Good and evil, reward and punishment, are the only motives to a rational creature: these are the spur and reins whereby all mankind are set on work, and guided.

People were free to do as they wished. However, people learned from their experience that it was better to join with others, to improve their survival chances and to make a better world together. By giving up some of their *freedom* people gained *liberty*, the advantages of a good community. The key point is that people, not God, made government.

Locke wrote much of his theory to counter works of two earlier English theorists, Hobbes and Filmer, who were royalists and defended the traditional notions of divine right. As political events in England were complicated by tensions between the monarch and the Parliament, more politicians turned to Locke's ideas and infused them into political positions. The attention turned to matching the nature of people, their tabula rasa attributes, and the right kind of government. William and Mary, for example, had taken the throne in 1689 at the "invitation" of Parliament. The notion of representative (not, one man one vote) government, of the community forming the government that would best serve its needs grew out of Locke's ideas.

Across England, aristocrats and the upper middle class met in their homes and at Parliament to discuss and refine new ideas about how government should be organized. Parlors and salons were places of heated arguments over concepts that once were only spoken of in secret places. Politicians like Henry St. John Bolingbroke invited poets and writers like Alexander Pope and Jonathan Swift to join in. The literature of the day reflected the furious debate. Pope's *Essay on Man* became popular not only in England but also on the continent and across the ocean in the English colonies. Swift's many writings, from *Gulliver's Travels* to *A Modest Proposal*, sometimes dripping with sarcasm, suggested ways to improve society. These Tory Poets, even though they were conservatives, provided not only entertainment but criticism of government and traditional institutions like the church.

A reading public wanted more knowledge. By now, printing presses were almost everywhere, and cities and towns had weekly and bi-weekly newspapers. By the beginnings of the eighteenth century, local gathering places, such as taverns and inns, became the focal point of discussions about the proper role of individuals and the right form of government. People read local, national, and international news although most papers were mainly filled with advertisements. Conversation focused on reform and progress, two new concepts in a world that had been bound by ancient rites. London developed coffee houses where conversations were as heated as those in the private salons of the wealthy.

In sections of London, particularly Grub Street, dissidents gathered, debated and wrote about injustices in society. The book by Peter Pinkus, titled: *Grub Street stripped bare: the scandalous lives & pornographic works of the original Grub Street writers, together with the bottle songs which led to their drunkenness, the shameless pamphleteering which led them to Newgate Prison, & the continual pandering to public taste which put them among the first almost to earn a fitful living from their writing,* alone, defines the growing numbers of popular writers who took political and social theories and presented them to the public.

As opposed to the group around Bolingbroke, these individuals were mostly Whigs, which meant in the early eighteenth century that their party was now in power. The Whigs, however, were not beyond corruption and included the first Prime Minister of England, Robert Walpole. They built the power of the Prime Minister and of Parliament around George's I inability to rule a country where he could not even speak the language. He had come from Germany and never learned English. There were several scandals, including the South Sea Bubble, where many lost their fortunes from poor investments. During Walpole's tenure his critics, Whig or Tory, were ready to condemn him and his compatriots.

In a small London neighborhood, John Trenchard and William Gordon became well known for their political articles. Their most famous pieces, called *Cato's Letters,* were short and to the point and were published in the English press. They touted freedom of thought as well as freedom of speech as sacred privileges. They used many of Locke's theories, such as the value of property (i.e., the results of a person's labor) as a yardstick for a people's contribution to their society and to their right to participate in government. For Trenchard and Gordon, liberty was a gift from God and no person or government could take it from the individual. History was a struggle between liberty and power and if liberty did not win, then individuals had not fulfilled their God-given role.

In 1722, *Cato* wrote a prophetic statement that showed how the ideas about people and their government had slowly changed from a purely divine system. The Newtonian concept of natural order is clearly shown in the description.

> *Government is political, as a human Body*
> *is natural, Mechanism:*
> *Both have proper Springs, Wheels, and a*
> *peculiar Organization*
> *To qualify them for suitable Motions,…*
> *the first Principle of all*
> *Power is Property: and every Man will*
> *have his Share of it in Proportion as he*
> *enjoys Property, and makes use of the*
> *Property,*
> *Where Violence does not interpose.*

THE NEW IDEAS SPREAD THROUGH EUROPEAN SOCIETY

These ideas filled the newspapers of England and then the English colonies. Some were smuggled to France where the government of Louis XIV condemned such notions. In Paris and in the countryside, a few French began to think that the despotism of Louis was not only unjust but corrupt and unbearable. If the English could formulate a government to suit their needs, why not the French?

In the sixteenth and seventeenth centuries, France was the center of European culture, fashion, and power. Even though the English controlled the seas and their colonies were growing rapidly, European political forces looked to France for leadership. Overseas colonies contributed to the French fashion monopoly, supplying furs from the New World. But the seeds of discontent were stirring.

Although the French political court was embedded in the traditions of monarchy and aristocracy, and the long reign of Louis XIV had made all French society center around his personality and whims, a small and growing group of French writers criticized the system. In the 1640s, when England was fighting against its king, the French experienced the Fronde uprising. However, Louis' government prevailed. What Louis did to stabilize his control brought controversy to the national conversation. He ended the toleration of Protestants, denied the middle class political power, and kept the nobility off balance by changing his favors among various families. The disapproval of the king's techniques grew despite political oppression. Louis' funeral was a welcomed event in the lives of many French people.

Francois Marie Arouet was born on November 21, 1694, in Paris to a family outside the power group that fluttered around Louis. He was educated in a famous Jesuit school and through a number of contacts, worked his way into a group of Parisian aristocrats. Witty and bright, Arouet could compose verse quickly, which pleased his new friends. In 1717, however, he recited a poem that ridiculed the French government, and he spent eleven months in the Bastille. When released, he continued to write but adopted the pen name "Voltaire" to hide his identity.

Voltaire was a multitalented writer frequently using sarcasm and wit. His quote "to hold a pen is to be at war" expressed his philosophy toward his own writing.

In 1726, Voltaire insulted a powerful young nobleman and went into exile in England. Here he read Locke and Newton and was fascinated by their ideas. After three years abroad, he returned home and quickly went back to writing. His *Letters on the English*, published in 1733, praised the ideas about liberty and a limited monarchy, but again he was censured. He then fled to the countryside and boarded with the first of many female supporters, Marquise du Chatelet. After her death, he was invited to Potsdam (near the present day city of Berlin, Germany) by Frederick the Great, the King of Prussia, who studied Voltaire's ideas and tried to implant some of them into his own style of "benevolent dictatorship."

In 1759, Voltaire purchased a small French estate called "Ferny" on the French-Swiss border. Soon his home became the "capital of the Enlightenment" and European intellectuals made their way to visit "the sage of Ferny." It is here he wrote, and among his works were the famous *Candide* (1759) and the *Dictionnair Philosophique* (1764). Voltaire was not optimistic about the nature of people and many of his works criticized society. In *Candide*, the central figure continually suffers from the selfishness and cruelty of society. However, he believed people were resilient and would find a way to live a peaceful life.

For Voltaire, free speech was crucial to a good society; his own suffering to keep this freedom alive in French society was well documented throughout his life. Although educated by priests, he was anticlerical and believed that French society should not be dominated by the clergy. He thought that a limited monarchy, an "enlightened despotism," was the best kind of government because he was unsure about the ability of average people to handle political power properly (for the good of all). He did have faith in the individual to do good if the right conditions were supplied. His famous closing of *Candide*, "and we must all cultivate our own garden," in some ways parallels Luther's and Calvin's notion of each person's calling, but Voltaire was concerned with living in this world, not the next.

When Voltaire was 83, he returned to Paris and was greeted by crowds praising him as a great man, almost a hero of the time. The celebration was so impressive that the old man wore himself out greeting people and died in the city that had so many times rejected him. His long and productive life set the stage for a social shift in France. His ideas, which lived long after him, would strike the political scene with the French Revolution.

A small, almost subculture, arose in France along with the fame of Voltaire. The death of Louis XIV and the weakness of the two Louis that followed him, provided a small gap in the political and intellectual landscape that would be filled to the brim by others who speculated on the nature of things, people, and government. As long as these ideas stayed in the "salon" society, they were tolerated, but, as with most intellectual commentary, they slowly seeped into general society, and then change—social and political revolution—appeared.

Voltaire's contemporaries were of varying interests. Denis Diderot and his associate, Jean la Rond D'Alembert, began a project to collect and coordinate all human knowledge. Their famous *Encyclopedia* summarized knowledge, with the resulting prescription that the lessons of history showed government needed to be reformed to allow for civil liberty for each citizen. On the conservative side, Charles Louis de Secondat, Baron de Montesquieu, defended monarchy but discussed the idea of the balance of power between the parts of government. In the *Spirit of the Laws* he described how the executive, legislative, and judicial branches needed to be divided into almost competing sectors so that no branch could control all, thus eliminating liberty from society. Both Montesquieu and Diderot saw, as Locke did, that power and liberty were at war and a concentration of power would destroy liberty.

Another contemporary of Voltaire was Jean Jacques Rousseau (1712-1778). He somehow always seems to be much younger than the others. Perhaps it was Rousseau's boyish style, as he spent much of his time wandering around France, living off the fortunes of adoring women, and immortalizing himself in his educational treatise, *Emile*, as a young dedicated teacher.

Rousseau was born in Geneva, the home of Calvinism. His family had migrated there generations before, after religious wars tore France apart. Rousseau's mother died soon after he was born from complications during birth. His father left him in the care of his uncle, who tried apprenticing the unruly child to several tradesmen, but the boy finally ran off. His passion was not for manual work but for writing. While quite young, he spent time with a young woman and fathered several children, all of whom were sent to the orphanage as he had no intention of supporting them. Much of his life, with few apologies, was catalogued in his *Confessions* that he began as a young man and completed later in his life.

This "free" life Rousseau lived was the basis of his theories about human nature. Luck and benefactors seemed to follow and find him. In 1749 he entered a contest about whether the arts and sciences had helped or hindered human's moral progress. His essay won first prize. His theory was that society had corrupted humankind from their original good nature. Supporters encouraged him, and he lived off their good

Rousseau enjoyed the beauty of Switzerland. Common people were inspired by Rousseau's attitudes toward equality and nobility, but ironically Rousseau despised commoners.

will and presents. He wrote an operetta, *The Village Socerer*, which met great success. He wrote articles for Diderot's *Encyclopedia*, and his career was set. Soon he won another contest with his *Discourse on the Origin of Inequality*.

Now famous as a literary figure, Rousseau earned his income from well-wishers, particularly women. In 1762, he produced his two most famous works, *Emile* and *The Social Contract*. These books praised the character of the individual in the natural state, definitely the opposite of the theories of the English writer, Thomas Hobbes. He said the state of nature was where people had lived in simplicity and in harmony (as opposed to the Hobbesian model where people were brutal). To improve the quality of life, early humans had joined into society by a voluntary contract. Unfortunately, the complicated society that had evolved after this simple agreement had corrupted people and now their only chance was to find a way back to the natural way of life.

The educational theory of *Emile* provided a way for a person to make this return. Instead of books of theory and complicated scenarios, a child should experience the natural world of goodness. The teacher should let children investigate, although protect them from harm. This way, the goodness and pureness of human nature would reappear. It is particularly out of this book that Rousseau lays part of the foundation for nineteenth-century Romanticism.

The world caused conflicts for Rousseau, and many of his ideas contradicted each other. While he glorified the "natural man," he advocated education. In praising the individual, he called for both democracy and totalitarianism. His most famous ideas, that of the noble savage and the general will, described a frenetic competition between the individual and society. He argued with his benefactors, often losing them to more rational writers. He wandered again, finished his *Confessions*, and tried to support himself by copying music. Meanwhile he began suspecting that every one was against him. Finally he settled in a small French town and kept to himself. On July 2, 1778, he suddenly died, some say by his own hand.

TOO MUCH CHANGE?

European women benefited from the changing assessments of the new epistemology, but it was a hard fought and complicated path that allowed a female role in science and philosophy. Women previously were not accepted in intellectual circles, and many "enlightened" men, including Voltaire, believed that these fields were beyond the needs, as well as the intelligence, of the "ladies." The specter of Eve, the corrupter of humankind, was an ever present memory in Western Civilization. In 1485, at the bequest of the Pope, Heinrich Dramer and James Sprenger, two Dominican monks, produced *The Mallelus Malificarum* or *The Witch's Hammer*. Since the time of the Black Plague, women had been under suspicion that they had consorted with the devil to cause evil. Now the Inquisition sought to identify and punish these horrid women.

The *Malleus* made it quite clear that women were against the stability and safety of society.

> *All wickedness is but little to the wickedness of a woman. . . What else is woman but a foe to friendship, an unescapable punishment, a necessary evil, a natural temptation, a desirable calamity, domestic danger, a delectable detriment, an evil nature, painted with fair colors. Women are by nature the instruments of Satan.*

The witch craze of the sixteenth and seventeenth centuries in Europe was a horrible period in a world struggling to break free of old ideas and traditions. The Reformation threatened the Roman Church; political theses threatened the monarchy and the aristocracy; art forms and music changed. It seemed as though all of Europe was convulsing and many believed it was not for the good of anyone. Each proponent looked for its opponent, and an "enemy" had to be found.

The hunt for witches, sometimes referred to by historians as "The Burning Times," was mostly a central European phenomena. It often occurred where the Church was vulnerable to the new ideas of the "protestants." In both Germany and the East, Catholic and Protestants saw evil in their attackers. There were many male witches, but as a whole, the verdicts of torture and death were handed down against women. Estimates of the executions range from 50,000 to 9 million over a period of three hundred years, but these estimates in the "campaign" against women are clouded and confusing. Many of the accusers were women themselves. In fact most women were safe from the long arm of the authorities. Although interviewed (the *Malleus* included investigation techniques and standardized questions) by Church officials, most were tried in secular courts. It is, however, true that the majority of those prosecuted were women, particularly older women who were without a husband and without children. These were, to some degree, "untraditional" women who did not fit the standard roles prescribed by society. On the other hand, in France, where far fewer trials were held than in Germany, about half the accused were men who seemed to be involved in political opposition rather than religious controversy.

There is no doubt that the *Malleus* provided the impetus to the hideous types of torture: thumbscrews and toe "smashers," the iron lady (a metal type coffin in which the live "witch" was placed until she confessed), the witch's cart (so all could see a caged witch), the disrobing of the accused so she had to appear in court naked, and so on. These "shows" of the "unacceptable" in society were popular, and the frenzy increased. Most trials and investigations were conducted by men, and even if women made the original accusations and testified, the attention they got was secondary to that males. Even if only a smaller number of women died, an attitude was slowly growing that a diversity of women should be more acceptable and that force would not limit differences that reason might see as new ideas. As a settlement of religious conflict turned towards political disagreements, the witchhunts died out. Women, however, still paid at least lip service to their traditional roles if they wished to be accepted.

FROM THOUGHT TO PRACTICE IN THE EUROPEAN COMMUNITY

The speculations of the "philosophes," as the French intellectuals came to be known, provided the subject matter for the universities and social groups of French society. Members of the traditional aristocracy often withdrew into ultra conservatism and defended the absolute monarchy, simply trying to save their privileged positions. A few supported conversations about the new theories, hoping to build a safe world for themselves by moving with change.

Across the European landscape, the new ideas began to affect many thinkers. Blaise Pascal (1623-1662) had a short but productive life. He was a child prodigy who helped his father, a tax collector for the city of Rouen, by inventing a calculating machine that made his father's job much easier. He also used the experiments of others to prove what Aristotle said could not exist, a vacuum. Although he was an innovator in many areas, Pascal was bound to the old notion that God was the prime mover of all that existed, and humans could only discover what He wanted them to know.

Georges-Louis Buffon (1707-1788) was a naturalist who classified all the inhabitants of the animal kingdom that he could discover. He believed that there was "progress" in their development; his 44 volume *Natural History* claimed that the European animals, being the oldest forms, were superior to all others.

In another field, Cesare Beccaria (1738-1794) became involved with a small group of Italian intellectuals. At the age of 26, Beccaria wrote *On Crimes and Punishments*, a treatise calling for rational treatment of criminals. His theory was based on the idea that a criminal was not an evildoer requiring punishment but rather a misdirected soul needing rehabilitation in the hopes of some day rejoining society. These ideas spread across Europe and created some reform.

Adam Smith defined the natural laws that he said governed commerce. The first law, he argued, was the law of self-interest.

In France, a group of economists called the "physiocrats" preached the notion of "laissez faire," which encouraged governments to let the economy develop without any intervention. The Scot, Adam Smith, visited these thinkers and returned home to spend ten years writing *The Wealth of Nations*. His basic notion was that there was only so much wealth in the world and there was much competition for it. He maintained that if the economic market place operated without interference, an "invisible hand" would guide each competitor so that the best products would be sold at the best price. He believed that there were natural laws that framed the economic world as there were for the universe at large.

In Germany, Immanuel Kant (1724-1804) stressed the idea that people must be free to discuss and disagree. Like Locke, he advocated political liberty and the importance of experience in critically analyzing the world. He believed that knowledge came from two sources: one from the senses and one from the mind. These notions would be the basis of the nineteenth-century philosophy of transcendentalism in both Europe and the United States.

David Hume (1711-1776), also Scottish, expanded the use of scientific principles into the realm of human morals. In *An Inquiry Concerning the Principles of Morals* he set the stage for a rational approach to understanding human behavior. He questioned the notion of causality, which claimed that for every effect there must be a particular cause. Hume claimed that there was no proof that one thing "caused" another thing to happen. This, of course, questioned the existence of the Prime Mover, or First Cause, which Christian Churches defined as God.

Hume was not alone in questioning the existence of God. From Voltaire through many of the Enlightenment figures, the idea of a Supreme

Immanuel Kant believed that humans had an innate sense of right and wrong. This served as a reason to believe in God.

Force who constantly watched and interfered with the world was the subject of heated conversations and disagreements. The "new" religious attitude was called Deism, where the "godhead," if he existed at all, sat back and let the laws of nature run the universe. Humans needed to study humans, and the introspection into divine things was left to the church.

THE ARTISTS

New ideas in science and the nature of human beings began to be seen not only in the written word but in art, architecture and music. In the middle of the sixteenth century, a new style was seen and heard. It was called "baroque" from the Portuguese word "barrocco," meaning "irregular pearl." The works of this period were complicated, uneven, asymmetrical, and almost confusing.

In response to the Reformation, the Roman Church sought to reaffirm its leadership across the European landscape. As they had in the Renaissance, the Popes sought to become the cultural patrons of the early sixteenth century. The Counter-Reformation encouraged art, literature and architecture that simplified the Church's message so all could see its truth. The opposing group supported a different style. They looked for compositions that emotionally connected the reader, listener, and viewer to their message. Soon the Church saw the advantage of this type of media.

Philip Neri, later canonized for his contribution to Church music, led small groups of laypeople to engage in spiritual conversation, study, and prayer. They met in prayer halls called oratories, becoming known as the Oratorians. Vocal music, although there was sometimes background music, was part of their devotions, and this form of music slowly grew into an accepted format, "oratorios."

Another Italian contribution to music was *opera*, the first being written by Claudio Monteverdi (1567-1643). These compositions were dramatic stories set to music. This new format met great success. There was a stage presentation, a play with music and voice rather than a script or dialog. Soon others were using the new medium. One of the most prolific was Antonio Vivaldi (1674-1741) whose famous *Four Seasons* is still a "popular" classical piece.

Beyond Italy, the most famous writer of *oratorios* was George Frederick Handel (1685-1759). Most of Handel's work was not in Latin but in English. His oratorios later included another new form, *arias*, songs set to an orchestral arrangement. Handel's most famous work was the *Messiah*, which used the text of the Bible as its message. Handel was an organist for many Protestant churches.

Another great Baroque figure, Johannes Sebastian Bach (1685-1750), was the master of a number of instruments, including the organ on which he could spontaneously play complicated pieces such as a *fugue,* a musical piece composed of three or four independent parts where one part, usually a voice, begins a theme, and then the other voices imitate it. The first voice, however, continues on a different "note" in a style called *counterpoint.* These multiple voices form a display of chords known as *polyphonic music.* Bach also introduced the *cantata,* which is a work of one or more singers accompanied by instruments.

These forms in music were echoed in painting and architecture. Whereas the Renaissance painters added dimension to painting, the Baroque painters "complicated" dimension with the shadings of light patterns and with an emphasis on the ordinary rather than simply the religious. Competition to win the various patrons was fierce, and the Church again led the way to successful reputations. Once more there was an emphasis on achieving an emotional response from the viewer.

One of the most famous early Baroque artists was Michelangelo Merisi (1573-1610) who quickly changed his name to Caravaggio after the town he came from. He is known for *tenebrism,* where the light and dark contrast. Usually, in his paintings, the light comes from above, centering on the main figure of the piece. One of Caravaggio's paintings, *The Entombment,* hangs in Philip Neri's Church in Rome.

One of the most fascinating painters of the period was Artemisia Gentileschi (1593-1653). Her father was an artist who introduced his young daughter to painting and she quickly outperformed him. She painted in the style of Caravaggio, but concentrated on women. Her *Judith Slaying Hologernes* contains the drama of a woman protecting her people by slaying the leader of an invading army; the picture is violent and produces an immediate emotional response.

Beyond Italy, the Dutch excelled in the Baroque techniques. The famous Rembrant van Rijn (1606-1669) also painted in the Caravaggio style. Instead of having the Church as his patron, Rembrant painted for wealthy citizens and the town fathers. His *The Night Watch* was a public commission from the Amsterdam Civic Guard. Jan Vermeer (1632-1675) used light to show the texture of clothing, materials and even architecture. Vermeer never left his hometown, Delft. His 35 paintings were only for local patrons and of mostly secular subjects.

The German Peter Paul Rubens (1577-1640) moved to Flanders and began a successful career, painting his own works and collecting those of others in the area: Titian (whose students copied Versallius' anatomical drawings into bright colors); Tintoretto, Van Eyck, Bruegel, and Raphael. The Baroque period was as active artistically as the Renaissance, and many supported themselves through wealthy patrons who desired paintings of their families, their homes, and simply anything that they could display and use to impress their friends.

GRAND BUILDINGS

The Roman Church attempted to reassert its power in rebuilding St. Peter's Cathedral. Michelangelo had created the great dome, but additions to the building made it the greatest architectural piece in Europe. (Remember that in 1453, the Muslims had conquered the city of Constantinople and converted the Hagia Sophia, the huge cathedral and center of Eastern Christianity, into a mosque.)

Papal support for the new improvements for St. Peter's demanded the spectacular. The cathedral itself was expanded, and within its walls, Gianlorenzo Bernini (1598-1680) built a magnificent canopy, or *baldaccino*, which stood almost 100 feet high. Ornate in design, it was decorated with the bees that symbolized the family of Pope Urban VIII. Outside the cathedral, a grand square and an arched colonnade designed by Bernini led the pious to the great church. A frontal Romanesque façade 147 feet high graced the cathedral, and figures of saints lined the roof. All of this composes St. Peter's square.

Perhaps Bernini's work is a good example to show the change in style. Michelangelo's famous statue of David is of a tall, powerful, but innocent youth. Bernini's David is an angry, aggressive young man poised for action. Statuary was no longer static and still but conveyed motion and action. So too did the architecture of the day, with towering obelisks and high ceilings, all decorated with massive art pieces that were full of crowds, activity, and the baroque counterpoints. Across Europe this new style was infused into old and new buildings.

FRENCH SALONS AND THE ROLE OF WOMEN

Upper class society in the seventeenth and eighteenth centuries had a kind of baroque quality. The traditional aristocrats craved recognition from their monarchs. Lavish parties, drinking excesses, and illicit affairs were practically the norm. In England, after the grayness of the Commonwealth period theaters reopened. Ribald plays attracted a wide variety of attendees, and the court was filled with festivities. In France, the court of Louis XIV, the Sun King, demanded excesses that made the English look prudish. The two kings who followed, Louis

XV and XVI, liked to party more than they liked to rule, so the aristocrats played along, again looking for attention by being ostentatious.

In French society some women were tiring of their traditional roles as objects of men's needs and prizes to be won on the marriage market. These women turned their role of hostess into an intellectual environment and created what is known as French salon society. Some were ladies with aristocratic connections and created circles of conversation that led not only into discussion but articulate articles and long distance contributors, making Paris the center of new ideas.

A few women led untraditional lives, especially young and hopeful ladies who wanted to do more than be a picture perfect lady. Madame Tencin was rumored to have escaped the convent her parents had placed her in, produced an illegitimate child (she was the mother of Diderot's collaborator, D'Alembert), and set up a salon, a place where individuals could discuss almost any idea that pleased them. On the one hand, women who enjoyed the conversation of men and attracted them to their homes were suspect because of their unconventional behavior. On the other hand, males—philosophes, scientists, physicians, and mathematicians—who flocked to these meetings often unwittingly made women important assets to French social and intellectual development.

Educational opportunities were minimal for women in France. The best that could be done was for a daughter to be sent to a nunnery where basic information, mostly about the Church and its saints, was conveyed. A few wealthy women were fortunate to have tutors or brothers who were educated at home and received a basic education. Even people who agreed that women should be educated had a hard time finding teachers and funds to pay for such an extravagance.

Educated French men and women gathered in salons like this one and listened to authors read or discuss topics of interest.

Many women were passionate in their search for knowledge and went to great lengths to expand their thoughts. In some ways, the salon was the perfect fit for this need. Women could throw parties and invite people who talked about the latest theoretical, artistic, and scientific information. As they wandered among their guests, they learned from and contributed to the conversations. Many wrote down their ideas, and although most were dismissed, it provided an opening for women to use their intellectual powers.

The names of intellectual salon women are not well known. Madames Geoffrin, Necker, Genlis, Rambouillet, and others have largely been overlooked by modern scholars. They were, however, instrumental in providing the rooms (salons) in which men, as well as women, felt free to speak about seemingly forbidden (and sometimes actually forbidden) topics, ranging from the way humans reasoned to the way government should be.

CENTRAL EUROPE

As reform and change occurred in France and England, the rest of Europe did not ignore the new ideas. The Scientific Revolution had been built by a community of people who lived all around the continent. Their common Latin language enabled many in the sixteenth and seventeenth centuries to communicate with each other, and they traveled and exchanged ideas with a certain ease. As French became the continental language, the Enlightenment slowly found its way to the cities and countries of Central Europe.

The map of Europe was quite different than it is today, with broad areas defined as Germany (mostly called the Holy Roman Empire), Poland, Russia, Austria and Hungary, but with borders that were vague and often disputed. Monarchs in these areas still clung to the notion that God had appointed them to rule, but they were interested in the ideas of progress and social change that the philosophes discussed. Voltaire had visited the King of Prussia. (He left after they argued about Frederick's god-given "rights.") Kant lived in a small German town where he was born; Leibnitz traveled through Germany, Italy and went to other eastern areas.

The West, really meaning France and England, and by the latter seventeenth century, the Dutch, had organized their countries around a "national" interest, the idea that a certain group of people had joined together (almost in Rousseau's Social Contract sense) in a political

Europe at the Beginning of the Enlightenment

organization. The Central European countries still consisted of a variety of people who were basically involved in agriculture rather than trade (at least international trade). Literacy was low, and most individuals did not travel far from their homes. Serfdom, particularly in Russia, was still part of the social and economic system.

In the midst of the intellectual critiques of European politics and society, much of the first half of the eighteenth century was embroiled in a complicated series of struggles that led to a situation of on and off wars. These involved the notion of "nationalism," where a particular area used history to justify its political organization. England and France had long turned to their past to justify their own governmental structures, but in Eastern Europe, the border still fluctuated and control was complicated by the agrarian nature of the population. When Charles VI of Austria died in 1740, he had ruled over a grand diversity of subjects and left a document, the

Pragmatic Solution, where he claimed the right to determine that his subjects remained united, and that his daughter, Maria Theresa, be the sole ruler.

Most of the European powers agreed to Charles' arrangement, but some were looking towards a future when they would be the most powerful area in Central Europe. One of those was Frederick II, King of Prussia, whose aggressive nature put him in direct conflict with Maria Theresa's claims. Frederick invaded Silesia to take it as his own. The War of the Austrian Succession (1740-1748) followed. The war was actually an international war, fought not only in Europe but also in the English and French colonies of North America. There was even conflict as far away as India. The British supported Maria Theresa, but their real intent was to break the continental power of France. With all the major powers of Europe engaged in warfare, shifting alliances brought about a new map in Europe.

In 1749, peace negotiations were set at Aix-la-Chapelle (once the seat of Charlemagne's empire) with Europe settling back to pre-war territories, except that Silesia stayed in Prussia's hands. The war had been a stalemate, with the British in control of the seas and the French dominating the land. After many bitter battles, nothing really seemed resolved, and a new conflict occurred 1756.

Alliances were now reversed. The English supported Prussia, and the French sided with Austria. The Seven Years War involved a new player, Russia, who feared a strong alliance between Britain and Prussia would damage both Austria and Russia and give Germany control of central Europe. This too was an international and intercontinental war, with the French fighting the British on both fronts. The Prussian-British alliance was a key factor, for the Prussians kept the French at bay in Europe while the English defeated them in North America. When the war ended in 1763, the British were in control of the American colonies, both French and English, and Prussia had grown to be the most powerful country in central Europe.

THE ENLIGHTENED DESPOTS

Rulers of Central European areas wished to retain supreme control over their subjects but to be respected by their Western counterparts. The result was a mix of new ideas with the old power structures. This was called "enlightened despotism," surely an oxymoron. The rulers of Prussia, Austria-Hungary, and Russia are classic examples of Enlightened Despots.

Frederick II (1712-1786), King of Prussia, grew up under the fierce and cruel criticism of his father. It was so horrendous that Frederick tried to run away to England. When he was captured and brought back, one of his punishments was to watch his friend and accomplice beheaded. He was forced to marry at the age of 21. Within a short time, he left his young bride, never to be closely involved with anyone else the rest of his life. After his death, his nephew took the crown.

Frederick spent lonely hours writing. His *Anti-Machiavel* was a rebuttal of the Renaissance writer's great work, *The Prince*. During these years, he wrote to Voltaire and the philosopher wrote back, beginning a correspondence that lasted many years and brought the Frenchman to Potsdam. When Frederick's father died, he assumed the throne.

Paternal domination affected Frederick's character. He was extremely reserved. He did, however, establish a small, intimate court at his home, San Souci, where discussion was more important than partying and drinking. These friends were mostly Frenchmen involved in the Enlightenment, men such as D'Alembert, La Mettrie, and others. Frederick admired the French and could speak and write French.

A strong military leader, Frederick engaged in both the War for Austrian Succession (associated with the Second Hundred Years War between the French and English), and the Seven Years War (that was, again, part of the Anglo French conflict). He was successful in adding territory to Prussia and made it dependent on his military style of leadership.

Frederick believed that the people, in general, were incapable of ruling or even suggesting the kind of government that might make their country grow and prosper. Under his initiatives, however, he set up trade monopolies, created new industries, effected legal and penal reforms, improved canals, constructed drainage projects, and built roads. It was his job, he believed, to make his country better, but he did not think the masses could help, except to obey his dictates.

In 1763, at the end of the Seven Years War, Frederick saw that the power of Russia could easily overcome the Prussian state so he formed an alliance with the Tsar, another enlightened despot. Catherine the Great (1729-1796) was a product of Central Europe. Born in what is now Poland, she was pledged to marry the Russian crown prince, Peter Feodorovich. A Lutheran by birth, Catherine not only changed her name (from Sophia Augusta), she converted to the Orthodox Russian Church to marry the heir to the Russian throne.

Catherine was strong, and intelligent. She quickly adopted the ways of the court and learned Russian. Peter was weak and not popular. In June 1762, she dressed as an Imperial Guard and led her troop to capture the Tsar. He was deposed and assassinated a few days later. Her role in the murder is unclear, but the villain was the brother of her lover so collusion probably occurred.

Catherine's reign was one of the most progressive and aggressive periods in Russian history. She instituted revisions in the political system without giving up her power; she improved roads and expanded cities, especially St. Petersburg; she took away church lands; she waged wars against the Ottoman Turks to Russia's south and, in her success, added a warm water port to Russia's territory, which now included the areas along the Black Sea. Literary criticism, like Novikov's journals which satirized Russian society, met with Catherine's approval and she allowed their publication. She even encouraged colonization, with the first colony in Alaska being established in 1785. A woman with almost endless energy, Catherine dominated the Russian court until her death in 1796.

Another strong and domineering monarch, Maria Theresa of the Austro-Hungarian empire, typifies the concept of enlightened despot. She gained the throne through a proclamation by her father that she should succeed him. Maria Theresa ruled the Austrian duchies, the Austrian Netherlands, Bohemia, and Hungary, or the heartland of Europe. Frederick II considered her a weakling and seized some of her lands in Silesia, but Maria Theresa fought back and gained a treaty with him to preserve the rest of her lands. Frederick had believed that her husband would co-rule, but Maria Theresa was the primary force in the government structure. After the Treaty of Aix-la-Chapelle, which ended the War of Austrian Succession, she and her chancellor turned the tables on Frederick and joined in an alliance with France who had been their traditional enemy. Slowly, however, the power of the Germanic areas passed to Frederick.

Maria Theresa turned her attention to her possessions. She enforced a series of agrarian reforms. Then, she centralized the government over her lands. Although she thought about the needs of her subjects, Maria Theresa was fully convinced they were her inferiors and should do as they were told. Her summer palace, Schonnenbrun, was so grandiose that even today, it is one of the most glorious palaces in Europe. Perhaps Maria Theresa's greatest contributions to history was that she produced 16 children, among whom were Joseph II (with whom she jointly ruled when he became of age), Leopold II, Marie Caroline of Naples, and Marie Antoinette of France.

THE PARTITION OF POLAND

Frederick, Catherine and Maria Theresa were convinced that they knew the best way to govern. The ruler of Poland was not so fortunate. Although Stanislaus II, King of Poland, had a small following, much of the government was in chaos. Whereas the Russian and Prussian states had solidified behind their monarchs, the Polish monarchy had strong opposition from various forces within the country. The system in Poland was that powerful nobles, called magnates, elected the king, and throughout the seventeenth and eighteenth centuries, the Polish kings had been too weak to keep the country together. Stanislaus decided to lead reform in Poland, setting the stage for constitutional changes that could have turned Poland into something like the English limited monarchy. He encouraged educational reforms and established the Zalulski library in Warsaw.

With pressure building from within, and with the powerful neighbors dismayed by the King's progressive notions, Frederick and Catherine decided to partition Poland. They convinced Maria Theresa to join them and annexed territories along their borders. Each

seemed satisfied that Poland was reduced to an insignificant territory. However, in 1772 events in the rest of the world temporarily turned their attention away from Poland. More divisions came in the 1790s as Poland tried to incorporate enlightenment ideas.

PUTTING THE ENLIGHTENMENT INTO PRACTICE

Discovery and settlement of the "New World" had created an opportunity to change the Old World. In the English colonies of North America, the traditions of English history, from the Magna Carta to the Civil War and the Glorious Revolution, had culminated in a society protective of its political liberties. These were the concepts that had been glorified by the European Enlightenment thinkers. Frenchmen, Poles, and many other Europeans came to defend them and to drive the "oppressive" and "unenlightened" English from their colonies. It was not a long war, following the many wars of the sixteenth and seventeenth centuries, but it was a war fought for ideals that a new generation of heroes believed would be the way of the future.

A new constitution was adopted in Poland in 1791, and the Russian army invaded in 1792. The Prussians followed. Soon only a tiny part of Poland was left, and the Russians supervised its government. In 1794, Thaddeus Kosciusko returned from the United States to his native Poland, inspired by the American victory and ideals for which he had fought. He led a national uprising against foreign troops. The French Revolution was beginning and the Russians and Prussians were not about to take the chance that Poland would be a shining star for political liberalism in Central Europe. In 1795, all of Poland was divided between Russia, Prussia and Austria and disappeared from the map of Europe.

CONCLUSIONS

The Renaissance of the fifteenth century laid the foundation for investigations and theories that became the Scientific Revolution and then the Enlightenment. Across Europe old ideas were being challenged and overturned. A new reliance on people's ability to understand was changing the way they saw their world and their role in it. Less attention was given to getting to heaven and more was given to living life here on earth. The universe had to conform to certain rules, natural laws, which guided the stars as well as human's actions. Even God had to conform to this system.

The first investigators were wed to the Church, and their success depended on their submission to its rules and traditions. As emphasis was increasingly placed on an individual's role and actions, the scientists, those who could prove their theories through mathematics or observation, became independent of their religious supervisors. This produced a alternate to religious explanations. Now the stage was set to reorganize society and to set up the modern world by rules people discovered worked for a broader majority of society.

Suggestions for Further Reading

Nicholas Copernicus, *On the Revolutions of the Heavenly Spheres*

D'Alembert, Diderot, *Encyclopedia*

Galilei Galileo, *Dialogue on the Two Chief World Systems; The Starry Messenger*

James Harrington, *Oceana*

John Henry, *The Scientific Revolution and the Origins of Modern Science*

Margaret C. Jacob, *The Enlightenment, A Brief History with Documents*

David Jacobson, *The English Libertarian Heritage*

Johannes Kepler, *Astronomia Nova*

John Locke, *Essay on Human Understanding; Two Treatises on Government*

Paula McDowell, *The Women of Grub Street: Press, Politics, and Gender in the London Literary Marketplace, 1678-1730*

Alexander Pope, *Essay on Man*

Jean Jacques Rousseau, *The Social Contract; Emile*

Charles Singer, *A Short History of Science*

Adam Smith, *Wealth of the Nations*

Jonathan Swift, *Gulliver's Travels; "A Modest Proposal"*

Andreas Versalius, *On the Structure of the Human Body*

Voltaire, *Candide; Dictionnaire Philosophe*

Eugen Wellesz, editor, *The Age of the Enlightenment, 1745-1790*

The French Revolution and Napoleon Bonaparte, 1789-1815

Napoleon Bonaparte

Louis XVI, formerly king of France, was taken from the prison in which French revolutionaries had held him back to the palace from which he had previously ruled. In the courtyard stood a scaffold with a guillotine ominously perched atop its wooden platform. A huge crowd numbering in the thousands had assembled to watch the guillotine do its nasty job. The carriage carrying the ex-king stopped before the platform. Guards took Louis from the carriage and attempted to partially undress him in preparation for the execution. Louis, however, refused to allow the guards to touch him. In an attempt to maintain his dignity the king, according to an account of the execution left by Englishman Henry Essex Edgeworth, a Catholic who witnessed the gruesome event, "untied his neck cloth, opened his shirt," exposing his neck to the guillotine's sharp blade. Likewise, when guards attempted to tie his hands Louis responded, "No! I shall never consent to that: do what you have been ordered, but you shall never bind me…." Almost immediately afterwards the king's neck was placed under the guillotine and with one blow the monarch's head was severed from his body. A guard then picked up the head by its hair, holding it aloft for the crowd to see while he paraded around the execution scaffold. At first, the spectators were silent as if they could not believe what they had just witnessed. Then someone among the multitude shouted "Vive la Republique!" Within a few minutes the entire crowd had taken up the cry, celebrating their victory over what many viewed as an oppressive monarchy.

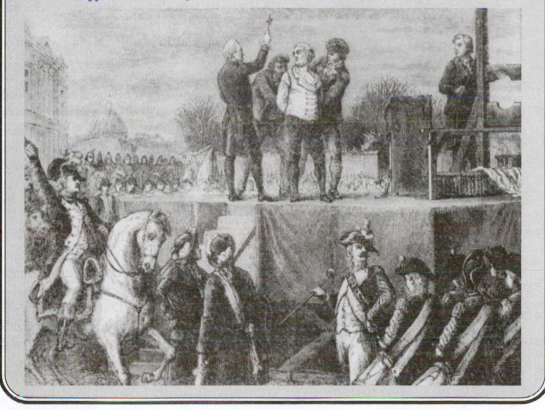

Chronology

1789   French Revolution Begins; Estates General Opens; Tennis Court Oath Bastille Falls; Declaration of the Rights of Man and Citizen

1790   Civil Constitution of the Clergy New Constitution accepted by Louis XVI

1791   Declaration of Pillnitz

1792   France and Austria go to war

1793   Louis XVI and Marie Antoinette are executed; The Constitution of 1793 is adopted; *Levee en masse* is instituted; Cult of Reason declared in effect.

1794   Robespierre falls and is executed

1795   Directory established

1796   Napoleon begins to have military successes

1797   Treaty of Campo Formio

1798   Nelson defeats the French at Abukir

1799   Consulate created in France

1801   Concordat with Papacy

1802   Treaty of Aminens

1804   Code Napoleon issued

1806   Battle of Trafalgar; Continental System Established

1807   Treaty of Tilsit

1808   Spanish Revolution

1812   Russian invasion begins

1813   Battle of the Nations at Leipzig

1814   Congress of Vienna meets

1815   Waterloo

1821   Napoleon dies on St. Helena

The execution of Louis XVI was part of the French Revolution, the most important political event of the eighteenth century in all Europe and throughout most of the world. Forces unleashed by this seminal event shaped events for the next two centuries, forever changing the world. When the revolution erupted in 1789, nobody could forecast all the twists and turns it would take or that it would give way ten years later to dictatorship under Napoleon Bonaparte.

CAUSES OF THE FRENCH REVOLUTION

Although the causes of the French Revolution are complex, it was financial bankruptcy within the French monarchy that provided the spark that ignited the rebellion. Louis XVI inherited a large debt from his predecessors. Yet, he did nothing to bring France's budget deficit under control. Instead, he presided over a government that tripled its national debt from 1774 to 1789. Louis XVI's decision to aid the American revolutionaries in their fight against England added to an already large government debt. French support for the American colonists cost the monarchy three times the amount of its yearly tax collections. France's financial problems became so acute by 1788 that interest payments on the national debt consumed about half the government's income.

Controversy within the government about how to best solve France's financial problems complicated matters. As early as 1785, Anne-Robert Turgot, the Physiocrat economist who briefly served as Louis XVI's chief minister, predicted a financial crisis if France's deficit spending was not brought under control. For a brief period Turgot was allowed to reduce government expenditures, but a group of special interests led by Queen Marie Antoinette persuaded Louis to dismiss Turgot. His replacement, Jacques Necker, maintained that if expenditures devoted to the American Revolution were subtracted, France's budget would show a surplus that could be applied to the national debt. Necker's figures, however, were incorrect.

By 1786 the French government had borrowed all that creditors would allow to hide the deficit. Bankers, convinced that France would never be able to pay its national debt, refused to loan the government any more money. Their refusal caused Louis to revive Turgot's earlier plan of austerity and increase taxes on the French population. The finance minister, Charles Alexandre de Calonne, hoped to promote economic growth by stimulating manufacturing, lowering some taxes, and requiring nobles and clergymen to pay money to peasants for services rendered. Calonne's most important proposal to deal with France's financial crisis was enactment of a new tax on land that would be paid by all landowners regardless of social class. In 1787 Calonne asked the Assembly of Notables to accept his plan. This body, which consisted of France's highest-ranking aristocrats and church officials upon whom the tax burden would be most heavy, refused to support Calonne's proposal. Louis then dissolved the Assembly of Notables and fired Calonne, replacing him with Etiene Charles Lomenic de Brienne, the Archbishop of Toulouse and chief opponent of Calonne in the Assembly of Notables. After taking office, Brienne discovered that the financial crisis was as bad as Calonne had said and thus adopted the land tax of his predecessor. The Parlement of Paris, a local governing body, refused to endorse the tax, insisting that only the Estates General could impose a new tax on French landholders. Brienne then appealed to the Assembly of the Clergy, asking them to fund interest on the French debt that was coming due.

The church responded by cutting payments to the government by about 83 percent. The Parlement of Paris then passed a resolution declaring the new tax to be illegal. Louis took the matter to the Royal Appellate Court, which like the Assembly of Notables, rejected the tax hike. Consequently, the French financial crisis deepened.

At about the same time, rioting broke out in several French cities. Aristocrats, clergymen, and middle class bourgeois insisted that under French law only the Estates General could impose new taxes on French citizens. Faced with little alternative, and desperate for money, Louis XVI reluctantly called into session the Estates General, a national legislature that had not met since 1614. The Estates General was comprised of representatives from three broad social classes legally defined within France: the First Estate consisting of clergymen, the Second Estate made up of aristocrats, and the Third Estate that included everybody else—peasants, bankers, business owners, farmers, lawyers, doctors, etc.

Each of the three estates had its own class interests that did not always coincide with interests of the other classes. Thus, class fighting often occurred in sessions of the Estates General. Social tensions between the three estates contributed to the outbreak of revolution in France. The first two estates represented only a small faction of France's population. Less than 3 percent of French residents were aristocrats or clergymen. About 97 percent of the population belonged to the Third Estate. Yet, the First and Second Estates had traditionally exercised much control within French government and society. The disproportionate control and social status exercised by the First and Second Estates had caused problems in French society for centuries. Although they comprised only 1/2 percent of the population, clergymen controlled 15 percent of France's land. This inequitable situation created resentment within the Third Estate. Anger and disgust simmered beneath the surface of what from outward appearances seemed to be a tranquil society. Many ordinary people despised the 10 percent tithes they had to pay the church every year. Tithes, on top of heavy taxation by the government, left many citizens destitute. French citizens also disliked the fact that the church was largely exempt from taxes. Instead of being officially taxed, church officials had agreed to donate money (the *don gratuit*) to the government. In the eyes of Third Estaters, the *don gratuit* was too small. French citizens in Paris and other towns recognized a need for governmental social services in urban areas that could not be provided because the church's *don gratuity* was so low. Even though the average French man and woman remained loyal Catholics and respected the parish priest, they disliked the wealth, social status, and privileges accorded to high-ranking clergymen.

Nobles that comprised the Second Estate also provoked resentment from most members of the Third Estate. The aristocracy, which comprised about 2 1/2 percent of France's population, controlled about 20 percent of its land. Like the clergy, nobles were generally exempt from taxes and were given privileges and rank within French society. Members of the Second Estate usually controlled the army and church by virtue of being granted commissions and ecclesiastical office. In addition, Third Estaters had to pay various tariffs and duties to aristocrats. The nobility, however, was itself divided into different classes. At the very top were "Nobles of the Sword," families whose position was inherited from generation to generation. Some families were descended from royalty or feudal barons of the Middle Ages while others had been made nobles by the king at a later time.

These aristocrats tended to look down upon everybody else, including lesser aristocrats. Beneath the Nobles of the Sword were the "Nobles of the Robe." They had achieved their position by purchasing it from the monarchy. Most Nobles of the Robe were originally merchants willing to buy a higher social status. The lowest level of the Second Estate contained the *obereaux*, aristocrats who were not wealthy and who exercised little influence within French society. Like their more lofty brethren, the French population also despised these small estate owners because they supported themselves by collecting ancient feudal dues from peasants and workers.

Anyone who was not an aristocrat or clergyman belonged to the Third Estate. The largest majority of the Third Estate were peasants who held small amounts of land. These people were generally impoverished, barely managing to eke out a meager existence from day to day. Peasant resentment against nobles and clergy was generally pronounced. From the peasant perspective, the First and Second Estates lived lavish lifestyles as a result of collecting high taxes, fees, and tithes from poor peasants who barely survived.

Economic and social conditions contributed to peasant social unrest. Inflation, caused by the government's debt, hurt peasant farmers and artisans. Prices paid for goods they sold did not keep pace with products they had to buy. In addition, profits were used to pay a wide array of taxes and fees—church tithes, feudal dues, property taxes, income taxes, poll taxes, and others. After paying all these taxes and fees members of the Third Estate often had little left.

Agricultural practices and policies also contributed to the peasant farmer's misery. Much French land was not farmed at all; other fields lay fallow every other year because modern methods of fertilization were not used in France prior to 1789. A rapidly growing population added to peasant problems. After paying all the taxes and fees and feeding the increasing number of family members, peasant farmers had only a small agricultural surplus to sell. Famine often engulfed local populations within France. These famines could have been prevented had the government lifted restrictions on the free movement of grain within the country that had been enacted during the Middle Ages to keep local grain prices high. Such laws prevented regions that produced a bumper grain crop from selling to regions hurt by excessive drought or insect infestations. After facing a crisis or two, peasants often had to sell their land and move to cities in search of work or turn to crime to survive. These conditions created a revolutionary fervor among peasants. They perceived their class as being in decline. The only thing, most believed, that would reverse their fortunes was a redistribution of land and a reduction of taxes, tithes, and other fees assessed against peasant farmers.

Not all members of the Third Estate were peasants. Urban workers and middle class bourgeoise businessmen, doctors, lawyers, and scholars were also part of this class. Like peasants, the bourgeois were also resentful of the status and privileges nobles enjoyed and were affected by economic conditions within France. Laborers were particularly discontented. Wages did not increase at the same rate as inflation, which hurt workers' ability to support themselves. Even though French law forbade workers to form unions, labor often engaged in strikes to protest rising prices. These strikes hurt production in fledgling industries and contributed further to economic woes workers faced. Moreover, it was difficult for workers to advance in their profession. Apprentices and journeymen found their path blocked by archaic laws and customs that were holdovers from the medieval guild system.

Within urban areas a class of displaced workers who were permanently unemployed developed. Discontent among such workers had slowly fermented for decades. Things were so bad in French cities that workers, who previously had been divided into separate groups—skilled, semi-skilled, artisans, day laborers, etc.—developed a class consciousness. Despite their differences in skill level or trade, all urban workers came to fear unemployment and starvation. This fear united all laborers.

In the French Revolution the bourgeois took advantage of worker discontent to take away the status and privileges enjoyed by the clergy and nobility. Middle class merchants, bankers, lawyers, factory owners, doctors, storekeepers, and others, who often were wealthier than nobles and clergymen, also resented the status and privileges enjoyed by the First and Second Estates. Bourgeois members of the Third Estate ultimately provided leadership for the French Revolution and molded agitated workers into a political force. Even though the bourgeois did not experience the economic hardships peasants and workers faced, their tax burden was still heavy, especially in comparison to that of clergymen and aristocrats. Because of these inequities the middle class readily criticized the French monarchy. In particular, bourgeois merchants complained about excessive taxes, duties, and laws the medieval guild system placed on commercial activity. French businessmen wanted these ancient laws and taxes that restricted free trade abolished. Another complaint voiced by the bourgeois was that they were treated as second-class citizens by the government. Aristocrats looked down upon the bourgeois even though many merchants, bankers, doctors, lawyers, and others in the entrepreneurial classes were far wealthier and more talented than either Nobles of the Sword or the Robe. French law and customs prohibited bourgeois from holding prominent positions in the church, government, or military, which were reserved for members of the Second Estate. Faced with such inequality, it is not surprising that the bourgeois would lead the French Revolution. More articulate, better educated, and wealthier than the peasants, the middle class provided the voice for Third Estate concerns. When the Estates General met in 1789, the Third Estate formulated a set of grievances, which were presented to the Estates General after it was called into session.

THE REVOLUTION

Once the Estates General met, social and political forces were unleashed that nobody in France could control. Before things settled, the monarchy was overthrown, a republic was created, radical views took hold throughout France, hundreds lost their lives, and a dictatorship emerged under Napoleon Bonaparte.

Even before the Estates General met conflict between the three estates erupted. The clash began when representatives from the Third Estate refused to allow church officials and aristocrats to make decisions about how the legislative assembly would be organized. Aristocrats representing the Second Estate tried to limit the power of the Third Estate by insisting that each estate have the same number of representatives regardless of its population. If this proposal were accepted, a type of legislative malapportionment would plague the Estates General. Nobles and clergymen would have far more influence in the legislature than warranted by their population. Adding to the controversy was a ruling by the Parlement of Paris, dominated by aristocrats, in September 1788 that each estate in the Estates General should have only one vote. If this procedure was followed it meant that aristocrats and clergymen of the First and Second Estates, who tended to have common interests because church officials were usually drawn from ranks of the nobility, could combine their votes and always prevail over the Third Estate. Such a procedure certainly was not democratic, nor was it fair. The Third Estate, as might be expected, refused to accept either of these ideas. The lawyers and merchants who largely represented the Third Estate were already suspicious about the motives of the aristocrats. For years, the middle class had suffered as a result of political, economic, and social discrimination at the hands of nobles. Attempts by the aristocracy to limit the Third Estate's power and dominate the legislature only increased middle class resentment.

The dispute between the First, Second and Third Estates was settled when Louis XVI's royal council decided that giving the Third Estate more power in the Estates General would make it easier for the monarchy to increase already existing taxes and impose new ones on clergy and aristocrats. So long as the First and Second Estates dominated the Estates General, it was unlikely that they would vote to raise taxes on themselves. Thus, in December 1788 the Royal Council doubled representation from the Third Estate. This meant that the middle class, if each representative was allowed one vote, could determine the type of taxes imposed by the Estates General and, more importantly, on whom they were imposed. However, the question of how votes would be cast, by head or by Estate, was yet to be resolved.

When delegates assembled at Versailles in May 1789, representatives from the Third Estate presented Louis XVI with a long list of grievances. These *cahiers de doleances*, as they were called, had been compiled by local electors and included complaints about corruption within the church, high taxes, unfair fees, and privileges such as hunting rights aristocrats enjoyed but others were denied. The *cahiers de doleances* also contained various demands such as regular meetings of the Estates General, fair and equitable taxes, a national system of weights and measurements, government subsidies for business, freedom of the press, more autonomy for locally elected government officials, and equal rights under French law for all male citizens.

Before action could be taken on the list of grievances, the previous question of how voting would occur had to be decided. Louis XVI, bowing to pressure from influential aristocrats, decreed that each estate would sit separately and cast one vote. The Third Estate refused to follow this edict, insisting that each representative be allowed to cast one vote. For several weeks the three estates confronted each other over this issue. Neither side would give in to the other. Then, without warning, on June 1 the Third Estate asked aristocrats and clergymen to abandon the Estates General and join together to form a new national legislature. With the exception of a few low ranking nobles and clergymen, the First and Second Estates ignored this invitation. Despite lack of participation from aristocrats and clergymen, on June 17, 1789, members of the Third Estate formed a new legislature that they named the National Assembly. Three days later, delegates to the National Assembly, meeting on a tennis court because they were accidentally locked out of their usual meeting hall, swore an oath not to adjourn until France became a republic governed under a constitution. Known as the famous "Tennis Court Oath," this vow was one of the most important events in the French Revolution. It ultimately meant the end of the Old Regime (the name given to the government of Louis XVI prior the 1789) that controlled France. After hearing about the Tennis Court Oath, Louis XVI condemned the National Assembly's actions, ordering it to disband.

Despite the king's order to disband, members of the National Assembly honored the Tennis Court Oath, continuing to meet on a regular basis. Several days after the Tennis Court Oath, relations between Louis XVI and members of the First and Second Estates deteriorated so badly that most nobles and clergymen joined the National Assembly. On June 27, Louis bowed to popular pressure, replacing the Estates General with the National Assembly. The few representatives of the First and Second Estates who had refused to join the National Assembly were ordered to do so. Within the National Assembly, which later renamed itself the National Constituent Assembly, votes were cast by individuals rather than by social class. France's government was forever changed. Gone were the days when hereditary aristocrats and clergymen ruled the country, enjoying privileges others were denied.

Perhaps the most celebrated event in the French Revolution was the fall of the Bastille, a prison fortress once used to house enemies of the monarchy. On July 14 over eight hundred residents of Paris marched to the prison's gates searching for weapons. Fearing for his life, the prison superintendent ordered troops guarding the fortress to fire upon the crowd. Nearly a hundred people were killed when the soldiers opened fire. The attack angered the mob, which then stormed the prison, broke down its gates, released the prisoners housed within, and killed the superintendent and troops guarding him.

Precipitating the attack on the Bastille was Louis XVI's dismissal of Necker, his chief financial minister, and the assemblage of royal troops in Versailles and Paris. French citizens believed that the king was going to attack the National Assembly and end the revolution. Residents of

Paris, who largely supported the revolution, became anxious when royal troops entered the city. Adding to their anxiety was a shortage of food that had produced riots during the winter and spring of 1789. Necker's dismissal, along with the presence of royal troops, was seen as the beginning of a conservative assault upon the liberal revolution. To protect the National Assembly, Parisians formed the Militia of Paris, which eventually developed into a national guard. It was members of the Paris Militia that stormed the Bastille searching for arms that could be used to outfit its various companies. One day after the Bastille fell, the Paris Militia persuaded the Marquis de Lafayette, hero of the American Revolution, to take command of the organization. Lafayette accepted command. One of his first acts was to create an insignia for the militia, red and blue stripes that represented Paris separated by the white stripe of the monarchy. Revolutionary leaders later adopted Lafayette's flag as the primary symbol of the French Revolution.

Violence similar to that which rocked Paris soon spread to other towns and cities. Louis XVI realized that popular pressure was going to prevail. As a sign that he was willing to allow elected assemblies to control French towns and provinces, Louis visited Paris a few days after the Bastille's fall. Clad in the revolutionary colors designated by Lafayette, the king decreed that officials elected by popular vote constituted the official government of Paris. Louis also proclaimed that the National Assembly was the legitimate government of all France and that Lafayette's National Guard was its legitimate defender. For all practical purposes the French monarchy as a governing authority was destroyed.

In July and August 1789, panic, known as the Great Fear, spread across France. The panic began when travelers from Paris brought news about riots in the city to rural districts. Rumors began to spread that royal troops would be dispatched into the countryside. Peasant after peasant relayed the news that the "brigands were coming" to subdue a rural uprising that had started in the spring. Rural inhabitants reacted by arming themselves to protect homes, family, livestock, and crops. Within weeks the uprising intensified. Peasants turned on nobles, burning manor houses, destroying public records, and refusing to pay feudal dues. Peasants also seized food and property they considered rightfully theirs and reclaimed privileges that aristocrats had previously taken. The peasant uprising ultimately served to destroy remaining vestiges of the feudal regime.

The National Assembly tried to restore order by dealing with peasant grievances. On August 4 several representatives, in a prearranged move, surrendered rights and privileges that peasants had already taken from them. Among the privileges surrendered were hunting rights, fishing rights, special exemptions from taxation, banalities, seigneurial privileges, and judicial authority. Serfdom and slavery were abolished. Manorial dues, along with church tithes, were also ended, but peasants were required to pay compensation to former manorial lords. In most cases, nobles received little money because peasants could not afford to pay. Later, in 1793, the National Assembly repealed the law requiring compensation for manorial obligations. The most important result of August 4 was that all French citizens became equal under the law when the feudal regime was abolished.

Reforms undertaken on the "Night of August 4" led to issuance of the Declaration of the Rights of Man and Citizen on August 26, 1789. This document, which was influenced by the

Declaration of Rights adopted by the American state of Virginia in 1776, set forth individual and group rights the government would respect. Article I, for example, declared that all "men are born and remain free and equal in rights." Moreover, the declaration proclaimed that all men had the natural rights of "liberty, property, security, and resistance to oppression." French citizens were also granted religious freedom, due process of law, the right to run for and hold public office, equal employment rights, freedom of thought, the presumption of innocence until proven guilty, the right to own land, and taxes apportioned according to the individual's ability to pay.

The Declaration of the Rights of Man and Citizen also set forth principles of government. Ultimate sovereignty resided with the national government. Law was declared to be the expression of the general will, and taxes could only be imposed and increased by the consent of the people. Government officials were to be held accountable for their behavior while in office. Private militias were outlawed; all military forces could act only on behalf of the nation. Private property could be taken through eminent domain but only if fair compensation was offered. Governmental power was divided among the executive, legislative, and judicial branches, and a system of checks and balances was instituted to prevent one branch of government from becoming too powerful.

Thousands of copies of the Declaration of the Rights of Man and Citizen were printed and distributed throughout France. Frenchmen often framed the document and hung it on their walls. It became the most powerful symbol of the French Revolution, ranking as important as Lafayette's flag and the slogan "liberty, equality, fraternity."

Women and the French Revolution

Even though the Declaration of the Rights of Man and Citizen espoused lofty ideas, it was biased against women. The word "man" in the title was deliberately included. The document's authors did not intend to grant women equal rights. Reflected within its content was the view that males were suited for citizenship and public life while women were fit only for domestic life and childbearing. Women certainly were not accorded the same rights as men.

Despite not being given equal rights, French women played an important role in the 1789 Revolution. On October 5 a mob of Parisian women, sporting knives, guns, sharp sticks, and swords, marched on Louis XVI's palace at Versailles demanding that the monarch do something to alleviate the bread shortage that gripped Paris. This crowd, which numbered between six and eight thousand, marched around the palace for the entire night. Louis, intimidated by the protestors, agreed to honor laws enacted by the National Assembly. His deference to the legislature, however, did not satisfy the Parisian women. Suspicious of the monarchy, they demanded that Louis and his family return to Paris where the people could monitor his actions. On October 6, Louis, Queen Marie Antoinette, and their children followed the women protestors back to Paris. Historians generally view the "March of the Women" as the first time popular sovereignty triumphed over the monarchy in the French Revolution.

Some women, angered at the denial of rights in the Declaration of the Rights of Man and Citizens, sought to bring women's rights to the forefront of the revolution. One such woman was Olympe de Gouges, a prominent playwright who published *The Rights of Women* in 1791. Modeled after the male Declaration of the Rights of

Man and Citizens, its seventeen articles applied the same rights to women that men had previously received. In addition, de Gouges insisted that women be given the right to divorce husbands, control of marital property after divorce, access to institutions of higher education, and opportunities to pursue employment outside the home. De Gouges's *Rights of Women* led Mary Wollstonecraft, an English woman, to publish a similar document, *Vindication of the Rights of Women,* in 1792. Wollstonecraft's treatise included many of the same demands that de Gouges made. Despite the protests de Gouges and Wollstonecraft raised, women's demands were generally ignored when French men reformed the government. Women were not given equal rights when the 1791 Constitution was written.

The 1791 Constitution

After the revolution had begun, the most important task facing the National Assembly was drafting a constitution by which France could be governed. This document is known as the 1791 Constitution. It decentralized the French government, dividing the country into eighty-three departments of roughly equal size. These departments replaced ancient provinces such as Burgundy, Anjou, Marche, Lorraine, and Picardy, which were officially abolished. Each department was small enough to have its capital located within one day's travel of outlying areas. Examples of the new French departments include Nord, Marne, Allier, Dordogne, Indre, Lot, Aude, and Gers, to name but a few. Each department was subdivided into districts called *arrondissements*. The districts were further divided into cantons and communes. Elected councils controlled each division of local government and enjoyed a great deal of autonomy.

The central government the 1791 Constitution established included the principle of separation of powers. Law-making bodies of the Old Regime were replaced by an elected national legislature. Courts and other judicial bodies that existed under the monarchy were abolished. Replacing them was an elected judiciary. An executive branch, headed by the king, was created. The monarch's power was somewhat reduced. His authority to issue edicts, for example, was taken away. All decisions the king made were subject to approval of his ministers. Yet, because most ministers owed allegiance to the king, they tended to uphold most of his decisions. The monarch also had limited veto power; he could only block legislation passed by the legislature for four years. The 1791 Constitution abolished most aspects of the Old Regime. Government bureaus, ministries, taxes, titles of nobility, parliaments, regional laws, and geographical boundaries disappeared. Louis XVI had lost the status of absolute monarch. Reflecting this change, he was forced to adopt the title "King of the French," (previously his title had been King of France) to show that he no longer owned all property in the country. France was also given a new legal code that was uniform throughout the country. The new legal code made many changes in the law, declaring, for instance, that marriage was a civil contract rather than a religious sacrament and provided for free public education for all French men.

Even though the 1791 Constitution was more democratic than the absolute monarchy France was previously governed under, it did not give France full democracy. Many people were denied suffrage. The constitution created two classes of citizens—active and passive. Only active citizens, defined as males who paid taxes equivalent to three days of wages at the local labor rate, could vote. Active citizens themselves did not make laws or vote directly for legislative representatives. Instead, they voted for electors who then chose members of the legislature. Most Frenchmen were not qualified to be electors or members of the legislature because they did not meet the necessary property qualifications. Of France's total population of twenty-five million, only about fifty thousand owned enough property to serve in the legislature or as electors. Women and passive citizens, who paid little taxes, enjoyed the complete protection of the law but could not vote or hold public office. Propertied interests still dominated the French government. The difference was that the 1791 Constitution took political power away from aristocratic land-owners and clergymen, distributing it to non-aristocratic property holders. The poor were still not politically empowered.

RADICALISM AND THE SECOND REVOLUTION

The move toward moderate constitutional government did not save France from radicalism. Moderates in the National Assembly were eventually pushed aside by extremists. Weakening the moderate position was passage of the Civil Constitution of the Clergy. This document, necessary to complete confiscation of church lands, made the Roman Catholic Church a branch of the secular government. The number of bishoprics was reduced from 135 to 83, and diocese borders were made to fit into boundaries established by the departments. Priests and bishops were required to stand for election and became salaried employees of the government. Church and state were not separated in France. Passage of the Civil Constitution of the Clergy was perhaps the biggest mistake the National Assembly made. Relations between the Catho-

lic Church and the French government deteriorated. Opposition within the Church surfaced because neither the Roman Pope nor French clergy were consulted about changes prior to their approval. In an attempt to control the clergy, the National Assembly declared that all clergymen were required to swear an oath to support the 1791 Constitution. Most clergymen refused to take the oath. The National Assembly then declared that clergymen who refused to support the constitution were "refractory priests" or outlaws and officially removed them from their positions of authority. Church reaction was swift. Refractory priests refused to step aside, and in February 1791 the Pope denounced the French Revolution. He condemned both the Civil Constitution of the Clergy and the Declaration of the Rights of Man as being heretical. The Pope's attack upon the French Revolution created a dilemma for ordinary citizens. How could they be both loyal Catholics and loyal French citizens? Religion and politics became incompatible for many French people. Some French citizens continued to support the outlawed priests while others supported the state church. Moderates in the government nevertheless saw their support eroded by this religious issue. Supporters of the refractory priests could not in good conscience support any government official, no matter how moderate their views might be.

Moderates also faced problems because they were unable to develop an effective party organization due to opposition from a radical minority called *Jacobins*. The Jacobins wanted to create a republic with universal suffrage and completely abolish the monarchy. To accomplish these goals, they created a network of political clubs across France. Working through these clubs, Jacobins gained control of most local and departmental governments. They then used local elections to eventually gain control of the national government.

On October 1, the first and only meeting of the legislature created by the 1791 Constitution occurred. Unfortunately, the brief session of the Legislative Assembly was plagued by factionalism. No one group held enough seats to enact its policies. However, the radical Jacobins, often called *Girondists* because they originated from the Department of Gironde, captured leadership positions within the assembly by forming an alliance with centrists delegates (usually called Plain or Marsh representatives). Jacques Brissot, a liberal attorney and journalist, led the Girondists. Brissot and his Girondists followers used nationalism to claim power in France's legislature. They portrayed France as being victimized by a conservative foreign conspiracy. According to Girondists, French *émigrés*, nobles who had fled the country during the revolution, aided by refractory clergy, the royal family, and foreign powers, were planning to overthrow the revolutionary government.

There was some truth to Girondists fears. On August 27, 1791, a group of émigrés pressured Austrian Emperor Leopold II, the brother of Marie Antoinette, and Frederick Wilhelm II, the King of Prussia, to issue the *Declaration of Pillnitz*. Both monarchs agreed to send military forces to restore the French monarchy if other European powers agreed to support intervention. Likely, intervention would not have occurred because England was unwilling to support Austria and Prussia. Nevertheless, Girondists interpreted the *Declaration of Pillnitz* as threatening the revolution and appealed to French patriotism to preserve the changes. Consequently, on April 20, 1792, Girondists persuaded the Legislative Assembly to declare war on Austria. Prussia soon entered the conflict to aid its Austrian ally. This war continued on and off for the next twenty-three years.

Oddly, both radicals and conservatives in France favored war. Girondists believed the conflict would make the revolution safe from its enemies abroad. In contrast, monarchists, including Louis XVI, wanted war because they believed foreign troops might defeat revolutionary forces, roll back changes within French society, and restore the Old Regime to its former glory.

Initially, the war went badly for France. Many experienced military officers had left the country as émigrés, and the army had trouble repelling Austrian and Prussian invasions. Food shortages were acute in many parts of the country. These difficulties led to a second revolution that was far more radical than the first.

War with Austria and Prussia radicalized the French population, producing the second revolution that overthrew the monarchy. Jacobins, using war as a cover, plotted a more radical revolution. Because they appealed to French patriotism, Jacobins gained a loyal following from within the military and from citizens angered over the shortage of food and the government's use of *assignats*, worthless paper notes used to pay its debts. Throughout the summer of 1792 Jacobins took control of Paris's forty-eight districts. On August 9 and 10 Jacobins used their control of local municipal districts to oust city officials and install a new municipal government. Jacobins, aided by the military, attacked Louis XVI's palace, killed the king's guards and forced the royal family to seek shelter with members of the Legislative Assembly.

After attacking the royal palace, Jacobins then held a rump session of the Legislative Assembly. While conservative and moderate deputies were absent, radical Jacobins passed legislation that stripped Louis XVI of his office, imprisoned the royal family, and ordered the con-

An engraving depicts the violence of the "September Massacres" in Paris in September 1792.

vening of a convention to write a new constitution. Until this constitutional convention could meet, France was to be governed by a ministry headed by Georges Danton and comprised mostly of Girondists.

Things got out of hand in Paris after Louis XVI was deposed. Jean Paul Marat, the leading Jacobin propagandist, worked crowds frightened by food shortages and news that Prussian troops had invaded northern France into a frenzy. The crowds' hysteria led to the September Massacres. On September 2, mobs of Parisians began to attack jails and prisons that held individuals thought to be enemies of the revolution. Prisoners were taken from cells, tried, and executed. The executions continued for five days. Neither military nor civilian authorities could halt the bloodshed. Over one thousand victims were executed, including many ordinary criminals like thieves and prostitutes, along with aristocrats, refractory priests, and others who had the misfortune of being imprisoned during this time. Most victims of the September Massacre were innocent of the treason they were charged with.

The violence was a prelude to even more violence that awaited France.

Election of deputies to the Constitutional Convention in 1792 marked the beginning of the First Republic. Even though all male citizens were allowed to vote in these elections, only about 10 percent actually cast ballots. The convention met and declared France to be a republic on September 21, 1792.

Maximilien Robespierre, a political extremist, dominated the convention. Two factions, the Gironde who favored federalism and the Mountain (the name came because these delegates were seated in the meeting chamber's balcony) who opposed federalism, vied for control of the convention. Eventually, the Mountain faction defeated the Girondists, gaining control over the proceedings. Robespierre, as chief spokesman for the Mountain, demanded that France create a "Republic of Virtue." After a lengthy voting process Robespierre and his Mountain faction forced conservative and moderate delegates, by a vote of 361 to 360, to declare that Louis XVI was guilty of treason. He was then sentenced to the guillotine. On January 21, 1793, the French monarch was beheaded.

The execution shocked the European continent. Leaders in other nations quickly denounced the violence. Edmund Burke, an Irish-born writer and British statesman, was particularly critical of the French Revolution after Louis was executed. In a publication entitled *Reflections on the Revolution in France*, Burke argued that the French Revolution represented application of a blind form of rationalism that posed a danger to all European society. He maintained that the revolution's disregard of historical realities, political developments, and social relations would lead to vast upheaval not only in France but also throughout Europe.

Robespierre cemented Mountain control of the convention when delegates rejected a Girondists constitution written by the Marquis de Condorcet. This constitution, which limited governmental power through a system of checks and balances, was rejected by the Mountain in favor of dictatorship. Robespierre and his colleagues established dictatorship with the help of international war and common Parisians known as *sans-culottes*, working people who suffered because of high inflation. After France declared war on Spain, England, and Holland in February 1793, a wave of patriotism swept the country that enabled Robespierre to garner support for his policies. Strengthening Robespierre's hand was the fact that Prussian troops defeated French troops, driving them out of Belgium, and that General Dumnoriez, the Girondists commander, fearing for his life after the Mountain gained control of the country, deserted to the enemy. Armed bands of *sans-cullottes* began to use violence to demand strong government. Faced with high unemployment, food shortages, and inflation, the *sans-cullottes* demanded that the government enact legislation to control prices and ration food. When Girondists rejected these measures, *sans-cullottes* attacked the constitutional assembly and abducted twenty-nine Girondists representatives. Robespierre and the Mountain faction, wholly supported by armed *sans-cullottes*, sentenced Girondists to the guillotine, beginning the infamous "Reign of Terror."

Reign of Terror

Now that Robespierre and the Jacobin Mountain faction controlled France, they moved to institute their views of government on the whole country. Since Robespierre was a great believer in "virtuous" government, he was determined to lead France on the righteous path. His goal was to create a democratic nation populated by citizens who exhibited an unselfish public spirit and civic zeal and who personally led a morally upright life. Even though Robespierre's goals were lofty and sounded morally pure, he was unable to achieve them.

Robespierre faced an emergency that pushed his views on democracy aside. France was at war, and its enemies were rapidly advancing. The National Legislature created a twelve-man Committee of Public Safety to govern France during the wartime emergency. Even though the Mountain faction had written and voters had approved a constitution in 1793 that provided universal manhood suffrage and a strong unicameral legislature, the document was never put into operation. The Committee of Public Safety had, in effect, established a dictatorship. Prominent members of the Committee of Public Safety included Robespierre, Jacques Danton, and Lazare Carnot.

Other than winning the war, the Committee of Public Safety's most immediate goal was repressing counterrevolutionary forces within France. To accomplish this goal, the Reign of Terror was instituted. It consisted of revolutionary courts convened to try "enemies of the state" and a Committee of General Security to hunt down opponents of the revolutionary regime. The Terror, as the period from 1793 to 1794 was popularly called, witnessed the execution of between thirty and forty thousand people. Victims of the Terror included Queen Marie Antoinette who was beheaded on October 16, 1793, royalists, aristocrats, Girondists leaders, and even some Mountain Jacobins who previously helped initiate the Terror. The largest number of victims came from the lower classes. Approximately 70 percent of Terror victims were peasant farmers or urban workers. Eight per-

An opponent of the Reign of Terror is led to the guillotine.

cent of its victims were nobles, 14 percent were middle class bourgeois, and 6 percent were clergymen. Executions occurred in a variety of ways. Important aristocrats, clergymen, and government officials were usually tried by revolutionary courts and sentenced to the guillotine while peasants and workers accused of harboring subversive ideas were killed by mob violence. Two thousand people, for example, were tied on barges at Nantes and deliberately drowned as part of the Terror.

To win the war with Austria and its allies, the Committee of Public Safety instituted a *levee en masse*, or military conscription program. All single or widowed males between the ages of eighteen and twenty-five were called to arms. The draft significantly enlarged France's armies. By the summer of 1794 France had about 800,000 men in uniform. This was the largest military force ever assembled by a European country up to that time. The military represented all socio-economic classes. Officers no longer came exclusively from the ranks of aristocrats. Members of the Third Estate rapidly achieved officer rank. Promotion in this new conscript army was based on merit, not heredity or class. Moreover, French soldiers, with nationalistic spirit, fought more zealously than did enemy soldiers who were largely serfs, peasants, or mercenaries who cared little about the cause they were fighting for.

Revolutionary armies were so successful that by the end of 1793 all foreign troops had been driven from France. In June 1794 French forces won the Battle of Flanders in Belgium. Afterwards, they marched throughout the Low Countries, taking Amsterdam by Christmas and replacing the Dutch provinces with a new revolutionary Batavian Republic. However, things did not proceed so well in Eastern Europe. Russian and Prussian armies defeated French forces supporting an attempt to establish a revolutionary regime in Poland.

A central feature of the Reign of Terror was an attempt to de-Christianize France. In 1793 the government attempted to destroy Catholicism. Churches were closed, artwork and ornate windows were destroyed, and buildings were converted into military barracks and administrative offices. A new calendar, dating from day

A revolutionary print of the "Republican Calendar,"

one of the French Republic, replaced the Christian calendar. Twelve months, named for the seasons and climate, with thirty days each comprised this calendar. Sunday was no longer a day of rest; instead, every tenth day was proclaimed a holiday. In November, a law was issued that made churches "Temples of Reason." Priests were sometimes forced to wed. Secular police were dispatched into rural areas to enforce de-Christianization policies.

De-Christianization produced much opposition within France. Even Robespierre opposed the reforms. He believed that the Republic of Virtue should acknowledge the existence of a supreme being who set moral standards. To alleviate criticism, in May 1794 the government declared that "the French people recognize the existence of the Supreme Being and the immortality of the soul." On June 6 Robespierre, attempting to placate angry Christians whom he feared had been alienated from the revolution, burned in a public ceremony three figures representing vice, folly, and atheism and unveiled a statue of wisdom. Even a declaration by the Committee of Public Safety that all peaceful Catholics should be tolerated did not help matters. Catholics distrusted the revolutionary government and regarded Robespierre as the anti-Christ. This would later help to bring about his downfall.

Perhaps the most revolutionary aspect of the Terror was reflected in drastic social, economic, and cultural changes imposed on France. Slavery was abolished in all French colonies. "Citizen" and "Citizeness" replaced traditional forms of address, "Monsieur and Madame." The metric system, a new system of weights and measures, replaced various systems in use under the Old Regime. Clothing changed as the revolutionary cockade replaced traditional male headdress. Art reflecting revolutionary themes was produced. The Terror issued decrees that regulated prices and wages. Meat, bread, and other foodstuff were rationed. The use of expensive bleached white flour was forbidden. Patriots were ordered to eat plain brown wheat bread called *pain d'egalite*, or equality bread. In 1794 laws were enacted authorizing government seizure of all property of émigrés and state enemies and its redistribution to landless friends of the revolution.

French women also became caught up in the revolutionary spirit that gripped the nation during the Terror. In May 1793, Pauline Leon and Claire Lacombe organized the Society of Revolutionary Republican Women. Like their male Jacobin Club counterparts, their goal was to oppose enemies of the revolution. Leon and Lacombe saw their organization as a woman's militant society. Initially, Robespierre and other male leaders welcomed the Republican women. However, after the Society of Revolutionary Republican Women began criticizing the government by demanding stricter controls on food prices and laws to prevent hoarding of food, male revolutionaries began to oppose their female counterparts. After the women insisted that they be allowed to wear the revolutionary cockade worn by male citizens, the Committee of Public Safety banned all women's revolutionary organizations. Olympe de Gouges, author of the *Declaration of the Rights of Women*, was beheaded after she opposed the Terror and accused Jacobin leaders of corruption. Robespierre's Republic of Virtue, like earlier governments headed by males, denied women the right to participate in public life.

De-Christianization, coupled with radical social reforms that displeased many people, caused Robespierre to lose support within the National Convention and the Committee of Public Safety. Moderate leaders became tired of the Terror and finally turned against Robespierre.

Robespierre is arrested at the National Convention.

The Reign of Terror ended on July 27, 1794 when Robespierre was not allowed to address the National Convention. After hearing shouts of "Down with the tyrant!" the National Convention had Robespierre arrested. He was sent to the guillotine on July 28, the victim of the same death he had sentenced so many others to. Robespierre's execution marked the beginning of a moderate to conservative stage of the French Revolution that Crane Brinton in his book, *Anatomy of a Revolution,* labels the Thermidorian Reaction. The most radical stage of the revolution had ended.

Thermidorian Reaction

After Robespierre's execution, moderate leaders, some of whom were formerly Jacobins, began to scale back or even undo many changes wrought by the revolution. The number of executions lessened. The Terror subsided. Powers given the Committee of Public Safety were retracted. The Revolutionary Tribunal and other courts that had tried enemies of the state were closed down. Jacobin Clubs in Paris and elsewhere were outlawed. Price controls and other economic regulations enacted by previous governments were rescinded. Girondists members of the legislature that had survived the Terror were allowed to take their seats in the assembly. Political prisoners were released from jails. Priests were again allowed to celebrate Mass; however, the government supervised all religious activities and the Catholic Church no longer received financial support from the state. Individual freedoms, which had been stifled by Robespierre's Republic of Virtue, were restored. Consequently, prostitutes again began applying their trade on the streets of Paris. Freedom of the press was restored. Theaters once more were allowed to perform plays. Families of victims of the Terror held memorial parties in which they shaved hair from their necks and tied red scarves around them to commemorate the deaths.

Even though the Reign of Terror was over, violence associated with the French Revolution had not completely ended. Enemies of the Terror often got revenge. In Paris, for example, moderate to conservative members of the middle class bourgeois, known as *jeunesse doree* (gilded youth), carried long sticks they used to beat people suspected of harboring Jacobin views. An event known as the White Terror engulfed parts of France. Southern and western provinces in particular witnessed the execution of individu-

Violence associated with the French Revolution did not end after the Reign of Terror. Rival factions were suspicious of one another.

als who had participated in the Terror. Members of the Mountain faction, along with people who had bought land confiscated from the church and aristocrats, were especially vulnerable. They and others believed to have supported the Reign of Terror were often executed as quickly as victims of the Terror had been. Like those guillotined during the Reign of Terror, victims of the White Terror were not given much chance to prove their innocence. In many cities, including Lyons, Toulon, and Marseilles, the *jeunesse doree* raided prisons, taking suspected Jacobins from their cells and murdering them in much the same fashion that Royalists were slaughtered in the September 1792 massacre.

Inflation caused by the repeal of price controls also produced violence. When food prices increased by one hundred times what they had been in 1790, riots ensued. Adding to the misery of rioters was that French currency was worthless. Merchants refused to accept the *assignats*. Consequently, suffering among common people was widespread. In the winter of 1794-95 half starved Parisians demonstrated against the government but were forcefully put down by military forces.

Royalists who had survived tried to use the popular discontent to restore the monarchy. On October 5, 1795, Royalists encouraged discontented people in sections of Paris they controlled to rise up against the Thermidorians. Like previous riots, this one was also forcefully suppressed. Napoleon Bonaparte, a young general in the French army, fired into the rioters with cannon, easily dispersing the crowd. This event was known as the Vendemiaire Massacre.

France made peace with some of its foreign enemies during the Thermidorian Reaction. The Treaty of Basel in March 1795 ended the war with Prussia and Spain. Yet, France remained at war with Great Britain and Austria. Despite the international difficulties, Thermidorians had not completely abandoned the revolution. They decided to once more attempt to institute constitutional government in the country.

The Constitution of 1795 and the Directory

The Thermidorian Reaction produced another constitution for France. This constitution, which replaced the 1793 democratic social contract that had never been implemented, reflected Thermidorian ideas on government. It rejected both democracy and constitutional monarchy in favor of a republic. France's government was comprised of a bicameral legislature. Representatives of the upper house, called the Council of Ancients, were required to be married or wid-

Napoleon Bonaparte fired into the rioters with cannon, dispersing the crowd. This event was known as the Vendemiaire Massacre. He established the army as a major player in France's political conflicts.

owed males over forty years of age. The lower body, referred to as the Council of Five Hundred, was comprised of males who were at least thirty years old. Because they feared both radical Jacobins and conservative Royalists, authors of the 1795 Constitution required that at least two-thirds of the newly elected legislature had to be members of the Constitutional Convention. Daily governmental operations were entrusted to an executive committee of five persons called the Directory. The five directors were not elected by French citizens but chosen by the Council of Ancients from a list selected by the Council of Five Hundred. With the exception

of military personnel, only landowners were accorded suffrage.

Once established, the new government faced numerous problems. The most immediate was social unrest left over from the Thermidorian period. In Paris, Gracchus Babeuf and his followers protested against inequities in French society. They demanded a redistribution of national wealth and more democracy. Babeuf and his followers criticized the Directory and new constitution because it permitted the rich to monopolize property and government while the "poor toil like slaves, languish in misery, and count for nothing in the state." The Directory quickly suppressed this revolt, known as the Conspiracy of Equals. Babeuf, along with some of his followers, was arrested and later executed.

Even though the Directory successfully suppressed the Conspiracy of Equals, problems within France were too much for it to overcome. Thus, the republican constitution and Directory government lasted only four years, from 1795 to 1799. Its chief weakness was that its base of support was extremely narrow. For the most part, only the propertied class had a vested interest in its survival. The poor were disenfranchised and saw the government as oppressive. At the same time, the republic faced enemies on both the right and left. Royalists in Paris and elsewhere openly worked to restore the monarchy. They even infiltrated the legislature. Working through the Clichy Club, Royalists communicated with Louis XVIII, the Count of Provence and brother of Louis XVI (Louis XVI's son, Louis XVII had died in prison), whom they regarded as the legitimate heir to the throne. Louis XVIII had fled France for Italy to escape the revolutionary violence. At Verona he used British money to produce propaganda designed to undermine the revolution and support monarchial restoration. In 1795 he issued the Declaration of Verona, in which he proclaimed his aim to overthrow the Republic, punish all revolutionaries, and reinstall the Old Regime to power.

Radicals were also unhappy with the Directory and 1795 Constitution. They believed the government had suppressed democracy. They wanted to overthrow the Directory, give all males the right to vote, decree equality under French law, and abolish private property. In short, leftists generally favored creating a Socialist-Democratic Republic.

Contributing to the demise of the Directory was that the government continued the foreign wars France was involved in. Authors of

LOUIS XVIII

the 1795 Constitution incorporated Belgium into France even though the Habsburgs had not agreed to give the "Austrian Netherlands" to France. Inclusion of Belgium as part of France meant that the Directory was forced to fight Austria and England, which refused to accept French control of Lowland territory. War with Austria and England demanded resources and energy that the Directory could better have employed to consolidate its power within France.

The beginning of the end for the Directory came with the political crisis of 1797. Under the 1795 Constitution the first elections were scheduled for March 1797. Unfortunately for the Directory, conservative Royalists and constitutional monarchists won a majority of legislative seats in these elections. Republicans feared that the Old Regime would be restored and Louis XVIII would execute those who helped overthrow the monarchy as he had promised in the Declaration of Verona. Republicans could not allow restoration of the monarchy, even if they had to violate the constitution to prevent it.

On September 4, 1797, the Directory staged the Coup d'etat of Fructidor. To ensure that the coup was successful, the Directory appealed to Napoleon Bonaparte, the popular general then commanding the Italian campaign, for help. Napoleon sent General Augereau to command troops supporting the Directory. Bolstered by military force, the Directory voided the March elections and ousted Directors who opposed their actions. Director Lazare Carnot, a strong constitutionalist, was exiled to England. The Republican Directors, aided by Napoleon, had snubbed democracy and imposed dictatorship on France.

After securing power the Fructidorian government increasingly became dependent upon Napoleon for its survival. Consequently, Napoleon dictated foreign policy to the Fructidorians. On October 17, 1797, France signed the Treaty of Campo Formio with Austria that incorporated Napoleon's ideas. Austria accepted French annexation of Belgium, control over the Left Bank of the Rhine, and domination of the Cisalpine Republic Napoleon had established in Italy. In return, France, acting on Napoleon's orders, allowed Austria to annex Venice and most of Venetia with the exception of the Ionian Islands, which went to France. Acceptance of Napoleon's ideas had brought a temporary peace on the European continent. With the exception of England, France's enemies had been neutralized. Even though France remained at war with Great Britain, the English were so weak economically that it was impossible for them to support armies in a continental campaign against France.

After the Treaty of Campo Formio was negotiated, French republican revolutionary ideas, aided by Napoleon's armies, spread throughout Italy and into other regions of Europe. The Papal States were taken from the Pope and made into the Roman Republic. Genoan rulers were overthrown, and Genoa became a Ligurian Republic, modeled after France. In southern Italy Napoleon established the Parthenopean Republic as Swiss reformers, under French guidance,

created a Helvetic Republic. German princes now under French control on the Left Bank of the Rhine were forced from their lands. As compensation they were given church lands in Germany that lay east of the Rhine.

NAPOLEON: RISE TO POWER AND DICTATORSHIP

France faced chaos after the Fructidor Coup. The constitutional republic envisioned by revolutionaries never materialized. More riots were quashed; more executions occurred as politicians who criticized the revolution were purged. The Directory functioned as a dictatorship but could never gain complete control of the country. France's economy continued to experience trouble. Guerilla attacks on government posts occurred in western France. When refractory priests condemned the government, the Directory had them arrested, deepening the religious schism.

Napoleon, however, took advantage of the chaos to seize power. Born in 1769 to a poor family of minor nobles at Ajaccio, Corsica, he became one of the most powerful rulers the world ever produced. Because France annexed Corsica in 1768, Napoleon received French citizenship, which allowed him to attend French schools. He pursued a career in the army after graduation from a military academy. In 1785 he received a commission as an artillery officer in the Bourbon army. When the French Revolution broke out, Napoleon adopted Jacobin ideas. As a Jacobin officer, he drove England out of Toulon, recovering the territory for France. Robespierre and other leaders of the Terror rewarded the young Jacobin by making him a brigadier general. After dispersing a Royalist demonstration in 1795, Napoleon was again promoted and given command of French forces in Italy.

Napoleon was the most successful general the French Revolution produced. After taking command in Italy he led two brilliant campaigns against Austria that crushed Austrian and Sardinian forces, securing northern Italy for France. Against orders from the French government, Napoleon negotiated the Treaty of Campo Formio.

Buoyed by successes in Italy and Switzerland, Napoleon returned to France in 1797 as a conquering hero. He was given command of all French forces in the war against England. Because he believed an invasion across the English Channel was too difficult to undertake, Napoleon decided to attack English interests in the Mediterranean. If France could take Egypt, Napoleon believed he could drive the English navy from the Mediterranean, disrupt communications with India, harm England's international trade, and bring the island nation to its knees.

Napoleon's invasion of Egypt did not have the desired results. Even though French forces successfully overran Egypt, Admiral Horatio Nelson isolated Napoleon's army by destroying the French fleet at Abukir on August 1, 1798. The French army was completely cut off. It had no supplies with which to continue the campaign in North Africa and the Middle East and could not return to France. The situation became even worse for France. Russia, Austria, and Ottoman Turkey had interests in North Africa, the Balkans, and the Middle East. Napoleon's invasion of Egypt alarmed these nations who joined with Britain to form the Second Coalition against France. In 1799 Russian and Austrian forces defeated France, taking control of Italy and Switzerland. Their victory placed them in position to invade France.

Faced with chaos in France and a threatening international situation, Napoleon left his army in Egypt and returned to France where he was hailed as a conquering hero despite his military failures in North Africa. In France, Napoleon joined with Abbe Sieyes and other Directors who were planning to launch a coup d'etat that would give them control of the government. On November 9, 1799, the coup of Brumaire was launched. Napoleon's troops, armed to the hilt, drove legislators from their chambers. Directors not part of the coup were forced to resign, and Napoleon was named military commander of Paris. Shortly thereafter, France got a new government headed by three Consuls. Napoleon was named First Consul.

Sieyes, Napoleon, and the Consulate in December 1799 gave France its fourth social contract, which was called the Constitution of the Year VIII. While this constitution gave the illusion of democracy, it in effect consolidated power into the hands of one man, Napoleon. Even though three Consuls theoretically shared power, Napoleon left the other two with little power. The First Consul also controlled the legislature, which was comprised of four houses. The Council of State proposed legislation; the Tribunate debated merits of proposed laws but could not vote on them; the Legislative Corps voted on laws but was not allowed to debate; and the Senate could veto laws enacted by the Legislative Corps. Although it appears this legislature had some power, in actual practice Napoleon dominated all four chambers because he appointed most members. Those he did not appoint were indirectly elected by a process Napoleon manipulated. The legislature was designed to only enact laws First Consul Napoleon decreed. The Constitution of the Year VIII, in another democratic façade, was submitted to French voters who "officially" accepted it by a vote of about three million to fifteen hundred.

After gaining popular acceptance of the constitution, Napoleon increased his power. In 1802

Napoleon Bonaparte wears the robe and laurel of an emperor in this lithograph.

the legislature abolished the constitution's limit of a ten-year term of office for the consulate and named Napoleon First Consul for life. He also was empowered to name his successor and to change the constitution whenever doing so suited his needs. In 1804 Napoleon had the Senate name him emperor. On December 2 he was coronated at Notre Dame Cathedral in an elaborate ceremony. When the Pope, who blessed the proceedings, attempted to place the crown on Napoleon's head, the emperor snatched it from the Pontiff's hands and crowned himself. Like Charlemagne centuries earlier, Napoleon crowned himself to show that no one, God, the Church, or the Pope, gave power to him.

Napoleon's dictatorship ended the French Revolution. The middle class had achieved most of what they wanted by 1799. Hereditary privi-

leges had been abolished. Individuals could now pursue careers that their innate talent suited them for. Property interests had been made secure. Even French peasants seemed satisfied with the revolution's results. They had acquired ownership of small plots of land and saw oppressive feudal taxes and obligations abolished.

Bureaucrats from all political backgrounds staffed France's government under Napoleon. Napoleon cared little whether a government worker was a Jacobin, a Royalist, or from the Mountain. What did interest the Emperor, however, was having a centralized administrative structure to implement his laws. Napoleon paid government workers high salaries to buy loyalty to his regime. He also eagerly endowed numerous French citizens with aristocratic titles, creating hundreds of Dukes, Counts, and Barons. Generals loyal to the Emperor were promoted to the rank of Marshall. Napoleon created the Legion of Honor to reward soldiers and established military pensions for retirees. What Napoleon had in effect done was to give the middle class the trappings of aristocracy. "Aristocracy always exists," Napoleon said. "Destroy it in the nobility, it removes itself to…the middle class."

Napoleon's Internal Policies

One of the most important legacies from Napoleon's rule was a series of changes in France's legal system that declared all people equal before the law regardless of wealth or status. Called the Code Napoleon, these series of changes enacted from 1804 to 1810 gave France a uniform legal system that reformers and revolutionaries had demanded but been unable to achieve. The Code Napoleon protected private property, abolished hereditary privileges, allowed individuals to pursue careers of their choosing, hired civil servants on the basis of merit rather than allowing them to purchase office, and provided for religious freedom.

Even though the Code Napoleon improved French law, it did not grant citizens full civil liberties. In general, individual freedoms were subservient to state interests. Torture, for example, was allowed in criminal proceedings. Napoleon did not tolerate free speech and expression. Instead, he tried to control information. The government closed about 80 percent of all newspapers operating in Paris prior to Napoleon's reign and demanded that playwrights only compose works that inspired patriotism. Divorce by mutual consent was permitted, but women lost some ground under the Code Napoleon. Revolutionary laws protecting wives, minors, and illegitimate children were repealed, and the Code Napoleon declared males to be the head of the household. Slavery was also restored in French colonies. All judges were selected by Napoleon, and the Emperor's advisors selected jurors.

Although French citizens were given religious freedom, Napoleon viewed religion as being under control of the state. Consequently, in 1801 he signed a concordat with Pope Pius VII and the Roman Catholic Church. This agreement required all priests, both refractory and non-refractory, to resign. The Pope would then choose replacements but the state chose bishops. The government paid salaries of bishops, and one priest in each parish. The concordat declared that "Catholicism is the religion of the great majority of French citizens," which acknowledged the dominance of Catholicism in the nation. It also allowed Catholic parades through French streets and the establishment of seminaries. In return for these concessions, Pope Pius VII recognized the legitimacy of Napoleon's regime, gave up rights to collect tithes, and dropped claims for church lands confiscated by former revolutionary governments.

Even though the 1801 concordat shocked Napoleon's anticlerical supporters, it represented a brilliant political move. Napoleon disarmed counterrevolutionaries who opposed his regime because they thought it and the Emperor were godless. No longer could opponents tell citizens the regime was atheistic.

Napoleon was probably godless. He viewed religion as a tool to be used when it served his purpose. In Egypt, for example, Napoleon claimed to be Muslim; in France he was Catholic; and when at the Institute of Paris, he was an atheist. The Emperor was willing to compromise with the Catholic Church because he understood the importance of religion to the masses. Since refractory clergy financed by England largely led the counterrevolutionary movement, Napoleon signed the concordat with Pius VII to rid himself of the conservative refractory priests. In signing the concordat he said, "Fifty émigré bishops, paid by England lead the French clergy today. Their influence must be destroyed. For this we need the authority of the pope."

In 1802 Napoleon enacted the Organic Articles to further regulate the Catholic Church. Under these laws the government got authority to subject Church activities to normal state police regulations. Napoleon's regime could, for instance, forbid the publication of papal bulls, supervise seminaries, determine the content of catechisms, and control Catholic education.

Napoleon abolished schools established by the revolutionary government, replacing them with a number of state-controlled institutions known as *lycees*. Whereas the previous schools operated by the revolution were open to most French students due to the low tuition they charged, Napoleon's lycees accepted a small number of students due to the high tuition students had to pay. As with religion, creation of the lycees had a political motive. Napoleon intended for the lycees to produce efficient administrators who were loyal to his regime. Students at these institutions wore military uniforms, marched in parades to military drums, and were indoctrinated with Napoleonic patriotism in the classroom.

Napoleon pursued effective economic policies. Nobody in France was exempt from taxes due to heredity, social status, or special privileges. Every French citizen was taxed to some degree, and the government actually collected taxes it levied. Governmental accounting methods improved, and financing was centralized in the treasury. No longer did French officials take money from numerous funds administered by different agencies. All expenditures came from the centralized treasury. France began to operate on a national budget, which Napoleon largely balanced with plunder from foreign wars. The Emperor also established the Bank of France in 1800 to provide for the nation's monetary needs. French currency was stabilized when Napoleon adopted the Directory's abolition of inflated, almost worthless paper currency in favor of specie. Labor unions and strikes were prohibited, and workers were required to carry a national identification *livret* denoting their occupation.

The Napoleonic Wars and the French Empire

Napoleon, from 1804 to 1814, did what only Julius Caesar had previously done—conquer virtually all of Western Europe and bring it under the control of an empire. The French conquest altered the European map, astonished the world, and unleashed nationalism throughout the continent. Had Napoleon and France not overreached, world history might have run a vastly different course in the nineteenth, twentieth, and

twenty-first centuries. In France, Napoleon was largely viewed as a conquering hero while continental Europeans and Englishmen saw him as Satan incarnated into human form.

After he was named First Consul, it appeared that Napoleon would quickly bring peace to France. He negotiated peace treaties with France's enemies from the revolutionary period. In 1801 Austria signed the Treaty of Luneville, which broke up the coalition of countries on the European continent arrayed against France. Likewise, England and France signed the Treaty of Amiens in 1802, temporarily ending hostilities between the two nations. During 1802 and 1803, for the first time since 1792 no European country was at war with France.

Unfortunately, peace did not last long. Napoleon was unwilling to accept a stable, tranquil Europe. He had imperial interests that he wanted to pursue. England and other European nations became concerned when Napoleon began to expand French influence around the world. Particularly upsetting to the British was Napoleon's attempt to reestablish the French empire in North America that England had destroyed during the French and Indian War from 1754 to 1763. Napoleon sent a large military expedition to Haiti to stamp out rebellion in that French colony and reassert control in the Louisiana Territory Spain had ceded to France in 1800. England viewed French colonization in North America as threatening British interests in the Caribbean. Napoleon also reorganized the Helvetic Republic, giving himself control over the Swiss Confederation, turned the Cisalpine Republic into an Italian Republic with the French Emperor as president, and dispatched representatives to oversee the reorganization of Germany. He further aroused British ire when he imposed high tariff duties on imports from Britain, hurting England's economy.

As a result of tensions produced by Napoleon's actions, England and France again went to war in 1803. Early on, England fared well. The British navy disrupted communications so successfully between France and its colonies in North America that Napoleon abandoned plans to reestablish a North American empire. Adding to French problems was that Haitian forces under Francois Toussaint L'Overture and Jean Jacques Desalines, both former slaves, resisted Napoleon's efforts to once more impose slavery on Haiti. The Haitian freedom fighters, along with an epidemic of yellow fever, devastated French forces until Napoleon decided to sell the Louisiana Territory to Thomas Jefferson and the United States in 1803, forever ending the French desire to gain control of North America.

England began to seek nations on the continent to form an alliance against France. By 1805 both Austria and Russia had joined with Britain in the Third Coalition against France. Francis II of Austria did not like the destruction of the Holy Roman Empire that Napoleon's reorganization of Germany had brought about. Francis II incorporated Danubian territories into Austria and established the Austrian Empire to counter the French Empire of Napoleon. Russian Tsar, Alexander I, grandson of Catherine the Great, completed the Third Coalition when he brought Russia into its fold. Alexander had been shocked when in 1804 Napoleon violated the sovereignty of Baden by taking control of the Duchy. From Alexander's perspective, Napoleon was an outlaw ruler willing to upset international security and risk war to achieve imperial goals. Thus, Alexander signed an agreement with England in April 1805 to enter the war against Napoleon's France.

After hostilities erupted, Napoleon began making plans to invade England. He stationed over one hundred thousand troops on the French side of the English Channel from 1803 to 1805. These troops were supported by over a thousand ships and landing barges designed to ferry them across the English Channel. French troops also practiced amphibious maneuvers to prepare for the invasion. Prior to launching the cross-channel invasion, Napoleon planned to have the French navy lure British naval forces away from the English Channel. In 1805 Admiral Pierre de Villeneuve was dispatched to the West Indies to fake an attack on British colonies there. While the British Admiral Horatio Nelson was searching for the French fleet in the Caribbean, Villeneuve was supposed to slip back to France to help with the invasion. Unfortunately for France, Napoleon's plans went astray. Villeneuve was unable to elude Nelson. Rather than coming directly back to France as Napoleon had ordered, Villeneuve docked at a Spanish port. Nelson found the French fleet there and forced it into battle off Cape Trafalgar in October 1805. At the Battle of Trafalgar, Nelson destroyed more than half the French fleet without losing a single British ship. Even though Nelson was killed, his victory gave England undisputed control over the ocean. Napoleon would be unable to transport French troops across the English Channel and had to abandon plans to invade Great Britain.

Following the defeat at Trafalgar, Napoleon concentrated his military efforts on the European continent. His goal was to dominate the continent, secure its resources, and use them to construct a navy larger than England could muster. Thus, Napoleon moved most French forces from the English Channel to Austrian lands on the upper Danube. On October 15 Napoleon's army surrounded 50,000 Austrian troops at Ulm, Bavaria, forcing them to surrender without firing a shot. From Ulm, Napoleon moved east. On December 2, 1805, French

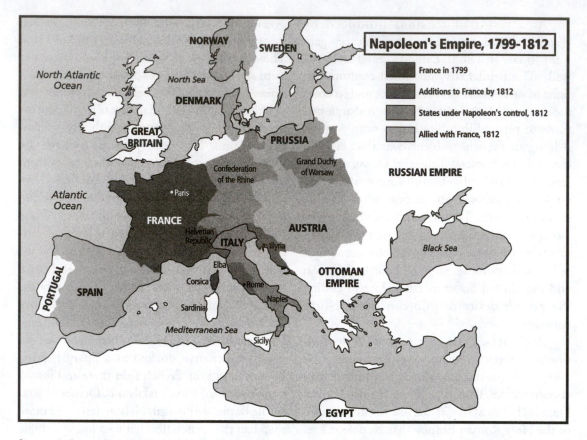

Napoleon's Empire, 1799-1812

- France in 1799
- Additions to France by 1812
- States under Napoleon's control, 1812
- Allied with France, 1812

forces defeated Austrian and Russian forces in Moravia at the Battle of Austerlitz. Russian forces withdrew into Poland, and Austria sued for peace, signing the Treaty of Pressburg, which allowed Napoleon to add Venetia to his Italian kingdom. Shipyards throughout Italy soon began building ships for the French fleet that would challenge England's naval superiority.

Napoleon's actions in Germany, however, angered Prussia, which had refused to join the Third Coalition. In 1806 Napoleon officially dissolved the Holy Roman Empire. He replaced it with the Confederation of the Rhine and named himself its "protector." Prussia initially fared little better than Austria. At Jena and Auerstadt in October 1806 French forces easily defeated the Prussian army.

After defeating Prussia, Napoleon turned his attention to Russia. French forces found the Russian army in eastern Prussia. At the Battle of Friedland on June 14, 1807, Napoleon's army decisively defeated Tsar Alexander I's forces. Rather than retreating into Russia to regroup, Alexander, unsure of the loyalty of Russian nobles and fearing a serf insurrection, opened negotiations with Napoleon. The French Emperor and Russian Tsar met on a raft floating in the Niemen River at Tilsit in July 1807. There the two rulers signed the Treaty of Tilsit, dividing Europe between Russia and France. Alexander agreed to French control over western and central Europe. In return, Napoleon pronounced Alexander the "Emperor of the East," meaning France recognized Russian desires on Ottoman territory in the Middle East.

Napoleon did not demand Russian territory at Tilsit. Yet, he did take Prussian territory. While Napoleon and Alexander negotiated on the raft, Frederick Wilhelm I, the Prussian king, waited ashore to learn the fate of his kingdom. When negotiations had concluded, Prussia lost about half its land. Prussia's Polish territory was given to Napoleon who made it into a French satellite called the Duchy of Warsaw. Prussian lands on the Elbe River were ceded to Napoleon, and French troops were sent to occupy Prussia proper.

Napoleon's victories against Austria, Russia, and Prussia mark the zenith of French power. Following the Treaty of Tilsit, Europe was divided into three political regions. The French empire included France and all lands conquered since 1789, along with puppet kingdoms such as the Duchy of Warsaw governed by Napoleon appointees. Austria, Russia, and Prussia formed the second division. Defeated militarily, these countries were forced to ally themselves with France. The only countries in Europe that remained outside French influence were England, Sweden, and the Ottoman Turks.

The Continental System

After the defeat at Trafalgar, Napoleon realized his plans to invade England must be scrapped. Yet, he believed France's empire could never be secure so long as England controlled the seas. Faced with this situation, Napoleon decided to bring England down with economic warfare. He planned to use French control of the European continent to disrupt England's economy while simultaneously increasing trade with France.

Napoleon put his Continental System into operation with issuance of the Berlin Decree in November 1806. This edict outlawed the importation of British goods into any European nation and ordered officials to immediately arrest and confiscate property of all British citizens doing business on the continent. Napoleon believed that the Continental System must be enforced in all European countries before England could be totally defeated. Thus, in the Treaty of Tilsit, Russian and Prussia were forced to follow the Berlin Decrees. Napoleon even ordered neutral nations like Denmark and Portugal to forbid importation of British products into their lands. When Portugal refused to obey, Napoleon invaded the country. After Napoleon devised the Continental System, England sent a fleet to shell Copenhagen because it feared the loss of the Danish trade. After a four-day battle, the English navy captured the entire Danish navy. The outraged Danes then voluntarily allied with France and joined the Continental System. In an attempt to tighten the vise more, the French Emperor forced Austria, Russia, and Prussia to declare war on England. Napoleon had imposed an economic blockade on England throughout Europe.

England responded by issuing the Orders of Council, which required all neutral ships carrying trade goods for France or a satellite nation to stop at a British port and pay custom duties. England thus shared in profits of goods bound for Napoleon's Europe. Napoleon retaliated by issuing the Milan Decree in December 1807. This edict ordered the French navy to capture all neutral ships that complied with the Orders of Council.

Napoleon's Continental System almost completely engulfed Europe. However, the Emperor encountered difficulties in Spain. In 1808 Napoleon deposed the Spanish royal family through a series of deceptions and installed his brother, Joseph Bonaparte, on the throne as a puppet ruler. The Spanish population did not easily accept Napoleon's ruler. They regarded French troops as godless fiends who violated Spanish laws and customs. On May 2, 1808, Spanish citizens in Madrid revolted. Although Napoleon brutally suppressed the Madrid uprising, it marked the beginning of a bloody war known as the Peninsular Campaign that lasted for five years. Napoleon was never fully able to resolve the Spanish problem, and it marked the beginning of his fall from power.

French forces fighting the Peninsular War encountered a new kind of warfare. Guerilla bands harassed French troops, severing communication, using hit and run tactics to destroy military units before melting into the general population. England, recognizing that Spanish resistance might succeed, dispatched an army commanded by the Duke of Wellington to assist the guerillas. Even though Napoleon committed three hundred thousand troops to the Peninsular War, they were largely ineffective. At Baylen in July 1808 a French general surrendered an entire army—the first time in Napoleon's reign that an entire army had been lost without a shot being fired. By 1812 England had defeated France in Spain. Joseph Bonaparte left Spain, and Napoleon pulled large numbers of French troops out to meet military needs elsewhere on the continent. Wellington then invaded southern France.

Not only was southern France being bombarded, Napoleon faced troubles elsewhere in Europe. Austria had risen up in April 1809, hoping that German princes would join with them to throw off French domination. Because German states remained neutral, French forces easily marched through Austria, winning a victory at Wagam in July. By October the war was over. Even though Austrian forces did much better than in previous wars, for the fourth time in twelve years, Austria had to sign a disadvantageous peace. Napoleon took Austrian coastal lands on the Adriatic Sea and the Polish province of Galicia in the Treaty of Schonbrunn. He also took parts of Dalmatia, Slovenia, and Croatia in the Balkans, making them into the Illyrian Provinces.

Napoleon's Decline

Napoleon and France peaked between 1809 and 1811. Territorially, Napoleon influenced practically the entire European continent. Lands that had not been annexed to France proper were either allied with or dependent on Napoleon. The Continental System was in operation, and even though actual hostilities were not occurring, Napoleon had forced Prussia, Austria, and Russia to declare war on Great Britain. The Emperor had divorced his childless wife, Josephine, and married Marie Louise, daughter of the Austrian emperor. She bore him a son who he made King of Rome. When Pope Pius VII protested, Napoleon imprisoned the Pontiff in Paris.

Life did not get any better for Napoleon. A military campaign against Russia in 1812 and 1813 signaled the onset of Napoleon's decline. Russian nobles did not like Alexander's alliance with France because the Continental System prohibited timber sales to England, an enterprise that had previously enriched Russia's aristocracy. Tsar Alexander himself became wary of Napoleon when France provided no help in subduing the Ottoman Empire as Russians believed the Treaty of Tilsit obliged France to do. Also, Russians disliked Napoleon's creation of the Grand Duchy of Warsaw. When the French satellite was enlarged after Austria's defeat in 1809, Alexander became incensed. Tensions between France and Russia increased when Napoleon, in violation of the Tilsit Treaty, annexed Holland.

After Napoleon named the French Marshall Bernadotte as the future King Charles XIV of Sweden and married Austrian princess Marie Louise, Alexander took Russia out of the Continental System.

Napoleon decided to invade Russia. His purpose was twofold: end Russia's military threat to France and bring Alexander back into the Continental System. For the invasion Napoleon raised an army of between seven and eight hundred thousand men through use of conscription. About two-thirds of these troops were non-French draftees forced to fight for Napoleon.

Logistical problems surfaced soon after the invasion began. Napoleon found it impossible to supply such an enormous number of troops so far from home. The Russian army complicated Napoleon's problems by adopting a scorched earth policy. Russian forces destroyed all food and supplies as they retreated before the advancing French army. In particular short supply was horse feed. All fodder and grain supplies were purposely destroyed so the French could not use them. The lack of food for army horses became so acute that many were euthanized. Nor did the weather cooperate. French troops had to withstand torrential rains and oppressive heat before the severe Russian winter set in.

Napoleon's plan was to wage a short campaign and defeat Alexander's forces in a decisive battle. However, Russia refused to fall into Napoleon's trap. Russian commanders, with only about one hundred seventy thousand troops, realized that a pitched battle favored France. Therefore, Russian armies, like Spanish rebels earlier, used guerilla tactics against the superior French forces while retreating toward Moscow. In September 1812, Napoleon got the battle he wanted. Russian public opinion forced Alexander and his General Mikhail Kutuzov to meet French troops at Borodino in the bloodiest battle of the Napoleonic campaigns. About ninety thousand soldiers were slaughtered in this battle (thirty thousand French and sixty thousand Russians). Even though Napoleon emerged victorious, he had not annihilated the Russian army. The Russians set Moscow on fire but the inferno did not prevent Napoleon from occupying the city for several weeks during September and October, hoping to force Alexander to capitulate.

The situation worsened for France. Napoleon presented Alexander with several peace offers, but the Tsar refused them all. Illness, coupled with starvation, forced Napoleon to order a retreat toward France. Russian forces launched relentless guerilla attacks on the retreating French armies. Making matters worse for Napoleon was the harsh Russian winter. French soldiers lacked adequate clothing to endure its subzero temperatures and horrific snow storms. Less than one hundred fifty thousand French troops survived the retreat.

Russian successes encouraged other European countries to resist Napoleon. In 1813 practically every nation in Europe participated in a coalition against France. Russian, Prussian, Austrian, and English forces attacked France from all sides. Even though Napoleon had used military conscription to raise another army of three hundred fifty thousand men, he could not replace the weapons and other equipment lost in the disastrous Russian campaign. Napoleon's army, even though it lacked combat experience, defeated enemy forces at Dresden. However, the victory was not decisive. Napoleon's army was itself defeated by coalition forces in the Battle of the Nations in October 1814. French forces then retreated into France. Thousands of foreign soldiers drafted against their will deserted. The German and Italian states that previously had

Wellington characteristically rode in the thick of his troops. His highly visible presence gave comfort to his men and improved their morale.

supported Napoleon drifted away. The mystique of Napoleon's invincibility was shattered. The once mighty emperor was on the run. Coalition forces invaded France, reaching Paris in April 1814. French citizens became restless. When Napoleon's generals refused to continue the war, the Emperor consumed poison in an effort to commit suicide. The suicide attempt failed because the poison, which Napoleon had acquired in case he was captured by Russian forces in the earlier campaign, had lost its strength. Napoleon then abdicated and coalition forces exiled him to Elba, a tiny island off Italy's northwestern coast.

Napoleon's defeat and exile did not mark the end of his career. On March 1, 1815, the Emperor surprised representatives of coalition forces gathered at the Congress of Vienna when he returned to France. French troops remained loyal to Napoleon, enabling him to briefly be restored as emperor. Coalition leaders were unwilling to accept Napoleon's restoration. They declared him to be an international outlaw and sent troops to end his reign. The Hundred Days,

as the period of Napoleon's restoration is called, alarmed European powers. They feared Napoleon would again try to conquer Europe.

British forces under General Wellington and Prussian troops commanded by Field Marshall Gebhard von Blucher defeated French forces at Waterloo in Belgium on June 18, 1815. Again, Napoleon abdicated and was exiled to St. Helena in the South Atlantic where he died in 1821. Napoleon's second reign caused coalition powers to extract a harsher settlement from France. France lost some territory, was required to pay war reparations, and was forced to accept an army of occupation on its soil.

CONCLUSION

With Napoleon's demise, troubles that enveloped Europe from the onset of the French Revolution in 1789 ended. The victorious nations that had defeated Napoleon at Waterloo created the Concert of Europe, an international structure that maintained general peace on the continent for most of the next century.

Europe had certainly undergone many changes and much trouble since the financial crisis faced by France's Old Regime touched off the revolution in 1789. Between the onset of the French Revolution and Napoleon's defeat at Waterloo, European nations had experienced great turmoil. Monarchies were toppled, republics created, the Reign of Terror cost France thousands of lives, Robespierre rose and fell, conservatives unleashed a Thermidorian backlash, and Napoleon became emperor. As emperor, Napoleon conquered most of Europe, instituting many changes such as the Code Napoleon, the Continental System, and the use of military conscription to create large armies. The forces of nationalism and democracy were also unleashed. These forces would profoundly change the world in the nineteenth and twentieth centuries.

Suggestions for Further Reading

Hannah Arendt. *On Revolution* (1963).

T. C. W. Blanning, ed. *The Rise and Fall of the French Revolution* (1996).

Crane Brinton. *Anatomy of Revolution* (1961).

Jacques Ellul. Autopsy of Revolution (1963).

Paul Higonnet. *Goodness Beyond Virtue* (1998)

George Rude. *The Crowd in the French Revolution* (1959).

Albert Soboul. *The Sans-Cullottes: The Popular Movement and Revolutionary Government, 1793-1794* (1972).

T. Tackett. *Becoming a Revolutionary* (1996).

Alexis de Tocqueville. *The Old Regime and French Revolution* (1856).

Gwyn A. Williams. *Artisans and Sans-Culottes* (1969).

THE INDUSTRIAL REVOLUTION 1760-1850

In February 1812, a boy named Charles, the second of eight children, was born into a debt plagued family of Landport, England. At the age of ten, Charles saw his father arrested and committed to debtors' prison in London. Although small for his age, Charles was put to work labeling bottles in a blacking factory to help his family. Charles hated the factory—the smells, noise, perpetual black stains on his hands and skin, and the bullying from the older boys and the bosses. On Sundays, his day off, he often visited his father in prison. To his immense disappointment, Charles' parents forced him to continue working in the factory after his father's release. Luckily, Charles was allowed to attend night and weekend classes, taught himself shorthand, and at age sixteen became a parliamentary reporter. Charles had an uncanny ability to make acute observations of people and human nature, and he developed a remarkable talent for writing. At age twenty-four, he published his first book, **Sketches of Boz**. From this humble start, Charles Dickens went on to become the Victorian era's most beloved and widest read author.

Working in the blacking factory made a deep, bitter, and lifelong impression on Dickens, and this showed in his writings. His very first book described an impoverished working class neighborhood and depicted milliner's apprentices as "poor girls!—the hardest worked, the worst paid, and the often, the worst used class of the community." In his tenth novel, **Hard Times** (1854), Dickens scathingly attacked the evils of industrial society—the physical assaults of smoke, soot, grime, noise, odors, and the body-breaking effects of repetitious, heavy labor, and the soul-destroying drudgery, boredom, and poverty of working class life.

Yet, when Dickens died in 1870, the English working class was the most prosperous, peaceful, and upwardly mobile in Europe. An Education Act of that year greatly extended school opportunities to workers' children. Their diets regularly included meats, butter, and jams, rarities in Dickens' childhood. They could travel under the city of London in the world's first "underground" subway. On their weekends off, extended by the Bank Holidays Act of 1871, workers could visit new city libraries and parks, lit by gaslights, or travel by train to seaside holidays enhanced by modern peers, bath houses, and hotels. And the Reform Bill of 1867 gave the highest skilled workers the right to vote. All these remarkable changes in Dickens lifetime were made possible by the Industrial Revolution.

Chronology

1733 John Kay invented the "flying shuttle"

1763 James Watt's Steam Engine invented

1767 "spinning jenny" invented by James Hargreaves

1776 *Wealth of Nations* published by Adam Smith

1800-30 England hit the "take-off" stage of industrialization

1810-15 Luddite riots in Midlands, England

1820s Textiles England's number one industry, employer, and export

1832 Great Reform Bill granted the vote to the very wealthiest English middle class
First passenger train service began in England

1833 England's first Factory Act passed to regulate child labor

1848 England's Public Health Act enacted
The Communist Manifesto published by Marx and Engels

ORIGINS OF THE INDUSTRIAL REVOLUTION

The term "Industrial Revolution" was coined in England in the 1830s to describe the phenomenal increase in production then underway and its attendant social and economic changes. The origins and legacies of the Industrial Revolution are subject to unending debate. Yet, the Industrial Revolution was the greatest shaper of our modern world and is still ongoing today.

The origins of the Industrial Revolution were present in the last decades of eighteenth-century Britain. British production doubled between 1780 and 1800 and hit the "take-off stage" during the following three decades, with output quadrupling between 1800 and 1830. The increase of production slowed slightly over the next two decades and leveled further after 1850 with England's arrival as a "mature" industrial nation. Every country that has had an industrial revolution followed England's pattern—an initial acceleration of production, then a drastic "take-off," followed by slower industrial growth, then the mature plateau stage.

A combination of factors made England the first industrial nation. England had a strong base of mercantile capitalism, an economic system based on trade and exports. As an island nation, England had a long history of trade. The British government's policies of colonization, a national Bank of England (established by Parliament in 1694) that provided credit and a stable currency, no internal tariffs, and a strong merchant navy and Navigation Laws (requiring imports be carried on English ships) all encouraged commerce and a thriving middle class. The Puritans' work ethic and association of material success with God's favor helped establish capitalist ideas and profit-motive as divinely approved.

England also enjoyed advantages of geogra-

Many families moved from farmland in the country to the city during the Industrial Revolution.

phy. Water transportation was the cheapest and easiest way to move goods, and no spot in England was farther than 70 miles from the coast, or 50 miles from a river. A canal-building boom in the late 1700s greatly facilitated internal trade, and England's merchant marine provided reliable contacts with her colonies and the outside world.

England also had an agricultural revolution in the late seventeenth century, as much of the old open farmlands were enclosed into more efficient, productive fields. The enclosure of farmland, improved technology and methods of planting and harvesting, and advancements in new hybrid seeds yielded unprecedented crops. Additionally, cross-breeding of livestock produced enormous new specimens of cattle and pigs. As Britain's food supply rose, the number of agricultural workers needed to produce the food fell sharply. Thousands of rural, land-less poor migrated to the new industrializing towns and became the "labor pool" of the Industrial Revolution.

England's cottage industry was another factor in the origins of the industrial revolution there. Also known as the "domestic industry," the cottage industry entailed workers making home-made goods for suppliers and contractors for piece-wages. The cottage industry created both a supply and demand for these products, and the wages earned by the workers increased the money supply in circulation.

England was also blessed with an abundance of raw materials such as coal, iron, tin, and other natural resources necessary for industrialization. Coal-mining was a crucial industry due to the

Cottage industries could not match the productivity of the new factories.

near depletion of England's woodlands during the middle ages.

The final ingredient that catapulted England into the industrial era was technology, especially the steam engine. Thomas Newcomen invented a crude steam engine in the early 1700s to pump water from coal-mines. In the 1760s, Scotsman James Watt redesigned the steam engine, building several models with condensers and rotary shafts. In the 1780s, Watt teamed up with a financial partner, Mathew Boulton, and their Boulton-Watt steam engine became the catalyst and power-supply of the Industrial Revolution.

The Textile Industry

The textile industry was the world's first mechanized industry, and textiles became England's largest industrial enterprise, export, and employer. Mechanization sprang from the flurry of new inventions and innovations. John Kay's 1733 "flying shuttle" allowed one person to operate a loom efficiently. The "spinning jenny," invented by carpenter James Hargreaves in 1767, allowed one machine to spin multiple spools of thread. In the same decade Richard Arkwright's "water-frame" harnessed looms to water power. In 1790, Richard Crompton created the first steam-powered loom called "the mule."

American Eli Whitney's "cotton gin," invented in 1793, had a profound effect on both sides of the Atlantic. His machine allowed one worker to clean (de-seed) as much cotton as fifty workers could do by hand. The cotton gin made cotton the "king crop" of the American South and enhanced the demand for slave labor and westward expansion for new cotton-growing land. Cotton became America's primary export and England's number one import. By the 1820s, cotton textiles was England's number one export and number one industrial employer, as roughly one-fifth of all factory workers toiled in cotton factories.

The demand for textiles reached an historic high in the late eighteenth century due to England's exploding population and the military demands of the French Revolutionary and Napoleonic Wars for uniforms, tents, and ships's sails. Napoleon even allowed French companies to violate his economic boycott on Britain and import English textiles for his own military needs.

The Factory System

Massive buildings were required to hold the large machines and their scores of operators. These structures were called "manufactories," or "factories" for short, and operated under the "factory system." Often several stories tall, they housed hundreds of workers who labored up to eighteen hours per day, performing repetitious tasks with few breaks and little pay. The early factories were cold in winter, stifling in summer, and sooty, noisy, and dangerous all year round. Due to the terrible working conditions and low pay, the earliest workers were the lowest of society—children, particularly orphans, and women. The great advantage factories had over hand-

The spinning jenny was an improvement over the spinning wheel and flying shuttle because it could produce many threads at a time, instead of just one.

A single cotton gin could process as much cotton as fifty workers.

made and cottage industry goods was "economies of scale," which allowed for the mass production of cheap goods. Gradually, adult men were forced into factories as family, "hand-made" businesses were driven out of business by the cheaper, factory-made items.

IMPACT OF THE INDUSTRIAL EVOLUTION

Population and Urbanization

One common result of industrial revolutions is a population explosion. England's population between 1780 and 1850 rose over 230 percent, from roughly nine million to 21 million people. In one decade, from 1821 to 1831, England's population increased 16 percent. Since young children were employable assets, the larger the family the more wage earners to contribute to the family income. The marriage age also fell to the mid-to-late teenage years (the husband being slightly older than the bride), since working couples, unlike their rural counterparts, did not need to wait to inherit property before marriage.

Improved diets, sanitation, and medical care assisted in the population growth in the later nineteenth century but had little impact in the first decades of England's industrial revolution.

Every country that industrialized experienced a population explosion. (However, Ireland, which did not industrialize along with England, interestingly had a population boom at the same time as England did).

Urbanization was another major consequence of the Industrial Revolution. Factories and jobs were concentrated in towns and attracted thousands of rural migrants. Seemingly overnight, the populations of many northern English towns exploded. In 1800, England had fifteen towns with 20,000 or more people, but in 1851 sixty-three towns had populations of 20,000 or greater. Manchester, Leeds, and Bradford were typical towns that grew on average over 50 percent in the 1820s alone. Britain's 1850 census revealed that for the first time in her history as many persons lived in cities as in the countryside.

Living conditions in the new industrial cites were squalid and wretched. Overcrowding was endemic. Families often crammed into one or two rooms, or packed into attics and cellars with total strangers. If lucky, one might sleep in a bed used by several persons on a rotating basis. The cities lacked any amenities for comfort or safety. Police, fire, health, water, or sanitation services did not yet exist. Raw sewage ran through the streets in open sewers. Often pigs roamed about and ate the refuse, while horses and other animals deposited their contribution to the filth and stench. Londoners living near the Thames River kept their doors and windows tightly closed year-round due to the smell of the river. Inside bathrooms, called "earth closets," were usually located in cellars and were little more than indoor "outhouses." The Romantic poet Lord Byron was known to avoid hotel "earth closets" and publicly relieved himself in hotel hallways.

Because clean, drinkable water was rare, cheap gin became the drink of choice for the working class, making alcoholism a chronic problem of the working poor. Other rampant urban problems were prostitution, crime, and disease.

Things were little better for the dead. Overcrowded cemeteries led to the practice of putting several coffins in the same plot, with only a few inches of dirt between them. On occasion, rats, cats, and dogs dug through a lightly covered grave for a feast. Coffins were also stacked in church crypts from floor to ceiling, and churchgoers occasionally fainted from the odor of the dead. As precautions, women would tie nose-gays of dried flowers or perfumed handkerchiefs around their noses.

English doctors and Poor Law Administrators led the fight against urban filth and squalor in the grass-roots "Public Health Movement." They eventually pressured Parliament into making modest reforms.

The Middle and Working Class

The emergence of an industrial middle class (*bourgeoisie*) and working class (*proletariat*) was one of the greatest consequences of the Industrial Revolution. The old landed aristocracy, which dominated the earlier, agrarian-based economy and held residual political power from the middle ages, was slowly pushed aside by the emergent middle class. The term "middle class" was first used in England in 1815 to describe the new, upwardly mobile, business-oriented professionals. The greatest historical movement of the nineteenth century was the political rise of the middle class, followed by the working class.

In Britain, their political ascent occurred slowly over several decades of gradual, peaceful reform, starting with the Great Reform Bill of 1832. In France, middle and working class gains were won via violent revolutions (1830 and 1848 respectively).

The Revolution in Transportation and Communications: The Rail-Way Age 1830-60

The Industrial Revolution's steam engine produced fantastic advances in transportation and communications. In 1807, American Robert Fulton used a Boulton-Watt steam engine to power the first successful steamship, *The Clermont*, on the Hudson River between Albany and New York City. By 1830, hundreds of steamships were plying the waterways of America (especially the Ohio and Mississippi Rivers). In the 1840s, the Cunnard Line was the first transAtlantic steamship service to connect America (Boston) with Britain (Liverpool).

During the 1830s the Railway Age exploded upon Britain, France, Belgium, Germany, and the United States. English miners had earlier discovered that horses could pull heavier loads of coal if their wagons were pulled upon tracks, and by the 1820s, steam-powered locomotives ("iron-horses") had replaced the horse-power. In 1830, George Stephenson opened England's first passenger railway service. Stephenson's Manchester–to-Liverpool Line ran for only twelve miles, and his locomotive, the "Rocket," never exceed sixteen miles per hour. Nevertheless, after the opening ceremony for its debut trip, the Rocket hit and killed Lord Huskisson, a former member of the British Cabinet, as he stood too close to the track with his back to the approaching locomotive.

The spread and impact of the railway was swift and momentous. By 1840, England led the world with seven thousand miles of track. By 1860, trains crisscrossed England at an unthinkable sixty-miles per hour. Railways drastically expanded markets, especially for perishable farm goods, which sustained the thriving industrial cities. The construction and operation of railroads employed thousands and stimulated many parts of England's economy. Iron and coal production skyrocketed, as iron output increased twelve-fold from 1806-1844, and coal production quadrupled between 1830 and 1850.

The railways eroded social barriers, as persons of different classes intermingled at train stations. Of course, the English class system was preserved by the separation of passengers into first, second, and third class carriages. First class carriages provided heat, cushioned seats, and glass windows; second class fare offered wooden benches and open windows; and on some lines, third-class passengers stood on open-air platforms, buffeted by rain, smoke, and coal-soot. Parliament in the 1840s established requirements of the so-called "Parliamentary Trains"—all third class passengers were to be seated in enclosed carriages and could be charged no more than one cent per mile. The "Parliamentary Trains" made travel safe and affordable for the masses.

Trains also carried information. London newspapers and journals sent by ship or conventional horse-carriages over land routes could take weeks to reach Edinburgh or Glasgow, but trains could deliver these articles in less than a day. The same was true for personal or business mail. Before the railways, mail-service was slow, expensive, and unreliable. Trains allowed the British government in the 1840s to introduce the penny post, whereby common workers could afford to communicate via a cheap and dependable mail service.

In summary, the train became the symbol of the new industrial age—of speed, progress, and the rapidly changing world. Glorified in art, literature, and song, trains also attracted critics. Many landed aristocrats refused to allow them within sight or sound of their manor houses, and Oxford University delayed for years the establishment of a train-station at Oxford, fearing they were haunts of prostitutes, pickpockets, and other lowlifes. When a station was finally built in Oxford, the university advocated the arrest of any student caught loitering there.

George Stephenson's locomotive steam engine, the Rocket, could average 16 mph.

The world's first "underground" transportation service was built in London in the 1860s. Many of the tracks and station-stops used today date back to the original Victorian era, and London's underground was the model of many of the world's subway systems.

The telegraph also revolutionized communications. Several inventors had created similar devices of electronic communication, but the invention of Samuel Morse, a Scottish immigrant to the United States, prevailed over the competing machines. Morse's telegraph had an advantage of its simple to use "Morse Code" of dots and dashes, created by breaking or completing the electrical connection. During the 1840s, scores of cities within America and in Europe were connected via wires, which usually paralleled railway lines. In the 1860s, trans-Atlantic cable connected America with Britain and from there the rest of Europe. Messages that had taken months by overland or overseas routes now flashed within minutes across oceans and continents.

REACTIONS TO THE INDUSTRIAL REVOLUTION

Government and Worker Responses

Most early industrialists and governments embraced the ideas of "Classical Economics" as expressed by Adam Smith and David Ricardo, especially the principle of *"laissez faire,"* or nonintervention in business affairs. For example, in the 1790s, the British Parliament, frightened by the ongoing French Revolution, outlawed labor unions as radical, dangerous, unfair combinations against employers. Yet, French labor unions were also outlawed during the French Revolution as infringing on the individual rights of workers to determine their own relationship to the employer. The policy of *laissez faire* was usually a policy of neglect, benefiting employers and denying rights to workers.

Workers initially reacted to the industrial revolution with hostility. Unable to legally form unions, and denied the right to vote and gain reforms through Parliament, workers turned to violence.

The Luddite Riots of 1810-15 were the most destructive and violent worker reactions to the Industrial Revolution. The Luddites were mainly hand-weavers and hand-loom operators of Midlands, England, put out of work by textile factories. Their name came from anti-factory handbills signed by "King Ludd" and "General Ludd," although some sources attribute their name to a teenage, illiterate leader, Nedd Ludd. On their nighttime raids, these "machine-smashers" wore masks, burned factories, and broke up machinery. After soldiers shot several of the Luddites, they retaliated with murder and terror. Parliament reacted by declaring the destruction of machinery a capital crime and dispatched the army to put down the Luddites. Several clashes ensued, and the movement waned after seventeen leaders were hanged and six others shipped to Australia in 1813.

The British governments resisted for years escalating calls for legislation to regulate child labor. After numerous Parliamentary committee investigations and mounting public pressure, Parliament finally enacted the Factory Act of 1833, the first in England's history. This law limited the workday for children under age twelve to nine hours and the workweek for thirteen to eighteen year-olds to 69 hours, and set the minimum age for miners at eleven years old. But the law provided for only two inspectors for the entire country.

Parliament was even slower in addressing the public health conditions of the new industrial

Child labor began to decline around the mid-1800s. Conditions for children who did work improved with laws like the Factory Acts.

cities. Doctors and Poor Law Administrators spearheaded a Public Health Movement in England in the 1830s and 1840s. The Public Health Movement sought government action in providing clean drinking water, clean streets, and other sanitary reforms of the filthy, overcrowded cities. Parliament ignored an 1842 report by Dr. Edwin Chadwick that predicted dire consequences if health issues were not addressed. Chadwick's warning came true four years later when a cholera epidemic killed thousands of Londoners. Parliament responded with the Public Health Act of 1848, which allowed, not required, municipalities to use tax money for public sewers and sanitation.

Capitalism and its Critics

The Industrial Revolution occurred under an evolving economic system of "industrial capitalism," which sprang from the earlier "mercantile capitalism." Mercantilism was an economic policy practiced in England, France, and the Netherlands as early as the mid-seventeenth century. Mercantilism relied on production and trade, especially exports. Colonies were a vital component of the trade network, supplying raw materials and buying finished products from the mother country.

Before the outbreak of the French Revolution in 1789, economic thinkers called "Physiocrats" advocated mercantilist policies. (Their critics called them "economists," a mildly derogatory name at that time.) The Physiocrats were often ministers to the French monarchy. They endorsed strong government, tax reform, and opposed government intervention on prices or wages, beginning the use of the term "laissez faire" ("let alone").

It was in England, however, that the "fathers of classical economics" shaped the basic ideas and concepts of industrial capitalism. The most important of these thinkers was Adam Smith (1723-90), a Scottish economics professor. Smith was a contemporary of the Enlightenment, the cultural and intellectual movement of the eighteenth century that maintained the existence of universal natural laws. In his landmark 1776 book, *Enquiry into the Nature and Causes of the Wealth of Nations*, Smith explained what he thought were the universal laws of economics. He set forth many of the basic tenets of "liberal" or "classical" economics—the law of supply and demand, private ownership of property, free enterprise, competition, and open markets (free trade). Smith explained the capitalist doctrine of separation of capital and labor. The *entrepre-*

neur (French for "undertaker") would put up the capital—machinery, buildings, raw materials, hire the labor, etc., and "undertake" the risks of losses but also reap the profits. Under the "wage-labor" system, the workers sold their labor for wages and had no liability for losses.

Smith argued that if governments followed a policy of *laissez faire* and did not intervene in the marketplace, the natural laws of economics would automatically work to everyone's progress and benefit. Thus, capitalism would lead to full employment, rising wages and profits, and worldwide prosperity and peace (since war would be to everyone's economic detriment). By 1800, *The Wealth of Nations* had been translated into every major language of Western Europe except Portuguese.

Thomas Malthus, an English minister, contributed to the canon of classical economics with his influential 1798 book, *Essay on Population*. The drastic population explosion greatly alarmed Malthus. In the *Essay on Population*, Malthus argued that the growth of population and food supply had till then increased arithmetically, but that the historic checks on population—war, famine, and disease—had been canceled by the Industrial Revolution. Therefore, the food supply doubled arithmetically, while the population increased geometrically. Malthus advocated abstinence to check population growth. The "Malthusian Theory" of mass starvation due to overpopulation did not materialize, due to the unexpected attendant increases in the food supply.

The fear of overpopulation was taken very seriously at the start of the nineteenth century and led English economist David Ricardo to formulate the "Iron Law of Rents and Wages." Ricardo was the son of an Italian immigrant to England who made a fortune as a speculator. Ricardo urged landlords to charge tenants the highest possible rents and employers to pay the lowest possible wages on the premise that overpaid workers would squander excess money on drink and sex, which would lead to earlier marriages and larger families. Thus, to avoid the hunger, unemployment, and social-political tensions of overpopulation, the working class should be kept poor. The pessimistic views of Ricardo and Malthus caused the study of economics to be called "the Dismal Science."

Utopian Socialists

The Utopian Socialists were critics of capitalism and the Industrial Revolution. They advocated a more just, fair, and equitable society through "social planning"—hence the term "socialism." Capitalists called them "Utopian" because the perfect world the socialists sought was unattainable. Utopian Socialists proposed various alternatives to capitalism, such as communal ownership of property, the abolition of inherited wealth, and government-supplied workshops under workers' control. The origins of Utopian Socialism can be traced to the days of the French Physiocrats before the French Revolution, and France was the early center of socialist thought.

Count Henri de Saint-Simon (1760-1825) was the "father of French Utopian Socialism." An aristocrat who fought with the Americans during their War of Independence, Saint-Simon was best known as a patron of the arts after his return to France. When the French Revolution began, he applauded the political changes and made a fortune as a land speculator. However, his business partner absconded, leaving Saint-Simon financially ruined. Forced to earn a living as a copy clerk in a pawnshop, Saint-Simon turned to writing on political and economic issues. Saint-Simon proposed placing regulatory powers in the hands of "Social Planners" who could coordinate the needs of society with labor and production. He urged the abolition of inheritance and the creation of an authoritarian-state "technocracy," which would glorify labor and manual talents. Saint-Simon greatly influenced Guiseppe Mazzini, Louis Blanc, and Auguste Comte, and his impact on socialism went far beyond France.

Charles Fourier (1772-1837) was another French Utopian Socialist and a severe critic of capitalism. A humble shop worker, Fourier was shocked at the wide income gap between wealthy industrialists and low paid workers, or by the fact that an apple in Paris cost one hundred times more than the same apple in the countryside. In his 1820 book, *Le Nouveau Monde* (*The New World*), Fourier denounced all existing social institutions and proposed that society be organized into small 400 acre units called phalanges. Comprised of 1,600 persons, these communities of half men and half women would live in a communal structure (phalanastere) and labor together in a cooperative system of shared work and profits. Government or legal institutions would be unnecessary, and as the community grew, it would splinter and create new phalanges. In this utopian world, Fourier envisioned workers enjoying five meals a day and living until the age of 140 years old.

French workers made several failed attempts to create Fourier's communal utopia. The 1833 community at Conde'-sur-Vesgres was perhaps the most famous failed socialist community. In America, several utopian societies were founded before the Civil War. A group of New England Transcendentalist authors founded Brook Farm, near Roxbury, Massachusetts, in 1842. Emerson and Thoreau were among its residents before it burned in 1847. The Oneida Community of New York was a rare economic success, and religious groups like the Shakers and Mormons cre-

ated utopian communities removed from secular, industrial society. Some Shaker communities survived until the early twentieth century.

The French Utopian Louis Blanc (1811-82) proposed in his *Organization and Work* (1839) that governments create worker-controlled "social workshops." As a member of the 1848 French Revolution's ruling "Council of Ten," Blanc saw his idea put into practice as the "National Workshops."

The father of English socialism was Robert Owen (1771-1858). An extremely religious and industrious man, Owen began his career as a common laborer. He saved and borrowed to buy his own textile factory in New Lark, Scotland. Distressed to find his workers were mainly young orphans, Owen refused to employ workers under eleven years old, paid the men relatively good wages, and limited the workday to eleven hours a day. Owen also provided his workers housing, company stores, and schools for their children. In 1825, Owen transported these ideas to America and built an ideal worker community, "New Harmony," on the banks of the Wabash River in Indiana. Owen's employment of immigrant labor and unusually generous practices earned the distrust of the local community, and New Harmony ended in failure in 1830. Owen returned to England to champion social reform and peaceful trade unionism.

Marxism

Karl Marx (1818-83) was undoubtedly the greatest critic of capitalism of all time. Marx and his colleague Friedrich Engels (1820-95) were the fathers of communism. Both Engels and Marx were both born into German middle class families. Engels' father was a textile manufacturer, and he sent young Engels to England to observe British textile manufacturing. The harsh factory conditions in Manchester deeply affected Engels, and he was drawn to the workers' Chartist Movement (1837-48), which demanded the vote and other political reforms. In 1844, Engels wrote *The Condition of the Working Class in England*, a harsh expose on the factory system. Engels claimed that since the workers were responsible for the worth of finished goods (the "added value theory"), that profit was really "theft" by the capitalist from the underpaid workers. Engels is best known, however, as the junior partner and patron of Karl Marx.

Karl Marx was born into a Jewish family of Prussia in 1818. Marx's favorite uncle was an aristocrat, the Baron von Westphalen. Both his grandfathers were rabbis, but Marx's civil servant father became a Lutheran for the good of his career, a move that made the young Marx cynical about religion. At eighteen, Marx began studies at the University of Bonn, but he earned poor grades. Marx's father decided to send him to the University of Berlin, known for academic rigor rather than the rowdiness of Bonn. Marx was attracted to law, philosophy, and economics but soon dropped out of college, never to earn a degree (although he later received an honorary degree from the University of Jena).

In 1842, at age 24, Marx began his career as a journalist for the *Rhinish Zeitung*. Marx was proud, vain, thin-skinned, egotistical, and a severe critic of contemporary society. In his articles, his favorite targets were the monarchy, nobility, church, and capitalism. Within a year, Marx had radicalized the paper, become the editor, and drastically increased its circulation. Marx and his paper caught the attention of the Prussian King, Frederick William IV, who had the paper closed and ordered Marx's arrest.

With his new wife, Jennie von Westphalen (his cousin and daughter of Baron von Westphalen), Marx fled to Paris and took a job as co-editor of the *Franco-Deutsch Jarbuch* (*French-German Yearbook*). His unrelenting attacks on monarchy, aristocracy, and capitalism led the French government to shut down his paper in 1845, and Marx fled to Brussels. There he met other European exiles and radicals, including Friedrich Engels.

Marx and Engels dismissed the utopian socialists as idle dreamers. They advocated a more militant ideology and co-founded in Brussels the first Communist League. In 1847, they co-wrote *The Communist Manifesto,* one of the most significant books of the nineteenth century. They published their book, written in German, in London in January 1848. The first translation was into Russian, and the first English translation did not appear until 1888, forty years after it was written. Although it never sold many copies in any language, this small work had a tremendous impact on European political thought and history.

Marx was the primary author of the *Manifesto,* which expressed a few simple but profound ideas. Marx postulated that everything in life and society was determined by economics ("economic determinism" or "economic materialism"). Second, Marx argued that history was an ongoing class struggle between the haves and have-nots (or the owners and workers, masters and slaves, etc.). Marx's view of history as an ongoing struggle was deeply influenced by the German philosopher, Hegel. Hegel had taught at the University of Berlin and died shortly before Marx became a student there. Hegel maintained that every idea, or *thesis*, was opposed by its opposite, the *antithesis*. The clash between the *thesis* and *antithesis* produced a *synthesis*, which in turn became a new *thesis*, and the cycle continued.

Marx also explained that due to the Industrial Revolution, the bourgeoisie had won the most recent class struggle: the middle class had overthrown the landed nobility and replaced feudalism with capitalism. Marx predicted that the final, inevitable stage of history would be the overthrow of the middle class and capitalism by the workers and the triumph of communism. Marx felt that this unstoppable event would lead to a perfect world, where all would be equal owners of the means of production, and the church and state would wither away. Marx urged workers to bring about the proletariat victory through violent class revolution.

Although Marx's *Communist Manifesto* has been lauded as a significant synthesis of history and economic theory, it contained several flaws. Marx incorrectly assumed a brotherhood of the proletariat, ignoring the power of nationalism, which gave workers many distinct and disparate identities. Marx also failed to believe workers could achieve political and social gains—the vote, better wages, and benefits— through peaceful unionism or government legislation. And Marx felt that the communist/proletariat victory could only be realized in a mature industrial, capitalist, middle class society. Yet the first "Communist" revolution occurred in 1917 Russia, a still greatly rural, agrarian society. Ironically, Marx had belittled the "idiocy of the peasants."

Marx returned to Germany briefly during the 1848 revolutions. When these revolutions failed, Marx resumed his exile in London. He spent the remaining thirty-five years of his life writing and leading the International Workingmen's Association, a conglomeration of communist and socialist groups and parties (known as the First International 1864-83). In 1867, Marx published what is considered to be his greatest work, *Das Kapital*. Writing this major economic treatise exhausted Marx, and his work greatly declined after 1867. His colleague

and financial helper, Engels, finished the second volume of *Das Kapital* not long before Marx died in 1883.

WOMEN IN THE INDUSTRIAL ERA

The Industrial Revolution had a profound impact on women. As noted above, girls and young women were the earliest factory workers and continued to make up the majority of laborers until the 1830s. Women also married younger and had larger families. The birth rate increased dramatically in the early years of the Industrial Revolution, since young children could become wage earners as young as five or six years old.

Rural women were also drawn to the bustling cities for occupations besides factory work. Prostitution flourished in Victorian England. At mid-century (1850), it is estimated that England had 50,000 women working as prostitutes, of which 8,000 were in London.

Ironically, the Industrial Revolution made domestic service the number one occupation of women in nineteenth-century England. The employment of domestic servants was the paramount symbol of Victorian middle class status and success, and having a household staff was the major distinction between the middle and working class. The typical middle class household employed three female servants. A male footman or coachman was common for the nobility but rare for the middle class family.

From 1801 to 1851, the number of household servants rose from 600,000 to 1.3 million, making domestic service the second largest profession, outnumbered only by agricultural laborers. Thirty years later, domestic service employed 2 million persons, the vast majority of which were women.

Church and school attendance was influenced by social class. The working class usually worked or rested on Sundays. Most working class youths rarely attended school before the 1870 Education Bill but spent their entire lives in factories, mines, or as domestics. However, as workers moved upward into the middle class, church attendance was not only made possible by having the time off but also came to be a sign of middle class status. Likewise, putting children into schools rather than into employment was another sign that a family had crossed from the working into the middle class. However, the working class still constituted roughly 80 percent of the population of England at the end of the nineteenth century.

CONCLUSION

The Industrial Revolution touched every aspect of European life, and dramatically changed forever European society, politics, class system, distribution of wealth, and even art, the landscape, and environment. It democratized and secularized society, gave rise economically and politically to the middle class, followed by the workers, and eventually women. The mass production of cheap goods and unprecedented numbers of better-paid workers led to a higher material standard of living and greater opportunities for education for millions of Europeans. By the end of the nineteenth century, the advances in production and technology allowed Europeans to amass global empires, construct the Suez Canal, produce x-rays, the radio, and the internal combustion engine for automobiles, airplanes, and submarines. The social changes, inventions and technology that began in the industrial era shaped our modern world, and these changes are ongoing today.

Suggestions for Further Reading

Isaish Berlin. *Karl Marx: His Life and Environment* (1965).

Charles Dickens. *Hard Times* (1854).

Shelly Dugan, and David Dugan. *The Day the World Took Off: The Roots of the Industrial Revolution* (2000).

MacKenzie. *Dickens: A Life* (1979).

Karl Marx, and Friedrich Engels. *The Communist Manifesto* (1848)

Charles More. *Understanding the Industrial Revolution* (2000).

Kirpartick Sale. *Rebels against the Future: The Luddites and their War on the Industrial Revolution: Lessons for the Computer Age* (1996).

Peter N. Stearns. *Interpreting the Industrial Revolution* (1991).

Philip Taylor. *The Industrial Revolution in Britain: Triumph or Disaster?* (1970).

E. P. Thompson. *The Making of the English Working Class* (1968).

Caroline Tuttle. *Hard Work in Factories and Mines: The Economics of Child Labor During the British Industrial Revolution* (1999).

Francis Wheen. *Karl Marx: A Life* (2000).

Jeffery Williamson. *Coping with City Growth During the British Industrial Revolution* (1990).

E. Wrigley. *Continuity, Chance, and Change: The Character of the Industrial Revolution in England* 1990

REACTION, REFORM & REVOLUTION, 1815-1848

Alexander I, Imperial Czar of all Russia, was a controversial ruler. He often advocated democratic reforms but ruled as an autocrat. Troubling divisions within his family likely caused contradictions within the czar's life. His parents, Paul Romanov and Maria Fyodorovna, the Princess of Wurttemburg, did not get along with his grandmother, Catherine the Great. At birth, Catherine, the Russian Empress, took him from his parents and raised him as her son. Groomed to be heir to the Russian throne, Alexander, a blond, handsome, and intelligent child, was manipulated by his parents and his grandmother for their own ends. He always felt caught in the middle between the warring factions. The conflict within his family taught Alexander how to manipulate people to get what he wanted. Early in life he developed the ability to change his views and personality to fit in with those around him. He would agree with Catherine the Great when in her presence and with Paul and Maria when around them.

Alexander's education probably also contributed to the contradictory personality he developed. Even though Catherine the Great was an autocrat, she chose the Swiss philosopher, Cesar La Harpe, a man who openly expressed republican principles, as Alexander's tutor. Catherine apparently had no fear that Alexander would become indoctrinated with republican ideas. She seemed to think that providing the young prince with a broad-based liberal education would better prepare him to make wise decisions when he ascended to the Russian throne. La Harpe taught Alexander many subjects, including history, philosophy, culture, and communication skills, and Alexander became an admirer of the Enlightenment and its emphasis on reason. He much preferred to think in terms of abstract, theoretical principles and tended to ignore the mundane, ordinary things a ruler needed to master to be an effective leader.

In 1793, when at the age of seventeen Alexander married a fourteen-year-old princess, Elizabeth of Baden, Catherine gave him as a wedding present the Alexander Palace, an estate larger than that his father lived on. Catherine intended to show that she favored her grandson over her son. This act produced further alienation within the Romanov family. When Catherine died on November 6, 1796, Paul became the Russian czar. He almost immediately issued a series of edicts undoing most of what Catherine had done during her reign. Unfortunately, Paul's actions upset the Russian nobility who plotted to murder him. Alexander was apparently aware that a plot to murder his father was underway and gave his tacit approval. The assassination occurred on March 11, 1801, in Mikhailovski Castle at St. Petersburg. Alexander then succeeded his father as czar. Because of his role in Paul's murder, Maria refused to speak to the new emperor for many years and never entirely forgave her son.

At first, Alexander tried to rule as an enlightened despot. Numerous restrictive police measures imposed by Paul were repealed. The Charter of the Nobility and the law of 1775 were reenacted. The hated security police that enforced government decrees since the time of Peter I were abolished. Alexander even put together a group of liberals, called the "Non-official Committee," to write a constitution for Russia. However, little came from the committee's work other than renaming various governmental ministries. After two years the Non-official Committee gave up. Frustrated by the lack of progress and the difficulty of accomplishing true reform within the framework of the

Russian governmental bureaucracy, Alexander began to use his vast powers in more of a dictatorial manner because he apparently found it easier to get results this way. After he began using autocratic power, he became intoxicated with it, relying upon corrupt ministers to carry out his will. Often these men persuaded him to do something because it personally benefited them.

On November 19, 1825, Alexander I died in the Russian town of Taganrog on the Sea of Azov. His death was as controversial and contradictory as his life. News of his death did not reach the Russian capital until eight days after it occurred. Since he died childless, Alexander was supposed to be succeeded by his brother, Constantine, who was next in line to the throne according to the law of 1797. However, Constantine had divorced his first wife, a German princess, in 1820 and married a commoner. He was allowed to marry a commoner only if he agreed to renounce his right to the throne in favor of his younger brother, Nicholas. Unfortunately, this agreement was kept secret from the Russian public and officials. Chaos broke out in Russia and produced the Decembrist Uprising. Adding fuel to the chaos were rumors that persisted about Alexander having faked his own death. According to these tales, Alexander did not actually die in 1825. Instead, some people believe he became a hermit monk named Fedor Kuzmich who wandered the forests of Siberia until his death in 1864. In the 1920s the government of the Soviet Union fueled the flames of this rumor when Alexander's tomb was opened but found to be empty.

Chronology

1815	Congress of Vienna
	Holy Roman Alliance formed
	Quadruple Alliance
1819	Carlsbad Decrees
	Peterloo Massacre
1820	Greek Revolution
1823	Spanish Revolution crushed
1824	Decembrist Revolt
	Charles X becomes French King
1830	French Revolution of 1830
	Four Ordinance issued
	Louis-Philippe becomes King of France
	Belgian Revolution
	Polish Revolution
1831	English Reform Bill passed
1838	Chartism begins in England
1839	Belgium independence recognized
1848	Revolutions of 1848
	Bloody June Days
	Louis-Napoleon Bonaparte elected leader of France
	Second Republic falls
	Austrian Revolution
	Metternich resigns

THE CONGRESS OF VIENNA

After the Napoleonic Wars ended, Europe was in a state of chaos. Thousands were dead, farms were ruined, food production had declined, commercial shipping had been disrupted, industrial output had decreased, and governments had fallen. The outlook for the continent was dismal when representatives from European nations gathered at Vienna, Austria in 1814 and 1815 to reconstruct Europe after Napoleon's final defeat. This Congress of Vienna, as the meeting was called, was dominated by Prince Klemens von Metternich (1773-1859), the Austrian foreign minister from 1809 until 1848, and Czar Alexander I, the Russian monarch from 1801 to 1825. Including Alexander, six European rulers personally attended the meeting: the Austrian emperor, and the kings of Prussia, Denmark, Bavaria, and Wurttemberg. England sent Lord Castlereagh and the Duke of Wellington while the infamous minister Charles Maurice de Talleyrand represented France.

The primary goal at the Congress of Vienna was to restore national and international peace, order, and tranquility after the frightful experiences Europe had endured during the French Revolution and Napoleonic Wars. Since most European rulers, with the exception of Alexander I, believed liberalism created by the French Revolution had produced the Napoleonic Wars, they wanted to create a system that would halt the advance of liberalism. Thus, the primary concern of delegates to the Congress of Vienna was to ensure that Europe would never again experience the revolutionary upheavals that had produced the French Revolution and given rise to Napoleon. To accomplish this objective, European leaders tried to create a permanent peace that would ensure international stability. Within the context of this lofty objective, delegates tried to advance national interests and claim new territory. Sometimes their actions even conflicted with the overall purpose of the Congress of Vienna.

With the exception of decisions regarding Germany and a few other territories, the central ideas that guided delegates at the Congress of Vienna were the principles of legitimacy and restoration. These principles meant that whenever feasible, European monarchs, or their heirs that had ruled prior to the French Revolution and Napoleonic Wars, should be restored to their thrones and that each nation should regain the same territory it held prior to 1789. Consequently, agreements reached at Vienna restored Louis XVIII, brother to Louis XVI, to the French throne. The king's brother was chosen because Louis XVII, the young son of Louis XVI and Marie Antoinette, never reigned after dying (1795) under suspicious circumstances a few years after his parents were executed. Likewise, Bourbon monarchs in Spain and the Two Sicilies were also restored to their thrones. Although the Congress of Vienna required France to pay 700 million francs in war damages to England and its victorious allies, France's boundaries changed little from pre-Revolutionary days.

Even though France was allowed to retain its boundaries prior to 1789, delegates to the Congress of Vienna took steps to ensure that France stayed within those boundaries and could not attempt to conquer its neighbors in the foreseeable future. The Dutch Republic, which Napoleon had conquered in 1795, was reestablished. Named the Kingdom of the Netherlands, the House of Orange was restored as its legitimate monarchial family. The Netherlands was given Belgium, which before the Napoleonic Wars had been controlled by Austria. Delegates believed that the Netherlands would act as a buffer between France and neighboring countries. In addition, the west bank of the Rhine River was given to Prussia while Austria was given territory in northern Italy. Delegates believed this readjustment in European territorial boundaries would prevent future French expansion.

Because Western European nations feared Russian expansion, the Congress of Vienna did not apply the principles of legitimacy and restoration to German states conquered by Napoleon. Even though ruling families pleaded with delegates to restore boundaries to pre-1789 days, European leaders agreed to accept German boundaries established by Napoleon. In particular, delegates retained Bavaria, Wurttemberg, and Saxony, three kingdoms Napoleon created within Germany, as an anti-Russian bulwark.

War almost erupted in Europe again after Alexander I demanded that the Congress of Vienna reconstitute Poland and make him its legitimate monarch. During the 1790s Poland had ceased to exist as a sovereign nation, having been divided by Russia, Austria, and Prussia. Prussian delegates agreed to support Alexander's demands in return for Russia agreeing to allow Prussia to add Saxony to its territory. This Russo-Prussian deal caused Metternich to fear that Austria would be threatened by both Prussian and Russian expansion. To counter this threat, he made a deal with Talleyrand and Castlereagh that Austria, France, and England would declare war on Prussia and Russia to prevent them from acquiring Poland and Saxony. Fortunately, war was averted when delegates reached a compromise allowing Russia and Prussia to annex parts of Poland and Saxony.

England also got territories as compensation for its losses in the Napoleonic Wars. Since Britain was a far-flung colonial empire, it was not interested in European territories. England, however, wanted to increase its overseas colonial holdings. Thus, delegates to the Congress of

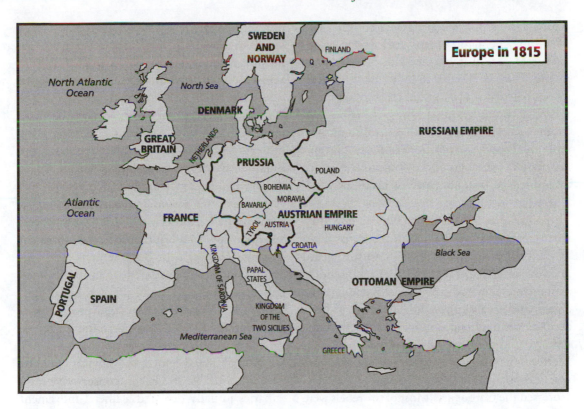

Vienna agreed that England would receive French territories in South Africa and South America along with the island of Ceylon (Sri Lanka). The territories enlarged England's commercial empire around the world.

The most important part of the Vienna settlement was not territorial acquisitions by various nations but an attempt to bring a permanent stability to Europe. This effort created what historians call the Concert of Europe. To prevent future revolutions from erupting, England, Austria, Prussia, and Russia created the Quadruple Alliance in 1815. Three years later France was admitted to membership in the group, making it the Quintuple Alliance. All five nations promised to act in concert to quell any rebellion designed to overthrow a legitimately established government or fight any na-

tion that threatened to take by war any territory of another country. The Concert of Europe was generally successful. With the exception of relatively short-lived conflicts, such as the Franco-Prussian War, Europe was free from international war for the next ninety-nine years. It was not until the First World War erupted in 1914 that Europe again experienced disastrous destruction. This extended period of peace between nations was largely brought about by the conservative destruction of liberal reform movements in country after country if these movements or their leaders threatened to throw the continent into war.

Revolution and Reaction

In the years immediately after the Congress of Vienna, conservative, reactionary governments crushed liberal movements across Europe. Two of the first liberal movements stifled by reactionary forces were in Italy and Spain. These movements, which originated in Italy and were led by secret societies of army officers that called themselves Carbonari, forced kings in Naples and Spain to agree to accept liberal constitutions similar to the French constitutions of the revolutionary period. Members of the Quintuple Alliance assembled at Troppau, Austria in 1820 to decide what to do about the Carbonari. At the Troppau Conference Russia, Prussia, and Austria agreed to aid each other in the suppression of the Carbonari. Even though both England and France agreed that the Carbonari should be suppressed, they did not formally endorse the agreement because they did not want to limit actions they might take individually to meet this renewed threat liberalism presented to Europe. Metternich, aided by Russia and Prussia, and with no opposition from England and France, repressed the Carbonari. Most of the rebels were exiled, imprisoned, or executed.

When liberal forces again threatened Spain in 1822, over 200,000 French troops were dispatched to Spain to crush a rebellion against King Ferdinand VII. Spanish liberals objected to Ferdinand's efforts to destroy the elected parliament in Spain. French troops, assisted by Ferdinand's forces, easily crushed the rebels. The Spanish monarch, thereafter, could rule as he pleased without interference from an elected legislature.

An effort to create a liberal democracy was also repressed in Germany. King Frederick William II did not fulfill a promise to give the Prussian people a constitution. With the exception of Weimar and a few principalities in the south, autocrats without benefit of a constitution ruled most German states. The lack of democratic constitutional government in Germany caused

university students to form *Burschenschaften,* or unions of students, to work toward constitutional democracy for Germany. Burschenschaften from across Germany met every year to work toward their goal. In 1817 Burschenschaften at the University of Jena met to celebrate the three hundredth anniversary of Luther's posting of the Ninety-five Theses. At this meeting the Burschenschaften burned books written by reactionary authors who opposed democracy. Two years later, after a student assassinated August von Kotzebue, a conservative writer who also was a Russian spy, Metternich ordered government officials to suppress the Burschenschaften. This oppression was orchestrated when the German Diet enacted the Carlsbad Decrees in September 1819. These laws increased press censorship, outlawed the Burschenschaften, and restricted academic freedom at universities.

Not all liberal reform movements could be crushed so easily. In Greece, conservative reactionaries initially defeated a liberal movement led by Alexander Ypsilanti, a Greek soldier who wanted to reestablish the Greek empire that had existed in antiquity. Ypsilanti, however, revived his movement and raised a force sufficient to fight against Turkey, which controlled Greece after the Napoleonic Wars. Turkey easily defeated the Greek forces but was unable to crush the spirit of the reformers. Five years after Ypsilanti's defeat, Greek rebels narrowed their goals from establishing a Greek empire to merely obtaining independence for Greece. They achieved their goal when England, France, and Russia sent naval ships to the Mediterranean and when Russian forces invaded the Balkans. Greece became independent and was governed under a liberal constitution. Greek independence indicated that the reactionary alliance created by the Congress of Vienna had cracks in it. In particular, Austrian and Prussian conservatives could not always count upon England, France, and Russia to act to preserve Europe's status quo. Liberalism's triumph in Greece was perhaps an indication that the ideology had survived and was a harbinger of its importance as a force on the European continent after 1830.

Liberalism also produced a revolt in Russia during the 1820s. The Decembrist Revolt of 1825 occurred after the death of Czar Alexander I. The Czar's last years witnessed the establishment of military colonies that upset liberals. Liberal ideas, however, spawned by the French Revolution permeated Russian society. Free masons and other secret societies that flourished in Russia after 1815 spread these ideas. Secret rites and rituals connected with freemasonry and other organizations created a sort of leveling process in Russia. Nobles and commoners met on equal terms in these lodges, participated in the same rituals, and shared ideals. In addition, Russians were concerned about the contrast between France, England, and Western European nations and Russia. The Czarist realm, despite its vast size and abundant natural resources, was backward economically and culturally when compared to Western nations. Military officers who had fought in the Napoleonic Wars were particularly aware of this contrast as a result of their service in foreign nations. They formed the Northern Society in St. Petersburg. This secret organization wanted to make Russia into a federation of states similar to the United States. The Czar's power would be limited, serfs would be freed but would not receive land, and provincial governments would gain more autonomy. Another more radical organization, the Southern Society, was formed at Kiev. Southern leaders wanted Russia to create a republic with a highly centralized and powerful national government. This organization also proposed freeing the serfs but demanded that they be given land.

Whereas the Northern Society advocated achieving its goals peacefully, the Southern Society urged that the Czar be assassinated.

Both organizations seized the opportunity presented by Alexander's sudden death in December 1825 to try and implement their goals. Confusion erupted throughout Russia because Alexander had no son to inherit his throne. Normally in such a case the throne would have passed to the Czar's oldest surviving brother, Constantine, the Polish Viceroy. Constantine, however, had given up his claim to the throne. He had signed a secret document conveying the throne to Nicholas, a younger brother. Unfortunately, the document was so secret that even Nicholas did not know of its existence. When Alexander died, Constantine immediately declared that Nicholas was the new Czar while Nicholas proclaimed Constantine to be the Czar. Russians were confused. While authorities were sorting out the mess, the Northern and Southern Societies initiated a revolt. When government officials ordered soldiers to take an oath recognizing Nicholas as the new Czar, military commanders who were members of the Northern Society ordered troops at St. Petersburg to rebel. While most soldiers recognized Nicholas as the new Czar, about three thousand revolted. The uprising was short lived, lasting about two days. On December 26 forces loyal to Nicholas crushed the rebellious garrison.

After this incident, Nicholas moved to crush all secret organization in Russia. Leaders of the Southern Society and all other secret fraternal organizations, including the Free Masons, were arrested. These arrests prompted the Southern Society to revolt early in January 1826, but without leadership the uprising was doomed before it began.

Czar Nicholas (1825-1855) was so alarmed that he decided to become more autocratic than

Alexander had been. Several Decembrist leaders were executed, and over a hundred others were exiled to Siberia. Once again, reactionary forces had subdued liberalism. Yet, conservative reactionaries could not permanently snuff out the flames of liberalism. Later in the nineteenth century liberalism would have more success.

English Reaction and Reform

England, like nations on the continent, experienced changes wrought by the forces of reaction and reform. The French Revolution and Napoleonic Wars caused both the Tory and Whig Parties to become more conservative. Neither party expressed much support for democratic movements in continental nations. Both tended to support the status quo when revolution threatened established government.

When riots broke out in England after 1815 due to economic depression and massive unemployment that engulfed the nation (England was industrializing, which made the recession following the Napoleonic Wars worse), Parliament enacted repressive laws, and governmental officials used militant tactics to quell the disturbances. Police used informants to gather evidence against radical leaders who agitated the rioters. One of the most serious episodes of repression was the Peterloo massacre that occurred at Manchester in 1819. A crowd in excess of 75,000 persons was demonstrating at St. Peter's field for increased representation in Parliament. When the protestors became unruly, police fired into their ranks, killing eleven and wounding over 400. British radicals, in a play upon the Battle of Waterloo, dubbed the massacre Peterloo. Later, Parliament passed legislation called the Six Acts to prevent demonstrations such as those that led to Peterloo. The Six Acts prohibited publica-

Nicholas I vowed that a Russian revolution would not occur during his reign. When the Decembrist Revolt broke out, Czar Nicholas crushed the rebellion and executed its leaders.

tion of seditious and blasphemous literature, placed a stamp tax on newspapers, restricted rights of citizens to hold public meetings, and allowed police to search private homes for weapons.

Despite governmental opposition to liberalism and efforts to suppress reforms, British leaders were able to compromise to prevent revolution. George Canning, the British foreign minister, and Robert Peel, the home secretary, understood the need for economic reform. Liberal manufacturers were demanding reform to help them make more profits from entrepreneurial activities. Under their leadership England became less active in the Quintuple Alliance and recognized the revolutionary governments that freed South and Central American countries from Spanish colonialism. At home these Tory politicians also instituted reform. They abolished the death penalty for over a hundred crimes and liberalized the Corn Laws. The Corn Laws, designed to benefit English landlords, levied a high tariff on grain imported into England, raising the price of bread and other grain-based foods. For manufacturers, the Corn Laws meant that they had to pay higher wages so that workers could afford the expensive bread and grain products. Liberal factory owners, along with wage laborers, supported the Tory politicians who lowered duties imposed by the Corn Laws. The same conservative Tory politicians who liberalized the Corn Laws also brought about reform in other parts of English society. One important change was the abolition of laws that prevented non-Anglican Protestants and Roman Catholics from holding public office. When these laws were abolished, Baptist, Congregationalist, Methodists, Catholics, and members of other religious sects could participate fully in public life.

One reform English conservatives resisted was to change the system of representation in the House of Commons. Liberal reformers wanted change because Parliament represented the interest of landowners rather than manufacturers. Nearly 70 percent of representatives in the House of Commons owed their election to the wealthiest landowners in England. Numerous parliamentary electoral boroughs that sent representatives to the House of Commons were controlled by landed gentlemen who used economic pressure and bribery to elect candidates who would look after their interests. Such districts were called "rotten" or "pocket" boroughs because they were believed to be firmly in the pockets of the rotten landowners who controlled them. Landowners argued that it was not important that elections were often bought or that only a few Englishmen (about 1 of 100) could vote. They maintained that despite these prob-

lems, Parliament had served England well, looking after the national interests fairly and consistently.

Members of the manufacturing middle class who owned little land, however, saw things differently. They argued that parliamentary electoral reform was necessary before the national legislature could truly represent all the people and look after the interest of the entire nation, not just the propertied class. Manufacturers had, for example, maintained that the Corn Laws were not in the national interest. Because these laws kept grain prices high, they worked in the interest of landowners while working against the interests of the nation at large by raising food prices and wages. Middle class liberals insisted that Parliament be reformed so that members were chosen to represent the interests of industrialists and landowners. Of course, manufacturers believed that their representatives would also look after the interests of their workers, firmly holding that if industry prospered labor would likewise prosper. Thus, they were not arguing in favor of electoral reform to achieve democracy but because they wanted government to protect industrial interests. Most reformers opposed extending representation to workers because they feared the changes workers might bring to England.

The movement for parliamentary reform intensified after 1830. Manufacturers, artisans, and workers formed an alliance, which toppled the Tory government and put the Whigs in power. Under the leadership of Lord Charles Grey, Whig members of Parliament introduced an electoral reform bill. Conservatives were afraid that the alliance of industrialists, artisans, and workers would provoke revolution in England. Numerous organizations sprang up across England to promote electoral reform. In Birmingham, for example, Thomas Attwood, a middle class banker, formed the Political Union of the Lower and Middle Classes of the People. Similar organizations existed in Glasgow, Manchester, Liverpool, Sheffield, Newcastle, Coventry, and other English cities. King William IV feared revolution, writing to Lord Grey that "miners, manufacturers, colliers, and labourers, are ripe for revolution."

To prevent revolution and stifle unrest, Lord Grey's government accommodated liberals by introducing the Reform Bill of 1832 into Parliament. This bill made two important electoral changes. First, it extended the franchise to English middle class males. Control of property was still necessary for voting, but the amount of land controlled and the length of time it was owned decreased. Outright ownership of prop-

Lord Charles Grey, England's prime minister from 1830-1834.

erty was no longer a requirement to vote. Renters of farmland in rural areas were given the franchise. Second, the Reform Bill of 1832 provided for redistribution of parliamentary seats. One hundred forty-three seats in the House of Commons were reallocated from the rural, agricultural south of England to the urban, industrial north. The political representation and power of the manufacturing middle class was thus increased. Likewise, the political clout of manufacturing centers such as Birmingham, Manchester, and Leeds also increased.

Unfortunately, the Reform Bill of 1832 did little to help the English working class. Because workers did not own or rent agricultural lands, few were enfranchised. Nor did the bill destroy the political influence of landed aristocrats, although it did reduce their clout to a degree. The industrial middle class benefited most from passage of the Reform Bill of 1832. Afterwards, they became a partner with the landed gentry that had controlled England for centuries. The two groups found common ground, working within Parliament to enhance the interests of the upper class of landowners and manufacturers at the expense of the working class poor.

After the Reform Bill of 1832 failed to grant them the right to vote, working class artisans, concerned about their limited economic opportunities, began to organize to protect their social and economic interests. The most important effort was Chartism. In 1836 William Lovett and other radical London artisans formed the London Working Men's Association. Two year later the group presented a charter demanding that Parliament enact six reforms: universal male suffrage, annual elections for the House of Commons, the secret ballot, equal population electoral districts, abolition of property ownership for election to Parliament, and salaries for members of the House of Commons.

Chartism spread across England. Proponents agitated for passage of the reforms for more than a decade. Upon three occasions the Charter was introduced into Parliament. Each time it did not receive sufficient votes for passage. Millions of people signed petitions demanding that the House of Commons pass the Charter. Trade unions called strikes in support of its passage. The Chartist Movement even published a newspaper, *The Northern Star*, to convince English people to support passage of the Charter. The Chartist Movement failed, however, because a split occurred between those who wanted to use violence to achieve reform and those who wanted to use peaceful tactics. When economic prosperity returned to England in the late 1830s and early 1840s, many English workingmen and women lost interest in the reforms.

THE 1830 REVOLUTIONS

France, the country that had awakened Europe to revolution in 1789, would again undergo revolution in 1830. This second French Revolution, however, was not as radical, all encompassing, or bloody as the first one had been. As was the case in England, the entrepreneurial middle class was its primary beneficiary.

The revolution was touched off by reactionary policies initiated by Charles X, the ultra-royalist brother who succeeded Louis XVIII as King of France in 1824. After the Congress of Vienna put Europe back together, French King Louis XVIII (1814-1824) realized that it was impossible to return France to the days of absolute monarchy. Thus, he agreed to abide by a charter issued in 1814 that made France into a constitutional monarchy. Although the charter's preamble asserted that governmental authority in France resided in the monarch, the document created a bicameral national legislature. While the upper house, the Chamber of Peers, was appointed by the king, the lower house, called the Chamber of Deputies, was elected. Even though only about one hundred thousand of France's thirty million population had the right to vote for deputies, there was, at least within France, the illusion of democracy. Moreover, the charter kept many changes brought by the 1789 revolution, including religious toleration, limited freedom of the press, the Code Napoleon, equality of all before the law, equal access to military and civil office, and the redistribution of property from the first revolution.

Ultra-royalists, including Charles X, disliked the charter. Particularly disturbing to these aristocrats who had escaped the guillotine in the 1789 revolution was the charter's acceptance of the property divisions created after the first revolution. Ultra-royalists were determined to recover all property and privileges they and the church had lost after 1789. In the early 1820s the ultra-royalists briefly won control of the Chamber of Deputies and began to pass legislation designed to undo the liberal reforms that Louis XVIII had accepted in the French charter. The pace of these changes accelerated after Charles became king in 1824. The ultra-royalist king and legislature enacted statutes that further restricted the already narrow suffrage, gave indemnities to aristocrats whose land had been confiscated by the state, allowed the Catholic Church to reassert its previous exclusive right to teach in French classrooms, encouraged Jesuit activity even though the religious order was legally banned throughout the country, and reduced interest paid on government bonds from 5 to 3 percent. While all these changes disturbed the middle class, the reduction of interest rates on securities was particularly troubling because it was the middle class that held most of the bonds.

The French middle class responded to the ultra-royalist changes with revolution. Middle class bondholders widely believed that the reduction in interest rates was used to pay the indemnities aristocrats were receiving for land that had previously been confiscated. Resentment over interest rate reductions allowed liberals from the middle class to gain a majority in the Chamber of Deputies. After gaining control of half the legislature, middle class revolutionaries began to demand reforms that would mark the onset of the Second French Revolution.

Fueling the flames of revolt was the appointment of the Prince de Polignac as Charles' chief minister. De Polignac, an ultra-royalist who claimed to receive mystical visions from the Virgin Mary promising victory for France, attacked Algiers and other cities along the Barbary Coast. His victory over Algiers on July 5, 1830 enabled France to begin establishing a colonial empire in North Africa. The liberal majority in the Chamber of Deputies immediately attacked de Polignac, saying his military activities were illegal and unconstitutional because the legislature had not approved his appointment as the king's chief advisor.

In March 1830 the Chamber of Deputies passed a vote of no confidence in the government. Charles, as the monarch was empowered to do under the French constitution, dissolved the Chamber of Deputies and scheduled new elections. When these elections gave liberals an even larger majority, Charles, encouraged by de Polignac, issued the Four Ordinances of 1830, which dissolved the newly elected legislature, strictly censored what the press could report, disenfranchised the middle class opposition to his government, and ordered new elections under the restricted suffrage. Charles X and de Polignac believed military victories in North Africa would stimulate sufficient patriotism that

the public would accept the Four Ordinances with limited opposition.

Charles and de Polignac had seriously underestimated the depth of opposition to changes they had tried to slip in under cover of military action. Liberal republican workers, artisans, students, writers, factory owners, and others aroused by protests from newspaper reporters, who were angry that the government had clamped down on the press, rioted. During the "three glorious days of July" (27 through the 29) rioters erected barricades throughout the French capitol and defied both the police and army. After the police force and army refused to fire upon the boisterous mob that had captured city hall and Notre Dame Cathedral, Charles X abdicated. He realized that without support from the military the ultra-royalist cause was lost. Charles voluntarily exiled himself to England, and his grandson, the Duke of Orleans, ascended to the throne as King Louis-Philippe (1830-1848).

After Charles' abdication, the revolutionaries could not agree upon the kind of government they wanted. Some, led by an aging Marquis de Lafayette, wanted a true democracy similar to that in the United States. However, the middle class power brokers—bankers, factory owners—feared democracy. They much preferred a limited constitutional monarchy that allowed only a few to vote. The power brokers agreed to support Louis-Philippe after extracting a promise from him to abide by the 1814 constitution. Even though the franchise was expanded, after 1830 only about 200,000 French citizens could vote. Property ownership was still necessary for exercise of the franchise. Ordinary French men and women benefited little from the 1830 Revolution. Its primary beneficiaries were the middle class. Changes in France after the revolution were hardly noticeable. The Chamber of Deputies revised parts of the 1814 charter, and the revolutionary red, white, and blue flag of the French Revolution became the official flag of France, replacing the white flag that symbolized the Bourbon monarchy. In short, the July Monarchy, as the new government was called, did not realize the liberal ideas of liberty, equality, and fraternity that French people desired.

France was not the only country to undergo revolution. Belgium, Spain, Poland, Italy, and the German states were also swept along on the revolutionary tide during the 1830s. Shortly after the July Revolution in France, a similar event occurred in Belgium. Rioting broke out in Brussels on August 25, 1830. Students, influenced by the July uprising in Paris, began to demonstrate against rule by the Netherlands. In particular, Belgian students were upset that King William I ruled the Netherlands in a despotic manner. Even though residents of Belgium's Waloon province spoke French, William made Dutch the official language of all Netherlands territory. He refused, moreover, to rid the nation of legislative malapportionment. Belgium, which had about one and a half million more residents than the Dutch provinces, was allocated the same number of seats in the national legislature as their Dutch neighbors. The student protesters demanded that the more populous Belgium provinces be given additional seats. Also irking to the students was William's refusal to make the Catholic Church the official religion in Belgium even though most residents of the territory remained Catholic. Equally galling to Belgian Catholics was William's insistence that the state regulate the education of Catholic priests.

Shortly after the riots began, industrial workers, unhappy with low wages, poor working conditions, and frequent unemployment, joined the fray. The more articulate business middle class, however, soon began to lead the Belgium revolt

and exerted much influence in the Belgium National Congress that revolutionaries convened in November 1830. Representatives at the National Congress declared that Belgium was independent of the Netherlands and instituted a constitutional monarchy headed by Leopold of Saxe-Coburg (1831-1865) as king. The new constitution gave the Catholic Church special status but also mandated tolerance for other sects, allowed local governments more autonomy, limited the government's power to regulate religious education, and broadened the franchise.

William I fought to bring Belgium back into the Netherlands in 1831 and 1832 but failed because Britain and France sent military units to defend the new government. In 1839, the Netherlands finally agreed to recognize Belgium independence. The liberal Belgian middle class had successfully established a constitutional monarchy that protected its entrepreneurial interests. Liberal forces in Spain, Italy, Germany, and Poland would also try to institute democratic reforms. A few would be successful. Most, however, would fail in the face of substantial opposition.

Liberal forces in Spain brought reform to the Iberian Peninsula. Middle class entrepreneurs formed an alliance with Queen Maria Christina, widow of King Ferdinand VII, to make Isabella, the Queen's daughter, ruler over Spain. Even though Maria was no liberal, she did not hesitate to accept the principles of reform to gain support of the urban middle class in her quest to secure the monarchy for her daughter. When Don Carlos, the late Ferdinand's brother, refused to acknowledge middle class grievances, business leaders threw their support behind Maria. From 1834 to 1840 Spain engaged in the Carlist Wars. During this time liberal entrepreneurs backing Maria and

Isabella forced them to grant Spain a constitution that favored middle class interests. The Spanish constitution created a legislature controlled by business interests. More radical reformers within the lower middle classes that contained workers and artisans were denied power within the legislature because the constitution did not give them the right to vote. Eventually, fear of the more radical lower classes resulted in the entrepreneurial classes accepting a government that was autocratic but that did not directly threaten the interests of the upper and middle classes.

While liberal forces in Spain successfully achieved reform, those in Poland, Italy, and Germany failed. In fact, liberalism took a step backward in Poland. After the Napoleonic Wars ended, Poland had the most liberal government and constitution in all Europe. In 1815, under Czar Alexander I, more Poles could vote than in any other European country. The Code Napoleon formed the basis of the legal code, and the Diet had substantial legislative powers. By 1835, however, the Polish democracy had disappeared; the country became a dependency of the Russian Empire. The last years of Alexander's rule were marked by political strife. Government ministers often used repressive tactics against Poles. When Nicholas I replaced Alexander as Russian Czar, Poland's troubles intensified. Initially, Nicholas respected the constitution Alexander had given Poland. Within a few years, however, nationalist fervor swept across university campuses in Poland. Nationalistic students began to demand that Lithuania, White Russia, and the Ukraine, territories that had previously belonged to Poland, be returned. Carbonari type societies arose within Poland, Lithuania, White Russia, and the Ukraine and began to instigate revolution in hopes of forcing Russia to return the former Polish provinces.

One of these Carbonari societies launched a revolt in Warsaw during November 1830. Students, artisans, and workers took to the streets, insisting that Russia return the Polish territory. Polish nobles quickly gained control of leadership positions within the revolution. Unfortunately, the nobles did not want true revolution to occur. They had no intention of freeing Polish peasants whom landlords that largely came from the ranks of the nobility had oppressed for centuries. Because the noble leadership was so conservative, radicals in Warsaw and elsewhere disrupted the revolutionary movement. Radical forces demanded that land and wealth within Poland be redistributed. This splintering within the ranks of the revolutionaries caused the movement to collapse in 1831. Russian forces, aided by an outbreak of cholera (the first time this Asiatic disease was noted in Europe), which killed or sickened thousands of peasants, took control of the Polish government. Czar Nicholas I abolished the Polish constitution, closed all colleges to stifle nationalism, and used Russian troops to impose martial law in Warsaw and other Polish cities. Revolutionaries were arrested and imprisoned, exiled, or executed. Many left Poland for safe havens in other European countries.

In Italy, liberalism was also crushed by foreign troops. When news of the July Revolution in France reached Italy, radicals began to organize. Rebels took control of the Duchies of Parma and Modena along with a sizeable portion of the Papal States in 1831. The revolutionaries, led by Italian business interests, hoped France would assist them. Unfortunately, France was not willing to risk war with Austria. When it became apparent that France was not going to get involved, Metternich sent an army to crush the rebellion and restore governments the Congress of Vienna had established throughout Italy. Metternich relied upon the legal system to crush revolt in the German states. After 1830, several princes in northern German states, including Saxony and Hanover, gave in to public pressure and granted their subjects liberal constitutions.

As a result of these limited successes, over thirty thousand revolutionaries met in the Palatinate in 1832. Their ranks included liberal college students and exiled Polish rebels. The rebels demanded German unification and a democratic constitution. One year later, professors and students revolted in Frankfurt, the capital of the confederation of German states and the city where the Diet met. Metternich filed charges against the students under German law, and thousands of people involved in the uprisings were arrested, tried, and convicted of insurgency. At the direction of Metternich, long prison terms were meted out by German courts. The harsh sentences served as a warning to future revolutionaries in German states. Yet, fear of imprisonment did not prevent liberal reformers from trying again at a later date. Another round of revolutions would sweep across Europe in 1848.

THE 1848 REVOLUTIONS

Europe again experienced a series of revolutions in 1848. While these uprisings had no singular cause, similar conditions across the continent likely produced them. Severe shortages of food, economic depression, unemployment, inadequate welfare systems, horrible living conditions in cities, and displacement of artisans, laborers, and farm workers all contributed to the violence that erupted in 1848. Nationalism was another common factor in many of the 1848 revolutionary movements.

As in previous revolutions, the middle class, rather than the working class, fostered the changes. They wanted governments to broaden

civil liberties, increase middle class representation, and lessen economic regulations. Even though the liberal middle class preferred initiating change through peaceful means, violence often resulted when reformers appealed to urban workers for support. Most common laborers had little interest in liberal reform; instead, they wanted an immediate improvement in living and working conditions. Some workers even favored emerging socialist solutions to their problems. Such oppressed people did not hesitate to employ violence to effect change. The 1848 revolutions shocked Europe. Never before in a single year had Europe experienced so many revolutions. Yet, the revolutions generally failed when different groups that were part of the uprisings turned on each other. The different goals of the middle and working classes eventually drove a wedge between the two groups and doomed the revolutions to failure.

France, the mother of revolutions, was the first hit by revolution. Liberal republicanism leftover from the 1789 and 1830 revolutions still simmered beneath the surface of the July Monarchy. In addition, politics and government within France was corrupt and generally undemocratic. Such a small percentage of the French population was represented in the national Chamber of Deputies that issues important to the country as a whole were seldom investigated. Most middle class citizens lacked representation in government—only one man out of every thirty Frenchmen could vote. The French government was so centralized that most officials readily followed orders issued by the Interior Ministry. Graft and corruption were so common that they had become a normal part of the political order.

Dissatisfaction with the limited franchise initially led to upheaval. A movement to give more people the franchise arose. Radical reformers wanted the government to enact universal suffrage and establish a republic while more moderate liberals wanted suffrage extended under France's current constitutional monarchy. Louis-Philippe, the French king, and Francois Guizot, his prime minister, absolutely refused to consider any changes. Revolution might have been avoided had more people been given the right to vote as moderate reformers wanted.

When the king and prime minister refused to extend suffrage, reformers called for a meeting and demonstrations in Paris on February 22. One day before the meeting was scheduled, Louis-Philippe banned such meetings. Leaders of the reform elements decided to go ahead with the meeting despite the ban. To combat police, barricades were erected in the narrow, winding streets of working class neighborhoods throughout Paris. Guizot ordered the French army to remove the barricades but to no avail. When the military refused to attack the demonstrators, Louis-Philippe promised electoral reform. His promises, however, did not satisfy the more radical reformers. Workers marched to Guizot's house where they began to demonstrate against the prime minister. Apparently one of the demonstrators shot at the guards surrounding the house. The sentries shot back, killing twenty demonstrators. Leaders of the radical movement placed the corpses on a cart and paraded them throughout Paris, inflaming and agitating thousands of workers. Working class people became so enraged at the spectacle that an enormous riot occurred in the French capitol. Louis-Philippe became so frightened that on February 24 he abdicated and, like Charles X, went into voluntary exile in England. The 1848 Revolution, like its predecessor in 1830, had forced a monarch from power in only a few days.

After Louis Philippe's abdication, revolutionaries established a provisional government headed by the poet Alphonse de Lamartine. A national election was set for April 23, 1848, to choose a National Assembly that was authorized to write a constitution for a permanent government—France's Second Republic. In this election the entire adult male population was allowed to vote, which represented the first time any European county had extended the franchise to all adult males. About eight million of the nine million eligible voters participated in this election. The election gave conservative republicans a resounding victory. While Frenchmen wanted to abolish the monarchy, they had little interest in electing radical socialist legislators who proposed to abolish private property rights.

France's new legislature met on May 4. Its first act was to abolish the provisional government and replace it with an executive board headed by Lamartine. Louis Blanc, a socialist leader who had served in the provisional government, was ousted, angering radical revolutionaries in Paris. Parisian radicals refused to abide by the will of conservative voters in the countryside. On May 15 they stormed into the National Assembly, demanding that a new provisional government be created. Elected members of the National Assembly fled in fear of their lives while the radicals created a new government and made plans for social revolution across France. Members of the National Assembly, however, used the National Guard to arrest the radicals and return the elected legislature to power. In an attempt to rid France of socialism, the legislature abolished the National Workshops established by the provisional government to appease socialists after Louis-Philippe's abdication. These National Workshops had amounted to a welfare project that provided government financial assistance to over one hundred thousand displaced workers in Paris. Radicals, like Blanc, used this organization to disseminate socialist views among the masses. Workers dependent upon the National Workshops for their livelihood were given a choice between working in outlying provinces or joining France's army. Paris' laboring classes were unwilling to accept closure of the workshops. They revolted on June 23, 1848.

From June 23 to June 26 a horrible class war engulfed Paris. Thousands of men and women erected barricades throughout the city, stubbornly defending their turf with firearms. These "Bloody June Days," as the event became known, saw urban guerilla warfare conducted throughout Paris. French troops brought to the city from conservative rural areas fought in hand-to-hand combat with angry Parisian workers. By the time General Louis Cavaignac subdued the revolutionaries, over ten thousand people had been killed or wounded, including several army generals. About eleven thousand rebels were captured. The National Assembly harshly punished the prisoners by ordering that they be exiled to Algeria and other French colonies overseas.

The June Days Revolution alarmed propertied classes throughout Europe. They saw the event as a revolution where the unemployed tried to redistribute the wealth of a capitalistic society and they reacted accordingly. Socialist organizations and newspapers were outlawed, and Blanc moved to England. Martial law was imposed in Paris, and Cavaignac operated as a military dictator. After the failure of the June Days Revolution the conservative National Assembly wrote a conservative republican constitution for France. This constitution for the Second Republic gave France a strong national executive in the form of a president elected by the male populace. In addition, the constitution gave French citizens the right to own private property and the right to elect a president every four years and a legislature every three years. But the constitution did not include a right-to-work provision that socialists had wanted.

The National Assembly decided to hold the presidential election before the constitution was finished. French voters had to choose from four candidates—Lamartine, Cavaignac, Ledru Rollin, and Louis-Napoleon Bonaparte, the nephew of the legendary Napoleon. Tapping into the Napoleonic legend that had developed in French popular culture, Louis-Napoleon easily defeated the other candidates in the December 1848 elections, receiving about five and a half million votes to Cavaignac's (the second place finisher) one and a half million.

The election of Louis-Napoleon spelled doom for the Second Republic. He dissolved the constitution three years later and declared himself to be Emperor Napoleon III. Ironically, the second French Revolution, like the first one in 1789, created a republic brought down by a Bonaparte dictatorship.

Austria, like France, also experienced revolution in 1848. Nationalism played an important role in Austria's revolutions. The Austrian Empire in 1848 consisted of four principal divisions—Austria, Bohemia, Northern Italy, and Hungary. Within each of these geographical areas lived a myriad of ethnic groups. Each had a distinct culture and often spoke a different language. The ethnic groups included Germans, Italians, Magyars, Czechs, Poles, Ruthenians, Slovaks, Serbs, Dalmatians, Croats, Slovenes, Rumanians, and other peoples. Some parts of the empire were populated almost exclusively by one ethnic group, but in most areas two or more groups lived in close proximity to each other. Neighboring villages separated by only a mile or two of land often spoke different languages.

After the Congress of Vienna in 1815, Metternich evaded the nationalistic question in Central Europe for about thirty years. His iron rule had discouraged nationalism. Metternich believed that if nationalism were allowed to take root in the Austrian Empire it would result in *bellum omnium contra omnes*, the war of all against all. At a time of growing national identity, Metternich and the Habsburg rulers of Austria could only offer diverse ethnic groups in the far-flung regions of the empire the idea that a benevolent ruler who had no connection or relationship with his citizens should rule over subjects who need have no connection with each other. Nationalistic revolts had occurred in Austrian territory prior to 1848, but such revolts in Italy and elsewhere had generally been brief and futile.

In March 1848 serious trouble erupted in Austrian lands. When news about the revolution in Paris reached Budapest, the Hungarian diet that had been in session for several months debating constitutional reforms urged Hungarians to revolt. Louis Kossuth, the Diet leader, spoke eloquently on the need for Hungarian liberty on March 3. His speech, which was printed in Hungarian newspapers, caused workers and students to rise up against their Austrian leaders. The cry for liberty in Hungary was also heard in Vienna. After Kossuth's speech was translated into German and read in Vienna newspapers, Austrian workers and students revolted on March 13, barricaded streets, battled with soldiers, and stormed the imperial palace. Metternich was stunned. He resigned and fled to England in fear of his life.

After Metternich's resignation, the Austrian Empire experienced chaos. Revolution swept across much of the land. The Hungarian Diet on March 15 enacted the March Laws, which constitutionally separated Hungary from Austria but still recognized the House of Habsburg as Hungary's constitutional monarchy. The Austrian Emperor, Ferdinand, terrified and

shocked at events, granted Bohemia essentially the same status as Hungary a few days later. From March 18 to the 22, Italian rebels fought Austrian troops, driving them out of Milan and other territory in northern Italy. Venice and Tuscany declared themselves independent republics. Sardinia declared war on Austria and invaded Lombardy and Venetia in an attempt to gain territory. Italian troops from central and southern Italy came north to join Sardinia and its ruler, Charles Albert, in what Tuscany, Naples, and the Papal States perceived as an Italian war to drive the Austrian occupiers from northern parts of the peninsula. Within one month the Austrian Empire was on the verge of collapse. Various ethnic groups were demanding independence, laws were passed abolishing serfdom, conventions were meeting to draft constitutions, and people were demanding the right to vote.

The initial success of the revolutions would not last. After Emperor Ferdinand and his family left Vienna for the Tyrol in May, a revolutionary council controlled the government. The revolutionary council issued a decree that freed peasants from their obligations to work for the landlord. This liberal decree, however, stopped the revolutionary momentum throughout the empire. Peasants lost interest in further revolution, as their main objective had been achieved. Middle class revolutionaries had lost the bulk of their support.

Further eroding the revolution was trouble between the Czechs and Germans. In June 1848 Czech nationals met at Prague in a Pan-Slavic conference to unify Slavic peoples within the empire against their German oppressors. The primary Slavic demand was political autonomy similar to that Hungary had just achieved. When the Vienna government refused to recognize Slavic autonomy, riots occurred in Prague. Soldiers and civilians fought in the streets. After five days the military defeated the revolutionaries and put Prague and Bohemia under martial law. The Prague victory marked the beginning of a counterrevolution that within a short period regained control of wayward territory for the Habsburg rulers. Flush with success in Prague, Habsburg armies marched into northern Italy, defeating Charles Albert, the Sardinian king, and took back Austria's Italian lands in July.

Hungary also was forced back into the empire. The liberal constitution and other reforms Kossuth gave Hungary benefited Magyars at the expense of other ethnic groups. The Magyar language, for example, was declared the official language within Hungary, replacing Latin. More than half the Hungarian population, however, was non-Magyars. The Slovaks, Rumanians, Germans, Serbs, and Croats resisted this change. Each ethnic group wanted to preserve its language and identity, fearing that the Magyar majority would dominate the country. Minority groups called upon the Habsburgs for protection. The Croats, who had been given special liberties by their Austrian rulers, revolted against the Magyars. In September, Count Jellachich, the provisional governor of Croatia, began a civil war in Hungary to overthrow the Magyar rulers and return Hungary to Austrian control. Emperor Ferdinand then commissioned Jellachich the Austrian military commander in Hungary. Supported by over half the Hungarian population, Jellachich easily defeated Magyar forces, took control of Hungary, and restored Austrian authority in October 1848. Magyars continued to fight until 1849. After the Hungarian parliament declared independence in April 1849, the Russian Czar, Nicholas I, fearing that the revolutionary fervor gripping central Europe might invade his domain, sent troops to crush the Hungarian rebels and destroy what was left of the Magyar Republic.

In Vienna, Austrian revolutionaries were also crushed. Rebel leaders who had been successful in March called the people into the streets because they feared that Habsburg forces, after subduing the Magyars, would march on Vienna. Initially the mass demonstration was successful. Emperor Ferdinand was driven from the city. Unfortunately for the revolutionaries, the Austrian General Windischgratz attacked Vienna, laying siege to the city for five days. On October 31, Vienna surrendered. The Austrian revolutions were over. Most revolutionary reforms were retracted with the exception of the edict abolishing serfdom. One important reason the revolution failed in Austria is because peasants, who were an important source of agitation, were generally satisfied and no longer supported revolution once serfdom was abolished.

Counterrevolutionary leaders, including large landowners, Catholic clergymen, and military officers, decided to depose Ferdinand. On December 2, 1848, he abdicated under pressure. His nephew, Francis Joseph, an eighteen-year-old lad, became Austrian emperor. He ruled the empire until his death in 1916. Prince Fleix Schwarzenberg, the man who had arranged Ferdinand's abdication, became the Austrian prime minister. He declared that Francis Joseph would not follow the policies of his predecessor. Various German states also underwent revolution in 1848. Rebels in various German states, including Wurttemberg, Saxony, Hanover, Bavaria, and Prussia, demanded constitutional government. Nationalism and liberalism both played important roles in the German revolutions as they did elsewhere in Europe. Liberalism and nationalism had early successes in Germany but eventually succumbed as a result of factional fighting among the rebels themselves and Austrian resistance.

Revolution in Germanic territories began in March 1848 when liberals in western provinces demanded constitutions and civil liberties. The rebels largely came from the ranks of the working and middle classes—artisans, industrial workers, peasants, and university professors. Most were moderates, wanting constitutional monarchies, more unity between the German states, and freedom from Austrian repression. King Frederick William IV (1840-1861) of Prussia became a hero to German rebels when he refused to attack rebel rioters in Berlin on March 15. Frederick William's refusal to attack Berliners was rooted in his belief that foreign agitators had caused the disturbances. He promised rebels that he would honor his father's unfulfilled pledge to give Prussia representative government under a constitution. When Frederick William was slow to move on his promises, rioters stormed the royal palace demanding that the king accept liberal ideas. Fearing for his life and position, Frederick William capitulated. He called a convention that would meet in Frankfurt to write a constitution, issued an edict stating that Prussia was part of a larger Germany, and declared himself king of a unified Germany.

On May 18 the constitutional convention met. The 830 delegates elected to attend this convention did not represent German society in its entirety because most representatives were chosen by an Electoral College system dominated by the wealthy, conservative classes. Frederick William intended for the Assembly to write a moderately liberal constitution that would unite all German states. Eventually, the Frankfurt Assembly gave Germany a fairly liberal constitution that included federalism and parliamentary government. German states would give up much of their power to a larger national government. The German Congress would consist of an upper chamber chosen by state legislatures and a lower house elected by the German population. All males were granted the right to vote while the franchise was denied to females. The legislature would choose the German cabinet, and the German emperor would rule as chief executive over the republic. Delegates to the Frankfurt Convention, as expected, elected Frederick William as Germany's first constitutional emperor.

Problems also arose over German unification. Delegates to the Frankfurt Convention generally fell into two camps—those who favored *grossdeutsche*, an all inclusive Germany, and those who wanted *kleindeutsche*, a small, isolated Germany. The all-inclusive Germans favored the inclusion of Austria and Bohemia with its large Czech population along with Prussia's and its Polish lands into a unified Germany whereas the small, isolated German adherents opposed inclusion into Germany of any people whose language and heritage was not German. The convention reached something of a compromise on this issue. Delegates voted to exclude Austria's Bohemian territory but accepted Prussia's Polish provinces. Austria, because it would lose much territory, rejected unification. Because Austria rejected unification and because conservatives opposed most of the economic and political reforms proposed at the meeting, the German attempt to create a unified republic failed. Conservatives convinced workers and artisans that the liberal commitment to free trade and hostility to protection of the guild system afforded labor would harm the working class. These issues caused a split to develop between labor and liberal reformers. Conservatives exploited this split for the rest of the nineteenth century to prevent real reform from occurring in Germany. After it became clear that the convention had failed, Frederick William rejected the offer to become emperor because he feared Austrian power.

ROMANTICISM: LITERATURE, ART, MUSIC, AND PHILOSOPHY

Romanticism, a broad cultural movement of the late eighteenth and early nineteenth centuries, played a role in European political developments as well as influencing art, music, literature, and philosophy. Romanticism was such a broad movement that it practically defies definition. More than anything, romanticism was a reaction against the eighteenth century Enlightenment. Whereas the Enlightenment emphasized the use of reason to acquire knowledge, nineteenth-century Romanticism stressed the role of emotion along with rational thought. While intellectuals produced by the Enlightenment understood the human mind as a blank slate that developed by adding knowledge gained through external sensual experiences, Romantic intellectuals believed that part of a person's knowledge was innate. This did not mean that Romantics rejected reason as a basis for knowledge. Rather, they believed in the importance of emotion. Romantic intellectuals insisted that each individual had a unique personality that was inherited at birth. Thus, the human brain contained information that had been present from birth. According to Romantics, people just instinctively knew some things without ever having learned them. Knowledge, then for Romantics, was acquired from both rational thought and external sense data as well as from innate feelings. This philosophy would be influential in the literature, art, music, and philosophy that Romantics produced during the nineteenth century. Of particular importance was the emphasis on the individual and individual creativity that resulted from the interaction of each person's unique personality and external sensory experiences.

Romantic writers, artists, and musicians also looked to the past as they protested against rationalism produced by the Enlightenment. These intellectuals championed things valued by earlier generations, including religious faith, emotional feeling, traditional ways of life, and other things associated with past eras. Romanticism was clearly present at the Congress of Vienna where, after Napoleon's defeat, European leaders largely rejected revolutionary changes and reestablished the balance of power system. The Enlightenment's emphasis on reason and natural law, according to Romantics, produced the Reign of Terror, Napoleon's dictatorship, and the reactionary movements of the first half of the nineteenth century. Romanticism, along with the protest and reaction associated with it, is usually dated from about 1780 to 1830; however, it reached its height from about 1815 until 1830.

Romantics rejected what they perceived as an undue emphasis on logic and confining rules in prose and poetry as well as history, science, music, and government. William Blake, an English artist, for example, criticized Isaac Newton. Rather than viewing Newton as a scientific genius, Blake argued that he was a narrow-minded technician who thought everything in the universe could be measured and quantified. Romantics like Blake maintained that while reason and logic were important, they were subservient to emotion and intuition.

Romanticism's rejection of logic and its emphasis on emotion contributed to the development of liberal ideas important in revolutions in the 1830s and 1840s while its focus on the past made nationalistic movements stronger. At the same time, the link between Romanticism and the past was used to support traditional

In *The Sorrows of Young Werther,* by Johann Wolfgang von Goethe, (pictured) the hero is so sensitive and emotional that he takes his own life.

monarchies and to oppose republicanism, anticlericalism, and liberalism. Many of these themes are present in prose and poetry produced by Romantic writers.

Literature

Romantic themes appeared in literature produced in most European countries by various authors. One of the most important Romantic writers was the German, Johann Wolfgang von Goethe. His novel, *The Sorrows of Young Werther,* made him famous overnight. Widely translated into many languages, including Chinese, the book represented a break from the Enlightenment's emphasis on logic and reason. The themes of self-destruction (The hero commits suicide because the woman he loves is married to another man.) and self-pity were repeated over and over in other Romantic novels. Goethe's most famous work, *Faust,* which some scholars

believe is the greatest of all German books, is also filled with Romantic themes. This long poetic drama, which took sixty years to write, emphasizes emotional values the Enlightenment had rejected. In the story *Faust,* an old man tired of intellectual pursuits, sold his soul to Satan to be young again. After an allotted time to enjoy his youth, Faust would then burn in hell. In the end, Faust is saved from eternal damnation because he comes to understand that personal selfish interests must be put aside for the welfare of the community.

Other countries also produced Romantic authors. The French philosopher Jean Jacques Rousseau's novel, *La Nouvelle Heloise,* also focused on Romantic themes of love and duty. Heloise, tempted to commit adultery, died before the sexual act could occur. England produced many Romantic writers. English poets were especially important. Whereas the Enlightenment had rejected most poetry as lovesick mush, Romantics embraced poetry from the past and produced new lyrics of their own. Lord Byron, Percy Bysshe Shelley, John Keats, William Wordsworth, and Samuel Taylor Coleridge are but a few of the poets Romanticism produced in England. The *Lyrical Ballads*, written by Wordsworth and Coleridge, represents one of England's greatest contributions to Romantic poetry. Coleridge's "Rime of the Ancient Mariner," a poem about a sailor who kills an albatross, which results in him being cursed, is particularly noteworthy for its Romantic themes. He later attacked scientific reason in "Kubla Khan." Rather than presenting a world ordered by logic, Coleridge has Kubla Khan exist in Xanachu, a place where feeling is more important than logical order. Wordsworth's poems, likewise, emphasize the emotional qualities of the individual and the connection between the human spirit, nature, and God. Sir Walter Scott was one of Britain's most well known Romantic poets and novelists. He collected folk poems and composed over thirty historical novels. *Ivanhoe*, a historical novel set in the context of the Medieval Crusades, is his most famous work.

Music

Romantic musicians, like writers, stressed nationalistic themes, rejected restraints liberalism imposed on music, and looked to the past for substance. Unlike literary figures who largely rejected eighteenth-century authors, Romantic musicians did not ignore the great composers of the previous century. Instead, they built upon music left by eighteenth-century masters.

Ludwig van Beethoven (1770-1827) was perhaps the most important Romantic composer. He built upon classical compositions by changing tempo from fast to slow to all speeds in between. The skillful change in tempo added life,

passion, and movement to Beethoven's compositions. His use of the piano and a wide variety of other instruments, especially winds, percussion, and brasses, broke with tradition, making his music much admired. His various symphonies are considered some of the best Romantic compositions ever produced.

Other Romantic composers made use of the piano. The Polish master, Frederic Chopin (1810-1849), composed music exclusively for the piano. His work was influenced greatly by Polish folk music. For example, he wrote many *polonaises* designed to allow peasants to dance to lively tunes. In general, Chopin's compositions were difficult to play because of the demanding techniques musicians had to master. However, his music made the piano into the most popular instrument of the nineteenth century.

Hector Berlioz (1803-1869), a French composer, emulated Beethoven's use of a wide array of instruments. His *Requiem* used, in addition to a full orchestra, a pipe organ, four brass choirs, and a chorus that numbered two hundred. His orchestra included over 450 instruments.

Franz Schubert (1797-1828), like Beethoven and other Romantic composers, used both chorus and instruments in his musical works. He is most famous for writing over six hundred songs that drew upon various poems. Seventy of his songs were based upon poetry written by Goethe.

Johannes Sebastian Bach, Carl Marie von Weber, Mikhail Glinka, and numerous other composers wrote musical compositions that drew from the Romantic Movement. Their use of the piano accompanied by a myriad of instruments, as well as the human voice, stimulated an interest in music and made Romantic composers some of the most important musical personages in European history. The longing for the past and nationalistic themes present in Romantic

The London House of Parliament along the edge of the Thames River is an example of Romantic architecture.

musical compositions are evident in European musical heritage today.

Art and Artists

Art and artists did not achieve the same level of acclaim as did music and musicians during the Romantic period. Romantic art represents a transitional period between the neoclassical style of the seventeenth century, which stressed form, line, and perspective, and Impressionism of the late nineteenth century, which emphasized light and color rather than form. Official recognition was first given to Romantic art at the Paris exhibition of painting in 1824. Two Romantic artists—Englishman John Constable and

Frenchman Eugene Delacroix—showed paintings in that exhibit. Delacroix, in particular, believed that art should be created "to strike the imagination rather than to reproduce scenes from the natural world."

Francisco Goya, a Spanish artist, is perhaps the best-known Romantic master. His paintings and etchings reveal deep-seated emotions that neoclassical works had refused to deal with. Human emotions and feelings are particularly evident in portraits he painted of figures like Charles II and in an etching depicting the French suppression of Spanish revolutionaries during the Madrid uprising of May 1808.

Romantic architecture tended to look toward the past for ideas. Structures designed by architects during this period tended to make use of ancient Greek, Roman, and Medieval designs. Nineteenth-century architects did not merely reproduce Ancient or Medieval structures but rather adapted their features to needs of the 1800s. The London House of Parliament is a good example of Romantic architecture. The structure had incorporated into its numerous Gothic towers classic features such as symmetry, balance, and harmony. Many buildings erected in Paris and other European cities during the nineteenth century make use of Roman and Greek architectural features such as columns and arches.

Philosophy

Georg Wilhelm Friedrich Hegel (1770-1831) dominated Romantic philosophy. This German philosopher introduced the idea of the dialectic. Hegel theorized that events occurred as a result of a dialectical process arising out of conflicting ideas. Two conflicting ideas, which Hegel called the thesis and antithesis, collided to produce a new idea called the synthesis. The synthesis then became the accepted order until it was challenged by a different antithesis, producing a new synthesis. This process, which had repeated itself over and over throughout human history, was the way history moved forward. Thus, a cyclic process produced linear movement over time. Eventually, Hegel theorized, the dialectical historical process would enable human beings to achieve a kind of heaven on earth. All human problems would be solved given the passage of sufficient time.

Karl Marx (1818-1883), another German philosopher, was heavily influenced by Hegel's ideals. *The Communist Manifesto*, written in 1848 by Marx and Friedrich Engels (1820-1895), used Hegel's dialectical process to theo-

rize that the working class would stage a revolution that would create a near perfect society in which the private ownership of property was abolished. This communistic society, according to Marx and Engels, would result from the clash of rich capitalists who controlled most wealth in industrial nations and working class proletarians who had little but the ability to labor. After the clash occurred, Marx and Engels said, a new society controlled by workers would result. In this new society, everyone would be economically equal, producing as much as they could and consuming only as much as they needed. For Marx class struggle was the dialectic element in the cyclical process of change. Once communism had achieved the perfect society the evolution would stop because with no more classes, there would be no more class struggle to drive the

German political philosopher Karl Marx believed that a democratic society could be achieved only when the industrial workers revolted.

change. Eventually, there would be no need for government and the state would wither away.

While the ideas of Marx and Engels sound good, they do not work well in practice. A fundamental flaw in their philosophy is that it does not take into account fundamental human nature. Not all humans will follow rules of society. Some people tend to be greedier than others and want to accumulate and hoard wealth, material possessions, and power. This human tendency negates the utopian ideas of Marx, Engels and other adherents of Communism.

Other Romantic philosophers included Friedrich Schlegel (1772-1829), Friedrich von Savigny (1779-1861), Samuel Taylor Coleridge (1772-1834), and Francois Rene de Chateaubriand. Schlegel and von Savigny opposed the importation into Germany of foreign institutions. Instead, they argued that national institutions must be developed from within a country according to ideas and customs prevalent within a society. Coleridge, an English philosopher and literary figure, argued much the same idea. He maintained that religion and government, for example, resulted not from universal principles but from peculiar circumstances faced by a particular group of people at a certain time. Thus, he opposed utilitarian ideas that were being introduced into the English government and church. Chateaubriand, a French conservative, agreed with Coleridge in *The Genius of Christianity*. He maintained that the past is so much a part of the present that foreign ideas and institutions cannot be forced on a people without destroying the society present within a nation.

In general, Romantic philosophers provided the intellectual underpinning for the nationalistic movements that were part of the numerous revolutions that swept across the European continent during the first half of the nineteenth century. Nationalism itself, in part, resulted from Romantic ideas about history, past events, and future destiny. Nations, for example, began to develop national archives to chronicle their glorious past.

CONCLUSION

European history during the first half of the nineteenth century was marked by revolution after revolution. After the Napoleonic Wars ended, representatives from various countries met to put Europe back together again. The guiding principles at this meeting were legitimacy and restoration. For the most part, agreements reached at the Congress of Vienna restored boundaries in European that had existed prior to Napoleon's conquest of the continent. Even though European leaders after 1815 wanted to extinguish the flames of liberalism produced by the French Revolution and Napoleonic reforms, they were not completely successful. From time to time liberal ideas would surface, often producing revolutions. Serious uprisings occurred in European countries in 1830 and again in 1848. Art, literature, music, and philosophy reflected the themes of reaction, conservatism, nationalism, and reform present in Europe throughout the first half of the nineteenth century. The turmoil that engulfed Europe following the Congress of Vienna along with the liberal revolutions that broke out and their suppression by reactionary conservatives paved the way for the industrial development and liberal reforms that were part of the industrial age that enveloped Europe during the last half of the nineteenth century.

Suggestions for Further Reading

Frederick B. Artz, Reaction and Revolution, 1814-1832 (1969).

Irene Collins, *Government and Society in France, 1814-1848* (1971).

Jacques Droz, *Europe Between Revolutions, 1815-1848* (1980).

Crane Brinton, *Political Ideas of the English Romanticists* (1926).

John B. Halsted, ed., *Romanticism: Problems of Definition, Explanation, Evaluation* (1965).

Eric J. Hobsbawm, *The Age of Revolution, 1789-1848* (1962).

Eric J. Hobsbawm, *Nations and Nationalism Since 1780: Programme, Myth, Reality* (1992).

Mary D. R. Leys, *Between Two Empires* (1955).

Peter Manent, *An Intellectual History of Liberalism* (1994).

Lewis B. Namier, *1848: The Revolution of the Intellectuals* (1964).

Harold Nicholson, *The Congress of Vienna* (1970).

David H. Pinkney, *The French Revolution of 1830* (1972).

Reuben J. Rath, *The Viennese Revolution of 1848* (1975).

C. A. Rudd, *Fighting Words: Imperial Censorship and the Russian Press, 1804-1904* (1982)

Guilaume de Sauvigny, *Metternich and His Times* (1962).

J. L. Talmon, *Romanticism and Revolt, 1815-1848* (1979).

Albert B. Ulam, *Russia's Failed Revolutionaries* (1981)

Mack Walker, ed. *Metternich's Europe* (n.d.).

NATIONALISM & REALPOLITIK

1848-1871

A British cookhouse during the Crimean War

Giuseppe Garibaldi: The Story of an Italian Patriot

Giuseppe Garibaldi, the great hero of Italian unification, was born in Nizza on July 4, 1807. Even in his youth he was a courageous young boy who at age eight rescued a woman from drowning and at age thirteen saved his friends from the harrowing circumstances of a shipwreck. He had a need for adventure and a desire to experience a physically challenging lifestyle. Garibaldi undertook several shipping voyages from age fifteen, experiencing many seafaring adventures and meeting several interesting individuals. Many of these people were influential in creating patriotic sentiments in the young Giuseppe Garibaldi.

In 1833, Garibaldi met Giuseppe Mazzini, a fearless fighter for Italian liberation, and set off on the first of many revolutionary adventures. This soon ended, however, in a flight for refuge under a false name. With his need for adventure not yet satisfied, Garibaldi traveled to South America where he lived for 12 years. His political interests overshadowed his weak attempts at business enterprise, and he moved into a revolutionary republican movement, eventually fighting in Brazil, Argentina, and Uruguay. His South American exploits made him the symbol of a great hero of freedom and a patriot in the hearts of Italians who saw him as a hero of Two Worlds.

Giuseppe Garibaldi returned to Italy to lead the challenge of reorganizing the revolutionary movements for the unification of Italy. Although this attempt failed miserably and, once again, Garibaldi narrowly escaped into exile, a deep republican spirit and love of his Italian heritage remained with him. Indeed, the political energy of revolution and love of liberation action never left him. Once again, he returned to Italy where in the Kingdom of Piedmont-Sardinia, the Chief Minister Cavour and the King Victor Emmanuel placed him at the head of the army with the rank of general, and he soon commenced military campaigns against the Austrians. Even after his resignation from the rank, he continued to provide support for insurrectionary action in central Italy.

In May 1860, with revolutionary excitement strong in Italy, Garibaldi returned to action and organized a military expedition to Sicily. On May 11, 1860, his campaign docked at Marsala harbour and moved toward Calatafimi to attack the Bourbon defenses. In a violent and mismatched battle of 1200 Italian patriots against a defense twice this size, Garibaldi and his volunteers took the position. Garibaldi relied on the ever-present revolutionary spirit, determination, courage, and tactical intelligence that had inspired so many of his followers and admirers. After successfully conquering all of Sicily, he crossed the Straits of Messina and moved on Naples. After a bloody and horrific battle at the fortress of Capua and Gaeta in the battle of Volturno, the Austrians were defeated.

After a plebiscite appointment on October 21 the two regions were joined to King Emmanuel's lands. At Teano, the heroic patriot Garibaldi is met by the king who is greeted as the king of Italy. The patriotic hero, Garibaldi, had succeeded in the reunification of Italy.

Chronology

1848	Liberal and Nationalistic revolutions in Europe
1851	Coup d'etat by Louis Napoleon in France
1853-1856	Crimean War
1858	War between Kingdom of Piedmont-Sardinia and Austria
1860	Garibaldi leads Italian invasionary forces against Kingdom of the Two Sicilies
1861	Victor Emmanuel of Piedmont is proclaimed the King of Italy
1862	Tsar Alexander II of Russia emancipates the Serfs
1863	Maximilian crowned emperor of Mexico; Prussians and Austrians at war with Denmark
1866	Seven Weeks' War between Austria and Prussia; Italy acquires Venetia
1867	The Hapsburg Empire Reorganized as the "Dual Monarchy"; Emperor Maximilian executed
1869	The opening of the Suez Canal
1870	The Franco-Prussian War; Italy annexes Rome
1871	William I becomes the Kaiser of Germany; German Empire proclaimed; Paris Commune

EUROPE AFTER THE REVOLUTIONS OF 1848

The failures of the revolutions of 1848 convinced many people that popular uprisings and rebellions were ineffective means of changing society. Yet, the spirit of change lived on while undergoing serious reassessment and, whether consciously or unconsciously, a practical transformation.

Clearly, the historical period of reaction, reform and revolution from 1815-1848 influenced Western Civilization after the revolutions had ended in disastrous outcomes. The romantic preoccupation with revolutionary dreams of mass uprisings had passed. Romanticism and high-minded idealism were replaced by an intense devotion to practical work for the sake of progress and change. A new generation of reformers replaced the mythological quest for liberation with a hard-nosed recognition of political reality. These individuals were devoted to a new kind of practical leadership required for effective change. This was the era of a new nationalism introduced "from above" and the applications of "Realpolitik." Practical considerations ascended over ideals and ethical concerns.

CAVOUR AND THE UNIFICATION OF ITALY

By 1848, reforming liberals had been unable to unify the Italian nation by defeating and expelling the Austrian Empire and the Hapsburg dynasty from their lands. But the dreams of liberation and Italian national unification lived on. Hopes for independence and liberty were kept alive by old revolutionaries and the memories of secret societies. The most significant of these underground revolutionary clubs were "the Carbonari," which had sections in every Italian state. Inspired by the Carbonari-led insurrec-

Prime Minister Cavour of Sardinia aired his grievances against what he considered to be the authoritarian rule of the Austrian Empire over lands in which Italian people lived. This was an important step toward achieving Italian independence, which came to fruition in 1871.

tions of 1831-32 and the determined mass uprisings led by charismatic patriots, a new generation of patriotic Italians refused to accept the reality of a divided Italy and continued the struggle for liberation. One important leader was Count Camillo Benso di Cavour (1810-1861).

The Italian revolution lived on driven by fervent nationalists like Count Cavour. After 1848, it was Cavour, the chief minister of Piedmont-Sardinia, who became the architect of a new nationalist movement in Italy. As a cautious and practical political manager, Cavour worked to transform Piedmont into a modern progressive Italian state. He reorganized the economy, innovated the transportation infrastructure, and attempted territorial expansion.

In foreign policy, Cavour crafted expanded alliances with England and France and promoted anti-Austrian sentiments among his people. In addition, he successfully negotiated a secret agreement with Napoleon III of France to match Austrian aggression with a powerplay intended to provide Piedmont-Sardinia with Lombardy, Venetia, and parts of the Papal States. In exchange, France would gain Nice and Savoy from Piedmont.

In the end, Piedmont only gained Lombardy. But the victory over Austria had inspired the seizure of power in Parma, Tuscany, Modena, and Romagna by nationalist forces. The new governments opted to join with Piedmont in the creation of unified Italy. Soon after Piedmont's successes, revolutionary activity broke out in the Kingdom of the Two Sicilies, where Giuseppe Garibaldi remained determined to liberate all subject nationalities in the cause of Italian national unity.

Napoleon III (Emperor of France)

Experiencing success in the liberation of Sicily in 1860, the charismatic Garibaldi invaded the Italian mainland, seizing Naples, and prepared for victory as he and his legions pressed on towards Rome. In Rome, Garibaldi's forces met with easy military success. Finally, Garibaldi had advanced the much longed-for liberation of Italy.

Garibaldi did not seek personal grandeur or reward for his military successes. He soon ceded his dominions to King Victor Emmanuel of Piedmont who was declared king of Italy in 1861. Even after Cavour's death in 1861, the movement for national unification continued. At the conclusion of the Austro-Prussian War in 1866, Italy was rewarded the state of Venetia for its alliance with the victorious Prussians. In 1870, during the Franco-Prussian War, Italian troops replaced the withdrawing French garrisons, and Rome was declared the Italian capital city. The unification of Italy had finally become a reality.

THE UNIFICATION OF GERMANY

During the German revolutionary wars of 1848, those who had struggled for liberal reforms and progressive change failed to weaken the power of monarchy and aristocratic tradition. The movement for a unified Germany also failed. The Old Order had prevailed after the failed revolutionary insurrections. Liberal ideals were quickly abandoned. The flames, however, of revolution were not completely extinguished among Germans. The dreams of legal equality, parliamentary reform, liberal politics, and economic opportunity for the bourgeois class, peasants, and artisans remained.

The realities of power called for something new and different. A new respect for practical work towards change overtook the more romantic spirit of revolutionaries left disenchanted but hopeful. Indeed, transformation would come from the "politics of reality" and reforms imposed from above.

After the French defeated the Prussians at Jena in 1806, high-ranking German army officials and ranking bureaucrats pushed for governmental reforms to create a more unified and devoted country. Although significant reforms were made, as with the abolishment of hereditary serfdom, Prussia failed to provide people a constitution and parliamentary institutions. The power of the monarchy and traditional aristocratic order remained. The state remained strengthened by the power to grant reforms from above without a check and balance of its authority from a liberal opposition.

In 1834, under the direction of Prussia, the collection of thirty-nine German states, with the exception of Austria, established a customs union known as the Zollverein, which abolished tariffs between the states to stimulate commercial activity, profit, and greater German unity. The

Zollverein provided the economic basis for the unification of Germany and the state of Prussia with the authoritative position of political leadership in the movement for unification.

During the revolution of 1848, German liberals had pursued ideas of political liberty, legal equality, civil protections, free speech, and laissez-faire economy. Liberals, however, had failed to weaken the power of the monarchy and aristocracy. Frederick William IV (1840-1861), rejecting a revolution of commoners, did not accept the crown offered to him by the Frankfurt Assembly. A conservative approach to unification followed in 1849 when Prussia fashioned plans for a German union.

Prussia forfeited plans for an expansive German union when Austria resisted. The Austrians rejected the unification campaign due to concerns that a Prussian-led unification plan would diminish the primacy of Austrians in German affairs. The German confederation was reestablished in 1849. Diplomatic activity intended to consolidate German national unification had ended in collapse and failure.

Frederick William IV transferred control of the Prussian government to his brother in 1858. Upon Frederick William's death, his brother became William I (1861-1888), the new king of Prussia. Intent on expanding his power, William recognized Austria as the chief opposition to Prussia in the extension of its influence in Germany. In a strategy designed to strengthen the Prussian state, William implemented plans to reorganize and expand the Prussian army. The strategy, however, met with opposition from liberal elements in the Prussian parliament who viewed the potential army reforms with concerns and suspicion. The parliament successfully blocked institution of the reforms for fear that this implementation would expand the power of the monarchy and the military regime.

William, angry and frustrated, withdrew the army reform bill from the upper chamber and requested additional funds from the lower parliamentary chamber to cover government expenses. When parliament granted these funds, William quickly used them to institute the proposed army reforms. In 1862, the chastened lower chamber refused to approve the new budget without a specific itemized breakdown. A critical conflict had arisen between the monarchy and a liberal majority in the Prussian parliament.

Otto von Bismarck (1815-1898)

An unyielding supporter of the Prussian monarchy, Otto von Bismarck (1815-1898) was called upon by William to lead the battle against recalcitrant liberals in the Prussian parliament in 1862. For Bismarck, preservation of divine right, monarchical power, and aristocratic order were the keys to a stable Prussia. With liberal elements in the lower parliamentary chamber withholding funds for military reforms, Bismarck moved with characteristic authoritarianism to dismiss the chamber, arrest outspoken liberals, impose censorship on free speech, and remove active reformists from the government.

Bismarck determined that the main instrument for success in German unification was foreign policy. In addition, he recognized this instrument to be critical for the dominance of the Prussian state over German affairs. With an appreciation for the machinations of foreign policy, Bismarck worked to remove Austrian influence in German affairs. In an orchestrated dispute over the division of Danish territory, Prussia and Austria went to war in 1866. Prussia won, decisively defeating Austrian forces at the Battle of Sadowa at the conclusion of the Seven Weeks' War. Austria allowed annexation of Schleswig, Holstein and other German states. As Prussia securely organized a confederation of north German states, notably leaving Austria out, Prussia emerged as the major power in Germany. This not only expanded the power of Prussia but also the fervor and spirit of nationalism.

Bismarck had successfully orchestrated the nationalist unification of Germany through his adoption of the practical politics of conservative rule. With the liberal struggle for parliamentary reforms greatly weakened through "realpolitik," victory belonged to the Prussian military and a Prussian authoritarian state. The conservative approach had succeeded where liberal traditions had faltered. National unification was achieved.

At the end of the Austro-Prussian War, Prussia was the leading power in the German Confederation. The Prussian king had primary control of the affairs of confederation members. The union still was not complete because the south German states remained resistant to Prussian authoritarianism. South German states feared the weakening of the Catholic tradition within their boundaries and the loss of identity in a broader German union.

Bismarck and Napoleon II

The pretext of war between Prussia and France delivered a nationalist cause with which to pursue the grander goal of unification. This was a war that Bismarck clearly invited and had secretly hoped for. With France increasingly threatened by the creation of a strong north German Confederation under the leadership of an increasingly powerful Prussia, Napoleon III heeded the advocates of battle. The main motivation for war came with the conflict over succession to the vacated Spanish throne. In this debate over succession, France opposed the candidacy of Prince Leopold of Hohenzollern-Sigmaringen, a relative of Prussian King William I. France was concerned that the succession of Prince Leopold would extend the control of Prussian authority into Spanish dominions. Hoping to avoid war, the Prussian king requested that Leopold withdraw his candidacy. Unfortunately, tensions did not end there.

Ems Telegram

Soon after, France requested formal guarantees that no potential candidates to the Spanish throne would be of Hohenzollern connection. William refused to acquiesce. The quarrel escalated further. When the Prussian king informed Bismarck of the rejection of the French ambassador's formal request in a telegram sent to Berlin from Ems, Bismarck edited the message to create the impression that William and the Prussian throne had been formally insulted. The altered telegram also suggested that William had returned the favor of insult to the French ambassador. News of this exchange of slights created an uproar in both countries. Patriotic indignation demanded immediate remedy. War fever broke out as France mobilized its armed forces. In Prussia, the response to French mobilization produced similar results.

Prussian forces decimated the comparatively weak and disorganized French. Just as Bismarck had anticipated, the south German states quickly came to the assistance of the powerful Prussian army. The fervor of patriotism combined with German nationalism was too powerful to resist for the south German states. Prussian leadership again proved to be key in the advance of German power.

With Napoleon III defeated and imprisoned, the Prussian army moved on Paris. With the residents of Paris placed under a siege, the city formally surrendered to the Prussians in January

1871. France was forced to cede the provinces of Alsace and Lorraine to the German Confederation and pay a significant indemnity. A victorious German Confederation rejoiced at its success against the French Empire.

Just as Bismarck had hoped, the nationalist fervor created by the Franco Prussian War secured the unification of Germany with the inclusion of south German states. At Versailles on January 1871, William I was granted the title of German emperor. The unification of Germany had created the most powerful military and economic empire in central Europe.

NAPOLEON III AND THE
PARIS COMMUNE

In 1848 in France, after the disastrous "June Days" of revolutionary violence, resulting from working-class radicalism, a conservative reaction countervailed. In December 1848, Louis Napoleon Bonaparte (1808-1873), the nephew of the emperor Napoleon Bonaparte, was elected the president of the Second Republic. The overwhelming support for Louis Napoleon reflected the great disdain of the French people for continued social disorder. The rest of France was simply terrified of radicalism and unsympathetic to both working class poverty and socialist ideology.

In the middle of the nineteenth century, in an election where all French adult males could vote, France embraced Louis Napoleon, and within three years, he became a dictator-emperor. Louis Napoleon soon changed the landscape of France and its government. Over time, the Second Republic was summarily destroyed and this action ratified by plebiscite in manipulated elections. Eventually, Bonaparte's authoritarianism successfully guaranteed his domination of French affairs, both domestic and foreign. His destruction of the republic was advanced with his support for Catholics in Rome, his imperialism, and national glory.

With a curious blend of nationalist, democratic, liberal, and authoritarian ideas, Bonaparte slowly but meticulously created an empire under stable rule. He was a brilliant political tactician. Opposition to his rule was suppressed. The press was controlled through censorship. Liberal voices in parliament went unheard, as the assembly was rarely convened. Most critical debates and elections were strategically manipulated for practical purpose. Nepotism resulted in a closely guarded circle of admirers and sycophants culled from relatives and friends.

After 1860, some controls were loosened. In 1869, when members of the liberal opposition party were elected to the parliament in overwhelming numbers, Bonaparte approved a new constitution that provided liberal individual rights and protections for citizens.

As the French armies and popular resistance were overrun by Prussian armies, the people of Paris rose up in defiance. The Paris Commune rejected the Second Empire as corrupt when it concluded peace with Prussia. The radical republicans, or "communards," refused to follow the new government and its edicts. These insurrectionary actions were supported by a diverse collection of people. They ranged from followers of republican sentiments to ordinary patriots and from radical socialists to anarchists. The communards waged battle for two months in Paris before the provisional government ordered French troops to attack Paris. The violent and bitter battles ended in defeat for the insurrectionary communards. The defeated were dealt harsh consequences. Twenty thousand French civilians were executed without formal trial, while others received sentences of death after manipulated trials or life in the hellish prison colonies.

Across Europe, aristocratic and bourgeois classes were concerned and alarmed by the insurrectionist violence of the Paris Commune. Fearful of anarchy and socialist advances, the bastions of tradition supported strong reactionary counter-measures from their respective leaders.

France faced a difficult reality. For the government in 1871, the combined circumstances of foreign war, civil war, social violence, heavy debt, indemnity, and the historic loss of Alsace and Lorraine were a heavy political burden.

This crisis resulted in the establishment of the longest-lasting republic in French history, the Third Republic of France from 1871-1940. In this government, republicans ruled with a traditional strong bicameral legislature, a prime minister, and a figurehead president.

THE AUSTRO-HUNGARIAN EMPIRE

The nationalist spirit also touched the Austro-Hungarian Empire and eventually caused the collapse of the old aristocratic tradition of Hapsburg rule. A great diversity of ethnicity, language, and tradition characterized life in the Austro-Hungarian Empire. Although Germans comprised the dominant national group, many minority groups were moved to assert their rights and nationalistic interests. These various minority groups included Czechs, Poles, Jews, Magyars, Croats, Slovaks, Ruthenians, Italians, and Romanians, to name a few. Each valued its own historical tradition and exhibited ethnic pride.

Having suppressed the Magyar, Czech, and Italian attempts at independence in 1848-1849, the empire used the combined instruments of authoritarian rule and German bureaucratic domination to prevent successful change. Additionally, the centralization of government combined with censorship, coercion, suppression, and secret police actions preventing liberal and nationalist voices from being heard. Among the minority nationalities, however, this inflamed conflict and resentment.

The Prussian defeat in 1866 had resulted in serious changes for the Austrian Empire. Under the Settlement of 1867, the Austrian Empire had to divide its dominion into two separate territories of Austria and Hungary with a common ruler, Franz Joseph (1848-1916). Francis Joseph retained the title of emperor in Austria but only the title of king in Hungary. Hungary held independent power over governmental bureaucracy, domestic policy, finances, and the army. Thus, the Austrian Empire had been forced by defeat to concede to the dominant non-German minority, the Magyars, significant independence in internal affairs.

In Austria, nationalist conflicts soon challenged the state. In general, Austrian political and social institutions respected the equal right of ethnic groups within the state. The attitude of ethnic and cultural superiority among German Austrians, however, was evident. This conflicted with the advancing spirit of national pride and consciousness among the South Slavs and Czechs. The determined control and domination of Austrian affairs by German Austrians was objectionable and insulting in the view of emerging cultural groups.

Czech and German conflict intensified in Bohemia. The emerging role and stature of Czechs in Bohemian society created problems. As Germans remained intent on political, economic, and cultural predominance in Bohemian affairs, the Czechs countered with challenges to German superiority.

In Hungary, other non-Magyar nationalities quickly challenged Magyar domination. The Magyars, although the largest individual minority group, represented less than half the total

Hungarian population. Nationalist fervor inflamed the complaints and frustrations of Serbs, Slovaks, Croats, Jews, and others demanding recognition.

In Hungary, Magyar culture and tradition overruled other nationalist considerations. Non-Magyars had limited rights of citizenship, as they were excluded from voting and bureaucratic office. The Hungarian government moved to impose repressive measures against recalcitrant minorities, including measures for social control, political exclusion, press censorship, and severe punishment without trial for protestors. Cultural organizations were severely restricted and suppressed. As a further insult to minorities in the Hungarian state, public school instruction remained largely in the Magyar language. This was the case even in areas where students were from predominately non-Magyar ethnic populations. Indeed, in the former Austro-Hungarian Empire, the spirit of independence and nationalist urges were intensifying rather than weakening.

Nicholas I

RUSSIA AND THE CRIMEAN WAR

In the early nineteenth century, the czarist Empire of Russia faced challenges and conflicts similar to other European lands. Although Russia was a vast empire, it remained weak and backward, as it had been for much of its history. Russia had remained essentially untouched by progressive movements of Western Europe. The Enlightenment, the Reformation, the Renaissance, and the great revolutions in science had transformed the history of other European states but did not significantly impact Russia. Russian ideology was practical, purposeful, and delivered with czarist authority.

The official ideology was intended to be an all-encompassing expression of Russian supremacy. The ideals of Russian patriotism and nationalist spirit were offered as a vital reinforcement of Russian political unity and social stability. The czarist Russian nationalism was an official ideology that instructed the Russian people to reaffirm the divine-right rule of autocracy, celebrate the Slavic traditions and cultural history, and re-energize spiritual devotion to the Orthodox Russian church. Nicholas I soon transferred the demonstrations of Russian civic and cultural pride to foreign policy. In this case, the event was the Crimean War (1854-56). With the Crimean War, the great powers witnessed nationalism translated into imperialism.

In the Crimean War, Nicholas was determined to demonstrate Russian supremacy to expand the influence of his empire in the eastern Mediterranean. Russia fought France and England to expand its power and influence. Meanwhile, France and England fought Russia to protect Turkey and their own interests in the Near East from an aggressive czarist.

This is a depiction of the fated Charge of the Light Brigade showing the determination of the cavalry as they proceeded toward mass suicide. The doomed Light Brigade rode down a valley, fired upon by Russian gunners on both sides. Those who made it through the valley crashed into Russian battery at the far end. Dead and dying horses littered the valley floor.

The alliance between France and England in the Crimean War successfully countered the Russian advance. Critical strategic errors, however, were committed on both sides. Russia soon faltered as the French and English military forces frustrated Russian actions. In the end, the Russian Empire failed to get its political spheres of influence in the eastern Mediterranean, and the victorious western European states had to resolve the future of the Turkish Empire through compromise and discretion.

In the aftermath of the Russian defeat in the Crimean War, a new successor to the throne was named. Alexander II (1855-1881) faced the challenges of deep crisis and dislocation in Russia. Alexander mostly adhered to the tradition of czarist rule and respected the ideals of a monarchy of divine right authoritarianism. Yet, he wanted to make Russia into a stable state where progressive methods of rule would strengthen the government. The challenge was to do this without threatening the sanctity of the old order. Clearly Alexander faced a formidable task. He met the challenge with conviction and authority.

In 1861, Alexander freed the Russian serfs. Emancipation, however, had its limits. This reform liberated a vast majority of peasants from perpetual servitude to the noble land-owning classes, however, liberty did not extend much further. The emancipation decree restricted individual freedom by limiting individual land ownership. Former serfs were only allowed to collectively own land. With this limitation, the power of the old order was left relatively untouched. Former serfs wanted more change.

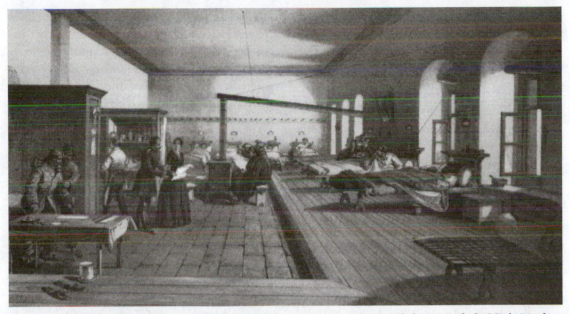

Florence Nightingale organized a group of nurses to go the Crimea to aid the wounded. Nightingale advocated clean conditions and open windows.

Soon, other social classes also demanded expanded rights and privileges from the czarist regime.

Florence Nightingale

Under the directive of Alexander II, several domestic bureaucratic reforms were designed to transform Russia into a progressive state. With these reforms, the tsar intended to energize the Russian economy, promote free enterprise, stimulate individual business, and end centuries of economic stagnation.

Closer connections were forged between eastern and western Europe. The borders between western European states and Russia were opened to trade. Transportation was advanced with the construction and expansion of railroads. This was a positive development for the Russian import and export of agricultural and manufactured goods. These economic changes created new business opportunities for the Russian bourgeoisie in commerce, industry, and capital.

Reforms in the Russian bureaucracy were also instituted by Alexander. In some select regions, a form of limited self-government created opportunities for free enterprise and urban growth. Additional reforms addressed civil protections. The pervasive political and social repression against non-Russian minority groups was weakened. Provisions for trial by jury and protections of civil courts were implemented.

The various reforms initiated by Alexander, however, were blunted by the realities of authoritarian rule in Russia. For example, free speech remained suppressed. Censorship of the press was strictly enforced. Open criticism and defiance of authoritarian rule was not tolerated. A secret police disrupted the potential outbreaks of civil unrest and rebellion. The liberal and educated Russian "intelligensia" had limited input into the process and activities of reform. Any potential influence of these progress-minded individuals was consistently and methodically thwarted. It was clear that intolerance reigned under the guise of enlightened rule. In Russia, along all social class distinctions, the frustrations of the csar's subjects only intensified.

In the late 1870s, organized secret societies began to ferment political rebellion and social revolution against the Russian regime. In 1881, the reign of Alexander II ended with his assassination.

MID-CENTURY IMPERIALISM

England

National unification and patriotic fervor held other consequences for the nations of Europe. By the middle of the nineteenth century, patriotic tradition and nationalist glory inspired new actions to demonstrate state grandeur and power. New markets and consumptive habits were mined as state economies transformed with the expansion of commerce, industry, transportation, and agricultural production.

As western states competed against each other with progressive economies, this competi-tion had a marked effect on economic timelines and tactical strategies. The rush for riches intensified existing competition among western nations for securing profitable new markets, raw materials, and spheres of political influence. The efforts made among the major powers to expand the boundaries of "empire" seemed to come from irresistible forces. Efforts to secure and sustain more and greater imperialist dominions and monopolies in the rest of the world intensified. Many of the reforms instituted in various states had created new wealth and capitalist vigor for state economies. Europe began to search outward to satisfy the needs of competition.

Some of these actions resulted in Western "imperialism," or world domination for the purpose of economic exploitation. Imperialism was motivated by the search for new markets, capital, and raw materials. These developments created extensive profit from overseas expansion into Asia, Africa, and the Middle East.

The Western states expanded into these other territories during a period of intense imperialist activity. The underdeveloped parts of the world found the combination of comparatively powerful western economies, industry, and superior military technology impossible to resist.

The British added India to their extensive dominions in the race for empire and profit. In the beginning of the nineteenth century, the British had effectively brought the richest regions of India, including the Punjab, Bombay, Calcutta, and Madras, under its control. This domination was secured through direct annexation of territory and the use of military force. Soon, the India Office of the British central government established extensive direct administration of British India. This was in response to challenges faced by the English East India Company, a commercially chartered trading monopoly. The Sepoy Rebellion of 1857 made it evident that more British authority and intervention was necessary in India. The violent rebellion was waged by the native army of the English East India Company in response to the belief that the company was imposing British ways on the natives to the detriment of their own culture and traditions. Europeans were massacred during this rebellion. The British military intervened, and the uprising was finally brought under control. After this incident, the British Empire directly took control over business enterprises of the East India Company, including all land and capital securities. In 1858, the Crown proclaimed that this would be the limit of British territorial annexation in India.

England soon added to its empire through annexations in Southeast Asia and in the Pacific. The successful exploitation of raw materials and goods for the manufacture of rubber and tin expanded in places such as Malaysia. The British Empire played a significant role in European expansion into China. With the establishment of political spheres of influence, military superiority, and forced trade-concessions from the Chinese, the British reigned supreme in the imperialist competition for Asia. The Chinese resisted the foreign interference. The most famous was the "Opium War." In the Opium War of 1841, the Chinese attempted to maintain control of the trade in opium against the efforts of British merchants to establish a monopoly in this lucrative trade. By 1842, the dominance of the British Empire in the China trade was secured over the resistance of the Chinese. The British gained important port facilities and Hong Kong for the advance of its empire.

France

In 1854, by the initiative of France, Said Pasha, the viceroy of Egypt, proposed building a canal to connect the Mediterranean to the Red Sea. The construction of the canal was undertaken by La Compagnie Universelle du Canal Maritime de Suez, especially formed for the building project. Owned by both French and Egyptian interests, the company was given authority to build the Suez Canal and to administer it for ninety-nine years. At the end of this time period, administrative jurisdiction and ownership of the canal would go to Egypt. Following the French initiative, the British were the first major financial investors in the project. The British Empire provided much of the capital and technological knowledge essential to the success of this formidable project. Actual construction of the Suez Canal began in April 1859. On November 17, 1869, the Suez Canal was opened for navigation with great celebration and fanfare. The Egyptian stocks of ownership in the Suez Canal were purchased by the British government in 1875.

During the nineteenth century, France increasingly expanded its participation in the competition for empire among European states. The French imperialist adventure took place most notably in Latin America. In 1867, Napoleon III initiated the conquest of Mexico. Military and technological superiority led to an easy French victory against Mexican resistance. With the domination of Mexico successfully achieved, the French emperor moved to place the Austrian Archduke Maximilian upon the throne as his titular representative. The Mexican subjects were outraged by the audacity of this action and the humiliations of defeat. Soon, Mexicans were driven by intense patriotic feelings to oust this bogus emperor and "pretender" from the Mexican throne. Back in France, Napoleon III realized the dangers and missteps of his imperialist machinations in Mexico. He ended the French military campaign to secure Maximilian's enthronement. With his chief protector abandoning him and with key military defenses in disarray, Maximilian was the victim of unfortunate circumstance. The victorious Mexicans, inspired by an intense nationalism, soon defeated, captured, and executed Maximilian.

ART, LITERATURE, SCIENCE, AND PHILOSOPHY: THE ADVENT OF "REALISM"

In Europe in the late nineteenth century, the focus was on practical actions and empirical reality. This applied not only to the politics of nationalism but extended to the arts, science, literature, and philosophy. This was a reaction against the spirit of romanticism and elevated emotion that had marked the history of Europe. The continued secularization of European society was a contributing element, as the changing currents of everyday life resulted in changed intellectual perspectives. Progress in science, technological innovations, industrial expansion, and practical bureaucracy reflected an empirical focus.

The art and literature of late nineteenth century Europe opposed the romantic sentimentality of previous times with a focus on the stark realities of life. This practical current was called "Realism." This was a clear departure from the romantic focus of the human spirit and imagination.

Many novelists wrote from a "scientific" perspective. Writers of "realism" made specific note of the transformative and practical effects of the material environment upon human social conditions and behaviors. In this way, the "realist" approach in literature was marked by an interest in ordinary human behaviors as influenced by the natural environment.

Within the literary genre of "realism," the daily experiences of common people are charted, and the interactive or "cause and effect" scenarios that result in specific human behaviors are chronicled. From the study of social conditions of life, realism constructed a science of causal relationship in a literary venue. French novelist Gustave Flaubert brilliantly used the realistic approach in his novel, *Madame Bovary* (1856), with the detailed depictions of the tragic life of a desperately neurotic aristocratic woman. Another French novelist, Emile Zola, used a natural "realism" in his literary representations of life among coal miners in his greatest novel, *Germinal* (1885). Realism was prominent in the work of Russian novelists, such as Leo Tolstoy in *Anna Karenina* (1873) and in *War and Peace* (1863), where Tolstoy chronicles the devastating impact of Napoleon's invasion of Russia. The Norwegian playwright, Henrik Ibsen, in *A Doll's House* (1879) analyzed and described in great detail and scientific accuracy the foibles of human society.

For the artists and painters of realism, the common everyday world was the purest source of inspiration for artistic depiction. With a practical style, realists like Gustave Courbet (1819-1877) portrayed the common people engaged in the basic rudimentary patterns of life. Courbet did not recoil from depictions of the abject or familiar. His subjects included peasants, prostitutes, laborers breaking stone, beggars, and families in funereal ceremonies. Realists, such as Courbet, depicted the ordinary social realities and conditions of life directly and honestly. This was certainly not painting in a grand or glorifying vein. This was art as a direct reflection of life with all of its mundane and ordinary content.

The focus on scientific method and technical detail carried over to other intellectual areas of study. Philosophy adopted the processes and clarity of scientific analysis. Many philosophers fashioned a science of ideas and human understanding, positivism. For Positivists, the purest form of human knowledge was directed by empirical inquiry rather than metaphysical insight. For Positivists, truth, or the ultimate understanding of the world, could only be derived from the application of reason, strictly directed by principles of empirical inquiry. Auguste Comte (1798-1857) was a leading practitioner of the scientific method or positivism in philosophical thought. Comte asserted that the human mind and intelligence had progressed through three specific historical stages that included the theological, metaphysical, and scientific. In the highest stage, which Comte associated with the "modern' mind, humans have perfected their intelligence to follow a higher order of thought by basing their society and future on the foundations of science and on the observations of an empirical reality.

CONCLUSIONS

In the early part of the nineteenth century, romantic ideals stirred the imaginations and desires of Europeans for affirmations of liberty and equality. Some essential components of the Romantic Movement had inspired and stimulated nationalist passions. In the last part of the nineteenth century, nationalism and unification were dominant historical movements in Europe. The romantic and liberal ideals of freedom, liberty, and equality were transformed by these movements into practical quests. Nationalism became a kind of mission—a collective quest for political/social unification, cultural advancement, and historical reverence. With the invocation of "realpolitik," or the politics of reality, European rulers often overrode considerations of individual rights and liberties in the "higher" struggle for nationalist rights and unification. In Europe, between 1848 and 1871, nationalism often led to brutal wars of expansion and political extrem-

ism. This new political "realism" resulted in considerable changes and transformations in the political, economic, social, and cultural history.

Suggestions for Further Reading

Derek Beales, *The Risorgimento and the Unification of Italy* (1971)

Crane Brinton, *The Anatomy of Revolution* (1957)

J.H. Clapham, *The Economic Development of France and Germany, 1815-1914*, (1936)

T. S. Hamerow, *Restoration, Revolution, and Reaction* (1958)

Hans Kohn, *Nationalism: Its Meaning and History* (1955)

Walter Langer, *Political and Social Upheaval, 1832-1852* (1969)

Arno Mayer, *The Persistence of the Old Regime*, (1981)

George L. Mosse, *The Crisis of German Ideology* (1964)

R. R. Palmer, *The Age of the Democratic Revolution Volumes I and II* (1959)

Otto Pflanze, *Bismarck and the Development of Germany* (1963)

John E. Rodes, *The Quest for Unity: Modern Germany, 1848-1970* (1971)

D. Mack Smith, *Italy: A Modern History*, 1959); *Garibaldi* (1956)

D. Mack Smith, Cavour and Garibaldi, *1860: A Study in Political Conflict* (1954)

A. J. P. Taylor, *The Struggle for Mastery in Europe, 1848-1918* (1954); *Bismarck: The Man and the Statesman* (1955)

J. M. Thompson, *Louis Napoleon and the Second Empire* (1954)

A. J. B. Whyte, *The Making of Modern Italy*, (1944)

Gordon Wright, *France in Modern Times*, (1974)

Chapter 19

LA BELLE EPOCH: EUROPE'S GOLDEN AGE

1871-1914

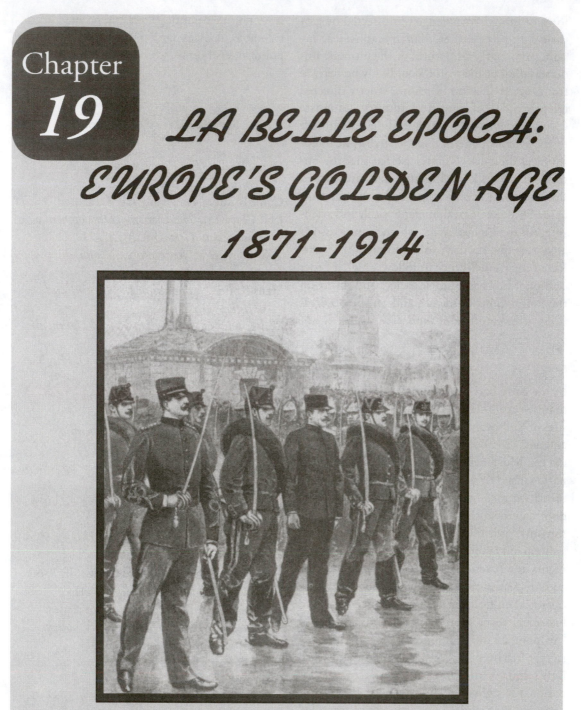

Alfred Dreyfus, stripped of his rank, marched in front of troops in Paris.

Alfred Dreyfus was born in 1860 to a Jewish family in Alsace. This was a French territory that was acquired by Germany in 1871 after the Franco-Prussian War. Though he was already financially secure because of his personal wealth and a prosperous family business, Dreyfus decided to devote himself to a career in the military. Dreyfus was a French patriot, and he wanted to serve his country. He rose to the rank of captain in the army, earning many favorable evaluations along the way.

What seemed to be a charmed life changed drastically in 1894. A French agent obtained information that had been sent to a German official working in Paris. This evidence seemed to indicate that someone had been giving the Germans military secrets on a regular basis. It would come to light much later that, in fact, the information was not that sensitive, nor was it very difficult to obtain. But, these revelations would not come soon enough for Dreyfus. The investigators needed a culprit, and Alfred Dreyfus fit the bill. Captain Dreyfus was accused of the crime and charged with treason. As the case unfolded, there was clearly not enough evidence to convict him. A sample of the case made against Dreyfus was as follows: It was alleged that his handwriting matched that found on the documents. When this was disputed, the investigators admitted that it looked different but only because Dreyfus had disguised his handwriting. The case was so poor that it probably would have been dismissed had not the allegations become public. The case brought about a wave of anti-Semitism and became too controversial to drop. Perhaps the most damaging public attacks on Dreyfus came from anti-Semitic newspapers like *La Libre Parole* and *L'Intransieant*, which repeatedly printed lies about the captain and his case. Since the editors hated Jews and they wanted to sell a lot of papers, the Dreyfus affair was an ideal situation for them to exploit. To stand up for Dreyfus was to make oneself a lightning rod for anti-Semitic abuse. The issue became bigger than one man's career, as others in the press, liberals, accused the army of a cover up. Conservatives, inside and outside of the army, tried to contain the problem and defend themselves against the liberals' attacks. For some, this was just one in a long list of heated disagreements between liberals and conservatives.

Dreyfus was convicted and sentenced to life imprisonment on Devil's Island. The years he spent there damaged his health. Devil's Island was located off the coast of South America, and it became a one-man prison for Dreyfus for four years. His guards would not talk to him, and no allowances were made for recreation or visitors. He had no news of the outside world because his mail was censored. Before he was freed, he had no idea that people had continued fighting on his behalf. Perhaps the most courageous champion for Dreyfus was the celebrated author, Emile Zola, who attacked the government and the army for covering up Dreyfus' innocence. Zola actually wanted to be put on trial for libel, so he could use that as a forum to present evidence on behalf of Dreyfus. Eventually, Zola was successful. Dreyfus was freed in 1899, but the legal battles continued until he was finally pardoned in 1906. Despite the unfair treatment he received, Dreyfus remained a French patriot. His health problems kept him from resuming his career in the army for several years, but when World War I started, Dreyfus was allowed back in the service.

Chronology

1870-1871	Franco-Prussian War
1871	Empire of Germany created Charles Darwin's *The Descent of Man* published
1876-1877	Edgar Deggas creates *The Star or Dancer on Stage*
1871-1940	France's Third Republic
1876	Auguste Renoir creates *Dancing at the Moulin de la Galette, Montmartre*
1881	Alexander II of Russia assassinated
1883	Karl Marx dies
1884	Greenwich Mean Time adopted
1884-1885	Suffrage for all English male householders
1891	Pope Leo XIII issues *Rerum Novarum*
1894-1895	Sino-Japanese War
1894-1906	Dreyfus Affair
1896	Abyssinians crush Italian invasion attempt
1900	Boxer Rebellion First flight of Baron von Zeppelin's dirigible
1902	Anglo-Japanese Treaty
1903	First flight of the Wright brothers' biplane
1904	Claude Monet creates Water Lilies
1904-1905	Russo-Japanese War
1905	France separates Church and State
1908	Austria annexes Bosnia and Herzegovina
1914	World War One begins

The Dreyfus case was symptomatic of the tensions swirling through Europe in the era from 1871 to 1914. These included such conflicting and contradictory forces as nationalism, liberalism, conservatism, imperialism, industrialism, and modernism. Between 1871 and 1914 discoveries in the sciences fueled the Second Industrial Revolution. Innovations in the social sciences increased as well. Europe's primacy of place in global politics became well established in the late nineteenth and early twentieth centuries. Europeans brimmed with assurance of their ability to mold the future, both at home and in the larger world. They felt that the continuing material progress must inevitably lead to human progress in which all of humankind's problems could be solved. However, even as many Europeans were winning new rights and opportunities at home, colonies around the world were denied freedoms. This might have been a "golden age" for Europeans, but it was hardly that for other people over whom they ruled.

THE SECOND INDUSTRIAL REVOLUTION

The period of 1871-1914 was characterized by dazzling economic growth, a Second Industrial Revolution that altered the human environment. Innovations included the typewriter, telephone, portable camera, phonograph, Bessemer process for steel manufacture, and the beginning of the chemical industry. This revolution was distinguished by a much greater reliance on electricity and the internal combustion engine. The growth of industry in the leading nations surged. In Germany, for example, the production of coal and lignite more than tripled during Europe's Golden Age, and steel production increased by more than fifteen fold. Germany, in fact, was replacing Great Britain as the industrial leader

This illustration from 1879 shows a landlord visiting a tenant family in their London apartment. The poor constantly struggled to pay rent and buy basic necessities.

of Europe, particularly in newer areas of manufacture. Europeans became less dependent as a whole on agriculture and more reliant on industry for their livelihood. Between 1871 and World War I automobiles began to revolutionize transportation. The year 1900 saw the lift off of Baron von Zeppelin's dirigible. Three years later, the Wright brothers' biplane took off at Kitty Hawk, North Carolina. Major cities were redesigned and, in the case of Paris after the destruction of the Commune, rebuilt. Department stores and apartment buildings were constructed, and the Eiffel Tower was built for the international trade exposition of 1889. Machines began to play a larger role in agriculture, reducing the need for laborers. A downside to all of these technological advancements was that nations were able to kill people much more efficiently.

Although the modernization and industrial growth created a feeling of optimism, this was not merely a period of uninterrupted economic growth. A severe economic collapse hit many industrial nations in 1873. This was followed by thirty years of economic recessions and recoveries. These economic fluctuations led to business bankruptcies and extended periods of unemployment that radicalized workers. There was a quickening pace of collective actions to gain better working conditions and pay. The numbers of strikes by workers greatly increased (289 in France in 1890 alone). In 1888 even the desperately poor London matchgirls struck to end the system under which they would lose a day's pay for being a minute late to work. Their plight moved philanthropists and writers, and they won their strike.

The Second Industrial Revolution had a profound impact on the lives of women. Upper class women continued to guard their status and domesticity, but the expanding middle class began opening doors to opportunities in college and social action to help the poor. In the 1880s, for example, Aletta Jacobs, a Dutch physician, began the first birth control clinic, promoting the use of a new device, the diaphragm. New job opportunities for the daughters of the middle class included sales clerks, secretaries, and telephone operators. Working class women, often desperate to supplement their husbands' scanty earnings, were easily exploited as marginal pieceworkers in their own homes or in "sweatshops." The surplus of working women led some to become prostitutes to survive. Prostitution was legal in most of Europe and was subject to government regulation.

For all the strife that was experienced around the world during this era, there was still some world unity displayed regarding a very significant matter: time. Localities based their clocks on their own assessment of astronomical conditions. It did not really matter much in the past when countries differed in their calculations, because travel was slow and regions were isolated. But the proliferation of railroads and transoceanic shipping that began even before the Second Industrial Revolution necessitated a more uniform method of time keeping. A British citizen named Sir Sandford Fleming persuaded representatives of the major countries in the world to adopt Greenwich Time as their benchmark. The powers agreed at a conference in Washington D.C. in 1884. The globe was divided into 24 time zones. Moving west from the Greenwich time zone, one would adjust one's watch to one hour earlier and so on for each subsequent time zone.

POLITICAL TRENDS AND IDEAS

The rapid economic changes and industrialization led to the development of a "mass society." As the working classes gained voting rights, political parties and ideologies developed to deal with the new realities.

Liberalism

The growth of political democracy led to the development of liberal political parties. Traditionally, "conservatism" is the belief that it is best to resist change because history and tradition were the best guides to public order. The deepest ideal of "liberalism," earlier in the nineteenth century, was the liberty of the individual person. This stress on the sovereignty of the individual contributed to the growing movement for political rights for all, including women. Liberals, by the end of the century, had come to believe that government could be an agent for making society better. In the late nineteenth and early twentieth centuries in America, liberals were referred to as "progressives," because they saw government as an instrument for progress. During this same time period in Europe there was a struggle between liberals and conservatives for the future of their countries.

In some ways, Germany was a leader in Europe in improving life for its citizens. Pensions and insurance were first extended to workers in Germany. These practices then spread to the other Western powers. By extending these benefits, the German government was undercutting support for the more extreme left wing groups. The spread of male suffrage throughout Western Europe was also a victory for liberals. Life certainly was not perfect, but liberals had some justification for being optimistic about the future.

Liberalism made inroads throughout Western Europe. Labor unions were gaining strength, and they agitated for more rights for the people. The great unifier of liberalism—and the great unifier of the unions that gave some liberals their strength—was the common desire for greater male suffrage. When that objective was achieved, liberals began to lose their cohesiveness and consequently their effectiveness. In Great Britain, Prime Minister Benjamin Disraeli, a member of the Conservative Party, undercut the Liberal Party's agenda in his country by co-opting the suffrage issue. In 1867, he called for greater suffrage than the Liberals had been suggesting. It took several years for Disraeli's proposal to pass, but in 1884-1885 the Reform Act gave all male householders in Britain the right to vote. Many people in Britain were left out, particularly women, but this was a major breakthrough in the movement for greater suffrage.

As Liberal politicians gained some of their objectives and power, some of them became more interested in maintaining the status quo. They wanted people to have the power to usher in their programs, but then the Liberals feared that the people might be influenced in supporting too radical solutions. As far back as the end of 1879, the coalitions of moderate Liberals (i.e. those who favored greater suffrage) and left wing Liberals (those who favored major changes in society) began to erode. The more moderate politicians began to join their former adversaries, the Conservatives. By the late 1880s the Liberal Parties that had dominated in Great Britain and influenced Germany were out of power.

As more men gained a voice in government, and labor parties began to display strength between election days by showing a willingness to strike, government leaders had to change their attitudes towards those over whom they governed. The rich and powerful who tended to dominate governments had to demonstrate more concern over the less well-to-do. Education was made more readily available, welfare was increased, and pensions for the aged were discussed. France used social services to foster loyalty to the Third Republic. British and German Conservatives felt the need to compromise with Liberals to maintain Conservative control overall, particularly on voting rights and education. In power in Britain from 1906 to 1914, Liberals began a substantial program of social welfare to win the support of workers. Thus liberalism, which had long argued that "the government that governs least governs best," was transformed into its more modern, activist form.

Marxism and Socialism

Radical thinkers continued to believe that tinkering with "welfare capitalism" could not alter the basic inequities of the capitalist system. Karl Marx and his friend, Friedrich Engels continued to refine the ideas they had expressed in the *Communist Manifesto* (1848). In *Das Kapital Capital* (1867-94), they argued that the advance of the working class to socialism was scientifically inevitable. Workers would overthrow bourgeois control of the "means of production," leading to a classless society in which all were treated equally. Marx worked to achieve this goal through the International Workingmen's Association. The destruction of the Paris Commune with its proletarian base, and conflict within its ranks, led to the dissolution of this "First International."

Working class parties developed throughout Europe and grew in political influence, particularly in Germany and France. In 1889 the various socialist parties formed a Second International. International socialism, however, suffered major splits. The Marxists continued to believe

Lenin led the Bolshevik revolutionaries who called for rapid changes in Russian government.

believed that a tightly disciplined revolutionary party could lead Russia right into socialism, despite the absence of a large working class. (Marx had argued that only a large, sophisticated working class could lead the revolution.) At a 1903 convention of Russian Marxists, Lenin's supporters won a fleeting majority. He then cleverly called his group the *Bolsheviks* ("majority"), even though that status was short-lived. The more moderate social democratic group was forever labeled *Mensheviks* ("minority"), although they were the larger group. The Socialist Revolutionaries, who believed in organizing the peasants to overthrow the government, had the most followers. However, it took the upheaval of World War I to destroy the Czarist government and lead to Lenin's eventual triumph.

Anarchism

that the collapse of capitalism was at hand. These orthodox Marxists, however, were challenged by a new group of "revisionists" who argued that socialism could be accomplished by evolutionary, rather than revolutionary, means. Nationalism proved to be an even more divisive issue. National loyalties outweighed workers' class loyalties. World War I, supported by workers and socialists in their respective countries, demonstrated the triumph of nationalism over socialism.

Russian socialists remained resolutely revolutionary since, unlike Western Europe, there was no way they could gain any political legitimacy in an unbending autocratic government. The foremost Russian Marxist was V.I. Lenin. Lenin

As socialists and trade union leaders seemed to be less revolutionary in methods and goals, some people, particularly in less modernized and democratic nations, turned to anarchism. Anarchists believed that existing forms of government could not be improved; they needed to be destroyed. The anarchists believed that the state was by its very nature oppressive, which was a logical conclusion for people to draw given the number of autocratic emperors then ruling in Europe. Anarchists tended to espouse one of two notions. Some anarchists, sometimes referred to as libertarians, advocated the extreme freedom of the individual. They believed that real freedom could come only when the state and all social institutions were abolished.

Other anarchists believed that society was best served by replacing governments with associations among individuals or groups. Two anarchists who were early leaders in propagating this belief were Russians Michael Bakunin and

Lenin called for a socialist government that would, in theory, distribute the nation's wealth evenly among the population.

Peter Kropotkin. These anarchists believed that in the absence of the state, society could be most efficiently and fairly run if people formed collectives. Within these collectives, the needs of the individual would be subordinate to the needs of the group as a whole. Bakunin and Kropotkin were associates of one another who not only published writings in defense of anarchism but set up secret societies throughout Europe.

Given the attitudes of the anarchists towards traditional forms of government, it is not surprising that there was quite a bit of hostility directed at anarchism by the existing powers. This hostility was not only generated by the beliefs of the anarchists; it was also generated by the anarchists' actions. While many were peaceful, others agreed with the Italian anarchist who declared, "We want to overthrow the government with violence since it is by the use of violence that they force us to obey." Small terror cells of trained revolutionaries could cause the collapse of the state by well-timed acts of violence, according to Bakunin and his followers. Anarchists sometimes resorted to assassination on behalf of their cause. Their victims included the president of France in 1894, Elizabeth, the wife of Austrian Emperor Franz Joseph, in 1898, the king of Italy in 1900, and President McKinley of the United States in 1901. Despite these actions, however, none of the governments collapsed.

THE ARTS

Cultural life reflected the same powerful tensions that stirred up economies, society, and social thought. Artists rebelled against traditional styles, particularly as the now popular photography could produce more realistic portraits than most artists could. The newest trend in art in this era was born in France. French artists like Camille Pisarro, Eduard Manet, and Claude Monet introduced a style of art that became known as "Impressionism." The aim of Impressionism was to suggest rather than describe. They rejected studios and went directly out into the countryside. They tried to catch their impressions of the changing effects of light upon nature. Colors were blurred to create a more subjective experience on the part of the viewer. Several other artists rose to fame with this style, including Paul Cezanne, Edgar Degas, and Auguste Renoir. Critics were not impressed at first. The subjects of Impressionist art were more mundane than the subjects depicted during the Romantic Movement. In other words, the Impressionists were much more likely than the Romantics to paint a picture of a field, or water lilies, or some trees. The color choices of the Impressionists favored creativity over authenticity. Post-Impressionists like Vincent van Gogh went even further in stressing structure, form, and color to reveal their inner feelings and personal image of reality. Despite the grumbling of the critics, Impressionism eventually became quite popular. By the turn of the twentieth century artists, led by such important figures as Pablo Picasso, moved even further from obvious reality in movements like Cubism and Abstract Impressionism.

Modernism also impacted the music of the day. Just as Impressionist painters used visual combinations that had not been used before, Impressionist musicians used tone combinations that previous composers would have dismissed as "unnatural" or dissonant. The chief Impressionist composer was Claude Debussy. Other composers, such as the Czech, Antonin Dvorak, and the Norwegian, Edvard Grieg, gave expression to the rising tide of nationalism. Richard Wagner, an anti-Semitic and reactionary composer, was the most renowned of this group. His powerful expression of a triumphant German nationalism was enormously influential and reflected troublesome currents flowing under the surface of the world of modern Europe.

In literature, the realism of authors like Emile Zola, began to give way to modernism, which, while equally trenchant in rejecting middle class society and its morality, was not as concerned with social issues. Marcel Proust, Virginia Woolf, and others adopted a stream-of-consciousness approach to uncover the human psyche. Realism continued its central importance in the theater. The Norwegian playwright, Henrik Ibsen, attempted to dismantle the façade from middle-class morality, assailing its false sentimentality and cult of domesticity in such plays as *A Doll's House* and *Hedda Gabbler*.

The twentieth century also saw the birth of a new type of art: movies. One of the major problems with proclaiming that movies were a new art form was that the accessibility of movies contradicted the established perception of what art was. The conventional wisdom was that art could only be truly understood and appreciated by the educated elite. Since movies were available to commoners, some critics argued that movies did not meet the criteria of art. Although movies reached their heights in later eras, they began in this time period and achieved great popularity even before World War I.

SOCIAL SCIENCES

Interest in the workings of the human mind is as old as humanity. Since humanity developed the ability to write, there have been people who have made observations about their society or were interested in reading about the past. The mid to late nineteenth century, however, was the first time people would try to seriously treat sociology, psychology, and history as "sciences."

People may have been making observations about the societies in which they lived for centuries, but the first man to use the term "sociology" as a label for the study of society or social institutions was Auguste Comte, who thus became known as the Father of Sociology. The trend towards applying scientific standards where none had been applied before, begun by Comte earlier in the century, extended into the fields of psychology and history in the late 1800s.

The Austrian Sigmund Freud became the Father of Psychoanalysis with his 1900 book, *The Interpretation of Dreams.* Freud's theories undermined the Enlightenment optimism about the rationality of the human mind. He argued that all sorts of urges were hidden in the "unconscious." The human personality was a battleground for the ego, the center of reason and reality, the superego, the site of conscience and moral values, and the id, where unconscious drives and sexual energies dominated. Later, Freud focused on the irrational human attraction to death and destruction, challenging earlier views of the inevitability of human progress. He believed that World War I confirmed this pessimistic view of human nature. Although some of the details of Freud's work were later proven to be incorrect, the impact of his ideas on the study of the human psyche has been incalculable.

During the Middle Ages, history had been the province of court propagandists and religious men who saw the world through the lens of their theological beliefs. Frequently, a given historian would find himself in both categories, since, for the most part, Church officials of that era were the only ones who knew how to write. In the modern era, rich men in need of indulging in a hobby began to write histories. During the latter half of the nineteenth century, colleges and universities throughout Europe and the United States produced professional historians. While these professional historians, predominantly teachers, professors and writers, were not unbiased—historians never are—they were generally more objective than their predecessors. Standards were raised in the way research was done, which improved analyses and conclusions. The

accuracy of the information conveyed by historians was thus improved. Two of the leaders in the effort to make the study of history more accurate were Leopold Von Ranke and Jacob Burckhardt, both of Germany. Von Ranke is especially noteworthy because of his efforts to bring together as many records as he could find of medieval Germany. The idea was that historians could get a more accurate picture of what took place in the lives of Germans in the Middle Ages if they were not limited in their access to the sources. Von Ranke's collection of sources is entitled the *Monumenta Germaniae Historia.*

RELIGION, SCIENCE & PHILOSOPHY

Religion still played a big part in the culture of the West during Europe's Golden Age. Several countries, such as Britain and Spain, maintained their traditionally close connections between church and state. But the influence of religion was on the decline. In France, the Catholic Church's decision to continue to support conservatives alienated many people who were sympathetic to the liberals who were in power at the dawn of the twentieth century. The heated disputes between the liberals and conservatives led the authorities to mandate the separation of church and state in 1905. The French government declared the right to authorize any and all teaching organizations. By withholding this authorization, the government closed thousands of religious schools. The percentage of French children who were not baptized rose from 2 percent to 40 percent between 1905 and 1914. Also by 1914, more than half of the weddings were civil rather than church ones.

One reason for the general decline of religious influence in Europe was the continuing popularity of the philosophical outlook derived from Enlightenment thinking. Those who espoused Enlightenment thinking believed that humanity was basically good (contrary to the Christian view of original sin), and bad things usually occurred as a result of ignorance. If the masses could be educated properly and shown the right way to live, society would improve. Nietzsche's famous quotation, "God is dead," was a succinct way of expressing what Marx, Comte, and others were writing about religion. They believed that organized religion was outdated, and humanity could improve itself without God. Of course, the two World Wars gave people second thoughts about the basic goodness of humanity.

Christianity had more to contend with than just eighteenth-century thinking. Protestant and Catholic leaders struggled with how to respond to the changing conditions in society. Did industrialists exploit their workers? If so, was the proper response to embrace Marxism? As with other major events in history, Christians found themselves on all sides of the issue. Pope Leo XIII (1878-1903) issued an encyclical in 1891 called *Rerum Novarum*, which urged Catholics to acquire a social conscience that could lead to unity among all social classes. Leo was limited by the recent history of the papacy. In 1864 Pope Pius IX had sent out an encyclical, attacking what Pius believed were the evils of modern society. Among other things, Pius railed against socialism, the separation of church and state, freedom of the press, and public schools. In 1870, the Catholic Church declared that when the Pope was acting in his official capacity, he was infallible. Thus, it would have been difficult for Leo to be too pro-liberal after Pius' conservatism, even if Leo had been so inclined. Predictably, Leo rejected Marxist-socialism as being too extreme. He stressed that business leaders had to deal justly with their employees and

came out in favor of the right of workers to unionize and bargain collectively. Catholic democratic political parties and Catholic trade unions were organized throughout Europe based on the pronouncements of Leo XIII. Leo, however, was followed by Pius X (1903-1914) who resisted modernism and attempted to restore traditional Catholic life.

Charles Darwin struck another mighty blow against traditional Christianity. Darwin followed his landmark 1859 work, *The Origin of the Species,* with *Descent of Man*, published in 1871. It made the case that evolution by natural selection applied to humanity, which evolved from lesser species. Of course, this contradicted a literal reading of humanity's origins described in the Bible. Some religious people then, and even today, believed that Darwin's teachings were an attack on their faith. Many liberals believed that the Bible should not be taken literally. Religious conservatives disputed this, and, furthermore, they believed the Bible was infallible. Despite the strongly held positions on opposing ends of the spectrum, however, there was a middle ground. In fact, some scientists were theistic evolutionists who believed that, because of the diversity in the world, God must have been the guiding influence in the evolutionary process.

Not all scientific breakthroughs created religious turmoil. British, Dutch, French, German, Russian and North American meteorologists were issuing daily weather bulletins and making weather forecasts by the 1890s. This breakthrough was the result of weather balloons and weather stations that were linked by telegraphs.

Social Darwinism

"Social Darwinism" captured the imagination of many European and American conservatives.

Charles Darwin's theory of evolution contradicted the prevailing belief that humans were created by God.

This was an application of Darwin's axiom of "survival of the fittest" to individuals' social status and societies at large. Herbert Spencer was the leading proponent of this type of thinking. He argued that human society progressed only through this "struggle for survival." It was wrong for the government to pass laws dictating better terms for workers because that would interfere with the laws of nature. Nature was neutral, and so was society, Spencer and his followers reasoned. So, if some men became wealthy and many remained poor, then that was their proper place. Thanks to this interpretation of Darwin by Spencer and others, conservatives could say they were not being selfish or cruel. They were simply defending natural selection.

Politicians applied "survival of the fittest" at the international level. The nations that were the most fit would win the "struggle for existence" and become great powers. Of course, there were different ways to measure greatness. One could assess military strength, technological advances, or the amount of land and people in a given country. But, generally there were some nations that were seen as superior, like Great Britain, France and the newly created Germany. Others, like Turkey, were seen as being in decline. The misuse of Darwinian concepts strengthened racism and justified the romantic nationalist idea of a "superior" Aryan race, which was most popular in Germany and most dangerous for the future.

Anti-Semitism

By the end of the nineteenth century this potent mixture of nationalism and racism produced a reactionary political movement directed against the Jews that reached its zenith during Hitler's reign. Anti-Semitism was certainly not new. It had been something Jews had struggled against for centuries. In Europe since the Middle Ages, Jews were harassed because their religion and culture differed from the majority. Jews were depicted as murderers of Jesus whose only god was money, and mob violence and restrictions to physically separate ghettoes victimized them.

The French Revolution of 1789 ended some of the more overt types of discrimination against the Jews, first in France, then in the German states as Napoleon's armies swept through. Laws granted Jews legal, though not necessarily social, equality. By the nineteenth century the Jewish population of Germany, France, or Britain was not very large but large numbers lived in Russia. In the late Middle Ages, many Jews had migrated to Poland at the invitation of the Polish monarchy, seeking economic progress. When Russia swallowed up the eastern part of Poland, the Jews found themselves in a different situation.

Jews were discriminated against in Russia as a matter of public policy. The majority of Jews were confined to an area in western Russia known as the Pale of Settlement. Jews were victimized by pogroms in Russia as early as 1871. Pogroms were riots directed at Jewish communities, resulting in murder and looting. Russian authorities encouraged and abetted these attacks, rather than responding to cries for help. In the early 1880s things got even worse for Russian Jews. Czar Alexander II was assassinated, and some of the people involved were Jews. As a result, more pogroms occurred in 1881 and 1882. Over the next several years, new laws were passed against the Jews. There were quotas on the percentage of Jews in the student bodies of universities. Though they were eligible to be drafted into the military, they could only rise in rank to the position of a non-commissioned officer.

Because of the harsh treatment of Jews in Russia, and the history of better treatment in France, thousands migrated to France from Russia during Europe's Golden Age. (Many hundreds of thousands more fled to the United States.) By 1914 France had a Jewish population of roughly 100,000, which was double what it had been just a few decades before. The French, however, grew uncomfortable with this influx of Jews, and there was an upsurge of anti-Semitism. One early result of this anti-Semitism was the Dreyfus affair, which was described at the beginning of this chapter. Many Jews wondered if this was the price of citizenship and assimilation.

Some began to believe that the solution to their problem was to have a home of their own where they would not be a persecuted minority. An organization that called itself "Lovers of Zion" was created to help make this dream become a reality. The Hebrew word for "Zion" is a synonym for Jerusalem, the capital city of the an-

The Dreyfus case triggered a rash of anti-Semitism in France, prompting Zionists to reassert the need for a Jewish nation.

cient Jewish kingdom and their holy city. There were already about 50,000 Jews living in Palestine—descendants of those who had never left and those who had trickled back over the centuries. But, the local Arabs outnumbered the Jews by about 10 to 1. Both Arabs and Jews in Palestine were under the control of the Ottoman Empire. From 1881 to 1903 small numbers of European Jews made their way to Palestine, but most remained in Eastern Europe. The Zionist movement benefited from the leadership of Theodor Herzl, an Austrian Jewish journalist who was jolted into action when he covered the Dreyfus trial in Paris. He was able to appeal to both the sympathetic and the racists when he said that the solution to "the Jewish Problem" was to give Jews a land to call their own where they would be in control outside of Europe. Herzl suggested it should be in Palestine.

Though this seemed like a good solution to many of the interested parties, there were some

Zionist Theodore Herzl decided that European Jews would never merge into the gentile mainstream.

significant obstacles. More assimilated Western European Jews were not interested in leaving their comfortable homes and those in Eastern Europe were too poor and perhaps somewhat fearful of the unknown. In addition, Palestine was part of the Ottoman Empire, which was not sympathetic to the movement. Despite this, by 1914, about 85,000 Jews had resettled there.

A problem that was not addressed in the nineteenth century was the response of the indigenous population to this influx of European Jews. The local Arabs (or Palestinians) were uncomfortable with having a large number of Jewish immigrants coming into their land. Most of the local Jews were very conservative in their religious beliefs and thought the newcomers were not pious enough. The newcomers dreamt of becoming a nation one day. To the orthodox believers, this was blasphemous since they believed Jews would have their nation only when their messiah came and provided it for them. But these were issues that would not take center stage until after the Second World War. After Hitler's Holocaust, there was far greater pressure for a safe Jewish homeland than there had ever been before.

THE NATION-STATES 1871-1914

The development of the mass society challenged the governments of the nation-states to evolve in ways that would cement national loyalties, build mass armies, and accept greater responsibilities for the welfare of their citizens. While political democracy grew in Western Europe, authoritarian forces remained more powerful in Central and Eastern Europe.

FRANCE'S THIRD REPUBLIC

France had been through periodic upheavals throughout the nineteenth century until the Third Republic was created in 1871 and produced the constitution of 1875. Despite the class divisions and tears in the structure of society shown by the crushing of the Paris Commune, the Third Republic lasted until 1940, making it the most stable government of France since the 1789 revolution. The Third Republic government sought to protect the French economy from foreign competition. France could afford to be less reliant on trade with other European powers because she had colonies around the world to serve as trading partners. Overall, this economic stability and foreign policy allowed France to avoid the governmental turmoil it experienced during other eras.

Despite this relative constitutional and economic stability, France did have some conflict. Charles De Gaulle, later the leader of France, once lamented, "How can you govern a country with two hundred forty-six varieties of cheese?" His point—only partially in jest—was that the French had a hard time agreeing with each other. Though their constitution survived, the French argued over politics even more passionately than they argued over cheese. Initially, monarchists, with a majority in the National Assembly, believed that if France had a strong central figure to act decisively and rally the people, then France would be an even more imposing power. However, they quarreled among themselves over who should be king and, even more absurdly, whether the revolutionary tricolor flag should be replaced by the white flag of the Bourbons. There were also anti-Republican nationalists who believed that France needed to assert itself more in Europe and around the world and that the Republicans had failed them. But, these anti-Republicans did not think that a monarch was the answer. Both conservative groups were discredited by their actions in the Dreyfus case.

Republicans dominated central France and tried to win over the rest of the country to their ideals. They believed that despite the way the other major powers were governed in Europe, France was better off without a monarch. They provided free public education to promote their Republican agenda. French leaders were also concerned about the lack of industry. France was an agriculturally-based country, and it embraced the growth of industry rather slowly compared to other places in Europe, like Britain and Germany. The industrial strength of Germany was of particular concern to the French. The Third Republic perceived anything that made the Germans stronger as a threat.

This situation led the French to form a defensive alliance against Germany. According to the terms of the Franco-Russian Alliance, an attack against either power would be treated as an attack on both. The Franco-Russian Alliance seemed logical since these countries were on either side of Germany; both felt the German threat and were positioned in a way that made war less desirable for Germany. Everyone recognized the difficulties of fighting a two-front war. Also, the colonial interests of Russia and France did not conflict since the Russians were interested in northern Asia, the Middle East, and Eastern Europe, while France's interests were centered on Southeast Asia and Africa. The alliance helped contain Germany for awhile, but by 1914 Germany had grown too strong to be intimidated by it.

The relationship between labor and government was another concern for the French. The leaders of the labor movement were divided between moderates and revolutionaries. Even those who favored revolution were divided: some were Marxists and some were not. There were people who believed that France's fortunes would improve if relations were improved with the Catholic Church. Finally, there were people in the rural areas who agitated against the central authorities, not because those authorities were Republican but simply because these rural dwellers did not like central authority. The Third Republic surprisingly survived corruption scandals and abortive attempted coups by would-be military strong men. Despite all of these problems, France still remained relatively stable in this era.

GREAT BRITAIN

A look at a 1900 map indicates that Great Britain was the most powerful force in the world. The British controlled roughly half of the continent of North America (Canada) and the entire continent of Australia. Britain also had extensive holdings in Africa, and the British ruled India, which was commonly known as the jewel of the empire and one of the most heavily populated regions in the world. In addition to its land holdings, Britain's naval policy was to have a fleet of ships greater than the next two largest fleets in the world combined, a policy the British referred to as the "two power standard."

British schoolchildren were taught that the British Empire would last forever. On January 1, 1877, Queen Victoria was proclaimed the Empress of India, which seemed to underscore the permanence of the British presence there. The idea for this came from Victoria herself. She wanted to put to rest the notion held by Bismarck and others that Victoria was a second-class monarch because she was a queen, limited in power. Now she possessed an imperial title like the rulers of Germany, Russia, and Austria. But, things were not as secure for the British Empire as they seemed to be. Such extensive holdings meant that there were many different areas that could become trouble spots. For example, Britain had to trust the United States completely. By the end of the nineteenth century, Britain had to believe that the United States was no longer interested in taking Canada by force, as it had been earlier in the century. The British simply could not afford to do otherwise since the United States-Canadian border was extensive, and Britain could not spare the resources to defend it. Britain also had to patch up its differences with France, a powerful country with forces around the world. In Africa, for example, both Britain and France had extensive holdings. Britain had another rival to worry about: Russia. Russia was a potential threat to India and to the British-controlled Suez Canal. The British did not trust the Russians, who were

guilty of the same greed for land belonging to others as the British, French, and Germans.

Britain tried to maintain its worldwide house of cards, not only by creating warm relations with the United States and France but also by sharing some of the responsibility for running the empire. Britain granted Dominion status to several locations, granting self-government to whites. The Dominion countries controlled their own affairs regarding most internal matters, but foreign policy was dictated by Britain. Dominion status was given to Canada, Australia, New Zealand, and the Union of South Africa. While this was a positive development for the whites involved, it obviously did nothing to address the situation of the natives living in British-controlled Africa and India. South Africa was the exception to this policy. South Africa had been formed after the British joined their colony on the cape of South Africa and Natal with two republics they had recently defeated in the Boer War (1899-1902). South Africa with its minority contingent of British colonists and Dutch descendants, known as Afrikaners, was granted Dominion status anyway. The majority population of blacks was brutally oppressed by the minority whites.

Britain also had to deal with the issue of rights closer to home. The majority of the Irish craved home rule and viewed the involvement of Britain in their country with great hostility. England had invaded Ireland hundreds of years before, but most Irish Catholics never accepted English rule despite the centuries that had passed. Catholics in Ireland demanded independence. Protestants in Northern Ireland did not want Britain to turn its back on them. The Protestants feared that they would be at the mercy of an angry Catholic majority. The harsh treatment of Irish Catholics by the British led to the formation of the Irish Republican Brotherhood and later the Irish Republican Army. Both adopted terrorist tactics to achieve their agenda of freedom from Britain. Britain was extremely reluctant to give up control of what they viewed as their domain, especially in response to violence. Great empires advanced; they did not retreat. Of course, not all of the Irish pursued their agenda through violence. Some directed their efforts at promoting Irish culture. Organizations like the Gaelic League, which encouraged the native Irish language, and the Gaelic Athletic Association, which organized uniquely Irish sports, helped advance Irish nationalism. The Home Rule Bill was submitted to the House of Commons in 1912, but the legislators deliberated over the bill without resolution. Any decision would have provoked heated dissent. Britain was able to put off the issue when World War I began.

Within Britain itself democracy advanced. An 1872 law introduced the secret ballot, reducing the influence of employers and landlords in elections. The Reform Bill of 1884 gave the vote to all men who paid rent or taxes, doubling the electorate. Britain had embraced the idea of extending democracy through gradual reform. At the same time, however, about half of the population of Great Britain were denied rights since women were not allowed to vote. This was not the only way the society treated women differently than men. At the beginning of the twentieth century, a woman earned on average one-third of what a man earned at the same industrial job. Women demonstrated against these injustices, and Great Britain had the most advanced women's movement in Europe. Women who demanded the right to vote were scornfully called "suffragettes." Emmeline Pankhurst and her two daughters were the best known radical feminists. By 1909, angered over their failure to win government support, they launched a vio-

British suffragette Emmeline Pankhurst and her two daughters founded the radical women's Social and Political Union.

lent campaign that included vandalizing postal boxes, smashing windows, arson, slashing works of art, and chaining themselves to the gates of Parliament. One woman even threw herself in front of the king's horse at a race, dying to dramatize her protest. Suffrage marches and demonstrations led to brutal attacks by furious male opponents. The demonstrators were often imprisoned and responded with hunger strikes that the authorities countered with force-feeding. Despite these confrontational tactics, British women did not receive the vote until 1918, supposedly as a result of their war efforts. For all the issues that it struggled with, Britain was still probably the leading power in the world and the most stable major democracy in Europe.

British suffragettes parade in front of Parliament's Big Ben in London, 1910. On November 18 of that year, there was a riot outside the House of Commons at which 120 women were arrested.

THE GERMAN EMPIRE

The Hohenzollern line of Prussian kings ascended to the imperial throne of the newly unified German Empire. The first German Kaiser was Wilhelm I. Because of Wilhelm's advanced age—he was 74 years old in 1871—the driving force in Germany was its dynamic chancellor, Prince Otto von Bismarck. Though Germany had demonstrated its military strength with its recent victory over France, politically Germany was still quite unsettled. The imperial constitution was deliberately vague regarding certain issues of sovereignty and government because that was what Bismarck wanted. He was not interested in creating a democracy; his goal had been to unify the German states under Prussian control. In Bismarck's opinion, parliaments and free presses could not solve Germany's problems. Instead the answers could be found only by, as Bismarck put it, "iron and blood." He admittedly rushed through a constitution as quickly as he could. The need for unity was felt strongly by his fellow Germans, and the opportunity was there in the wake of the Franco-Prussian War. Bismarck's conservatism, demonstrated by suppression of freedom and representation, was tolerable to the people because he appealed to their nationalism. Bismarck was creating a strong German empire so people were expected to sacrifice democracy. Many Germans were willing to live with this since Bismarck had been so successful.

The northern German states had been bound to Prussia by Bismarck's maneuverings back in the 1860s. When the southern states were added, it seemed to the liberals like the perfect opportunity to address some of the existing problems. As far as the liberals were concerned, the main problem with the new empire was that the government ministries were only accountable to the emperor and the chancellor. The Bundesrat, which was a council made up of delegates from the various German states, had no input. Members of the Bundesrat could voice opinions, but there were no checks and balances

Known as the Iron Chancellor, Otto von Bismarck launched an era of military strength and industrialization.

built into the German constitution like those in the American constitution. Despite the wishes of the Bundesrat, Bismarck resisted any fundamental changes to the constitution because he had nothing to gain from such changes. Fearful of the growing influence of the Roman Catholic Church in southern Germany, he launched a *Kulturkampf* (culture war) against the Church based upon nationalist sentiment. He succeeded only in provoking Catholic resentment and turned on his liberal allies in the "struggle." The successes of the Social Democratic Party in winning the support of the working class led to legislation outlawing the party. He believed that the antimilitary, antinationalist, and anticapitalist views of the socialists endangered the empire.

He also tried to win the workers away from socialism by enacting the first extensive social welfare program in history, including old age pensions and workmen's compensation. (This was 50 years before America's New Deal.) In 1888, a brash and impulsive young (he was 29) emperor ascended to the throne. By 1890 an ungrateful Kaiser Wilhelm II had dismissed his aging chancellor to push for his own policies.

AUSTRIA-HUNGARY

Although the creation of the dual monarchy of Austria-Hungary in 1867 had also introduced a constitutional parliamentary system in theory, Emperor Franz Joseph ignored the system in practice and tended to rule by personal decree. In the arena of foreign affairs, the emperor was in an uncomfortable situation. Italy and Germany had only recently become nations, and Germany, in particular, was seen as a rising power. Franz Joseph did not want to be known to posterity as the emperor who presided over the decline of an empire. His family line, the Habsburgs, had ruled kingdoms and empires for roughly five hundred years. Cut off by German expansion and pushed out of previously held areas of Italy, Franz Joseph turned to the Balkans as a possibility for recapturing some lost glory. This drew the Austrian emperor into conflicts of interest with both the Turks and the Russians and was the spark that set off World War I.

Ethnic nationalism was a problem in the Austro-Hungarian Empire just as it was a problem in the Ottoman Empire. The Austrians were able to hold their empire together until the end of World War I because the Austrians were more sensitive to the needs of their people than the Turks. Some historians have referred to Austria-Hungary as a "prison of nations," but, despite not being a democracy, it was not as oppressive as Russia or the Turkish Empire. As a result of the revolution of 1848 and the unrest that existed for years afterward, the Hungarians had their own constitution. Franz Joseph served as the only remaining official connection between Austria and Hungary as the emperor of both. Although ethnic Germans who ruled the empire made up only one-third of its population, Austria only allowed for a limited self-government in its other ethnic enclaves. Minorities, such as Czechs, Poles and Slovaks, did have rights that were respected by the rule of law. This was far from an ideal situation, and there was unrest in the empire as a result.

A man who might have eventually helped the empire through this time of turmoil was the son and heir of Franz Joseph, Rudolf. The emperor's son was a man noted for his intellect, charm, and good looks. His most remarkable characteristic, however, was his liberal political outlook. He thought the end of the monarchical system was inevitable, and he favored greater autonomy for all of his empire's minorities. Perhaps Rudolf's political views were irrelevant, given that his father lived to see his empire enter World War I (after which all of the Eastern European empires were dismantled). We will never know for sure because Rudolf had a self-destructive tendency that manifested itself in drug abuse and in his suicide. With the death of Rudolf, his cousin, Franz Ferdinand, became heir to the throne. Ferdinand had expressed some liberal views regarding Slavic representation, but he, too, did not live long enough to rule.

RUSSIA

Industrialization

Russia experienced an industrial revolution in the late nineteenth century that was even more dramatic than that in the rest of Europe. From 1890 to 1914, Russia's industrial growth rate was the highest in Europe. In southwest Russia, large deposits of coal and iron were discovered, leading to a considerable upsurge in iron production, and the textile industry also saw rapid growth. Russia was such a massive country that even though its industry surged, most Russians did not benefit from these developments. In fact, the new factories created an industrial working class that lived and worked under the same appalling conditions that had accompanied the emergence of industrialization everywhere. Conditions among the debt-ridden peasants remained desperate. Reformist impulses were brutally suppressed, particularly after the assassination of the reformist Czar, Alexander II in 1881. Alexander III (1881-1894) increased the repression and expanded the power of the secret police. He was followed by Nicholas II who declared, "I shall maintain the principle of autocracy just as firmly and unflinchingly as did my unforgettable father." He was, however, a much weaker ruler, and revolutionary movements flourished. Despite Russia's size and the growth of its industry, in 1913 it was still only the fifth leading power in the world behind the United States, Germany, Great Britain, and France.

Russian-Turk Relations

Tension between the two powers existed long before Russia declared war on Turkey in World War I. Perhaps one could trace the hostility between the Russians and the Turks as far back as 1453 when the Turks toppled the remnants of the Byzantine Empire. The Russians and Turks were still adversaries in the late nineteenth century.

The Ottoman Empire, the European portion of which was also known as Turkey, had one strong similarity to Austria-Hungary. Both empires were trying to hold together ethnically diverse peoples who were chafing for independence. The troubles in the Balkans that exist today have long historic roots. The Serbs, Bosnians, and Croats have detested each other for hundreds of years for territorial, religious, and ethnic reasons. In addition, they opposed Turkish rule. A Russian underground in the Balkans, encouraging the subversion of Turkish rule, made it even more difficult.

The Russians were interested in Turkey for several reasons. Two of the ethnic minorities under the control of the Turks (the Serbs and Bulgarians) had an ethnic connection with the Russians: they were all Slavic peoples. The rulers of Russia saw themselves as leaders of a Pan-Slavic empire, and they saw these ethnic minorities as future members of this empire. There was also the common religious heritage of the Eastern Orthodox Church, whereas the Turks were Muslims. Finally, the Russians felt a powerful need for a warm water port. Economic strength was a key component to being a world power. Russia needed a warm water port so it could conduct trade on a year-round basis, and Turkey had long blocked Russian access to the Black Sea. If Russia could pry the Bulgarians and the Serbs away from Turkey, those peoples would understandably be, at least somewhat, sympathetic to Russian interests.

Bosnia revolted against Turkish rule in 1875. The Russians were delighted. Bulgaria followed Bosnia down the road to rebellion, and all the empires of Eastern Europe watched with great anticipation. The Turks received a message from Russia, Germany, and Austria supporting the rebels. Austria-Hungary's stance might seem surprising, since any success by the minorities in the Ottoman Empire might serve as an inspiration to Austria's minorities. But, the Aus-

trians supported the rebels because they might weaken a rival. Austria was interested in expanding, and if independence-minded minorities succeeded in carving up Turkey, the Austrians thought they might pick up some of the pieces.

The Russians, Germans, and Austrians had hoped that their fellow Christians, the British, would add their voice against Turkey, but the British had other concerns. The British absolutely did not want the Russians to dominate the eastern part of the Mediterranean Sea and did not trust Germany's Bismarck. But mostly, British policy in this matter had to do with its own interests. Understandably, Britain placed great importance on clear lines of trade with India and Australia. The only overland route to India was through Turkey, so the British obviously did not want to antagonize the Turks or see the Turkish Empire split up. The best route by sea went through the British-run Suez Canal, which would be vulnerable if Russia took over parts of Turkey and had a presence in the Mediterranean.

By 1877, Russia decided it was time to attack the Turks. In addition to all of their other incentives to fight, there were stories of atrocities committed by the Muslim Turks against the Christian Bulgarians. There were stories of massacred children, raped women, and young girls sold as slaves. The British were ambivalent about the situation. Prime Minister Benjamin Disraeli was skeptical of stories of Turkish war atrocities and unsympathetic to Russian interests, but British officials in Turkey confirmed the stories. Nevertheless, Disraeli was still against supporting Russia against Turkey. He did not condone war atrocities, nor did he care much about the Turks. He was involved in the "Great Game" of competing for control of the area. Queen Victoria wanted to go to war on the side of the Turks. Like her prime minister, she saw Russia—and the prospect of its expansion—as the real threat to her empire. But the British Cabinet had no interest in intervening in the war, especially on the side of the Turks. Much to Victoria's frustration, Britain stayed out of this conflict.

Without British involvement, Bulgaria was freed from Turkish rule in 1878. This ended roughly five hundred years of Turkish domination over the Bulgarians. Bulgaria would have been twice as large if Russia had gotten its way. Russia had forced a treaty on Turkey that would have removed all Turkish influence from Europe and given Russia the unimpeded access to the Mediterranean that it so desperately craved. But Britain's Disraeli told Russia that was unacceptable, and Britain began to prepare for war. The Russians relented, and the Ottoman's European presence was maintained. Russia was kept from controlling land and waterways connected to the Mediterranean. The Russians simply could not afford to fight another enemy after facing the Turks. The Russians were also intimidated by the specter of the large number of Indian troops the British were prepared to use.

The Russians would have preferred controlling their destiny in the Mediterranean, but they could live with relying on the permission of the weakened Turks to get to the sea. Russia wanted the Turks weak enough so that they could not afford to be belligerent with Russia but not so weak that another power might think of attacking them. Unfortunately for Russia, the situation in Turkey became more and more unstable in the succeeding decades. In 1908, Austria formally annexed two former Turkish provinces it had already been occupying, Bosnia and Herzegovina. Italy fought the Turks in 1911 and grabbed Libya. The next year several of the Balkan states—Serbia, Bulgaria, Greece, and Montenegro—attacked and quickly defeated Turkey. The defeat of Turkey and the fighting next year among the Balkan states are known collectively as the Balkan Wars. Serbia claimed a significant amount of territory, but the great powers supported Austria's position that Serbian gains should be limited. Austria did not want to face a Serbian threat down the road, and the Austrians were always interested in the possibility of gaining new lands for themselves. After this diplomatic conflict between Austria and Serbia, the Serbs turned to Russia for support, and Austria looked more and more to Germany for reassurance. The conflicts also stirred up increasing nationalism among Austria's subject peoples. Some of the seeds of World War I were sown.

THE RUSSO-JAPANESE WAR

The Russo-Japanese War was fought when the Russians decided to expand into Asia. Specifically, they made inroads into Manchuria, a territory that Japan had coveted because of its abundant resources and proximity to Japan. The Russians built the Trans-Siberian railroad through Manchuria and encouraged anti-Japanese groups in Korea, which seemed to Japan like "a dagger thrust at the heart of Japan." Then Russia built a naval base at Port Arthur, which the Japanese had earlier been forced to return to China. The Japanese wanted to negotiate with the Russians, but that was an embarrassment to the Russians who, like most other Europeans at this time, were highly racist. They referred to the Japanese as "baboons" and treated the Japanese diplomats with considerable disrespect.

Fortunately, for Japan, it had signed a treaty with Britain in 1902, which enabled Japan to buy some warships from Britain and agreed that both countries would look after each other's interests in Asia. Because of this, the Japanese were confident that they could start a war with Russia without all of the major powers of the West joining forces against them.

The Russo-Japanese War began with Japan sinking Russia's entire Pacific fleet at Port Arthur on February 8, 1904. The Japanese then attacked Russian land forces. Japan gained ground, but Russia with its huge population had so many troops for reinforcements that Japan could not win a complete victory. On the other hand, Russia was unable to defeat Japan, despite the numerical superiority of the Russian army. Russia was handicapped by the fact that the most expedient way to get troops from the West to the fighting in the East was via the Trans-Siberian railroad. The distance that needed to be traveled was enormous, and the railroad operated on a single track, part of which was not finished.

The Russians sent their antiquated Baltic fleet to engage the Japanese. The question at this point was what would Britain do? Some people wondered if Britain would interpret its treaty with Japan to mean that the British were obligated to fight alongside the Japanese against Russia. This was a real possibility, especially after the Dogger Bank incident. In Dogger Bank, near the British Isles, many British fishermen earned their living. Early one morning, as Russia's Baltic fleet was passing through the area, they saw British commercial ships. Believing that they were part of a Japanese attack fleet, the Russians fired on the civilian ships. The British were outraged. Britain never did attack Russia over this incident, but tensions ran high.

The Russian fleet had to split up at the Mediterranean. Some of the ships went down around the southern tip of Africa, and others sailed through the Mediterranean with the intention of cutting through the Suez Canal. The ships that took this second route were too rick-

ety to risk going through the storms that were common near the southern tip of Africa. The Suez route was, of course, much quicker. Britain controlled the Suez so the entire fleet did not want to cross through it. The Russians were not positive Britain would let any Russian ships through, but the British decided not to be an impediment to Russia's war effort. The Baltic fleet finally made it to Asia about seven months after setting out. The Japanese, led by Admiral Togo, sunk the majority of this fleet over the course of three days at the Battle of Tsushima on May 27-29, 1905, Russia's worst naval defeat of all time.

Both sides were looking for a way out, but neither wanted to lose face by negotiating with the other. Behind the scenes, Japan asked the President of the United States, Theodore Roosevelt, to step in and offer to mediate an agreement. Russia and Japan signed the Treaty of Portsmouth in August 1905, bringing the war to an end. Roosevelt received a Nobel Peace Prize for his efforts.

Japan could not afford to lose any more troops. It needed peace almost as badly as the Russians did. So both sides made compromises. Among other things, Russia removed its troops from Manchuria, but the Russians balked at Japanese demands for a large indemnity and Russia's withdrawal from the strategically important island of Sakhalin. The two powers agreed to divide control of the island, and Japan relented on the demand for money.

Japan had censored many events concerning the war. The Japanese had heard about all of the damage inflicted on the Russians, but they did not know about the losses they had experienced. The Japanese citizens felt that their negotiators had given away too much. So, people in Japan rioted. Despite this, the war opened a period of Japanese domination in East Asia. It was the first modern victory of a non-European country over a European power. One amazed British General noted, "I have today seen the most stupendous spectacle it is possible for the mortal brain to conceive – Asia advancing, Europe falling back."

The Revolution of 1905

The Russians, like the Japanese, had been censoring reports from the Far East. So, most Russian citizens had no idea how badly the war had gone for them. When the details of the peace agreement became public, the people were amazed at the concessions their government had made. There had already been a great deal of unrest in Russia, and with this latest frustration the people were pushed over the edge. People rioted over what they perceived to be the incompetent leadership of the czar. There was no other explanation that made sense to the Russians of this era, since their population was much greater than that of Japan, and the Russians were white. Russia's performance against Japan was not the only reason that things were tense in the czar's palace in 1905. On top of earlier discontents, the war caused a breakdown of the transportation system that led to massive food shortages in Russian cities. Trade unions were not allowed in Russia, but associations of "loyalist" workers did form. These associations were supposed to be overseen by men who were loyal to the czar, as instruments to promote the image of a benevolent ruler who only cared about the well being of his people. But one of the associations became a springboard for dissent and labor strikes. Father Georgei Gapon, a man who had been working on behalf of the government, organized a mass protest. On January 9 (Orthodox calendar), thousands of workers marched to the Winter Palace in St. Petersburg to air their grievances. A young tourist reported watching, "a slow-moving human flood. It was a mute and terrible procession. . . ." Many of them were dressed in their Sunday best, carrying icons and pictures of the czar, and singing the imperial anthem, "God Save the Czar." Cossacks (members of the Russian cavalry) rode into the crowds, killing and maiming their victims with swords, while Russian soldiers fired indiscriminately at the people. Hundreds of Russian citizens were slaughtered in what started out as a peaceful demonstration. The czar's image as a peaceful, loving ruler would never recover from the day known to Russians as "Bloody Sunday." As one historian noted, it "raised a blood-stained barrier between the Russian masses and the dynasty."

Rioting continued in Russia over the summer of 1905 and into the fall. There were strikes, peasant uprisings, revolutionary activity among ethnic minorities, even turmoil within units of the military. In response to all of this, Nicholas II issued the October Manifesto. This document promised civil liberties to Russians—but not to other minorities like the Jews—and it created a parliament known as the Duma. Technically, Russia had just become a constitutional monarchy, but the reality was different than the rhetoric. The compromises split the Russian opposition as some liberals were pleased, and others remained unconvinced. After things had calmed down, Nicholas cracked down on leading dissidents and began to disregard the will of the Duma. In the end, he was as autocratic as ever, relying on his army and the bureaucracy to maintain his rule. But the seeds of revolution had been sowed and they would flower in World War I.

THE NEW IMPERIALISM

From the 1880s European nations launched a frenzied drive for overseas territory described as the "new imperialism." Prior to 1914, only about one third of the people in the world were not ruled by Europeans or their descendants. Nationalistic competition and arrogance led many countries to believe that they needed colonies around the world. From a strictly economic standpoint, the Great Powers keenly felt the need for colonies. Colonies were the most favorable of trading partners, and they served as an outlet for emigration when unemployment threatened to be a problem. These concerns were especially sharp in the prolonged economic slump from 1873 to 1896. Countries were desperate for a return to the good old days of prosperity and for a chance to increase revenue for government programs without increasing taxes. Europeans also believed that they needed the resources these colonies provided and had to keep these resources out of the hands of their rivals. Colonies also provided important bases and ports for navies and shipping industries, two of the basic components of world trade.

To explain and justify their position of dominance, Europeans developed a racist model that they based on the theories of Darwin and Spencer. Whites were fit to rule the world, because they were naturally superior. Browns (Asiatic Indians) would become fit to rule over themselves at some distant point in the future. Until then, it was, in the words of the poet Rudyard Kipling, the "white man's burden" to guide these lesser people. Blacks were seen as even less capable than browns. Yellows presented a problem for the racists. China was a country with an incredible number of people, but Europeans were able to dominate them. The astute players in world politics on the other hand saw Japan as a potential threat. The people of Japan would not be easy prey for the West. Since Japan fit outside the model, it was not treated uniformly by the West. By the twentieth century, Britain and the United States negotiated with the Japanese as equals.

It would be unfair to say that colonial efforts were only exploitative. Infrastructures were improved upon, education and technology was provided, and medical practices were modernized. Many Europeans had a paternalistic attitude that was well intentioned, even if it was condescending. Missionary work was, in some cases, facilitated by aspects of colonialism. Our postmodern society might view missionary work as another example of Western arrogance, but it was, at the very least, usually the result of good intentions.

It is, however, almost impossible to create a pleasant picture of colonialism. As the European powers congratulated themselves on their benevolent oversight of the less gifted, the colonies were being bled dry of resources. Even after the occupations ended, these native populations had to deal with the consequences of being in lands that were far poorer in resources than when their would-be saviors arrived. And, when the locals strained against the inequities and lack of freedom under colonial rule, they were brutally suppressed.

AFRICA

The renewed interest in colonization was manifested in the early 1880s by new encroachments into Africa. France annexed Tunisia, and Britain occupied Egypt. Germany, Belgium, and Italy all tried to improve their standing through involvement in African territory, though Italy's ineptitude hurt its cause. The Italians wanted to connect their African colonies by taking over the land between them. This land was Abyssinia—later called Ethiopia—and it was one of the few independent African nations in existence in the late nineteenth century. Italy invaded

Abyssinia, but despite the military superiority of the Italians, they were crushed by the Abyssinians. Italy lost out on resources and territory, and, perhaps most importantly of all in racist Europe, Italy forfeited prestige. The Italians' inability to defeat a native African army made them a second-rate power in the eyes of Europe. Despite the "whiteness" of the Italians, they seemed racially inferior to the British, French, and Germans. Not even snatching Libya from the enfeebled Ottoman Empire in 1911 could completely remove the stain of Italy's humiliation. This failure also left Italians more open to the tough talking rhetoric that Benito Mussolini offered in the 1920s.

Tensions between France and Germany flared anew over Morocco. France wanted to attach Morocco to the growing French Empire in Africa that already included Tunisia and Algeria. The French had also been interested in Egypt, but the French acquiesced to British control of Egypt in exchange for Britain's approval of French policy regarding Morocco. Germany demanded access to Morocco in 1905. The Kaiser had been reluctant to push the issue before this because of France's alliance with Russia, and the Germans were reluctant to engage in a game of brinkmanship that might lead to fighting a two-front war. Obviously, they overcame this reluctance by 1914. Germany pressed its case against France in 1905 because Russia was in the midst of its difficulties with Japan. Germany was considering going to war over the matter, but the ubiquitous Teddy Roosevelt intervened. He persuaded the Kaiser to agree to arbitration over the matter. Roosevelt persuaded the French to agree by promising to use his influence to see to it that French interests were preserved. Because the Kaiser had agreed to abide by the arbitration, he did not feel he could continue to press the issue at that time. Looking back on the matter, Roosevelt later said that he believed that he delayed the coming of World War I with his actions regarding Morocco.

ASIA

Like Africa, Asia was a target of European colonial interest. The Chinese with their massive land holdings and enormous population considered themselves to be the center of the world. Their ancient culture was a source of their pride and belief that they were superior to the other peoples of the world. But the Chinese had trouble dealing with the changes that occurred in the second half of the nineteenth century. When Britain demanded trade concessions, the Chinese were not able to hold out against them. The Chinese Army was poorly trained and poorly provisioned and fared badly against Britain in what was known as the Opium War of 1840-1842. Merchants from Britain and later the United States were shipping opium into China. The profits from the sale of the drug were used to buy Chinese goods and resources.

Several European powers (Germany, France, and Russia) followed Britain's example and carved out their own areas of influence in China. China's assets were offset by its lack of unity. The current imperial family in China, the Manchu dynasty, actually belonged to an ethnic minority. Chinese citizens who were already unhappy about being ruled by this family were frustrated by the emperor's inability to deal effectively with the Europeans. As a result, many of the provinces strained against the emperor's authority, and they had little incentive to sacrifice themselves on behalf of the imperial family.

Nevertheless, there were many people in China who were impacted by the invasion of foreigners. Many Chinese resented the modern technology and industry that took away jobs.

Spiritually minded Chinese believed that modern telegraph machines, mining, equipment, and steamboats disturbed the spirits of air, earth, and water. Also, Christian missionaries were converting scores of Chinese. Many felt that the worst of the converts were the so-called "rice Christians," the Chinese who traded their spiritual allegiance for a decent meal.

In 1900 a secret society known as the Boxers rebelled violently against Western domination. The foreigners, because of the martial arts routines the revolutionaries practiced, derisively referred to these Chinese revolutionaries as "Boxers." The "Boxer Rebellion," as it was called, was put down ruthlessly. Even after the Chinese were once again forced into submission, many were killed. For the most part this was the work of the Germans, but the other occupying nations also participated in the killings. Officially, they were rooting out Boxers, but many of the people who were killed were not a part of the uprising. In addition to their suffering, the Chinese were supposed to pay the occupying forces for the losses that the foreigners incurred during the rebellion. Chinese forts were destroyed, and the outsiders annexed more land. This entire episode only deepened Chinese resentment of the West, and this resentment still impacts relations between China and the West today.

Japan was also in danger of being dominated by the West at the dawn of the twentieth century but were not, ironically, though they were smaller than China. Japan was able to consolidate more easily than China. Japan also benefited from the fact that the Japanese had always been willing to learn from their enemies. Japan's leaders attempted to modernize their nation by imitating the West, adapting military techniques, industrial and financial organizations, and administrative organizations to suit Japanese needs.

They created a parliamentary system in form that was autocratic in practice.

By doing this, Japan created a strong military state. Japan fought its way into controlling its own sphere of influence in China in 1894. In 1902 Japan negotiated an alliance with Britain. It was the first time a European power made an alliance with an Asian power without any fighting as equals. Most whites did not yet concede that the people of Japan were their racial equals, but the British and the United States respected the military strength that Japan possessed and treated Japan with respect. Russia would have benefited from following this example. If the Russians had done so, the Russo-Japanese War and the Russians' humiliating defeat might well have been avoided. Japan had certainly proved that it too could win in the white man's imperialistic playing fields. But those fields were now crowded by all the major powers and conflict seemed inevitable.

CONCLUSION

During the era from 1871-1914, the optimism of many of Europe's leading citizens was easy to understand. People were benefiting in this time period from technological breakthroughs and governments that seemed to be more benevolent—at least to their own citizens—than they had been in the past. More rights were extended, and countries had shown the ability to work together where their interests corresponded, as was the case with the adoption of Greenwich Time and in dealing with the threat of the Boxer Rebellion. Despite this, there were also signs of the dark days to come. Europe dominated much of the world, and this dominance was characterized by a combination of greed, arrogance, and contentiousness. The mixture of these traits would lead the world to war in 1914.

Suggestions for Further Reading

Clark Blaise, *Time Lord: Sir Sandford Fleming and the Creation of Standard Time* (2001).

Dave Breese, *Seven Men Who Rule the World from the Grave* (1990).

Gordon A. Craig, *Germany: 1866-1945* (1978).

Clifton Daniel, *Chronicle of America* (1993).

John Darby, *Conflict in Northern Ireland* (1977).

Niall Ferguson, *The House of Rothschild: The World's Banker 1849-1999* (1999).

Carter V. Findley and John A. M. Rothney, *Twentieth Century World* (1998).

Rovert I. Fitzhenry, *Barnes and Noble Book of Quotations: Revised and Enlarged* (1987).

Martin Gilbert, *The First World War: A Complete History* (1994).

Raymond J. Haberski, Jr., *It's Only a Movie! Films and Critics in American Culture* (2001).

Richard Hough, *The Fleet that had to Die* (2001).

Joel Krieger, *The Oxford Companion to Politics of the World* (1993).

Barnet Litvinoff, *Weizmann: Last of the Patriarchs* (1976).

Joseph Machlis and Kristine Forney, *The Enjoyment of Music* (1999).

Arthur Marwick, *Britain in Our Century: Images and Controversies* (1984).

Andre Maurois, *Disraeli* (1980).

Lee Cameron McDonald, *Western Political Theory: Part 3, Nineteenth and Twentieth Centuries* (1968).

Nathan Miller, *Theodore Roosevelt: a Life* (1992).

Wolfgang J. Mommsen, *Imperial Germany 1867-1918: Politics, Culture, and Society in an Authoritarian State* (1997).

R. R. Palmer and Joel Colton, *A History of the Modern World Since 1815* (1984).

Diana Preston, *The Boxer Rebellion* (2000).

Nicholas V. Riasanovsky, *A History of Russia* (1977).

Jacques Rupnik, *The Other Europe* (1989).

Hillel Schwartz, *Century's End: A Cultural History of the Fin de Siecle from the 990s Through the 1990s* (1990).

Bruce L. Shelley, *Church History in Plain Language* (1982).

J. Kelley Sowards, *Makers of the Western Tradition: Portraits from History, Vol. II, Seventh Edition* (1997).

John G. Stoessinger, *Why Nations go to War* (2001).

C. L. Sulzberger, *The Fall of Eagles* (1977).

Chapter 20

THE GREAT WAR
1914-1919

June 28, 1914, was a hot morning in the Bosnian town of Sarajevo, a spot on the globe virtually unknown to Americans. (Eighty years later, when it again led in the news, Americans would still be unable to locate Bosnia on the map.) The city's balconies were hung with banners and colorful carpets to welcome Archduke Francis Ferdinand—heir to the throne of the large and troubled Austro-Hungarian empire—and his wife, Sophie. The Archduke intended it to be a day of celebration and validation for his more lowly born wife on the occasion of their fourteenth wedding anniversary. He and his wife entered an open car at 10:00 A.M. for a triumphant procession.

Waiting among the milling crowds, however, were seven young Serbian nationalists. They were a disorganized and crudely armed group of conspirators, seeking a Greater Serbia. The Archduke's chauffeur, misunderstanding his instructions, took a wrong turn. When he realized his mistake, he braked and stopped the car less than five feet from Gavrilo Princip, the most determined of the assassins. Princip fired two shots. One hit Francis Ferdinand in the neck; the other struck Sophie in the abdomen. Observing his beloved wife crumpled in a heap, the dying Archduke cried, "Sophie dear...don't die. Stay alive for our children." His last words were a response to questions about his own suffering, "Es ist nicht." (It is nothing.) By 11:00 A.M., both were dead.

As the Bolshevik leader, Leon Trotsky, would say later, "History had already poised its gigantic soldier's boot over the ant heap." In a little over a month, a complex system of alliances would escalate the responses to the assassination into the most terrible war the world had yet seen, the "Great War." Princip's act also helped bring about a whole new era of conspiracies and assassinations. Serbians embraced him as a folk hero. In the newly established nation of Yugoslavia, after the war, a black marble tablet was placed on the wall opposite the curb where the royal car stopped. It read: "HERE ON THIS HISTORIC SPOT GAVRILO PRINCIP WAS THE ANNUNCIATOR OF LIBERTY. . . ."

On that bright Sunday day decent families all over Europe were attending church, secure in their belief in an unchanging world with the father as master of the family, the monarch as leader of the nation, and a benevolent God overseeing all. Later that day, they would go on to other innocent Sunday enjoyments: bands playing in the parks, swimming at the beaches, bicycling down country lanes, and having afternoon teas. The president of France was at the races with beautifully dressed gentlemen and ladies. Kaiser Wilhelm II of Germany was spending a lazy day aboard his yacht.

It was hard to believe that "the good years" might be coming to an end. Technological advances and the decades of relative peace had created a feeling of optimism. Sir Edward Gray, the British Foreign Secretary, had a more realistic intimation that an age was about to end. Watching a London lamplighter at work on the evening of August 4, 1914, he commented sadly to a friend, "The lamps are going out all over Europe; we shall not see them lit again in our lifetime."

Chronology

1871   End of the Franco-Prussian War creating the German Empire
Germany annexes Alsace and Lorraine

1873   The Three Emperors' League (Germany, Austria-Hungary, and Russia)

1878   The Congress of Berlin

1879   The Dual Alliance between Germany and Austria-Hungary

1882   The Triple Alliance (Germany, Austria-Hungary, and Italy)

1887   The Reinsurance Treaty between Germany and Russia

1888   Wilhelm II becomes Kaiser

1890   Bismarck is dismissed as Chancellor

1894   Alliance between France and Russia

1904   Entente Cordiale: France and Great Britain

1905   The first Moroccan crisis

1907   The Triple Entente (Britain, France and Russia)

1911   The second Moroccan crisis

1912   The first Balkan War

1913   The second Balkan War

1914   Assassination of Archduke Francis Ferdinand
World War I declared
Battle of Tannenberg
First Battle of the Marne

1915   Battle of Gallipoli
Italy enters the war on the Allied side
Germany sinks the *Lusitania*

1916   Battle of Verdun
Battle of the Somme

1917   Germany resumes unrestricted submarine warfare
Russian Revolution overthrows the Czar
United States enters the war
Bolshevik Revolution in Russia

1918   Wilson outlines his Fourteen Points
Treaty of Brest-Litovsk
Final German offensive in the West
Second Battle of the Marne and Allied Counteroffensive
Armistice ends the war (November 11)

1919   Paris Peace Conference
Treaty of Versailles signed

THE ROUTE TO WAR

"Some damned foolish thing in the Balkans," Bismarck had once supposedly predicted, would set off the next war. The Archduke's assassination fulfilled his prophecy. The ominous storm cloud of war had been looming over Europe for several years. For almost a century there had been no wars involving all of the major European powers. Many "experts" predicted that war, a discreditable by-product of a "barbarous" past, would never again rear its ugly head. In 1914 an English group was making elaborate plans to celebrate the centennial of the Battle of Waterloo on June 18, 1915. Their real commemoration was not only that victory but the fact that it would be 100 years since the British army had fought in Western Europe. But below the seemingly placid surface, many young European men, partially inspired by the writings of Nietzsche, believed that their society had become decadent, uninteresting, and dangerously soft. They longed for the excitement of war, an experience they believed would build character and create a new "superman," sweeping away the rotting remains of a decaying civilization. "Like men longing for a thunderstorm to relieve them of the summer sultriness, so the generation of 1914 believed in the relief that war might bring," an Austrian official noted. The theme of the *Rite of Spring*, a ballet that premiered in Paris in 1913, was the ritual allure of death. Self-important thinkers distorted the biological theories of Charles Darwin about "the survival of the fittest" and argued that nations must organize all of their efforts to defeat rivals either in commerce or in war.

Strategists still asserted that a balance of power in Europe would maintain the existing system because no nation would be dominant enough to risk war. The balance, however, rested precariously on competing forces of nationalism, imperialism, and militarism. The European powers had constructed a complex system of alliances that eventually divided into two camps: the Triple Entente (Great Britain, France and Russia) and the Triple Alliance (Germany, Austria-Hungary and Italy). As we have seen in Chapter 19, the imperial ambitions of Britain, France and Germany clashed in the race for markets and resources in Africa and Asia. These divisions became far more dangerous in light of a growing arms race. Germany had succeeded in creating a united nation out of many principalities only in 1871. Under the leadership of Kaiser Wilhelm II, it boldly pursued national greatness and military might, seeking to overwhelm France's army and to challenge British naval supremacy.

Bismarckian Diplomacy

The old "Iron Chancellor," Otto von Bismarck, had been a consistent exponent of *realpolitik* (politics grounded in realities, rather than ideology) in international affairs. He understood that the rise of a united Germany in 1871 had upset the delicate balance of power that had been established at the Congress of Vienna in 1815. He realized that the humiliation the French suffered in 1871, including a triumphant march by the victorious German army down the empty, hushed, black-draped Champs Elysees, might pose a danger to peace. He had even opposed the annexation of Alsace-Lorraine that had been insisted upon by the German military, arguing that it would be "the Achilles' heel" of the new German Empire. This new Germany was changing more rapidly than any nation in Europe with an expanding population, the fastest rising per capita wealth, and booming industrial and military capacity.

Bismarck sought to reassure the rest of Europe that Germany was "satisfied" and would seek no further territorial expansion. He attempted to soften French bitterness by supporting French colonial ambitions. At the same time, he wanted to prevent a French alliance with any other European power. To that end, he forged an agreement with the other two conservative empires of Austria-Hungary and Russia. It was known as the Three Emperors' League. The Austro-Russian rivalry in the Balkans, however, led to the collapse of the league. Bismarck considered himself an "honest broker," attempting to prevent a war between Austria and Russia over the decaying Ottoman Empire that might draw in Germany despite its national interest. "The Eastern question," he declared, "is not worth the healthy bones of a single Pomeranian musketeer." After Russia's success in defeating the Ottomans in 1876, the 1878 Congress of Berlin, under the presidency of Bismarck, reduced the territory of Bulgaria, a Russian client-state, by two-thirds. Austria was allowed to "occupy and administer" the provinces of Bosnia and Herzegovina. Although Germany gained no territory and seemed to be motivated by a desire to maintain peace,

Russia felt humiliated and deeply resentful. To counter Russian alienation, Bismarck signed an alliance with Austria in 1879 that was joined by Italy in 1882 to become the Triple Alliance.

Although this agreement seemed dangerous to German interests by tying them to the unstable Austro-Hungarian empire, Bismarck was well aware of its liabilities. He commented that every alliance contains a horse and rider, and Germany must be the rider. He thought of the alliance as strictly defensive and flatly asserted, "For us, Balkan questions can never be a motive for war." He was careful to allay Russian fears by signing a Reinsurance Treaty with Russia in 1887. Bismarck hoped that this would preclude the possibilities of a threatening Russian-French alliance. This elaborate diplomacy seemed to be working well to continue both peace and the status quo. In 1890, however, Kaiser Wilhelm II used a supposed conflict over domestic policy to dismiss Bismarck. The nature of European diplomacy was abruptly altered by this event.

Kaiser Wilhelm II

Wilhelm II ascended to the German throne in 1888 at the age of twenty-nine. He was pretentious and impulsive. The Kaiser was born with a withered left arm that had repelled his cold and distant mother. She was the eldest child of Queen Victoria of England, and he was the eldest grandchild of the Queen. His unrelenting struggle to compensate for his disability distorted his character, cultivating an image of "militaristic belligerence." He enjoyed hunting and massacring vast numbers of animals and maintained a wardrobe of two hundred military uniforms. One historian has noted that, although Wilhelm was a religious man, it wasn't always clear to him, "just who was the senior partner in his unique relationship with God."

As a child and young man, he visited England virtually every summer where he expressed great pride at being "half an Englishman." His mother's rejection of him probably helped explain his conflicted feelings about England. Although he came from a landlocked country that neither needed nor had a navy, he developed a love for ships and the sea on his visits to his mother's homeland. He admired and envied the British navy and pushed for a navy bill to build a high seas fleet to earn Germany the respect he craved. He demanded Germany's legitimate "place in the sun." Wilhelm had an unfortunate tendency to make rash comments that scandalized Europe and made him seem like a dangerous bully. Expounding on the Hague Peace Conference of 1898, he blurted out: "I trust in God and in my unsheathed sword and I *** on all resolutions of international conferences." In his infamous speech to German troops departing to help squash the 1900 Boxer Rebellion, he proclaimed, "Give no quarter. Take no prisoner. . . . Even as a thousand years ago when the Huns under King Attila made such a name for themselves as still resounds in terror. . . so may the name of German resound . . . for a thousand years. . . ." These unfortunate comments made it possible for Allied propagandists to fix the label of Hun on Germany during the war.

Alliances and Crises

The Kaiser's decision to drop the Reinsurance Treaty with Russia was an even greater blunder. Its consequence was exactly what Bismarck had feared: an isolated and capital-poor Russia turned to an equally apprehensive France. The French were happy to encourage investments in Russia, and in 1894, a defensive military alliance was concluded between the two nations. The austere and reactionary Czar Alexander III had swallowed his distaste for republican France even to the point of standing at attention for the revolutionary national anthem, the *Marseillaise*. Nicholas II, a weak-willed and poorly educated absolute ruler who was controlled by his emotional, unstable wife, Alexandra, succeeded him. (Like Wilhelm, she was a grandchild of Victoria.) Although the Kaiser believed that Czar Nicholas was "only fit to live in the country and grow turnips," he attempted to repair his mistake through letters to Nicholas. The letters, written in English, were addressed to "Dearest Nicky" and signed "Your affectionate friend, Willy." The French republic had been built on the blood of kings, he solemnly informed the Czar. "Nicky, take my word for it, the curse of God has stricken that people forever." This personal diplomacy failed to split Russia away from France, especially since Alexandra had developed a fervent hatred for the arrogant Kaiser.

Britain had become crucial in the international balancing act. The British might seem to be a natural ally of the Germans. They were traditional enemies of the French, particularly in colonial contests for Africa, and had long been suspicious of Russian ambitions in central Asia. The Kaiser, with his ambivalent feelings toward Britain, altered the equation. His insistence on building a great German fleet to counter British naval supremacy antagonized the British and succeeded only in squandering German resources and precipitating a naval arms race. He also angered the British by congratulating a Boer leader in South Africa for repelling a British assault. An interview that the Kaiser had set up with a British newspaper further inflamed these feelings. In it, he declared, "You English are mad, mad, mad as March hares" and insisted, "Germany must have a powerful fleet to protect. . . her manifest interests in even the most distant seas." In 1904, the British dropped their traditional hostility to the French and concluded the *Entente Cordiale* in which the two nations settled all their colonial disputes. Britain recognized French claims in Morocco in return for France's agreement to British control of Egypt. Still, when the British allied themselves with Japan at the time of the Russo-Japanese War, it seemed unlikely that the British and Russians could ever get together.

The Kaiser responded to the Entente by attempting to split up the two new allies. He landed in Morocco in 1905 and challenged French supremacy there. He then insisted on an international conference to resolve this First Moroccan Crisis of 1905-6. Despite Wilhelm's blustering, French control of Morocco was confirmed by the powers at the conference, and Germany gained nothing. In fact, German threats drove Britain and France closer together. The British and French general staffs began to coordinate their naval and military plans, making them practically, if not officially, allies. Russia's growing uneasiness about German ambitions led to an agreement with Britain in 1907, which settled disagreements in central Asia and called for closer cooperation. Thus, the Triple Entente, an informal but strong coalition of Britain, France and Russia, now faced the Triple Alliance. When France took complete control of Morocco in 1911, the Germans set off a Second Moroccan Crisis by dispatching a gunboat to a Moroccan port and demanding concessions. No nation backed Germany's actions. The French and British drew even closer together in formulating specific, binding military plans. Wilhelm and his advisors had succeeded in destroying the balance that Bismarck had worked so hard to achieve. They had made his nightmare of a Germany encircled by enemies into a reality.

The Balkans Again

As it is today, the Balkan area was the most volatile part of Europe. The Ottoman Empire, the "sick man of Europe" had continued its inevitable decay. The vultures circled, eager to feast on its remains. As nationalism grew among the south Slavic peoples (Yugoslavs), independent Serbia hoped to unite them in a single nation under its leadership. Russia viewed itself as the protector of its "little brothers," the Slavs, and hoped to replace the Ottomans as the predominant power in the region. In 1908, a group of modernizing activists, the Young Turks, revolted and gained control of the empire. Their movement endangered European plans by resuscitating the Ottoman corpse. Austria quickly annexed the two Slavic-speaking territories of Bosnia and Herzegovina. The Austrians feared that an enlarged Serbia would jeopardize the unity of their own empire with its large number of Slavic inhabitants. Germany forced a humiliated Russia to accept the Austrian actions, further inflaming the resentments of the Russians and the Serbs.

The smoldering embers in the Balkans erupted into a fire in the First Balkan War (1912). The Young Turk leaders of the Ottoman Empire advocated extreme nationalism and a policy of repression of subject nationalities, even reviving the horrific massacres of Armenians. They succeeded in getting the Balkan countries of Serbia, Bulgaria, Montenegro, and Greece to unite to drive the Ottomans out of the region. The victors quickly had disagreements over how to divide their spoils: Macedonia and Albania. In 1913 a Second Balkan War broke out in which Greece, Serbia, and Romania were joined by the Turks to attack Bulgaria. Bulgaria was stripped of much of its earlier gains. Although Macedonia was divided between Greece and Serbia, Serbian ambitions in Albania to gain an outlet to the Adriatic Sea were thwarted by the successful Austrian move to create an independent Albania. Increasingly, Serbian nationalists saw Austria as an evil empire blocking their road to greatness. The Russians felt discomfited by their inability to affect events in the area. The Austrians continued to believe that Serbia was a deadly menace to their empire that eventually had to be annihilated. The system of alliances led Germany to give Austria its unconditional support while the British and French drew closer to each other and realized that they had to bolster their humiliated Russian ally.

The Arms Race

As tensions escalated, so did the military buildup. European nations, except for Britain, began to draft ordinary citizens into large mass armies. By 1914 Germany, Russia, and France were each calling up, at least, 250,00 men per year. Between 1890 and 1914, European military capabilities doubled in size. The French and Germans each had armies of 900,000, while the Russians could field a force of 1.3 million men. Defense expenditures consumed an increasing percentage of national budgets, rising to 45 percent in Germany.

Technology also transformed the nature of modern weaponry. Alfred Nobel, a Swedish arms manufacturer, developed dynamite and a smokeless gunpowder that could propel shells and bullets. Long range artillery could hit targets six miles away. Howitzers, quick-firing field guns, and machine guns were stockpiled. The 1906 launching of the British warship, *Dreadnought,* with its unprecedented gun range and size and engine power, led to an intensified naval construction race with Germany.

The military buildup stimulated the economies of the nations involved. The public was increasingly convinced that their nation's importance and economic stability depended on military power. This, in turn, increased the influence of military leaders. They developed complicated plans to rapidly mobilize vast armies and supplies for war. They contended that these plans could not be changed in any way. Never before had so many men and so much material been gathered for battle. Once the order to mobilize had been given, it was considered impossible to change or delay the process. The conviction that the armaments race would deter conflict had given way to the certitude that war between the two alliances was now inevitable. Rather than devoting themselves to preventing armed conflict, the leaders of Europe seemed more interested in assuring that when war came, it would be at the right time and over the right question to fulfill their nation's strategic plans. No wonder that a perceptive American observer in Europe commented on the feeling of electricity: "Everybody's nerves are tense. It only needs a spark to set the whole thing off."

THE WAR ARRIVES

When Archduke Francis Ferdinand was assassinated on June 28, 1914, many Austro-Hungarian leaders were secretly relieved. The Archduke was unpopular with these conservatives because he had espoused a federal system of government that might have raised the status of minority nationalities in the empire. They were so detached that they neglected to provide a state funeral and even botched the meager ceremony that was provided. This led one historian to comment that not only could Austria not produce a single diplomat with Metternich's tactical skills, "it was no longer capable of producing even a

good funeral director." Although they issued official statements expressing outrage and denunciation of the assassination, most world leaders expected a muted response. This kind of political murder had, unfortunately, become a kind of "occupational hazard" for important political leaders of the era. The series of crises between 1908 and 1913, however, had heightened tensions and mutual mistrust. Diplomats had increasingly demonstrating a willingness to take ill-considered risks and bring their nations to the brink of war to uphold some supposed national honor. Austrian leaders, who had long opposed Francis Ferdinand's accommodating policy toward the Slavs, saw his assassination as an opportunity to "render Serbia impotent once and for all by a display of force," as Austria's foreign minister acknowledged. Most Europeans believed, with good cause, that Serbian officials directed the Black Hand, the terrorist organization responsible for the assassination. The joy expressed in Serbian newspapers after the slaying reinforced this perception. Despite the inclination to take strong action, Austrian officials realized that they needed German support if and when Russia intervened to defend Serbia.

The Germans responded to the Austrian leaders with the infamous "blank check." They assured the Austrian emperor that he could "rely upon Germany's full support." They went even further, insisting "that this action must not be delayed" and pledging that, should this lead to an "unavoidable" war with Russia, "Germany, our old faithful ally, would stand at our side." Historians have long debated over whether the Germans deliberately encouraged the crisis to implement their long-standing war plans. When the Austrian ambassador returned to Vienna with the German blank check, Francis Ferdinand, the old Austrian emperor, responded with a resigned sigh, "Now we can no longer turn back. It will be a terrible war."

The Austrians sent an ultimatum to Serbia so extreme that it would have undermined Serbian independence. The stunned Russian foreign minister told the Austrians, "You are setting Europe ablaze." The Serbians astonished the Austrians with a reply that was so accommodating that even the volatile Kaiser exclaimed, "A great moral success for Vienna! All reason for war is gone." The Austrians by this point, however, were so determined not to turn back that they used the one Serbian reservation of the ultimatum's demands to declare war on Serbia on July 28, 1914. Many Austrian diplomats believed, with Germany backing them, "Russia would protest and France would growl," but both would back down as they had in the past. The Russians were determined not to retreat. Pan-Slavic nationalists pressed Czar Nicholas II to act to protect their Serbian "little brothers." The French might well have restrained Russian impulsiveness, but the Austrians had timed their ultimatum to arrive when the French president and prime minister were at sea after a meeting in Russia. The Czar cautiously ordered a partial mobilization of his army. At this point the inflexibility of military plans came into play. His General Staff told him that any attempt at partial mobilization would create turmoil in the army. Even though he realized that the Germans would consider this an act of war (or use it as an excuse), the Czar ordered full mobilization. The Germans were already about to mobilize but were able to use the news of Russian mobilization to paint the latter as aggressors and declare war on August 1.

Unfortunately, the only German plan for war insured that the conflict would spread. The Schlieffen Plan had been developed in 1905 after France and Russia had formed their alliance. It assumed a two front war in which there would only be minimal initial action against a slow-mobilizing Russia in a gamble to concentrate on and quickly defeat France first. This meant that any struggle between Germany and Russia would automatically involve France and that German mobilization must inevitably be followed by war. The Plan, as revised, called for rapid incursion into western France through Belgium. Both Germany and Britain had guaranteed Belgian neutrality in an 1839 treaty. On August 2 Germany demanded that Belgium allow German troops to pass through its territory. The following day, Belgium rejected this ultimatum, and Germany and France declared war on each other. Many British politicians hoped that Britain could avoid involvement in the continental European power struggle, and the French feared that they would. But Britain insisted that Germany must ensure Belgian neutrality or the two nations would be at war. On August 4, the British declared war. The rueful German Chancellor Bethmann-Hollweg exclaimed, "Just for the sake of a scrap of paper Great Britain is going to make war on a kindred nation." Many people felt that this comment reflected German unawareness of public opinion in Britain and America. The mercurial Kaiser, signing the order to start his armies rolling, was unexpectedly clear-sighted as he remarked to his military leaders, "Gentlemen, you will live to regret this."

Public Reaction

The public was not nearly as regretful. After the constant crises, the war seemed a release for the increasing tensions. In every capital vast crowds singing patriotic songs celebrated the war. Resurgent patriotism swallowed up class and other internal conflicts. Even socialists, who had always scorned "imperialist war," dropped slogans

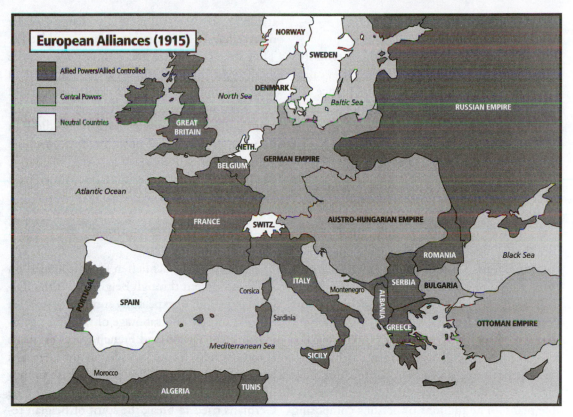

European Alliances (1915)

- Allied Powers/Allied Controlled
- Central Powers
- Neutral Countries

NORWAY
SWEDEN
DENMARK
North Sea
Baltic Sea
RUSSIAN EMPIRE
GREAT BRITAIN
NETH.
BELGIUM
GERMAN EMPIRE
Atlantic Ocean
FRANCE
SWITZ.
AUSTRO-HUNGARIAN EMPIRE
ROMANIA
Black Sea
PORTUGAL
SPAIN
Corsica
ITALY
Montenegro
SERBIA
BULGARIA
ALBANIA
GREECE
OTTOMAN EMPIRE
Sardinia
Mediterranean Sea
SICILY
Morocco
ALGERIA
TUNIS

of working class solidarity to support the war efforts. The recruiting offices in Britain, where there was no conscription, were overrun by enthusiastic volunteers who worried that they might be too late to get into the battles. Most people, recalling conflicts since 1815 (and forgetting the four-year American Civil War of 1861-5), thought the war would be over in a matter of weeks.

In the first few weeks of August millions of soldiers throughout Europe boarded railway carriages chalked with slogans like "To Paris" or "To Berlin" as woman, children, and old people cheered. Their rifles were often adorned with flowers. An actor watching the troops leave in Vienna wrote, "Old heroes have reemerged from the books of legends. A mighty wonder has taken place, we have become *young*." Even the usually sober Sigmund Freud fervently remarked, "My whole libido goes out to Austria-Hungary." The collective enthusiasm was even greater in Berlin. "The general feeling among the Germans," wrote the American ambassador, "is that their years of preparation would now bear fruit." A German student told his parents that they should be proud to "have the privilege of sending those you love into so glorious a battle." All over Europe recruits paraded to triumphant music and shouted to their loved ones, "We'll be home at Christmas." They believed this would be, in the words of one writer, "romantic, a wild manly adventure." They didn't want to miss "this most wonderful and exciting experience of their lives," so they rushed to join and "shouted and sang in the trains that carried them to the slaughter."

THE EARLY BATTLES

The two great alliances faced each other in implacable combat. The Triple Entente, now called the Allies, consisted of Great Britain, France and Russia, joined by Balkan allies, Serbia, Romania and Montenegro. (Later, Italy, Japan, and the United States entered on the Allied side.) The Triple Alliance became known as the Central Powers. The Ottoman Empire and Bulgaria joined Germany and Austria-Hungary. (Italy changed sides in the course of the war.) The major powers each had a complex plan for mobilization linked to an operational plan for deploying troops. Once the order was given, these plans would unfold automatically, and military leaders argued that any change or delay was impossible. "As a result," observes one historian, "the first weeks of World War I presented the amazing spectacle of vast human machines. . . operating in a truly inhuman fashion and moving. . . according to predetermined and irreversible plans. The millions of persons composing the rival machines behaved almost as though they had lost individual will and intelligence." These plans, however, suffered under a common delusion: that a decisive offensive battle could be successfully launched. The consequence of this "deadly illusion" was the blood sacrifice of millions of young men.

For the first six weeks of the war, the military leaders followed the plans that had been concocted before the war began. It quickly became clear, however, that these plans were defective. Even after the trench system was improvised, the generals continued to assure their governments that if only they had enough equipment or men, they could break through enemy lines. It would seem to be obvious that if you march into machine gun fire, you are likely to be cut down. Military men of this era, however, had been trained to believe that a cavalry charge was the most effective operation an army could take. They were convinced that ordinary men in the infantry or manning the machine guns lacked the spirit and bravery of the cavalry and would run away when the latter charged them. Of course, they soon discovered that soldiers in trenches or barricaded positions with machine guns could effectively resist any kind of charge. But in August-September 1914, many men paid for that lesson with their lives.

The Western Front

The success of the Schlieffen Plan depended on rapid movement through Belgium, but the Belgians put up an unexpectedly stiff resistance with guerilla snipers and sabotage of rail lines, gaining time for British and French forces to arrive at the northern front. In addition, the Germans had underrated the ability of the British to mobilize and move their troops to the front. The Germans tried to break the spirit of Belgian resistance by shooting civilians, including 600 men, women, and children in the village square of Dinant, and burning villages. The most infamous case was the ancient town of Louvain with its collection of priceless medieval manuscripts. These atrocities succeeded only in providing material for Allied propaganda.

Meanwhile, the French, whose military theorists had preached that troops with *elan* and *cran* (guts) could overcome artillery, streamed across the German-French border into Lorraine with bugles sounding, colors flying, wearing baggy red trousers, blue jackets, and white gloves. Well-situated machine guns and artillery mowed them down. This defeat, however, released troops for deployment against the main German army advancing on Paris. The continuous miles of summer marching under fire had taken their

A German cavalry regiment parades through Berlin in August 1914. Thousands of soldiers such as these led the German invasion into Belgium. The Schlieffen Plan called for the German armies to march through Belgium and Luxembourg and invade France.

toll on the German soldiers. Under the command of French General Joseph Joffre, the British and French forces counterattacked at the *First Battle of the Marne* in September 1914. Although the Germans fell back, neither side was able to finish off the other. The casualties of the Battle of the Marne reached 40 percent in the first three months or more than 1.5 million men. Armies totaling more than 3.7 million crowded into two lines of trenches in the narrow front between Switzerland and the English Channel.

The intensity of the destruction led many men on both sides to seek cover. Soldiers began to look to drainage ditches and holes in the ground to dig primitive trenches to find safety in the mud created by continuous September rains. At night they might dig links between their foxholes. Over a period of time from November to December 1914 they gradually developed a more elaborate system. The trenches eventually became more complex and up to thirty feet deep. Attempted offensive actions bogged down as artillery fire could not destroy infantry and machine guns deeply entrenched in shelters. Attacking soldiers could not breach trench systems that were defended by strategically placed machine gun nests. For the rest of 1914 and 1915 neither side was able to dislodge the other from its established position.

The only respite occurred on Christmas morning, 1914. British troops could hear the Germans in their trenches singing "Stille Nacht, Heilige Nacht" (Silent Night, Holy Night). The British responded with their own carols. Soldiers applauded each other's singing. Finally, someone sent a message saying, "Let's have a party. Let's meet in the middle," promising not to shoot. Soldiers from both sides began to cautiously emerge between the lines. Gradually it spread through the lines. Soldiers shook hands and traded buttons, badges, and cigarettes for two or three days. This was never repeated in the war. One historian has described the "Christmas Truce" as "the last gesture of the 19th century idea that human beings are getting better..."

War in the East

The huge old-fashioned Russian "steam-roller" army advanced quickly into Austrian territory, inflicting substantial casualties. Soon, however, the Germans, under the command of Generals Paul von Hindenberg and Erich Ludendorff came to the aid of their Austrian allies. They completely crushed an entire Russian army at the *Battle of Tanenberg* and defeated another at the Masurian Lakes. The Russians were pushed back 300 miles into their own territory and sustained well over two million casualties in one year. Still, the very success in the east helped provide the final blow to the Schlieffen Plan by diverting troops from the western front to the east and, despite its horrendous losses, Russia remained in the war.

In 1915 Winston Churchill, first lord of the British admiralty, suggested that the Allies break the deadlock in the West by attacking the Dardanelles and capturing Constantinople. Victory in this campaign would drive Turkey from the war and help the hard-pressed Russians. Success in this battle of *Gallipoli* required an amphibious invasion with a level of preparation and resources the British did not possess. The narrow beaches and steep cliffs provided perfect cover for the Turkish defenders. Savage fighting was followed by ghastly trench warfare. Unendurable summer heat and dysentery gave way to unexpected November freezing and 15,000 cases of frostbite. By the end of the month the Cabinet decided to evacuate. Nothing had been accomplished, and the Allies suffered casualties of over 50 percent of the 500,000 troops who served

General Paul von Hindenburg (left) and General Erich Ludendorff (right) talk strategy with Kaiser Wilhelm II at German General Headquarters. The Germans scored a victory at Tannenberg on the eastern front that pushed the Russians back.

Australian troops charge a Turkish trench on Gallipoli. The Australia-New Zealand Army Corps (ANZACs) suffered brutally.

there. Despite this, the campaign proved the heroism of Australian and New Zealand troops. Anzac Day (April 25, the day of the first landings) is still a national holiday in those two nations. The campaign also created a military legend for the junior Turkish officer who rallied his men on the heights of Gallipoli, reorganizing its defenses and establishing military discipline. Mustafa Kemal would build on this legend to change the future of Turkey.

THE SLAUGHTER INTENSIFIES
1916-1917

By 1916 the system of trenches had developed into elaborate structures, defended by concrete machine-gun nests, mortar batteries, and barbed wire. Troops lived in the ground. The area between the opposing lines of fences was known as "no man's land." Despite this, generals continued to order fierce attacks on the enemy positions. Throughout 1915 the French had at-tempted to dislodge the Germans from their positions in northern France. Little was accomplished beyond casualty rates of more than 100,000 per battle.

The Allies had also suffered severe losses in the east. With the help of the Germans and Bulgarians, three-quarters of Serbia's army was destroyed, and one-sixth of the entire population was lost. Austria had finally realized full retribution for the assassination of the Archduke. Things seemed so bleak for the Allies by the end of 1915 that General Joffre wrote, "Our armies had everywhere been checked or beaten—the enemy appeared to have succeeded in all his undertakings."

Verdun

Commanders on both sides were convinced that they knew how to break the stalemate at the beginning of 1916. Their solution was found in the heavy artillery gun firing high explosive shells. They believed they could smash the trenches of their enemy and pound their barbed wire and machine gun nests if they used these shells on a scale never before attempted in battle. Neither side, however, had nearly enough guns or shells to accomplish the desired results.

The new German Chief of Staff, Erich von Falkenhayn, hoped to take advantage of Allied weaknesses to force them to sue for peace by further disabling them militarily and ending their will to continue the struggle. He wrote to the Kaiser, "If we succeed in opening the eyes of her (France's) people to the fact that in a military sense they have nothing more to hope for, that breaking point would be reached and England's best sword would be wiped out of her hand." To achieve that goal, he launched a massive assault on the French stronghold of Verdun beginning in February 1916.

The attack came as a complete surprise to the French High Command. The Germans also had an immense advantage in artillery, particularly heavy guns. They fired as many as a million shells a day in the furious assault. Unlike the failed French offensives of 1915 that had lasted only a few weeks each, this onslaught continued through June and, to a lesser degree, into December. The heavy bombardments destroyed the ordinary trenches, leaving only pieces of trenches. Soldiers felt alone, utterly forsaken, lacking food, letters, or even stretcher-bearers. The battlefield became an enormous slaughterhouse, littered by corpses. A French soldier wrote, "You ate beside the dead. You drank beside the dead. You relieved yourself beside the dead. You slept beside the dead." Eventually, the Germans had to divert three of their divisions to bail out their Austrian allies who were being annihilated by the Russian army in the east. Verdun had held. Its commander, Henri Petain, was dubbed a French national hero and

This unshaven French soldier rests in a trench behind the lines. French soldiers were commonly called "poilus," meaning "the hairy ones."

his slogan, "They shall not pass," became the symbol of French bravado. In the words of one observer, "There was no battle before, and no battle after, which was so important in the French memory." In ten months at Verdun, in a struggle over a few miles of contested territory, 700,000 men were killed or wounded.

The Battle of the Somme

In June 1916, in response to Joffre's urgent appeal to alleviate the German pressure on Verdun, the British launched a major offensive to try to break through the German defenses along the River Somme. Unlike the other combatants, the British had to create a mass army after the war began and arrange to

These Canadian troops climb "over the top" and charge across No-Man's-Land in 1916. Junior officers often led the attack, resulting in six times more deaths than enlisted men.

supply almost a million and a half men. They had, amazingly, succeeded in doing that in less than two years. An "over-educated officer class" who had learned about war from Greek and Roman literature and expected it to be "brave and heroic" led them. It was a great shock to these English officers to discover that war was actually "horrible and nasty and dirty." The British army recruited its regiments by counties or towns, promising those who joined in a group that they would be kept together. These were called "Pals Regiments" because the slogan was "Join up with your pals or your chums." The unfortunate result was that neighborhoods of young men went off together and got killed together. By summer 1916 these new regiments, which had first drilled with broomsticks the year before, felt they were ready to fight. Yet, one commander wrote in his diary that his men, "are still not PROPERLY TRAINED, although full of courage. . . ."

On July 1, 1916, British troops climbed "over the top" (out of their trenches) shoulder to shoulder along an 18-mile front. The Germans had constructed an ingenious trench system that included shell-proof deep shelters for their men. German artillery and machine guns mowed down the waves of British soldiers. Their bodies piled up by the uncut barbed wire. More than 57,000 men fell on that one day, 19,000 of them dead, "swept away by a curtain of fire." It was the bloodiest single day in British military history. Local British newspapers in the next few weeks were filled with pages of pictures of local men who died on the Somme. The Allies fired millions of shells in a relentless barrage. The roar of the guns was "so loud you could hear it in England." The British commander had expected to demolish the German defenses. Instead, he barely dented them. The offensive dragged on until November. A shortage of doctors and stretcher-bearers made the situation even worse. It was difficult to get wounded men to tented casualty stations, and once there, they might lie on stretchers or the ground for days until they could be seen by the handful of exhausted doctors. Over 1.2 million men were killed or wounded on both sides, but the stalemate continued.

France had already suffered more than 3.5 million casualties by the end of 1916. Despite this, there were no calls to pursue peace talks. Most French people were just as determined as ever to dislodge the Germans from their land. In 1917 the French chose Georges Clemenceau as premier. He announced, "Home policy? I wage war! Foreign policy? I wage war! All the time I wage war!" A few months earlier David Lloyd George had become War Premier of Britain with the declared mission of delivering "the knock-out blow" to Germany. In spite of these declarations, the offensives launched by both sides on the western front in 1917 proved to be just as futile as those of the previous years.

The War on Other Fronts

Troops on the eastern front were no more fortunate than the armies in the west. The battered empires staggered as they traded punches. In 1916 the Russians mounted a successful offensive against the Austro-Hungarian armies to relieve the pressure on Allied forces at Verdun and the Somme. Their advances, however, were halted by the intervention of the German army. The Austrians had reached such a level of hopelessness that they were recruiting men in their mid-fifties. The Russians, however, were enduring staggering casualties—7.5 million by 1917, and thousands of desperate peasants, plagued by hunger and disease, were fleeing the eastern front areas.

Meanwhile, the war's impact was widening. In the Far East, Japan, honoring its treaty with Britain, entered the war on the Allied side. They used the opportunity to conquer German possessions in the area and to enhance their own power in relation to China.

In the Middle East, a colorful British officer known as Lawrence of Arabia encouraged Arab princes to revolt against the Ottomans with the promise of support for their own independent states. In December 1917, British forces conquered Jerusalem, a "Christmas present" to cheer up the British people after the grim losses of the previous year. By 1918, using forces from India, Australia, and New Zealand, the British had succeeded in destroying the rest of the Ottoman Empire in the Middle East.

Life in the Trenches

As the war dragged on, the defensive systems became more elaborate. On each side there were two or three consecutive lines of deep trenches connected by passages and strengthened by sandbagged fortifications and snarled thickets of barbed wire. The "no man's land" between the two sides was generally no more than 100 or 200 yards, sometimes no wider than the width of a city street. Bloody petty conflicts frequently broke out over a few yards of terrain. After each engagement rotting corpses and remnants of bodies lay between the lines or entangled in the wires. "Do you want to find your sweetheart" ran the chorus of a cynical British army song. "I know where he is: Hanging on the old barbed wire."

Between sorties each army disturbed the enemy trenches with erratic fire that might land a shell, killing or crippling the occupants. When there was no attack, there was nothing to do all day but listen to the constant noise as shells exploded everywhere. Some active areas in the western front endured an average of a ton of steel and explosives per square yard. At any time, if a soldier poked his head above the parapet, a sniper might kill him. Naturally, this led to feelings of unrelenting anxiety that wore men down. Many men suffered from "shell shock." (Today we call this "post-traumatic stress disorder.") To prevent this, the army tried to restore soldiers' psyches by leaving them in the front line for no more than a week at a time; moving them to reserve trenches for a week, sending them behind the lines for two weeks, and then bringing them back to the front line trenches for a new cycle.

While leaders spoke of war as "kill and be killed," troops in the trenches often developed a system of "live and let live." They made arrangements not to fire on latrines or attack during mealtimes. A German soldier wrote about trenches where "friend and foe alike go to fetch straw from the same rick to protect them from cold and rain —and never a shot is fired." Opposing troops occasionally exchanged mementos or even played a game of soccer. They often buried enemy dead in graves with their own men, perhaps feeling a greater closeness to those who shared the same dreadful experiences than to uncomprehending civilians. Trench life also reinforced bonds of male comradeship, overcoming the usual obstacles of class differences in what one soldier described as the "wholly masculine way of life uncomplicated by women." These men, thrown together in such close quarters, began to take care of each other and even grew to love each other, occasionally passionately.

The horrors, however, outweighed any positive experiences. There was no place to lie down when a soldier was not on duty, so he lay in the mud. Open latrines and rotting bodies gave off horrendous smells. It was, one author-soldier

The Germans used chlorine gas, which affected the nose, throat, and lungs. Later the Germans used other types of gas, including mustard and phosgene. Eventually the Allies also used gas. These carrier pigeons are being stowed in gas-proof cages by German soldiers.

remarked, "the absolute zero of discomfort." In misery, "we fed like pigs, we stank like pigs." Rats and lice invaded the trenches. Rats, "the size of cats," ate corpses and food and nestled next to sleeping soldiers. One poet wrote of his daybreak encounter with a "queer sardonic rat" of "cosmopolitan sympathies," which having touched an English hand "will do the same to a German."

In April 1915 the Germans started a new chapter in total warfare. They opened cylinders of poison (chlorine) gas to try to break through the Allies' defenses. French and Canadian troops watched in horror as a green cloud descended

A German pilot drops a bomb. Such crude bombing methods frequently missed their targets.

nated, rather than killed in combat as it had been defined in the nineteenth century.

It was a great cultural shock to many young men to discover that war was neither heroic or noble. A gas or artillery shell didn't know if a soldier was a coward or a hero when it killed him. As one historian has noted, it was more like "industrial murder." The misery of trench life led some men to almost long for a chance to scramble over their ramparts and break through the enemy lines decisively. Yet, each attempt to do so collapsed in fruitless massacres through 1917. One of the worst was a four-month British offensive in Belgium, known as "Passchendaele." The Allies had 400,000 casualties, and nothing of any significance was accomplished. In World War II a unit's morale was considered to be severely damaged when it lost 10 percent or more of its men in an attack.

on them, burning out their lungs and causing frightful deaths. Gas warfare added another level of cruelty to the war. The great British war poet, Wilfred Owens, tried to convey the horror of death by poison gas:

> If you could hear, at every jolt, the blood
> Come gurgling from the froth-corrupted
>   lungs,
> Obscene as cancer, bitter as the cud
> Of vile, incurable sores on innocent
>   tongues...

Both sides began to use gas warfare. Industry was geared up to produce gas shells so that by 1918 one in every four shells on the western front was a gas shell. Soldiers who couldn't flee their trenches and lacked protection were extermi-

French soldiers spray liquid fire at the enemy. Horrible new weapons were used in World War I, including flamethrowers, poison gas, barbed wire, and machine guns.

In World War I regiments might lose three-fourths of their men in the first hours of an assault and still keep fighting. Increasingly, the ordinary soldier saw himself, in the words of one, as an ingredient for the "sausage machine" because "it was fed with live men, churned out corpses, and remained firmly screwed in place."

Although most common soldiers continued to fight on, many became embittered and despairing of their leadership's ability to ever win this seemingly unending war. A German soldier on the Somme wrote, "Hans is dead. Fritz is dead. Wilhelm is dead. There are many others. I am now quite alone in the company. God grant we may soon be relieved. Our losses are dreadful. . . If only peace would come!" After the particularly disastrous French offensive at Champagne in 1917, "Spontaneously, whole regiments and divisions revolted," a French foreign ministry observer reported. "Alas, this is the price of our military policy of the last three years—2,000,000 casualties. . . . We are heading towards peace by revolution. . . . " He almost proved to be right when mutinous divisions from the Champagne front began to march on Paris, singing a Socialist anthem. They were stopped short of the capital and, in an attempt to restore discipline to the disheartened French Army, French military courts randomly sentenced 253 soldiers to death. Although only a few of the sentences were actually carried out, the incident revealed the level of desperation felt by many soldiers. ("Paths of Glory" is an excellent film about this incident.) Even in Britain, where there were no similar occurrences, many disillusioned soldiers agreed with the words of Siegfried Sassoon in his poem *Attack*:

> And hope with furtive eyes and grappling
> fists,
> Flounders in mud, O Jesus, make it stop!

THE HOME FRONT

As the war continued on, it increasingly involved all of the people in the warring nations. It became the first "total war" in which governments had to organize industries, economies, and even public opinion. War ministries set up boards to regulate factories, control wages and prices, and ration food and vital supplies. Vast bureaucracies arose to mobilize their nations' resources, leading to planned economies. Most European countries had already instituted mass military drafts of millions of young men. Even Great Britain, which had traditionally depended on a volunteer army, instituted conscription in 1916.

Political Mobilization and Public Opinion

Many governments passed sedition laws that made criticism of governmental policies a criminal act. Even socialist parties that had once declared, "the worker has no country," demonstrated their eagerness to support the war effort. The power of central governments dramatically expanded, even in democracies like Britain and France.

This was all the more the case in Germany where the Kaiser had declared, "I no longer recognize (political) parties. I recognize only Germans." By the end of 1916, the Kaiser himself had been reduced to a mere figurehead. The government had become a military dictatorship, controlled by the brutal and arrogant General Erich Ludendorff who completely bent his supposed superior, Commander-in-Chief von Hindenberg, to his will. They decreed that all men between the ages of seventeen and sixty could be subjected to conscription or required to work only in jobs that were essential to the war effort.

From its gun platform mounted on top, a German Zeppelin fires on a fighter plane.

The Germans instituted the first action that sensationally illustrated that the old differentiation between civilians and their armies no longer existed. In 1915 German Zeppelins began bombardment of the civilian population in London and elsewhere in the previously impregnable British Isles. That year, these raids killed over 100 people, including kindergarten children in London's East End. There was little damage to British morale, but, coupled with German submarine sinking of passenger liners, the raids reinforced the popular perception of the Germans as immoral murderers of civilians who must be resisted at all costs. Public feeling was further outraged by more extensive Zeppelin forays in 1916. By the end of the war there had been 52 such raids, killing 852 civilians and shredding the nerves of a population unused to the deaf-

ening blasts of bombs and antiaircraft guns. By this point, British aircraft, equipped with machine guns loaded with a new kind of explosive ammunition, began to shoot down the giant airships. Their awesome plunges to the ground over British territory, enshrouded in spectacular flames, gave British civilians a great feeling of satisfaction. (One couple, who had just witnessed such an event, named their newborn daughter Zeppelina.) Later in the war, the Germans developed gigantic guns, called "Big Berthas" (after the wife of their manufacturer), that had a range of 75 miles. They used them to bombard Paris, reinforcing the lesson that there "were no noncombatants in a total war" and further inflaming Western public opinion about Germany "savagery."

Wartime governments actively employed propaganda to drum up greater enthusiasm. The Germans were the first to press the new medium of moving pictures into war service. They welcomed newsreel cameramen to the battlefield. Their editors, according to a film critic, "rapidly became skilled in using newsreel footage to carry a propaganda weapon, and their war reports became a powerful psychological tool at home and in neutral countries." The British quickly realized the value of this new medium for propaganda. *Britain Prepared*, produced by the British War Office, was a great worldwide success, despite its three-hour running time, and played to capacity houses in America. This led to hundreds of British propaganda films, many with captions in foreign languages. British authorities even brought over the famed American director, D.W. Griffith, who used German newsreels in his fictional film, *Heart of the World*. The film portrayed a French village under brutal German occupation and ended with the American film star, Lillian Gish, barely avoiding rape by a beastly German officer.

British propagandists were particularly active in circulating tales about atrocities committed by the German "Huns," especially against the Belgians. The Germans had, counter to the rules of war at the time, forcibly deported many French and Belgian civilians to work in German factories and mines. Although most of these were men, pamphlets and posters implied that there were women sent to become sex slaves. For example, one poster depicted a clearly virginal young woman being led away by a huge, leering German soldier. (German propaganda was equally outlandish in warning that French African troops would rape German women if the Allies won the war.) One Allied atrocity story described German "corpse factories" that made soap out of the dead. The obvious falsehood of this propaganda, revealed after the war, unfortunately caused many people to disbelieve accounts of the real German atrocities committed in the World War II era.

Women and the War

One of the objects of propaganda was to win the support and encourage the work of women. Feminists were divided as to whether they should maintain their traditional opposition to militarism. In Britain, the militant Pankhursts were so fervent about the war that they changed the name of their suffrage paper to *Britannia*. In it they condemned men who would not protect English womanhood from the brutality of the "Huns." They even launched a campaign to humiliate "cowards" who didn't enlist by publicly presenting them with white feathers. Men, returning from the front wounded and traumatized, were taken aback by the ardor of women's support for the war. One enthusiastic jingle by a female writer declared, "Oh, its you have all the luck, out there in the blood and muck."

Some men protested that women were "sending men to the slaughter." An angry poet expressed these disillusioned soldiers' resentment at this seeming female obliviousness to the real war:

You love us when we're heroes, home on
   leave,
Or wounded in a mentionable place.
You worship decorations; you believe
That chivalry redeems the war's disgrace.
You make us shells.

Posters that were placed throughout public spaces portrayed patriotic working women, devoted to their absent men. Many more women did, in fact, join the work forces. Many found it a "genuinely liberating experience" to support the war effort. Probably most, however, worked to support their families in the absence of male breadwinners. For the first time, they drove trucks, conducted streetcars, and put on police uniforms. As increasing numbers of men left for the trenches, women began to work at jobs in munitions factories and heavy industries, work formerly considered beyond the "capacity of women." As the war's toll continued to grow, even the armed services opened up to women. Although they did not go to the front, they took over many behind-the-line tasks such as typists, cooks, drivers, telephone operators, and mechanics. By 1917, there were over 100,000 women in British auxiliary services like the WAACs (the Women's Auxiliary Army Corps). The unease of society at these enlistments was reflected in the sexual innuendoes directed at the motives of the women who served in the armed forces. Thousands more served as nurses, often dealing with men whose limbs had been smashed or lungs had been destroyed by poison gas.

More than 900,000 British women and almost 700,000 French women got jobs in armaments plants. By 1918, 38 percent of the workers at the giant German Krupp Armaments Works were women. Women munitions workers faced great danger. There were several big explosions, killing or wounding women workers. Wartime censorship prevents us from knowing the exact number of casualties in these accidents. The TNT being produced in these factories was even more dangerous, as it was absorbed through the skin and inhaled. Women turned yellow, and their hair became orange. They would be given a few weeks off and told to drink milk, and they eventually looked better. But, in fact, the long-term consequences included serious illness and even death.

In general, women did their best to cope. Some were desperate. A photo from Berlin shows a line of women waiting to sell their long hair. Although many found jobs in the expanding war economies, their wages never equaled those of men. Men often expressed resentment at this perceived challenge to traditional gender roles, decrying the loss of femininity. On the other hand, young munitions workers were denounced for wasting their new income on jewelry and fur. More importantly, these jobs were considered to be temporary. When the war ended, governments rapidly moved to displace women from the jobs they had once been urged to fill.

Despite this, the war seemed to have a direct impact on the struggle for women's rights. Women were given the right to vote in Great Britain shortly before the end of the war and in Austria and Germany right after the war. Many observers noted the greater independence and social freedoms exercised by young women, particularly of the upper and middle classes, as a result of their wartime experiences.

Other Social and Economic Consequences

Domestic service was probably the chief loser when women entered the workforce. In Britain alone more than one-quarter of female domestics left their jobs. In general, it became more difficult to keep the "serving class" in its place. The battlefield had been a "social leveler" since exploding shells could not distinguish between classes. In fact, aristocratic junior officers who led charges across "no man's land" were three times as likely to be killed as other soldiers were. The chapel of St. Cyr, the French military academy, memorialized the dead of World War I with a single tablet inscribed "the Class of 1914."

Many people believed that class conflict had been eliminated by the war-induced sense of national communities. This certainly did not happen. In fact, the war exacerbated class divisions. The major capitalists made enormous profits from war production, creating public resentment. Skilled workers were often exempted from military service, and the prestige of their unions increased as the governments sought their cooperation in ensuring continued production. The war increased inflation, hitting unskilled workers and middle-class people on fixed incomes the hardest. Their dissatisfaction would be a significant factor in the postwar years.

Discontent and Revolution

As the casualties of the war mounted and civilian deprivations got worse, nations on both sides experienced growing discontent. The British blockade led to serious food shortages in Germany. By 1917, food rations were down to a mere 1000 calories, barely enough for subsistence. Poor people were living on turnips when potato production plummeted. It has been estimated that 750,000 German civilians starved to death during the war. The number of strikes increased dramatically, culminating in an April 1917 strike by 200,000 Berlin workers protesting reduced rations. Socialists and some liberals in Germany and Austria called for peace negotiations.

Strikes also increased in Britain and France, as did opposition to the war. The British government began to censor newspapers. In France, after the army mutiny, the government worried that dissent might weaken the will to win. One editor of an antiwar newspaper was actually executed for treason. Clemenceau's government drafted other critical newspapermen. Rising opposition to the war by civilians in Italy led one leader to warn in 1917, "We are living on a volcano."

Irish nationalists saw the struggle against Germany as an opportunity to win independence. On Easter Sunday 1917, Irish rebels occupied government buildings in Dublin. After six days, the "Easter Rebellion" was crushed, fifteen of its leaders executed, and many more imprisoned. Although this event was barely noticed by the British public, it was an important step in the eventual independence of southern Ireland.

Nationalist groups in the Austro-Hungarian Empire were more successful in thwarting the war effort. Czechs, Poles, and others vigorously worked for their own self-determination, rather than for Austrian war aims. Francis Joseph, the old Emperor, died in 1916 after a 68-year reign. His people, suffering severe food shortages, barely noticed. In fact, conditions had grown so bad that an Austrian official warned, "if the monarchs of the Central Powers cannot make peace in the coming months, it will be made for them by their peoples."

Even though the belligerent governments rejected any move to negotiated peace as "defeatism," anti-war activists made their way to peace conventions at the neutral site of The Hague in the Netherlands. Militant socialists who revived earlier opposition to "workers killing workers" began to meet in Switzerland, led by Vladimir Lenin.

Despite all this tumult, Europeans in most nations continued to bear the hardships of the war and fought on. The collapse that many had prophesied for all of Europe actually took place in Russia where conditions were the most desperate.

REVOLUTION IN RUSSIA

One historian has commented that the Russian people and army, by 1917, had suffered nearly nine million casualties (other observers put the number between seven to eight million). "The real problem," he notes, "is not to explain why they finally revolted or why the revolution took such a catastrophic turn, but why it was so long in coming."

When Russia first declared war there was a tremendous outburst of patriotic zeal and fidelity to the Czar and his regime. It seemed as if Nicholas II was being given a second chance to reconcile his government with the mass of his people even after the disastrous policies that had followed the Revolution of 1905. Conservatives and Pan-Slavists viewed the war as a chance to erase the humiliation of the Russo-Japanese War and to emancipate their Slavic "little brothers" in the Balkans. Reformers and liberals hoped that fighting on the same side as France and Britain, modern democracies, would bring basic changes to Russia once the war was won.

Unfortunately, Russia's leaders were not capable of dealing with the tribulations of modern warfare. As a result, the war simply intensified the defects of the regime. The Russian army would often take the offensive to relieve pressure on its Western allies, even under the most adverse conditions. One such battle in 1916, designed to divert German troops from Verdun, took place in knee deep mud. Infantrymen, lacking food and ammunition, slogged ahead until an Arctic wind came in, freezing the wounded to death before they could be evacuated. The result of this disaster was 250,000 casualties. The red tape and corruption endemic to the Czarist bureaucracy caused the front to be chronically short of weapons. There were many battles in which two-thirds of the Russian soldiers had nothing more than a bayonet on a stick. They waited for others to fall to pick up their rifles. A Russian infantryman told a visiting Englishman, "You know sir, we have no weapon except the soldier's breast." Another added, "This is not war, sir. It is slaughter." The incredibly heavy early losses suffered by the Russian Army also annihilated a generation of competent young

Rasputin, a self-proclaimed spiritual healer, was embraced by Alexandra, who believed he could help heal her son.

professional officers who might have been an effective barrier against revolution. The necessities of the front aggravated the deterioration of the Russian economy in rural areas and cities.

Even as conditions worsened, the Czar refused to consider any reform of his absolute rule. Paradoxically, the least competent monarch ruled the most autocratic government in Europe. His most positive quality, absolute devotion to his family, ironically reinforced his worst flaws. His wife, Alexandra, a German-born princess, was headstrong and shallow. She, in turn, was under the sway of the "monk," Rasputin, a combination of holy man and con man. Using his seeming ability to control the bleeding of their hemophiliac son and heir, Rasputin exerted his power to cause the dismissal of enlightened and competent officials and even the dissolving of the Duma (Parliament). "Russia loves to feel the whip. . . . How I wish I could pour my will into your veins, " Alexandra wrote her husband, "Be the Emperor, be Peter the Great, Ivan the Terrible. . . crush them all under you—Now don't you laugh naughty one. . . ." Nicholas replied with, "Tender thanks for your severe written scolding," and closed his letter, "Your poor little weak-willed hubby."

Finally, even conservative aristocratic supporters of autocracy had enough. They assassinated Rasputin in December 1916. (The murder was particularly grisly as it required a huge dose of cyanide, shooting, and stabbing to do away with the resilient monk.) This accomplished little as Alexandra clung more adamantly to her devotion to absolutism. It was far too late to save the regime.

The March Revolution

The revolutionary leader, Leon Trotsky, remarked that, although both the regime and its adversaries had long been expecting revolution, both were caught by surprise when it actually erupted right in their faces. A police report had warned in November 1916, ". . . the industrial proletariat of the capital is on the verge of despair. . . the smallest outbreak due to any pretext will lead to uncontrollable riots." February 23, 1917 (March 8 on our calendar) was International Women's Day. On that day, thousands of women in Petrograd (formerly St. Petersburg) started a bread riot. They were tired of waiting in long lines for bread. By 1917 the ordinary working woman was spending 40 hours a week in those lines, often sleeping outside bakeries overnight to be first in line. The shortage of coal and firewood was an added grievance. The presence in the capital of thousands of demoralized soldiers and ex-soldiers, who would rather destroy society than return to the front, added to the combustibility of the situation.

As the women marched through working class districts, thousands of male factory workers joined them. By the time they reached the city's center, there were, at least, 100,000 people in the mob. In the next few days, thousands more, students, curious spectators, officers, as well as workers, flowed into the churning throngs. Shouts of "Down with the Autocracy" or "Down with the German Woman," (the Czarina) echoed through the streets. The chief of the military district was incapable of dealing with the situation. On March 11, obeying the command of the Czar to stop the "disorders," he turned a chaotic demonstration into a revolution by ordering his soldiers to fire into the unarmed civilians. Thousands of troops mutinied, horrified at the idea that they might be ordered to shoot at women and children. They marched from the Garrison, occupied key government buildings, arrested government ministers, and opened prison gates. Even the Cossacks, "age-old subduers and punishers," in the words of Trotsky, refused to fire on their comrades.

The recently dissolved Duma met and agreed to establish a Provisional Government on March 12. At the same time, a rival authority was set up as lower class radicals and soldiers resurrected the workers' soviet (council), a product of the 1905 revolution. Nicholas, heading to the front to rally his troops, was intercepted by railway workers. Soldiers detained him and his family. On March 15 the Czar abdicated. The 350-year-old Russian monarchy had collapsed in one week.

The Provisional Government

The Provisional Government was initially in the hands of the Constitutional Democrats, moderates who hoped to establish a liberal republic. Unfortunately, they also believed that Russia's honor required it to live up to its obligations to the Allies by continuing the war against the Central Powers. Soviets sprang up throughout the nation in rural area, factories and cities, and even in army units. They competed with the Provisional Government for authority and were quickly organized by various socialist groups. Peasants began to seize land from the aristocracy. Food shortages persisted in the cities. Meanwhile, the military situation continued to disintegrate. Order No. 1, issued by the Petrograd soviet, created further mischief by destroying military discipline. It encouraged soldiers to replace their officers with committees of "elected representatives of the lower ranks."

The deteriorating situation led the Provisional Government to give the position of prime minister to the moderate Socialist Revolutionary Alexander Kerensky, an outstanding orator who was "the darling of the Petrograd intelligencia." The theatrical Kerensky was adored by many young women who sent him love poetry. He believed that he was the man destined to lead Russia out of disorder into salvation. But Kerensky was too young (in his thirties) and inexperienced for such a momentous task.

In the summer of 1917 Kerensky decided to launch a military offensive despite the warnings of his generals that the army was too undisciplined and weakened, as well as badly supplied, to sustain an attack. When he toured the front, an ordinary soldier ran up to him and observed, "You say we should go and fight the Germans so that we, the peasant soldiers, can go home to our villages and divide up the land. But, what's the use of my fighting Germans if I'm dead and there's no land to have?" However, Kerensky ignored this warning. The resulting July offensive was a total failure. Masses of peasant soldiers deserted and returned to their villages to participate in the seizure of lands, voting, as Lenin later put it, with their feet.

VLADIMIR LLYICH ULYANOV—LENIN

The Bolshevik Revolution

In April 1917, hoping to subvert the Russian government, the Germans sent the brilliant Bolshevik leader, V.I. Lenin, and several of his followers in a sealed train from his exile in Switzerland through Germany to Petrograd. Lenin had become a fanatical opponent of the Czarist State at the age of seventeen when his beloved older brother was executed for his part in a plot to assassinate the Czar. He developed into a dedicated Marxist who chose exile in Switzerland after serving some time in Siberia. As leader of the Bolshevik faction of the Russian Social Democratic Party, Lenin argued that a revolutionary "vanguard" of activists must be formed to bring the destruction of capitalism and the Russian government.

When Lenin emerged from his railroad car, he issued his "April Theses." In this document he maintained that Russia must withdraw from the war; the soviets must overthrow the government; private land must be redistributed to the peasants and factories put into the hands of committees of workers. Simple, but effective, slogans summarized his program: "All Power to the Soviets," and "Peace, Land, and Bread." Rising agitation by the Petrograd soviet, stirred up by Lenin's close associate, Leon Trotsky, led the government to round up Bolshevik leaders. Lenin had to flee to Finland. An attempted military coup, however, forced Kerensky to turn to the Petrograd soviet for support and to release the Bolsheviks. This series of events discredited and exposed the weakness of the Provisional Government. The Mensheviks and Socialist Revolutionaries, old socialist opponents of the Bolsheviks, had destroyed their credibility by being part of the incompetent government.

Now that the Bolsheviks had obtained majorities in the Moscow and Petrograd soviets, Lenin decided that the time was ripe to overthrow the Kerensky government. It was important to accomplish this before elections to the planned Constituent Assembly that might stabilize the government. Crowds of Bolshevik supporters stormed the Winter Palace, now the seat of the Provisional Government. In the basement, much to their delight, they found a supply of the Czar's finest wines. The looting of the cellar and resulting carousing continued for several weeks. The Bolsheviks were forced to impose martial law on Petrograd. By the new year, the city "perhaps with the biggest hangover in history," awoke to a new order under Bolshevik control.

The Bolsheviks (now called Communists) had to deal with the newly elected Constituent Assembly convened in January 1918. The Bolsheviks had been badly defeated in the free elections by the Socialist Revolutionaries. Lenin immediately dissolved the Constituent Assembly by force, declaring that the assembly had engaged in "a most desperate struggle against the Soviet power. . ." To win the support of the masses, Lenin proclaimed that land (that the peasants had already seized) was to be nationalized and turned over to rural peasant soviets. Factories were to be placed under the direction of workers' committees. Although Lenin considered both of these actions to be interim expedients, they did help build popular support, as did social reforms protecting women's rights.

In Petrograd on May 1, 1917, crowds celebrate the collapse of the czarist monarchy.

Most importantly, Lenin had promised peace to the weary Russian people. The Germans, having the upper hand, imposed the Treaty of Brest-Litovsk in March 1918. Russia was forced to yield eastern Poland, the Ukraine, Finland, and the Baltic lands and to pay a heavy indemnity to the Germans. The Germans showed how uncompromising they would be in victory. To Lenin this disastrously high price was unavoidable as he needed time to bring order to a shattered and chaotic Russia. He also firmly believed that communist revolutions would soon spread through Europe, rendering the treaty moot.

Real peace did not come to Russia, however, as the nation dissolved into civil war. Trotsky's newly organized Red Army faced a "White" Army created by army officers loyal to the czar and supported by the varied opponents of Lenin, including liberals, socialists and aristocrats. In 1918, the Allies sent in thousands of troops to different parts of Russia with the initial goal of bringing their former ally back into the war. In the summer of 1918 the Bolsheviks slaughtered the Czar, his wife, son, four daughters, their doctor, three servants, and even their little dog. By 1921 the Communists had succeeded in taking firm control of Russia and in setting up a centralized dictatorial state.

Russia's withdrawal from the war made it possible for the Germans to concentrate all their troops on the western front. This might have resulted in a German victory, but another element entered the equation. The original March Russian Revolution meant that all the Allies were now democratic, reinforcing American sympathies for the "forces of freedom."

AMERICA ENTERS THE WAR

Initially, Americans were shocked and dismayed by the Great War. "Civilization is all gone, and barbarism come," one writer lamented. President Woodrow Wilson declared neutrality and

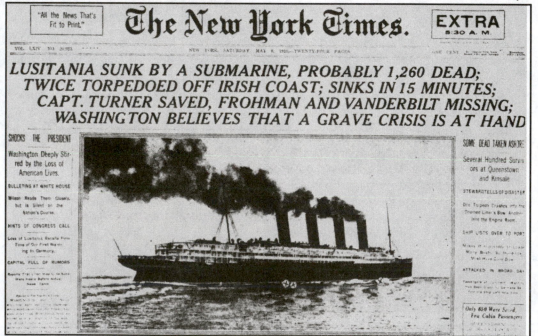

Black German submarines, U-boats, lurked beneath the ocean's surface. They preyed on defenseless British and French cargo and passenger ships during the early years of World War I.

urged Americans to be impartial "in thought as well as in action," to show "the dignity of self-control." Despite the feeling expressed in a popular American song, "I didn't raise my boy to be a soldier, to kill some other mother's darling boy," many American leaders felt emotional ties to the British. Wilson himself believed that a German victory "would change the course of our civilization and make the United States a military nation." British propaganda made effective use of these sentiments by emphasizing the "atrocities" committed by the barbarous German "Huns" against innocent civilians in neutral Belgium.

Britain was determined to use its naval superiority to cripple Germany economically. The British, "ruling the waves and waiving the rules," stopped American merchant ships and seized their cargoes bound for Germany. In violation of international law, the British even planted deadly mines throughout the North Sea. American ships may well have been sunk if the U.S. had chosen to challenge the British by sending them into the area unescorted. Instead, the presi-

dent protested in a formal note. He never entertained any serious notion of action against the Allies since he believed, as he told his advisors, "Gentlemen, the Allies are standing with their back to the walls fighting wild beasts."

German violations that, unlike the British actions, destroyed both life and property, aroused far more anger. The Germans had developed a frightening new weapon: the U-boat, a submarine equipped with torpedoes. In February 1915, determined to weaken the blockade and disrupt Allied trade, Germany announced a war zone around the British Isles where ships were likely to be sunk. The Germans felt that Wilson's resulting protests were unfair. Their submarines were fragile and so small that they had crews of only a few men. If they surfaced to give warnings, as Wilson demanded, they could easily be rammed and destroyed. They sank several ships culminating in the sinking of the British luxury liner, the *Lusitania* in May 1915. Among the 1,198 dead were 128 Americans. Americans were outraged, declaring, "The torpedo which sank the *Lusitania* also sank Germany in the opinion of mankind." (Historians later discovered that the ship's cargo had included ammunition.) Wilson demanded that Germany pledge to end unrestricted submarine warfare.

For a while it appeared that Wilson's approach, resolute but restrained, was working. German Chancellor Bethmann, dismayed by the anger of the American public, wanted to abandon submarine warfare. German naval leaders opposed him. The Kaiser shifted between these views. After some further sinkings, Wilson warned Germany that "the United States can have no choice but to sever diplomatic relations" if German attacks continued. This threat caused the Germans to back down and pledge that they would no longer sink merchant vessels without warning.

By 1917, however, German military leaders were winning their argument that the U-boat, their best weapon, should be used to its fullest extent. They contended that, even if America declared war, they could defeat the British by cutting off supplies before American troops could reach the front. The German Foreign Secretary, Arthur Zimmermann, even held out hope that "America will do nothing because Wilson is for peace and nothing else." The Chief of the German naval staff assured the Kaiser that Americans were "disorganized and undisciplined" and pledged, "I give your Majesty my word as an officer, that not one American will land on the continent." Bolstered by this counsel, the Kaiser sent a secret message to his navy declaring, "I order that unrestricted submarine warfare be launched with the greatest vigor on February 1." Wilson then broke off diplomatic relations, as he had promised.

Despite this, the German policy of victory at any price appeared to be paying off. In February alone, U-boats sank 781,500 tons of Allied shipping. In March two German submarines torpedoed clearly marked American ships. America declared war on April 2, 1917. Meanwhile, the German U-boat attacks had succeeded in reducing Britain to a six-week supply of food. When American Rear Admiral William Sims concluded, "Looks as if the Germans are winning the war," his British counterpart replied, "They will unless we stop these losses." Sims convinced the British that the way to counter this menace was to send merchant ships in swarms, guarded by circling destroyers—the convoy system. The convoys rapidly cut the rate of loss in half, convincing military planners that the German submarines would not be able to stop the flow of American troops to France. These troops would be crucial since, after years of terrible trench warfare, the Allies were on the verge of collapse.

A symbolic division of the regular American army had been rushed to France by July 1917 in time to participate in celebrations in Paris. As they paraded through the streets of Paris, they were welcomed tumultuously by the French people to whom they represented the promise of an end to the war. The ecstatic crowds shouted, "Vive les Teddies!" A brief ceremony was held at Lafayette's Tomb. There an aide of American General John Pershing pronounced the slogan that would capture French and American imaginations: "Lafayette, we are here!" It was clear that the French army, physically and morally wounded, required a summer of rest. There would be no great offensive for the rest of the year, giving Pershing time to build up American forces for 1918. Although there were fewer than 300,000 American soldiers in France in March 1918, by July Pershing had a million men under his command. The arrival of hundreds of thousands of fresh American troops caused the Allies to regain numerical superiority. (By the end of the war they had 600,000 more men un-

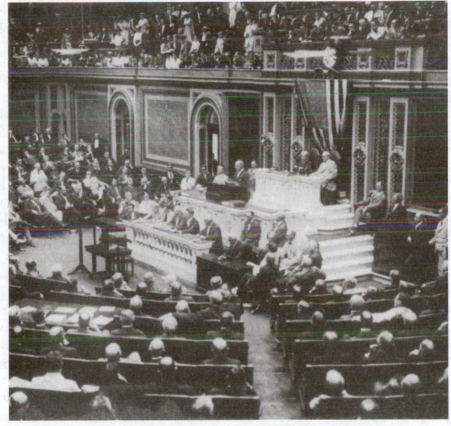

President Woodrow Wilson addressed Congress on February 3, 1917. Wilson announced that the United States was breaking diplomatic relations with Germany,

der arms than the Germans.) This, along with material aid from American farms and factories, was a key factor in the ultimate Allied triumph. The German gamble had failed.

THE END OF THE WAR AND THE SEARCH FOR PEACE

1918: The Last Offensive

Despite rising restlessness among the German population, the withdrawal of Russia from the war persuaded General Ludendorff and the German High Command to gamble on one last grand offensive in the west. Ludendorff hoped to drive the British back hundreds of miles from

the Somme to the sea. He expected that this would cause the French to collapse before vast numbers of Americans could arrive. Historians have characterized the war as "the blind war," one that had lost any direction. The means employed were no longer proportional to the ends that could be achieved, but the war went on and on like a machine with no controls. Ludendorff, like most of the generals, had no sense of where he was going or how to stop it. Instead, he continued to launch another offensive to gain the "mythical breakthrough." The Germans initially did drive the British back a considerable distance all the way to the Marne. They moved so fast, however, that the infantry outran their supporting artillery, ultimately dooming the foot soldiers. Like the British and French, the Germans were running dangerously short of manpower. Yet Ludendorff was trying to end the war by killing large numbers of soldiers. It was, in the words of one historian, "lunacy—a prescription for disaster." The Allies launched a counteroffensive at the Second Battle of the Marne in July 1918. By this time, they were able to utilize to some degree the newest weapons: tanks supported by airplanes. The Allies were also bolstered by the arrival of 140,000 fresh American troops. They began an inexorable advance toward Germany. The disintegrating German armies had suffered more than two million casualties between the spring and summer of 1918.

The German war machine had collapsed. Germany faced the unenviable prospect of an unending supply of American troops and equipment. Mutiny had spread among its armed forces and starving urban dwellers. Turkey and Austria-Hungary, its allies, had sued for peace. Wilson, backed by the Allies, declared that he would negotiate only with a "democratic Germany." The unhappy Kaiser was forced to abdicate and flee to neutral Holland where he took up gardening. The new government quickly agreed to Allied terms, hoping for a peace based upon Wilson's idealistic declarations in favor of a "peace without victory." Firing did not cease immediately. More soldiers on both sides died in the few days left to reach the symbolism of ending the Great War at 11:00 A.M. of the 11th day of the 11th month (November 11, 1918). Pilots who flew over the war zone watched the great guns being silenced. Men broke into tears and wild cheering. Enemies cautiously approached each other and began exchanging food and souvenirs. Corporal Adolf Hitler, however, sitting with his eyes covered with bandages, was shocked to hear about the German defeat. Right then and there, he vowed to find those "November criminals," responsible for the "stab in the back" that was the only possible explanation for Germany's loss.

The Fourteen Points

The combatants had accepted President Wilson's Fourteen Points as the basis of the peace negotiations. Well before America's entry into the war, the Allies had signed agreements to gain territory and indemnities at the expense of the Central Powers. The new Bolshevik government in Russia had threatened to publish the terms of these secret treaties. Wilson hoped to create a new and better world order.

In a January 1918 address to Congress, Wilson presented his Fourteen Points, which were designed to ensure a world "made fit to live in." One of the central ideas was "open covenants, openly arrived at." This implied a rejection of the self-serving secret treaties that many perceived to be a cause of World War I. The new moral order would also include freedom of the seas, freer trade, disarmament, readjustment of colonial claims to reflect the interests of the peoples involved, and "self-determination" for the subject peoples of the former Austro-Hungarian and Turkish Empires. The new boundaries would be based on the language spoken in each area. (Such "linguistic nationalism" proved difficult to achieve in the intertwining of peoples of Central and Eastern Europe and remains problematic even today.) In Wilson's view, the fourteenth point was the most important. It called for a "general association of nations" (or League of Nations) to maintain world peace. The idealistic Wilson believed that these points were "the moral climax of this final war for human liberty," and Germans assumed they would be the basis for the peace treaty to be negotiated.

The Big Four (left to right) British Prime Minister David Lloyd George, Italian Prime Minister Vittorio Orlando, French Prime Minister Georges Clemenceau, and U. S. President Woodrow Wilson.

The Peace Conference and the Treaty of Versailles

Wilson decided to personally lead the American Peace Commission delegation, risking his personal prestige. On December 4, 1918, delighted Americans lined the docks to cheer the first American president to go to Europe while in office. The war-weary people of Europe also responded enthusiastically to his eloquent prescriptions for peace. He was met with joyful frenzy in a march up the Champs-Elysees in Paris. At the docks in England, children threw flowers in his path. Passionate Italian crowds shouted, "Viva Wilson, king of peace." One ardent adherent even compared his arrival to the Second Coming of Christ.

The other Allied leaders, who met in the peace conference at Versailles Palace, near Paris, in January 1919, were less enthusiastic about Wilson's moralistic ideas. The war had caused their nations far more grievous damage than the United States. Britain's tough Prime Minister, David Lloyd George, had helped his party win victory with the slogan, "Hang the Kaiser." He was committed to British colonial expansion and reparations from Germany. France's "tiger" Georges Clemenceau, whose nation had suffered the most, was resolute in his conviction that Germany mush be punished and prevented from ever making war again. The Italians and Japanese pressed for territorial advantage. The other world leaders were not impressed by Wilson's vision of a new world order. The cynical Clemenceau best expressed their views when he supposedly observed, "God gave us the Ten Commandments and we broke them. Wilson gave us his Fourteen Points—we shall see." At the conference, Wilson was forced to compromise the idealism of the Fourteen Points to per-

The Versailles Peace Treaty signed in 1919 required Germany to relinquish land, make cash reparations, and keep its armed forces at a minimum.

suade skeptical European statesmen to place the covenant of the League of Nations in the treaty. He convinced himself that any faults in the treaty could be corrected later by the League.

On June 28, 1919, the Germans reluctantly signed the Treaty of Versailles that had emerged from negotiations. It stripped Germany of all its colonies. The French, who had pushed for a permanently divided Germany, settled for a return of Alsace and Lorraine (which had been taken from them in the 1871 Franco-Prussian war), control over the coal-rich Saar Basin for fifteen years, and a demilitarized zone in the Rhineland. In the east, the newly recognized Polish state was given a corridor to the sea that cut off Germany from its eastern section and created resentment. Wilson's plan for universal disarmament applied to Germany alone, which was

limited to an army of 100,000 and forbidden any heavy armaments.

Treaties with the other Central Powers (Austria, Hungary, the Ottoman Empire, and Bulgaria) created a series of new nations in Central and Eastern Europe out of the old empires. These new nations included Finland, Poland, Latvia, Estonia, Lithuania, and Czechoslovakia. Austria was separated from Hungary, and the latter lost three-quarters of its territory. Serbia was rewarded by being able to form a new south Slav state, Yugoslavia, combining Serbs, Croats, and Slovenes. Many of these new nations were inherently unstable. The people of eastern Europe were so intermingled that neat divisions along ethnic lines was unattainable. Almost every new state had minority problems that endangered future peace in the region. Unhappy

Europe After World War I

Newly Created Nations

Other Territorial Changes

Germans in Poland and Czechoslovakia became the source of future conflict. The unstable combination of peoples in Yugoslavia has continued to create problems to this day. Austrians, with their empire gone and their economy shattered, hoped to merge with Germany, but the treaty specifically prohibited such a solution. In the Middle East, the Arab lands of the Ottoman Empire were divided up and awarded to the League of Nations that, in turn, gave them to Britain and France to administer as "mandates." This was simply a thinly-disguised form of imperialism that went counter to Wilson's promise of self-determination and Allied wartime statements assuring recognition of independent states in the region.

The Allies, who had been devastated by the war, wanted the Germans to pay huge, unrealistic "reparations" for war damages. The treaty did not set a total for reparations. As a compromise, it was decided that a future commission would determine the sum, which would be substantial. (The Germans ultimately paid less than one-quarter of the amount the commission set.) The treaty included a "war guilt" clause to justify the reparations. Under this clause the Germans "accepted the responsibility" for the damages of the war, caused by "the aggression of Germany." Most Germans saw this as an attack on their honor and blamed the hapless new democratic government for accepting these onerous terms. It provided an opening for later demagogues. Yet millions who had lost their loved ones needed to feel that those who they considered responsible were somehow paying the price for their actions.

If the purpose of the Treaty of Versailles was to prevent future wars and end the German menace, it was not successful. In practical terms, it was either too harsh or too lenient. Certainly it was too severe to be considered a "peace without victory." It created resentments in Germany that would undermine its newly created democratic government and would help lead to the rise of Hitler. On the other hand, its terms were not nearly as onerous as those the Germans would have imposed on the Allies had they won (as shown by the Treaty of Brest-Litovsk with Russia). The treaty did not destroy German economic and military strength as the French had hoped. Thus, it succeeded in creating the worst of both worlds—an embittered Germany that could again disrupt the peace of the world. Some historians have contended that the real problem with the peace settlement was lack of enforcement rather than its terms. This failure was insured when the United States, which had become the leading economic power in the world, declined to accept the responsibilities that its new role implied by refusing to ratify the Treaty of Versailles or join the League of Nations. Perhaps, in the words of a British historian, the competing goals of "revenge and reconciliation are incompatible. They tried both and got neither."

CONCLUSION

The most conservative estimates are that 10 million young men died on the battlefields of World War I, and, at least, 30 million more were wounded, many horribly mutilated. Many were incapable of ever again functioning normally in societies that sought to ignore them. Most Eu-

ropeans (and Americans) did not want to be constantly reminded of the true nature of war. Returning soldiers, expecting great changes in their societies, as a result of the sacrifices of war, were quickly disillusioned. Postwar poets and writers reflected these feelings of cynicism and festering anger at the meaninglessness of the conflict and their sacrifices. In Great Britain alone 2500 war poets were published. Most gave voice to their grief for:

> The unreturning army that was youth;
> The legions who have suffered and are
> dust.

The war was an enormous tragedy, not just because of its horrendous toll in human life but also because of all the unfinished business that remained. It never really settled the issue of the balance of power in Europe and the role of Germany. Once Germany was rebuilt, it would again become the most powerful nation in Europe. Another war ultimately had to be fought to finally bury this issue. The yearnings of the millions of returning veterans for the sense of community and comradeship they had experienced in the front lines helped fuel the Fascist movement that arose after the Great War.

On a practical level, the first total war led to increasing centralization of government power. The age of the dominance of Western Europe over world affairs came to an end. The Russian Revolution created a new center of power, and the pivotal role of the United States demonstrated its ascendancy on the world scene. America, however, refused to accept the responsibilities that its new role implied, and the Soviets, as a result of international pressure and domestic exigencies, turned inward. A resurgent and dangerous Germany filled the power vacuum thus created.

The Great War, on a deeper level, permanently changed the way people thought about war. The terrible cost in human life and misery made it difficult for people to believe in the same unqualified patriotism they had felt at the beginning of World War I. People became more suspicious of ringing rhetoric like "the war to end all wars" or "the war to make the world safe for democracy." On the other hand, the growing numbers of dead and wounded numbed people to feelings of horror about the deaths of soldiers and even civilians. What one historian has called, "the banalization of violence" can be traced to World War I. People still question why the wholesale killing was needed in the Great War and in conflicts today as well. In the end, the story of the war may be one of "idealism betrayed."

Suggestions for Further Reading

Gail Braybon, *Women Workers in the First World War: The British Experience* (1981).

Robert H. Ferrell, Woodrow *Wilson and World War I, 1917-1921* (1983).

Franz Fischer, *War of Illusions* (1975).

Sheila Fitzpatrick, The *Russian Revolution* (1982).

Martin Gilbert, *The First World War: A Complete History* (1994).

Maurine W. Greenwald, *Women, War and Work* (1980).

Samuel Hynes, *A War Imagined: The First World War and English Culture* (1991).

Jurgen Kocka, *Facing Total War: German Society, 1914-1918* (1984).

Bernadotte E. Schmitt and Harold C. Vederler, *The World in the Crucible, 1914-1919* (1984).

Leonard *Smith, Between Mutiny and Obedience: The Case of the French Fifth Infantry Division During World War I* (1994).

Edmund Taylor, *The Fall of the Dynasties* (1963).

Barbara Tuchman, *The Guns of August* (1962).

Trevor Wilson, *The Myriad Faces of War: Britain and the Great War, 1914-1918* (1986).

J.M. Winter and R.M Wall, *The Upheaval of War: Family, Work, and Welfare in Europe, 1914-1918* (1988).

THE INTERWAR ERA
1920-1939

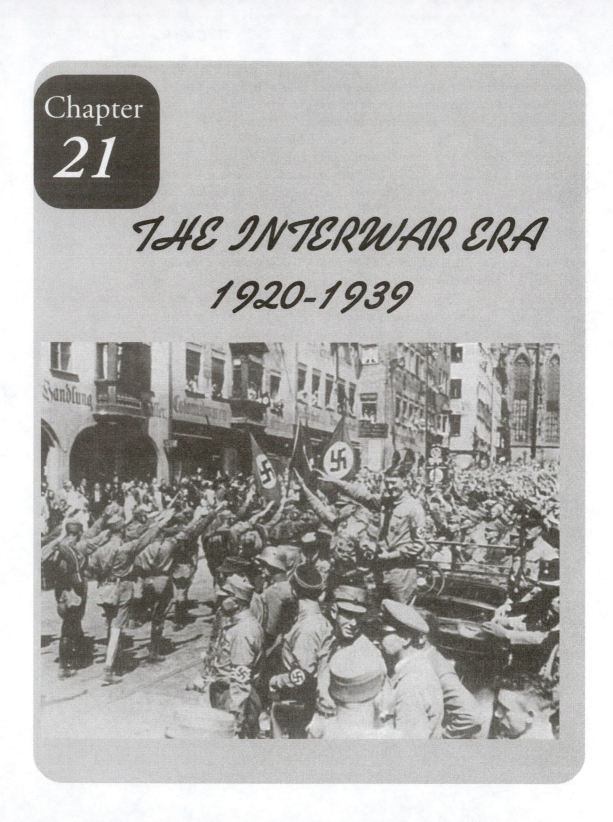

Leni Riefenstahl was born in Berlin, Germany, in 1902. Before Leni's thirteenth birthday in 1915, the first of two world wars had engulfed Europe and caught up in its camaraderie and destruction millions of young men, including an Austrian named Adolf Hitler who served the German army in a Bavarian regiment. In 1918, as the First World War drew to a close, Hitler lay in a hospital, temporarily blinded by a poison gas attack, and was dismayed to learn of Germany's surrender in the November armistice. For Hitler, the shock of 1918 led him eventually into politics and the rise of the Nazi party. For Leni Riefenstahl, 1918 was a year that transformed her life as well. Only sixteen years of age in 1918, the young, pretty, and athletic daughter of a strict father began secretly that year to take dance lessons against his wishes. She had found her calling. When her father found out about Leni's dancing, he sent her off to boarding school. At the boarding school Leni was able to act and to write film scripts, sports articles, and short stories. She was also secretly able to continue dancing. When Leni graduated at twenty-one years of age, she began a career in professional dancing with her father's belated and reluctant acceptance.

Leni developed into a highly talented dancer, touring Europe and delighting audiences. She was her own choreographer and costume designer, and she selected her own music. But then in 1925, as Adolf Hitler tried to revive his political movement after its disastrous 1923 failed coup, Leni cracked her knee while dancing in Prague, Czechoslovakia. After consulting several specialists, Leni was still not certain of her prognosis or her future in dancing. While waiting for a train to take her to another doctor, Leni saw a movie poster advertising **The Mountain of Destiny**, a film directed by Arnold Fanck. Instead of catching her train, Leni went to see the movie and was so captivated she looked up Fanck and convinced him to star her in his next film. While Leni recovered from her knee injury, Fanck wrote the script for **The Holy Mountain**, one of many in a genre of mountain adventure movies for which he was famous, with Leni in mind as the lead actress. Between 1926 and 1933, as Hitler and his Nazi Party grew increasingly successful, coming to power by 1933, Leni Riefenstahl starred in five Fanck mountain films and attained national and even European-wide fame.

By 1932, Leni had moved into other aspects of filmmaking. In that year she directed her first film, **The Blue Light**. She not only directed the movie, she was producer, editor, and lead actress. In 1933, two fans of Leni's films called her to meet them in Berlin: the new German Chancellor, Adolf Hitler, and his propaganda minister, Joseph Göbels. At their meeting, Hitler asked Leni to oversee the artistic content of German films and to begin filming the annual Nazi Party rallies held at Nuremberg. Leni, at first, refused both requests, citing her lack of political awareness due to having been out of the country filming movies and her inexperience with documentary filmmaking. But with no other work in sight due to Nazi policy in the film industry, and with the assurance that she *would have her own film crews, Leni agreed to film the party congresses. She made three Nazi Party rally films, **Victory of Faith** (1933), **Triumph of the Will** (1934), and **Day of Freedom** (1935). The most famous of these was **Triumph of the Will**, in which Leni expertly developed techniques and effects of camera angles, shot selection, musical accompaniment, and camera movement that depicted the 1934 Nazi Party rally in such dramatic, powerful fashion that her documentary work became powerful propaganda, at least in the eyes of countries suspicious of Hitler.*

*In 1936 the International Olympic Committee commissioned Leni to film the 1936 Berlin Olympic Games. The resulting film, **Olympia**, won international acclaim as documentary film but also was considered by many as an example of more propaganda. Although for her the films were artistic efforts, not political inspirations, Leni's service to the Nazi state won for her a great deal of criticism, suspicion, and outright hostility after World War II. She faced arrest, imprisonment, and questioning before being cleared of war crimes. While Hitler's rise to power brought Germany to the brink of destruction, Leni Riefenstahl's association with Hitler brought the near-destruction of her career. Her work since the war has had to proceed without financial support due to the taint of Nazism.*

Chronology

1918 Russian civil war begins, pitting Reds vs. Whites

1919 Weimar constitution adopted in Germany
Germany accepts the Versailles Treaty

1922 Käthe Kollwitz paints *The Survivors*
Germany and Russia make the Rapallo agreement
Mussolini's March on Rome

1923 Ruhr crisis
Hitler's failed Beer Hall Putsch

1924 Dawes Plan adopted ending Ruhr crisis
Lenin dies, Stalin moves for power

1925 Locarno pacts signed

1926 Germany admitted to the League of Nations

1928 Kellogg-Briand Pact

1929 Young Plan adopted
All Quiet on the Western Front published
Wall Street stock crash heralds Depression

1931 Vienna bank, Creditanstalt, fails as the Depression engulfs Europe

1933 Adolf Hitler becomes Chancellor of Germany

1934 Adolf Hitler becomes Führer of Germany
Stalin's Great Purge begins
Nazi purge of the S.A. carried out

1935 Hitler announces German rearmament
Italian invasion of Ethiopia

1936 Remilitarization of the Rhineland
Spanish Civil War begins

1938 Anschluss of Austria
Kristallnacht attacks on German Jews
Munich Accords dismember Czechoslovakia

1939 Remainder of Czechoslovakia seized
Nazi-Soviet Non-Aggression Pact
German and Russian armies invade Poland

Europe emerged from the horror of the Great War and the endless wrangling of the Paris Peace Conference to face an uncertain world and a troubled future. While many war-weary people hoped to return to a normal life, this would prove to be an elusive dream. In the post-war world there would be no normal existence, at least no normality comparable to pre-war life. Everything it seemed had changed. Three ancient dynasties that had shaped European affairs for centuries were no more: the Hohenzollerns of Germany, the Habsburgs of Austria, and the Romanovs of Russia all had been dethroned and replaced by new, untested governments and states. The self-assurance and dominant position of Europe in the world had been shaken as Western powers expended their financial resources on the great conflict and poured their population of young men into the meat grinder of modern warfare. The map of Europe was replete with new countries like Czechoslovakia, Yugoslavia, and Poland. Hundreds of square miles of territory along the trench lines of the Western front were barren of all vegetation, pockmarked and tortured by millions of artillery shells expended in the war.

Millions of an entire generation of European men lay dead in cross-sprouted and star-speckled cemeteries or at the bottom of the ocean, or their bodies lost in the mire of battlefields, or blown to bits along the trench lines and battle fronts in Flanders, along the Somme River in France, in Galicia in the east, in the mountains of northern Italy, on the peninsula of Gallipoli, or a hundred other places. Hundreds of thousands of others who survived the terrors of the battles served as constant reminders of the war's suffering by their blank stares, their uncontrollable facial tics or twitching arms, or their maimed bodies. Amputees were everywhere, missing an arm or leg or maybe both or all. The

These crippled German soldiers with artificial limbs are at work in a shop making bandages.

"men without faces," their countenances horribly disfigured by mine or artillery shell explosions, were particularly pitiful victims of the war's horrors. Men only blinded by poison gas attacks could count themselves lucky.

In these ways and countless others, in the twenty years between the end of the Paris Peace Conference in 1919 and the beginning of a second, even greater world war in 1939, the Great War affected Europe and its people. It loomed over their consciousness, permeated their subconsciousness, and impacted society, culture, their economies, politics, and relationships with other nations. While many people sought to avoid ever going to war again, others worked to start war anew. Only the coming of a new generation and the even more profound impact of the Second World War pushed the Great War

from its domineering position as the shaper of the European world. Indeed, most of the attention paid to the interwar period is in an effort to understand the coming of the Second World War.

Unfolding in the stark shadow of the First World War, the history of the two decades between that conflict and the beginning of World War II can be divided into three basic phases. First, in the immediate aftermath of the war, until the mid-1920s, Europe faced numerous postwar adjustments, converting from a total war production mode to a peacetime economy, to settling into a new international and political environment, to figuring out how to move on with life. Second, by the mid-1920s Europe began to recover economically, move toward resolution of international problems, and, otherwise, op-

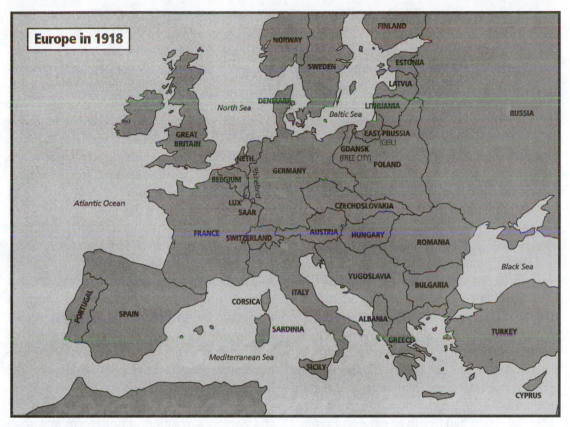

Europe in 1918

erate on a more stable, hopeful basis. This period of hope, economic success, and potential for international cooperation came to an end with the beginning of the Great Depression in 1929. This marked the beginning of a third phase, marked by a tumultuous series of events that engulfed Europe and culminated in the start of World War II in 1939. Though not all was despair in this third period and some countries either were not as heavily affected by the Depression as others or were able to deal with it more effectively, the economic crisis helped revive international tension and stir political problems in various countries, most prominently in Germany where the Nazi Party of Adolf Hitler was able to rise to power. In the tension and strain of the depression years, international events swept Europe toward the Second World War with aggressive nations like Nazi Germany and Fascist Italy contributing much of the impetus to the direction of events.

SOCIETY AND CULTURE OF THE INTERWAR YEARS

Understanding why a Second World War developed a mere two decades after the first involves understanding the particular social and cultural climate of the interwar period, a climate produced by the direction of culture and ideas before the Great War, the impact of the war itself, and particular new developments after the war. The Great War happened at a time in European history when peace, prosperity, and progress had seemed to be within the grasp of Europeans to control and secure through science, industry, and the application of reason. A sense of optimism characterized most people's attitude about the future as the rough transition to an industrial economy during the early and mid-nineteenth century had given way to a maturing industrial economy near the turn of the century that brought material benefits to life, increasingly even to the lives of most ordinary Europeans. Newtonian science offered the possibility of knowing and understanding the physical world, and the Enlightenment heritage in thought and society promised the rational solution of human problems, a promise that seemed to be confirmed by such liberal achievements as the growth of parliamentary government and the extension of democratic rights.

The horror and futility of the Great War and the disappointment of the Paris Peace completely shattered the optimistic spirit of the prewar *belle epoch*. Yet, even before the war came along, intellectuals, including the emerging social scientists, and artists had begun to sense and explore a disturbingly uncertain, unhopeful, irrational side of modern life. In the wake of the Great War, these recent intellectual and cultural developments would in many ways seem confirmed and would wash over European culture, heavily influencing it just as the older, rational Enlightenment and scientific views were submerged by the deep sense of disillusionment and pessimism the war left behind.

The turn-of-the-century challenges to the rational Enlightenment tradition combined in the interwar years with additional intellectual and cultural developments to produce a set of ideas, a mindset, and a cultural milieu that affected many in the generation and helped give expression to the feelings of the age. Some of the approaches to understanding modern life

were effectively adopted or adapted by individuals and groups like Mussolini and his Fascists, Hitler and his Nazis, and Stalin and his Communists, who sought to manipulate and dominate mass society and established totalitarian dictatorships in the postwar period. Other of these cultural developments provide sources to understanding the mindset of societies that produced, allowed, or failed to meet the challenge of the rise of totalitarian dictatorships. It is important, therefore, to examine some of these intellectual and cultural developments.

Challenges to the Enlightenment Tradition

The Enlightenment tradition basically held that through using human reason, orderly principles that governed the physical world or human society could be discovered, rational approaches to life and society operating in accord with these principles could be developed, problems of the human condition could be solved, and progress could be attained. Although the conservative and Romantic reaction to Enlightenment liberalism had challenged this notion, by the late nineteenth century the Enlightenment tradition had become dominant, in no small part because of the achievements of science. By the time of the Great War, this sense of certainty and firm belief in the basic rationality of humans and life had come to face a new set of challenges. One early example is found in the work of Fyodor Dostoevski, a Russian author who posed in *Notes from Underground* (1864) the idea that humans are not necessarily purely rational beings. While this was not an original idea, Dostoevski pointed out that the irrational part of humans is what makes them individuals and that people will do irrational things to demonstrate their uniqueness; they may even choose pain, receiving from it some gratification. If irrationality then is a key part of the human makeup, if people do not necessarily choose the rational path, then the fundamental workings of a reason-based system, like democratic government, could be called into question.

One of the most influential individuals in the late nineteenth-century criticism of the rational tradition was Friedrich Nietzsche (1844-1900). Nietzsche, a German philosopher and son of a Lutheran minister, emphasized the human irrational side in his unsystematic, poetic philosophical writings that critiqued and belittled the fundamental values of liberal, rational society and traditional Christian morality. Arguing that intellectual development hindered the cultivation of the will and of instinct, basic human faculties that he saw as responsible for creativity and meaningful life, Nietzsche condemned things such as Christian moral restrictions that inhibited spontaneous, vigorous life. To him, Christianity's egalitarian uplifting of the weak, meek, and humble denied and suppressed the superior forces of pride, strength, and power. He said that no rationally discernible standards of morality or behavior existed, so superior humans, "overmen," should forge their own path, ignoring rules, and ruthlessly asserting their strength to make their lives meaningful in the acquisition of power. This higher human could dethrone the power of inferior humans, follow instinct and will to revive and invigorate European society.

Such ideas gained force in an age of increasing uncertainty that the Great War helped along. The proponents of the Nazi movement in Germany saw themselves as Nietzsche's superior humans, using force, power, and will to reform a world in decline, according to their own instinctual designs, and claimed that Nietzsche, in essence, prophesied them and philosophically validated their movement. Although Nietzsche opposed German nationalism, notions of German racial superiority, militarism, and glorification of the state, all of which were key components of Nazi ideology, his denigration of humane, democratic, rational principles and his reveling in power and force certainly found common ground with aggressive, emotional, irrational movements like Nazism that tapped emotional response through myths and proposed action-oriented solutions to the many problems of the uncertain postwar world.

Other intellectuals who contributed to the growing interest in or concern with the irrational included Georges Sorel (1847-1922) and Sigmund Freud (1856-1939). Significantly, Sorel argued that the nonrational power of myth could move the proletariat to decisive action. He posed the political possibilities of using myths to motivate the masses to achieve some end, one of the approaches used in the three primary totalitarian movements of the interwar years.

Freud also explored the potential of the irrational in humans but with a great concern for the problems it created, rather than its potential political usefulness. The irrational actions people take may come without their awareness or understanding, driven to the surface from within. Freud developed techniques like dream analysis and free association to try to explore the subconscious and determine the true source of disorders. Though he wanted to deal with human irrationality through scientific study in order to control it, he saw its great potential power to overrule the rational mind and, thereby, threaten civilization. Nazism and the other totalitarian movements certainly demonstrated the threat that irrational forces posed to civilization.

In turn-of-the-century Europe, the new social sciences like sociology, although they used rational, science-based approaches, also contributed to an understanding of the basic element of irrationality in humans, as well as the problems confronting modern society. Some of the social analyses produced in the early century profoundly influenced the formulation of Fascist and Nazi ideas and provided useful methods and approaches for attracting followers. Frenchman Gustave Le Bon (1841-1931) studied "crowd" behavior, the dynamics of large groups like a mob or political party, and determined that in a group individuals' ideas, beliefs, or rational thoughts get lost and swept up in a group mentality that is driven primarily by unconscious instinct. He argued that the more effective leaders of crowds used emotion, action, and will rather than logical argument to persuade and move.

Similarly, the Italian Vilfredo Pareto (1848-1923) argued that social behavior is not rational, rather it is based on fundamental feelings and instincts. People devise rationalizations for their actions after the fact, rather than taking an action based on a rational decision. Finding that natural inequality among people and scarcity of material goods mean that a few, whom he called the elite, will have more ability and goods than everyone else, whom he labeled the masses, Pareto believed that the superior elite should use force, appeals to emotion through propaganda, or trickery to dominate the masses. Both Mussolini and Hitler took the lessons of Le Bon and Pareto to heart and went to great lengths to appeal to emotion and to cultivate the mind of the instinctual crowd rather than the rational individual.

Another French sociologist, Emile Durkheim (1858-1917), in attempting to devise an approach to preventing the disintegration of modern society, argued that in modern life, due in part to its emphasis on individualism and loss of religious focus, people have no sense of purpose in life, do not feel a part of a community, and, therefore, are unhappy and alienated. In different ways, the totalitarian dictatorships all played on this missing ingredient in life and tried with great success to create a sense of purpose and belonging, to incorporate people into a larger whole, a movement in which they could feel rooted and connected. Max Weber (1864-1920), a German thinker and student of society, while affirming the benefits of the rational approach, also saw that the rational and anti-religious nature of modern life deleted the meaning and purpose from life. Additionally, he believed that it led to bureaucratization and mechanization of human life that might result in irrational reaction. Interestingly, he paid particular attention to the possibilities of a leader using appeal of personality and charisma to unify and sway the people, thereby describing the very phenomenon that the totalitarian regimes would exhibit.

The move toward the nonrational, the collapse of certainty, and the destruction of older values and standards seen in philosophy and social thought was echoed in the world of art and in the physical sciences. In art post-impressionists or expressionists like Vincent van Gogh (1853-1890), Paul Cezanne (1839-1906), and Henri Matisse (1869-1954) left behind the emphasis that realism and impressionism had placed on depicting physical, visible reality and moved toward expressing inner, nonvisible emotion or feeling that objects evoked for the artist. The rational, representational approach to art was giving way to the nonrational, abstract. Pablo Picasso (1881-1973) took things further by establishing the cubist movement. Cubism avoids traditional, realistic methods of depicting three-dimensional objects on a two-dimensional canvas (such as perspective) and uses, instead, lines, angles, and overlapping planes to show various aspects of an object on one two-dimensional surface. Like expressionism, cubism depicts feeling and imagery, not what the eye sees. As these artistic developments caught on and gained wider acceptance, modern art was born, and traditional artistic standards and ideals were challenged.

Developments in science also contributed to the collapse of certainty. The science of Newton was the bedrock of the Enlightenment rational tradition, holding forth the idea that the physical world, being composed of indivisible blocks of matter called atoms and operating according to mathematically expressible, consistent, mechanical principles could be known and understood through fact-based experimentation and observation. Using the scientific approach, Western science seemed near figuring out all the mysteries of the physical world and solving most material problems. Charles Darwin's theory of evolution, well accepted among the educated elite of Europe by 1900, explained how the species evolved. Telegraph and rail had revolutionized communication and transportation, and science had developed seemingly limitless power sources with the electric dynamo and internal combustion engine. Science had even eliminated darkness with the incandescent light bulb. Just as these immensely practical benefits of science were impacting everyday life in Europe, new developments in physics in the late nineteenth and early twentieth centuries shook the smug certainty of Newtonian science and opened up the frightening possibility that one could never exactly know or predict the physical world.

The discovery of x-rays and the electron demonstrated that the atom was divisible. The development of quantum theory demonstrated that energy radiation was not constant and predictable as Newtonian science believed but rather occurs in spurts. Radioactive decay was shown to be unpredictable. Albert Einstein showed that

Albert Einstein predicted the results of what became known as nuclear fission; he also warned that the technology could be used for mass destruction.

time and motion were relative to the observer and, therefore, were fundamentally unknowable in absolute terms. Even if science continued to open doors of understanding, the new physics called into question old certainties and challenged the notion that humans understood or could understand the world.

The Cultural Impact of the Great War

Taken together, all of these developments in thought and culture that were underway by the time the Great War began marked a massive shaking of confidence and certainty in European culture and contributed to the general climate of disillusionment and uncertainty that pervaded Europe after the Great War. But the experience of war itself was in many ways most responsible for these feelings, particularly among the larger society. Building on the earlier trends but shoved forward by the dramatic impact of the Great War, cultural developments occurring in the interwar period reflect the profound impact that the war had on the psyche of Europe and help explain the rise of totalitarian regimes and the coming of the Second World War. Various cultural developments illustrate the ways that Europeans tried to find answers or deal with the lingering effects of the cataclysmic war.

Intellectuals were some of the most deeply affected by the uncertainty of the age. While some intellectuals like Jose Ortega y Gasset (1883-1955), Julien Benda (1867-1956), Erich Fromm (1900-1980), and Ernst Cassirer (1874-1945) tried to reclaim rationality and the Enlightenment tradition, others found themselves despairing the future of society and reason, turning in response to the development of a loosely defined philosophical movement called *existentialism*. Existentialism is the general term used to describe a philosophical approach that saw individual action and decision as the path to finding meaning in life. With traditional "compasses" such as God (for atheists) or reason having been shattered as reliable guides, the individual had to strive for consistent, responsible choices in life to achieve morality or meaningful existence. Though no well-ordered, commonly accepted set of existentialist beliefs developed, thinkers such as Martin Heidegger (1889-1976), Jean-Paul Sartre (1905-1980), Albert Camus (1913-1960), and Karl Jaspers (1883-1969) forged the basic existentialist approach of individual responsibility for defining values and existence.

While many existentialists were atheistic and Friedrich Nietzsche had declared God dead, the role of God and religion in European life was not dead. Christianity provided another choice for those seeking answers in an uncertain post-war world, as many returned to the fundamentals of both Catholic and Protestant Christianity. For these people, faith in God and the tenets of religion provided the hope and anchor that were lacking in an anxious, uncertain world. Many intellectuals revived their interest in or converted to religion, including Protestant theologian Karl Barth, Catholic existentialists Jacques Maritain and Gabriel Marcel, historian Arnold Toynbee, poets W.H. Auden and T.S. Eliot, physicist Max Planck, and authors Aldous Huxley and Evelyn Waugh. Among common people in the United States, Protestant fundamentalism thrived in the interwar period, providing a strong counter-current to the direction of modernity. Religious belief also flourished in other ways in Europe as some people, including Sir Arthur Conan Doyle of Sherlock Holmes fame, sought comfort in spiritualism, a movement that promised communion with spirits of the dead; contacting lost loved ones through a medium and rituals could assuage grief.

While philosophy and religion provided answers for some, other people in the post-war climate of uncertainty and anxiety tried to leave worries and the war behind by seeking release or escape by indulging in frivolity and modern amusements. The Jazz Age, so much a part of the 1920s culture of the United States, with its night life, fast-paced music, and modern values, also raged among some classes in Europe as jazz and American style were imported to the continent. Paris, already a center of avant garde culture since the late 1800s, continued along this line, embracing American jazz and blues music in cabarets like the Moulin Rouge, adoring African-American entertainers like Josephine Baker, and attracting alienated American intellectuals and writers such as F. Scott Fitzgerald, Ernest Hemingway, and Gertrude Stein, those whom

Stein called the "lost generation." Berlin, Germany, without having a history of cultural leadership to rival that of Paris, also became the scene of a lively and vibrant night-life culture. Prostitution houses, restaurants, cabarets, and music spots became common, and hundreds of bars where gays and lesbians gathered punctuated the modern culture evolving in Berlin.

For other people, the war loomed so large in their life that they could never leave it behind. For these people, the horror, grief, and despair of the war lived on, contributing to a deep desire to avoid future conflict, making appeasement or peace at any cost seem like good ideas in the 1930s. Examples of the war's grim impact lingering on include the work of German artists Otto Dix and Käthe Kollwitz and author Erich Remarque. Otto Dix, who as a front-line soldier had seen the grisly human carnage and misery in the trenches, painted intentionally shocking and horrifying images of the death, decay, and destruction as a way to try to exorcise the war from within himself. Käthe Kollwitz was a German artist and mother who lost her son in the war and continued to feel the grief and loss as constant companions thereafter. Struggling for years to produce sculpture to be placed at her son's grave, she finally created two stone figures: a grim father on his knees clutching his folded arms and a kneeling mother, her head bowed in grief. Kollwitz's painting, *The Survivors* (1922), depicts in stark, contrasting shades a group of hollow-eyed, grieving, shocked survivors of the war. Significantly, the survivors portrayed include the elderly, a mother, and several young children, three of whom the mother is protectively holding close. The only representatives of the generation of young adults who had fought and died in the war are two blinded men with bandages covering their eyes. Erich Remarque, an author from Osnabruck, Germany, who fought and was wounded in the Great War, spoke movingly against war and its effects through the characters in his works. His 1929 novel *All Quiet on the Western Front* depicted the tragic fate of a group of German soldiers who had enlisted together. Leaving Germany for Switzerland in 1931, Remarque continued to explore the effects of war in other novels like *The Road Back* (1931) and *Three Comrades* (1937). For these three artists and many ordinary citizens, the pain of the war never ended.

Another element of European society found they could not leave the war in the past either. This group consisted of the soldiers who had fought in the Great War but who saw the war as a positive experience on the whole, an episode in their lives that seemed real, vital, and meaningful, making all that came after pale in comparison. Millions of former soldiers faced the trials of returning home to a civilian existence in a profoundly altered, much more complex, and uncertain world. The soldier's life had offered a simpler, more meaningful existence. Ex-soldiers throughout Europe shared these sentiments, and many tried to recreate the camaraderie and sense of defining purpose military service had provided by forming volunteer, paramilitary units usually under the direction of former officers. In Germany and German-influenced areas in the new states of eastern and central Europe these groups were called *freikorps* (volunteer corps). The first freikorps formed in post-war Germany was the Volunteer Territorial Rifle Corps, organized by General Ludwig von Maercker, who envisioned, as many members of freikorps did, these units as the military embodiment of the citizenry who served to protect order in society.

In Germany, the freikorps were called on to put down rebellions the provisional government faced in 1919; later, some of these units were incorporated into the 100,000-man army the Versailles Treaty allowed for Germany. Others officially disbanded but moved into right-wing political movements like the Nazi Party's S.A. stormtroopers or the communist Red Front. In Italy, similar units formed the basis of Benito Mussolini's Fascist movement. Elsewhere in central and eastern Europe and in Portugal and Spain, freikorps-style units were popular among ex-service men. In the western and northern European democracies, including France, Great Britain, and the Scandinavian countries, however, this phenomenon did not become established. Nonetheless, where these groups formed, they represented an important reaction to the end of the war and the end of the purpose that war had provided. The men that comprised the groups understood that they influenced history before and could do so again.

As this examination of cultural responses indicates, Europeans turned in many different directions for answers as they experienced the disillusionment, anxiety and uncertainty of the interwar period. Another more troubling response combined elements of the various cultural responses with the power of politics to create organized mass movements that swept authoritarian and totalitarian regimes into power and/or provided the basis of support for them. Political movements like Fascism and Nazism were calculated to appeal to those seeking connection, identity, and a sense of belonging and purpose in the anxious, uncertain interwar world. They also offered satisfying-sounding solutions to some of the very concrete problems and grievances Europeans had—such as economic woes, dissatisfaction with the peace settlement, and national jealousies. The Communists offered an identity in party and ideology; the Fascists and Nazis, also based on party organization, offered an identity tied to the state, the nation, and the leader, with the Nazis having a caustic racial element in their definition of nation. Fundamentally nonrational, these movements evoked powerful emotional or instinctual responses that did not require complicated thought or decision making. This ominous development provided the force behind the rise of totalitarian regimes in Italy, Russia, Germany, and Japan. The response of Europeans to these movements and the rise of these movements to political power is crucial to an understanding of the coming of World War II and is integrally connected to the post-war political and international climate, as well as the related economic and international crises of the interwar period.

POSTWAR POLITICAL AND INTERNATIONAL CLIMATE

Eastern and Central Europe

Virtually all European nations experienced the effects on culture and society described above: disillusionment, anxiety, uncertainty, intense grief and sense of loss, and "displaced soldier phenomenon." In this social and cultural environment, the countries of Europe and their governments had to move forward into an uncertain peace in a Europe that was politically very different from the Europe that had marched naively and joyously off to war in August 1914. War and the peace settlement dramatically altered the map of Europe, and completely new political systems were in place in most areas from Germany eastward. These countries were burdened by issues the peace settlement had left unresolved, by problems such as reparations and international jealousies that the settlement helped create, and by new, unfolding situations and challenges.

One of the new situations that Europe faced was the result of internal developments in Russia during and immediately after the war. The Russian and Bolshevik Revolutions of 1917 had deposed the ancient Romanov dynasty and ended the imperial monachy it had ruled. In its place a fledgling Communist dictatorship was emerging that fought and eventually won a civil war in 1918-1921 and also reconquered territory that had been temporarily lost: the Dneiper Ukraine, Belorussia, Georgia, Armenia, and Azerbijan. In this bitter civil war, Western European powers and the United States intervened in a fruitless attempt to oppose the Communists. On the other hand, the Bolshevik leaders of Communist Russia (by 1922 called the Union of Soviet Socialist Republics or U.S.S.R.), headed by V.I. Lenin, organized the Communist International, or Comintern, and called upon workers and Marxist movements worldwide to begin communist revolutions in their respective countries.

While permitting the survival of the Bolshevik regime, the heavy territorial losses accepted in the Treaty of Brest-Litovsk weakened the Russian state in the interwar period and provided a source of instability as desire to regain the losses grew. Instability was also fostered because the Communist dictatorship of Lenin, succeeded in power eventually by Josef Stalin, was an untested, uncertain regime that was shunned and isolated by the Western European powers and the United States. The climate of mistrust and hatred between the West and Communist Russia would undermine the possibility of a lasting peace in the interwar era and allow Germany, also shunned and isolated diplomatically in the immediate postwar period, to find a friend and partner in secret efforts to rearm and undermine the peace settlement. The efforts of the Russian regime to foment revolution in western countries led to no end of hysteria over the threat of Communist insurrection. In fact, the Western fear of Communism contributed to toleration and even support of the Nazi movement in its rise to power both within Germany and in the Western democracies because the Nazis were vehement rivals of the Communists: an anti-Communist German government could protect middle class Germans' economic position and could potentially insulate and protect Western Europe from Bolshevism.

A major consequence of the Paris Peace Settlement was the creation of an entirely new state system in eastern Europe. Among these states, the entirely new countries, Poland,

Joseph Stalin drove Russia into misery with his failed economic policies and his use of the brutal secret police.

Czechoslovakia, Austria, Hungary, and Yugoslovia, posed an important challenge to a stable Europe since they, like the new Soviet Russia, were untested. Ruled under monarchy before the war, all of these countries adopted governments that were variations of parliamentary democracy on the Western European model, with elected parliaments serving as law-making bodies and the executive functions being carried out by ministries responsible to the parliaments and, in some cases, to a head of state. These new parliamentary governments operated in a very unstable environment since ethnic rivalries, economic problems, and other contentious issues tended to divide the electorate and, therefore, the membership of the parliaments. The survival of these governments was in question from the beginning.

In addition to lacking tested political systems, none of these countries had an existing national economy, so economic patterns both within the countries and with other nations had to be worked out. In many cases it was questionable whether the countries had the necessary combination of ingredients to establish effective economies at all. For example, the new Austria was primarily rural and agricultural, but its capital was the great city of Vienna that had thrived as the cultural and political center of the Habsburg Empire but did not mesh very well economically with the small rural environs that now composed its country. The economic problems were compounded by economic requirements of the peace settlement: Austria, Hungary, and Bulgaria were by treaty supposed to pay reparations to the Allied Powers, and Poland, Rumania, Yugoslavia, and Czechoslovakia signed interallied agreements in 1919 to make payments toward the "expenses of liberation," the cost to the Allies of defeating Austria-Hungary and Germany that had allowed the creation of the new states or had benefited them territorially. While little or none of these payments were ever made, the issue contributed considerable uncertainty to the economy of the region.

Finally, these relatively small countries had to survive in an international situation that was also new, untested, and especially dangerous for them. Not populous or industrially strong enough to face alone the potential military strength of Russia to the east or Germany to the north and west, these countries depended on support from other powers. This support from early was very uncertain. The United States ultimately refused to support the peace settlement and dramatically reduced its involvement in European affairs. At the same time, unsatisfactory territorial divisions in the peace settlements led several of these eastern states to desire territory held by neighboring countries, sentiments that threatened peace and stability to be sure. Likewise, both Germany and Russia desired the return of territories in the region lost in the war. Germany, in particular, resented the loss of German-inhabited territory to the new Poland and also felt that Germans had been treated unfairly in regard to the idea of national self-determination since German-speaking areas had been given to non-German states and the union of Germany and Austria (primarily German-speaking) had been prohibited by the treaty. All these political, economic, and international forces contributed to making the postwar period in Eastern Europe uncertain and unstable.

Germany

In Germany, when the military high command had determined that the war was lost and washed their hands of the matter, Wilhelm II abdicated and fled to Holland, leaving a provisional civilian government to do the dirty work of signing the armistice that surrendered German arms in November 1918 and the worst job of accepting the Versailles Treaty, or Versailles Diktat ("dictate") as the Germans called it. This provisional government was the forerunner of the Weimar Republic, the parliamentary government formed at Weimar in central Germany during the summer of 1919.

The Weimar constitution established a government for Germany similar to the parliamentary, democratic governments set up in the successor states of central and eastern Europe, with several features seen as particularly democratic. The government consisted of a president, a two-house legislature or parliament, and a chancellor and cabinet of ministers controlled by the lower house and appointed by the president. The election of president was by a direct vote of the people, with the winning candidate needing a majority of the vote; otherwise a second election would be held in which a plurality of the vote would suffice. The president was mainly seen as a titular head of state but had key powers to appoint the chancellor and cabinet and to rule by decree in times of emergency, two powers that contributed to the Nazis' rise to power. The upper house of the legislature was the *Reichsrat*, composed of representatives from the eighteen state governments in Germany, with more populous states receiving more representation. The Reichsrat served in administrative capacities and voted on legislation. The *Reichstag*, the lower chamber of the parliament that was designed to be the main legislative and executive body, could pass a law over the objection of the Reichsrat with a two-thirds majority vote, rescind presidential decrees, amend the constitution, enact laws, and controlled the ministry (cabinet of ministers).

Elections for the Reichstag, in which men and women at least 20 years of age were eligible to vote, were conducted by the Baden system of proportional representation that gave political parties a number of seats in the Reichstag proportionate to the number of votes the parties received, with each 60,000 votes earning a seat. This type of proportional representation gave political parties significant power since the party prepared lists of candidates in each of 35 electoral districts and Reichstag seats were given (assuming the party polled enough votes) to the people on the party list *in the order in which they were listed*. Leftover fractions of 60,000 party votes from various districts ("unused" votes since it took 60,000 votes to earn a seat) were pooled to select additional Reichstag members, including selection from a national list of candidates that usually included the top party leadership and ensured that the party leaders would always be included in the Reichstag. This system of representation meant that the size of the Reichstag depended on how many people voted, and, therefore, encouraged party support and party loyalty, both of which the Nazi Party proved effective in generating.

Although most of the various segments of the German political spectrum eventually worked within the Weimar system, including Hitler and the Nazis, the constitutional government did not enjoy very deep-rooted support. Conservatives from various classes admired and respected the authority and tradition represented by the Hohenzollern monarchy and wished for its return. Moreover, for many Germans, such as a young Austrian German named Adolf Hitler who had served in a Bavarian regiment during the war, the Weimar government was tainted from the start with blame for losing the war. This blame was unfairly placed because neither the provisional nor the Weimar governments had anything to do with the loss of the war and had no alternative but to accept the Versailles Treaty

Hitler joined the German military at age twenty-four. He was devastated by his country's defeat. He and others scapegoated the Jews for the economic conditions after World War I.

since thousands of Germans faced desperate hunger as the Allies continued a total blockade of then disarmed Germany. Still, many believed (with encouragement from the military) that Germany had been "stabbed in the back" by traitors at home. Support was not strong for the government, tainted as it was with the stench of the Versailles Diktat that blamed Germany for the war, reduced its revered military to a mere token force, took away territory in Europe and colonies abroad, reduced it to inferior status in trade and international affairs, and demanded reparations payments.

In these circumstances, the new German government had to face several monumental problems. Soon after the end of the fighting, in January 1919, the "Spartakist rising," a radical socialist uprising in Berlin, threatened the provisional government headed by the Social Democrat (moderate socialist) Friedrich Ebert. Ebert's defense minister called on the remnants of the German military to put down the rebellion. Anti-revolution volunteer freikorps units headed by pro-monarchy officers of the old Imperial Army crushed the workers' rebellion and assassinated Rosa Luxemburg and Karl Liebknecht, two leaders of the radical socialists. This incident demonstrated the dependence of the provisional government on monarchists and other conservative opponents and divided the socialist support for the government at the same time.

The Spartakist rising had been fueled in part by another of the new German government's major problems: economic crisis. This economic crisis, which continued after the Weimar constitution was implemented, stemmed partly from the dislocations of converting from a total-war economy to a peace-time economy, the return home of hundreds of thousands of soldiers seeking employment, and the continuing Allied blockade of Germany that stifled all external trade. Once the Versailles Treaty was implemented, the blockade was lifted, but economic problems were compounded by the terms of the treaty; among other things, Germany lost its colonies, had to accept disadvantageous trade terms, and faced the looming threat of soon-to-be-imposed war reparations. The demand for war reparations to be paid to the Allies, primarily France, Belgium, and Great Britain, was established in theory in the Treaty of Versailles and given a concrete reality on May 1, 1921, when the Reparations Commission announced that $33 billion was due in reparations plus the total Belgian war debt of about $1.4 billion and the cost of occupation armies. This was a major financial burden for the troubled German economy and one that from the start Germany argued it could not possibly pay. Regardless of whether the amount was realistically payable or not, the fledgling German democracy was caught in a difficult position between international pressure to pay the reparations, internal demands to refuse payment, and the economic consequences of either course of action.

Spain

Spain had remained neutral in World War I and escaped the negative effects of the war, benefiting economically from war demand, especially in its electrical, textile, iron, and coal industries. Nonetheless, Spain also experienced turmoil in the interwar period. The end of the war brought an end to foreign demand for Spanish products, creating economic depression. Industrial workers faced low wages. Farmers earned little from their labors since most worked as tenants, paying high rents to large estate owners. Over half of Spain's land was owned by less than 1 percent of the population.

Despite industrialization and modernization that had impacted Spain, in some areas much more so than in others, long-standing powers like the large landholders, the military, and the Catholic Church continued to hold their grip on Spanish life under the Bourbon monarch Alfonso XIII (1885-1931). In the last years of Alfonso's reign, from 1923-1930, General Miguel Primo de Rivera held power with the king's consent as a virtual dictator, ruling by decree under martial law. In 1931 a moderate, virtually nonviolent revolution ousted Alfonso and established Spain's Second Republic, setting up a democratic government. Elected reformist elements in the new government implemented policies to separate church and state, take control of education from the Church, outlaw the Jesuit order, and begin the process of redistributing some land from large estates into the hands of peasants. The political left in Spain divided as extremists believed the pace of change was too slow; meanwhile conservative elements opposed what they saw as radical policies. After rightist and conservative political parties gained control of the government in 1933, halted reforms, and used brutally repressive measures against a miners' revolt and a Catalonian separatist movement, left-wing parties won elections in 1936 and pushed ahead with reforms. From February through July 1936, supporters of the right clashed violently with supporters of the left as both sides fought and murdered. In July 1936, an element of army leaders, headed eventually by fascist General Francisco Franco, organized a rebellion against the republican government, initiating a bloody civil war that lasted until 1939. The instability and turmoil in Spain brought one more element of tension to the already shaky European situation. The Spanish Civil War also proved to be a critical event in the series of international problems that led to the Second World War.

The Western Democracies: France & Britain

In most of the countries with parliamentary democracies, one of the fundamental political weaknesses of the interwar period was the divided nature of politics. Sizeable support for extremists at both ends of the political spectrum or having the vote spread among several parties of widely differing views, which required frequently shaky coalition governments, tended to paralyze governments because securing majority votes in parliaments on important issues proved difficult or impossible. Tough issues might not be addressed at all or only weak action might be taken; this was especially true in matters of foreign policy where fear of war made consistent, firm policy difficult and frequent turnover in cabinets and ministries ensured inconsistency.

France was particularly hard hit by this problem. Deeply divided politically since the French Revolution between right and left, the French government exchanged hands numerous times in the interwar period, with increasing frequency in the late 1930s. Tensions between conservative, monied classes and the working classes, socialists, and communists drove political turmoil that broke out in violence on different occasions. From 1919-1924 a coalition of conservative parties controlled the government, followed by France's first socialist government in 1924. In 1926, Raymond Poincaré headed a right-leaning national coalition until 1929. In this period, France confronted major post-war adjustment problems. France had suffered tremendously in the war. Among major countries in the world, France had the lowest birthrate and with a population of under 40 million people lost 1.4 million military dead and a high rate of civilians in the war, a combination of factors that resulted in the country having a smaller population in 1918 than it had in 1914. Physical devastation affected 10 percent of French territory, as much as four years of fighting in the west had occurred on French soil. Germany had also devastated France further as the Kaiser's forces retreated in 1918, rendering coal mines useless and cutting down orchards. Massive war debt, much of it owed to the United States, and continuing huge military expenditures created fiscal burdens that France hoped to offset with German reparations payments. France insisted on reparations and kept its own military level high because it felt the Treaty of Versailles had failed to provide security for France. The United States and then Great Britain failed to keep promises to form a military alliance with France. The League of Nations established in the peace treaties was untried, and France viewed it with extreme skepticism, especially after the United States failed to join. Germany retained most of its pre-war territory, and its growing population of over 60 million outpaced France's considerably. In this situation, France felt betrayed by the peace settlement, and its international anxiety and insecurity led France to see its survival as being tied to stringent enforcement of the Treaty of Versailles, flawed though it might be, and keeping Germany isolated and disarmed. Inflation plagued the economy, especially hurting those with savings or living on fixed incomes, as the franc fell from a 1914 value of 20 cents to the dollar to a mid-1920s value of two cents. Colonial woes also confronted France as the country found it increasingly difficult to hold on to territories like Algeria, Senegal, and Indochina (Vietnam) where independence sentiments ran high.

By the late 1920s, France had managed to recover economically and was confronting the international situation with more confidence and hope. The Great Depression, internal political scandals, the growing threat of Nazi Germany, and continuing political rivalries and colonial problems, however, served to make the 1930s an increasingly paralytic and tumultuous period for French government. Revolving door ministries governed the country as one coalition followed another: France had six cabinet changes in two years in the mid-1930s. The Depression hit France as it did other European countries, although somewhat later. Fortunately for France, however, traditional family businesses continued to dominate the economy despite growth of big business and economic concentration in the 1920s. While small firms did not enjoy the efficiencies of scale that favored large operations, they could survive economic depression much more effectively and had a much smaller impact on the national economy if they went under or cut back than did large conglomerates. Partly as a result, French unemployment only reached 5 percent, compared to 20 percent in Britain and, at least, 25 percent in the United States, where mergers and combinations had drastically concentrated the economy in the hands of a relatively few corporations. Still, economic woes were a powerful force in the political turmoil of the decade. In 1936-1937 a Popular Front government of leftist parties under moderate socialist Leon Blum managed to enact a sweeping set of reforms, including nationalization of some industries and a 40-hour work week plus two weeks of paid vacation for workers. Rightist opponents, however, were able to oust Blum in 1937 and reverse many of the Popular Front policies, though no consistent alternative policy surfaced.

Great Britain also faced a problematic post-war adjustment. The British Empire had suffered a major human cost in the war, with about 900,000 military fatalities plus about twice that number wounded. Although this was a tremendous loss of life, it was not quite on the level of the continental powers, and Britain had escaped the physical devastation of the war. Still, the British lost much economically, and economic woes proved to be the fundamental political problem the country faced in the interwar period. British national debt had increased tenfold over 1914 with huge obligations owed to the United States. The country had lost about 40 percent of its valuable merchant marine fleet; it spent a wealth of foreign investments and other assets to fund the war; and British merchants lost many trade ties and markets during the war as firms in the United States and elsewhere pursued opportunities presented by British preoccupation with the war. After a brief post-war boom, the British economy went bust, with over 2 million men, roughly 20 percent of the workforce, being out of work by the summer of 1921. The economy improved by the mid-1920s, but persistent problems plagued it. When the Depression came in the early 1930s, further problems accompanied it.

British politics in the interwar period revolved around debate between the Conservative, Labour, and declining Liberal Parties over what direction policy should take on economic matters. Labour generally preferred socialistic solutions, like nationalization of key industries, while the Conservatives sought to help British industry through protective tariffs and favorable trade deals with members of the British Commonwealth, such as Canada and New Zealand. Although Labour was in power under Ramsay MacDonald for ten months in 1924 and again from 1928-1931, the fact that they depended on support from the Liberal Party limited their freedom of action. For most of the interwar period, the Conservatives dominated the government, including the national government coalition of the early-to-mid-1930s. Although Conservative policies failed to solve Britain's economic troubles, the party continued to enjoy strong support.

Other than economic problems, the most important domestic issue of the interwar period was the "Irish question." After the war, from 1919-1921, often violent agitation by Irish groups seeking complete independence from British rule for Ireland led to the formation of the Irish Free State, comprised of the counties of southern Ireland (apart from Ulster) that were given dominion status, including their own parliament. Some Irish groups wanted the entire island to be included and continued agitation. After 1933, the Irish cut the remaining ties to British rule, including abolishing the oath of loyalty to the British crown. When World War II came along, Ireland clearly demonstrated its independence by remaining neutral, refusing to assist Great Britain.

INTERWAR ECONOMY AND INTERNATIONAL CRISES OF THE 1920s

The economic impact of the war and the economic provisions of the Treaty of Versailles, such as the demand for reparations, contributed a great deal to the economic woes of Europe, as well as the instability. Determined, ruthless leaders and political movements like the Nazis could and did play upon the social and cultural anxiety, uncertainty, and rootlessness that existed in the interwar period. But they also played on concrete economic problems, grievances, and jealousies in arousing public support for their dramatic proposals for action. Their actions helped push Europe down the road to another world war and, therefore, the economic crises have to be seen as a major cause of the breakdown of the peace and the coming of the Second World War.

The anxiety and uncertainty that post-war Europe experienced in cultural and intellectual aspects of life were echoed in economic matters and international relations. The peace settlement intended to ensure stability and security, with the League of Nations being established to provide collective security through the promise of concerted action against aggression. Instead, mistrust, suspicion, and insecurity prevailed. The new state system created by the Paris Peace Conference was untested. The treaties ending the war had not created a climate of security, particularly for France, which felt the settlement had not been harsh enough on Germany. Britain began to believe the opposite, feeling remorse for the treatment of Germany. Germany seethed with anger over the terms of the peace. Italy felt it had not received just compensation for its contribution to the war on the side of the Allies. Russia, under communist rule, had not participated in the peace settlement negotiations. Both Germany and Russia were not admitted to the League of Nations and were ostracized from the diplomatic arena. The United States not only failed to join the League of Nations but rejected the entire set of peace treaties as well, eventually forming separate treaties with the defeated powers.

As Europe experienced the difficult transition from wartime economy to peacetime economy, economic issues tied to the peace settlement undermined the potential success of the settlement. Prevented from trading on even terms with most European nations, Germany turned to the other outcast nation in European affairs, Russia. In April 1922, Germany and Russia signed a treaty drawn up in Rapallo, Switzerland. The Rapallo agreement formally established diplomatic relations between the two countries, provided terms of a trade agreement, and, in a secret military protocol, established a military deal in direct violation of the Treaty of Versailles. In the secret military provisions of the Rapallo agreement, Russia allowed Germany to set up factories in Russia to produce military hardware, such as tanks and aircraft. In exchange, Germany would help train Soviet officers. This agreement was most important for it demonstrated German intention to violate the Versailles Treaty disarmament provisions. The economic isolation of both Germany and Russia, however, provided the cloak used to obscure the military violations.

Much more directly, an economic problem in international relations stemming from the peace settlement was the reparations issue. John Maynard Keynes, a British economist who had served on the British staff at the peace conference until he quit, published a scathing critique of the negotiators and the economic provisions of the peace settlement entitled *The Economic Consequences of the Peace*. Keynes argued that the reparations bill demanded from Germany would so harm the German economy that it could not possibly generate income sufficient to continue paying reparations. He predicted that reparations would mean disaster for other nations' economies as well: Britain could not expect to sell goods to Germany if German income was drained to pay reparations. Keynes' predictions were fairly accurate, and his work influenced the easing of British desire to enforce reparations provisions of the Versailles Treaty, a development that further strained the French view of British trustworthiness.

France, feeling betrayed by Britain, sought security elsewhere, by forging a set of individual alliances with several states of eastern Europe: Poland and the "Little Entente" countries, Czechoslovakia, Romania, and Yugoslavia. But France also continued to demand full payment of reparations as a way to finance continued

military strength and to keep Germany weak. Germany, as the Rapallo agreement showed for military matters, did not want to abide by the treaty and make the payments. This, in combination with France's insistence on German fulfillment of the reparations obligation, led to the first major post-war international crisis.

When the Reparations Commission (chaired by France) presented the final reparations bill of $33 billion to Germany in May 1921—after a heated debate that had increased international tensions—Germany reluctantly began making payments. In August 1922 the British, feeling guilt over the terms of the Versailles Treaty, proposed that all reparations payments from Germany to Britain, France and the other Allied countries, as well as all loan payments from Britain and France to the United States, be cancelled. France, feeling further betrayed by the British, adamantly refused the proposal, as did U.S. President Warren Harding, who insisted that U.S. loans be repaid. In December 1922, Germany failed to make a scheduled in-kind payment of telephone poles. France convened a meeting of the Reparations Commission, which with Belgian and Italian support declared Germany in default. With the idea of securing reparations directly, France and Belgium moved troops into the Ruhr region of Germany, the center of much of Germany's industrial activity, to appropriate the production from German factories. This began the Ruhr crisis, an episode that threatened the peace and stability of post-war Europe.

Without a military capable of resisting French and Belgian forces, Germany turned to passive resistance. With Weimar government encouragement and support, German workers refused to produce goods for the French and Belgians to appropriate. Factories and other industrial operations shut down. Some violence was involved with more than 70 Germans and

20 occupation troops being killed. The Weimar government met the financial burden of supporting workers and reduced tax revenues by continuing to print paper currency. Although the reparations issue had already caused serious inflation, the Ruhr crisis and German handling of it led to ruinous, astronomical inflation. The pre-war value of the German mark had stood at about 4 marks to one U.S. dollar. After the skyrocketing inflation, the value was about four *trillion* marks to the dollar! Those in Germany who had worked hard to save their money, which included most of the middle class and the upper working class, saw their life savings become absolutely worthless. Scenes that played out all over Germany included children playing with bound stacks of currency like they were toy blocks, women using bundles of paper money as firewood in cookstoves, and a German carrying a wheelbarrow filled with paper money to the store to buy a loaf of bread. Conditions within Germany were so tense that Adolf Hitler and the Nazi Party he had been organizing in Bavaria attempted a coup, known as the Beer Hall Putsch, with the support and involvement of German war hero Field Marshal Erich von Ludendorff. This coup failed, in part due to poor planning and execution. In the end, the passive resistance foiled the French and Belgian plan to extract reparations and made those countries appear as vindictive bullies, but at a tremendous cost to Germany. The stability of the international financial system was severely strained, and, more importantly, for the future of Germany, the Weimar Republic earned the hatred of many Germans who, although they supported resistance, had lost the fruits of their labor in the inflation. Later, when the Nazi Party began to transform the Weimar constitution into a dictatorship in the 1930s, few of these disgruntled Germans came to its defense.

Eventually, the obvious failure of the Ruhr occupation, the growing international discontent with French policy, and a change in the German government's public attitude led to a resolution of the Ruhr crisis and a general improvement in the international situation. In 1923, German statesman Gustav Streseman became foreign minister in a new German cabinet and adopted the "fulfillment policy" in September 1923. This involved Germany abandoning open resistance to reparations and making a good-faith effort to fulfill the reparations obligations in hopes that Germany would become better accepted internationally and other states would soften their policies toward Germany. The approach paid off. In November 1923, a commission headed by U.S. banker George Dawes began meeting to restructure the reparations and international loan payments system. This committee produced the Dawes Plan in April 1924. Under the terms of this plan, the occupation forces were evacuated from the Ruhr and reparations payments were scaled back and tied to the performance of the German economy—in prosperous years, the payments would be larger. Additionally, the plan revamped German currency with the new currency unit called the Retenmark, set up a special bank to oversee reparations payments, and loans to Germany from the United States were organized to help the German economy and energize the payments flow.

The Dawes Plan created a circle of payments in which Germany made reparations to Britain and France, the reparations payments allowed Britain and France to repay loans from the U.S. made during the war, and new U.S. loans to Germany made the reparations payments possible. This international payments system depended entirely on U.S. credit and created an unstable situation that could easily collapse. On the positive side, the plan did resolve the Ruhr crisis and helped begin the "Five Good Years," a period of improving international relations characterized by harmony and cooperation. A general recovery of the European economy, although it did not benefit all industries or regions, helped create this period of harmonious international relations by making it easier for countries to get along with one another.

One hallmark of this improved international climate was German efforts to make good on the reparations obligation. In 1927-1928, Germany paid $1.3 billion in reparations. Another indication that Europe was looking more hopefully toward a future of peace was a series of efforts to strengthen the League of Nations. The League of Nations had been the brainchild of U.S. President Woodrow Wilson at the Paris Peace Conference and the other major Allies viewed the international organization with great skepticism. When the United States Senate rejected the Treaty of Versailles and League membership, thus removing the major supporter of the League from involvement in it, the League seemed doomed to failure. The basic premise of the League was that if the nations of Europe acted collectively, they could deter aggression or successfully stop it if undertaken. This collective security principle depended on the ability of the League to get its members to take action in the face of aggression. The original charter of the League, however, provided little means of requiring members to support League decisions. In 1924 and again in 1925, diplomats worked out draft agreements that would have given the League broader authority to take action in situations that threatened the peace. In both cases, the British Parliament refused to support the agreements, and the measures were not put in place, giving the French more reason to view Britain as undependable. Although the efforts to strengthen the League ultimately failed, the attempt itself demonstrated that international relations were being conducted on a more positive basis in the mid-to-late-1920s.

Another development indicating improving relations and efforts to resolve problems was the effort in various conferences and discussions in the 1920s to devise a disarmament scheme to reduce the chances of war by reducing the physical ability of nations to wage war. The diplomatic development that best illustrates the improved international climate, however, was the set of agreements reached at the Locarno Conference held in 1925 in Locarno, Switzerland. Germany, in improved standing due to the fulfillment policy, was invited to attend this international conference that discussed a variety of European issues, particularly border questions. With German agreement, a pact reached at Locarno fixed the Belgian and French borders with Germany and provided an international guarantee of these borders. Germany received a payoff with an international agreement that its eastern border, where it had lost territory in the Versailles settlement, could be changed by peaceful means. This effectively meant that the Versailles territorial settlement was no longer viewed as permanent. Another benefit was that Germany was admitted to the League of Nations with a permanent seat on the chief council in 1926. The cooperation and harmony achieved at Locarno among foreign policy leaders like Gustav Streseman and France's Aristide Briand seemed to epitomize the spirit of the times so well that people spoke of the "Spirit of Locarno." In secret, however, Streseman continued the Rapallo arrangement between Germany and Russia, signing a German-Russian defensive military alliance of sorts in which both sides promised to continue trading with one another in the event of war and pledged neutrality if either became involved in a war.

The continuation of the spirit of Locarno was evident in the signing of the Paris Peace Pact, more commonly known as the Kellogg-Briand Pact, in August 1928. This agreement originated when French foreign minister Aristide Briand suggested to U.S. Secretary of State Frank Kellogg that France and the U.S. should renounce war as an instrument of foreign policy between the two nations. Kellogg proposed that such a treaty be opened up to other nations. After discussions and an international invitation, fifteen major powers, including Japan, signed the pact. In the wording of the pact, the signatories simply condemned using war to settle controversies, renounced the use of war in relations with one another, and promised to use peaceful means to resolve disputes. On the surface, such an agreement seems to be an important step toward doing away with war. The fact that such an idea was taken seriously by the statesmen of Europe and that the pact was agreed to indicates the strength of the spirit of Locarno. In terms of practical reality, however, the pact was meaningless since the signatories made exceptions for "defensive" wars, wars to protect national interests whether at home or in overseas areas of concern, and in other specific circumstances. As political scientist Edwin M. Borchard put it, "it would be difficult to conceive of any wars that nations have fought within the past century, or are likely to fight in the future, that cannot be accommodated under these exceptions." The pact, nonetheless, marks the high point of the Locarno spirit, the cooperation, and the pacifism of the Five Good Years.

A final fruit of the Locarno spirit was the further revision of German reparations payments in 1929 under the Young Plan. In 1928, as the European economy began to slow somewhat and German reparations and interest payments under the Dawes Plan began to prove increasingly burdensome, another American financier, Owen D. Young, and an international committee were charged with addressing the reparations issue. While the Dawes Plan had reduced the annual payments Germany had to make, it had not set an end date or total payments figure. The Young Plan did both. Germany was to make payments, reduced further from the Dawes Plan level, until 1988. Though this was a lengthy payment series, the total Germany would have paid by 1988 was not quite one-third of the $33 billion the Reparations Commission set in 1921. In addition to payment restructuring, the Young Plan also involved more loans for Germany and provided for the evacuation in 1930 of Allied occupation troops that were present in the Rhineland of Germany under terms of the Versailles Treaty. This evacuation was four years ahead of treaty schedule.

Despite the anxiety and uncertainty of the interwar years, the Spirit of Locarno and the Five Good Years in European international affairs seemed to offer hope for a permanent peace. While the early 1920s saw great tension exemplified by the Ruhr crisis, the latter part of the decade saw cooperation and resolution of problems. Part of what made this possible was the improved European economy, which reduced competitive pressures between nations. In 1929, however, the United States economy, already slowing, began to collapse in the midst of a financial panic on Wall Street. The fall of the U.S. economy into the Great Depression eventually dried up the source of loans Germany relied on to make reparations payments, led to other U.S. investments in Europe being sold off, and shrank U.S. demand for European goods. The shaky structure of international payments fell apart and, eventually, the European economy was drawn into the Depression. In 1931, the failure of the financial giant, the Vienna-based bank Creditanstalt, set off a chain reaction of bank and business closures that confirmed the spread of the Depression to Europe. These developments led many states to try independent, competitive policies like high protective tariffs, generally called economic nationalism, which encouraged international tensions and worked directly against cooperation. One of the most important ways in which the Great Depression impacted international affairs, however, was that it helped Adolf Hitler and his Nazi Party into power in Germany. Hitler established a totalitarian regime and led the country in a series of aggressive international moves that in many ways led to the start of the Second World War.

TOTALITARIANISM

Adolf Hitler was not the only architect of totalitarianism in interwar Europe. Benito Mussolini in Italy and Josef Stalin in Soviet Russia also forged totalitarian governments. All three of these countries and their totalitarianism provided important ingredients that, along with poor responses from other nations such as Britain, France, and the United States, helped create World War II. Examining these regimes will help more fully explain how the interwar era led to the Second World War.

Before exploring the origins and nature of these three totalitarian regimes, it is important to clarify what totalitarianism is. Europe turned to authoritarian political systems where the government was usually headed by a strong leader who could wield power and authority without being restricted by the opinions of the larger populace or parliamentary bodies. By 1938 authoritarian dictatorship had become the rule. Seventeen of twenty-seven European countries were by that time governed by a dictatorship (as was Japan). In the ten countries preserving

democratic-style government—Norway, Denmark, Sweden, Finland, Czechoslovakia, Switzerland, Holland, Belgium, France, and Great Britain—active right-wing groups promoted authoritarianism.

In three countries this authoritarianism became even more extreme, with ominous consequences for the general peace. Russia, Italy, and Germany developed political systems so thoroughly authoritarian that they are called *totalitarian*. Totalitarianism is basically a political system where a dictator controls the state, and the state uses its power to try to control virtually all aspects of life, including the thinking and expression of the citizens. Absolutely total control in this sense is not possible, but totalitarian regimes went far in trying to achieve it. These totalitarian regimes confronted the democratic Western European states with a collective will, wielded by powerful leaders, that the democracies could not, at first, match in the crisis-ridden interwar period. Subject to divided political bases and a strong inclination to avoid war, the Western democracies did not meet the threats posed by the totalitarian regimes.

Fascist Italy

Although Soviet Russia under V.I. Lenin's leadership might be classified as totalitarian, it would remain for Josef Stalin to create thoroughgoing totalitarianism in that country. Before Lenin died and Stalin worked his way into power in Russia, however, Italy shocked the democratic world when a former Socialist and school teacher, Benito Mussolini, seized power in 1922, established an authoritarian government and attempted to implement totalitarianism. Although Mussolini was less successful than either Stalin or Hitler in his totalitarianism, he was the first to use the word "totalitarianism" and promote it ideologically. Mussolini also served as an important and admired model for Hitler, and so he must be considered in analyzing the rise of totalitarian dictatorships and the coming of World War II.

In all three European totalitarian regimes of the interwar period, a key element was the glorification of the leader as hero, as an exalted figure who embodied the will of the whole. The title of Mussolini in Italy and Hitler in Germany was simply "the Leader," which in Italian is *Il Duce* and in German *der Fuhrer*. The identity and nature of the regimes, therefore, were tied very closely to the identity and nature of the individual leaders. Benito Mussolini was born in Dovia, Italy, on July 27, 1883, the son of a school teacher (his mother) and a blacksmith. Expelled as a teenager for bad conduct from a school operated by the Salesian Friars, Mussolini went on to become an elementary school teacher himself. In 1902 Mussolini spent some time as a laborer in Switzerland where he got in trouble with the police for vagrancy and fighting. Moving back to Italy in 1904, he did his term of compulsory military service and then taught for a short stint again in 1907-1908. In 1909 he began involvement with socialist newspapers and became a radical agitator, also reading and being influenced by works by Nietzsche and Sorel. When World War I broke out, however, Mussolini became a nationalist warmonger, recalling Italy's glorious past and demanding that Italy join the fight on the Allied side and seek to reclaim Italian territory then controlled by the Austro-Hungarian Empire. He was kicked out of the Socialist Party for his pro-war stance. When Italy did enter the war on the Allied side, Mussolini joined the army, eventually rising to the rank of corporal, and fought in the trenches from September 1915 through February 1917, when he was wounded.

After the war, as Italy was experiencing postwar problems similar to those in other countries—war debt, an economic slump, strikes, political turmoil—Mussolini became involved in the *freikorps* phenomenon. He organized in March 1919 a group of men, most of them former soldiers like himself, into a *fascio di combattimento*, a fighting "bunch" or band. *Fascio,* which meant "bunch" or "bundle," also played on the term for the ancient Roman symbol of authority, the *fasces*, an axe surrounded by a tied bundle of rods. When the Paris peace settlement failed to give Italy all the territory it had been promised by the secret Treaty of London (1915), many Italians, Mussolini included, felt that Italy's sacrifice of over 600,000 lives in the war had been wasted. Using his dramatic speaking ability, his strutting, boastful demeanor, his flair for flamboyant gestures and charades (He jumped through a hoop of fire to demonstrate his machismo.), and his fiery personality, Mussolini developed his Fascists into a larger group with an identity as a political party as well. Roman salutes, chants of "Duce, Duce, Duce," and black shirt uniforms created a sense of belonging, of immersing oneself into a group that was larger and more potent than the individual. The Fascists, nicknamed the Blackshirts, engaged in street fighting against Communists, Socialists, Christian Socialists, workers, and other opponents in this restive time. Mussolini, the former socialist revolutionary, now cast his Fascists as saviors of law and order, fighting against communism and labor agitation. The Fascists beat people, forced them to drink doses of castor oil, set fires, and committed murder. Conservative Italians, who were scared of radical workers and communists and increasingly favored the use of force to crush such groups or other strong measures to protect the existing order, began supporting the Fascists.

Fascists rallying in Rome at the conclusion of the March.

Although any real danger of revolution in Italy had passed, fear of leftist groups persisted, and in October 1922, Mussolini took advantage of this fear and the parliamentary government's general inaction over the past years (The government had been content to let the Fascists subdue the leftist groups.) to threaten a coup to secure order. With Mussolini staying in Milan, Blackshirts from various parts of Italy converged on the capital in the "March on Rome." The king of Italy refused to oppose the Fascists, the Italian government resigned, and Mussolini was named premier. Although given only a year of emergency power to restore order, Mussolini and the Fascists moved to consolidate their power and established a dictatorship that lasted until 1944.

The totalitarian aspects of Fascist Italy can be seen in the way power was wielded. Mussolini and his council of party leaders assumed the key posts in the Italian government. The press was controlled, all political parties other than the Fascists were outlawed, and a fascist labor union replaced all others. Economic controls were imposed to increase Italian self-sufficiency. Public works projects, such as hydroelectric dams, had similar goals as well as providing economic stimulus. Fascist propaganda permeated textbooks, education, art, plays, and movies. Secret police worked to discover and deal with all opposition to the Fascists. Eventually, to assert the Italian nationalism, Mussolini embarked on imperialistic adventures in the Mediterranean world and North Africa that contributed to the coming of the Second World War.

The ideological basis of Italian Fascism involved several elements. First, it was action-oriented, being focused on practical results. In terms of policy Fascism did not bind itself to a specific doctrine or agenda, but it pursued what seemed to have the best chance of working at the moment. Mussolini wrote that "Fascism was not the nursling of a doctrine worked out beforehand with detailed elaboration; it was born of the need for action and it was itself from the beginning practical rather than theoretical." Second, force, violence, and police power were glorified and used to get and keep power. The Fascist Party served as an elite element of society that held the power. In 1938 Fascist Italy was organized into syndicates, or "corporations" (bodies), of workers and producers that, according to theory, planned and governed the economy and state. This led to the term "corporative state" to describe Fascist Italy. In reality, however, power remained in the hands of Mussolini and his top party officials. Third, nationalism was a part of Fascist ideology. The Italian nation was glorified, with heavy reference to the ancient Romans. In an effort to tie imperialistic goals to the past glories of the Roman Empire that had ruled the entire Mediterranean world for a time, Mussolini called the Mediterranean Sea *Mare Nostrum*: "Our Sea." National power and glory were ends for which Italians should strive. Fourth, Fascism championed the state over the individual. The individual was to forego personal desires and efforts and instead focus on the good of the state. The state was a spiritual force that individuals could contribute to and participate in by subsuming themselves to it. Of course, the will of the state, what was good for the state, was expressed by the leader of the state, *Il Duce*, who was Mussolini.

Mussolini and Fascism contributed a great deal to the coming of the Second World War. The example of tough-talking, nationalistic, action-oriented leadership set by Mussolini provided Adolf Hitler with a concrete model to imitate. Mussolini helped make Hitler more acceptable by paving the way for totalitarianism and by casting himself as a defender of order against radical or communist activity; Hitler was viewed in a similar light by many Europeans who might disagree with tactics but applauded the seeming results. Mussolini eventually provided Hitler with a like-minded ally and was important in demonstrating the ineffectiveness of the League of Nations in the face of aggression.

Communist Russia

Although the basic communist system in Russia originated before Josef Stalin came to power and, therefore, was not tied to the totalitarian leader in the same way Fascism and Nazism were, the special character and personality of the Communist regime under Stalin was in many ways a result of the influence of the man. Josef Stalin was born Iosif Vissarinovich Djugashvill on December 21, 1879, in the town of Gori in the Russian province Georgia. He changed his name to Stalin, meaning "man of steel," in 1913. The son of a shoemaker, Stalin proved to be a bright student as a child and was able at the age of 14 to go on scholarship to a religious seminary in

Tiflis where he studied for the priesthood in the Georgian Orthodox (Christian) Church. While at the seminary Stalin was punished several times for reading forbidden books and became interested in the socialist ideas of Karl Marx, joining a secret Marxist group in 1898. After being expelled from seminary for missing an exam, Stalin devoted more time to revolutionary Marxism, writing pieces for radical papers and organizing worker strikes.

In 1903, after being jailed the previous year for his radical activity, Stalin was exiled to Siberia by the Czarist government. That same year, Marxists in Russia split into two factions. The majority, or *Bolsheviks,* favored revolution as the means to socialist change as opposed to the minority, the *Mensheviks,* who favored a gradual approach of working within the system. The Bolsheviks believed the party should be composed of an elite cadre of dedicated revolutionaries. Escaping from exile, Stalin joined the Bolsheviks and met V.I. Lenin, the group's leader, for the first time in Finland in 1905. He continued his radical activity over the next dozen years, spending the majority of the time in prison or exile. Lenin included Stalin in the Central Committee of the Bolsheviks (the party's governing body) in 1912. During World War I, Stalin spent most of the conflict in Siberian exile, having been rejected for military service by the Russian army for physical reasons.

Under the strains of the war, the czarist monarchy collapsed in 1917 as a liberal revolution established parliamentary government. The provisional government released Stalin from exile, and he returned to his political activism, becoming editor of the Bolshevik (Communist) newspaper *Pravda* ("Truth"). The provisional government itself was overthrown later in 1917 by the Bolsheviks under the leadership of Lenin. The Bolsheviks pulled Russia out of the war with Germany with great cost in the Treaty of Brest-Litovsk, a move that incensed the Western Allies who now had to face Germany in a one front war. The Bolsheviks also had to fight a two-year civil war to remain in power, all the while facing major economic crises. Stalin served the Bolshevik revolution in various ways during this period and became General Secretary of the Communist Party in 1922, a very powerful position that Stalin used to good advantage, maneuvering and scheming to increase his own personal political power.

Lenin eventually decided that he wanted Stalin removed from this position because of the Georgian's machinations and abuses of power. Lenin, however, suffered a stroke in 1923 and died the following year without having ousted Stalin. There was no clear successor to Lenin and a power struggle played out over the next few years, primarily waged between Stalin and Leon Trotsky, another committed Bolshevik who had played central roles in the revolution and Lenin regime. The two figures disagreed on policy in addition to competing for power. Stalin favored consolidating the revolution in Russia as the Bolsheviks' first priority, believing that "socialism in one country" was possible. Trotsky, on the other hand, wanted to focus on fomenting revolution in other European countries, believing that Russia needed other socialist nations to help sustain the revolution. Stalin used his party influence and great skill as a political infighter to isolate Trotsky, eventually ejecting him from the party and Russia as well. Stalin was firmly in control of the party and the Soviet Union by the end of 1927. His iron-fisted dictatorship in that country became thoroughly totalitarian and lasted until his death in 1953.

The Communist regime of Josef Stalin naturally incorporated much of the ideology of Karl

Marx's socialist theory. The term Communist, however, is perhaps not the most appropriate to use. Marx had argued that socialism, a dictatorship of the proletariat established after the workers' revolution, would evolve into a perfect state he called communism in which no classes existed and the state (government) disappeared as well. Stalin's communism was in many ways Marx's socialist phase of this evolution stuck permanently in place. Under Stalin, the state owned and controlled the means of production. The state (controlled by Stalin) centrally planned the economy, deciding what to produce, how much to produce, and who did what in the process. A good example of this is the series of five-year plans that Stalin proposed and implemented beginning in 1928. The 1928 plan involved excising capitalism completely, industrializing the economy, collectivizing and mechanizing farming, and providing for national defense.

The government of the state was a totalitarian dictatorship that relied on various techniques to enforce conformity to the rules. Secret police units monitored citizen loyalty and enforced conformity. The GPU (Chief Political Administration), which became the NKVD (People's Commissariat for Internal Affairs) in 1934, was a primary secret police agency. Opponents of the state were ruthlessly eliminated. Terror—threat of death, imprisonment, exile, disappearance, or worse—kept many people in line. The forced changes involved in implementing the five-year plans were wrenching and demonstrate the totalitarian nature of Stalinist communism. For Soviet agriculture to be collectivized, i.e., organized into huge farms operated collectively by the peasants under state control, tens of thousands of individual plots of land privately owned by the *kulaks*, as these freeholding peasants were known, were forcibly taken by the state and the owners forced to work on the collective farms. Those who resisted, as some two million did, were removed to Siberia or killed.

Stalin's use or application of terror followed no logical pattern. There was no way to be completely safe from it because the victim might have done nothing to deserve punishment. In many cases, Stalin's paranoia of possible threats to his power resulted in exiles and executions. The best example is the Great Purge of the 1930s, a four-year period of terror beginning at the end of 1934. In this episode, the Communist Party, the Red Army, secret police organizations, and other units of the state were cleared of suspected opponents of Stalin, of those who helped "identify" the threats, of those who did not help, of eventually the purgers themselves. Without rhyme or reason, Soviet citizens were imprisoned, exiled, and forced into labor camps by the millions. By 1938 Russian prison facilities and labor camps were filled with about 8 million people, some of whom died, all of whom suffered terribly. The Red Army was particularly (and illogically) hit hard. Executed in the purge were all 11 Deputy Commissars for Defense, 3 of 5 Field Marshals, 13 of 15 army commanders, and tens of thousands of middle-rank officers. The purge of the army, occurring mainly in 1937, seriously weakened the Russian military on the eve of the Second World War and contributed to the military disaster Russia experienced in 1941 at the hands of Germany, a disaster that nearly led to Russian defeat. Although the Great Purge cost the lives of about 300,000, in the final result, it is impossible to say with accuracy how many *millions* were either killed outright or died in labor camps or concentration camps under Stalin's dictatorship. But in terms of sheer numbers killed, Stalin's record makes Hitler and the Nazis seem tame in comparison.

As in other totalitarian states, propaganda, ideology, and party control impacted the arts, sciences, and education. If a style of art or music was deemed capitalistic or bourgeois, it was censored. In some cases even scientific ideas were censored. In one case a Soviet commissar determined that the Mendelian law of genetics, well accepted in the scientific community, conflicted with party ideology. Russian scientists, therefore, had to repudiate the theory. Though conformity to ideology was enforced, Soviet education effectively trained people to fill all manner of needed positions, from engineers and scientists to artists and musicians.

Reordering of society was also pursued by the totalitarian Soviet state. Women received legal equality in marriage, could vote in the Soviet elections, received equal pay, and had the same educational and occupational opportunities as men. Politically, however, women did not share equally. Religion was eliminated from public life, with education being strictly secular. Churches were not allowed to carry on organized religious instruction. Church property was confiscated. Many class distinctions were eliminated, but party membership created a new caste. The Communist Party became an elite element in Soviet society, with members often having privileges that the ordinary Russian did not enjoy. On the other hand, party membership had its negative consequences. In the Great Purge, party members were the main targets. In 1935, there were 2,358,000 party members. In spite of continual recruitment efforts, the party membership was 1,920,000 in 1938.

Communist Russia contributed to the coming of World War II in various ways. One of the more important was that through the hysteria generated in the West by Comintern efforts to foment revolution in the West, anticommunist right-wing dictatorships like Mussolini's and Hitler's had enough tacit approval in the West to survive until they themselves had become threats to the peace. By casting themselves openly as enemies of the Western capitalistic system, the Communists made Mussolini and Hitler valuable as bulwarks against Communism and made them look like a preferable alternative. The mistrust generated by Comintern activity and the way the Communists had pulled Russia out of the First World War, leaving the Western Allies alone in the fight, made it difficult for the West to trust Russia and created a split in European diplomacy of which Germany took full advantage. Finally, Stalin's Red Army purges and other brutalities severely hurt Russia militarily, making the country a weaker deterrent to Nazi aggression. The impact was in some ways similar to the effect of pacifism in the West. Hitler believed the West would not act against him because they lacked the will to do so, while he believed Russia was too weak militarily to effectively act against him. In both cases, the aggressiveness of the dictator was tempted.

Nazi Germany

As with Fascism, the origins and rise of Nazism are inextricably tied up with the life of the movement's leader. In many senses, Adolf Hitler was Nazism. This is not just because Hitler's ideas and attitudes were so well-reflected in Nazi ideology but because the Nazis were so effective in establishing a totalitarian regime tied to its leader that Hitler literally embodied the movement. Adolf Hitler was born on April 20, 1889, at the town of Brannau-on-Inn in Austria, just across the Inn River from Germany. The German-speaking border town was a natural location for Hitler's birth because of his father's occupation as a career customs official in the Austrian civil service. The geographic circumstances of Hitler's birth and childhood in Linz, also near the German border, are significant in another way. As a cultural and linguistic German born and raised just outside the then newly formed German Empire (the Second Reich) at a time of intense German nationalism, Hitler experienced a more powerful sense of nationalism than someone inside the Reich. Hitler was a German inside the polyglot Habsburg Empire of Austria-Hungary where many ethnic groups and nationalities lived. German cultural identity could seem much more important in that circumstance.

Hitler's father, Alois, had been born the illegitimate son of Maria Schicklgruber but was legitimized and took the surname of his claimant father, Johann Georg Heidler. Alois spelled the name Hitler. If there is anything in a name, Adolf Hitler's later political career benefited tremendously by Alois taking Hitler instead of Schicklgruber. Adolf's mother, Klara, was Alois'

Alois Sr. was not a loving father. He was an abusive alcoholic with little patience.

third wife and second cousin. At the time of Adolf's birth, Alois was over 50 years old and Klara was under 30. To this unpromising family setting was added the tension of conflicting aspirations for young Adolf. Alois wanted his son to follow him in the civil service, but Adolf wanted to pursue the dream of becoming an artist. This conflict, combined with arguments over Adolf's poor grades, made disputes between father and son an important backdrop to Hitler's childhood. He found relief and was indulged by his mother after father Alois died in 1903.

Hitler went through the usual education and Catholic instruction. He served as a choirboy in the local Catholic Church and even toyed with the idea of becoming a priest at one time. Eventually Hitler and a friend from Linz went to Vienna, the lively capital of the Austro-Hungarian Empire, to go to the art academy. Hitler was crushed when he was denied admittance to

Hitler's mother showed him affection and was very protective.

the Academy of Fine Arts in 1907 and again in 1908. His mother having died in 1907, Hitler spent the period from 1909 to 1913 in a hand-to-mouth existence, working odd jobs, painting advertising placards for money and postcards that he sold to tourists, living in hostels, barely getting by. During these tough years in Vienna, Hitler spent a lot of time reading. He soaked up the anti-Semitic and extreme/racial German nationalist literature that was quite common in German-speaking areas like Vienna at this time. In Vienna he observed in action the anti-Semitic politics of Karl Lueger's Christian Social Party and the mass-party, mass-propaganda political tactics of the Austrian Social Democrats. He also attended the opera when he could and loved the operas of Richard Wagner. Wagnerian opera was generally nationalistic in theme, evoking strong emotional images of the mythic, Germanic past. Hitler came out of his Vienna experience with a strong grounding in anti-Semitism and German nationalism, as well as political tactics, ideas that proved central to the Nazism he later shaped.

By the time World War I began in August 1914, Hitler had left Austria and moved to Munich, Bavaria, in southern Germany. Enlisting in a Bavarian regiment, Hitler served with distinction on the Western front, primarily as a dispatch runner, a very dangerous position. He won the Iron Cross First Class and Second Class for his bravery, attained the rank of lance-corporal, and was recovering from temporary blindness sustained in a British poison gas attack when the war ended. After the war, he continued to serve the army in Bavaria as a political instructor of sorts and found that he had the gift of oratory. In this capacity, he was sent to check on a small group called the German Workers Party, one of many politicized groups meeting in the beer halls of Munich in the troubled post-

The swastika, on the NSDAP flag, symbolized the German people's struggle "for the Aryan man."

war period. Ernst Röhm, a captain in the German army, and other army and ex-army elements were attracted to the group. In the context of this little organization, Hitler became enthralled by politics, and by April 1920 he resigned from the army to devote himself full time to politics and this party. By July 1921, Hitler had become the leader, or *führer*, of the party.

In this period the party changed its name to the *Nazionalsozialistichedeutschearbeiterpartei* (NSDAP), National Socialist German Workers Party, usually shortened to Nazi, from the first four letters of the German word for "national." The Nazi Party adopted a flag that used the white, red, and black of the German Empire's flag and a *hakenkruz* (hooked cross), or swastika, that was a symbol of mythical "Aryan" racial purity. A political program was also adopted that, among other things, called for the repu-

The SS units, originally formed to serve as Hitler's personal security force, became the most feared branch of the Nazi organization.

diation of the Versailles Treaty, an anti-Semitic racial policy, the unification of Austria and Germany (forbidden by the Treaty of Versailles), agrarian reform for the peasants, and a strong, centralized, authoritarian government.

Hitler worked tirelessly in building up the party, using his hypnotic speaking ability to spellbind listeners, playing on their prejudices against Jews, their hatred for the treaty of Versailles, and their distrust of the Weimar politicians. He established a party newspaper for propaganda purposes, adopted the "heil" greeting and Roman salute, and formed a freikorps-style group of roughhousers to control party meetings and to fight opposing parties like the Communists. This para-military group was the S.A., short for *Sturmabteilungen,* or "Storm Detachment," who wore brown shirts and mimicked Mussolini's blackshirts. Ernst Röhm, an intensely loyal Hitler supporter, was the man behind the S.A. and its long-time leader, though not its first

leader. An elite bodyguard was also formed, which evolved into the S.S., short for *Schutzstaffel,* or "Protection Squadron," who wore black uniforms and a runic double-lightning-bolt symbol. Other early supporters and party members included Rudolf Hess, who had served in the same regiment with Hitler in the war, and Hermann Goring, a tall, dashing flying ace who had shot down twenty Allied planes in the war. Both of these men were key figures in the Nazi regime once Hitler rose to power in the 1930s.

By November 1923, with tension and economic problems besetting the country due to the Ruhr crisis over reparations, Hitler felt that the time was right to take dramatic action, like the Fascists' March on Rome, and attempted a coup in Munich. He had enlisted the support of Erich von Ludendorff, eminent field marshal and war leader during World War I. Apparently, Hitler expected a spontaneous response in Ber-

On trial for their part in the 1923 Beer Hall Putsch, General Ludendorff (far left) and Hitler (second from left) await the verdict of the court. Hitler was sentenced to five years in prison but served only nine months.

lin and elsewhere in Germany to rise up in support of the Nazis, once they had seized power in Bavaria, and sweep the party into power. The Nazi Party had little presence outside Bavaria and even in Munich plans for the coup were not well thought out. The coup (putsch in German) attempt is known as the Beer Hall Putsch because Hitler was able to initially take control of the Bavarian government by bursting into a political rally the government was holding in the Buergerbraukeller, a Munich beer hall.

After achieving momentary surprise and brief control of the Bavarian government, the coup fell apart when the police and army moved against it. Hitler was eventually arrested and tried for treason. The trial gave Hitler national attention, as people tuned in to see what the funny-looking Austrian with the toothbrush moustache had been up to. He was able to use his oratorical skills to good effect, however, and made a favorable impression on many. As an indication of how little respect the Weimar government had, treason against it was not taken too seriously. Hitler was sentenced to a mere five years imprisonment in comfortable Landsberg Prison and would serve less than half the sen-

tence. More importantly, however, the Nazi Party was dissolved (at least temporarily) by the government, its property seized, and Hitler was banned from speaking in public for a period of time.

The failed putsch was a major setback and caused Hitler to rethink his strategy. While in prison, Hitler dictated to Rudolf Hess most of the book that became *Mein Kampf*, "My Struggle." *Mein Kampf* was Hitler's and, therefore, the Nazis' political manifesto, explaining their beliefs and goals. Nothing of importance was hidden or left unspoken: the anti-Semitism, desire for territorial expansion, plans to throw off the Treaty of Versailles. All of what Hitler eventually attempted was spelled out in *Mein Kampf*. Hitler also decided to change tactics; instead of trying to seize power by means of a coup, he decided the Nazis should pursue power through the Weimar system by trying to win seats in the Reichstag in the electoral process. This did not mean, however, that the Nazis would give up violence and other underhanded tactics.

After leaving prison, Hitler steadily rebuilt the Nazi Party. But, after several years of effort, in the 1928 elections the Nazis managed to win only 12 seats in the Reichstag. The prosperity and international cooperation of the Five Good Years made extremist approaches, such as Nazism, less attractive. In 1930, however, the Nazis won 107 seats, and in 1932 they won 230 seats, some 37 percent, making the Nazis the largest party in the Reichstag. The coming of the Great Depression had made the difference. German unemployment stood at 2.2 million in March 1930. In March 1932, unemployment was over 6 million. As times got hard, people were more willing to listen to the Nazi approach and its call for strong leadership. In fact, by 1933, the Weimar government itself had already become quite authoritarian by resorting to the constitutional provision that allowed the president to rule by decree in times of emergency. The aging President Paul von Hindenburg, field marshal of World War I fame, went through a series of chancellors and cabinets based on shaky coalitions in the Reichstag. Eventually, the size of the Nazi vote combined with political maneuvering by Franz von Papen, a close associate of Hindenburg who thought he could control Hitler, led to Adolf Hitler being named chancellor of a coalition cabinet in January 1933. Only two other Nazis were included in the cabinet, but one of them was Hermann Göring and he was named as the Minister of the Interior, a position that controlled police forces.

Hitler and the Nazis set out to consolidate their power. After calling for another round of elections to be held in March, Hitler used a fire that burned the Reichstag building and was blamed on the Communists as an excuse to suspend civil liberties. Hitler and Goring used government power then to lock up opponents and control the press, speeches, assemblies, and the mail to Nazi advantage in the elections. The Nazis won 288 seats or 44 percent of the vote. This was still not a majority and certainly was

The aging German President Paul von Hindenburg did not want Adolf Hitler to be chancellor.

not a two-thirds majority needed to change the constitution. However, by excluding Communist delegates from the Reichstag, by intimidating other delegates, and with the supporting votes of the Catholic Center Party in the Reichstag, Hitler had a two-thirds majority that passed the Enabling Act on March 24, 1933. This law authorized the chancellor to rule by decree. With the power to make law in the chancellor's hands, the Reichstag became a rubber-stamp body with no real power. Hitler proceeded to legislate the Nazis into power and establish a totalitarian regime. He Nazified the trade unions, made the Nazi Party the only

After being sworn in as chancellor, (pictured) Hitler set out to seize absolute power.

legal party, and brought the state governments directly under the national government's control. When the aged President Hindenburg died in August 1934, the offices of president and chancellor were merged, and Hitler became the sole leader, assuming the title of *der Führer*. Hitler was now dictator.

One major obstacle to complete success remained. The German army, with its aristocratic officer corps and its long and glorious heritage, viewed the Nazis with suspicion and often with disgust, particularly because the Nazi S.A., with its ruffian character, seemed to be organized as a replacement for the German army. In fact, Röhm, head of the S.A. since 1931, had built the organization into a force of a million members with the idea that its members would fight for the party as it rose to power and then be rewarded by becoming the core of a revived German army as the military restrictions of the Versailles Treaty were cast away. Another problem for Hitler was that many army leaders wanted a return to the Hohenzollern monarchy, not rule by an upstart Austrian corporal. Hitler

needed to win the support of the army if he was to be in complete control and if he hoped to achieve his foreign policy goals. To achieve this, first, Hitler promised the army that he would no longer follow the Versailles Treaty military limits and would rebuild, revive, and rearm the German military. Second, Hitler showed his capacity for extreme ruthlessness by literally sacrificing the S.A. to satisfy the army of his commitment to them. Beginning on June 30, 1934, a purge of the S.A. and Nazi Party was conducted on the orders of Hitler. Key leaders of the S.A., including Ernst Röhm, who was one of Hitler's closest associates and longest supporters, were summarily executed. The opportunity was used to assassinate old political enemies outside the party as well. In all, at least 78 and perhaps as many as 400 people were murdered as a part of the organized purge. With its leadership gone, the S.A. was rechanneled in the party, losing its former role and promise. Shocked, but satisfied that their position was secure, the German army moved into line behind the Hitler regime. Nazism could now be extended into all aspects of life.

This 1934 photo of the Nuremberg rally shows the strength of the Nazi Party after Hitler made himself dictator of Germany's Third Reich.

Ideologically, Nazism was much like fascism in its glorification of violence and force, its desire for action, its celebration of the nation, and its emphasis of the state over the individual. But there were important differences between the two movements. The meaning of the words National and Socialist in the Nazi Party name point out some of these differences. The idea of the nation for Nazis was one of a racial nation, or *volk* (people), based on birth. What made one German to the Nazis was blood. The glorious, superior characteristics of the German were inherited. Racial purity, avoiding intermarriage with inferior nationalities (races to the Nazis), and even destroying those polluting races, was necessary to preserve the strength and vitality of the nation, the volk. The "Socialist" in National Socialism did not involve the socialism of Karl Marx in which the state owned the means of production and rewards were distributed according to need. Instead, the Nazis referred to the idea of a community of racial kin working together for the greater good of the society. The Nazi slogan, *Gemeinnutz vor Eigennutz,* illustrates this idea: the slogan translates as "Community good before individual good." Germans, united by blood (race) were to work for the good of the nation (*volk*). In this sense the state was not the ultimate force but rather the *volk* was. Nazis believed, however, that the interests of the *volk* were served best by having a powerful state controlled by one leader (*führer*). This *führerprinzip*, or "leader principle," further held that the will of the leader was the will of the state and the will of the nation; therefore, the leader must be followed.

As implemented in Germany, Nazism pursued many policies, involving state control of most activities and aspects of life and thus illustrates the totalitarian nature of Nazi government. For Hitler and many other Nazis, the most important aspect of life to be controlled was the racial situation. Jews were held to be the most inferior "nation," representing the opposite characteristics of what Germans represented. German Jews were, therefore, targeted early in the period of Nazi control. The Nuremberg Laws of September 1935 set the tone. Jewishness was defined based on the degree of Jewish parentage one had. Sexual relations and intermarriage between Jews and Gentiles (non-Jewish) were forbidden. Jews were stripped of their German citizenship. Jews were barred from the professions and many occupations. Jews could not employ "Aryan" females under the age of 35. In addition to official laws, a powerful unofficial anti-Semitism policy was encouraged—general discrimination against and humiliation of Jews.

A guard stands outside a Jewish business to
enforce the 1933 boycott.

Additionally, Jews were required to wear a yellow Star of David emblem on their clothing, a practice that had its origin in Church policy of the Middle Ages.

One of the worst episodes of anti-Semitic harassment before the outbreak of World War II and the Holocaust was *Kristallnacht*, the "Crystal Night," i.e., the Night of the Broken Glass. November 7, 1938, the Nazi regime unleashed an organized pogrom, or attack, on Jews all over the country. Organized by Reinhard Heydrich, head of the Nazi Security Service and the Gestapo secret police, Nazis vandalized, pillaged, or burned thousands of Jewish stores and synagogues. The damage estimates for the broken glass alone was 5 million marks. Several Jews were killed, and thousands were arrested and imprisoned in concentration camps set up to incarcerate various "enemies" of the state. Jews

were fined one billion marks for this episode, they were forced to pay for the damages, and any insurance money they received was confiscated. Hereafter, Jews were forbidden to own businesses. The ultimate extension of these policies was the Holocaust that was carried out during the Second World War. All of these policies were implemented despite the fact that virtually all German Jews were German in their language, culture, loyalty, and heritage and represented only about 500,000 people in a total German population of over 60 million.

Other Nazi policies affected the economy and other aspects of life. The Nazis set up a mandatory labor service that organized all workers. A public building program provided jobs and constructed facilities the government deemed necessary, including the *Autobahnen*, a national highway system that served military transport needs as well as civilian. A housing program constructed over 300,000 homes by 1937. All existing labor unions were outlawed, and a single Nazi-controlled union, the Labor Front, was created. The state did not abolish private ownership of factories but controlled

The Hitler Youth camps provided an opportunity
for more influence over the lives of members.

Hitler Youth members, ten- to eighteen-year-olds, salute their leader.

what was produced. A "Four Year Plan" to move Germany to economic self-sufficiency was attempted. Education at all levels, including universities, was directly controlled by the state. Racial and Nazi indoctrination was incorporated in education. Nazi organizations, like the Hitler Youth, encouraged children to become a part of the Nazi movement. Propaganda was funneled through the government-controlled press, radio, movies, art, literature, and music, all coordinated by a Propaganda Ministry headed by Joseph Göbels. Secret police monitored citizens' activities and encouraged snitching. In these ways and others, the Nazis forged a highly totalitarian system in a few short years.

The foreign policy of Hitler and the Nazis is in many ways even more important because of the role it played in the coming of the Second World War. The particular foreign policy objectives of the Nazis were given the power and impetus of virtually the entire German nation because of the effectiveness of the Nazis in establishing a totalitarian regime. This is impor-

tant in understanding the connection between the First World War, the interwar period, the rise of totalitarianism, and the coming of the Second World War. These Nazi goals were intentionally, explicitly designed to undo the Paris Peace settlement reached at the end of World War I, restore Germany to a position of international power, and to extend German control eastward. This aggressive policy, when implemented piece by piece in the 1930s would be the driving force behind events leading to the Second World War.

INTERNATIONAL AFFAIRS OF THE 1930s AND THE PATH TO WAR

The security framework (or means of keeping the peace) incorporated in the Paris peace settlement involved two primary components: 1) a set of economic, military, and territorial provisions designed to prevent Germany from rising and making war again, and 2) an international organization, the League of Nations, designed to resolve disputes and provide a deterrent to aggression through collective security. The 1930s saw this security framework destroyed in a series of events that culminated in the start of a Second World War, marking the ultimate failure of the Paris scheme.

The first key development undermining the peace framework of the Paris settlement was the coming of the Great Depression. The economic distress of this crisis crushed the spirit of cooperation and international goodwill that had developed in the last five years of the 1920s. It also focused attention on internal matters in Britain and France at the same time that it helped the Nazis to power in Germany and gave that regime a concrete reason for challenging the Paris settlement. The Depression intensified fears in the West that communist revolution might be around the corner and enhanced support and toleration of right-wing authoritarian governments. On a potentially positive note, the Depression also did away with the thorny problem of reparations and war loans payments. The economic collapse made it impossible to pay either, and after U.S. President Herbert Hoover finally declared a moratorium on payments in 1931, the payments never resumed. On the other hand, reparations had been one of the ways that Germany's ability to wage war was limited.

At the same time that the Depression was making international relations more troubled, the League of Nations' response to an incident in Asia demonstrated the unwillingness of the Western powers to use the League to prevent or stop aggression. The "Manchurian incident" was a military incident staged by Japanese forces and designed to give the Japanese an excuse to assume greater control in Manchuria. The League of Nations sent a commission to investigate. The commission found the Japanese guilty of aggression, the League accepted the commission's findings and agreed that Japan was the aggressor, but the League took no action to prevent Japan from occupying Manchuria and incorporating it into their economic empire. The League could only deter aggression if it built a reputation for acting to stop it, and this development had the exact opposite effect. Japanese militarists, on their way to establishing authoritarian rule in their country, felt free to pursue further expansion. Would-be aggressors in Europe also took note.

Shortly after coming to power in Germany, Adolf Hitler dealt the next major blow to the peace settlement. After demanding and being refused parity of armaments, Hitler pulled Germany out of the World Disarmament Conference that was meeting in Geneva when Hitler became chancellor in 1933. He also pulled Germany out of the League of Nations, dealing the

league a symbolic blow, and announced that the military provisions of the Treaty of Versailles requiring German disarmament were no longer binding. These actions drew no response from Britain, France, and Italy. In March 1935 Hitler took the armaments issue a dramatic step further. He openly announced that Germany was beginning a rearmament program that included the formation of a 36-division Wehrmacht (army), the introduction of conscription, a naval building program, and the formation of the Luftwaffe (air force). All of these steps were blatant violations of the Versailles Treaty and struck at the heart of the peace and security structure of that settlement. Britain, France, and Italy protested and, at Mussolini's suggestion, formed an agreement called the "Stressa Front" to watch Hitler. But they took no action to enforce the treaty, and, in fact, Britain made a naval treaty with Nazi Germany limiting the size of the German navy relative to the British, an action that seemed to legitimize the end of Versailles restrictions on Germany.

One reason for Mussolini's offer to work with Britain and France to watch Hitler in the Stressa Front was that the Italian dictator was planning what became the next major blow to the League of Nations and hoped the British and French would not intervene. As part of his nationalistic agenda to restore Italy to greatness by acquiring colonies, Mussolini ordered an Italian invasion of the northeastern-African country of Ethiopia. As a member of the League of Nations, Ethiopian leader Haille Sallaise appealed to the League for collective assistance against Italian aggression. The League responded by denouncing Italy as an aggressor but took no military action to assist the hard-pressed Ethiopians. Economic sanctions were imposed that cut off trade to Italy for certain products like tin and scrap iron, but the most important item of trade for Mussolini, oil, was not included in the sanctions. Again the League was exposed as a weak force that would not be used to block aggression.

While Europe was distracted by the Ethiopian crisis, Hitler took another bold step in direct violation of the Treaty of Versailles that undercut a key security provision of the peace settlement. According to the Versailles Treaty, the strip of Germany that lay west of the Rhine River and bordered Belgium and France was to be demilitarized: Germany was allowed no troops or fortifications in this area. This was supposed to enhance French security by making it difficult for Germany to launch an attack on France without the preparations becoming noticeable. In March 1936, Hitler sent units of the German army into the Rhineland with orders to immediately withdraw if they met any resistance. The French and British once again did nothing. Germany began construction of the Siegfried Line defensive fortifications along the French border. The Treaty of Versailles had become worthless.

In July 1936, the Spanish Civil War broke out as army leaders, eventually headed by General Francisco Franco, fought to overthrow the republican government. Franco, backed by right-wing, conservative elements in Spain, including the fascist-styled *Falange* Party, was also supported by Nazi Germany and Fascist Italy until he eventually prevailed in 1939, becoming the dictator of an authoritarian regime that lasted until Franco's death in 1975. Mussolini contributed naval forces and over 50,000 troops to Franco's aid, and Hitler sent 5000 advisors and Luftwaffe units. In one of the first uses of aerial bombing against civilians, the Basque town of Guernica in northern Spain was heavily bombed, evidently by German planes. The devastation and grief of the event inspired Pablo Picasso's famous painting *Guernica*. Both Mussolini and Hitler used the civil war in Spain as a practice ground for their militaries, trying out equipment and techniques on the republican forces. The Soviet Union also intervened in the war, supporting the Republic but funneling that support through the Communist element fighting for the Republic. The Western democracies, however, did nothing to help the fellow democratic government against Franco, nor did the League of Nations, which adopted a policy of non-intervention based on the argument that the war was an internal Spanish matter. Volunteers from Western countries, including Ernest Hemingway from the United States, did fight for the republicans, but their governments avoided involvement and watched another democracy turn to authoritarian dictatorship.

Along with the Ethiopian crisis, the Spanish Civil War helped solidify a relationship between Mussolini and Hitler that bolstered their aggressive tendencies by providing one another an ally. This mutual support between aggressive nations not only bolstered those regimes' confidence but also heightened tensions in the troubled world. Not long after the beginning of the civil war in 1936, the two dictators formed an agreement called the Rome-Berlin Axis. In the informal October Protocols of 1936 that set the stage for the Axis, Hitler accepted Mussolini's conquests in Ethiopia and Mussolini accepted Hitler's desire to annex Austria, a move the Italian dictator had previously opposed. Another aggressive authoritarian regime became involved in the mutual support system. In November 1936 Germany and Japan signed the Anti-Comintern Pact to oppose the Communist International's efforts to spread Communism and oppose Fascism and Nazism. Italy also signed on to this pact in November 1937 and then in May 1939 formed with Germany the Pact of

Steel, a formal political and military alliance. A formal Tripartite Pact between Germany, Italy, and Japan was eventually signed in September 1940, finalizing a Rome-Berlin-Tokyo Axis of authoritarian powers.

While these diplomatic maneuvers played out, Europe proceeded down the path to war. By 1937, Japan, Italy, and Germany had demonstrated that the League of Nations was ineffectual in halting aggression, and Germany had rendered the Versailles Treaty meaningless. Germany also had allies and a rapidly growing military force. From this position of advantage, Hitler began to implement the nationalistic program of expansion he had set forth in *Mein Kampf* and in countless speeches: unite the German-speaking areas of Europe into one Reich and then acquire *lebensraum*, or living space, in eastern Europe for Germans to expand into. On November 5, 1937, Hitler met with the top leadership of the German army, navy, air force, war ministry, and foreign ministry and set forth to them his vision for the future. He told them he was ready to use force if necessary, which meant the risk of war, to achieve his expansion goals,

and the expansion needed to be completed by 1943-1945 at the latest since he believed the peak of German advantage in armaments would have been passed by then.

The first territory Hitler sought was Austria, a country that was home to six million Germans but prohibited by the Versailles Treaty from uniting with Germany. The Nazis had been at work in Austria for some time building up an Austrian Nazi movement. These Austrian Nazis assassinated the Austrian dictator Englebert Dollfuss in 1935 in a premature attempt to force the *Anschluss,* or union of Austria with Germany. At that time Mussolini had opposed the union and made military preparations to prevent it. By 1938, however, Mussolini and Hitler were allies, and Mussolini accepted Anschluss. In February 1938 Hitler summoned the Austrian chancellor, Kurt von Schuschnigg, to his home at Berchtesgaden and in a tirade browbeat the Austrian into agreeing to put Nazis in cabinet positions in the government and then hold a vote on the question of Anschluss. Schuschnigg attempted to derail Hitler's plan, but with German army forces moved to the border, set up

Residents salute German troops as they march through an Austrian town in 1938. Millions of Austrians supported the takeover.

the plebiscite vote and resigned. The German army moved into Austria without opposition in March, and the vote went overwhelmingly in favor of union. Hitler's homeland was now a part of the larger German Reich. Britain and France did nothing.

Feeling a surge of confidence and spoiling for a fight, Hitler next turned to Czechoslovakia. In order to give Czechoslovakia defensible borders when the country was created at the Paris Peace Conference, a mountainous area of predominantly German-speaking population, called the Sudetenland, was included in the Czech and Slovak-dominated country. As in Austria, the Nazis had earlier begun agitating within the Sudetenland, stirring up sentiment for union with Germany. Hitler mounted a public crusade arguing that the Sudeten Germans were being mistreated and were unfairly denied national self-determination. German troops were moved to the border in May 1938. The Czech government, headed by President Eduard Benes and Prime Minister Milan Hodza, were prepared to meet the Nazis with force. Czechoslovakia had an alliance with both France and Russia that gave them encouragement to oppose Nazi aggression, and the May crisis passed. The British government, however, headed at this time by Prime Minister Neville Chamberlain, was pursuing a policy of appeasement toward aggressive countries like Nazi Germany in an effort to avoid war. When tension over the Sudeten question increased again in September, Chamberlain was able to secure French support for giving Hitler what he said he wanted, the Sudetenland, but then Hitler demanded all German-speaking areas of Czechoslovakia. The appeasement deal fell through, and by September 23 war seemed imminent.

At this point Mussolini proposed that a conference be held at Munich to resolve the crisis.

Hitler received an enthusiastic welcome from the crowds after Germany liberated the Sudetenland from Czech rule.

Britain, France, Italy, and Germany conferred at Munich on September 29. Russia and Czechoslovakia were not invited to the discussions! The Munich Accords reached at this meeting gave to Hitler, without any consultation with Czechoslovakia's government, all that he asked for: the entire German-speaking territory of the Czech state. In exchange, Hitler gave Chamberlain his solemn promise that this was his last territorial demand in Europe. The Czechs were faced with a *fait accompli*. The deal had been struck, and their ally France was a party to it. Without French and British support, Russia would not assist the Czechs, so Benes and Hodza could do nothing. Chamberlain returned to England and declared that he had achieved "peace in our time." In less than a year Europe was at war.

The appeasement at Munich, rather than satiating the appetite of the aggressors, whetted it even more. In March 1939, Hitler proved himself a liar by seizing the remaining Czech rump state. With its defenses ceded to Germany in the Munich Accords, the Czech government was powerless to stop their final dismemberment. Feeling left out, Mussolini launched an Italian attack against the tiny country of Albania across the Adriatic Sea from Italy. Chamberlain was offended and shocked by Hitler's move and secured French agreement to offer treaties of guarantee to Poland and Romania, countries that were likely to be the next German targets of aggression. Chamberlain was through with appeasement. By this time, however, the past experience of the entire decade suggested that such promises of support carried little weight, and Hitler proceeded with his next objective of expansion, Poland. In a genuine effort to avoid war, the British Prime Minister had confronted a ruthless dictator willing to lie, break international agreements, and use force and had been found lacking. Appeasement was a failure, and Britain and France had to pay the price of surrendering numerous advantages to Nazi Germany. That price was paid as the remainder of 1939 saw the start of the Second World War.

Throughout the 1930s, the United States watched with growing alarm the events in Europe and Asia that were leading to another war. Isolationist sentiment ran high in America, however, and the country adopted a policy of neutrality, hoping to avoid getting involved in another European conflict. After 1932, the President of the U.S. was Franklin Delano Roosevelt who desired to be more proactive in checking aggression but his political instincts led him to restrain this desire lest it cost him support in the electorate. The U.S. became another Western democracy that presented objections but little action in the face of aggression. This was the case in regard to Japan's aggression toward China, an area of special concern for the U.S. since the adoption of the Open Door policy at the turn of the century, a policy that sought to maintain China's independence. The beginning of warfare in Asia when Japan invaded China in 1937 placed the United States in a cycle of growing tension with Japan that eventually led to the Japanese attack on Pearl Harbor in late 1941 and the transformation of the war into a total war of global proportions.

Suggestions for Further Reading

Franklin Baumer, *Modern European Thought* (1977).

Karl Dietrich Bracher, *The German Dictatorship* (1970).

Heim Bucheim, *Totalitarian Rule* (1968).

Alan Bullock, *Hitler: A Study in Tyranny* (1964).

Alan Cassels, *Fascist Italy* (1968).

Winston S. Churchill, *The Gathering Storm: The Second World War, Vol. I* (1948).

M.K. Dziewanowski, *A History of Soviet Russia and Its Aftermath* (1997).

Sheila Fitzpatrick, *The Russian Revolution, 1917-1932* (1982).

N. Greene, *From Versailles to Vichy: The Third Republic, 1919-1940* (1970).

H. Stuart Hughes, *Consciousness and Society* (1958).

John Keegan, *The Second World War* (1989).

W. Neuman, *The Balance of Power in the Interwar Years, 1919-1939* (1968).

A.J. Nichols, *Weimar and the Rise of Hitler* (1991).

Erich Remarque, *All Quiet on the Western Front* (1929).

H. Seton-Watson, *Eastern Europe Between the Wars, 1919-1941* (1962).

William Shirer, *The Rise and Fall of the Third Reich* (1960).

Aleksandr I. Solzhenitsyn, *The Gulag Archipelago*, 3 volumes (1973-1975).

R. J. Sontag, *A Broken World 1919-1939* (1971).

WORLD WAR II
1939-1945

WINSTON CHURCHILL

Mary Blavier was thirteen years old in September 1939 when she heard of the German invasion of Poland that began the Second World War. Living with her family in Liège, Belgium, a strategic point near the Belgian-German border, Mary remembers the fear of what might lay in store for Belgium and her town. That fear became more concrete in May 1940 as German forces attacked the Low Countries and France. Mary's family quickly packed a few bags and caught a train in an effort to flee to France, but a German airplane halted the train with gunfire before it had traveled many miles from Liège. The family stayed a couple of nights with friends before deciding to head back home. As they walked home, a loud rumbling sound met their ears. Suddenly a German tank appeared; Mary started to run, but her father held her fast. The tank passed them by, but the fear of that encounter remained impressed on Mary for the rest of her life. To get back home, the family had to cross a large river in a rowboat since the Belgians had blown up the bridge to impede the Germans. After finally reaching home, the family stayed inside the house for a week.

Living in German-occupied Belgium, Mary and her family faced various hardships. Food was scarce. During one particularly bad period, Mary walked quite a distance every day to her uncle's hotel where he helped her family by feeding her lunch. They occasionally received packages from the Red Cross, and Mary remembered what a treat it was to have the fresh fruit these packages contained. In 1943, a few months after her older brother, Joseph, turned eighteen, he was forced to go to Germany to work at a labor camp. After a few weeks, the family received word that Joseph was sick. Mary's parents decided to try to travel to the camp to check on Joseph. While they were gone to the train station, a man came to the house with the news that Joseph was dead. Mary hit the man and screamed hysterically; neighbors had to pull her away from him. When her parents returned home that evening, having been unable to travel, they were hit with the devastating news. Her mother took to her bed in a depression, and her father "went to pieces," both taking some time to recover. At the time, Mary's grandparents and another uncle lived with Mary's family because the grandparents' home had been bombed. Mary remembers going to the rooftop to watch Allied bombers fly over, cheering them as they went. The family also periodically helped people who were hiding from the Germans though Mary was not told the details of who the people were or why they were in hiding. One night when a man-in-hiding was in their home, German officials burst into the house, told everyone to get out of bed, and dragged her uncle, who was paralyzed from a pre-war construction accident, from his bed. Mary refused to get out of bed. Eventually, her parents were able to convince the officials they were not hiding anyone, and the officials left. The family also listened to the BBC, British radio, which was against the rules, and knew when the Allied invasion of Normandy was launched. Mary remembered people excitedly saying, "Ike is coming!" June 6, 1944, the day of the invasion, was "one of the happiest days" of her life.

It took some time for the Germans to be driven from Liège, but when they left, Mary and other teenagers went out to line the streets and watch them go. Mary's hometown was finally liberated from the Germans on September 8, 1944, and she remembers seeing her first GI (American soldier). He was riding alongside the river in a jeep and was "enormous" to Mary. The war was still not over, however, for Mary after Liège's liberation. The Battle of the Bulge threatened the Allied position in

Belgium. And German "buzz bombs" (V-1 rockets) fell on the town. Once, a buzz bomb exploded nearby, and Mary, who had been standing in a window, was thrown across the room by the force of the blast. Eventually, as the German war effort collapsed, threats to Liège declined, and American forces moved into the area in strength. The Americans used some of the buildings near Mary, and one GI in particular worked and lived right beside Mary's home. She married that GI in September 1945.

This memorial was erected in the Ardennes Forest by the citizens of Belgium in honor of the Allied soldiers who had died during the Battle of the Bulge.

Chronology

Sept. 1939	Germany invades Poland, starting World War II Russia invades Poland
Nov. 1939	Russia attacks Finland
Apr. 1940	Germany attacks Denmark and Norway
May 1940	Germany invades Holland, Belgium, and France
June 1940	France surrenders to Germany
July 1940	Battle of Britain begins
Oct. 1940	Italy invades Greece
Mar. 1941	Afrika Korps attacks British forces in North Africa
June 1941	Germany invades Russia in Operation Barbarossa
Aug. 1941	Atlantic Charter proclaimed
Dec. 1941	Japan attacks U.S. at Pearl Harbor
June 1941	U.S. defeats Japan at Battle of Midway
Nov. 1942	Allies land in North Africa in Operation Torch
Feb. 1943	German forces surrender at Stalingrad
June 1943	Tide turned against Germany in the Battle of the Atlantic
Sep. 1943	Allies invade Italy
Nov. 1943	Teheran Conference
June 1944	D-Day Invasion of Normandy in France
Aug. 1944	Russia refuses assistance to Warsaw uprising
Dec. 1944	Battle of the Bulge
Feb. 1945	Yalta Conference
May 1945	Germany surrenders
July 1945	Potsdam Conference
Aug. 1945	U.S. drops atomic bombs on Japan
Sep. 1945	Japan formally surrenders, ending World War II

World War II was the costliest, most lethal, and most destructive conflict in the history of the world. Beginning in Asia in 1937 as Japan invaded China and in Europe as Germany and Russia invaded Poland, the war involved two shifting sets of alliances that eventually opposed the twenty-seven countries of the Allies, or "United Nations," against eight members of the Axis. The Allies were dominated by the "Big Three," Great Britain, Russia (Soviet Union), and the United States of America. The primary Axis partners were Germany, Italy, and Japan. Because the major combatants had possessions and interests all around the globe, World War II was, indeed, a worldwide conflict fought on the seas, in the air, and on the land all around the world. Whereas the critical fighting in the First World War was concentrated in Europe, the critical battles of World War II were fought not only in Europe but also in North Africa and the Mediterranean, in the central and southwestern Pacific, and on the Atlantic Ocean. In Europe, major action extended into nearly every section and corner of the continent. The war was a total war, involving not only ground, air, and naval forces, but also, to an unprecedented extent, civilian populations. Civilians not only worked in factories, government bureaucracies, and scientific war projects but were also victims and participants in the fighting, most notably as aerial bombing brought the war literally into their homes.

ORIGINS OF WORLD WAR II

World War II began with a crisis provoked by Nazi Germany over German territory given to the newly created nation of Poland in the Treaty of Versailles. This crisis culminated a series of diplomatic and military moves by German dictator Adolf Hitler after he came to power in 1933. His foreign policy objectives from the start were to void the Treaty of Versailles, unite German-speaking areas in Europe under German rule, and then expand eastward, acquiring territory that would provide *lebensraum* (living space) for German growth. This agenda, especially the effort to throw off Treaty of Versailles restrictions on Germany, provided part of the attraction that Nazi rule had for many German people. The agenda also shows the close connection the First World War and the peace settlement that ended it had with the beginning of the Second World War. The resentment and dissatisfaction created by the way the First World War ended and by the peace settlement the victors devised were a powerful motivating force behind the international tensions of the interwar period that led up to World War II.

Although many particular issues are involved in the relationship between the end of the First World War and the start of the Second World War, the fundamental problem is twofold. First, since the armistice of November 1918 was signed before a single Allied soldier had invaded Germany and with U.S. President Woodrow Wilson's idealistic Fourteen Points as a proposed basis for peace, many Germans did not feel they had lost the war and hoped that Germany would emerge from the fight on an equal basis with the Allies. Yet, when the Paris settlement was presented, Germany was treated as a defeated nation and forced to accept humiliating punishments, such as the loss of its colonies, the loss of German territory, the emasculation of its revered military, and the demand for reparations. This created anger and resentment in Germany that proved to be a powerful political force the Nazis effectively tapped. Second, while the Versailles Treaty *was* humiliating and while its terms *were* harsh, it was not harsh enough to prevent Germany from rising again to power and seeking revenge or trying to overturn the settlement. Germany was left more or less intact as the most populous and potentially most industrially powerful of the advanced western European nations. In other words, the creation of a united Germany in the 1870s had upset the balance of power in Europe (which contributed to the coming of the First World War) and the Paris peace settlement did nothing to change that fact. A humiliated, resentful Germany had the potential resources and population to act on its resentment and avenge its humiliation. In this sense, the end of the Great War was not decisive. It failed to resolve the complex competitive forces that had led to the war in the first place. It did not convince the powerful German nation that it had lost the war. It punished Germany in a humiliating way but not harshly enough to prevent the country from acting on its resentment.

Even in these circumstances, however, the peace settlement might have worked if it had either been enforced or sufficiently modified to resolve German resentment. Blame falls on the Western democracies and the United States for not doing the things that might have kept an angry Germany from rising. They did not enforce the treaty when, even as late as 1937, they had the military advantage and power to do so. Great Britain is particularly at fault, for its leaders failed to support France in its early efforts at enforcement. The Western democracies also failed to use the League of Nations to halt aggression. The weakness they demonstrated in this only encouraged further aggression. Also, blame falls most heavily on Germany, particularly the Nazi regime and its supporters, for the Western democracies proved willing to modify the peace settlement in the second half of the 1920s. In supporting a violent overturning of the treaty and territorial settlement, rather than being satisfied to continue pursuing the peaceful resolution of problems that had greatly improved Germany's international situation in the late 1920s, Nazi Germany bears much of the blame for starting the Second World War.

Another major cause of the Second World War is the way that the leading victors of the First World War—Great Britain, France, and the United States—dealt with German efforts in the 1930s to destroy the peace settlement and with aggressive actions of other nations, such as Japan, Italy, and Germany. The response of the democratic victors was deeply divided and ineffective in meeting the challenge. Under Prime Minister Neville Chamberlain, Britain, suffering from remorse over the harshness of the Versailles Treaty, actively pursued a policy of appeasement that sought to give in to German demands so as to eliminate any cause for war. Meanwhile, the French, after years of being the only major power interested in enforcing the Treaty of Versailles, became so defeatist and so unsure of British support in the 1930s that they feared making any moves by themselves. The United States, though involved in international matters, was not willing to commit to any kind of security framework for Europe, preferring to maintain independence of action and taking steps in the 1930s to ensure its neutrality in any future European war.

This weak, ineffective response of the former Allies of World War I was tied to another cause of the Second World War: the rise of totalitarian dictatorships in the interwar period. Totalitarian regimes came to power in Italy, Germany, and Russia, and a militaristic authoritarian regime developed in Japan. The nationalistic aggressive foreign policy of the Italian and German dictators bolstered their support at home. Moreover, totalitarian regimes could be more nimble in foreign policy, making sudden shifts in direction that democratic governments would have to build up support for before making. Motivated by internal political factors and ideology to be aggressive, the totalitarian nations took advantage of the timid responses made by the peace-seeking democratic nations.

For the democratic countries, reacting effectively to aggressive moves by Japan, Italy, and Germany was difficult enough due to the maneuverability of totalitarian governments. Good response was made more difficult by the particular state of politics within the democratic countries during the 1930s. The Great Depression preoccupied the attention of these countries and their leaders. Also, a powerful pacifism gripped the Western democracies, and isolationism ran strong in the United States. Both pacifism and U.S. isolationism meant that any government move to block aggression was liable to provoke an outcry of opposition, and leaders already careful of politically dangerous issues tended to step lightly, if at all. Yet another factor was that in France, in particular, and to some extent in Great Britain, political division made consistent, effective response to aggression difficult. French politics was so polarized that cabinets were formed and dissolved in dizzying succession in the critical 1930s. Extremists on the right were soft on Nazism while leftist groups, like the Communists, were vehemently opposed to Germany. The many different political groups between the two extremes had just as many different views.

Meanwhile, the ideology of Fascism in Italy, Nazism in Germany, and the militarists in power in Japan glorified war, force, and power. Nations seeking to accomplish things by force as a demonstration of national worth were confronted by democratic nations in which peace was the objective and the desire to avoid war so strong that appeasing the aggressor nations was an acceptable choice. It was almost inevitable that the aggressors would continue to push until the peace-seeking nations' tolerance level was exceeded and war resulted. In this way, the cultural, ideological, and psychological developments of the early twentieth century and the interwar period also contributed to the causes of World War II. The anxiety, uncertainty, and psychic restlessness led to a variety of different responses, some of which advocated war while others recoiled from it. The clash of ideologies involved in World War II derives in part from the cultural and intellectual stew of the interwar period.

Finally, totalitarian Russia contributed to the international crisis. Coming to power by means of revolution, the Communist dictatorship that developed in Russia under Lenin and Stalin sought to export communist revolution to other countries around the world. Through the Communist International (Comintern), Communist Party activities designed to achieve communist control in other countries were coordinated and instructed from the Soviet Union. By the middle of the 1930s, when Stalin attempted to work

with the West against Hitler, the legacy of mistrust generated by the Comintern, Stalin's extreme brutality, and the nature of communist government were too powerful for the West to overcome. Working with Stalin would have meant working with a regime that was even more brutal and more alien to Western liberal ideals than Nazism or Fascism. Rebuffed by the West, Stalin made a deal with Hitler in the Nazi-Soviet Pact of 1939. Russia became a co-conspirator in the invasion of Poland, not only encouraging Germany to invade by eliminating the fear of Russian involvement in a two-front war if the West came to Poland's aid but also actively participating in the dismemberment of Poland by sending in the Red Army and taking over sections of Poland once the Germans had largely defeated Poland's military forces.

THE COURSE OF THE WAR

World War II can be divided into three basic phases. In the first phase, September 1939 through December 1941, Germany experienced spectacular success in conquest, controlling territory from the English Channel in the west to the environs just west of Moscow in Russia. From December 1941 to November 1942, in a second phase, a series of developments in three main regions—Russia, North Africa, and the Pacific—saw the war hang in the balance and then turn in favor of the Allies. The Allies took the initiative in the last phase. From November 1942 until the end of the war in Europe (May 1945) and in the Pacific (August 1945), the Allies slowly but steadily beat back the Axis forces in all theatres until victory was achieved. This global conflict involved not only the clash of army and air forces but also a naval war, critical diplomacy, and other facets, such as espionage, deception, and a technology race.

The First Phase:
September 1939 - December 1941

The first shots in the Second World War in Europe were fired in the early morning hours of September 1, 1939, as the armed forces of Nazi Germany unleashed the *blitzkrieg* ("lightning war") on Poland. Three major thrusts spearheaded by *panzer* (tank) units quickly drove deep into Poland from the north, west, and south. These drives were supported by tactical air attacks that quickly destroyed the tiny, hopelessly outdated Polish air force, hit transportation targets, pounded military targets, and harassed the mustering Polish army. The Luftwaffe's Stutka dive-bombers, which were equipped with an air-driven horn that reached a scream pitch as the plane accelerated in its dive, were particularly terrifying. The German infantry poured in behind the panzer units to secure gains and finish off disrupted Polish forces that had been cut off by the pincher movements of the initial panzer thrusts. This coordinated combination of air force, tank units, and infantry that comprised the German blitzkrieg technique was devastatingly effective and presaged that the Second World War would not bog down into the trench warfare that had characterized the Western Front in World War I. Although much of the German army's movement remained unmechanized with the age-old method of boot and hoof carrying most of the army in deployment, it was the dramatic use of motorized armor and modern aircraft that caught the most attention and transformed warfare.

By September 17, the Germans had encircled the Polish capital, Warsaw, and after ten days of heavy bombing it fell to the invaders on September 27. At German request, on September 17, the Russian Red Army moved in to seize eastern portions of Poland that the Nazi-Soviet

Employing *blitzkrieg* tactics, a motorized division of German troops drive through a ravaged town.

pact had promised Russia. By October 6, the fighting was over, barely a month after it had begun. The Polish government and about 100,000 Poles managed to escape and continue fighting bravely and skillfully as allies for the remainder of the war, with the government continuing to operate in exile eventually in London. About 910,000 Poles were taken prisoner, however, and of these some 217,000 were taken by Russian forces. In the spring of 1940, 12,000 imprisoned officers of the Polish army were murdered by direct order of Stalin and buried in

The powerful, quick-moving Panzer IV, with its impenetrable armor and firepower capability, gave Germany a great advantage at the beginning of the war.

the Katyn Forest near Smolensk in eastern Poland. The blatant aggression and conspiracy that the Russians exhibited, as well as the harsh treatment and murder they meted out to Polish prisoners of war, were largely responsible for the strained relations between the London Poles and Russia. Near the end of the war, this strife contributed to the development of the Cold War as Stalin worked to install a communist regime in Poland despite the existence of the legitimate London Poles' government.

After the battle for Poland was over, Stalin continued to press forward with aggression, using tactics of which Hitler would have been proud. He immediately began a campaign of intimidation, making demands for concessions, against the Baltic states of Estonia, Lithuania, and Latvia, which had been part of the Russian

Empire until 1917. He followed through with outright annexation of these countries in June 1940. The far northern nation of Finland, which had been under Russian control from 1809-1917, was also subjected to Russian demands beginning in October 1939. When intimidation failed to convince the tough and determined Finns, Stalin launched an attack against them in November. In this Winter War, the Finns, despite being hopelessly outnumbered, used ingenious tactics and literally ran circles around the confused Russian forces. After committing *one million* troops against the 175,000 Finns, Russia prevailed in securing its terms from Finland in March 1940. The Finns lost 25,000 killed to 200,000 Russians killed. The Winter War was significant in leading the Nazis and the West to underestimate the Russian war-making capac-

The Stuka dive-bomber, known as "the Shrieking Vulture" terrorized its victims with its screaming pitch as it accelerated in its dive.

ity, but it also meant that Stalin treated Finland with much greater care in the developments at the end of World War II. As a final bit of Russian aggression, in June 1940 the Soviet Union seized Bessarabia from Rumania. Russian aggression and collusion with Nazi Germany made the situation of the Western Allies more difficult and contributed to the disaster they faced in the spring of 1940.

When Germany invaded Poland at the beginning of September, both Britain and France presented Germany with an ultimatum, demanding a halt to the attack. When Germany pressed on, the two western democracies honored their treaties of guarantee with Poland and declared war. But other than mobilizing their military forces and implementing a naval blockade, Britain and France remained inactive in the West and were unable to provide any assistance to the Poles. After Poland was lost, the French

stood watch behind the Maginot Line, a series of fortifications along the German-French border, and the British moved their Expeditionary Force to France to be prepared when fighting should begin. But neither the western Allies nor the Germans made a significant move in that sector for six months after Poland was finished. This bizarre period of inaction that Chamberlain termed the "twilight war" was called more generally in Britain the "Phony War" or in Germany the "*Sitzkrieg*," or sitting war.

In April 1940, the lull ended as Germany turned its military to the north, on Scandinavia, with Norway being the primary objective. Denmark, a small and virtually defenseless nation bordering northwestern Germany, surrendered without a shot being fired on April 9. Further to the north, Norway put up a fight. Hitler targeted Norway primarily for two reasons. First, the Grand Admiral of the German navy, Erich

Civilians in Denmark resist the Nazi occupation by overturning a German police van to release Danish freedom fighters.

Raeder, urged Hitler to secure Norway for the German navy to use as bases of operation and to deny the same to the British and French. Second, the British navy was interfering with German use of Norway's territorial waters to shelter its transport of valuable food, timber, and mineral resources, particularly Swedish iron ore that was hauled across northern Norway and then shipped south by sea. The Germans quickly secured control of southern Norway, but the king and his government escaped to Britain. British and French forces, numbering 12,000, landed in the north, helping the Norwegian effort. However, defense against a German landing was inadequate, and the allied forces had to withdraw in defeat. Norway proved to be valuable to the Germans not only for naval and trade purposes but also as a base for the air war against Britain. On the other hand, the effort had been costly for the German navy, weakening it shortly before Germany was in a position to consider a cross-channel invasion of England.

Concern over the botched effort against German forces in Norway led to a debate in the British Parliament over the Chamberlain government's conduct of the war. As a result of this debate, Parliament failed to support Chamberlain's government and a new war coalition government was organized with Winston Churchill as Prime Minister on May 10, 1940. In one of many memorable and eloquent speeches, Churchill told Parliament that he could only offer them "blood, toil, tears, and sweat" and that he had but one policy, "to wage war, by sea, by land, and air, with all our might and with all the strength that God can give us." This soon proved necessary.

Winston Churchill was one of the most remarkable figures of any era in history and proved to be a crucial ingredient in the successful British and Allied war effort. Born on November 30, 1874, Churchill was 65 years old when he became Prime Minister and had a wealth of experience to draw upon. His father was the third son of the seventh Duke of Marlborough, making Winston a direct descendant of John Churchill, the original Duke of Marlborough, who had led alliance armies successfully in the War of the Spanish Succession against Louis XIV of France and who had been a chief adviser to Queen Anne. Winston attended Harrow School and the Royal Military College at Sandhurst, and he served in the British military in a cavalry unit, becoming involved in action in various parts of the British Empire, from India to the Sudan. He became quite literate after having a poor academic record as a child and youth and served as a journalist while in the military. After leaving the service, he continued as a correspondent in the Boer War in South Africa, becoming famous after being captured by the Boers, escaping, travelling 300 miles to freedom, and writing his story. He entered politics, winning his first seat in Parliament in 1901. Churchill sat in Parliament throughout most of the next 39 years, dramatically switching from the Conservative Party to the Liberal Party in 1904 and then back to the Conservative Party in 1924. He served in various cabinet-level posts, including First Lord of the British Admiralty. As First Lord in World War I, Churchill was blamed for the disaster at Gallipoli in which an effort to secure the Dardanelles Strait for the Allies failed miserably. After resigning his post, Churchill briefly fought on the Western Front before being called back to serve as Munitions Minister in 1917. In this capacity, Winston pushed the development and production of the armored tank, a weapon he had supported as First Lord of the Admiralty. While the weapon's full potential was not realized until the Second World War, Churchill's sponsorship had a decisive impact on future military tactics and strategy. After World War I, Churchill lost the 1922 election due to being incapacitated by appendicitis but was back in with the 1924 elections. From 1929 until 1939, Churchill became an increasingly vehement critic of the lack of military preparedness, of the inaction in the face of growing aggression, and of the appeasement policy. In Parliament in this period, he was a virtual outcast because his far-sighted views did not match the temper of the times nor the views of party leaders. When war came in 1939, Churchill's views were mostly vindicated, and Neville Chamberlain's government brought Churchill into the cabinet as First Lord of the Admiralty, serving there until becoming Prime Minister.

On the day Churchill became Prime Minister, Germany began its attack on the western front, with the defeat of France being the primary objective. As part of their strategy, the Germans first attacked the small neutral nations of Luxembourg, Holland, and Belgium enroute to France. On May 10, 1940, Nazi forces rolled over tiny Luxembourg and invaded Holland. Within six days Holland was finished, and Queen Wilhelmina fled with her government to England. Belgium, with the help of the British and French forces that moved forward into Belgian territory to meet what they thought was the main German invasion force, put up a solid resistance. However, the main German force was actually making its way along an unlikely route: the densely wooded and hilly Ardennes Forest of southeastern Belgium. Here the narrow, twisting roads made moving tanks, artillery, infantry and supplies seem impossible.

Nonetheless, the Germans did it. The road network was packed with a massive German force of 1800 tanks plus other motorized equipment moving along nose-to-tail in such a concentration that one German officer estimated it would have reached all the way to East Prussia if stretched out in one column. After securing bridgeheads across the Meuse River, the Germans broke through the French lines at Sedan on May 14. Sedan was the site of French disaster in 1870 when French Emperor Napoleon III surrendered to Prussian/German forces. It proved to be the site of another disaster. Although many French forces fought bravely, they were not the best of the French army, nor did they have sufficient numbers to meet the German force. Some French turned and fled upon seeing tanks coming or even hearing that tanks might be on the

The Allied army was trapped in the French seaport of Dunkirk. From forty miles across the English Channel, Royal Navy destroyers, ferries, fishing boats, pleasure yachts, tugs, and even motorboats evacuated the British army, including many French soldiers. Almost anything that would float was brought to the rescue. Navy regulars, civilian sailors, and volunteers helped with the retreat.

way. Some even ran when they saw *French* tanks approaching. With the panzer divisions leading the way, German forces pushed rapidly through the break at Sedan, driving west along the Somme River, and reaching Abbeville, where the Somme meets the English Channel, by May 20. The bulk of British and French forces were north of this line in Belgium and were thus trapped, cut off from the rest of the Allied forces and in no way able to defend France.

The scope of this monumental disaster was lessened somewhat by the miraculous evacuation of virtually all the British Expeditionary Force plus many French troops at Dunkirk, on the English Channel. After Hitler ordered a temporary halt on May 24 to the panzer advances from fear they were over extended, British and French troops pulled back to the coast. By the time the German tanks began to press forward again on May 26, the Allies were in a tempo-

rarily defensible position. From May 26 to June 4, hundreds of British vessels of all description, from navy destroyers to privately owned pleasure craft, worked under harassment of German aircraft to ferry soldiers from the French coast to England. In those few days some 337,000 soldiers were saved from capture, about 110,000 of them being French. While the Allies lost virtually all their equipment and the British had little with which to replace it, the force saved at Dunkirk was essentially all the army that Britain had. Without these men, armed or not, England would have been virtually without ground defense against invasion. The evacuation, though obviously the result of a major military defeat, gave some boost to morale and some reason to hope.

After Dunkirk, the British had little immediate help to offer, and the French war effort collapsed quickly. Various strategies were devised and debated, and some in the French military made notable efforts to stop the Germans as they turned back southward after securing Belgium. One example was Charles Andre Joseph Marie De Gaulle. Charles De Gaulle, born November 22, 1890, to parents with military and literary backgrounds, was a tall, lanky man at 6'4" in height whose very name epitomized French patriotism. ("Gaul" was the ancient Roman name for France and held nationalistic significance.) In his early service in the French infantry, De Gaulle had been nicknamed "Big Charles" and "Asparagus." In World War I De Gaulle was wounded 4 times and captured by the Germans at Verdun in 1916. Continuing to serve in command capacities in the French army between the wars, De Gaulle was an active proponent of mobile war and the use of tanks and mechanized equipment, as he argued in his 1934 book, *The Army of the Future*. Unfortunately for France, the army did not heed his advice. In the 1940 crisis, De Gaulle, placed in command of one of the French armored units, made a valiant but futile effort to confront the German panzers. He was promoted to general and became the Undersecretary of Defense as the situation in France worsened.

Between June 5 and June 10, France was for all purposes finished off: the government abandoned Paris, moving first to Tours, then Bordeaux. On June 10, Hitler's ally, Mussolini, finally, after 9 months of war, declared war and entered the fray by attacking southern France. There four French divisions easily held off 28 Italian divisions, losing only 8 men to 5000 Italian casualties. Despite this performance and the dogged determination of French fighters, such as the forces garrisoning the Maginot Line, the cause was lost. A new government was formed with Marshal Philippe Pétain as premier. Pétain had been the hero of Verdun in World War I and had saved the French army from collapse in the mutiny of 1917. In this war, he was the instrument of its surrender and leader of a collaborationist puppet government of France headquartered at Vichy. As Pétain arranged for peace discussions with the Germans, Charles De Gaulle left France for Britain where he continued the French war effort as a general and member of the government. From London, De Gaulle broadcast to the French people a call for them to continue fighting, saying "this war has not been settled by the Battle of France. This war is a world war...whatever happens the flame of resistance must not and will not be extinguished." For this, Pétain's government court-martialed De Gaulle. De Gaulle remained abroad and formed the center of the Free French, who continued the fight from Britain and some French colonies.

The peace terms that Pétain accepted were presented to his representative on June 21 near Compiegne at the same place that Germany had signed the armistice ending the First World War in 1918. An exultant Hitler had the same railcar in which the 1918 armistice was signed brought from a museum to the site for the festivities. Nothing more vividly demonstrated how closely the two world wars were connected. For Hitler, the first war humiliated Germany, and the second, thus far, avenged that humiliation. The peace terms he dictated to France and Pétain accepted, to take effect June 25, show the vengefulness clearly. Pétain's government was allowed to continue, but it ruled only a remnant of the former France plus the French colonies. Northern and western France, in a wide arc along the coast that included Paris, was occupied by Germany with occupation costs to be paid by Pétain's Vichy government. Vichy retained the French navy but had to confine the vessels to port. Germany kept as hostages, to insure Vichy's collaboration, the 2 million French prisoners taken

The RAF Halifax four-engine bomber, could carry 40,000 pounds of bombs. This bomber saw action through-out the war.

in the war. These men represented 5 percent of the total population and about 25 percent of men of prime adult age. Even with these terms, the Vichy government collaborated extensively with the Nazis, even helping them collect Jews as the Holocaust proceeded and ordering that U.S./British landings at Morocco in 1942 be resisted by Vichy French forces.

In six short weeks of fighting, Hitler added the Low Countries and France to his growing list of conquests. By July 1940, the world was reeling in disbelief at the seeming ease with which Nazi Germany came to rule most of the continent of Europe. Soviet Russia was a cooperating, if uneasy, friend in aggression to the east, and Japan was a friendly fellow totalitarian country. To the south, Italy was a firm, if incompetent, ally. The only country of great power status outside of Europe and Japan was the United States, which, gripped by the Depression, had only recently begun to grow concerned about Nazi power and was in no position politically or militarily to deal with the Nazi threat.

The only remaining European foe facing Hitler by July 1940 was the island nation of Great Britain. Britain had at its disposal a top-rate navy, the small but growing Royal Air Force (RAF), capable and determined leadership, the resources of a shrunken, though still considerable, empire, and the assistance of former colonies like Canada and Australia that were a part of the British Commonwealth of Nations. Britain also had the support of the President of the United States, Franklin Delano Roosevelt, and the limited, but growing, support of others in the United States. The situation facing Britain was critical, however, given that Hitler dominated Europe. The same empire that provided resources that could sustain Britain also demanded attention and defense, both of which were scarce in 1940 in Britain. The British army was virtually without vital equipment. Trained and equipped soldiers were scarce: Britain had one fully equipped division to Germany's 150. Churchill had gas masks issued to the population in case Germany used the internationally outlawed chemical weapons of World War I and ordered that British stocks of gas be used as a last resort in the event of invasion. Britain depended on imports that had to be brought through waters made perilous by German submarines patrols. The republic of Eire, i.e., Ireland, England's next-door neighbor and a former colony, was, at best, an unfriendly neutral.

In July, Hitler gave orders for his generals and admirals to prepare for Operation Sea Lion, the proposed cross-channel invasion of England. Hitler had never really contemplated the problems of a cross-channel invasion, being very continental in his thinking. He hoped Britain would recognize its hopeless plight and come to terms so that he could turn his attention eastward to the question of *lebensraum*. When the British, led by a defiant Churchill, refused to come to terms, however, Hitler pushed ahead with planning an invasion. Given the great superiority the British navy had over the German surface fleet, a successful invasion would depend on the German *Luftwaffe's* ability to achieve absolute control of the air over the English Channel. For the invasion to happen in 1940, this would have to be achieved in time to cross the channel before autumn gales made it impossible. The task of making the invasion happen fell to Luftwaffe commander, Reichsmarschal Hermann Göring, the old Nazi S.A. commander and World War I flying ace. Göring dismissed the problems of the task, believing that a few heavy blows would bring Britain to terms. The last time England had been successfully invaded by hostile forces was 1066, when William the Bastard of Normandy had conquered Harold Godwinson at Hastings. Göring would not break the streak.

The Battle of Britain, then, turned out to be the first major battle in history fought almost exclusively in the skies. The Luftwaffe had no strategic plan, relying instead on a series of improvised strategies. They began with an effort to soften up England's coastal defenses and naval forces on the southern coast of England. This effort lasted from July 10 through early August but failed to do much damage to the British navy. Then the Luftwaffe turned on August 13 to Operation Eagle, which was intended to overpower the RAF by hitting its bases, supply facilities, and production factories, as well as engaging its fighters to destroy them. The classic part of this operation lasted until August 18, when disappointing results and mounting losses led the Luftwaffe to shift focus to RAF airfields from August 24 through September 6. Unknown to the Germans, this effort had a devastating effect on the RAF, seriously straining their capacity and costing RAF fighter command 290 fighters to only about 190 German fighters. Had the focus continued on the airfields, the Germans might have prevailed, but Hitler and Göring wanted to force a decision with Britain more quickly and dramatically since favorable weather for an invasion would not last much longer. On September 7, the Luftwaffe shifted to attacks on London, hit in concentrated effort for the first time in this stage, that lasted through September 30. In this "London Blitz," the RAF cost the Luftwaffe dearly in planes. By September 17, Hitler decided to postpone Operation Sea Lion indefinitely. The critical period of the Battle of Britain was, therefore, over but not the fighting nor most of the damage. After September 30, the Luftwaffe continued to pound London, but increasingly relied on night raids to the point that by November, attacks were almost exclusively at night. From September 7 to November 13, London was hit on 67 out of 68 nights by an average of 160 sorties of German bombers. After November 13 through May 1941, London was hit only sporadically with other cities like Bristol, Liverpool, Portsmouth, Plymouth, Birmingham and Coventry bearing German attacks. Coventry, a city of 200,000 people, was virtually destroyed in a 10-hour raid on November 14, 1940. After January 1941, Hitler

The king and queen of England inspect the damage to Buckingham Palace after a bomb attack.

increasingly focused his attention on plans for an upcoming attack in the East. After May 1941, despite sporadic raids and the later employment of rocket-driven missile attacks, the worst was over. Hitler did not admit defeat, but in abandoning invasion plans and having failed to bomb Britain into submission, Hitler suffered his first significant setback of the war, leaving Britain standing as a base from which to eventually attack Hitler on the continent.

In meeting the challenge of German aerial attack, the British employed many tactics and countermeasures. Barrage balloons held cables aloft around London to ensnare German planes. Anti-aircraft batteries of "ack-ack" guns filled the sky with flak in an effort to damage and destroy enemy planes, though with very limited success. In London anti-aircraft fire could shoot down only one plane for every 4000 shells expended in January 1941. This was a major improvement over September 1940 when 30,000 shells had been required for every plane shot down. Blackouts at night were implemented to reduce the Germans' ability to find targets, but this took a toll on pedestrians and automobile passengers as accidents multiplied. Air raid wardens were employed to help ensure that the population followed blackout procedures and other safety measures. In London, "the Tubes," as the subway system was called, were opened to serve as air raid shelters. Despite the terror, destruction, and disruption the bombing caused, it did not destroy British morale; in fact, it had the opposite effect as people rallied to the cause. Life went on, disrupted as it may have been. Movie theatres and nude shows went on uninterrupted. More importantly, war production went on despite damage and disruption, a fact critical to the outcome of the battle.

Several factors lay behind Britain's victory in the Battle of Britain. For one thing, Britain was able to maintain production of aircraft at a greater rate than its losses throughout the critical period between August 11 and September 7. Moreover, in the summer of 1940, the British produced 500 fighters per month while the Germans could only produce 250 per month. This was an important key when combined with the success ratio of British and Allied pilots. While the Luftwaffe outnumbered the RAF 4 to 1, the RAF destroyed 2 German craft for every British plane lost in the battle. Thus, superior British production and pilot/fighter performance played a decisive role in the outcome. Other factors gave the British pilots an advantage, however, and proved key to their success. A network of observers helped gather information on enemy aircraft movement and numbers. The British had pioneered the technology of radar, an acronym for "radio detecting and ranging." Developed by Robert Watson-Watt of the National Physical Laboratory, radar enabled British Fighter Command, already a well-organized and efficient director of the fighter defense commanded by Air Chief Marshal Sir Hugh Dowding, to detect German planes as they crossed the Channel and North Sea. The tech-nology provided information on the altitude, direction, distance, and speed of the approaching craft, and, therefore, Fighter Command could direct British fighters to the most critical positions. Some fifty radar installations along the coast provided the data, but the Germans never made a concerted effort to destroy them. The British "ULTRA" project, which employed a captured German code device, enabled the British to decipher German instructions and proved valuable in anticipating where attacks would fall. Finally, another critical advantage was that the RAF pilots fought over home territory and many could be saved when their planes were lost, while the Germans lost not only their aircraft with each killed plane, but also their pilots and crews—either to capture, death in battle, or to drowning in the sea. The efficiency of pilot survival was crucial because the RAF could only add about 50 newly trained pilots a week to the 1450 they had in 1939, while the Germans started the war with about 10,000 pilots. Indeed, about 2500 pilots, most of them British but some Australian, Canadian, New Zealander, South African, Polish, Czechoslovakian, Irish, and American, provided the vital service that saved Britain and earned Churchill's admiration expressed in the House of Commons with the comment that "never in the field of human conflict was so much owed by so many to so few."

While Britain was engaged in its struggle for survival, Mussolini took advantage of the situation to move in the Mediterranean world to secure Italian objectives. In June 1940, the Italians closed the Mediterranean to British maritime traffic, a move that hurt the British severely because travel through the Mediterranean to the Indian Ocean via the Suez Canal was critical in their defense of India and other Eastern colonies, as well as in securing resources from these possessions since without this route, traffic had to pass all the way around the African continent. In September 1940, Mussolini moved on British positions in Egypt and on the Suez Canal from Italian-held Libya to the west and Ethiopia to the south. In late October 1940, he sent Italian forces from Albania into Greece. In both these adventures, however, the hapless Italians met disaster. The outnumbered Greeks under General John Metaxas beat the Italian forces, driving them in retreat out of Greek territory by November 30. In North Africa, Italian forces that earlier had moved into Egyptian territory were routed in a series of engagements beginning December 9, 1940, led by British General Sir Archibald Wavell. The British attacks pushed the Italians back 400 miles along the Mediterranean coast to Beda Fomm in two months and resulted in the capture of 130,000 Italians by February 5, 1941. British naval forces meanwhile had reduced the Italian navy's control in the Mediterranean and gave the British greater maneuverability.

In both misadventures, Greece and North Africa, Mussolini was rescued by German intervention. Hitler sent Field Marshal Erwin Rommel, a veteran tank commander of the Battle of France, to North Africa as commander of the Afrika Korps and he was prepared to launch a counter offensive by February 1941. Meanwhile Hitler moved to salvage Italian prestige in Greece, counter British assistance to the Greeks, and secure the Balkans before his planned invasion of Russia set for May 1941. Diplomatically, Hitler secured Hungary and Rumania as members of the Axis alliance in November 1940 and Bulgaria in March 1941. In April 1941, German forces attacked Greece, defeating that country and forcing the evacuation of British forces in three weeks, and Yugoslavia, defeating it in 11 days. In a dramatic move led by paratroopers, Germany in a brutal fight seized the Mediterranean island of Crete from the British in May 1941. In March 1941, Rommel launched the Afrika Korps in an offensive against the British forces that had reached Beda Fomm in February. By the middle of April, Rommel had reconquered virtually all the territory the British had taken from the Italians and reached the Egyptian border. The British, now under Claude Auchinlek, mounted yet another counteroffensive and by December 31, 1941, drove Rommel back to El Aghelia, a point further west than Beda Fomm. However, this British counteroffensive did not succeed in cutting off Rommel's forces, and Rommel retained a position of strength. By the end of 1941, the Germans had salvaged Mussolini's North African debacle and were in a position to make 1942 the decisive year in that theatre of the war.

With the problem of Britain proving insoluble by late 1940, Hitler turned his attention and the direction of the war to the east. The German activity in North Africa, the Balkans, and the Mediterranean in 1941 was pursued in part to shore up Mussolini as an Axis partner. The Balkan initiative in April and May, however, was also strategically important for securing the southern flank of Germany's position in central Europe so that Hitler could pursue his main project for 1941, the invasion of Russia. Codenamed Operation Barbarossa, the Nazi invasion of Russia was a massive undertaking that Hitler announced to his generals as early as July 1940, informing them that he wanted the attack to occur no later than the summer of 1941. As planning proceeded over the next several months, May 15 was set as the date by which to complete preparations for the attack. The German action in the Balkans complicated plans for Barbarossa, but as it turned out, a shortage of trucks and a longer-than-usual winter that delayed the spring run-off prevented the attack from happening until June 22, 1941, a delay that cut the available time for campaigning before the harsh Russian winter set in again.

As the Germans prepared for the impending invasion, Stalin refused to heed warnings from various sources, including Britain and the United States. He continued to abide by the Nazi-Soviet Pact and sent shipments of grain, oil and other products into German territory right up to the morning of the attack and refused to alert forward units of the potential threat. Stalin's military, although huge, was weakened by his purges of the officers in 1937-1938 that had eliminated a lot of the experienced, imaginative leaders, replacing them with Stalin loyalists but not military masters. The Germans amassed over 3 million troops, 3350 tanks, 2000 aircraft, and 7200 artillery pieces, which were launched on June 22 in 3 main spears along a 1000-mile front. The Germans caught the Russians completely off guard, and the Red Army suffered monumental losses. By July 9, the Germans were half way to Moscow and the center army group had captured 300,000 prisoners and 2500 Russian tanks. By July 19, the center group captured another 310,000 prisoners and 3200 tanks. At the end of July, as Moscow lay just 220 miles away, Hitler intervened and diverted effort from the main thrust to seize as much territory as possible in the south. This effort captured Kiev and some 665,000 Russian troops as well. By late September, nearly *three million* Russian soldiers had become prisoners of war. As the Russians retreated in this series of disasters, they followed a "scorched earth" policy, destroying anything of possible use to the enemy rather than leaving it behind. As the Russians retreated, they also exerted a monumental effort to remove industrial equipment and relocate industry to safer points further east, such as in the Ural Mountains. In the first three months

of the attack, Russian railroads shipped eastward the physical plant of 1523 factories. Stalin called upon the people to fight in what he called the "Great Patriotic War of the Fatherland." Political commissars attached to the army were given the authority to execute soldiers and officers for dereliction of duty. After the drive on Moscow was resumed on September 6, the Russians were able to stabilize their defenses and hold just as the Germans moved to within sight of the capital city. In December, as the Russian winter set in, the Red Army, which Hitler had expected to fall apart, counterattacked, and the Germans were able to stave off the attack only by extreme exertion. As 1942 arrived, the Germans had inflicted massive damage to the Soviet Union and had nearly captured Moscow. But the Russians had proven to be resourceful and resilient. Moreover, in attacking his former partner in aggression, Hitler drove Russia and Britain into an alliance that was potentially quite powerful. The ultimate decision in the war in the east would have to wait for 1942.

While Germany conquered Western Europe, brought Britain to the brink of collapse, dominated the Balkans, and overran much of the Soviet Union, the United States remained out of the war officially but had become increasingly involved in helping Great Britain materially and with naval support. The sudden collapse of France and the dire situation of Britain shocked isolationist America, and the nation adopted its first-ever peacetime draft in September 1940. President Franklin Roosevelt was able to secure large-scale support for Britain with the enactment of Lend-Lease early in 1941, which allowed the U.S. to supply the British without having to worry about payment. In 1941, Roosevelt met with Churchill and adopted the Atlantic Charter, which essentially outlined joint war aims even though the U.S. was not yet at war. By late 1941

Japan launched a surprise attack on the United States at Pearl Harbor on December 7, 1941. Hitler declared war on America four days after the Pearl Harbor attack.

the U.S. navy was helping escort shipping to Great Britain and had engaged in action with German warships. It appeared that outright war might eventually result from the naval conflict, but as it turned out, the U. S. became involved in the war in another way, a way that came as a shock to America, galvanizing support for involvement and throwing the tremendous productive capacity of the nation into the conflict against the Axis.

War engulfed America from the Pacific Ocean. Since 1937 Japan was involved in a full-scale war of aggression against China, seeking to control China for Japanese benefit. The U.S. had early in the twentieth century developed the notion that it was the protector of Chinese sovereignty and so made diplomatic protests to Japanese policy but not military moves. After the collapse of France in 1940, Japan invaded French Indochina to secure valuable natural resources and expand its influence and power in the region. The U.S. countered with diplomatic and economic pressure. Eventually, the Japanese decided to try to eliminate U.S. interference in the region by means of a surprise attack on Pearl Harbor, the primary base of the U.S. Navy's Pacific Fleet. This attack came on December 7, 1941 and caught the U.S. Army and Navy forces off guard. Suffering over 2000 deaths and the loss of a good portion of its Pacific Fleet, the United States declared war on Japan. In a bizarre development Hitler decided to honor the Tripartite Pact and declared war on the United States, as did Mussolini as well. With the sudden entry of the U.S. in the war, the balance of power shifted overnight. The U.S. now joined with Britain and Russia into what Churchill called the "Grand Alliance." Churchill believed that the U.S. entry ensured the eventual victory of the Allies. However, in many senses the outcome of the war hung in the balance as 1942 began. The Axis had momentum and was in a

position of advantage in most theatres of conflict. The United States brought tremendous industrial capacity and military potential to the Allies but the question was whether the U.S. could make a decisive contribution before it was too late. The year 1942 proved to be the pivotal year of decision as the war hung in the balance in the three main theatres of conflict.

The Second Phase: December 1941 - November 1942

Although the outcome of the war was still not certain after 1942 and much of the toughest fighting on both sides happened in the three years of war after November 1942, the year between December 1941 and November 1942 proved to be the turning point of the war as fortune turned against the Axis in three critical struggles, and the Allies assumed the initiative. The three critical struggles played out in three different theatres of conflict: the eastern/Russian front, North Africa, and the Pacific.

On the eastern front, deep in Russian territory, the Germans had ground to a halt outside Moscow by December 1941, having lost about one-third of their original Operation Barbarossa forces. When the Russians, well-equipped for the bitterly cold temperatures (-20 degrees Celsius!), counterattacked against the inadequately winter-equipped Nazis, only desperate fighting and the iron determination of Hitler, exercised in part by dismissing droves of German commanders who faltered in their determination to fight and assuming direct leadership of the army himself, saved the German position by mid-January 1942. By springtime, Germany had stockpiled and reinforced its eastern units and launched another massive offensive in June 1942, focused on the southern part of the front, designed to seize control of the Caucasus oil fields.

Franklin D. Roosevelt signed a war declaration against Japan after the attack on Pearl Harbor.

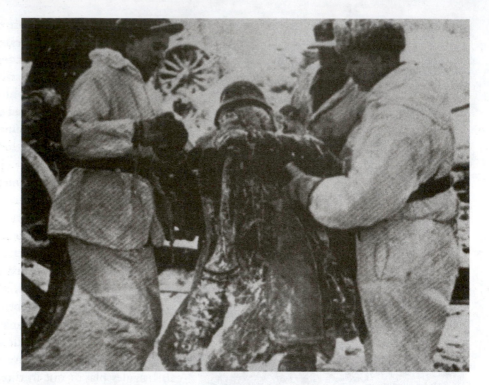

The Russian winter helped defeat the Germans who were not prepared for the cold. This nearly frozen German is taken prisoner.

Once again, the Red Army was dealt staggering blows as German forces drove into the Caucasus, as far south as the Caucasus Mountains and east to within a hundred miles of the Caspian Sea near the mouth of the Volga River. By August, Germany held some of the most populous, agriculturally rich, and industrially important parts of the Soviet Union in a line stretching from the Gulf of Finland near Leningrad in the north to the Caucasus Mountains near the Caspian Sea in the south. The Russians, however, had strengthened their forces over the winter as well and were receiving valuable supplies from Britain via the far northern port of Archangel, located on the White Sea, an extension of the Arctic Ocean.

The key point in the Germans' Caucasus campaign turned out to be the largest of several Russian cities named for the country's dictator, Stalingrad, a factory city located on the west side of a westward bend of the Volga River that approaches an eastward bend of the Don River. Stalin chose to garrison the city and defend it to the utmost. Hitler was determined to take the city. The Russians planned to draw the Germans into a fight for the city and then launch an encirclement offensive to surround and cut off the German forces. In late August, after the city had been bombed, the German Sixth Army under General Friedrich von Paulus launched its attack on the city, which the Russians defended street by street, ruined building by building, even room by room and in the cellars, in the toughest urban warfare the world had yet known. A German officer in a panzer division reported fighting 15 days over one bombed and burnt-out house. By October 18, the slow German advance halted, and the front that ran through the remains of the city stabilized.

The bulk of the German forces in this sector were concentrated at Stalingrad and lesser quality units of Italian, Rumanian, and Hungarian troops were left to defend the front to the north and south of the city. The Russians launched Operation Uranus on November 19 - 20. Under the command of General Zhukov, who had organized the successful defense of both Leningrad and Moscow in 1941, Russian forces punched through the poorly defended front to either side of Stalingrad and surrounded the 200,000 men of the Sixth Army, which Hitler had vehemently (and disastrously) ordered to stay in place. This November 1942 victory sealed the fate of the Germans at Stalingrad and marked a critical turning point in the war. Hitler had committed tremendous resources to Stalingrad and needlessly lost them all. For the rest of the war, the Russians maintained the initiative in the east while the Germans remained on the defensive. After being surrounded, the German Sixth Army held out, starving, freezing, and desperate, until February 2, 1943, when General Paulus finally disobeyed Hitler's orders and surrendered the 110,000 men who had managed to survive. Most of the captured Germans died as prisoners.

While the momentous events of 1942 played out on the eastern front, the war in North Africa also turned in favor of the Allies. By December 1941, Rommel's Afrika Korps halted the British attack led by Auchinlek and prepared another attack of their own. On January 21, 1942, Rommel began driving the British back along the Mediterranean coast over the same ground won and lost before. In mid-June the British were forced in a battle just west of the Libyan coastal town of Tobruk to withdraw to positions inside Egypt, leaving behind a trapped garrison at Tobruk and managing to make a defensive stand at El Alamein at the end of June. El Alamein was just 70 miles from Alexandria, and now once again the Suez Canal was threatened. If the Germans took the Suez, more was

Stalingrad was in ruins after the bombardment by the Luftwaffe and German ground forces.

British troops defeated Erwin Rommel at El Alamein in Egypt.

his troops for a major offensive that was launched, beginning with a midnight bombardment of German positions, on October 23. By November 4, British tanks broke through the German line and threatened to cut off Rommel's main force. Although Hitler refused to give Rommel permission to retreat, the "Desert Fox," as he was nicknamed, did so anyway and began what turned into a 2000 mile retreat along the North African coast to Tunisia. By the end of November 1942, the British had pushed Rommel's dwindling and poorly resupplied forces back to Benghazi, near Beda Fomm, and continued to press the attack. Meanwhile, since July, preparations had been underway for joint U.S.-British amphibious landings on the eastern end of North Africa, in Vichy France-held Morocco and Algiers. Codenamed Operation Torch and under the command of U.S. General Dwight Eisenhower, these landings began on November 8, 1942, and, despite setbacks, pushed German forces eastward toward Tunisia and the retreating Afrika Korps. Montgomery had turned the tide at El Alamein and the Operation Torch landings put the Allies in position to drive the Germans from the African continent in early 1943. The North African campaigns of 1942 gave the initiative in the west to the British and American allies and marked a turning point in the war.

The third critical area of operations that saw the war turn against the Axis in 1942 was the Pacific. For the first half of the year, Japan was triumphant. The Japanese attack on Pearl Harbor on December 7, 1941, was accompanied by moves on other U.S. holdings, like the Philippine Islands, as well as British and Dutch possessions, such as Singapore and Indonesia. By May 1942, Japan had met with spectacular success. In an unbroken series of victories they inflicted major damage to U.S., British, and Dutch

at stake than British access to the optimal travel route to India. Control of the Suez Canal would open the way for the Germans to drive into the Middle Eastern oil fields and link up with the German forces then driving into the Caucasus in Russia, thus encircling the Mediterranean and controlling crucial sources of oil.

Auchinlek was replaced as Commander-in-Chief, Middle East, by Harold Alexander, and the British Eighth Army in Egypt was given a new commander, Bernard Montgomery, who proved to be one of the more controversial figures among the Allied commanders due to his ego, his at times excessive desire to win glory for British forces (and himself), and his competition with the equally egotistical American general, George S. Patton. Montgomery prepared

naval forces and brought a vast swath of the western Pacific Ocean with its numerous island chains under Japanese control. Control extended south, including a portion of the island of New Guinea, which lies just north of Australia and was critical to the defense of that nation. With British and American strategy giving priority to the war in Europe and the defeat of Hitler, the Allied effort in the Pacific War had to be fought with more limited resources, a circumstance that made the Pacific situation in 1942 even more critical.

In May, the Allies began to turn the tide in the conflict. In that month, the Japanese pushed to secure control of New Guinea by sending a naval task force through the Coral Sea around to the southern side of this large island. Japanese success in sinking the new British battleship, *Prince of Wales*, in December 1941 had already demonstrated that air power could dominate traditional naval power. In the Coral Sea,

an Allied aircraft carrier force engaged the Japanese forces in a naval aircraft battle that forced the Japanese to turn back. Meanwhile Australian and American forces struggled in the steamy, bug infested tangle of New Guinea's jungle to halt the Japanese land advance toward Port Moresby. While these important developments temporarily lessened the threat to Australia, the major turning point in the Pacific occurred to the north, in the central Pacific. The Pearl Harbor attack, though it hurt U.S. naval power, had not dealt the Pacific Fleet a deathblow. In early June, Japan moved to finish off the American naval presence by sending a large aircraft carrier force to seize Midway Island, a tiny but critical U.S. base in the middle of the Pacific Ocean, and draw the U.S. fleet into battle to destroy it.

Due to successful decipherment of the Japanese naval code, called MAGIC, the United States was prepared for the move and sent its

The Japanese sunk both of the British warships, *Repulse* and *Prince of Wales*.

carrier force, which had been absent from Pearl Harbor at the time of the attack, to intercept the Japanese carrier strike force. On June 4, the Japanese attack on Midway began with carrier based bomber raids. American torpedo bombers from the U.S.S. *Hornet* were the first to find the Japanese carriers and, though they were unable to do damage themselves, other U.S. bombers from all three U.S. carriers involved arrived and destroyed three of the four Japanese carriers. The fourth escaped but was found later in the afternoon and sunk as well. The United States lost one carrier but destroyed four Japanese carriers along with many of their excellent pilots. The balance of power in the Pacific shifted significantly in this one engagement. Carriers already had become the crucial element of the World War II navy, and the heart of the Japanese carrier fleet was gone. Japanese objectives were foiled, and the Japanese Empire had reached

the largest extent of its power. The Japanese had also lost the initiative in the war. After Midway, the United States and its allies began the slow and excruciatingly difficult task of regaining the areas of the Pacific the Japanese had taken with such ease from December 1941 to June 1942. The war in the Pacific had turned decisively against the Japanese.

The Final Phase: November 1942 - August 1945

By the end of 1942, the balance of the war had shifted in favor of the Allies. The Axis powers were by no means beaten. The outcome of the war was still uncertain, and most of the worst fighting of the war still lay ahead. But in the three primary areas of fighting, the Allies were able to press forward until achieving victory against the Axis in 1945.

Survivors from a burning *USS Lexington* climb aboard a U. S. ship following the Battle of the Coral Sea, May 8, 1942.

Yugoslavian women fought alongside their husbands, brothers, and fathers against the Nazis.

On the Eastern European front, the Red Army built on its victory at Stalingrad. In the spring of 1943, the Germans had recovered from the shock of Stalingrad sufficiently to attempt another offensive, but the Russians quickly dealt with this attack and launched their own major offensive in July. The Russians had great success in reorganizing their war industries after the 1941 losses and produced tanks, airplanes and other vital war equipment in prodigious quantities. They were also aided tremendously by the material provisions and equipment, especially trucks and tanks, pouring into Russia from the United States and Great Britain by the end of 1942. Along the front between Moscow and the Black Sea, the Russians relentlessly pushed the Nazi army back to the west in the summer and fall of 1943. Reaching and crossing the Dneiper River on which Kiev in the Ukraine lies by October, the Red Army made further gains before winter arrived.

During the winter of 1943-1944, Russia pressed forward on the northern sector of the front, driving the Germans from Leningrad and Novgorod, while in the south freeing the Crimea of German forces by May 1944. The summer of 1944 saw more of the same steady offensive pressure from the Red Army. By August 1944 they had reached the Vistula River in southern Poland and drawn near to Warsaw. On August 1, the Polish resistance in Warsaw rose up against the Germans to help the advancing Red Army take Warsaw, expecting the Russians to soon arrive. But under direct orders from Stalin, the Soviet commander, Marshal Konstantin Rokossovsky, halted the Russian advance, and the army remained virtually inactive for 63 days while the Germans annihilated the Polish resistance. This betrayal of the Poles allowed Stalin to establish a subservient communist Polish government without having to deal with the involvement of the Polish resistance. The offensive was not resumed in Poland until January 1945. Throughout the late summer and fall of 1944 and into the winter of 1945, the Russians concentrated on the Danube Valley and the Balkans, moving through Rumania, Yugoslavia, and into Hungary, securing the surrender of Hungary by February 1945. After resuming the offensive in Poland in January 1945, the Red Army pushed across the pre-war German-Polish border, slaughtering German civilians as they went, across the Oder River, and into Berlin, entering the outskirts of the German capital in late April 1945.

While the mammoth battles raged on the eastern front, involving some 9 million men on both sides, the Western allies also pressed the war against the Axis—although not to Stalin's liking—in North Africa, the Mediterranean, and eventually in Western Europe. After Operation Torch landings in Morocco and Algiers and Montgomery's victories further east in North Africa against Rommel in 1942, the Americans, British, and other allies squeezed the German forces into Tunisia and then drove them from North Africa in May 1943, capturing 250,000 German and Italian troops. Stalin vehemently called for the British and Americans to open a "second front" in western Europe. Lacking sufficient shipping, equipment, supplies, and preparation for an invasion of France, but desiring to continue the pressure on the Axis so that Russia did not bear the burden of fighting Germany alone, the British-American effort turned next to an invasion of the island of Sicily and then the Italian peninsula. By this point, as in North Africa, the Germans had assumed control of the war in the Mediterranean from their disappointingly ineffective Italian allies, and so the Sicily and Italian projects did engage German forces and tax German resources. During the Sicilian campaign, Benito Mussolini was ousted from power and a new Italian government under Marshal Badoglio sued for peace, but the Germans secured control of Italy before the Allies, who had promised to accept only unconditional surrender, could decide whether and how to accept Italian surrender. Under General Eisenhower's direction, Sicily was cleared of Axis forces by the middle of August 1943 and Italian landings were made in early September. Due to tough German resistance that contested virtually every foot of ground and to mistakes by Allied leaders, the Italian campaign bogged down and progressed only slowly through the remainder of the war. Allied forces did not enter Rome until June 4, 1944, and fighting continued on the peninsula until the war ended.

Well before the Allied forces took Rome, Eisenhower was pulled from the Italian campaign, made Supreme Allied Commander in the Western European theatre, and given the task of overseeing the grandiose Operation Overlord, codename for the invasion of France. Extensive planning and a massive buildup of supplies and equipment in England preceded the invasion. Storage capacity was so exceeded that supplies lined roadsides in areas near embarkation points. Tanks, trucks, jeeps, munitions and weapons of all kinds, fuel, landing craft for the amphibious assault, and a myriad of other items were amassed and plans for the logistics of loading vessels, unloading them on the beaches, and supplying the various units of the invasion force were all carefully worked out ahead of time.

Just prior to the invasion, Allied bombers pounded transportation facilities and other targets behind the landing beaches on the Normandy coast in northwestern France. In the night prior to the attack, airborne troops parachuted in or used gliders to land behind the invasion beaches and attempt to secure key points. In the dark before dawn on "D-Day" June 6, 1944, a massive naval flotilla bombarded the coastal defenses of Hitler's "Atlantic Wall" as 4000 landing vessels moved to the 5 beaches, codenamed Utah, Omaha, Gold, Juno, and Sword. American forces went ashore on Utah and Omaha, the two westernmost beaches, while British and Canadians hit the other three. Despite some mistakes and ferocious German resistance at Omaha Beach, the initial landings

American soldiers land on the coast of France.

were a success, and by the next day ("D+1") over 177,000 troops were ashore. Continuing to pour men, equipment, and supplies onto the beaches in a massive buildup, the Allies met tough but undersupplied resistance. Eventually American forces in the western part of Normandy broke through the German lines near Avranches in late July, and the British and Canadians began to drive the Germans back with more success.

On August 15, Allied forces landed in southern France and drove north up the Rhone River Valley. Meanwhile, American forces drove southwest and east from the Normandy breakthrough, liberating Paris on August 25, and British-led forces drove northward into Belgium, capturing Brussels on September 3 and Antwerp on September 4. The quick capture of Antwerp gave the Allies port facilities that would have eased supply problems if Montgomery, commanding the British attack, had pressed forward to secure the estuary leading from the English Channel to Antwerp. Montgomery, however, failed to take advantage of the achievements, paused, allowed the Germans to regroup, and then made an ill-fated effort to seize a bridge over the Rhine River at Arnhem with an airborne attack to be followed by a drive forward from the main lines. This drive failed. Other attacks on the German lines ground to a halt by the end of October 1944, and the Germans held their "West Wall" defenses west of the Rhine River. Antwerp's port could not be used until late November. Despite some gains made by Allied forces in November and December, the Allies' sense of elation felt in August was replaced by disappointment.

Disappointment turned to concern when the Germans implemented Hitler's plan to reverse the course of the war in the west with a counterattack in the Ardennes Forest. Using a stockpile of munitions, equipment, and gasoline, remarkable because of the disruption being caused by Allied bombing, the German army attacked the western Allies in mid-December 1944 at their weakest point, in the same Ardennes Forest that Hitler had unexpectedly used in the Battle of France in 1940. As the Germans pressed forward, Waffen SS troops massacred American prisoners near Malmedy. The German attack drove as far as 65 miles into the Allied front but failed to break through. The bulge in the Allied lines led the Allies to call the struggle the "Battle of the Bulge." Critical de-

U. S. Army vehicles in the snow-covered Ardennes forest. Much of the Battle of the Bulge was fought under such conditions.

American troops form a chow line in the frigid weather while fighting in the Battle of the Bulge.

fense at key points, like St. Vith and Bastogne, along with effective countermeasures by Montgomery on the northern side of the bulge and Patton on the southern side, turned the German advance. By mid-January 1945, the bulge had been pushed back. Early German gains had been aided by cloudy weather that prevented the Allies from using their air power. General Patton had his chaplain say a particularly war-like prayer, and when the bad weather broke, he rewarded the chaplain with a medal.

In January and February 1945 the Allies steadily wore out German defenses and by early March reached the Rhine. At Remagen, German efforts to destroy a railroad bridge over the river failed, and the Allies captured the crossing on March 7, pouring men and tanks across as fast as they could. Farther south, Patton breached the Rhine with pontoon bridges on March 22 and rushed as many of his forces as possible into the heartland of German industry. Montgomery's forces pushed across the Rhine shortly thereafter. Hitler's armed forces were beaten, and the German citizenry put up little resistance as the British and Americans pushed eastward. American forces linked up with Russians driving in from the east on the Elbe River

on April 25. President Roosevelt did not live to see this, dying of a brain hemorrhage on April 12, 1945.

Russian forces took Austria in early April, and the German forces in Italy surrendered on April 29. Italian partisans captured former Fascist dictator Benito Mussolini, who had been under German protection since his fall from power, killed him and hung his dead body from a lamp post. The Russian assault on Berlin began April 16 and was complete by April 30. On that afternoon, Adolf Hitler was trapped in Berlin with aides and some close associates in his bomb-proof bunker buried deep beneath the Reichschancellery. Hitler and his newlywed wife, Eva Braun, committed suicide, as did Nazi propaganda minister Joseph Göbels and his wife, who administered poison to their children before taking their own lives. Their bodies were taken above ground, doused with gasoline, and burned. Just as the Nazi Empire went down in flames, so too did its Führer. Hitler had authorized that Admiral Karl Dönitz become commander upon his death. Upon receiving word that he was in command, Dönitz immediately arranged for surrender, which was signed on May 7, to take effect within 48 hours. May 8, 1945, was celebrated among the Allies as V-E (Victory in Europe) Day.

While the Allies pressed to victory in Europe, the war in the Pacific continued. After the Battle of Midway in 1942 had turned the fortunes of war against the Japanese Empire, the Allies, primarily behind the strength of American forces, began to move against the extended Japanese positions, beginning in the Solomon Islands just northeast of Australia where the U.S. Marines landed on Guadalcanal in August 1942. The navy fought a series of naval battles, and the Japanese withdrew from the island in February 1943. On the large island of New Guinea, Allied forces under the command of U.S. Army General Douglas MacArthur, who had been in command of U.S. forces in the Philippines before the Japanese onslaught of 1941-1942 forced his evacuation, pressed Japanese forces northwestward along the island in the summer of 1942. By April 1943 the plan was to continue this effort in New Guinea and at the same time move northwest along the Solomon chain, converging forces on the powerful Japanese base at Rabaul in the Bismarck Archipelago that lay between the Solomons and New Guinea. This

The Reichstag, Hitler's seat of government, was ruined during the fall of Berlin.

objective would set up the possibility of retaking the Philippine Islands from the Japanese.

By the middle of 1943, however, the Allied position, particularly in equipment and naval forces, was much improved, and Allied commanders adopted a change in strategy in August 1943. The Japanese stronghold at Rabaul was to be bypassed to cut it off from Japanese reinforcement and allow it to be bombed until it submitted or was neutralized. This by-pass technique, termed "island-hopping," was then used in *two* major drives in the Pacific. Combining carrier- and ground-based air power, traditional naval power, and amphibious ground forces, the Allies pushed toward Japan along two main lines. One drive, primarily under the authority of Admiral Chester Nimitz of the U.S. Navy, pushed through the central Pacific along island chains like the Gilberts, Marshalls, Carolines, and Marianas to draw near enough to begin bombing Japan, be in a position to move on the Philippines, and be able to acquire positions from which to invade Japan. In the other drive, which MacArthur commanded in the southwest Pacific, the Allied forces continued to push up the island of New Guinea until it was secured and then island-hopped to bases in the Admiralty Islands that isolated Rabaul and positioned forces for an invasion of the Philippines. By August 1944, key points in the central Pacific drive were in Allied hands, including Saipan, Guam, Tinian, and the Marianas, and MacArthur was in position south of the Philippines.

Although by this time Admiral Nimitz wanted to bypass most of the Philippines in a move on Formosa in preparation of an invasion of Japan, President Roosevelt supported MacArthur's desire to return the Philippines to U.S. control. The first important island in the Philippines to be invaded was Leyte, in October 1944. The Japanese, who needed to defend the Philippines, as well as Formosa and the Ryukyus to protect the shipment of oil from southeast Asia to Japan, made the Leyte invasion the occasion of their last major naval stand. The Battle of Leyte Gulf in late October 1944 was the largest naval battle in history, involving on the U.S. side some 800 ships (including 9 large aircraft carriers and 12 battleships), 1500 carrier airplanes, and 143,000 naval personnel, which was more people than were in the entire U.S. Navy before the war. The Japanese had 6 carriers and 9 battleships plus a host of attending vessels. Among the battleships at Japan's disposal were the two largest battleships in the world, the *Yamato* and *Musashi*, each displacing 70,000 tons, protected with 9" deck armor and 16" belt armor, and sporting nine 18" guns that could fire a 3000-pound shell 26 miles. Despite serious mistakes, the Allied force with luck turned Leyte Gulf into a crushing defeat for the Japanese. Japan's carriers and their complements of aircraft were virtually wiped out with the destruction of 3 battleships and 19 other major vessels, leaving Japan with little ability to continue to wage naval war. As a sign of the desperate position Japan faced, Leyte Gulf saw the first *kamikaze* ("divine wind") attacks in which suicidal Japanese pilots flew their planes, armed with explosives, into U.S. ships. Although the Japanese exhibited a tenacious, to-the-death fighting style throughout the war, the kamikaze attacks began because the Japanese had airplanes and explosives but few trained pilots and very little fuel, a condition that only worsened with U.S. domination of the seas achieved at Leyte Gulf.

With the destruction of Japan's naval capacity, the Allies proceeded to take Leyte and in January 1945, Luzon. In the spring of 1945, air bases already secured in the Marianas were supplemented by the conquest of Iwo Jima and

Okinawa, which lay much closer to the Japanese home islands. Taking these two islands required extreme sacrifice. At Iwo Jima, 6821 Americans died, and 20,000 were wounded, while the 21,000 Japanese defenders died almost to the man. On the 80-mile-long island of Okinawa, the Japanese pulled their 120,000 defenders back from the beaches to a series of interior defensive lines involving tunnels and strong points. The Japanese, having convinced the residents of Okinawa that the Americans would commit horrible atrocities, encouraged residents to fight to the death, as the Japanese tended to do. In addition, Japan had approximately 4800 aircraft ready for kamikaze missions at Okinawa. Air attacks on Allied ships, most of them kamikaze, killed 5000 men, injured another 5000, sank 30 ships, and damaged 368 ships. The U.S. lost 7000 men in fighting on the island. About 110,000 Japanese soldiers died in the desperate

defense; only 7400 prisoners were taken. At least 80,000 civilians died as well. These shocking death tolls seemed to provide ominous warning of what an invasion of the home islands would entail.

The end of the war in the Pacific came, however, without invasion. After securing bases sufficiently close to Japan, the U.S. began a massive bombing campaign that destroyed most Japanese cities with any industrial or military value as targets by the time Okinawa was secured. With the European war over after early May 1945, the Japanese could expect the full attention and brunt of American military power to be leveled against them. Despite the extension of tentative, unofficial peace feelers, the militarists who still dominated the Japanese government showed no sign of giving up the increasingly desperate fight. Meanwhile, in a top-secret program called the Manhattan Project that

The Japanese cruiser, *Mikuma*, under attack by American dive-bombers.

worked feverishly throughout the war, the United States with British support and involvement had developed the first-ever atomic bombs. These nuclear fission devices were exponentially more powerful than any previous high-explosive bombs, with one bomb having the power to level a moderate-sized city. The first successful test of the atomic bomb was conducted in the New Mexico desert at Alamogordo in mid-July 1945.

Although the atomic bomb was developed because it was believed the Germans were trying to do so, Germany had been defeated before the bomb was ready. After a brief debate over whether to use the weapon against Japan, U.S. President Harry S Truman decided that its use would end the war quickly and save American and Japanese lives, and, therefore, unless Japan surrendered immediately, it would be dropped. Target cities were chosen that had been preserved from other American bombing so that the effects of the atomic bomb could be analyzed. On August 6 an atomic bomb incinerated Hiroshima, killing over 90,000. The Soviet Union, fearing the war against Japan would end before it could stake a claim in the peace settlement, finally declared war against Japan two days later. On August 9 a second bomb was dropped on Nagasaki, killing another 35,000. With the personal intervention of the Japanese Emperor Hirohito, Japan surrendered, formally signing the instrument of surrender on September 2, 1945. The war was over.

The Naval War

A critical part of World War II was the naval conflict that raged around the world. Naval forces were used in traditional ways, as portable artillery to bombard coastal defenses, as escorts for merchant vessels, and as defenders against water-borne invasion. But the World War II navy also saw dramatic changes and adaptation to modern warfare. Since World War I, navies had become vulnerable to attack from airplanes, and with the construction of fleets of aircraft carriers, navies could use air power for defense, as well as attack. Amphibious water craft, small and large, involved navies in new ways in the invasion of enemy territory. Submarines, used for the first time to devastating effect in World War I, continued in importance and expanded their role as technology and tactics improved.

One critical role played by sea power in the Second World War was its impact on the supply of vital resources—from raw materials to war equipment to food stuffs—that gave combatants the physical ability to fight the war. For example, Russian industry was completely disrupted by the German invasion of 1941. Although the Soviets achieved remarkable results in relocating and regenerating their industrial capacity, much of their war-making capability in 1943 and 1944 resulted from supplies they received from the U.S. and Britain. From March 1941 to October 1945, the U.S. shipped 2000 locomotives, 51,000 jeeps, 375,000 trucks, almost 3,000,000 tons of gasoline, and 15,000,000 pairs of felt winter boots plus massive quantities of other items. These critical items kept the Red Army mobile and able to advance on the Germans. Supplies were even more important to island nations like Great Britain and Japan.

While control of coastal waters was crucial in preventing invasion of Britain by the Germans in 1941 and France by the Allies in 1944, for the European war as a whole it was the impact of naval activity on supply that proved to be the most important aspect of the naval war. After the war was over, Winston Churchill remarked that "the only thing that really frightened me during the war was the U-boat peril." In his memoirs he wrote that "this mortal danger to our lifelines gnawed my bowels." He was referring to the German submarine (*Unterseeboot* or U-boat) fleet that stood between the island nation of Britain and its main sources of supplies, most critically food in the Americas being sent to the British Empire. Britain imported all of its oil needs and half of its food supply, along with other necessary industrial raw materials. When the war began, the German *Kriegsmarine* (War Fleet) had 57 submarines, with 27 capable of oceanic travel. A massive submarine construction program brought the total fleet strength to 300 by July 1942, which sank shipping at an annual rate of 7 million tons, over five times the British construction rate. (The average pre-war merchant ship displaced about 5000 tons.) By that time, however, the British had the great assistance of American shipyards, which in 1943 built 1500 new ships (some of them 10,000- and 15,000-ton vessels), a total tonnage of more than three times the amount the Germans were sinking.

Still, the submarine threat was grave for the British. U-boats harassed shipping around the British Isles. After the fall of France in June 1940, U-boats began attacking shipping in the eastern Atlantic and along the route to South and West Africa. In mid-to-late 1941, the raiders preyed on the convoy routes in the central and western Atlantic and in the North Sea from Britain to the Soviet port of Archangel. Since the United States Navy was patrolling convoys on part of the route from the Americas to Britain, this submarine activity brought Germany and the U.S. into a shooting naval war before the two were even officially at war. The U.S. naval frigate, *Reuben James,* was sunk in October 1941 with the loss of 100 American lives. Once the United States was in the war, the U-boats had a "Happy Time" for several months in the Gulf of Mexico and along the Atlantic Coast of the U.S. before

the U.S. took countermeasures with its coastal shipping. Germany, however, continued to position as many as twelve submarines at any given time in these waters. From January through March 1942, U-boats sank 1,250,000 tons of shipping in waters near America. In November 1942, they sank 509,000 tons in the North Atlantic.

U-boats were especially successful if merchant vessels plied the trade routes strung-out individually because the submarines could wait for additional targets if they happened to miss one. The primary countermeasure against submarines, therefore, was the convoy system, running a group of merchant ships together in a zigzagging course, along with naval escorts that attempted to sink the submarines if detected in time. It was nearly as difficult to find a convoy on the open ocean as it was a single ship, and if a U-boat was out of position to hit a convoy, it might have to wait a long time before another came along. The German submarine admiral Karl Dönitz developed the "wolf-pack" tactic to improve success against convoys. By deploying a group of U-boats along trade routes, the Germans stood a greater chance of spotting a convoy, and with radio signaling the pack of subs could move in to attack. An effective countermeasure against the wolf-pack was a change of route. This tactic points out the importance for both sides of communication monitoring and cryptoanalysis. The Germans monitored radio communication, instructing submarines of changes in departures and courses. For a time, the British Admiralty continued to use an easier-to-crack book code rather than a tougher machine code in its instructions, and the Germans were able to send the wolf-packs to targets regularly. On the other side, British and American cryptoanalysts deciphered by December 1942 a new German code implemented earlier in the year in February, an achievement which greatly improved the Allies' ability to move against submarine deployments in 1943.

Just as 1942 was the critical year of the war in the three main theatres of ground action, the year was also pivotal in the Battle of the Atlantic, as Churchill called it, by the middle of 1943. Under the new leadership of Sir Max Horton, who was put in charge in November 1942, the British and Americans turned the tide. Breaking the new German code proved invaluable. The availability of new, longer range bombers gave the Allies crucial air cover over much of their convoy routes, and escort aircraft carriers provided some air cover as well, forcing the U-boats to submerge. In this condition they were much slower than on the surface. Improvements in Asdic, the technology of locating underwater craft by echo-sounding, and new depth-charge launchers improved the Allies' ability to destroy submarines. High Frequency Direction Finding (HF/DF) enabled the Allies to determine a U-boat's position by fixing on the submarine's outgoing radio communications. As important as any factor, however, was the overwhelming productive capacity of American shipyards, which kept bigger and faster replacement ships coming and added escort vessel strength. From September 1939 to May 1943, the Germans sank some 13 million gross tons of merchant ships, a total of 2452 vessels, plus 175 naval ships. Over the same period, however, the Allies sank 696 submarines out of a total 830 craft deployed. With these U-boat losses went the loss of 25,870 men of the 40,900 crew members deployed. Despite the great impact submarines had on Allied supply, Germany could not keep up this rate of loss, and Dönitz called off the wolves in May 1943, dramatically curtailing their operations in the open Atlantic. After August 1943, Allied monthly shipping losses in the Atlantic exceeded 100,000 tons in only one month and usually were around half that figure.

The activity of German surface raiders is an aspect of the Battle of the Atlantic that receives notoriety due to the drama involved. Early in the war, the German navy sent out into the Atlantic several surface vessels to attack British commerce. The *Atlantis*, for example, was able to sink 22 ships before being sunk itself in November 1941. Large German naval ships, like their pocket battleships, also raided the Atlantic. In November 1939, one of these ships, the *Graf Spee*, sank 9 merchant ships off the coast of South America. The British trapped the *Graf Spee* in December 1939 in the Rio de la Plata near Montevideo, Uruguay, and its captain ordered it scuttled to avoid falling captive to the British. This gave the British a positive victory in the depressing early stages of the war. Another British naval victory, more important for its morale and propaganda value, was the sinking of the massive German battleship, *Bismarck*, in May 1941. The Germans tried to challenge British surface fleet power by sending the *Bismarck* and *Prinz Eugen* into the Atlantic. But the ship was spotted and, after a dramatic mobilization of the British Home Fleet, was hunted down and sunk.

The Pacific theatre was dominated by naval warfare as carrier battles, submarine action, and amphibious operations combined with traditional naval activity to determine, in large part, the success of land operations. As in the Atlantic, supply was a critical factor in the Pacific, and the United States Navy used the submarine to great advantage against the Japanese. The Japanese wanted to expand toward southeast Asia to secure raw materials, like oil and rubber, that Japan's industrial economy required but had no sources of at home. As the war in the Pacific progressed, U.S. naval power, particularly aircraft patrols and its submarine fleet, constantly harassed Japanese efforts to supply its forces scattered across the Pacific islands. Eventually, after the Philippines were retaken in late 1944, the flow of supplies running from southeast Asia up the coast of China to the Japanese home islands was virtually halted. Before, in 1942, U.S. submarines sank 180 merchant ships for a total tonnage of 725,000. In 1944, the submarine fleet sank 600 merchant vessels of 2.7 million tons. As a result, by the time of the Battle of Okinawa, the Japanese had a good supply of aircraft but very little fuel with which to power them. The dramatic step of *kamikaze* flights taken by the Japanese was a testament to the importance of supply to the outcome of the war and of the naval forces in securing or denying that critical supply.

Wartime Diplomacy: The Grand Alliance

Because the three major partners of the Allied (or United) Nations, what Churchill called the "Grand Alliance," Great Britain, Russia, and the United States, worked together in cooperation and coordination, despite serious differences in ideology and strategic viewpoint, the Allies were able to defeat the Axis on the battlefield. The Grand Alliance was a marriage of necessity with a common enemy in Nazi Germany, which all believed must be completely defeated. Major disagreements, particularly over the so-called "second front controversy" and plans for the post-war world, challenged the Grand Alliance, but it held together and worked effectively to defeat the Axis. Throughout the war the military staff of the "Big Three" conducted ongoing conversations and conferences to iron out military issues. The most dramatic aspect of the Grand Alliance, however, were the wartime conferences held between the "Big Three" leaders themselves: Churchill, Stalin, and Roosevelt. At these con-

ferences, some involving two of the leaders and others involving all three, the Allies decided goals and strategies for the conduct of the war and, in an important departure from World War I, questions regarding the future of post-war Europe.

The first of these conferences, the Atlantic Conference, was held aboard the *Prince of Wales* in Placentia Bay off the coast of Newfoundland and involved Churchill and Roosevelt. This meeting, held in August 1941 just as Germany was driving deep into Russian territory in Operation Barbarossa, derived, in part, from a long-distance friendship that the two Western leaders had developed via telegram since Churchill became prime minister in May 1940. Meeting about four months before the United States entered the war, the two leaders, nonetheless, discussed general war objectives and principles to guide decisions about the post-war world. The most significant outcome of this conference was the signing and proclamation of the Atlantic Charter. The charter proclaimed that the U.S. and Britain sought no territory in the war, called for the destruction of Nazi tyranny, and laid out several principles they wanted implemented in the post-war world: 1) self-determination in establishing territorial boundaries and governments, 2) equal access to raw materials in world trade, 3) international economic cooperation, 4) freedom of the seas, 5) a peace that would ensure the safety and freedom from fear and want of all nations, 6) disarmament of the aggressor nations, and 7) efforts to reduce armaments in general. The charter also pointed to the establishment of a "permanent system of general security," and led to nine other nations signing the charter in September 1941.

Two weeks after Pearl Harbor, Churchill traveled to Washington, D.C. and spent three weeks as Roosevelt's guest in the White House. The two leaders met with Russian ambassador to the U.S., Maxim Litvinov, and discussed various issues, including Stalin's demand that the U.S. and Britain open a "second front" in the west to relieve the hard-pressed Soviets. Roosevelt and Churchill told Litvinov that a second front was impossible in 1942, which was the truth considering the tenuous position of Britain, the lack of military resources, and the Japanese onslaught against British and American holdings and forces already underway in the Pacific. Russia was unwilling to open a "second front" in the Pacific against Japan, upholding a 1941 nonaggression treaty with Japan. (Russia declared war on Japan in August 1945 when Japan lay devastated and on the verge of surrender.) The alliance held together, in large part out of necessity, but the second front issue remained controversial. Stalin apparently believed that the Western Allies were stalling, trying to make Russia bear the biggest share of the fighting against Germany, despite the fact that, as Churchill had pointed out, the Russians stood by as a partner to Nazi Germany and allowed Hitler to overrun France in 1940, thus closing the front he now demanded be opened again.

As a result of the meetings in Washington D. C. and the aspect of the Atlantic Charter pointing to a future international organization, a United Nations declaration was issued and signed in January 1942. The Declaration of the United Nations pledged the nations to the principles of the Atlantic Charter and to work together (no separate peace) for complete victory over the Axis. A total of 26 nations signed the declaration, including the U.S., Britain, and Russia. Inherent in the formation of the war coalition, the United Nations intended to form a post-war international organization to replace the failed League of Nations, a permanent United Nations organization. Discussions were conducted during the war, and a U.N. charter was more or less completed by the time the war ended.

In January 1943, after the Operation Torch landings in North Africa, Roosevelt and Churchill met at Casablanca in Morocco. Stalin was invited but refused to attend mainly because of his paranoia and insecurity regarding his own power in Russia. At the Casablanca conference, the next move in the west was settled. The British successfully argued that Italy should be the next step and that a "second front" invasion of France should be put off until later in 1943. Italy was made the next priority, given the American and British forces that were already in North Africa. The leaders decided to open a second front, but the decision of where and when to open it was postponed. In this discussion, Churchill suggested that after Italy, the U.S. and Britain should move on the Balkans. Churchill argued that this area was the "soft underbelly" of Nazi Europe, more easily won than better fortified areas in other places. Such a move would have also limited Russian influence in eastern Europe, an objective that Churchill wanted. Roosevelt felt that a Balkan front would unduly anger Stalin and rejected the idea. While there were good arguments for a Balkans campaign, there were also real problems, such as the rugged terrain and the proximity to existing Nazi forces opposing Russia. Knowing that Stalin would be upset at the postponement of a second front, Churchill and Roosevelt agreed to and announced their intention to seek *unconditional surrender* from the Axis powers. This would hopefully reassure Stalin that his Western Allies were committed to the complete defeat of Germany and would not settle separately with Germany while it still held Russian territory or was in a position of advantage. Although unconditional surrender might encourage tougher, longer resistance by the Axis, another reason for adopting it was to avoid the circumstances after World War I in which Germans could with some justification feel they had not truly lost the war because the 1918 armistice was signed while German territory was still free of enemy forces.

In May 1943, Churchill and Roosevelt met at the Trident Summit to finalize plans for the Italian invasion. At this meeting, the two leaders decided on a cross-channel invasion of France in spring 1944, with Churchill reluctantly giving up on the "soft underbelly" idea he still cherished. This postponed earlier hopes of a 1943 invasion and, done without Stalin's input, infuriated the Soviet ruler who refused to agree to the plan. After receiving an angry reply from Churchill, Stalin was angered once again, saying the Russian contribution to the war had been tremendous (which it had) and that the British and American contribution had been insignificant (which it had not). He recalled his ambassadors from London and Washington and put out peace feelers to Germany through Sweden. The German offensive in the summer of 1943, surprisingly mounted in the aftermath of their disastrous Stalingrad losses, gave Stalin reason to reconsider his treatment of his allies and calm down.

Churchill and Roosevelt met again in August 1943 at the Quadrant Conference in Quebec to discuss how to best take advantage of Mussolini's fall from power. They decided on four goals: to invade France in spring 1944, to stabilize the Italian front north of Rome, to increase the air war on Germany, and to increase operations in both the central Pacific and southwestern Pacific. The two allies also dealt with some post-war concerns and acknowledged some important disagreements. The U.S. pushed for decolonization, and Britain resisted the idea. Britain wanted a prominent place in the postwar world for France as a counter to Germany

and Russia, while the U.S. envisioned "four policemen": the U.S., Britain, Russia, and China. There was no place for France. Poland also arose as a postwar concern because the London Poles wanted to take the German territory of East Prussia and keep the portion of Czechoslovakia they got at Munich in 1938, both of which were likely to cause problems with the Russians.

After the Quadrant Conference, with his offensives against German forces having good success, Stalin was more conciliatory and friendly toward his allies and proposed a meeting of the Big Three to be preceded by a planning conference of the foreign ministers in Moscow. In pursuit of this, Anthony Eden for Great Britain, Cordell Hull for the United States, and Vyacheslav Molotov for Russia, along with other officials, met in October 1943 in Moscow. They repaired some of the rough spots in the alliance, although much disagreement remained. They discussed various topics, including Stalin's demand for a second front, the future of eastern Europe where Stalin wanted "unfettered influence," and Russian influence in France and Italy. Regarding the future of Germany, Stalin wanted reparations, and all parties agreed to war crime trials for the Nazi regime. Britain wanted to reach a unified agreement on the future of the Balkans, but the U.S. and Russia preferred to delay dealing with the issue, not seeing any possible agreement. Not much of substance was accomplished, but Britain and America assured Russia that plans were moving forward for an invasion of France in 1944. Russia agreed to enter the war against Japan as soon as they were able, and the Allies agreed to establish the European Advisory Commission (EAC) in London to plan for post-war Europe. Finally, at Stalin's insistence, the site of the proposed Big Three meeting was set for Teheran in Persia (modern-day Iran), which was close to the Soviet Union, something the paranoid and insecure Stalin seemed to need. The site also would be under Russian control, and they could monitor communications of the other allies.

When Churchill, Stalin, and Roosevelt met at Teheran in November 1943, problems in the alliance were all too visible. Stalin belittled Churchill's concern over the Balkans and was cool toward Roosevelt's desire to promote Jiang Jeshi (Chiang Kai-Shek) of China as a "fourth policeman" on a par with the Big Three. Despite tension and problems, however, the three Allied leaders reached several important agreements. Stalin promised to enter the war against Japan as soon as the European war was over. Churchill and Roosevelt agreed that the "second front" invasion of France would begin May 1944, and Stalin agreed to a simultaneous Russian offensive in the east. The three agreed in principle to a post-war United Nations international organization and that steps would be taken to prevent Germany from expanding again, with details to be referred to the EAC. The most serious question left unresolved was the future of Poland, which Stalin wanted to control by means of a communist pro-Russian government (which the London Poles exile government definitely was not), acquiring the Polish territory he had gotten in the Nazi-Soviet pact of 1939 and shifting Poland's borders westward.

During late 1943 and 1944 several steps were taken to create a more cooperative world for the future. The United Nations (referring to the coalition of Allies) Relief and Rehabilitation Administration was set up in November 1943 to take care of refugees and related problems. Allied representatives met beginning in July 1944 at Bretton Woods in New Hampshire to deal with long-range economic plans for the post-war world, hopefully to head off some of the economic problems that contributed to the coming of World War II. Participants at this meeting planned and established an International Monetary Fund (IMF) to stabilize exchange rates and the World Bank to create a pool of capital to lend or grant to liberated nations for economic restoration after the war. From August to October 1944, representatives met at the Dumbarton Oaks estate in Washington, D.C., to draft plans for a charter for the United Nations international organization. Despite these moves toward post-war cooperation, other developments tended to create tension among the Allies.

Between the Teheran meeting and the next Big Three conference at Yalta in February 1945, a great deal changed. Russian forces pushed all the way to the doorstep of Germany in the east. The U.S. and Britain had successfully invaded France and pushed German forces back so that they were also on the verge of breaking into the German heartland. Stalin had infuriated Churchill in August 1944 by refusing to help the Polish resistance in the Warsaw rebellion, allowing the Poles to be annihilated. In September 1944, Roosevelt convinced Churchill to support the "Morgenthau Plan" to completely de-industrialize the German economy and then turned about and withdrew the idea. In October, Churchill traveled to Moscow and made an informal deal with Stalin to give Britain and the U.S. majority influence over Greece, Russia influence over Bulgaria and Rumania, and equal influence in Hungary and Yugoslavia. Roosevelt, envisioning a "one world" setting in which old-style spheres of influence and power diplomacy would give way to democratic cooperation, wanted no part of the deal. In December, Stalin formally recognized the Communist "Lublin Poles" government he had set up in opposition to the London Poles.

In this environment, with Germany on the ropes and post-war matters becoming more ur-

Prime Minister Winston Churchill of Great Britain, President Franklin D. Roosevelt of the United States, and Premier Joseph Stalin of the Soviet Union (seated left to right) during the Yalta Conference in February 1945.

gent with every day, the Big Three met again in February 1945 at Yalta in the Crimea, once again on Stalin's terms and turf, this time actually in Russia territory. At Yalta, Churchill, Stalin, and Roosevelt confronted four main issues and tried to come to agreement on them: the United Nations (U.N.), Poland, Germany, and Japan. Regarding the U.N., the Allies set a meeting for April 1945 in San Francisco to work out the constitutional details, but the three leaders agreed to the basic governing framework in which the Big Three would each have veto power over actions of a security council charged with matters of collective security. Russia was given three seats in the organization's assembly. On Poland, which by the time of Yalta was entirely in Red Army control, the Allies agreed to move the country's boundaries westward, with Russia getting the eastern territory Poland lost and Poland getting German territory in the west in compensation. Stalin finally agreed to allow the London Poles to have a place in his communist government he had set up in Lublin and also to hold "free and unfettered" elections in accordance with the

Atlantic Charter's self-determination principle. Germany was to be temporarily divided into British, Russian, and American zones and militarily occupied, as was Berlin, which lay entirely within the Russian occupation zone. An Allied Control Commission was to make decisions for the whole of Germany. A reparations commission was established to work out the details of reparations with a starting figure of $20 billion, half to go to Russia. Regarding Russian assistance in the war against Japan, although Stalin had already agreed to enter the war, he now demanded a list of terms in exchange. He once again promised to enter the war against Japan but in return Russia got the Kurile Islands, the southern half of Sakhalin Island, Port Arthur (Vladivostok), railroad concessions in Manchuria, and influence in Korea.

At Yalta, Stalin received more than he promised to do in return. The U.S. and Britain had to concede on several points. Roosevelt was in very ill health at the conference and had declined markedly since Teheran. (He would be dead in two months.) His negotiating skills were undoubtedly hampered, and he has been criticized for giving away too much. The end of the war in the Pacific, however, still seemed a long and bloody distance away, and Stalin's help was seen as important. Moreover, since the Red Army controlled Poland, inclusion of the London Poles and promised elections seemed to be important concessions from Stalin. The key issue with Yalta, and the Cold War that eventually separated Russia against the other two allies, was not whether too much was conceded to Stalin but that Stalin did not do what he promised. Had he kept the promises, Yalta would have been viewed as more satisfactory from the British and American perspective. As it was, Stalin's failure to honor the promises he made contributed to the split of the wartime alliance after victory was achieved and the eventual development of the Cold War in the late 1940s. Not honoring the promises by the time of Potsdam contributed to the tension and lack of agreement during that conference.

The final wartime conference of the Big Three took place at Potsdam in July 1945 in the midst of great tension and change. The war in Europe had come to a surprisingly quick end, but the war with Japan still persisted. Franklin Roosevelt had been dead since April, replaced by Vice President Harry S Truman, a principled, matter-of-fact man without the diplomatic nuances of Roosevelt. During the conference, Britain held its first Parliamentary elections since before the war began, and Churchill's Conservative Party was defeated by the Labour Party. Prime Minister Clement Atlee replaced Churchill in the middle of the proceedings. Stalin's grip on power was as firm as ever, and he now was the senior statesman of the Big Three leaders. The realities of Soviet occupation of eastern Europe meant that Stalin could (and did) dictate policy in that region, and he was not ful-

filling the spirit of the Atlantic Charter nor later promises, especially regarding the Polish government and elections. Truman received word of the successful test of the atomic bomb in New Mexico while he was at the conference and hoped to impress Stalin into being more cooperative but to no avail since Stalin was already aware of the atomic project through espionage efforts. The atomic bomb did change the Pacific war situation, making Russian help less necessary while encouraging Russian intervention in order to make claims on the Yalta promises.

Despite the number of issues where no agreement was reached, the Big Three made several agreements on the disposition of Germany. They agreed to disarm, demilitarize, and de-Nazify Germany, specifically to hold war crime trials to deal with leaders responsible for Germany's aggressive war-making and its atrocities during the war. In all, 22 leaders were eventually tried in a special military court at Nuremberg in 1946-1947, and 19 were convicted, 10 of whom were hanged. One of those condemned to death, Reichsmarschal Hermann Göring, cheated the hangman by committing suicide in his cell. Many Nazi leaders committed suicide to avoid capture or escaped all together. The Allies also agreed to deindustrialize Germany to a level compatible with a peacetime economy. Reparations were tied to this goal, since reparations could be assessed in the form of removing industrial plants from the occupation zones of Germany to be taken home. Russia did this thoroughly in their zone and received some of the plants from other zones as well. Poland's boundaries were moved westward, pending peace treaties. East Prussia, a part of Germany, was divided between Poland and Russia. Finally, the Allies agreed that a foreign ministers conference would work out peace treaties with Germany's Axis war partners in Europe.

Treaties were signed in 1947 with Italy, Rumania, Hungary, Bulgaria, and Finland. For Germany, and much of Eastern Europe, no uniform peace settlement emerged. Instead, as the Cold War developed competing goals, mistrust and animosity between Russia on the one hand and the U.S. and Britain on the other led to each side making moves and countermoves in postwar Europe in the areas they influenced. The result was that Germany remained without a tidy peace treaty with all parties and remained divided between East and West. The whole of Europe was divided between the U.S.-influenced West and the Russian-dominated East. The West signed a peace treaty with Japan in 1951. Russia signed a separate treaty in 1956. The Grand Alliance had defeated the Axis Powers, but the disagreements and diverging post-war objectives seen in the alliance helped create the Cold War.

Other Facets of the War

World War II was waged in ways other than on the battlefield, in the skies, or on the seas. These other aspects of the war often proved crucial to the outcome. All major combatants made efforts to conduct espionage and to deceive the enemy. Cryptoanalysis proved invaluable for both the Allies and the Axis. Britain had a highly centralized system of intelligence gathering that organized efforts to collect information from German-held areas through agents on the ground and by monitoring radio transmissions. Counter-espionage efforts also monitored radio transmissions from within Britain and took measures to guard against or undermine spying. Through double agents, the Allies were able not only to use German spies to gain information but also to feed Germany false information. Feeding false information, such as fake messages or allowing false plans to fall into enemy hands,

proved useful. One of the most successful deception campaigns masked the British and American plans for the 1944 cross-channel invasion of France. A widespread effort created the impression in the German military that the invasion would land in the narrow Pas de Calais stretch of the channel, whereas it actually fell in Normandy. The deception helped delay German response long enough to secure a hold on the beach head. The military services of all combatants had their own intelligence branches to assess the enemy. In some cases the spying done against Allies proved to be as valuable as that against enemies. A Russian spy network infiltrated the top-secret Manhattan Project and gave the Soviet Union the benefit of much of the atomic weapon program of the United States and Britain.

The Manhattan Project is a prime example of another facet of the war: the technology race. The U.S. spent $2 billion on this long-term project to develop an atomic bomb, splitting the atom to release its energy. Various parts of the project operated at different sites like Oak Ridge, Tennessee and Los Alamos, New Mexico, in a top-secret mission on the cutting edge of science. The Manhattan Project was inspired by fear that the Germans would develop and use such a weapon. Ironically, German racial policy drove out top scientific talent like Albert Einstein, giving the U.S. the nuclear physicists it needed to successfully develop the weapon. Although the Germans failed in their atomic project, they were successful in other high-technology endeavors. Under the direction of Werner von Braun, the Nazis developed a rocket engine that powered the V-2 "vengeance weapons" fired from the continent at Britain. The V-2 and their non-rocket driven predecessors the V-1 were not decisive but caused considerable damage and might have been more decisive if employed earlier. Another major technological breakthrough by the Germans, the jet engine fighter, the Messerschmitt 262, was ineffective because it came too late. Radar technology, constantly being improved during the war, proved crucial for British air defense in the Battle of Britain, for German defense against Allied bombing, and for surface action on the seas, including detection of surfaced U-boats. Asdic and sonar technology improved the ability to destroy submarines. New weapons like the flame thrower, bazooka rocket launcher, and napalm (jellied gasoline) altered combat.

Low-technology produced effective developments. The Germans developed a schnorkel device for submarines that allowed them to use their diesel engines while submerged and thus avoid detection by aircraft. Had this been employed earlier, it could have altered the outcome of the Battle of the Atlantic. The LCVP was a cheaply produced landing craft that made possible amphibious assaults by large numbers of troops. Developed by Andrew Higgins, some 20,000 of these 36' x 10.5' crafts of plywood stern and sides with a metal front ramp were produced in New Orleans. In the air war, the British developed "Windows," a countermeasure against German radar that significantly cut British bomber losses for a time. Windows involved dropping strips of aluminum from planes to "blind" German radar by creating blips that appeared to be bombers. Thousands of other innovations brought ideas and endeavors into the war effort. The war also produced important innovations that benefited the post-war world, including medical achievements, such as the use of blood transfusions that saved countless wounded soldiers from death.

Women played an important role in the conflict in all the belligerent countries, Axis and Allied. While the political and military leadership establishments were overwhelmingly dominated by men, and women did not serve in direct combat roles in most countries, women did play active military roles and contributed in the civilian war. For American women, the Women's Army Auxiliary Corps, created in May 1942 and transformed into the Women's Army Corps (WAC) in 1943, and the navy's Women Accepted for Volunteer Emergency Service (WAVES), established in 1942, organized women military personnel for service, ranging from clerical and secretarial positions to pilots flying transport aircraft or ferrying bombers from America to combat areas. Some 17,000 WACs served overseas, and 40,000 "Air WACs" served at air bases in the U.S. Beginning in 1942 the German army used women volunteers called *Stabshelferinnen* as army clerks and truckdrivers to release men to fight on the front. The range of women's involvement was as broad as that of men. Women celebrities served as entertainers for military forces. Women also were partisans or spies operating behind enemy lines. Female traitors served enemy propaganda purposes, as did Mildred Gillars, an American known as "Axis Sally," who made radio broadcasts for Nazi Germany, and Iva d'Aquino, an American who did the same for Japan as "Tokyo Rose."

Women experienced the widest involvement in the war effort in Russia. In civilian roles, Russian women contributed a monumental effort to the defeat of Germany. In early 1940, before the Soviet Union was invaded, women already made up 41 percent of the labor force. As war engulfed Russia, women worked in munitions factories, labor squads, as air raid wardens, miners, welders, machine operators, and painters. "Special women's brigades" of painters painted artillery pieces on the rail flatcars as they were being transported to the front lines. Maria Meksandrovna, the first Soviet woman train en-

Russian women went into battle to fight the Nazis to help save their country.

gineer, drove "flying column" trains rapidly to the front. In militarized war industries women were subject to military discipline, which meant that absence without leave drew stiff prison sentences or worse. Women also carried on much of the agricultural labor, and, with most tractors being appropriated for use in the fighting, women were harnessed six to a team to pull the plows.

Russian women also served in military roles, including combat service. In the defense of Leningrad and Moscow in 1941, Russian General Zhukov mobilized city residents. Some 250,000 residents of Moscow, three-fourths of them women, went to work digging anti-tank ditches by hand. About 300,000 women worked in anti-aircraft defenses. At least 500,000 women served on the battlefronts as nurses, combat pilots, navigators, snipers, gunners, paratroopers, tank crews, laundresses, cooks, and sappers (mine-clearers). At least 100,000 women were involved as partisans behind enemy lines. An average of about 2000-3500 women served in front-line combat in each of the armies com-

prising the Red Army at large, and about 25,000 women served in the Soviet navy. Women served as 41 percent of the doctors in the Red Army and 43 percent of the medics who collected wounded in the heat of battle. Junior Lieutenant Aleksandra Boiko commanded a JS-122 heavy tank with her husband serving as driver-mechanic. The all-women 46th Guards Taman Women's Air Regiment flew wooden bi-plane bombers called *Lastochki* ("swallows") in night raids against the distressed Germans, who called them "night witches." As a combat pilot in this effort, Aleksandra Semyonova Popova flew 365 missions.

WAR HITS HOME

Total War

World War II was a "total war" in that all or most of the resources of the main combatants were committed to the war effort, and citizens were mobilized to serve in the military, in the war industry, or in other capacities in support of the war. The war was also total in the sense that in most of Europe and in some areas in other theatres of the war, civilians were directly victims of or participants in the fighting on an unprecedented scale. War hit home as never before as invading modern armies and bombing missions brought the war into the homes and lives of citizens in new and unique ways.

As countries prepared for war, their governments became increasingly powerful and assumed control of activities. Governments undertook rationing of products needed in the war effort, such as gasoline, butter, sugar, meat, rubber products, and metal items. In the United States the production of major consumer items like automobiles ceased altogether during the war. Production of war goods such as ammunition, small arms, artillery pieces, trucks, tanks, and airplanes was organized by government agencies that set production goals, allocated resources, and organized distribution. Government controls in these areas of life were similar in democratic and authoritarian countries. The War Production Board in the U.S. and the Ministry of War Production in Germany did essentially the same thing. Germany was not fully mobilized economically for the first two years of the war. Early in 1942, Hitler made Albert Speer Minister of War Production. Speer pushed the German economy to full war mobilization, organized it more efficiently, and implemented measures to disperse industry to minimize the impact of Allied bombing. Government administrative bureaucracy expanded dramatically to mobilize populations through conscription into armed forces, assignment to governmental and industrial jobs, and emergency work details. Russia, for example, called upon hundreds of thousands of citizens to help construct defensive works around Moscow and Leningrad as German armies approached. Governments regulated economic matters through wage and price setting, regulation of union activities, taxation, and borrowing. Several countries tried to control inflationary pressure by taxation, bond sales, and savings programs.

The entire society of many countries was mobilized. Entertainers encouraged the war effort. Films and radio programs stirred patriotism and presented favorable versions of the war to viewers and listeners. Music became part of the war effort with songs like Glenn Miller's "People Like You and Me," encouraging all to contribute to the war effort. Printed propaganda encouraged activities such as saving of scarce goods, buying war bonds, and working hard in industrial jobs. Propaganda also portrayed the enemy as evil, often with appeals to racist images, which were as common in Allied countries as in Axis states. Enemy leaders were lampooned in editorial cartoons and posters. People of all ages contributed in numerous ways from children helping collect scrap metal to housewives giving donations for the war to older persons serving in civil defense capacities as air raid wardens.

Fear also gripped nations at war and led citizens and governments to take action to enhance feelings of security. The threat of espionage led to tighter security, and police agencies like the Federal Bureau of Investigation in the U.S. and the Gestapo in Germany stepped up surveillance and monitoring of suspect individuals. One concern that citizens and governments shared was the fear of sabotage by traitors or enemy activists on the homefront. Suspect groups often were targets of reaction to these fears. Totalitarian regimes in Germany and Russia were notorious for aggressive action against groups based only on suspicion. While not violent nor conducted on the same scale as Nazi and Communist actions, reactionary measures were taken against suspect groups in democratic countries as well. In the United States on the West Coast, an intense fear of Japanese attacks, sabotage efforts, and other partisan activity focused on people of Japanese descent living in the United States. In February 1942, President Roosevelt issued Executive Order 9066 to round up and detain the 112,000 Japanese-Americans living on the West Coast. Two thirds of these people were native-born U.S. citizens. The Japanese Americans, imprisoned in internment camps in the American west, most of them for the duration of the war, lost their property and freedom, without trial, simply because of their ethnicity. No evidence of sabotage or disloyalty was uncovered to justify the action taken against them. Nonetheless, General John DeWitt, in charge of West Coast defenses, pressed for the removal and incarceration of the Japanese-Americans arguing that "the very fact that no sabotage has taken place to date is a disturbing and confirming indication that such action will be taken."

Civilians and the Air War

One of the most horrific ways in which World War II hit home for many in combat areas around the globe was through the air war. A major part of the war effort of both the Allies and Axis was the use of air power to control the battlefield, disrupt supply lines, destroy defenses and supply dumps, sink shipping, destroy air bases, and otherwise directly impact the military activities of the enemy. World War II, however, also saw air power used in the bombing of civilian areas. In the Spanish Civil War, German squadrons had attacked civilians at Guernica, and Japan had bombed Chinese civilians beginning in 1937, actions that brought forth a flood of negative world opinion. In World War II, bombing of cities was first done as the Germans did in the Battle of Britain in an effort to knock out industrial plants and, thus, the production of essential war goods. Eventually, however, as in the London Blitz and in Allied campaigns against Germany and Japan, bombing was used against civilians directly in an effort to undermine morale and reduce their ability to work in war industries and support the war effort. The main impact was to kill civilians.

The German effort in the Battle of Britain laid waste to large sections of many British cities and killed thousands of civilians, some 20,000 in London. The British repaid the Germans with their own bombing campaign. Early in the war, Britain's Bomber Command carried out raids on specific targets in Germany, focusing on nighttime attacks. These raids were extremely inaccurate, with a 1941 analysis showing only one out of every three bombers hitting within five miles of the target. They then shifted to "carpet bombing" in an effort to "dehouse" German workers. Under a new commander, Air Marshal Arthur T. Harris, Bomber Command improved its effectiveness in 1942. In May, 1000 British aircraft overwhelmed the night defenses of Cologne and destroyed 600 acres of the city. In July 1943 a raid on Hamburg, using incendiary and high explosive bombs, was perfectly executed and created a firestorm that sent superheated air aloft so quickly and sucked in surrounding air so fast that wind speeds reached 300-400 miles per hour. The temperature on the ground approached 1000 degrees, and four miles of the center was wasted. Some 30,000-40,000 people were killed.

The U.S. Army Air Forces were also employed against Germany. First arriving in England in the summer of 1942, the American bomber units concentrated on daylight attacks, with raids first reaching Germany in the summer of 1943. From August through October

A B-17 heads back to England after bombing the ball-bearing factories at Schweinfurt.

American bomber raids, largely unguarded by fighters, attacked specific industrial targets such as the Messerschmitt aircraft factory in Regensburg and a ball-bearing works at Scheinfurt. Despite heavy losses and limited effect on German industry, daylight bombing continued throughout the war with most German cities suffering major destruction. American forces also participated in raids on non-industrial targets. In February 1945, British Bomber Command ordered an attack on the German cultural center of Dresden. British night bombing and American day bombing created a firestorm even greater than that in Hamburg. Estimates vary, but at least 40,000 and perhaps as many as 135,000 people were killed, many of them dying of suffocation as the great fire sapped the oxygen from the air. American bombers also hit columns of refugees fleeing the city.

In the Pacific, the U.S. Army Air Forces conducted massive bombing campaigns against Japan once bases were secured on Saipan and Tinian in the Marianas Islands by late 1944, which brought the Japanese home islands in range of American B-29 bombers. At first, the American preference for attempted precision bombing was followed, which produced limited results since Japanese industry was spread out among scattered small factories. In February 1945, General Curtis Le May assumed command of the bombing in the Pacific and implemented incendiary attacks on Japanese cities where close-packed, wood and rice paper housing construction made excellent tinder. In a March 1945 night raid on Tokyo, American firebombs in the center of the city created a firestorm so hot that glass ran liquid in the streets and water in the city canals boiled. Sixteen square miles of the city were burned out, 267,000 homes were destroyed, and at least 83,000 people were killed. Le May continued with attacks on other cities so that by July all of Japan's major industrial cities were gutted.

An analysis of the effect of bombing on the war reveals mixed results. On the one hand, the accuracy of bombing in hitting strategically important targets was poor. By the spring of 1944 only 14 percent of American daylight bombers hit within 1000 feet of their target, and even after German defenses had been virtually neutralized in the spring of 1945, only 44 percent could hit the same window of accuracy. Axis war production continued; in Germany production of war goods continued to rise every month of the war until the very end. Bombing often destroyed buildings but not the equipment and material within. Countermeasures like anti-aircraft defense and spreading out and hiding factory operations had great success. To achieve the damage inflicted, the loss rate of bombers and personnel was staggering. In bombing operations in Europe through 1943, an average of nearly 30 percent of American bomber crews were lost each mission, which meant that bomber crews facing a standard 25-mission tour of duty could hold little hope for survival. Moreover, despite the sometimes extreme casualty rate among civilians, their morale did not seem to be negatively impacted by the bombing, which instead engendered hatred of the enemy and a determination to carry on just as strong in Germany as in Britain. Despite these problems, however, bombing did disrupt enemy industrial output, transportation, and efficiency. Resources, such as air power, had to be expended on homeland defense and were not available for battlefield action. For the British and Americans, bombing provided the only way to hit Germany directly until the Normandy invasion

of 1944 and helped sustain their own population's morale. Finally, in several critical areas, such as in German fuel production from 1944 to the end and in its atomic form in Japan, bombing crippled the Axis and proved decisive. The use of atomic bombs in Japan forced the timing of the Japanese surrender forward and may very well have saved more American and Japanese lives than it cost. Regardless of its specific impact on the war, the widespread use of bombing in civilian areas represented a new and terrible facet of modern warfare as citizens of nations at war could expect to be directly affected.

Nazi Occupation

Many people in Europe outside Germany were forced to live under Nazi occupation. As Germany conquered most of Europe, or overtook its allies (e.g. Vichy France, Italy), the Nazis militarily occupied the territory and implemented measures to enforce their rule. While most people in occupied lands attempted to go on with as normal a life as possible, Nazi policies led Eu-

Underground newspapers were published in all occupied countries, such as this Yugoslav printer.

Yugoslavian partisan leader, Tito, (right) and one of his officers.

ropeans into greater involvement with Nazi rule. Some of these people became active in the resistance to Nazi rule and worked as partisans to help the Allied war effort. At the same time, others actively and willingly collaborated with the Nazi regime. The inherent conflict in loyalties between the resistance and collaborators, as well as internal disputes within the resistance, created an important element in the post-war political development of nations liberated from Nazi rule.

All of the occupied countries developed some kind of resistance movement, in some cases unorganized, in other cases quite organized. The number of people directly involved usually was not very large: at its height, the French resistance could count about 116,000 armed individuals. The impact of these movements, therefore, was usually limited and mainly served to bolster morale. Partisans attempted sabotage, gathered information to be sent to Allied governments, produced underground newspapers, carried out assassinations, helped Allied pilots shot down over enemy territory, and carried out numerous other actions. On the whole, partisan activity did not cause the Germans to divert much attention or effort. In France, for example, the German military was deployed primarily along the coast, leaving the control of the rest of the country to security forces, which totaled only about 6500 men at maximum strength. In two areas of Europe, however, partisans did cause significant concern, in Yugoslavia and in the area around the Pripet Marshes in Poland. One of the most famous and most successful resistance movements was the partisan group organized and led in Yugoslavia by Josip Broz, known as Tito. Tito, a communist and Comintern agent, led a guerrilla war against Italian, German, and Axis satellite forces with assistance from the Allies. His group, numbering as many as 100,000, competed with other partisan bands, such as the Chetniks under Draza Mihailovic, and caused the occupation forces a good deal of headaches. After the war, Tito gained control of the Yugoslavian government and implemented a Communist dictatorship but refused to be dominated by Stalinist Russia, pursuing an independent communism.

Collaborators were more visible in occupied Europe. These people ranged from government officials who helped the Nazi rulers control occupied areas to business owners who sought the benefit of Nazi cooperation to informants who worked against the partisans or victims of Nazi racial policies like the Jews. For example, Celeste di Porto became a deadly informant in Rome, identifying over 50 Jews for German authorities to arrest, and with her dark hair became known as the "Black Panther." The Nazi conquest of Europe was aided by collaborators such as Vidkung Quisling in Norway who encouraged the Germans to invade and became the leader of the Nazi puppet regime there, his name, "quisling," entering the English language as a synonym for traitor. The most notorious collaborationist government was that of Vichy France, headed by Philippe Pétain and Pierre Laval. Vichy France refused to turn over its navy to the Allies, actually fought against the North African Allied landings of Operation Torch, and assisted the Nazi regime, including rounding up, *without German request*, Jews in their territory to be turned over to the Nazis. Once France was liberated, the Vichy collaborators faced reprisals at the hands of the French resistance and the Free French government set up under De Gaulle. Collaborators were arrested, publicly humiliated perhaps by having their heads shaved, and in many cases executed by the government or resistance members. About 50,000 collaborators were arrested and some 10,000 executed; the government carried out only 800 of the executions.

Nazi occupation policies created intense feelings and help explain the divided response among occupied peoples. Because of Nazi brutality and exploitation that involved severe reprisals for partisan activity, many people were

This Belgian woman, who collaborated with the Nazis, was marked with a swastika after her hair was shaved. Public shaming of collaborators was part of the post-liberation in some countries.

terrorized into obedience or used collaboration as a way to hopefully avoid Nazi violence. On the other hand, the nature of Nazi rule inspired others to resist at all costs and to view those who collaborated as guilty of the same crimes the Germans committed. Nazi occupation policies involved the implementation in Europe, by rule of force, of what Hitler called the New Order. The New Order was based on racial notions that classified ethnic or national groups as separate races, with some being of a higher order than others. The mythical "Aryan" race, equated by the Nazis with the Germans, was the supreme or master race, whose superior qualities suited them for rule over others. Beneath the Germanic people were Western Europeans like the English and French who were not extremely inferior but were to be ruled over by the Germans. At the lower levels were the *untermenschen*, the "subhumans," such as Slavs that were fit for slavery but were expendable. At the very bottom of the *untermenschen* were the Jews, who in the irrational Nazi belief were seen as a racial group that embodied all the typical anti-Semitic stereotypes of Jews, as well as what the Nazis saw as the worst characteristics of humankind, such as weakness and intellectualism. Because the Nazis believed these traits were not cultural (learned) but racial and, therefore, transmitted by blood to offspring, the only way to control the "problem" was to prevent intermarriage and to ultimately exterminate the Jews to remove their unremediable polluting effect from humankind. "Aryan" purity required the extermination of the Jews.

Hitler's New Order sought to set up his racial hierarchy into political and economic practice: Nazi Germany would rule over all of Europe and the other nationalities (races) would be put into the service of the Reich (empire) or exterminated according to their racial value. The implementation of this New Order involved three main elements: 1) plunder, 2) slavery, and 3) *Endlösung* or "Final Solution." As the Nazis conquered Europe, they plundered the states they took over. They seized gold reserves and cash, forced conquered governments like Vichy France to pay the costs of German occupation, removed industrial plant and equipment to Germany, and extracted payments of money or raw materials. The Nazis even seized cultural treasures. Hermann Göring personally organized the theft of over 20,000 works of art from western Europe alone for his personal art collection.

Nazis used the conquered people as slaves for the benefit of the Reich. By the end of September 1944, Germany was using 7.5 million non-German civilians as slaves and another 2.5 million prisoners of war. The slaves worked in war industries, as trade apprentices, domestic servants, and agricultural labor. Many of the noto-

rious German concentration camps used prisoners as the labor supply for adjacent factories. Some inmates of the Auschwitz camp in Poland slaved in an I.G. Farben plant and Krupp munitions factory. Living and working conditions and the treatment of slaves and other prisoners was horrible. French prisoners of war working for a Krupp factory in the west were kept in dog kennels, five men per cage, 3 feet high by 6 feet wide by 9 feet long. Prisoners were systematically underfed, sometimes by adding sawdust to bread dough to add bulk but no nutritional value to the food. The Germans provided inadequate shelter, insufficient clothing, and forced prisoners to work long and hard under pain of death. In this way, slavery was also used as an exploitative and gradual means of killing those considered to be racially inferior. Of the approximately 5.1 million Russian prisoners of war Germany captured, 3.3 million of them died by a combination of overworking, malnutrition, and murder.

Death by slavery was only one means used to implement the third element of the New Order, Endlösung. Meaning "final solution," Endlösung was a euphemism the Nazis used to refer to their organized, systematic, and ruthless effort to find and exterminate all the Jews of Europe, the Nazis' final solution to the "Jewish problem" as they saw it. Given the anti-Semitic racial ideology of the Nazis, the "Jewish problem" was simply that in 1939 some 11 million people in Europe were Jews and were alive. The Final Solution was ordered by Hitler, carried out primarily under the leadership and active support of Hermann Göring (Hitler's second-in-command during most of the war), Heinrich Himmler (head of the S.S.) and Reinhard Heydrich (head of the S.D., security forces), with the involvement of thousands of Nazi Party officials and German and non-German soldiers and officials, and with the complicity of many Ger-

**Prisoners were packed into railway cars and deported to unknown destinations,
where many met their deaths.**

man citizens. In a January 1939 speech, Hitler proclaimed that if a European war broke out, it would result in "the annihilation of the Jewish race throughout Europe."

The Final Solution was organized before the invasion of Poland as the Nazis began to round up some of the small population of German Jews and to make plans in the event of war. But true to Hitler's threat, the extermination of the Jews was not begun until after the war was started. Himmler and Heydrich organized *Einsatzgruppen* (Special Action Groups) that followed the Nazi troops into Poland and rounded up Jews into ghettoes in the cities in preparation for killing them. In the summer and fall of 1941, as the Nazis rolled across eastern Russia, the Einsatzgruppen followed and began carrying out the killings of Jews and political prisoners. The commonly used method in the early

stages was to have a group of those selected for murder dig a large hole and then line up along the edge to be killed by gunfire or lie down in the hole on top of earlier victims to be shot. On August 31, 1941, Heinrich Himmler ordered 100 prisoners killed by the above method so he could watch how it was done. The bespectacled former poultry farmer got sick watching the gruesome scene and went hysterical when two women did not die immediately from their gunshot wounds. In the spring of 1942 at Himmler's order the Nazis began killing women and children using special vans designed by a German business that funneled the exhaust into the cargo compartment. The victims were herded into the vans and driven around until they were asphyxiated. From 750,000 to 1,000,000 people, mostly Jews, were murdered by the Einsatzgruppen during the war.

The above methods used by the Einsatzgruppen proved to be too slow for the Nazis, as did efforts to kill Jews by working them to death on road work gangs. The Nazis carried out killing the Jews in the notorious concentration camps. As soon as the Nazis came to power, they set up several concentration camps where political prisoners, personal enemies, or anyone who might get out of line were sent. At the start of the war these camps held about 25,000 people. The number of camps and prisoners skyrocketed during the war. The Germans set up 20 main concentration camps and about 165 subsidiary labor camps. A few of these camps were erected to specifically carry out the mass slaughter of millions of Jews and other people. Most of these death camps, or extermination camps, like Chelmno, Belzec, Treblinka, Sobibor, and Auschwitz, were in Poland, and all were organized to efficiently process murder victims. The most effective, though not the only method of murder at these camps, were the gas chambers, which used poisonous hydrogen cyanide gas. After the victims were killed, many were disposed of by incineration in crematoria.

At Treblinka, the Germans developed a highly efficient and cruelly exploitative death

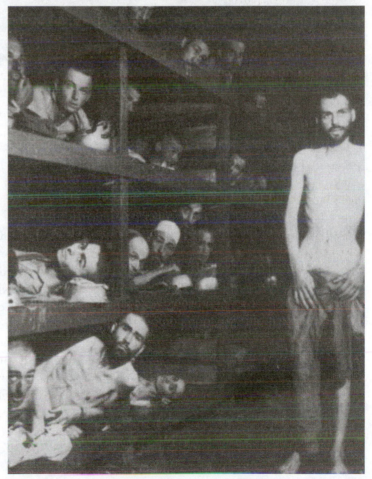

Prisoners look from their bunks at the Buchenwald concentration camp. Many died from disease, maltreatment, and starvation. The camp was opened in July 1937 and liberated by American troops on April 11, 1945.

A row of ovens reveals the cremated remains of the bodies of Jews sent to their deaths in gas chambers.

process. The Nazis brought Jews to the camp packed in railroad boxcars, sometimes having been locked inside for weeks, 10 to 15 cars at a time. Ukranian and Latvian guards, assisted by a few Jews, unloaded the cars and had the people disrobe, telling them they were going to be cleaned up. The men were separated from the women and children and walked naked up through a fenced path, screened by evergreens, that was called "the funnel," or the Highway to Heaven. At the end of this path lay the gas chambers, which were set up to resemble a large, communal shower. Before going into the gas chambers, the Jews had their hair cut by a team of Jewish barbers made to do the task. The guards herded the victims into the gas chamber, the gas was put into the chamber, and then after the victims died, a gang of Jewish workers

removed the bodies and cleaned up the chamber for the next group. In this way, the camp could "process" a trainload of 50 cars in two hours.

Although the specifics varied and not all the Jews were immediately killed, an organized process was used at all the extermination camps. Since Auschwitz served as an extermination camp and a labor camp, doctors examined the Jews coming out of the boxcars and picked out those who could be put to work. The Nazis at the camp still killed about 6000 people each day through their systematic murder process. The Germans' efficiency, however, was not restricted to the killing. From the mass murder victims, the Germans collected the shoes and clothing taken off before being "processed," personal articles like glasses and jewelry, gold tooth fillings

Clothes taken from the prisoners before being killed at Dachau are heaped on the ground.

and bridgework, and their shorn hair. The hair was used as stuffing and in some cases body fat was used in soap production. One notorious Nazi, Ilse Koch, even had human skin made into a lampshade.

The Final Solution was the targeted extermination of the Jews, but other groups were selected for a similar fate. The Nazis rounded up and murdered 250,000 Gypsies and 60,000 gay men, and they targeted the mentally retarded, Jehovah's Witnesses, Communists, and many Slavs. All told, the Nazis exterminated 11 million people, 6 million of these being Jews. The horror went on and on and is unimaginable and incomprehensible, but the records kept by the Germans themselves, the testimony of camp survivors and guards, information gathered by the Allied troops who liberated the camps, and photographs demonstrate the reality of the Final Solution. The Germans were most thorough in their genocidal effort in Poland, which makes the term Holocaust truly appropriate. In 1939 Poland had approximately 3,350,000 Jewish residents. In 1945, only about 50,000 remained.

"Holocaust," a term that means mass or complete sacrifice by fire, appropriately has become the most common name for the attempted genocide the Nazis perpetrated against the Jews of Europe. The term certainly applies well to the Nazis' nearly complete devastation of Poland's Jewish population. One of the most poignant examples of this "complete sacrifice by fire" is the fate of the Jews of Warsaw, who as is in other Polish cities had been rounded up early in the Nazi occupation and confined to a small, enclosed section of the city—the Jewish ghetto. The Warsaw ghetto also provides an important example of Jewish resistance to the Holocaust.

In late 1940, after about a year of Nazi occupation, the Warsaw ghetto was a walled-in section about 2.5 miles long by one mile wide into which were crammed some 400,000 Jews. Captive within the walls, living in overcrowded conditions, allowed few provisions, and with only

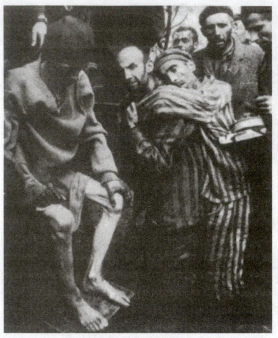

Concentration camp survivors liberatd from Nazi Germany were barely alive.

JEWISH POPULATION LOSS. 1939-1945		
	1939	**1945**
Austria	60,000	7,000
Belgium	90,000	40,000
Bulgaria	50,000	47,000
Czechoslovakia	315,000	44,000
Denmark	6,500	5,500
France	270,000	200,000
Germany	240,000	80,000
Greece	74,000	12,000
Hungary	400,000	200,000
Italy	50,000	33,000
Luxembourg	3,000	1,000
Netherlands	140,000	20,000
Norway	2,000	1,000
Poland	3,350,000	50,000
Romania	800,000	430,000
Soviet Union	3.020,000	2,500,000
Estonia	4,500	
Latvia	95,000	
Lithuania	145,000	
Yugoslavia	75,000	12,000

some being given employment in a few German munitions plants inside the ghetto, the Warsaw Jews faced slow death by disease and starvation. Most of the Jews in the ghetto, however, met a different fate.

In the summer of 1942, S.S. leader Heinrich Himmler ordered that the ghetto population be removed. Between late July and early October 1942, in what the Nazis called a "resettlement action," over 310,000 Jews were taken from the Warsaw ghetto and sent to extermination camps to be killed, with most going to Treblinka. By early 1943, only about 60,000 remained in the ghetto, which itself had been reduced to a small area about 300 by 1000 yards in size. These 60,000 remaining Jews had determined to resist being "resettled" by the Germans. They had managed to hoard, smuggle in, or make a few weapons and explosive devices and had fortified

various places, making good use of the basements and the ghetto's sewer system.

On April 19, 1943, the Germans, under the command of S.S. officer Juergen Stroup, began what was supposed to be a three-day "special action" to deal with the remaining Jews. Although the Germans used explosives, artillery, tanks, and fire, the Jews fought tenaciously and forced the Germans into a month-long, building-to-building struggle that involved setting fire to the ghetto's buildings to burn out the resisters. On May 16, 1943, the ghetto resistance was finally finished off, with nearly all of the 60,000 Jews being killed by the fighting, explosion, fire, capture (followed by immediate execution), or transportation to Treblinka. For the Jews of Europe, Nazi conquest meant a Holocaust indeed.

These Jews were captured during the final liquidation of the Warsaw ghetto and marched to a deportation site by armed Nazi soldiers.

OUTCOMES:
THE IMPACT OF WORLD WAR II

World War II impacted Western civilization profoundly in many ways, most of them difficult, if not impossible, to measure or describe adequately. The war ended with the complete and utter destruction of the two most important warmaking nations, Nazi Germany and Imperial Japan. With Germany eliminated as a force in international affairs, much of the resources of Great Britain used up, and France shaken by its rapid defeat and capitulation, the old powers that had shaped pre-war European international relations were in no position to resume leadership. In the resulting power vacuum, two powers, the United States and Russia, emerged as "superpowers." These two superpowers exerted their influence and tried to shape the postwar world in ways that suited their governments, economic systems, and foreign policy objectives. The conflicts between the Russian and American agendas, and the efforts of these two leading nations to build coalitions of other states, became the defining features of international relations in the post-war era and created the long, tense struggle known as the Cold War. In this setting, the United Nations organization never became the arbiter of conflict and basis of international security it was hoped to be.

The death and devastation of the war was one of its most horrific impacts. Estimates vary and the true figures can never be known for certain, but the war caused at least 17 million military deaths and another 18 million civilian deaths. Some estimates range as high as 50 million total killed. The Soviet Union faced the highest loss, around 20 million dead. With such figures, the human toll of the war is unfathomable. The cost of the war was even more difficult to measure. One estimate is that the war cost $1 trillion in military expenditures by all nations combined and $2 trillion in property losses. Perhaps a better way is to imagine the cost in comparison with something else. For example, the United States government from 1941-1945 spent over $300 billion on the war. This figure is *two times* the total amount the government had spent over the entire 152 previous years of its existence.

The physical destruction was massive and widespread. Europe was rubble. As a result of bombing campaigns by both sides, many European cities like Coventry, Berlin, Stalingrad, Warsaw, Dresden, Hamburg, Stuttgart, and much of London, were nearly destroyed. In Europe west of Russia, 5,000,000 homes had been destroyed. In Russia 25 million people were homeless. In damaged cities there was no water or electric service, sewer systems were disrupted, and food supplies were nonexistent. The continent literally stank from sewage, corpses, and general decay. People could smell the German city of Cologne 25 miles away. Rats thrived in this environment. Millions of people were on the move. These "displaced persons," or DPs, clogged the roads, taxed food supplies, and in-

cluded those fleeing from Russian occupation of eastern Europe, those released from concentration camps, liberated prisoners of war, and people seeking lost family members. The economy was shattered as war goods production ended abruptly and conversion to a peacetime economy proved extremely difficult in the midst of destruction and displacement. Transportation networks were destroyed or out of commission. The Rhine River was impassable; 750 barges were sunk in the river's channel. The river was uncrossable; no bridges were left standing.

The war produced innumerable other effects. Scientific advances like atomic power, radar, jet engines, mass production of penicillin, and blood plasma transfusions transformed the world. Oil emerged as the critical strategic material, and control of oil supplies would dominate much of post-war international affairs. The ending of European economic dominance in favor of American economic power helped drive Europe to make steps toward unification, at least economically: the European Economic Community or Common Market was made possible in the wrecked state of the economy. Finally, the war disrupted the hold of European countries on their overseas colonies, and in the years after the war most colonies in Africa and the Pacific became independent.

World War II shook Western Civilization to its foundations, destroying a great deal of the inherited legacy of the past in the death of millions of people and in the destruction of cities and buildings that had stood for centuries. The barbarism of Nazi tyranny and the cruelty of war threatened basic Western values and called into question even more emphatically than had the First World War the Western notion of progress. The emergence of another tyrannical and brutal dictatorship, the Soviet Union, as one of two world superpowers after the war seemed to beg the question as well. The nuclear age initiated by the use of atomic weapons, coupled with the origination of the Cold War, meant that the war helped create the possibility that humankind might utterly destroy civilization itself.

Suggestions for Further Reading

Rita S. Botwinick, *A History of the Holocaust: From Ideology to Annihilation*, 2nd ed.(2001).

Alan Bullock, *Hitler: A Study in Tyranny* (1964).

Winston S. Churchill, *The Second World War,* 6 vols. (1948-1953).

Winston S. Churchill, *Memoirs of the Second World War* (1959).

Conrad Crane, *Bombs, Cities, and Civilians: American Airpower Strategy in World War II* (1993).

A. Dallin, *German Rule in Russia, 1941-1945* (1981).

Robert Doughty, et al, *World War II: Total Warfare Around the Globe* (1996)

H. Feis, *Churchill, Roosevelt, Stalin: The War They Waged and the Peace They Sought* (1967).

Daniel Goldhagen, *Hitler's Willing Executioners: Ordinary Germans and the Holocaust* (1996).

B. Liddell Hart, *History of the Second World War* (1980).

Raul Hilberg, *The Destruction of the European Jews*, 3 vols. (1985).

R. Hough, *The Longest Battle: The War at Sea, 1939-1945* (1986).

John Keegan, *The Second World War* (1989).

G. Martel, ed., *The Origins of the Second World War Reconsidered* (1986).

H. Michel, *The Shadow War: The European Resistance, 1939-1945* (1972).

William Shirer, *The Rise and Fall of the Third Reich* (1960).

Albert Speer, *Inside the Third Reich* (1970).

John Toland, *The Rising Sun: The Decline and Fall of the Japanese Empire* (1970).

G. Wright, *The Ordeal of Total War, 1939-1945* (1968).

THE POSTWAR ERA
1945-1968

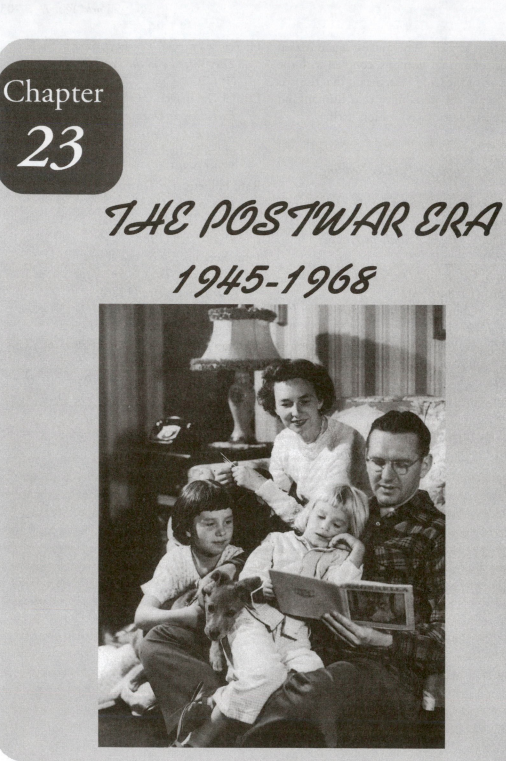

In the summer of 2000 Hans and Helga Schmidt (not their real names) flew to Granada, Spain to spend their fiftieth wedding anniversary. Sitting on a shady bench to rest on a hot summer day, they struck up a conversation with an American tourist, sharing life stories. Hans and his wife met and married after the war. Hans had served in the German army. Never very interested in politics, he had still volunteered to fight because he thought it was his duty to his country. He had been captured by the Americans during the war and spent a year in an American prisoner of war camp before being returned to Germany in 1946. Before the war he had worked in coal mines until they closed during the depression. After the war he and Helga became teachers, trained at government expense as part of the postwar rebuilding effort. Now, retired, he and his wife enjoyed a level of prosperity they never had dreamed of before the war. The economic and political issues that had led to devastating war a half century before were now to him another life in another world.

The reasons for the war—German nationalism, fascist ideology, European hegemony—no longer mattered to him or his family. He and his wife were in Spain, visiting one of their sons, who had married a Spanish woman and now lived in Granada, working for a company that had dealings across the whole of the European Union. The old battle cries of "Victory to the Fatherland" and "Deutschland Uber Alles" (Germany over all) no longer meant much to a man with family scattered across the European Union. Germany was no longer in conflict with the other European states. Since the creation of the European Common Market in the 1950s, cooperation between the states of Western Europe had replaced competition, and economic development had replaced military conquest. Three thousand years of war to determine the fate of Europe had been replaced by a half century of peace and stability.

"German, Spanish, French, Italian—it no longer matters to us," the old man smiled to the American. "We have had our wars. We are done with them. We are all Europeans, now."

Chronology

1945 (May 7)	Unconditional Surrender of Germany
1945 (Sept 14)	Unconditional Surrender of Japan
1946-49	Greek Civil War
1946 (Mar 6)	Churchill gives "Iron Curtain" speech
1946 (Oct 13)	Creation of French Fourth Republic
1947 (Mar 12)	Truman Doctrine proclaimed
1947 (June 5)	Marshall Plan announced
1947 (Fall)	Independence of India. First Indo-Pakistani war
1947 (Nov 1)	BENELUX created
1947 (Nov 29)	Partition of Palestine
1948 (June)	Yugoslavia breaks with Soviet Union
1948 (July 24)	Berlin Blockade; Airlift begins.
1948 (Nov)	Harry Truman reelected president
1949 (April 4)	NATO treaty signed
1949 (May 8)	Federal Republic of Germany (West Germany) laws enacted
1949 (May 12)	Berlin blockade ends
1949 (May 14)	State of Israel declared
1949 (May 15 -July)	First Arab-Israeli war.
1949 (Sept 12)	Konrad Adenauer elected Chancellor of West Germany
1949 (Oct 1)	People's Republic of China created
1949 (Oct 7)	German Democratic Republic (East Germany) created by U.S.S.R.
1949 (Dec 27)	Indonesia becomes independent from the Netherlands.
1950 (June 25)	Korean War begins.
1951 (Mar 19)	European Coal and Steel Community (ECSC) created
1952 (Nov 1)	U.S. tests first successful hydrogen bomb
1952 (Nov 4)	Dwight Eisenhower elected president
1953 (March 5)	Death of Stalin
1953 (June)	Protests in East Berlin repressed by pro-Soviet regime
1953 (July 27)	Armistice signed in Korea
1954 (Feb 25)	General Nasser becomes premier of Egypt.
1954 (May 7)	French fortress of Dien Bien Phu falls in Vietnam. French withdrawal
1954 (Dec 30)	West Germany enters NATO.
1955 (Feb)	Nikita Khrushchev consolidates power in the Soviet Union
1955 (April 6)	Anthony Eden becomes British Prime Minister.
1955 (Summer)	Algerian rebellion begins
1956 (Feb 16)	Khrushchev repudiates Stalin at Twentieth Party Congress
1956 (July 26)	Egypt nationalizes Suez Canal
1956 (Fall)	Suez Crisis
1956 (Oct 21)	Gomulka becomes leader of Poland
1956 (Oct)	Hungarian rebellion begins. Soviet Union invades
1956 (Nov)	Hungarian rebellion crushed
1957 (Feb 20)	Treaty of Rome signed
1957 (Oct 4)	Sputnik launched by Soviet Union
1958 (Jan 16)	European Common Market begins
1958 (May-June)	French Algerian Crisis; DeGaulle recalled to power

1958 (Sept)	French Fifth Republic created
1958 (Nov)	Beginning of Berlin crisis
1958 (Dec)	DeGaulle elected president of Fifth Republic
1959 (Jan 1)	Fidel Castro captures Havana, Cuba
1960 (May 5)	U.S. U-2 spy plane shot down by Soviet Union
1960 (Summer)	Congo Crisis
1960 (Nov 8)	John F. Kennedy elected president
1961 (Jan 3)	U.S. cuts ties with Castro regime in Cuba
1961 (April 17-19)	Bay of Pigs
1961 (Aug)	Berlin wall built
1962 (July 13)	Algerian independence
1962 (Oct. 22-27)	Cuban Missile Crisis
1963 (Jan 14)	British entry into Common Market blocked by France
1963 (Oct 15)	Leonid Brezhnev replaces Khrushchev
1963 (Nov 2)	Military coup in South Vietnam
1963 (Nov 22)	John Kennedy assassinated. Lyndon Johnson becomes president
1965 (Feb 7)	U.S. begins air strikes on North Vietnam
1966 (Feb 2)	France withdraws from NATO military command
1967 (June)	Second Arab-Israeli war
1968 (Aug)	Warsaw Pact troops invade and subdue Czechoslovakia
1969 (July 20)	Apollo XI makes first manned landing on the moon.

Such an outcome to the twentieth century, in which Europeans could increasingly set aside cultural and national differences and work together to create unprecedented peace, stability, and prosperity, seemed almost an impossibility in the ruined shadows of W.W.II. Yet, visionaries such as Konrad Adenauer in Germany looked at the ruin as a chance to wipe the slate clean and start anew, to build a new Europe out of the rubble. In the years immediately following the war, however, it looked as if Europe might revert quickly to business as usual, as renewed conflict on a continent divided between a communist East and a democratic West by two hostile atomic powers seemed imminent.

The seeds of unity and prosperity sown by European leaders tired of war, however, took root. The 1950s and 1960s saw the rise of an economically integrated Europe. By the end of the century Hans and Helga would be able to spend part of their time in Germany, part in Spain, and travel freely around the rest of Europe, visiting friends and family irrespective of national boundaries. Europe, always a historically vague concept, had become, for this and countless other European families, a simple matter of fact.

THE FALL AND RISE OF EUROPE

The outcome of the Second World War had a greater impact upon the global balance of power than the "Great War." After W.W.I the United States had firmly established itself as a great power while Japan positioned itself to be the first great modern Asian power, a rival to European influence in the region. After W.W.II the United States was not just *a* great power but *the* power, the single greatest economic and military force on the planet. Japan was a ruined imperialist state, but a phoenix-like So-

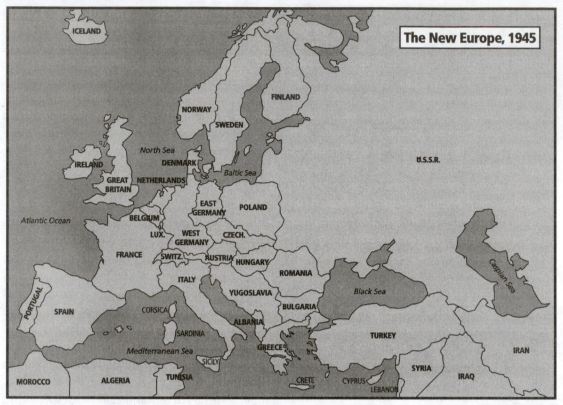

The New Europe, 1945

viet Union was rising to challenge American hegemony. Three great processes dominated European history for the next half century: the dissolution of Europe's colonial empires, the titanic cold war struggle, and the economic, social, and political recovery of a continent wrecked by war.

For European powers, the war's end meant the passing of not just conflict but of a half millennium of the continent's dominant position in global affairs. For the remainder of the twentieth century the most significant decisions affecting humankind would now be made in Washington and Moscow, instead of London, Paris, Berlin, or Vienna. The cost of two world wars proved utterly ruinous to the great European imperial powers. Within two decades of the end of the war Britain, France, and the other

European colonists were forced to grant independence to the bulk of their empires in the developing world. As Europe withdrew from the colonial periphery, new nations and new leaders, from Cairo to Delhi to Beijing, began to exert unprecedented influence on world affairs. Meanwhile, the stage had been set for confrontation between Soviet communism and American liberal capitalism with a hapless Europe caught between two nuclear global superpowers. The division of Europe agreed to at the Yalta and Potsdam Big Three summits created the front line for a new and potentially more devastating conflict than even the Second World War. During this new "Cold War" the former great European powers would be reduced to junior partners, proxies, and even pawns for the U.S. and U.S.S.R. Yet, at the same time, fear of direct war between the two major powers allowed Europeans to enjoy an unprecedented period of peace until the new Balkan wars of the late 1980s grew out of the chaos of the collapse of Yugoslavia.

Against this background of peace, Western European states would be able to achieve equally unprecedented levels of economic prosperity and political and social stability. With peace and prosperity also came the opportunity for continental cooperation and integration at levels unimaginable by Europeans during decades of war and conflict. With the collapse of the Soviet Empire and the end of the cold war, Eastern Europe for the first time stood on the brink of unity with its Western sibling. What Caesar, Napoleon, and Hitler could not accomplish through force of arms was now obtainable through fifty years of peace and cooperation: the real possibility of creating a unified, integrated community stretching from the Atlantic to the Asian steppes. Thus, out of the ashes of three great conflicts, Europe at the turn of a new century, shorn of its empires, stood stronger than ever before in Western history. Given the challenges and crises of the last half of the twentieth century, such an outcome was by no means certain, or even very conceivable, at the dawn of the cold war.

The Big Chill

"From Stetin in the Baltic to Trieste in the Adriatic, an iron curtain has descended across the continent. . . . From what I have seen of our Russian friends and allies during the war, I am convinced that there is nothing they admire so much as strength, and there is nothing for which they have less respect for than weakness, especially military weakness."

Winston Churchill, March 6, 1946

"Given the current situation, I am ceasing my activities as president of the U.S.S.R."

Mikhail Gorbachev, December 21, 1991

When Winston Churchill, himself recently rejected by the peacetime voters of England, stood before a crowd of students and academics at Westminster College in Fulton, Missouri and threw down his oratorical gauntlet, he understood that the world had entered a profound and dangerous period of struggle. The guns of World War II had scarcely fallen silent, and now a new conflict, made infinitely more dangerous by the advent of the atomic age, confronted humankind. Churchill's speech was meant as a warning to the Western powers, preoccupied by the challenges of peace and demobilization, that the goals they had fought the previous two global wars for had not fully been accomplished. War by other means would now continue. Thus, Churchill envisioned a titanic struggle between the liberal democracies of the West and the communist empire of the East, which could well define the future of humankind.

What Churchill could not envision was that forty-five years later Mikhail Gorbachev would resign his position thereby signaling the collapse of the Soviet Union and the end of a half-century ideological struggle. This, then, was the cold war (1946-1991). It is, of course, only with the utmost hubris that Americans, Europeans, and Russians can talk of a war as "cold" when, in reality, it would directly or indirectly cause a greater loss of life than World War One. The war did remain cold in the sense that, for almost half a century, its principle belligerents did not directly come to blows. The great danger of the cold war was precisely that with the advent of the atomic age, such a direct conflict could become very hot—nuclear hot—for all of humankind. The great success of the cold war, if it can be thought as such, was that this horrific outcome was avoided. For the over ten million people who perished in cold war related battlefields, from Guatemala to Vietnam to Afghanistan, however, this war was hot enough. Indeed, for them, the struggle amounted to World War III. How then, barely a year after the ending of World War II, did this World War III begin?

Causes of the Cold War

As with the Second World War, the seeds of the cold war can be found in the ending of the previous conflict. The principle roots of the conflict began with the division of Europe. The division of the Nazi empire into two zones, the western zone controlled by the armies of the U.S., Britain, and France and the eastern zone by the Soviet Red Army, was ostensibly driven by administrative necessity. The anticipated collapse of Hitler's government meant the defacto collapse of government of the occupied lands from the Pyrennes to the Ukraine. Of prime concern to the Allied powers were the simple matters of keeping the lights on, the water running, and the food delivered for the millions of soon to be liberated European peoples. On that point the big three powers agreed. The fundamental division in view between the U.S. and the U.S.S.R. was over what was to happen next.

For the U.S. and Britain, the division of the continent was a short-term expediency towards the longer term goal of creating a stable postwar Europe based on principles of national self-determination. Who should govern the Poles? The Czechs? The Germans? That answer was "self evident": they should govern themselves. Thus, the Anglo-American view of postwar Europe was one premised on liberal democratic values being triumphant from the channel to the Russian bor-

der: a free market of ideas and goods. For this end the war had been fought.

The postwar view of the Soviet Union, however, was markedly different. Marxist doctrine held that communism was not just a desirable system of government, it was an inevitable outcome of the very processes of dialectical materialism, dictated by the very laws of history itself. The peoples of Eastern Europe now under communist control must remain under that control, enforced, as necessary, by socialist military force; one did not need elections to validate the inevitable. Moreover, from a Russian strategic perspective (as opposed to a communist ideological one) there were tremendous advantages to keeping the Red Army in the middle of Europe in perpetuity. Three times in one hundred fifty years armies of western militarist powers—Napoleon's, the Kaiser's and Hitler's—had rolled across the plains of eastern Europe and slashed into mother Russia, the last time killing over twenty-five million people. The simple resolve of Soviet Russia was "never again." The next time armies of the west rolled east, they would exhaust themselves killing East Germans, Poles and Ukrainians before Russian civilians would die.

Thus, both sides, having fundamentally and, perhaps, irreconcilably different views of the future of Europe, were on a collision course. A series of crises between 1946 and 1948 would convince both sides that the other held not only different views but hostile intentions, making Churchill's warning of a perpetually divided Europe a reality for the balance of most of the twentieth century.

Postwar Crises

The first flashpoint was Austria. Occupied at the end of the war by both American and Soviet forces, Stalin had agreed to allow democratic elections to be held in late 1945 to determine the fate of the country. Soviet discontent over the victory of pro-democratic parties and the poor showing of the Austrian communists led to an increasingly intransigent position on further Austrian autonomy by Stalin. The result was a chill in diplomatic relations between the Soviets and its former allies and a growing feeling in Western capitals that cooperation with Stalin would be increasingly difficult.

The following year the Truman administration (1945-1952) grew to believe that Stalin had serious designs on Iran when it was discovered that the Soviets were meddling in the northern Iranian region of Azerbaijan. The southern most part of the Soviet-controlled Caucus was also called Azerbaijan; the czar's armies had been able to conquer half the Azer people in the nineteenth century. Now Stalin was offering the Azers in Iran a deal: declare independence from the pro-Western Shah in Tehran, and the Soviets would recognize their new nation, supporting it, as necessary, with military aid. (As a side note, this was the same ploy Teddy Roosevelt had used five decades earlier in triggering a rebellion in the Colombian province of Panama to create a new state more amenable to American canal-building interests.)

President Harry S Truman (1884-1972) directly warned Stalin off of this venture, even using America's atomic monopoly as a not-so veiled threat. Stalin backed down, but the U.S.-Soviet partnership of the war was now moribund. Resolving never to be caught at such a strategic disadvantage again, the Soviets committed to a crash program of atomic research and development that included, amongst other things, the use of spies such as Ethel and Julius Rosenberg (tried for espionage in 1951; both executed in 1953) in the United States to steal Western weapons' secrets.

The Greek Civil War finalized the rift. A Communist movement had been waging a guerilla war against the pro-British Greek government before the Second World War. During the war they had fought as partisans against the German invaders, broadening their popular legitimacy. In 1946, with support from the Soviet Union and the communist government of Yugoslavia, the guerillas resumed the civil war. The British, unable to bear the cost of supporting the Greek government, turned to the United States. The Truman administration's verification that the Soviets were directly supporting these rebels with arms and other materials proved to be the last nail in the coffin of American-Soviet cooperation.

Western Response

Possibly the single greatest lesson the United States took from World War Two, the one that most profoundly influenced its subsequent foreign policy, was the "Lesson of Munich." It was a centrally held principle of the postwar U.S. leadership that British and French appeasement of Hitler, culminating in the 1938 Munich conference where Czechoslovakian sovereignty was sacrificed for the illusionary promise of peace, was the single biggest cause of the war. Thus, if Hitler had been met with force early in his territorial ambitions, such as the occupation of the Rhineland in 1936, he would have been effectively contained, thus avoiding the greatest tragedy in human history. (Indeed, Nazi archives clearly show that reoccupation of the Rhineland had been a tremendous gamble; Hitler had expected the Allies to call his bluff by threatening force that would have forced his withdrawal. The subsequent political humiliation might well have led to the fall of his government.) The lesson of Munich was clear: only a credible threat of force

The Truman administration proposed a "European Recovery Program," more popularly known as the Marshall Plan, named for Truman's Secretary of State George C. Marshall.

would serve to contain the ambitions of a territorially aggressive bully. Hence, by 1947 the Truman administration felt compelled to draw a line in the sand.

Truman's response to the perception of Soviet aggression in Austria, Iran, and Greece was two-pronged. The first prong was to stop pro-Communist guerilla movements, such as in Greece, from taking power. In 1947 the United States pledged to intervene, militarily if necessary, to prevent pro-Soviet regimes from coming to power anywhere around the world. This policy became known as the Truman Doctrine, and Greece became its first successful application. By 1950, thanks to substantial American aid, the Greek government defeated the guerillas. The Truman Doctrine became the justification of American military and political interventions from Latin America to Vietnam.

The second prong was to directly "contain" the Soviet Union as an alternative to actual war. In 1947 an article entitled "The Sources of Soviet Conduct" appeared in the influential journal, *Foreign Affairs*, written by a noted diplomat, George Kennan, under the pseudonym "X." Kennan advocated a policy of containing the Soviet Union's apparent territorial ambitions by applying the "adroit and vigilant application of counterforce" around the Soviet frontier. Any direct Soviet military expansion would, therefore, run the risk of running into U.S. and British forces and potentially triggering a major war. Thus, the policy of "Containment" was born. Over the next decade a series of American- or British-led military alliances were created on the borders of the Soviet Union. The first of these would be the North Atlantic Treaty Organization (NATO), consisting initially of the U.S., Canada, Great Britain, France, Italy, Norway, Portugal, Greece, Turkey, the Low Countries, Denmark, and West Germany, created in 1949.

In 1947, to help speed up the recovery of Europe as both a humanitarian good and political necessity to undercut support of communist parties in Western Europe, the Truman administration also proposed a "European Recovery

Program," more popularly known as the Marshall Plan, so named for Truman's Secretary of State George C. Marshall (1880-1959). Originally envisioned as a program to provide economic development aid from the Atlantic to the Urals, Stalin quickly vetoed the distribution of aid in Eastern Europe. From the Soviet viewpoint this was simply an American strategy to subvert socialist Eastern Europe by promoting capitalist market systems. The Soviet rejection of aid further underscored the West's belief that the Russians had permanently grabbed half of Europe. The thirteen billion dollars in American aid that was given to seventeen Western European states (the equivalence of almost one hundred billion dollars today) made a tremendous contribution to the postwar European economic miracle.

The Soviet response to the increasing militant policies of the West was to harden its own positions. In addition to directly challenging the West in Berlin, Stalin saw the American move to rearm West Germany (part of the U.S. and NATO containment strategy) as incredibly provocative; less than four years after fighting the Russians, the German Werhmacht (army) was being resurrected, with many of its new officers culled from the ranks of the old Nazi officer corp. To directly counter NATO, Stalin created the Warsaw Pact (East Germany, Poland, Hungary, Czechoslovakia, Romania, and Bulgaria). Within five years of the end of W.W.II the European continent was, once again, divided into two heavily armed and hostile camps.

(As a side note, some historians have argued that the cold war was, perhaps, a wholly avoidable conflict brought on by the ignorance each major power had of the true desires and goals of the other side. Thus, these "Nations in Darkness" drifted into war almost by accident, much as historians in the 1950s and 1960s tended to see the outbreak of World War One as a result of the diplomatic confusion of August 1914. W.W.I, thanks to more detailed archival research, is now seen as a more deliberate conflict triggered by the direct actions and ambitions of the German high command. So, too, does the cold war now appear, under more systematic study of the archival sources, to be not a deliberate conflict but an inevitable one. Neither the U.S., preoccupied by the desire to return to a peacetime economy, or the U.S.S.R., with its twenty-five million, desired a direct conflict in 1946. Both sides, however, perceived conflict with the other as increasingly unavoidable in the years to come. Both sides had world views that were fundamentally contradictory: a world dominated by liberal capitalism versus a world dominated by Marxist communism. That two continental powers so diametrically opposed would not come into conflict, especially military conflict, was without historical precedent. That they did not destroy themselves and the world, in the process, was historically remarkable.)

A World Gone MAD

Unlike W.W.I and W.W.II, however, this time the two armed camps could not afford to fight each other directly. Humankind had entered the era of Mutual Assured Destruction (MAD), a doctrine wherein war between two parties would be so horrific in its cost as to make any measure of victory meaningless. By 1954 the United States moved from the atomic to the nuclear age with the detonation of its first hydrogen bomb. The atomic bomb that destroyed Hiroshima in Japan had the power of about ten thousand tons (or ten kilotons) of conventional explosives. To put that in perspective, it would have taken one thousand American B-29 Superfortress bombers to deliver the same explosive force as a single plane carrying one atomic bomb. The hydrogen bomb had the power of over a megaton (million tons) of explosives, or one hundred Hiroshimas. The Soviet Union detonated its first atomic bomb in 1949 and its own hydrogen bomb in 1953. Armed with weapons of unprecedented mass destruction, the U.S. and the U.S.S.R. moved beyond the realm of great powers to become the history's first true superpowers, nations that could dominate all other nations in international competition.

Coupled with advanced rocket technologies developed by the Nazis and perfected by the Americans and Russians, by the end of the 1950s both sides had the ability to hurl these weapons across continents. By the end of the 1960s each side had over ten thousand nuclear warheads distributed on bombers and intercontinental ballistic missiles (ICBMs). One submarine or one missile equipped with numerous warheads capable of hitting separate targets could each destroy a dozen or more cities. Thus, the rationale of MAD: if either side attacked the other, even if it succeeded in a surprise attack in destroying all of the other side's nuclear weapons before they could be used *except* for only one submarine or missile, the counter attack would kill tens of millions of the so-called victor's population. As a deranged computer would later say in the 1980s anti-nuclear war movie, *Wargames*, "The only way to win is not to play."

Even without nuclear weapons, conventional warfare had become devastatingly lethal. World War One killed some thirteen to fourteen million people with conventional weapons, World War Two over fifty million. A directly fought Third World War would kill easily over one hundred million even without the detonation of a single nuclear weapon. For the first time in history the game of war had become too dangerous to play. In the absence of a direct solution to the cold war confrontation, the two sides were reduced to an indirect struggle, one fought largely in the former colonial periphery—the developing world.

Some Like It Hot

During the Berlin Crisis (1948-1949) and the Cuban Missile Crisis (1962) the world came perilously close to testing MAD. Control of Berlin had been divided after the war between the U.S., British, and French (West) and the Soviets (East), mirroring the division of Germany proper. In June 1948 the Soviets responded to American plans to militarize West Germany by blockading West Berlin, severing all rail, river, and road links to the Allied occupied part of the city. Having essentially turned off the power and water to the city, the Russians now waited for starvation to force Western capitulation, thereby demonstrating Soviet capability and handing Stalin a major propaganda victory. Stalin gambled correctly in ordering the blockade that the U.S. would not risk direct war to liberate the city. Instead of attacking, however, Truman responded with an unprecedented military airlift, flying in all the supplies necessary to keep a city of several million people functioning. Truman gambled that Stalin would not order the planes shot down, thereby precipitating war. Stalin, not believing that the airlift could work, sat back and waited. When almost a year later West Berliners still stood defiant, the Soviets decided to end the blockade.

Many historians point to this as a Soviet capitulation and an American victory. This view is mistaken. For the Soviets, the blockade was a success for it demonstrated their ability to inflict serious cost to the Americans (to the tune of almost a quarter billion dollars) to maintain a presence in Berlin. The Americans were able to

President Kennedy and his brother, Attorney General Robert F. Kennedy, confer during the Cuban missile crisis. The entire world was frightened over the possibility of a nuclear conflagration that could be so devastating.

demonstrate their resolve to "pay any price" to protect their interests. Both sides, therefore, could claim victory and, ultimately, when the dust settled, things returned to the status quo. This became a necessary conclusion to all direct conflict during the cold war. Were either side to see itself as potentially "losing" a confrontation with its resulting loss of strategic position and "face," it would be tempted to escalate the conflict, hoping to make the other side "back down." Such games of geopolitical "chicken" were inherently unstable unless a formula could be found to provide each side with grounds to claim a victory.

Such was also the case with the Cuban missile crisis. Nikita Khrushchev (1894-1971), Stalin's successor, ordered intermediate range ballistic missiles placed in Cuba in 1962. He did this for four reasons. First, John Kennedy (1917-1963) had run for office in 1960 in part on a platform that the administration of Dwight D. Eisenhower (1953-1960) had allowed a missile gap to develop with the Soviet Union. To close this gap, Kennedy had ordered the construction of more American ICBMs. Khrushchev knew that it was actually the U.S. that possessed superior numbers of missiles in 1960, and Kennedy was only expanding this lead. Placing short-range missiles in Cuba provided the Russians with a temporary means of offsetting this deficit. Second, the U.S. had placed nuclear missiles in Turkey on the Soviet border. Soviet missiles in Cuba would offset this threat, as well. Third, Khrushchev had met Kennedy at a summit in 1961 and had concluded that the young, rich American could be pushed around.

The final reason concerned Cuba itself. Since its liberation from Spanish rule, Cuba had been largely a de facto political and economic colony of the United States. While Cuba had become one of the wealthiest countries in the region under American patronage, it also had some of the greatest division between rich and poor in the hemisphere. This social cleavage provided a foundation for the rise of Fidel Castro (1926-), a charismatic young socialist, who waged a successful guerilla insurgency against Fulgencio Batista (1901-1973) in the 1950s. In 1958, facing a spreading mass uprising, Batista and many of his supporters fled Cuba, ushering in the Castro regime.

Fidel Castro, the communist dictator that came to power in 1959, dealt President Kennedy a major foreign affairs defeat in 1961 with the Bay of Pigs.

The United States, uncertain as to the direction Castro would take the island, was at first neutral towards Cuba's new regime. When it became clear the pro-Soviet communist elements were gaining the upper hand in the new regime, American policy hardened against Castro, and the perception grew in the Eisenhower administration that the bearded revolutionary must go. A plan was developed and implemented by the American Central Intelligence Agency (CIA) to train an army of these Cuban exiles and assist them in invading Cuba, which, it was believed, would trigger a massive anti-Castro uprising across the island. In 1961 the newly elected administration of John F. Kennedy (1961-1963) authorized the CIA to carry out the invasion; thirteen hundred exiles subsequently landed in

Cuba at the Bay of Pigs. When no sign of a broader social uprising followed the landing, the Kennedy administration decided against providing previously promised American military support for the invaders, who were subsequently crushed by the Cuban Army.

Though the Bay of Pigs proved a fiasco for the Americans, the Soviets were concerned that further invasions might be attempted. The presence of nuclear weapons in Cuba could deter such an attack, thereby protecting the Soviet's *only* ally in the Western Hemisphere.

Learning of the missiles in October 1962, Kennedy could neither allow them to remain nor use direct military force to remove them, lest he trigger a general war. Instead, the U.S. erected a naval "quarantine" (blockade) of the island designed to keep the final shipment of parts necessary to make the missiles operational from reaching Cuba. If Soviet ships ran the blockade, they now risked war. When the Soviet vessels approached the quarantine, they did, indeed, stop rather than challenge the American line, which caused an advisor to President Kennedy to remark, "We were eyeball to eye ball and the other fellow blinked." Far from blinking, it turned out the Soviet freighters had turned to rendezvous with attack submarines and were then going to challenge the blockade, forcing the Americans to either back down or shoot. As the world slipped to the brink of war, a last minute, diplomatic deal was struck between Kennedy and Khrushchev. The Russians agreed to withdraw the missiles and pledged never to reintroduce them. In exchange the U.S. pledged to never again try to overthrow Castro and quietly withdrew its missiles from Turkey. Once again, the status quo was restored.

Such crises occasionally scared the two sides into taking steps to defuse the level of conflict. For example, following the Cuban missile crisis, the U.S. and U.S.S.R. negotiated and signed a treaty limiting nuclear weapons testing in 1963. Yet the shear number of weapons in each country's arsenal, expanding yearly through the arms race, worked to make the cold war world increasingly dangerous.

The Great Game Revisited

Without direct conflict as a means to resolve the balance of power between East and West during the cold war, indirect conflict became the principle vehicle of the struggle. The goal of this game was simple: between the 1940s and the 1980s the U.S. and the U.S.S.R. engaged in a great game of trying to put flags on the global map, that is to say, trying to create and support regimes friendly to themselves while trying to subvert regimes allied to the other side.

In this way the cold war resembled the "Great Game" of the nineteenth century where the major powers of Europe sought to demonstrate their power relative to each other by grabbing flags on the map (the partition of Africa, for example); the country with the most flags at the end of the game wins. Thus, the cold war became a sort of global game of RISK, with both sides trying to gain strategic advantage over the other. The American intervention in Greece in 1947 set the prototype for this sort of struggle. The Soviets supplied aid to the rebels; the United States aided the regime. The Korean War (1950-1953), the crisis in the Congo (1961), the Vietnam War (1957-1975), and the Afghani War (1979-1989) represented similar such conflicts.

The results of projecting the cold war into developing nations were to extend the division of Europe to a global level. The cold war divided the world into three parts: the United States, Western Europe and their allies; the Soviet Union and its allies in Eastern Europe, Asia (China, North Vietnam, North Korea) and Latin America (Cuba and, later, Nicaragua); and everyone else. The U.S. and its allies and the Soviet bloc sought to support their respective allies in the developing world by shipping them massive quantities of weapons. This arming of the emerging nations dramatically increased the destructive power of indigenous national conflicts and shifted precious resources in these countries away from economic development and into military spending. The long-term result of the conflict was the death of millions of people and billions of dollars in economic damage in developing nations, which directly further impoverished the poorest economies on the planet. At the same time that the ideological war of the industrial world was being transferred to the developing world, the former European colonial masters were being forced to divest themselves of their empires.

THE SUN SETS ON THE EUROPEAN EMPIRES

Just as the Second World War resulted in the U.S. and U.S.S.R. achieving positions of global dominance, the war also resulted in a decline in the global power and importance of Europe, proper. The phenomenal costs of recovering from the war and increasing pressures for independence in the developing world made continued possession of colonial empires by the major European states increasingly untenable. Within twenty years of the end of the war the global colonial empires European states had spent almost five hundred years conquering would be liquidated in the political equivalence of a going out of business sale. The great age of European hegemony had come to an end.

The unraveling of empires is never a well-planned or orderly event. In 1945 only five European states—Britain, France, Belgium, the Netherlands, and Portugal— remained as colonial powers. Both within the countries and within the colonies themselves, opposition to continued policies of colonial imperialism were developing or escalating. The political leadership of these nations, however, did not, at least in the immediate aftermath of the war, embrace the notion that the possessions they had fought to defend during the war should now be surrendered during the peace. The French and Dutch governments had made return of their Asian colonies, overrun by the Japanese, a major war aim. With the war concluded, the newly restored governments of both nations quickly moved to reoccupy and control their old colonies. As for those colonies in Asia and Africa that had not changed hands during the war, the European powers acted on the assumption that the colonial status quo would continue. Many within these colonial states had other ideas.

Independence Days

Four forces drove the dissolution of the European empires. The first was the simple weakness of these states, militarily and economically, to maintain the cost of empire. Two great continental wars within a generation of each other had effectively bankrupted the national treasuries, especially of Britain and France. Both entered the postwar period deeply in debt to domestic lenders and to the United States, in particular. The need to balance national accounts, meet debt obligations, and fund reconstruction efforts squeezed national treasuries, making the "luxury" of colonial ownership that yielded limited economic gain increasingly unaffordable.

The second force was the United States itself. Franklin Roosevelt reluctantly supported his European allies' goals of reestablishing their colonial presence, privately expressing his view that allowing the Europeans back into Asia would be a major mistake. U.S. resistance to European colonialism was, at least in part, based on idealistic opposition to the denial of self-determination to any peoples anywhere. It was also opportunistic. Liquidation of empires would break open traditional trade monopolies enjoyed by the European states, allowing the U.S. access to new markets. The U.S. had publicly chafed since the First World War at the preferential system of trade British colonial possessions provided Great Britain. Thus, while tacitly allowing the continuation of empire, American postwar attitudes and policies were increasingly inimical to colonialism.

The third and most significant force developed indigenously in colonial possessions around the world: anti-colonial nationalism. The nineteenth century had witnessed the rise of European nationalism and the fight for self-determination by ethnic and cultural groups across the continent. One of the by-products of nineteenth- and twentieth-century European colonialism was to help export such ideals to the very people over whom dominion was sought. Nationalist movements, which had been percolating since the First World War, grew dramatically in the years after the Second.

The final force was growing domestic opposition within the European democracies to the concept of imperial occupation of other people's lands. If World War Two had been a just war to end the threat of tyranny and advance the rights of self determination for the peoples of France, Belgium, the Netherlands, and Britain, how could the governments of these same countries deny these same rights to the peoples of Vietnam, the Congo, Indonesia, and Nigeria? The old colonial justifications of the racial and moral

Ho Chi Minh (left) meets China's Chairman Mao during his travels in Asia.

superiority of Europe over the world rang increasingly in European ears.

There were two general pathways to colonial independence—political negotiation or violent confrontation—with the latter, initially, being more common. Faced with increasing agitation for independence by its principle colony of the Dutch East Indies, the Dutch government responded with military repression. A four-year war (1945-1949) followed, which resulted in the Dutch withdrawal and the creation of the new nation of Indonesia.

Vietnam and the Algerian Crisis

The French encountered similar, bloody, opposition in its colonies in Indochina and North Africa. Even before W.W. II the French had been dealing with rising, armed resistance to the occupation of Vietnam. The leader of this movement, Ho Chi Minh (1890-1969), was an ardent north Vietnamese nationalist and socialist who sought the expulsion of the French and the unification of Vietnam under his northern rule. Ho's forces fought the Japanese occupation during the war. Indeed, at one point Ho tried to solicit American support in his efforts, but virulent French opposition prevented such a step. After the war, efforts to negotiate a political settlement towards independence, at least for northern Vietnam, collapsed in the face of French intransigence; the guerilla war resumed.

The struggle, however, proved increasingly untenable for the French government, which was forced to appeal to the United States for support. At first rebuffed by the Americans who

An American soldier on patrol along the Mekong Delta

held little sympathy for colonialism, the French government was able to swing the U.S. to their side by increasingly portraying the struggle in Indochina as not a colonial war but as an anti-Communist campaign. Ho Chi Minh's socialism and limited material support from Communist China and the Soviet Union were used to portray the struggle as part of the broader cold war in which Vietnam was now a domino in the struggle for communist domination of Asia. Even increasing American aid, however, proved futile. In 1954, the French suffered a catastrophic defeat when the guerillas laid siege to and captured the major French fortress of Dien Bien Phu.

Faced with military disaster, the French were now forced to find a negotiated settlement with Ho Chi Minh. The resulting 1955 accord led to a French military and political withdrawal, a temporary partitioning of the country between the communist-dominated north and the non-communist south, and the scheduling of internationally supervised elections to establish a single national government. When the southern candidate lost to Ho Chi Minh in the elections of 1957, the South Vietnamese, with American support, refused to certify the outcome. Vietnam would remain divided for the next eighteen years as the guerilla war for control of the country resumed, this time with the

United States replacing the French as the major foreign power fighting on the ground. The American expulsion from Vietnam in 1975 would result in the communist North finally becoming triumphant over the entire country.

The ability of armed nationalists to challenge their colonial masters in Asia mirrored similar actions in Africa. In the wake of Vietnam, the French found their North African colonies agitating for independence. France negotiated terms of independence for Morocco and Tunisia in 1956, but French public and political opinion would not tolerate similar treatment of Algeria, which had been under French control for over 120 years and where over a million Frenchmen had emigrated. French obstinacy resulted in another, even bloodier, conflict that cost thousands of lives and forced the commitment of over a half million soldiers. The colonial conflict resulted in dangerous political instability in France itself. In 1958, military officers committed to holding on to Algeria came close to staging a coup d'etat when they came to believe the civilian leadership might consider a negotiated settlement. Only a return to public life by Charles DeGaulle, the Caesar figure of modern French politics, ended the crisis. DeGaulle, the French nation's greatest war hero, headed the French provisional government from 1944-1946, from which he resigned in protest over political bickering between political parties within the government. These same parties dominated the postwar Fourth Republic of France and proved unable to deal with the crisis created by Algeria. By the sheer power of personality De Gaulle was able to defuse the military crisis, engineer the constitutional reforms that produced the more stable Fifth Republic, and negotiate a political settlement that resulted in Algerian independence by 1962.

India, Africa and the Middle East

The British decolonializing experience included both violence and negotiation. Controlling an area over 125 times larger than its own homeland, Britain was the dominant European colonial power. By the postwar period, however, Britain was an empire already in transition. While Winston Churchill had been an ardent pro-colonialist, the Labor government of Clement Attlee (1883-1967), which replaced Churchill in 1945, was far more suspicious of the benefits of continued empire; thus, Attlee quickly embarked on a policy of decolonialization after the war.

The most important element of this policy was the disposition of India, the crown jewel of the British Empire. Since the end of W.W.I pro-independence sentiment had been rising on the subcontinent under the primacy of civil rights leader Mahatma Gandhi (1869-1948). Gandhi's strategy of non-violent resistance to colonial rule had led the Churchill government to reluctantly make concessions towards Indian independence. The Attlee government delivered quickly on that promise after the war; Indian independence became fact in 1947. Unfortunately, the peaceful nature of the independence movement ran afoul of severe ethnic and religious tensions between Muslim-dominated western and eastern India and the Hindu-dominated Indian peninsula. In 1947, as independence arrived, war erupted between Muslims and Hindus, resulting in a partition of India into a Muslim-dominated East and West Pakistan and Hindu-dominated India proper.

Such a peaceful model of decolonialization was replicated in most of Britain's African possessions, such as in Nigeria and Tanzania. Disposition of some of Britain's other African and Middle Eastern assets, however, proceeded with

Nairobi in the early 1900s, under the rule of the British.

more complications. In Kenya, Britons who had relocated to the colony resisted the idea of independence. The resulting militant response of several Kenyan tribal groups to continued colonization became known as the Mau-Mau Rebellion (1952-1957), a bloody uprising that complicated the eventual negotiation of independence by 1964. In Rhodesia (Zimbabwe) similar agitation by white colonists delayed independence until 1980 and then only after prolonged internal conflict.

Britain maintained its occupation of Palestine until 1948 when, under increasing pressure from all sides, including the Russians, Americans, Arabs, and Jews, it announced plans to withdraw, turning over to the United Nations the mandate Britain had received after World War One to govern the territory. Years of vio-

lence by Zionist nationalists aspiring to the creation of a Jewish state in Palestine and Arab nationalists aspiring to their own state, directed mostly at the British, had produced deep-seated animosities in the region. The United Nations attempted to appease all parties by creating two new states, one Arab, one Jewish. Neighboring Arab states, seeing the vote in the U.N. as having been manipulated by European powers and, thus, an extension of European colonialism, refused to accept the legitimacy of this act and attacked the new Jewish state, only to suffer a quick and humiliating defeat.

The consequence of what was to be the first of four such Arab-Israeli wars in the twentieth century (1948, 1956, 1967 and 1973) was to produce thousands of Arab refugees from the Jewish territory, deep-seated hostility by Arab states towards the new state of Israel, and the rise of Arab nationalism. It was control of the land and conflicting nationalism, Arab versus Jewish, rather than religious differences, that lay at the root of the Arab-Israeli conflict and dominated the Middle East into the next century. In the short run, the humiliating defeat of the Arab armies in 1948 produced a series of such nationalistic coups in Syria (1949), Egypt (1952), and Iraq (1958), bringing militant anti-Western and anti-Israeli regimes into power.

Here, then, was a fundamental hallmark of European colonial withdrawal. Independence alone did not solve all of the problems of the former colonial world. Poverty, political instability, and ethnic and religious strife, some the product of indigenous forces, some the consequence of cold war struggles, some the legacy of decades of colonialism, continued to bedevil efforts to produce stable, prosperous societies in the former colonies. Whole new conflicts arose over the borders the colonial powers had imposed upon colonial peoples, borders that seldom reflected social and economic realities of the people upon whom they were forced. New nations like Nigeria, with its distinct religious and ethnic regions that had never co-existed within one state prior to colonization, struggled to function as real nation-states. The result was social and ethnic tensions that created political and economic instability for many former colonies throughout the remainder of the century. In many cases, these problems continue to persist, making their resolution one of the major challenges for the twenty-first century.

The Suez Crisis

The decline of British and French global status, both as colonial powers and global political pow-

ers, was underscored by the 1956 Suez Crisis. While Britain had granted ostensive independence to Egypt in 1922, it had maintained control of the precious canal and, even after W.W.II, continued to cling to it as a last vestige of global power and status. When, in 1952, General Abdul Nasser (1918-1970) overthrew the Egyptian monarchy and established a new, socialist military government predicated on the principles of Arab nationalism, continued British control of the canal became problematic. In 1954, Nasser pressured the British to turn control of the canal over to Egypt. Britain agreed to give up rights to the Suez Canal by 1956 on the condition that it then come under international jurisdiction. In 1956, however, impatient with the pace of change, Nasser nationalized the canal, expelling the British.

The conservative government of Anthony Eden (1897-1977), loath to accept such a blow to Britain's international stature, enlisted the aid of France and Israel to mount a military expeditionary force to retake the canal. While a fierce Egyptian defense was able to delay the invaders, it was the combined diplomatic opposition to the invasion of the United States and the Soviet Union that brought matters to a head. Both Eisenhower and Khrushchev understood the potential for such a peripheral conflict to lead to a direct confrontation between the superpowers should either side seek to support any of the combatants. Under this intense diplomatic pressure, the British-led coalition withdrew from Egypt in new humiliation. Thus, the two superpowers effectively demonstrated their ability to leash the old European powers. For the remainder of the century, no solitary European state would be able to act decisively in international affairs without the direct support of either the U.S. or the U.S.S.R. The age of European hegemony was truly past.

BEHIND THE IRON CURTAIN

At the same time the Western European powers were dismantling their empires, a new empire was being forged in Eastern Europe. At the end of W.W.II the Soviet Red Army held sway across the whole of Europe east of the Elbe River. The former Axis and Axis-occupied countries of Hungary, Czechoslovakia, Romania, Bulgaria, and Poland were wholly under Soviet military occupation, as were the eastern third of Germany and half the city of Berlin. In Yugoslavia, which alone had liberated itself from the Nazis under the communist partisan leader, Josip Tito (1892-1980), and in the former Italian territory of Albania, pro-Soviet governments held power without the direct aid of the Red Army.

From the Soviet perspective, perpetual occupation of Eastern Europe held three strategic advantages. First, as examined above, it provided the Soviet Union with a fortified buffer zone on its western frontier. Second, it provided a potential "launch" platform into Western Europe for any future military or political operations the Soviets might deem necessary. Finally, it provided the Soviet Union with a desperately needed source of resources and materials for economic recovery and potential markets for Russian surplus production once recovery had occurred.

This, then, was the economic imperative of Eastern European occupation, the creation of a Russian-dominated form of colonial mercantilism. Just as the colonial powers of Europe had sought colonies to provide cheap, secure raw materials to their home industries and a market for surplus goods, so too did Russian postwar recovery depend on control of Eastern Europe resources, skilled labor, and consumers. Following the war, accordingly, the Soviet armies saw to the establishment of pro-Moscow socialist regimes in each occupied country. In the im-

mediate months after the war, the Red Army systematically looted industrial equipment and resources from these newly acquired "colonies," sending them back to Russia proper to be used to rebuild from the Nazi invasion. In 1947 the Soviet regime rebuffed tepid overtures by the Americans to extend the Marshall Plan, with its free-market orientation, into Eastern Europe. Instead, the Soviets created a new economic organization, COMECON, to coordinate the collectivization and economic recovery of its satellite states. Under COMECON policy, Eastern European states were forced into vastly expanding trade with the Soviet Union, to the latter's direct advantage.

Postwar Stalinization

Stalin also sought to reinforce political control over both Russia proper and the newly acquired peoples of Eastern Europe in the years following the war. Indeed, the end of the war saw a second period of purges and arrests throughout the Soviet system, especially within the army, as Stalin sought to guarantee his iron-fisted control would continue without interruption. Hundreds of thousands of "unreliable" residents of Eastern Europe—resistance fighters and others who had sought their own nations' independence and self-determination during the war—and several million Soviet citizens who had either not fought hard enough against the Nazis or had actively helped them, seeing even Hitler as a preferable alternative to Stalin, were incarcerated and, in many cases, sent eastward to the Soviet gulag system of prison camps. Hundreds of thousands of Soviet prisoners of war, newly liberated from German camps, were immediately shipped to Siberia by Stalin, their crimes two-fold: cowardice in surrendering and also having been "contaminated" by having seen a world beyond Soviet control. All told, more than two million people ended up in forced-labor camps in which as many as half perished. The war had ended one form of totalitarian repression, Fascism, but the other form, Communism, emerged in many ways stronger than before.

The extension of Soviet control to the center of Europe, however, did not occur without challenge. Observing the systematic destruction of national autonomy under Soviet occupation in the rest of Eastern Europe, the Tito regime sought to limit Soviet influence in Yugoslavia. By 1948, Stalin, unwilling to let Tito's independent-streak become an example for other possessions, demanded Yugoslavia yield to total Soviet occupation and integration. Tito rejected these demands, in effect, declaring Yugoslav independence from Soviet hegemony. For the remainder of its existence, the Yugoslav communist regime would walk a delicate path of neutrality between East and West. Stalin, unwilling to provoke an uncertain response from the United States by invading the rebellious Yugoslavia, was forced to accept Tito's defection. This necessitated harsher repression in the rest of the Soviet empire to prevent further political dissidence inspired by Tito's example.

Khrushchev and Destalinization

Stalin's death in 1953, however, presented the Soviet Union and its empire with a significant challenge. Caesar was dead; who would replace him? Stalin's power had been based upon the utter, personal control of the three pillars of the Soviet State: the party, the Army, and the secret police known as the Committee of State Security (KGB). Stalin unexpectedly died of a stroke on March 5, 1953, while at his dacha outside of Moscow. So great was the personal fear he inspired in those around him, it was later reported,

that no one was willing to come to the great tyrant's aid as he lay unconscious on the floor of his room. His aides feared that, upon recovery, their glorious leader might repay their assistance with execution. There are conflicting reports as to what transpired at the top of the Soviet leadership immediately after all were sure that Stalin was truly dead. It is certain that a power struggle immediately broke out between Lavrenti Beria (1899-1953), head of the Commissariat for Internal Affairs (NKVD), forerunner of the KGB, and Nikita Khrushchev, bureaucratic head of the party. With a coup or civil war imminent, Khrushchev moved quickly to forge an alliance with the Red Army against the hated Beria and the secret police. Backed by the military, Khrushchev had Beria arrested and executed. (Some accounts have Khrushchev himself shooting Beria at the first Politburo meeting after Stalin's death.)

While having successfully avoided full-scale political violence, it would still take Khrushchev until 1955 to consolidate full control of the Soviet political system. Even then, he would never approach the degree of personal authority and terror wielded by his former master; for the remainder of its history the Soviet Union was governed by different coalitions of top party leaders instead of by one tyrant. The most remarkable feature of the transition to post-Stalinism was precisely that the culture of violence that had dominated Soviet history since 1917 was slowly replaced by a more procedural, if still totalitarian, system of authoritarian rule.

Khrushchev sought to end the violent excesses of the Stalinist past as a necessary means towards more efficiently motivating the party and the people to work towards the building of a modern, powerful, socialist world power. In his famed "Secret Speech" to the XXth Party Congress in March 1956, he denounced the crimes of "Stalinism," undercutting those hard-line elements of the Soviet government who wanted to maintain iron-handed repression; the age of purges and massive gulags were over. That is not to say that, from 1956 onwards, the Soviet Union became a model protector of human rights and political dissent: far from it. Rather, it marked a sophistication in method; no longer would entire populations be targeted for violent repression. Instead, such violence would be applied more specifically to individuals and groups. By the 1970s, for example, the KGB was abandoning the concept of gulags entirely. Instead, political dissidents would be sent to insane asylums under the impeccable logic that, as the Soviet State was always right, only the irrational could disagree with it.

Khrushchev also sought to soften relations with the Soviet satellite states where signs of chafing under the heavy-handedness of Soviet control were growing. In 1953, following Stalin's death, workers in East Germany started protesting the increasing levels of production demanded of them by both the U.S.S.R. and their own government leaders who were eager to please their Soviet masters. While the protests were suppressed, the reality of pro-nationalist sentiments across Eastern Europe could not be ignored. Rather than meet such predilections with overt force, Khrushchev pushed for a policy of limited accommodation, allowing more national control of economic production and allocation within the satellite states and even limited efforts at economic "liberalization," that is, moving away from a pure state-planned economy and tolerating the development of a very limited free-market sector.

In his 1956 speech Khrushchev even went so far as to suggest that the Soviet model was not the only model of socialism; different countries might take different paths to the same goal.

Khrushchev's commitment to "reform," however, was more rhetorical than real. As news of the "Secret Speech" worked its way into the Soviet satellites, expectations were raised amongst the peoples of Eastern Europe that greater autonomy and, even independence, might be in the offering. To his regret, Khrushchev soon discovered that when the lash is removed from the backs of a repressed people, they are not as much grateful as hateful for having felt the lash at all. Rebellion tends to follow. Such was the case in Poland and Hungary in 1956.

Polish and Hungarian Crises

In Poland, the expectation of coming change led to riots by workers demanding a greater voice in government and the economy. Rather than imposing a Stalinist-style crackdown, the Polish communist government acquiesced to public demands and released thousands of political prisoners, including the moderate communist Wladislaw Gomulka (1905-1982). Gomulka was quickly able to rise to power in the new pro-reform environment. Within months a new Gomulka-led government was in power, implementing publicly demanded labor and consumer reforms. Labor unrest and riots, however, continued into the fall with protests increasingly directed at the Soviet occupation of Poland itself. Outraged that limited liberalization should be greeted by nationalist protests, Khrushchev ordered a crackdown by Soviet troops, thereby restoring order and curbing the more progressive programs of the Gomulka government.

Similar protests by workers and students in Hungary exploded into quasi-revolution in October 1956, resulting in the rise to power of the communist reformer Imre Nagy (1896-1958). Inspired by statements of support by the Eisenhower administration, the Nagy regime pursued a policy of Hungarian independence, abolishing the one-party system, demanding Soviet troops leave the country, and announcing its international neutrality and withdrawal from the Soviet Warsaw Pact. Confronted by outright rebellion in Hungary, Khrushchev was again forced to resort to old methods; the Soviet Red Army invaded and deposed Nagy, killing thousands of Hungarian civilians whom fought the invaders in the process. Nagy and several thousand others were later executed, and a more secure, pro-Soviet regime was put into place. The results of the 1956 anti-Soviet uprisings were twofold. First, it compelled the Soviet Union to actually maintain some commitment to political and economic autonomy in Eastern Europe to avoid stimulating further rebellions. Second, it demonstrated that, no matter the rhetoric of destalinization, if ultimate Soviet control over any of its colonies was truly threatened, the response would be as brutal as in Stalin's time. Thus, for the next twenty years, Eastern European economic and social experimentation occurred within a very narrowly defined political space.

Sentries stood guard at the Berlin wall, erected by the East Germans and Soviets in 1961 to prevent East Germans from escaping to West Germany.

Before German troops arrived to seal the Berlin border, this individual made a dash to freedom through an opening in the barbed wire.

The Berlin Wall and the Prague Spring

This space would be tested two more times over the next two decades, Berlin in 1961 and Czechoslovakia in 1968. Berlin was the last major challenge during Khrushchev's reign. Until 1961 East Germans still held onto a political option unavailable to the other residents of the Soviet empire, the ability to vote with their feet. During the 1950s over two million East Germans (more than 10 percent of the population) made a dash to freedom, using Western-occupied West Berlin as an escape hatch. Faced with both a loss of labor and of political face, the East German government of Walter Ulbricht (1893-1973) moved in August 1961 to stop the flow of refugees by constructing a concrete partition between the two parts of the city. The Berlin Wall, as it was promptly dubbed, eventually grew into a barricade of steel, barbed wire, and watchtowers armed by troops ordered to shoot to kill anyone attempting to pass over it. Over the next three decades, more than eight thousand people tried to escape over the wall. Two hundred of them were killed in the attempt.

East Germans sealed windows that opened to West Berlin.

The Kennedy administration subsequently turned this heavy-handed act to American advantage. On a visit to West Berlin he stood before what was to become the Cold War's most visible symbol of Communist repression and expressed his and America's solidarity with the freedom-loving peoples on both sides of the wall by announcing *"Ich bin ein Berliner!"* That is, "I am a Berliner." Translated directly into the German vernacular of Berlin, he actually said, "I am a doughnut," the "Berliner" being a local name for a popular breakfast biscuit. The Germans understood what he meant, however, and tremendously appreciated the sentiment. For the remainder of the cold war, attempts by Soviet leaders to portray the communist system as clearly superior to the liberal-capitalism ran head on into the Berlin wall; a prosperous nation needs walls to keep people out, not in.

In 1968 the people of Czechoslovakia repeated the Hungarian experience. This time, reformists in the capital of Prague sought to pursue internal economic and political liberalization (creation of a free market and development of democratic institutions) within the context of continued Czech communism and participation in the Soviet bloc. Under the leadership of Alexander Dubcek (1927-93), "Prague Spring," as the movement became known, sought to thereby create "socialism with a human face." After months of hesitancy and intermittent negotiation with the apostate Czechs, the Soviet leader Leonid Brezhnev (1906-1982) decided that deviancy from orthodoxy was again too dangerous to be left unchallenged. Once independence of any sort was allowed within the Soviet system, it might spread to all aspects of communist life with the resultant threat of profound revolution.

Beginning on August 21, 1968, 500,000 Warsaw pact soldiers overran the country. Dubcek was removed (though not executed) and replaced with a reliable old communist. Thus, the Russians announced the Brezhnev Doctrine: once a communist state, always a communist state. Should any communist state express unorthodox (un-Soviet) desires, the Red Army would intervene and restore orthodoxy. This doctrine would become the basis for the disastrous Soviet invasion of Afghanistan a decade later.

While far less bloody than the repression of Hungary in 1956, the invasion of Czechoslovakia produced profound international condemnation of the Soviet Union, not just by the Western allies but by non-aligned states as well. Czechoslovakia was the first rebellion to be effectively covered by television, its images of Soviet tanks advancing on bloodied civilians broadcast around the world until the last Czech television station could be silenced by the invaders. A harbinger of similar scenes from Beijing twenty years later, the televised image of the individual struggling for liberty before armies of a repressive regime, became a globally motivating force that would haunt authoritarian states of all kinds, from the Russian and Chinese communists to Latin American militarists for the remainder of the century. The globalization of television meant that dictators would be increasingly unable to carry out their gruesome deeds in private; their dirty (and bloody) laundry could now be displayed for inspection by the entire world.

Peaceful Coexistence

On the international front, Khrushchev sought three goals. First, he sought to establish the Soviet Union as a clearly capable military power able to counter the American-led NATO forces by continuing the Stalinist military arms build up, especially in atomic weapons. At the same time he sought to lesson cold war tensions by advocating a diplomatic policy of "peaceful coexistence" between capitalism and communism,

meeting with American and European leaders and agreeing to work cooperatively on resolving various disputes, particularly the recognition of a neutral Austria in 1955 that allowed ten years of joint military occupation to end. Third, he orchestrated a major diplomatic offensive by the Soviet Union to win friends amongst the newly independent states of Africa, the Middle East, and Asia, portraying the Soviets as the natural friend and ally of nations that had endured the plight of capitalist colonialism. Thus, Russia sided with Egypt against Britain and France during the 1956 Suez crisis and anti-imperialist revolutionaries such as Castro in Cuba and Ho Chi Minh in Vietnam.

Finally, he sought to parlay Soviet domestic economic recovery into a global model of economic development to be followed by all nations. Thus, when Khrushchev stated of the West, "We will bury you," he was not referring to war as the final arbiter of the East-West struggle. Khrushchev made this point clear during the famed impromptu "Kitchen Debate" with U.S. Vice President Richard M. Nixon (1913-1994) during Nixon's visit to an international exhibi-

Flag-waving Czechs shouted protests as they passed a Russian tank following the 1968 Soviet invasion of Czechoslovakia.

tion on technology in Moscow. Standing in a mock up of an American kitchen, which was part of the exhibition, Khrushchev boasted that the Soviet system of superior economic production would out-produce the capitalist system within twenty years, burying it in cheap toasters, television sets, and automobiles. Precisely the opposite occurred.

The Khrushchev period ultimately failed to deliver on its twin promises of massively increased Soviet economic prosperity and manageable competition with the Western powers. His attempts at political and economic reform produced greater political stability within the Soviet Union itself—no purges or substantial political discord occurred into the 1960s. Moreover, the Soviet Union and its satellite states witnessed a profound recovery from the damages of the war. By 1960 most of the basic needs of the Soviet population (housing, food, clothing, energy, medical care) were being met; indeed, for many average Russians, the 1950s and 1960s industrial policy produced a higher standard of living than ever before. But, by the early 1960s serious problems, especially in agriculture production, began to develop, casting the future of economic expansion into doubt.

Indeed, for most of those in Eastern Europe, living standards remained below those of the pre-war period. Even in Russia, per capita living space would only reach its then woefully inadequate *pre-Revolution* levels in the 1970s. Khrushchev's economic rhetoric, however, had raised expectations of future prosperity, which many within the regime doubted could be reached. It was one thing to show economic growth when the starting point was utter devastation, as had been the case in the late 1940s. Conservatives within the Communist Party feared that, if economic growth slowed, there could be a significant popular backlash that the coercive arm of the Soviet regime, weakened by Khrushchev's political reforms, might not be able to handle. As large sectors of the Russian economy, especially the inefficient agrarian sector, began to show slower rates of growth in the 1960s than in the 1950s, rising economic discontent became a real possibility.

Khrushchev's foreign policy also produced mixed results. His relaxation of controls over Eastern Europe had almost resulted in revolution. His attempts to cool cold war tensions had clashed with his desire to expand Soviet power, leading to a series of crises: Suez and Hungary in 1956; an ill-conceived and ignored ultimatum to the Western powers to evacuate Berlin in 1958; the shooting down of an American U-2 spy plane in 1960; an angry split over the leadership of global communism with Mao Zedong's Chinese communists in 1960-1; the Berlin Wall in 1961; and the Cuban Missile Crisis in 1962. While Soviet military and political power grew through the period, these erratic series of crises gave the impression, both to the world and, increasingly, to conservatives within the Kremlin, that Khrushchev was unreliable. Khrushchev's personality also proved a liability. Essentially raised as a peasant with little of the formal polish expected of a world leader, he was given to often violent verbal outbursts of anger (one infamous example he pulled off a shoe while addressing the United Nations and began pounding a table with it), which led other members of the Soviet state to question his stability on more than one occasion.

From Peasant to Bureaucrat: The Rise of Brezhnev

In 1964, following reports that Khrushchev's agrarian reforms were failing, a troika (three people) of conservative Soviet leaders engineered his removal from power and forced retirement and confinement at his country dacha (summerhouse). Khrushchev's dismissal marked a somewhat positive milestone in Russian history: for the first (and last) time a change of leadership occurred without the previous leader having to have died or been killed; both during the period of the Czars and the Commissars, the only route to power was over the corpse of the previous power-holder. The Soviet Union had matured from simple tyranny to a more complex corporate form of dictatorship where leaders of the key interests within the Soviet state would share decision making.

Shortly after Khrushchev's removal, Leonid Brezhnev, new chairman of the Communist Party, emerged as the first amongst equals within the Soviet leadership. Brezhnev represented the conservatives who thought that Khrushchev's reforms had gone too far in weakening the control of the state. At the same time, there was no desire by the leadership to return the Soviet system to an all-powerful Stalinist regime where even those in the highest reaches of authority enjoyed no personal security; there would be no new gulags and purges. Instead, for the next two decades the watchword of the Soviet regime was a cautious perpetuation of the political and economic status quo. Brezhnev represented the triumph of the nomenklatura, the personalityless gray party bureaucrats who built careers upon the principle of not making waves.

Under Brezhnev, if people did not challenge the status quo, they would suffer no increased sanctions from the state; those that tested any limits would be harshly dealt with. Thus, the relatively mild dissent of the Dubcek regime in Czechoslovakia was harshly crushed, and social and political dissidents within the Soviet Union proper were subjected to increased political repression. At the same time, this devotion to the status quo had a chilling effect on economic performance and technological development. Risk-taking of all kinds was out of favor, hence industrial managers and workers became increasingly cautious in setting goals for economic productivity. By the 1970s real economic growth was in decline, setting up the political crises of the next decade. Even as the Russian tanks rolled over Prague, the most dynamic days of the Soviet Union were over. The Russian stone stopped rolling and became covered with the moss of stagnation, corruption, inefficiency, and decay. The next two decades would be a holding action by a Soviet regime dominated by increasingly old, cautious, and uncertain men.

THE EUROPEAN PHOENIX RISES

While the Soviet Union saw its political power rise even as its economic power waned in the decades following the war, the states of Western Europe saw precisely the opposite unfold. The loss of empire and the rise of the U.S. and the U.S.S.R. as the dominant global powers, as well as the rise of non-European powers such as Japan and China, clearly marked the end of European global political dominance. Shorn of the need to maintain the costly pretensions of imperial power and national rivalry, the European states could, for the first time in their history, focus solely on economic development and reap the benefits of mutual cooperation. In 1946, however, the apparent challenges to building such a prosperous and peaceful Europe seemed so great that the actual achievement of these goals within two decades of the war's end were often referred to as nothing less than a miracle. It was, in fact, three miracles: the miracle of economic recovery, the miracle of political integration, and the miracle of cultural unification.

Millions of civilians were displaced as they became refugees. Without food and shelter, many died of disease and hunger.

Challenges to Recovery

The economic miracle consisted of two parts: immediate postwar recovery and subsequent European economic integration. The war had left Europe shattered. By the end of 1945 industrial production had declined by 80 to 90 percent compared to pre-war levels across the whole of the Nazi-occupied territories. This decline was partly a result of war damage and even more a result of the collapse of political administration and markets. Across Europe, thousands of factories and millions of housing units had been destroyed. Hundreds of mines and thousands of acres of farmland lay idle, warehouses and stores were empty, and millions of refugees, some displaced by bombings and combat, many fleeing the advancing Russian army, were without basic necessities. Roads, bridges, dams, dikes, and canals were destroyed or impassable. The accumulated labor of decades-spent developing industrial economies was now squandered on the broken fields of war. Some historians have esti-

mated that W.W.II cost Europe, at least, thirty years of economic growth. Rebuilding this shattered hulk would be a major, costly undertaking.

This undertaking was further complicated by political realities. While the Allies moved to restore basic administration within their zones of occupation, the lack of true governing institutions hindered economic recovery. Even where there were governments, such as in Britain and newly restored France, treasuries across the continent were bankrupt. Things were even worse in Eastern Europe, where the occupying Soviet army was looting billions of dollars worth of industrial equipment as immediate "war reparations" while also pursuing Stalinist purges of their newly acquired populations. Moreover, the fundamental mistrust between the wartime allies that quickly arose once the raison d'etre of the alliance—the destruction of Hitler's Germany—was accomplished directly precluded the development of a coherent, continental reconstruction plan. Both the Soviet and Anglo-American occupiers had political imperatives—establishing ideologically compatible regimes within their zones of occupation—as their first order of business. Humanitarian and economic policies would be driven by these political goals first and foremost.

Europe also faced a fundamental internal cultural challenge towards recovery, the consequence of forty years of nationalism run amok. The post-World War I period had witnessed the economic recovery of the major combatants and, even, the restoration of political stability within the major national regimes. The period had not, however, witnessed any significant lessening of the national political rivalries, which had led to war. The central question left unanswered by the first war—which state or alliance would dominate central Europe—which helped lead to World War II—remained unanswered.

Early into the postwar period some European intellectuals and political leaders began to understand that such political considerations, however, begged the larger question of creating a stable, prosperous Europe. Europe had experienced centuries of warfare between rival nations and blocs trying to establish continental hegemony and only had devastation to show for it. Postwar leaders, especially in France and Germany, began to understand that the future security of Europe could only be premised on the ending of such nationalism-based politics.

The recovery of Europe, to these thinkers, could not be thought of in the context of the restoration of any one nation's national power and security. Instead, it must be talked about in the context of establishing *European* economic power and political stability. The Reformation had ended the cultural Christian unity of Europe; four hundred years of cultural, ethnic, and ideological nationalism had only deepened that rift. The postwar period would see the rise of a newly unified Europe, this time founded on the more material basis of economic efficiency and prosperity. No nation better demonstrated these processes than Germany.

The German Postwar Miracle

The first key to the recovery and pacification of Europe lay with Germany. The military division of Europe agreed to at Potsdam was, at best, a short-term remedy to a long-term issue: what to do with Germany? On that issue, even more than on any other, there was no consensus or even longer-term vision. Opinions varied on both sides of the Iron Curtain. Those fearful of Germany rising from the ashes as it had after W.W.I believed the country should be demilitarized and deindustrialized, essentially reduced to a large, relatively poor agrarian society, thereby preventing a reemergence of militarism. Such a policy would require the occupation of Germany into the indefinite future.

Both sides paid lip service to the notion of German reunification—integrating the Soviet-controlled East German zone with the Allied West Germans. For the Soviets, however, such a move would be predicated on German political and economic neutrality. The Americans and British feared that German neutrality could, as in Austria, be used as a cover for Sovietized eastern German groups and institutions to accomplish a national consolidation. Thus, the American and British governments gave no real strategic consideration towards short-term German unification and instead focused on a Western European plan of recovery dedicated to two ideals: the restoration of industrial market economies (i.e., capitalism) and the creation of liberal democratic political institutions. The Soviets meanwhile pursued their Sovietization of their occu-

Guarded by Allied military police, German leaders accused of war crimes sit in the defendant's dock during the Nuremberg trials.

pied territories with the goals of producing ideologically cloned satellite states.

So Germany and Europe proper would remain divided for the next half-century. In the west, European people would live under liberal capitalist governments influenced to various degrees by elements of democratic socialism. Choice would be made by the people in free (if government regulated) markets and free elections. Power would lie with the individual. In the east Europeans would live under state-controlled, communist totalitarian regimes. Choices would be made by Communist Party elite in centralized state planning institutions and by Politburo decree. Bullets would be resorted to more frequently than ballots; power lay with the regime. Starting at relatively equal levels of eco-

nomic devastation after the war, the West would rise up to levels of unprecedented prosperity; the East, after a modest recovery, would sink into a quagmire of stagnation and spreading poverty. No where else in history can one find such an almost laboratory environment to make clear and controlled comparisons between two rival ideological systems. The fate of the two Germanys is most telling in this regard.

The partition of Germany proceeded incrementally. Between 1945 and 1949 Germany was still technically one nation. Early on, German de-Nazification was a driving goal of both the occupying powers, as those who had held positions of authority during the Nazi period were arrested and the population as a whole was subjected to anti-Nazi reeducation programs. Between August 1945 and October 1946, a series of trials of two dozen major Nazi leaders (without the big four—Hitler, Goebels, Goering, and Himmler—who had not survived the war) were held in Nuremberg, Germany. Charged with "crimes against humanity" for their roles in civilian-targeted warfare and the genocide of the "final solution" targeted at European Jewry, all but three would be convicted, and ten would be executed. Lacking a real foundation in the international law of the time critics of the Nuremberg trials argued that the proceedings were simply a case of winners punishing the losers. Indeed, as American General Curtis Lemay (1906-1990), chief architect of the American strategic bombing campaign and the decision to "terror-bomb" German civilian population centers, later remarked, if the Germans had won it would have been people like himself, Truman, and Eisenhower in the war-crimes dock. On the other hand, the Nuremberg trials marked an important moment in the development of international law. For the first time major political powers formulated the concept of some foundation of international behavior that attempted to address the needs of all people rather than those of individual nation states. The old assumption that nations and their sovereign leaders were to be considered powers beyond some global sense of law was part of the dawning awareness that, in the nuclear age, actions of national leaders could affect the entirety of the human community. Throughout the remainder of the century this would become a global major question: where does the rights and sovereignty of a nation end and where does that of humankind, if such a thing exists at all, begin? De-Nazification was probably most effectively carried out in the Western zone, where liberal democratic ideals were advanced to replace the Nazi totalitarian dogma. The Soviet occupation,

itself advancing a totalitarian agenda, tended to co-opt the existing Nazi centralized governmental system to its own end. Many who had participated in lower levels of the Reich became functionaries in the new authoritarian Soviet East German regime, especially in the secret police, the Stasi (state security service). After the reunification of Germany in 1990, eastern Germany proved to be more fertile ground for the growth of neo-Nazi propaganda and interest groups. Even in the West, however, numerous Nazi and Nazi sympathizers were "rehabilitated" and allowed to participate in public life as part of the German military or economy under justification of the cold war's need to use all resources against the Soviets. Thus, despite the public trials such as Nuremberg, fascism and issues of war-justice continued to haunt Europe from the grave across the remainder of the century.

Between 1946 and 1949 government in western Germany was restored from the local levels upwards. Democratic processes of elections were restored, and utilities and other economic infrastructure were gradually shifted from military to civilian control. By 1948, as it became apparent that the partition of Germany was to be permanent, a coordinated program was begun to create an independent West German state. In September 1949, a special parliamentary council of pro-democracy German leaders adopted a new constitution, the "Basic Law." This act created the Federal Republic of West Germany that provided for a parliamentary system of democratically elected government and much greater regional autonomy for the "states" of Germany than had been the case under the highly centralized German states dating back to unification in the nineteenth century. Such a "federal" distribution of power, it was thought, would inhibit the ability of dictatorship or militarism to ever seize the central government of

Germany again. Konrad Adenauer (1876-1967), the former anti-Nazi mayor of Cologne and now leader of the majority Christian Democratic Union Party (CDU), became the first postwar chancellor (prime minister) of the FRG. Adenauer and the Christian Democrats dominated German politics for the next generation with a moderate agenda calling for political stability through economic security. The Soviet Union, in direct response to the creation of the FRG, proclaimed the creation of the German Democratic Republic (which being neither German in origin, democratic in process, or republican in structure was something of a misnomer) in October 1949.

Adenauer, with the brilliant guidance of his Minister of Economy, Ludwig Erhard (1897-1977), pursued a "mixed" economic model, where private ownership and investment in industry would be supplemented by state investment and even ownership of some key industries, thereby providing a safety net to the overall economy. Boosted by billions of dollars in largely American foreign aid and a German public vehemently committed to avoiding extremism of any kind, Adenauer's CDU government presided over twenty years of phenomenal economic growth—the *Wirtschaftswunder* or "Economic Miracle" of postwar Germany. By the mid-1950s the quality of life for average West Germans recovered to pre-war levels. By the mid-1960s these levels were dramatically exceeded. Within fifteen years of the war's end, West Germany reemerged as an international trading partner and a major European economic power.

The economic recovery of West Germany helped reinforce the commitment of the German public to centrist politics. German politics were dominated by the moderate conservative CDU government, which worked cooperatively with the Social Democratic Party, representing the moderate left. Extreme parties of the left (communist) or right (fascists) were barred from political participation by law. Government policies sought to create consensus-based politics in which all national debates would be resolved in such a way as to include and benefit all mainstream social, political, and economic interests. The radical success of these policies is born out by the comment by one major historian of the period that, "after 1949, West German politics was, frankly, unexciting." Gone was the age of the charismatic ideologue; in was the day of the slightly boring technocrat. Under this experience Germany would reach levels of prosperity that two wars denied them. Similar processes played out in the Low Countries, Denmark, and Norway.

This same tandem process of economic and political recovery played out across Western Europe. Denmark, Norway, and the Low Countries largely followed the German model in creating economic and political stability. In France and Italy, where politics never became quite as staid as in Germany, reestablishing stable democracy was a slightly bumpier path.

French and Italian Postwar Instability

In 1946 conservative war hero and Free-French leader General DeGaulle left power after serving for two years as premier. For the next decade French politics was mired in division between the conservative and socialist parties over the structure of postwar French society and economics, resulting in frequent changes in government (with prime ministers lasting about six months, on average). These political divisions were intensified by communist radicals and the ultraconservative *Poujadistes*, who used strikes and demonstrations to destabilize moderate politics. Repeated international crises in the Suez,

Indochina, and Algeria further undermined public support for the Republic. By 1958 political unrest and the resulting negative impact on economic recovery almost resulted in a military coup (see the Algerian crisis, above) that only the return of DeGaulle to public life thwarted. The Fourth Republic was replaced by the Fifth Republic, establishing a stronger chief executive directly elected by the people who could bypass the squabbling parliament and use public support to compel the development of national consensus. Thus, DeGaulle's tenure as president from 1958 to 1969 ushered in the period of political stability and economic prosperity that the Fourth Republic had failed to produce.

In Italy the same political divisions of the French Fourth Republic caused frequent changes in government for the next two generations. Unlike France, no DeGaulle-like figure existed to quell division. Having largely eliminated the core of Mussolini's fascist movement from political life, postwar Italian politics still experienced sometimes paralyzing division between leftist communists and rightist ultranationalists. The moderate-right Christian Democrats under Alcide De Gasperi (1881-1954) were able to maintain political dominance for much of the early postwar period, but as power seesawed between the CD and the opposition moderate-leftist Social Democrats, neither usually able to secure an outright majority in national elections, economic recovery lagged. Italy would remain economically backward compared to the rest of Western Europe into the 1960s, with southern Italy remaining one of the poorest regions of Europe to the turn of the century.

Postwar Economic Recovery

European economic recovery was driven by three factors: the creation of a stable global trade and financial system, the success of the American spearheaded recovery program, and the success of Western European economic cooperation as seen in the rise of the EEC. Following W.W.II, the peoples of the industrial liberal democracies in general enjoyed an historically unprecedented period of economic expansion and prosperity, producing the wealthiest societies in human history.

The Western European route to economic recovery differed from both the Soviet approach, with its total state control of the economy, and the American laissez faire system that still saw government interference in the free market with some suspicion, if not outright hostility, even with the experience of the New Deal and the war economy. The European mixed system called for the state to take the role of employer, consumer, and investor of last resort to guarantee economic stability. The social-welfare state, in which governments became increasingly involved in providing for the basic needs of its population, including medical care, education and economic subsidies, grew dramatically in the postwar period across Western Europe.

In France and Italy, for example, the government not only supported the rebuilding of domestic industries with favorable tax policies but directly sought state ownership of key producers or entire industries. Even in Great Britain, the originator of laissez-faire capitalism, there was a profound postwar shift to a social welfare mixed model under the Atlee Labour government that replaced the economically conservative Tories in 1945. Government control of core industries allowed it to shift resources where they could most effectively be used and, in times of economic down turn, cushion workers from unemployment. Government economic intervention, therefore, sought to offset the uncertainty of the market with its boom-bust business cycle with the guarantee that state resources could keep industries producing, labor working, and consumers buying.

Conventional laissez faire wisdom held that such government intervention in the economy would, in the long term, hinder economic growth because companies and workers, protected from the full competition of the market place, would become increasingly less efficient. From the 1940s until the 1980s, however, this model produced unprecedented economic growth and stability. Most Western European nations saw the lowest unemployment levels and highest economic growth rates up to that point in their histories. In part this was a function of the peculiarities of the times—millions of unemployed workers across the region willing to forgo high wage demands in return for guaranteed jobs, thereby keeping wage-driven inflation low. The huge demand for all manners of industrial and consumer goods generated by the recovering economies allowed private and public industry alike to maintain strong profit margins, which in turn led to more capital for investment and growth. The fostering of freer trade policies between European states and with the United States further opened economic opportunity. Until the rise of the increasingly interlinked competitive market system of the 1980s and beyond, however, the Western European mixed industrial model proved as capable as the laissez-faire model in promoting economic prosperity and political stability.

Only on the Iberian Peninsula would conservative authoritarianism continue. In Spain, Franco's nationalist regime remained in power until his death in 1976. In Portugal, the conservative authoritarian regime continued in power into the 1980s. In both cases economic growth remained far below that of the rest of Western Europe. By 1990 Portugal was the definition of poverty within the European Union.

The lesson of the economic recovery of postwar Europe dispels one of the great false dichotomies of history: that the authoritarian state is unfair but efficient, while the democratic state is fair but inefficient. Mussolini may have been a ruthless dictator, but he made the notoriously inept Italian trains run on time, so went the famous nostrum. By 1946, however, Mussolini's trains were so much smoking rubble. The reality of the next fifty years was that the democratic states proved themselves to be both fair and efficient. The economic recovery of Western Europe and its rise to unprecedented prosperity stood as an undeniable testament to the efficacy of the liberal democratic state, be it economically laissez faire or mixed, to the authoritarian state, be it communist or state-capitalist.

TOWARDS ONE EUROPE

Western European political and economic recovery provided the foundation for the unprecedented economic (and later political) integration that would mark the second half of the century. Two viewpoints towards the nature of "Europe" quickly solidified after the war. The "Europeans" believed the future of the continent lay in creating some form of a "European Federalism," in which nations would surrender some, if not most, of their sovereignty to a new trans-European political union. This viewpoint was prevalent amongst continental politicians and scholars, especially those within the various Christian Democrat Parties whose shared-Catholic tradition tended towards recognizing transnational authority.

The "Sovereignists" denied the need to sacrifice national sovereignty to such authority. Instead, stability could be achieved by working through the existing framework of independent nation-states. Traditional nationalists and communists fell into this viewpoint. This view was particularly strong in Britain, with its historic tendency to distance itself from continental affairs, considering itself a class apart—and above—from its neighbors. One should remember the famed nineteenth-century *London Times* headline when fog had closed the channel to crossing: "Continent Isolated!" This view was also shared by the American government, which, as the new global hegemon, was loath to advance ideas that might undercut its own sovereign power.

The desire to present a unified bloc in facing the Soviets during the cold war made some degree of political coordination among the western states critical. Cooperation in implementing the Marshall Plan (1947) facilitated this process. The Organization for European Economic Cooperation and the Council of Europe were created in 1948 to institutionalize such cooperation. While envisioned by European Federalists as a first-step in further integration, the British and Americans worked to minimize the ability of these organizations to take on a policy-making role. For the Americans, military coordination through NATO would be a greater priority than the development of transnational European political institutions. It was to be in economics, therefore, and not in politics, that the process of "building Europe" would first truly emerge.

First Steps: the ECSC and the EEC

The first major impetus to such integration came in the Low Countries of Belgium, the Netherlands, and Luxembourg. In 1947, they established the Benelux customs union. Integrating duties and tariffs, these nations calculated, would provide for a more efficient pattern of trade with the rest of Europe and the world. Cooperation, rather than competition, was now a recognized economic strategy.

In 1950, the French Foreign Minister Robert Schulman (1886-1963) and advisor Jean Monnet (1888-1979) put forth a plan to integrate European coal and steel production through the dropping of national tariff and trade barriers and the adoption of common state economic policies. Coordination of these policies would be carried out by a commission of members from each participating European state. The Schulman Plan was adopted by France, West Germany, Italy, Belgium, the Netherlands, and Luxembourg in 1952. This led to the creation of the European Coal and Steel Community (ECSC). By 1958 a free market for coal and steel had been instituted among the six countries; for these two commodities borders ceased to exist. This integration served two purposes. First, it greatly increased the efficiency and quantity of coal and steel production in the member states. Second, it bound the trading members into an economic relationship of *interdependency*: each state's economic performance was now intricately linked with that of its neighbors. Cooperation would positively affect each nation; conflict could prove ruinous. War, therefore, became less thinkable; an attack by any state on its neighbor would be the same as dropping bombs on its own factories—in other words, extraordinarily counterproductive.

Unity vs. Nationalism

The success of the ECSC quickly led to economic cooperation in a number of other areas. In 1957 the six nations of the ECSC formed Euratom to coordinate atomic energy policy. That same year saw the signing of the Treaty of Rome, establishing the European Economic Community (EEC) that soon became known more simply as the Common Market. The goal of the EEC was to extend the same principles of trade and cooperation beyond the coal and steel industries. The process first began with reducing trade tariffs and barriers between member states, with the ultimate aim of creating a single market area that might rival the United States in size and wealth. The more enthusiastic supporters of the EEC saw trade as the first step in even greater integration that could eventually include the free movement across borders of capital, labor, and even political power: a united Europe. Progress towards this vision, however, occurred in fits and starts. In the early 1960s negotiations proceeded to lower tariffs in a variety of industries, and trade among the members of the EEC almost doubled; annual overall economic growth rates for members soared above 7 percent.

Progress towards further integration was to be temporarily derailed by resurgent nationalism in the person of Charles DeGaulle. By the early 1960s DeGaulle increasingly viewed American influence in Europe as detrimental to the reassertion of European, especially French, global power and political autonomy. Europe, he believed, had needed America's shield in the 1950s during the process of recovery but now the patient was healed; it was time for the doctor to let the patient walk without help. The continued American tendency to treat European powers as minor partners in the Western alliance, as illustrated by the unilateral actions of American administrations over the 1961 Berlin and 1962 Cuban crises, underscored French resolve to reassert their political autonomy.

In 1966 France announced its withdrawal from the NATO military command structure; the United States could no longer count on automatic French compliance with American military decisions. DeGaulle's desire to reassert French sovereignty increasingly ran against the supranational direction of the EEC. France twice (in 1963 and 1967) blocked British admission to the Common Market as a political protest against Britain's close cooperation with the United States. The British government, seeing the economic advantage gained by other EEC members, had reconsidered its early decision to boycott the organization only to run into DeGaulle's veto. In 1965 DeGaulle precipitated a crisis over EEC agrarian policy that he believed would unfairly penalize French farmers. French intransigence provoked similar nationalist backlash in other member states.

While the Common Market survived the crisis, further integration took a back seat to nationalist interests for years to come. The failure to include the United Kingdom in the EEC created an effective limit to the efficacy of the Common Market, and global economic crises in the 1970s further undermined integration. It would take until the 1980s for additional substantial progress to occur on the road to European Unity. Yet, at the same time, the progress achieved by the 1960s was nothing short of phenomenal. In 1946 Europe lay shattered by two generations of war. By the 1960s Western Europe, at least, had established stable democracies, prosperous economies, and a common trade policy that helped underscore the political unity of their collective military policies. Europe was no longer a collection of separate, warring states; it was not one unified state, either.

THE NEW POSTWAR ORDER

European integration occurred against a backdrop of American-led Western political and economic integration arising out of the ending of World War II. By the end of 1945 the United States, controlling more than half of all global industrial production and the world's only atomic power, had achieved a level of economic and military superiority unprecedented in history. Maintaining this superior American position and establishing a more stable international order than had been the case since the outbreak of W.W.I was of paramount concern to the Roosevelt administration. Advisors to the president increasingly saw the debacle of W.W.II as having its origins, at least in part, in the collapse of a stable global trading order in the early 1930s. The collapse of world markets following the American stock market crash had dramatically intensified the resulting depression and, so these advisors reasoned, provided a breeding ground for the radicalization of European politics, which led to the rise of fascism. Avoiding a return to such unstable global conditions became the major American postwar aim.

U.S. Postwar Goals

To accomplish this task, four principle postwar American goals were established. First, the incredible domestic economic growth caused by the war had to be maintained, and economic recession, such as occurred after W.W.I, must be avoided. Second, European recovery had to be effected to build stable political allies with which to counter potential Soviet aggression. Third, a new international institutional structure needed to be created that could fulfil the role of international arbiter that the League of Nations never achieved. Fourth, a stable system of global finance and trade was needed to avoid a repetition of the economic cataclysm of the 1930s.

The first of these goals, as it turned out, ended up being self-fulfilling. Ten years of pent up American consumer demand coupled with the U.S.'s profoundly advantageous global trading position—all of its principle trade rivals lay bankrupt or in ruins—were more than sufficient

to offset a dramatic decline in U.S. government economic spending after the war. After a very short economic downturn in 1946, the American economy rebounded and rose steadily, with only minor interruptions into the 1970s. America's newly flush economy was more than up to the task of providing the huge sums of money that went into the Marshall Plan, the key to rapid Western European recovery.

Replacing the defunct League of Nations would be a new United Nations (U.N.). At American instigation, and with British and recalcitrant Soviet support, delegates from fifty nations ratified the charter of the new institution in June 1945. Unlike the League of Nations, the U.N. was not limited to the power to debate issues and pass non-binding resolutions. This would be the province of its General Assembly, to which all nations would belong. A new Security Council, however, would have the authority to mobilize member states to protect the global peace and to intervene, even militarily, to stop the aggression of one state against another. The principle winners of the war—the U.S., Great Britain, France, the Soviet Union, and China—were granted under the charter permanent seats on the Security Council and the power to veto any of its actions. Thus, if any one of the five dissented on any issue, the council would be prohibited from action.

Roosevelt had thought such a framework necessary to get the major powers to sign on to the venture. He also believed that, if the spirit of wartime cooperation perpetuated, the U.N. could play a decisive role in moderating international disputes. By 1945, however, it was becoming increasingly clear that there would be substantial differences in goals and viewpoints among the allies once the war was over. The rise of the cold war, in effect, neutralized the U.N. as the two blocs—American and Soviet—repeatedly vetoed actions called for by the other. The Security Council acted decisively only once during this time when, in 1951, it authorized the intervention of a U.N. army to stop North Korean aggression against South Korea, and then only because the Soviet delegation was boycotting the U.N. as an unrelated protest at the time of the war's outbreak. For most of the next forty-five years, the U.N. failed to play a major role in maintaining international peace and stability.

Bretton Woods

Establishing a stable international economic order was a complicated task. In 1944, as victory in the war became increasingly certain, the Western Allies met in Bretton Woods, New Hampshire (1944) to establish the foundation for this new economic order. Four crucial agreements were reached. First, the American dollar would now officially replace the British pound as the dominant global trading currency. A system of fixed exchange rates tied to a gold standard was adopted, with the dollar pegged at thirty-five dollars per ounce of gold. The currencies of the principle Western European states were tied directly to this dollar value, thereby providing every trading partner with the security of knowing the precise value of all future economic transactions, minimizing risk and thereby increasing trade.

The creation of three important new transnational economic institutions was also agreed to. The International Monetary Fund (IMF) was formed to provide short-term loans to national treasuries to guarantee they would always be able to meet debts owed to other national banks as a result of trade deficits. The International Bank for Reconstruction and Development (IBRD), later known as the World Bank, was created to provide capital originally for rebuilding Europe but later for development

projects in the newly independent colonial possessions. Finally, a process for multilateral trade negotiations, known as the General Agreement on Tariffs and Trade (GATT), was initiated. The goal of GATT was to lower global trade barriers, especially amongst the industrial economies, to increase trade and overall global economic efficiency.

Bretton Woods established, for the first time in modern history, a coordinated program for the world's wealthiest trading states to cooperate in maintaining a stable global market of capital and materials. The accords were far from perfect. The nationalist agendas of the major participating states frequently interposed themselves on attempts at cooperation, such as when the United State's refused to join the International Trade Organization, which would have been empowered to enforce GATT agreements, thereby dooming the venture to failure. Moreover, these policies tended to address the needs of the industrial states and not the emerging developing world. For twenty years Bretton Woods was, however, the foundation for an unparalleled level of stability in trade, which lasted until the global recession of the 1970s derailed the gold standard. Under this security, the U.S. and, later, European companies dramatically increased their levels of foreign direct investment in each other and in the developing world; by 1970 such levels were 600 percent higher than they had been in 1950. Thus, out of the World War emerged the economic foundation for the modern global economy and rising global economic interdependency.

THE RISE OF MODERN CULTURE

The postwar period witnessed a renaissance in Western European material existence, culture, and popular attitude. That such a renaissance was in the offing was not immediately apparent after the war. The years following the Great War had plunged Europe into a period of existential malaise. The first years following the Second World War saw a return of such intellectual and cultural despair. Europe, which had entered the twentieth century as global master, had, within a period of two generations, brought utter ruin upon itself. How could Europeans ever recover their former prosperity?

The Culture of the Absurd

Nineteenth-century European philosophers, such as Hegel and Marx, had tended to see the world as a potentially orderly place leading towards higher, more efficient forms of organization. Postwar philosophers, such as Albert Camus (1913-1960) and Jean Paul Sartre (1905-1980), saw the twentieth century as a world gone mad. The high European culture of the cathedral and the opera had turned into the horrors of the concentration camp and the fascist march. Now the world lay beneath the sword of nuclear Armageddon. The future itself looked equally bleak. The growing divide between increasingly well armed, hostile blocks led the novelist George Orwell (1903-1950) to envision a world a few decades hence (*1984*) locked in endless combat between three, all powerful fascist states, the life of men reduced to that of emotionless cogs in the great machines of war.

Life, under such circumstances, had become absurd. The struggle of the average man was, hence, to find meaning as he could, living and existing within the moment, taking no solace in past or future. This postwar European existentialism was further driven by conflict between Soviet communism and American capitalism, which seemed to take the future of Europe out of European hands.

Many existentialists associated the crisis of Europe with a failure of the "old" Western tradition of liberal values and middle class morality. It had been the middle classes of Italy and Germany, they argued, that had given the fascists the power they needed. Hence, Western "*bourgeois*" middle class values were to be challenged and rejected. The United States—the postwar bastion of such values—was, in turn, highly suspect to such thinkers, especially to Marxist intellectuals, increasingly referred to as "neo-Marxists," many of whom had established new credibility as resistance fighters during the war. The fusion of existentialism and Marxism became a powerful intellectual and cultural force in the decade following the end of the war.

To the postwar neo-Marxists, the American occupation of Western Europe took on the flavor of a cultural occupation as well, in which the rising American values of material satisfaction—shopping, big cars, and more consumer stuff as the measure of the good life—were to be imposed on the European masses. Only the movement to a class-free, post-bourgeois communal society such as foretold by Marx, the neo-Marxists believed, would restore sanity to Europe. Invigorated by such intellectual support, communist parties saw their membership increase strongly in Western Europe, especially in France and Italy. This time, however, the goal of the communist movement was to take power legally through the electoral process. Once in power, they would then effect social and political policies, such as state takeover of industry, limits to private property and income, and, eventually, a turn toward international neutrality in the cold war, which would be able to peaceably create communism.

By the late 1940s, as some semblance of normality returned, a cautious optimism began to rise amongst European leaders that, by the

1950s, had spread to the average person in the street. As living standards rose to and then exceeded pre-war levels, the material basis for much of the existential despondency dissipated. The revelations of the horrible excesses of Stalinism by Khrushchev further undercut the legitimacy of communism as an alternative to liberal capitalism. By the late 1950s, with the return of the conservative Gaulists to power in France and the presence of stable democracies in Germany and England, the rise of communism leveled out. The continued postwar economic boom and rising personal prosperity reinforced this process.

One World Divided

This prosperity, however, was not globally shared. The peoples under Communist governments in the Soviet Union and elsewhere saw limited economic expansion. By the 1960s the peoples of Eastern Europe and the Soviet Union had returned to, or exceeded, their pre-war standards of living. By the end of the decade, however, economic growth slowed down or ceased due to the increasing inefficiencies of the central planning system. The developing world also showed erratic patterns of economic growth. Parts of Latin America and the former colonies of East Asia, such as South Korea, Taiwan and Singapore, demonstrated robust economic expansion during the 1950s and 1960s. Central American, African, and Middle Eastern nations, however, showed far weaker levels of economic growth. Except for a rise in oil revenues for some Middle Eastern states such as Saudi Arabia and Iran, the reality of political independence did not easily translate into economic prosperity for most former colonies and protectorates.

The growing gap in wealth between these states led a French journalist to proclaim, in the mid-1950s, that there were now, in fact, three worlds. The First World consisted of the rich, Western industrial liberal democracies: the United States, Western Europe, and Japan. The Second World consisted of the Communist nations: the Soviet Union, Eastern Europe, North Korea, North Vietnam, China after 1949, and Cuba after 1958. Then, there was a Third World made up largely of the former colonial possessions. With economies dominated by agriculture or the export of natural resources such as metals and oil, the prosperity of these nations was ultimately dependent upon the price rich nations would pay for their exports. Market forces, as they had for the previous two centuries, always worked over the long run to lower the price of such raw materials, as industrial nations worked to cut the costs of production to increase the competitiveness of their goods.

This would lead to the accusation that, while the former imperialist states of Europe had granted political independence to their colonies, the continued domination of these new nations' economies by their former masters amounted to a new form of economic imperialism. Thus, political relations between the industrial and developing worlds continued to be soured by economic inequality. By the 1960s the Dependency Theory, blaming the industrial world for most, if not all, of the problems of the Third World, became a major argument advanced by leaders of the poorer states in an emerging global dialogue.

The Triumph of Science

The postwar period also witnessed an unprecedented revolution in technology in the Western world. The nineteenth century was an age of coal, steam and steel; the twentieth century was an age of oil and electricity. The postwar period saw the development of the age of the

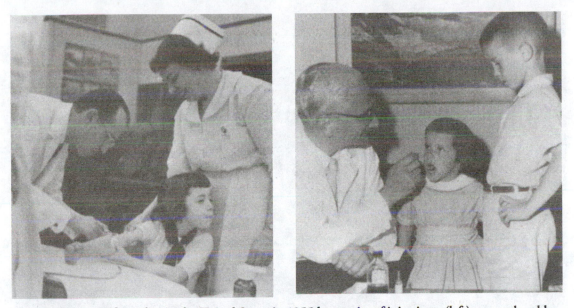

The Salk vaccine for polio, in the United States in 1955 by a series of injections, (left) was replaced by the Sabin vaccine, taken orally and in a single dose. (right)

atom, electronics, computers, space exploration, and plastics. So great was this increase in scientific knowledge and technological development that, by the 1970s, some would start to question its origins. Humans alone could not have come so far so fast, it was argued; the postwar technology boom must have had extraterrestrial sources, such as UFO's crashing in New Mexico. The true origins of this revolution, however, rested in the revolution in postwar science.

While the initial research into developing many of the significant postwar technologies can be traced back to the 1930s and even 1920s, it was during the war and afterwards that a true revolution in science and technology emerged. This was a direct consequence of a fundamental lesson Western nations, especially the United States, learned during the war. Prior to the war, the endeavor of science was basically privately funded. The Manhattan Project, however, demonstrated the utility of subsidizing the work of scientists and engineers with massive amounts

of public funds. The United States government provided its scientists a billion dollars; in exchange they developed the atomic bomb, making the United States the global military superpower. After the war, governments recognized the continued usefulness of directly funding scientific research. In exchange for this funding scientists and engineers produced a seemingly never-ending stream of the new and improved, from polio vaccines to color television to space travel and Tang, the instant breakfast drink.

As standards of living became inseparable from advances in science and technology, popular conception of science also went through a transformation. In the cinema of the 1920s and 1930s, for example, the dominant characterization of science was in the person of the "mad scientist": Doctor Frankenstein playing with the forces of nature and producing the horror of his "monster." It would be the common man, the villagers, who saved the world from the evils of science. By the 1950s the "mad scientist" was

Televisions became common in American homes by the late 1940s. Postwar Americans spent a good deal of their incomes on items that made the home comfortable and enjoyable: appliances, automobiles, and televisions.

still a cinematic cliché, but now this villain would be defeated by the "good" scientist. The heroic scientist saved humankind from colliding worlds to gigantic tarantulas. The rise of space exploration, meanwhile, produced a new cultural hero: the astronaut. The launching of the first man-made satellite, Sputnik, by the Soviet Union in 1957 reinforced the relationship between scientific ability and global standing. The need to "catch-up" to the Soviets scientifically led to a fundamental shift in education in the U.S. and Western Europe, with a renewed emphasis on science and mathematics and a corresponding rise in scientific literacy by populations as a whole. Thus, by the 1960s, the scientific secular values, which had been on the rise in the West since Copernicus and Galileo, were culturally triumphant. The great Age of Science had arrived.

Modern Life

These dramatic changes in technology had an equally dramatic change on the lives of people. Prior to W.W.II, life in the average household of Europe or America had only changed marginally over that of the later nineteenth century. By the 1930s most people still did not have tele-

England had been famous for her madrigals and church music during the reign of Elizabeth I, but not much of her music was popular outside the country since then. The breakthrough in popular music came when the Beetles took the world by storm in the 1960s.

phones, electric lights, or electric consumer goods; many did not have indoor plumbing. Refrigeration, where available, was provided mostly by ice delivered by horse-drawn wagon. Air travel was a luxury—in 1940 most people had never even seen a plane, let alone ridden in one. Few owned or rode in cars. During W.W.II, with the exception of the American and British armies, the vast majority of men and materials were transported by horse or donkey cart, as they had been since the time of the Roman legions.

The change in the standard of living after the war, by comparison to only a generation before, was almost unbelievable. By the 1960s the average citizen of the United States or Western Europe had access to almost all of the modern amenities of life, including an increasing array of laborsaving electrical appliances from refrig-

erators to toasters to washing machines. The radio was now as common place as shoes, and the new medium of television was quickly spreading into every household. Telephones, electric lights, and indoor plumbing were now considered amongst life's basic necessities. The car, at least in the United States, was also increasingly in the category of necessity. The average house of 1968, therefore, had far more in common with the house of 1998, or even 2008, than it did with the house of 1938. Rising economic prosperity allowed households to procure an ever-increasing variety of cheaper, better goods, the consequence of rising worker productivity and more efficient means of production, themselves the product of technological development. Mass production of everything from cars and housing to food and entertainment now

This post World War II housing project established on the edge of an American metropolitan area made housing affordable and produced a mass migration from the cities to the new suburbs.

allowed mass consumption on a scale never before seen in history.

The postwar period ushered in the great age of mass consumption and the modern consumer society. This was reflected in the arts and architecture where "traditional," meaning pre-war, was out, and "modern" was in. Utilitarian became the watchword of design, both in architecture and fashion. Architectural ornamentation, as well as fashion ruffles and bows, were stripped away. Clothes and buildings alike became sleeker, showing off the new materials of steel, glass, rayon, and polyester fiber.

The prototype of this new society was, of course, the United States, where bigger became synonymous with better and "keeping up with the Jones," meaning always having as much or more than one's neighbors, became something of the national past time. By the 1950s the availability of affordable single family housing had produced a mass migration from the cities to the new suburbs. Concentration of retail space, moving away from the mom and pop stores to national chains that could take advantage of economies of scale, created the shopping mall and reinforced fashion trends across all segments of society. It would take Europeans several decades to begin to fully emulate the American model.

Demotic Times

The postwar period ushered in the rise of what one historian called "Demotic times," meaning the rise of an inclusive mass society that sought to understand the fair position and relationship of all of its members. The existentialists, who had critiqued Western culture with an eye towards tearing it down, inadvertently helped give context to movements that would work within the Western tradition to improve it. As more groups placed increasing demands upon the governments of the West, the influence and scope of government increased. Thus postwar period prosperity and political stability produced its own complexities

The rising integration of Europe and the influence of the United States on European culture produced, by the 1960s, a nationalist backlash, especially in France. This was manifested politically by French obstinacy in economic cooperation and withdrawal from NATO. It was manifested socially by rising anti-Americanism. By the late 1960s and into the 1970s, demonstrations, especially by college students, against the American war in Vietnam, against the continued presence of hundreds of thousands of American soldiers in Europe, and against signs of creeping American cultural dominance grew. The continued rise of English language as the growing *lingua franca*—common language of international exchange—with its obvious Anglo-American bias, prompted further backlash. France, for example, began passing laws banning the use of English words from entertainment programs on French national television and from advertising. Thus, even as European integration occurred, nationalist sentiment also began something of a renaissance.

The challenge to Western values begun by the existentialists in the 1940s and 1950s was expanded by a new generation of social activists in the 1960s. Traditional values such as the assumed dominance of males in society, the assumed superiority of the traditional family structure of children within marriage, the assumed dominance of European and Western cultures and ethnicities over their nonwestern counterparts, even the assumed dominance of humans over nature, were all called into question. Between the 1950s and 1960s a number of social

and political movements began in the West, each challenging fundamental tenants of traditional Western culture.

The rise in prosperity had freed women from the necessity of household labor and, even more important, from that of procreation itself. The large family with children as a labor-source was no longer needed in the affluent consumer households. Indeed, having many children was increasingly seen as an economic drain as each child necessitated an ever increasing number of consumer purchases to maintain the accustomed lifestyle: more televisions, toys, clothes, and shoes needed be bought. The introduction of fairly safe and effective contraceptive methods by the 1960s furthered this process, ushering in the Sexual and Feminist Revolutions. Women in the U.S. and Europe began to organize to politically and socially promote greater equality, both in economic opportunity and social stature.

The Women's Movement built on the rising success of the quest by racial and ethnic minorities for greater parity in society and the economy. In the United States, African Americans began to petition and demonstrate for greater equality and protection of their constitutionally granted civil rights. Individual acts of defiance, such as Rosa Parks' (1913-) refusal to sit in the back of a Montgomery, Alabama bus, and charismatic leadership of activists, such as Malcolm X (1925-1965) and Martin Luther King (1929-1968), strongly influenced by the strategies of disruptive non-violence used by Gandhi in India, forced major political and social change. In 1954 the United States Supreme Court officially ended sponsored segregation in American schools. In 1964 the United States government passed its Civil Rights Act, which sought to end racially based discrimination in the political and social arena.

Black citizens picketed schools in St. Louis, Missouri, in the United States in 1963 protesting the policy of school segregation.

In academia the 1960s saw a rise in the debate over cultural relativism, the charge that Western-dominated science and philosophy had unfairly advanced its own values over those of other civilizations. As a new generation of non-European thinkers, such as Amilcar Cabral (1924-1973) of Guinea, came upon the scene, the proponents of value systems other than that of Western liberal capitalism or Judeo-Christianity, challenged the cultural and academic "hegemony" of the Western cannon of ideas.

So too did the Environmental Movement develop, challenging the traditional Western notion that man existed as master of nature. As the first pictures of earth—a small, blue orb in a sea of endless blackness—came back from early space exploration, the interconnectivity of humans to their environment took on new meaning. Postwar economic expansion had also meant a tremendous increase in the production of pollutants and trash. Rising global population also put an increasing strain on natural resources and on entire ecosystems. By the end of 1960s, the Age of Prosperity was giving way to the Age of Limits.

The social welfare state, rising in the nineteenth century to provide a minimum standard of living to workers in exchange for their political and social obedience, was now increasingly tasked with rising standards of living for all members of society and improving the quality of life in general. As the economies of the West moved in the 1950s and 1960s away from heavy industry and more towards providing consumer products and services, so did government in the postwar period become a "service" provider. In Britain and on the European continent pro-labor governments provided guarantees of employment to their workers, access to universal healthcare, and improved educational opportunities. Japanese workers were promised lifetime employment within the great national corporations in exchange for loyal service and dedicated hard work: the famous "salaryman" unselfishly giving 60 or more hours each week to the company good was born. Even in the United States, where laissez-faire principles ran truest, by the 1960s government had embarked upon a "War on Poverty" and established at least minimal universal medical care for the old and disabled. By the 1960s the world wars had receded into history, displaced by the current tensions of the cold war, and, for Western nations, the incredible prosperity of the postwar period. The issues left unresolved by the war—the divisions between East and West, between North and South, between rich and poor, between modern and traditional, had been subsumed during the 1950s by the struggle to recover from the cumulative affects of two world wars. Postwar economic and political stability, however, was to be increasingly challenged by the economic, political, and social upheavals of the later 1960s and 1970s, the product of these unresolved tensions.

Suggestions for Further Reading

Graham T. Allison and Philip Zelikow, *Essence of Decision: Explaining the Cuban Missile Crisis* (1999).

Christopher Andrew and Oleg Gordievsky, *KGB: The Inside Story* (1990).

Jacques Barzun, *From Dawn to Decadence: 500 Years of Western Cultural Life* (2000).

Bernard Lewis, *What Went Wrong: Western Impact and Middle Eastern Response* (2001).

John McCormick, *Understanding the European Union: A Concise Introduction* (1999).

James E. McClellan and Harold Dorn, *Science and Technology in World History: An Introduction* (1999).

John George Stoessinger, *Nations in Darkness— China, Russia, and America* (1990).

Birdsall S. Viault, *Modern European History* (1990).

Martin Walker, *The Cold War: A History* (1995).

Chapter 24

A NEW EUROPE & THE TWENTY-FIRST CENTURY

Margaret Thatcher (1925-) is one of the most prominent European woman of the twentieth century. She made her mark not merely by being Great Britain's first female prime minister, and one of the few women to lead a modern state, but by pursuing and implementing a conservative agenda that shaped the course of European politics in the 1980s.

According Mrs. Thatcher, it was her father who influenced her early years. Thatcher's father was a strict Methodist who ran an austere household. So parsimonious was he, that he refused to install hot water in the bathroom until after World War II. Margaret gained entrance to Oxford and upon enrolling soon found herself actively involved in campus politics. At Oxford she joined the student Conservative club, becoming the organization's president by her fourth year. Upon graduating with a degree in chemistry, she took jobs with a plastics firm and then with a company in which she tested cake mixes. The Conservative Party had opened its doors to women in the post-war years, and Thatcher became one of the first of her generation of women to not only join the party but to run for office. At the age of twenty-four, Thatcher lost her first bid for a seat in Parliament in a solidly Labour district.

In 1951 Margaret married Denis Thatcher, owner of a lucrative chemical company. Freed from the necessity to earn a living, Mrs. Thatcher returned to school to study law, passing the bar in 1953. Over the next few years, she practiced law, gave birth to twins, and spent her spare time seeking a politically "suitable" (a Conservative district) place to live where she could run again for Parliament and win. Thatcher had trouble convincing some Conservative clubs that a woman should get their nomination. In 1958, however, she outworked and outtalked two hundred aspirants for a solid Conservative seat, which she represented for the next thirty years.

Working her way up through the party hierarchy, she became party leader in 1975 and prime minister in 1979. Thatcher stood out and dominated the English political scene with combative assurance. She reiterated time and again how she wanted to return Great Britain to the days when the ethos of rugged individualism prevailed and had made England the most powerful, advanced, and secure nation in the world. When Argentine troops seized the Falkland Islands in 1982, she ordered her military to throw them out by force, which they did, to the rousing cheers of the British people. When coal miners struck, she stonewalled them into defeat. These forceful acts earned her the nickname "the Iron Lady."

Thatcher also inspired her countrymen, or at least a good portion of them. When dissidents in the Conservative Party voted a no confidence in her in 1990, she could and did look back on solid, if controversial, accomplishment. She privatized previously government-owned industry, totaling about 5 percent of the British economy; she curbed the power of the trade unions, which she thought had crippled British industrial productivity and innovation; she created millions of new homeowners by selling off public housing; and she had presided over a significant revitalization of the British economy. Had the rich got richer and the poor poorer? Had she blocked European unification? Had she turned loose a generation of self-serving nouveau riche? Margaret Thatcher dismissed such criticisms with contempt. Defiant, brazen, confident, tough, and able, Thatcher was Britain's most important and dominating leader since Winston Churchill.

Chronology

1968   Days of May uprising in France. Prague Spring reform movement crushed.

1969   Willy Brandt become West German chancellor.

1973   First OPEC oil crisis begins.

1978   Kidnapping and assassination of Aldo Moro in Italy.

1979   Margaret Thatcher becomes prime minister of Britain.
First direct elections to European parliament.

1980   Formation of Solidarity in Poland.

1981   Socialist Francois Mitterand elected president of France.

1982   Death of Leonid Brezhnev in the Soviet Union.

1985   Mikhail Gorbachev comes to power in Soviet Union.

1986   Explosion at Chernoybl nuclear power plant.

1989   Collapse of communism in east-central Europe.

1990   Reunification of Germany.

1991   Collapse of communism in Soviet Union; dissolution of the Soviet Union.
Beginning of fighting in Yugoslavia
Maastrict agreement expanding scope of the EC.

Attempted coup in Russia to over throw Gorbachev.

1992   Boris Yeltsin elected president of Russia.

1995   American intervention with bombing in Bosnian crisis.

1999   Escalation of violence in the Balkans; Serbian invasion of Kosovo and more American bombing of Serbian forces and strongholds.

2000   In closest election ever in United States history, Republican George W. Bush elected president of the United States.

2001   Most devastating terrorist attack ever, as two jetliners crash into the World Trade Center towers in New York City, killing thousands.

2002   Advent of the Eurodollar and the beginning of uniform currency system in Europe.

The second half of the twentieth century witnessed profound social, economic, intellectual, and political changes throughout Europe. One of the most important of these changes occurred with the creation of the European Economic Community and subsequent European Union. Other important transformations, overshadowed by the Soviet Union-United States rivalry, occurred quietly and with little fanfare. For example, Western Europe experienced unprecedented economic expansion; much of Western European and even Eastern European culture became "Americanized," as consumers in both regions increasingly enjoyed more goods and services than ever before. A second agricultural revolution made Europe still more urban, with fewer people living on the land. The role of women in the workplace and in the larger society became more important than during any previous historical era. A distinct youth culture emerged and continues to flourish, affecting economic, social, and political life. The Roman Catholic Church has become less dominant as increasing numbers of Europeans have found spiritual solace in more secular institutions and movements. Science has made remarkable advances in virtually every area of research. The effects of technology and industrialism, however, has created growing concern for the environment in Europe and the United States.

The last decades of the twentieth century saw astonishing and largely unexpected political changes that will bring still further social and economic changes. For example, after more than two decades of cold war, Europeans had become accustomed to a divided East-West Europe. A prosperous Western Europe had developed, closely tied to the United States, and stood opposed to a struggling and oppressed Eastern Europe largely under Soviet hegemony. The division of Germany symbolized this order. Within another two decades, however, this supposedly entrenched polarization convulsed into revolutionary upheaval first in the Soviet Union then reverberated throughout the former satellites leading to an end of communism, the cold war, and the division of Europe. By the 1990s, an era of cooperation developed between the former Eastern bloc and successor states of the former Soviet Union and the West. As result of the Soviet collapse, Germany again became united, the nations of Eastern Europe became independent, and, until recently, a bloody and vicious civil war had raged in the former Yugoslavia. A new Europe has clearly emerged after a period of flux and redirection that in recent history can only be compared with the period immediately after the Great War and World War II.

DEMOCRACY AND ITS DISCONTENT

Post-1968 European Politics

A kind of breaking point was reached in 1968 European politics, especially in the West. In many ways the upheavals of that momentous year mirrored those taking place in the United States. In both Europe and the United States it was disaffected and alienated youth that challenged the established order. Young people on both continents believed that traditional democratic assumptions had failed to bring about necessary social reforms, and, instead, a conservative elite had taken control of their respective societies, determined to preserve the status quo at all costs. This elite had also pursued an "imperialist" foreign policy—the Vietnam War for the United States and a senseless, arrogant, and aggressive foreign adventurism spearheaded by Charles de Gaulle's internationalism. Although democracy had succeeded remarkably well, by the late sixties a sense of political alienation had emerged that shattered over a decade of prosperity and stability. New economic difficulties also affected the European political mood, but the breaking point was reached earlier when prosperity was at its nadir.

The shock waves from the 1968 protest movements continued throughout the seventies, as new issues emerged and new political alignments and forms of political action developed. Even though reform efforts had accomplished much, expectations had been raised, and when continued reforms either were too slow in coming or were never implemented, frustration and alienation remained high. Often the challenges

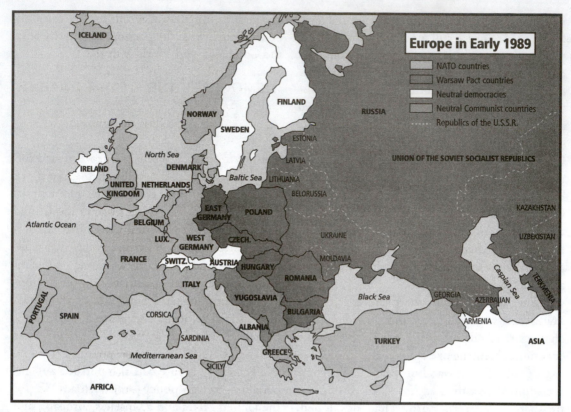

Europe in Early 1989

- NATO countries
- Warsaw Pact countries
- Neutral democracies
- Neutral Communist countries
- Republics of the U.S.S.R.

to traditional democracy were in the form of terrorist violence, and thus the ability of governments to maintain order became a major issue. It sometimes seemed that the postwar political consensus, the basis for two decades of success since the war, was about to unravel.

The most dramatic eruption of radical protest was the "Days of May" uprising that shook France during May 1968. Although initially failing in its revolutionary intent, it ultimately forced Charles de Gaulle's resignation as France's president in 1969. It also proved to be a watershed for the political left in France and elsewhere. The movement was partly a reaction against de Gaulle's Fifth Republic agenda, especially his preoccupation with France's international role. But it was mainly a reaction to the imbalance and inequities that had emerged in French society as a result of technocratic modernization, which was perceived by many to have caused a glaring discrepancy between the quality and quantity of French life. Student activists and New Left advocates believed that too few French citizens had benefited from post war prosperity and modernization and that poverty and political oppression were still too prevalent to allow French politicians to proclaim that France was a truly democratic country. De Gaulle's and his predecessors' economic agenda had produced impressive economic growth, but many Frenchmen felt they had not reaped any of the benefits, particularly in the areas of social services, as problems in housing and education continued or even worsened.

It was within French higher education that the above problems first manifested themselves.

Enrollment in French universities had quadrupled since 1939. Apart from a few highly selective *grandes ecoles*, the institutions of the state-run university system were open to anyone who passed the same entrance exam, and it was not considered politically feasible to limit enrollments by restricting access. Instead, the government simply physically expanded the system to keep up with demand. In the process the universities became vast, impersonal institutions with classrooms with too many students, professors who paid little attention to their students, and, worst of all, the universities were run by authoritarian, bureaucratic administrators determined (in the eyes of students and faculty) to crush any opposition to their view of what higher education should be or provide. Despite some changes in the curriculum, students still felt that universities were not providing an education relevant to student needs and the realities of the modern age. Increasingly students and faculty found the university a place void of intellectual creativity and academic freedom. Instead, universities had become the bastions of bourgeois values and conformity, imposing upon students and faculty a regimen of discipline and an irrelevant curriculum designed not to promote intellectual curiosity or independent thinking but rather to perpetuate the status quo by churning out yet another system "product": a technocrat. This discontent led to an outburst of student revolts in the late 1960s. In part these protests were an extension or amplification of the spontaneous disruption in United States universities in the mid-1960s, which were often sparked by student opposition to the Vietnam War. Many American students perceived their "multiversities" (vast, overpopulated, impersonal institutions run by myopic bureaucrats and administrators, who processed students through education "mills," churning out by the thousands every year, unthinking and uncaring "products") in the same light as their European counterparts. Indeed, as early as 1962, with the Port Huron Manifesto of the Students for a Democratic Society, many of the issues and demands that came to the fore in the 1968 student revolts in Europe were first articulated by American students in that declaration.

The "Days of May" first erupted at the University of Nanterre outside of Paris but soon spread to the Sorbonne, the main campus of the University of Paris. French students demanded a greater voice in the running of the university, took over buildings, and then expanded the scale of their protests by inviting workers to join. The students rather naively believed that industrial workers were just as alienated and victimized by "the bourgeois system" as they were. French radical students, like their American counterparts, were influenced by New Left political ideology, which asserted that an alliance could be formed between educated youth and workers, both of whom had the same oppressor: the bourgeois technocrats who controlled French politics and education. Though the student movement grew strong enough to shake the government, it failed in its hope to rally to its cause the working class and union activists. Though half of France's workers went on strike in May 1968, the de Gaullist government defused the potential for a student-worker alliance by giving workers a hefty wage hike. The workers returned to their jobs, and the police repressed the remaining student protestors. In the end, the students settled for relatively limited concessions. But their rising, like that of American students, brought home to the government that the university system needed a major overhaul and that faculty and students had to be involved in the reform process. Over the next several years, the Education Ministry moved forward on a significant reform

Student opposition to the Vietnam War sparked protests in many Western European countries as well as in the United States.

effort, breaking existing institutions into smaller, more manageable, responsive, and accessible entities. Also, faculty and students were granted a greater voice in institutional governance.

The French revolt spurred student protests elsewhere in Europe, although none of them succeeded in becoming mass movements. In West Berlin, university students led a protest against Axel Springer, leader of Germany's largest newspaper establishment. Many German students were motivated by a desire to destroy what they considered to be the corrupt old order, but their attempt at revolutionary violence backfired as angry Berliners supported police repression of the students. The student protest movement reached its zenith in 1968, although scattered incidents lasted into the early seventies. There were several reasons for the emergence of student radicalism. Some students were genuinely motivated by the desire to reform the university. Others protested the Vietnam War, which they viewed as the result of the military-industrial

complex and Western imperialism. They also attacked other aspects of Western society and culture, such as its materialism, and expressed grave reluctance about becoming technocrats or bureaucrats in the soulless and impersonal world of a corporation. For many students, the calls for the democratization of universities were a reflection of their deeper concerns about the direction of Western society.

In Italy comparable frustration with the political system developed during the sixties as many Italians, particularly working class, found themselves lagging far behind the middle class in material gains. As a result, increasing numbers of working class Italians gravitated to the left, swelling the ranks of the Socialist Party, which challenged the conservative to centrist Christian Democratic Party's hegemony of Italian politics. This clash between the left and the Christian Democrats unleashed a powerful wave of radicalism, manifested in labor militancy, which began during the "hot Autumn" of 1969 and continued into the early seventies. Beginning in the fall of 1969, workers demanded concessions, and if the companies for whom they worked failed to meet their demands, the workers did not hesitate to strike. Such unrest and militancy was especially prevalent in the industrial north, historically a hotbed of labor unrest and radical politics since the early twentieth century. Unlike the past, however, the strikes and labor actions of 1969 were notable for their new methods and demands. Workers sought not just higher wages but actual power or control over factory organization and work, including a major say in the investment decisions of the companies involved. The working class rank and file often took the initiative in these labor actions, reflecting a new determination to do things themselves instead of waiting for the established leftist parties or trade unions to issue the call to action. To many Italian workers, those traditional parties and organizations had become entrenched, unresponsive, impersonal, and elitist institutional bureaucracies, no different in attitude and policy than the corporations for whom they worked.

By the early seventies, the workers had won considerable concessions, including, in some industries like automobile production, actual control of the work place as well as shared decision-making with management. Their victories over management and their innovations in the work place attracted leftists and labor attention all over Europe. A sort of second "renaissance" had occurred in Italy, and this time it emanated from the bottom up rather than from the top down. Unfortunately, the gains made proved ephemeral. As the economic climate steadily deteriorated after 1973, employers regained control of their industries as workers, desperate to keep their jobs amid increasing unemployment throughout Italy and Europe, were willing to forfeit their earlier triumphs for the sake of job security. By the end of the decade (the 1970s), workers in Italy and the rest of Europe once again found themselves on the defensive.

At first glance, the parties of the Marxist left appeared the likely beneficiaries of the popular discontent of the late 1960s. But in France the 1968 uprising only deepened divisions within an already polarized Communist Party and initiated a growing disenchantment with Marxism among French intellectuals and radical youth. French communism seemed old and stale to many of those, especially young people, who believed the promise of 1968 could still be translated into substantial change. Many intellectuals and radical youth found new ideological solace in the New Left social philosophy of Herbert Marcuse and others. In *One Dimensional Man*, published in 1964, Marcuse argued that capitalism had undermined the dissatisfaction of the oppressed masses by encouraging consumption of material things. He proposed that a small cadre of unindoctrinated students could liberate the masses from the control of the capitalist ruling class. Once the masses realized that they had been "duped" by the capitalist bourgeoisie, they would join with the "enlightened" students and other disgruntled and alienated middle class professionals and overthrow (with the use of violence, if necessary) the bourgeois technocrats and bureaucrats who had economically and socially oppressed them for decades. Perhaps more important, Marcuse and other New Left advocates believed that the key player in the uprising was neither the students or the workers but rather the middle class professional or "white" collar worker who had been exploited emotionally, spiritually, and intellectually rather than materially, as in the case of the industrial working class. Once these individuals realized that their oppressors had stripped them of their humanity and creativity and had turned them into an empty, soulless automaton, then they would become the vanguard of revolutionary change and the leader of the new socialist order.

The French Socialist Party, overshadowed by the communists since the war, gained dramatically during the 1970s as it claimed the mantle of the New Left that had emerged in 1968. The situation in Italy was more complex but the forms of protest in 1969 indicated a growing alienation from a political establishment that now seemed to include the established left.

THE OIL CRISIS AND THE CHANGING ECONOMIC FRAMEWORK

As the Western European political scene became more volatile, events outside Europe dramatically illustrated how interdependent the world had become by the early 1970s. Perhaps more important, these events proved to be "comeuppance" for the West, for they showed that neither Europe nor the United States held all the trump cards. In the fall of 1973, Egypt and Syria attacked Israel, seeking to avenge the losses they suffered in the brief war of 1967. Although the invaders were defeated, in the aftermath, in a show of solidarity, the Arab nations of the oil-rich Middle East united to retaliate against the Western bloc for supporting Israel. By restricting the production and distribution of the oil they controlled, the Arab-led OPEC caused an oil shortage, which drove prices steadily upward, causing severe economic disruption in Western Europe, which was heavily dependent on Middle Eastern oil. By January 1975 the price of oil was six times what it had been three years earlier before the embargo. Inflated oil prices remained intact until the early 1980s. Perhaps most important, the immediate European response to the embargo dramatized that the Common Market was not as economically integrated as many believed. When OPEC imposed especially harsh sanctions on the Netherlands, which had strongly supported Israel in the war, the other members of the Common Market refused to stand by the Netherlands and, instead, negotiated separately with the cartel for their own benefit.

The 1970s saw the beginning of a new economic problem "stagflation," which was (and is) sharply reduced rates of growth combined with inflation and rising unemployment. The economic miracle that had transformed much of Western Europe in the previous decades had clearly ended. This was due, in part, because the European economies were affected by growing competition from non-Western countries, most notably Japan. Everywhere the labor movement was on the defensive because of increasing global competition, technological change, and high unemployment. These more difficult economic times deepened the disaffection evident by the late 1960s and intensified the challenge to the democratic political order.

THE WESTERN DEMOCRACIES IN THE SEVENTIES

How adaptable to the leftist challenges were the governments of France, Italy, and Germany in the 1970s? In Germany, the Socialists had been "co-opted" by the ruling SPD, becoming part of an integrated two-party system that shared power equally with the SPD by the mid-seventies. In France and Italy, by contrast, the left sought ways to escape what seemed increasingly sterile opposition. In all three countries there were also questions about the legitimacy or viability of the ruling conservatives.

In France, the central issue became whether the unique persona of Charles de Gaulle was essential to the functioning of the Fifth Republic and even to the cohesion of the conservative coalition that had governed France under de Gaulle's auspices since 1968. For ten years de Gaulle ruled France according to his own priorities, all of which revolved around making France a great power again, equal to the United States, Soviet Union, and England. The student protests, however, of 1968 nearly toppled his government and, in 1969 de Gaulle resigned after some minor constitutional changes he had proposed were rejected in a referendum. Even before de Gaulle's retirement, his eventual successor, Georges Pompidou (1911-1974), worked to move the informal Gaullist party and the regime away from exclusive identification with de Gaulle. Pompidou and his conservative to moderate successors cemented both the legitimacy of the Fifth Republic and the ongoing role of the Gaullist coalition. To be sure, the conservative Gaullists became increasingly unpopular during the troubled 1970s and were finally defeated in 1981. But opposition to the Gaullists emerged from within the Republic and the system, thus representing no radical challenge to the Republic's and system's foundations and functioning. Despite de Gaulle's departure, French political life became remarkably stable down to the present. In contrast to de Gaulle, his various successors, most importantly Valery Giscard d'Estaing (b. 1926), a Gaullist, and Francois Mitterrand (1916-1996), a Socialist, strongly supported European unification. Mixed electoral results have required the various French political parties to learn to cooperate and accommodate. Such an accord and co-optation has provided France with over two decades of political stability and peace.

The Italian situation was more dramatic. The severity of the economic downturn of the 1970s and the concomitant growth of terrorism produced a genuine crisis in the Italian body politic, which saw the ruling Christian Democrats continue to be mired in *trasformismo*—regionalism, shortsighted political patronage, and behind-the-scenes dealing. Italian public life desperately needed revitalization, yet only the Communists seemed strong enough to provide an alternative, or at least some novel departure. Since the war, the Communists had done well at organization and governance on the local and regional levels, so they had gradually attained a significant degree of credibility in postwar Italian life. In the 1976 parliamentary elections they won 34.4 percent of the vote, a new high.

Seeking to translate that support into a more significant national role, the Communists, under Enrico Berlinguer (1922-1984), offered what they called an "historic compromise." Knowing this new accommodation or "coopting" with the opposition would lose their more militant followers, Berlinguer, nevertheless, offered to participate in a coalition government with the Christian Democrats, sharing responsibility for the measures necessary to deal with the growing economic crisis. Though there was much negotiation talk, the Christian Democrats had no real intention of compromising with their long-time adversaries, and in the end the Communists were outmaneuvered and got little in return for their willingness to cooperate. Although Italian Communist were effective at the local levels, many were reluctant to entrust the party with power at the national level. The Communists' long-range goals for Italy were perceived as nebulous and doctrinaire. Also, a Communist role in the national government would surely raise questions about Italy's place in NATO.

By the end of the 1970s, the Communists' attempts at compromise with the Christian Democrats seemed futile. The Christian Democrats talked about the possibility, but in reality they remained as intransigent as before the decade. They knew that neither the United States or even other Western Europeans would welcome such a coalition, fearing not only NATO's security and stability but the welfare of the EEC as well. There also lingered a suspicion, despite Italian proclamations to the contrary, that Italian communists, especially if the more "hard-liners" gained control of the party, would drift into the Soviet camp.

By the late 1970s, support among younger people and intellectuals declined appreciably and the Communists Party's share of the vote in national elections fell from its 1976 peak. But if communism, for better or worse, could not mount a credible strategy for revitalizing Italian politics, Italy seemed saddled with an endless reshuffling of ministries dominated by Christian Democrats, a system that looked unstable on the surface but was in reality more stagnant than volatile. It was a system the bred increasing apathy, cynicism, and political alienation among the Italian electorate.

As the 1970s progressed, a new form of political action emerged in Western Europe, reflecting the sense of frustration and disillusionment many felt because of the stagnation and immobility of the established leftist parties. Unfortunately this new call to action advocated the use of violence in the form of terrorism to overthrow the conservative status quo, as well as to try to energize the left with a new radicalism. Such brutality grew to alarming proportions, especially in Italy and Germany, reaching a zenith of havoc in 1977 and 1978. In Italy the terrorist organization known as the Red Brigade assassinated a number of prominent public officials and businessmen, most notably the long-time Christian Democratic leader, Aldo Moro, in 1978. In Germany, the Baader-Meinhof gang perpetrated similar acts of violence. By the late seventies,

left and right-wing extremism fed each other, and it was right-wing terrorists who were responsible for the worst incident of the era, a bombing in the railway station in Bologna in northern Italy that killed eighty-five people in August 1980.

Political frustration did not always lead to violence and terror, as the majority of the disgruntled still believed in the "system" and continued to work within it to find new ways of battling the inertia. New coalitions developed around new politicized issues—from abortion to the environment—that had not been associated with the Marxist left. In Italy such popular initiatives from below led to referenda on particular issues, which provided the left with a new way of breaking the Christian Democratic stranglehold on Italian politics and simultaneously offer the electorate with a new leftist platform or vision that revitalized the movement. Use of the referendum tactic forced the Italian parliament to enact one of the most liberal abortion laws in Europe in 1978.

In Germany, the Green movement formed by peace and environmental activists during the late seventies, went to great efforts to avoid acting and developing into a conventional party. Its "platform" was interestingly nationalistic yet reflected a non-partisan, "universalist" facet as well. Concerned that Germany with its central location would end up the devastated battleground in any superpower confrontation, the Greens called for an end to the arms race as well as the stopping of any more deployment of United States' missiles on German soil. The SPD, as the governing party in an important NATO state, seemed unable to confront this issue effectively and lost members as a result, as increasing numbers of young Germans joined the Green movement and other apolitical organizations whose agendas transcended conventional issues and partisan politics.

REEVALUATING THE WELFARE STATE

After World War II, increasingly Western European governments accepted greater responsibility for their citizens' well-being. Of all the Western democracies, it was England's welfare system that was recognized as the most viable, stable, and entrenched. By the early 1970s, the percentage of the British economy allocated to maintaining the welfare system, public housing, and education was 18.2 percent. That figure was about average for the industrialized nations of the West. Sweden had the highest percentage of its public expenditure at 23.7 percent.

Sweden

In Sweden, as in Great Britain, the economy remained fundamentally capitalist, based on private ownership; its nationalized, or government-owned and managed sector, was not disproportionate by European standards. But Sweden's social insurance system was the most extensive in Europe, and the government worked actively with business to promote full employment and to direct the economy into areas deemed socially desirable. The Swedish welfare state came to be identified in the minds of many Swedes with the powerful trade unions, which secured for their workers relatively high wages and even the power of a quasi veto over legislation. Government welfare measures, however, were costly. By the early seventies, over 40 percent of Sweden's national income went for taxes to finance the system. Swedes paid the highest tax rate in the world. In Sweden, as elsewhere, the economic strains of the seventies made the welfare state increasingly more difficult to manage and maintain. By the mid-seventies, critics of the system emerged throughout the Western democracies, asserting that the welfare state had caused the decline in individual initiative and productivity essential for success in the increasingly competitive global economy. Sweden rather abruptly found itself less competitive, both because its wages were so high and because it was not keeping abreast of technological developments. Swedish efforts to adjust to the changing circumstances simply accelerated the dissolution of the postwar consensus that had sustained the welfare state. By 1980 unemployment and efforts to cut government spending led to the most severe labor unrest the country had experienced since the war.

Britain

In Britain, a dramatic assault on the welfare state developed simultaneously. Until the early 1970s, there was majority political, as well as popular, support for the British welfare system; even Conservatives had accepted the system's essentials, not dismantling any part of it when they returned to power from 1951-1954. By the 1970s, however, that consensus began to unravel.

During the 1950s and 1960s, the British economy grew at an annual rate of only 2.8 percent, less than half the rate in Germany and even Italy. Even as growth slowed all over Western Europe during the 1970s, the British economy continued to lag, indices showing only half the growth rate of the other Western industrial democracies. Between 1968 and 1976, the nation lost one million manufacturing jobs. By the mid-seventies economic decline threatened to shatter Britain's postwar settlement, because there was no consensus over how to apportion the pain of the greater austerity that the situation seemed to demand. During the decade, both of Britain's two major political parties—the Conservatives and Labour—made serious efforts to ameliorate the conditions, but to no avail. The Conservatives got their chance between 1970-74 with the Edward Heath government, but Heath failed even though he was an energetic moderate with a good deal of technocratic expertise. No matter what he tried, the end result was widespread strikes, the most debilitating being the coal miners' strike of 1974 that toppled Heath's government.

Labour did not fair any better when its turn came from 1974-79. Government efforts to limit wage increases soon produced an open rupture with the unions, the bread and butter support of the Labour Party since its inception in the 1890s. A wave of strikes during the winter of 1978 and 1979 battered the Labour government, contributing to its defeat by the Conservatives in the 1979 elections. The growing split between the Labour Party and the trade unions made the party's future course and existence precarious at best.

The Conservatives, by contrast, were united and prepared to offer Britons an alternative direction and series of policies to implement this new agenda. With the defeat of the moderate Heath in 1974, the Conservative Party moved to the right, away from consensus over the welfare state. The election of the "hard" Conservative Margaret Thatcher as party leader in 1975 was a turning point. When she became prime minister in 1979, it was clear that Britain was about to embark on a radically different course, which will be discussed later in the chapter.

FROM COLD WAR TO POST-COLD WAR

Toward a New World Order

By the 1970s, United States-Soviet relations entered a new phase called détente. This new accord was highlighted by a reduction of tensions and enmity between the two superpowers, which was largely the result of President Richard Nixon's trip to China (February 1972) to establish relations with that country and the fear among Soviet leadership that such a rapprochement between China and the United States could lead to much more substantive agreements between the two countries, even an alliance of sorts, all to the detriment of the Soviet Union. Even though such a Soviet foreboding never materialized, Soviet leadership concluded that it was now too risky to continue a hardline policy toward the United States. The Soviet Union would now pursue a course of amelioration of past tensions and even promote "peaceful coexistence."

A symbol of détente was the Antiballistic Missiles Treaty (ABM) in 1972. Despite some lessening of tensions after the Cuban Missile Crisis (October 1962), both the Soviet Union and the United States continued to expand their nuclear arsenals. In the 1960s both nations extended their missiles' destructive power by arming them with multiple warheads. By 1970, the United States developed the capacity to arm its intercontinental ballistic missiles (ICBMs) with multiple independently targeted re-entry vehicles (MIRVs) that enabled one missile to hit ten different targets. With such a United States advantage in first-strike capability, the Soviet Union proceeded to develop a similar, if not superior, weapons delivery system. Between 1968-1972, both sides also developed antiballistic missiles (ABMs), whose purpose was to hit and destroy incoming missiles. In the 1972 ABM Treaty, the two countries agreed to limit the production of these particular missiles.

In 1975, the Helsinki Agreements provided another example of détente between the superpowers. Signed by the United States, Canada, and all the European nations, these accords recognized all borders in Central and Eastern Europe that had been established since the end of World War II, thereby officially recognizing Eastern Europe as a Soviet sphere of influence. The Helsinki Agreements also committed the signatories to recognize and protect the human rights of their citizens. The later mandate became the raison d'etre of President Jimmy Carter's (1977-1981) foreign policy goals. Largely because of the Vietnam debacle, which finally fell to the communists in April 1975, the American people appeared, in the aftermath of such humiliation, to want a retrenchment of the nation's commitment to such active internationalism—a return, in effect, to a quasi-isolationist position. Even though the United States limited its presence and activism in world affairs, hopes nonetheless ran high during the Carter years for the continuation of détente. In the Soviet Union, however, the last of the cold warrior "hardliners," to be premier or First Party Secretary Leonid Brezhnev, saw the United States' retreat as the perfect opportunity for one final expansionist move. In December 1979, while the United States was dealing with the Iranian hostage crisis, the Soviet Union invaded Afghanistan, hoping to restore in that beleaguered country a pro-Soviet regime. All hopes of continued détente dissipated as a result of the Soviet invasion as relations between the two superpowers hardened. President Carter called for economic sanctions against the Soviet Union, which he hoped would force their withdrawal. The president even canceled American participation in the 1980 Summer Olympic Games held in Moscow that year as a symbol of American protest, as well as to demonstrate to the world that the United States was devoted to and determined to uphold the principle of human rights and self-determination, which he believed the Soviets had blatantly violated with their invasion of Afghanistan. Despite Carter's trade embargos and other gestures, the Soviet Union remained in Afghanistan. Carter failed to understand that no degree of pressure was going to force the Soviets out of that country. In the mind of Brezhnev and other party hardliners, Afghanistan was perceived to be a vital area of security for the Soviet Union. Moreover, Afghanistan's neighbor was Iran, at the time in political turmoil as a result of the toppling of the United States-sustained Shah. Iranians, led by Islamic fundamentalist clergymen, blamed the United States for the shah's brutal regime, and as a result, the peopled vented their rage against the United States by capturing its embassy in Teheran in November 1979 and holding as hostages its entire entourage. The Iranian revolution and subsequent hostage crisis was perceived by the Soviet leadership as the perfect time to invade Afghanistan. They believed that the crisis in Iran would immobilize the United States, and in the end the freeing of the hostages would take priority over the use of force or other measures to get the Soviets out of Afghanistan. Also, continued chaos in Iran would so weaken that country that it too could easily be invaded and occupied and become another Soviet sphere of influence, perhaps its most vital one because of its oil. After several months of watching such humiliation on television virtually every night, the Carter administration finally decided to act. In April 1980, a special forces contingent attempted a rescue operation, but it failed most embarrassingly in the Iranian desert, as rescue helicopters crashed into each other, momentarily stranding the rescue teams. This fiasco proved to be the final nail in Jimmy Carter's presidential coffin.

Campaigning on a jingoistic platform by promising a return to American preeminence in world affairs, Ronald Reagan crushed Jimmy Carter in the 1980 election. No sooner was Reagan inaugurated (on that day, January 20,

This picture, which showed Iranians parading their hostages from the U.S. Embassy, had a dramatic effect on foreign policy.

1981, as Reagan gave his inaugural address) than the American hostages in Iran were released, which the new administration took full credit for by asserting that the "new sheriff" in town would not have hesitated to use force to secure their release. All of the harsh rhetoric and practices of the pre-détente decades graphically and dramatically returned. Calling the Soviet Union an "evil empire," Reagan began a costly military buildup, especially in the area of nuclear missiles, that provoked another arms race. Reagan believed, however, that an arms race was precisely the way to an ultimate American victory in the cold war—something no previous cold war president would have ever assumed or asserted. The only other president to approximate such rhetoric was John Kennedy, who while campaigning for the presidency in 1960 claimed that a "missile gap" existed between the United

States and the Soviet Union, whereby our adversary had by far greater quantities of weapons of mass destruction. Upon taking office, however, Kennedy completely reversed his earlier declaration and rather embarrassingly admitted that indeed a gap did exist but in the favor of the United States.

Reagan and his advisors contended that the war in Afghanistan, as well as a faltering Soviet economy, which had been declining for years, would result in an inability of the Soviet Union to match the American buildup, missile for missile, as it had done in the past. The Reagan administration believed that such an attempt by the Soviets would have dire economic repercussions, perhaps even causing the economic and political collapse of the entire Soviet system. The president gambled that the Soviets would not undertake such a risk. In 1982 the Reagan administration introduced the nuclear-tipped cruise missile, whose ability to fly at low altitudes made it difficult to detect. Reagan also became a passionate supporter of the Strategic Defense Initiative (SDI), nicknamed " Star Wars." Its purpose was to create a space shield that would destroy, with lasers, incoming missiles. By providing military support to the Afghan rebels, the Reagan administration helped to maintain a Vietnam-like quagmire in Afghanistan that the Soviet Union could not win. Like the Vietnam scenario for the United States, the war in Afghanistan demonstrated that power of a superpower was limited in the face of a strong nationalist, guerrilla-type opposition.

The End of the Cold War

The accession of Mikhail Gorbachev to First Party Secretary in the Soviet Union in 1985 (see the Gorbachev era later in this chapter) eventually brought a dramatic end to the cold war. By the time of Gorbachev's accession to power, the Soviet system, economically and politically, was already reeling from years of corruption, decay, and obsolescence. Instead of continuing to pursue an aggressive, expansionist foreign policy like his predecessors, Gorbachev decided it was time to examine those policies and their viability before they led to his country's demise. His "New Thinking," as it was called, opened the door to a series of stunning foreign policy changes. For example, in 1987 Gorbachev initiated a plan for arms limitation that led to an agreement with the United States to eliminate intermediate-range nuclear weapons (INF Treaty). Both sides had incentives to curtail the expensive arms race. Gorbachev hoped to make extensive economic and internal reforms while the United States had serious deficit problems. During the Reagan years the United States became the world's greatest

debtor nation, a position it had not witnessed since before the Civil War and certainly at no time during the twentieth century. By 1990 both countries realized that their large military budgets—the arms race, in effect—was making it difficult for them to address their mounting socioeconomic problems.

The years 1989 and 1990 were pivotal in the ending of the cold war. The postwar settlements that had become fixed in Central and Eastern Europe began to unravel as mostly peaceful revolutionary changes swept through Eastern Europe. Gorbachev's policy of allowing greater autonomy for the Communist governments of Eastern Europe meant that the Soviet Union would no longer come to the rescue with the use of military force for those regimes threatened with internal revolt. The unwillingness of the Soviet regime to militarily suppress indigenous reform movements to maintain the status quo, as it had in Hungary in 1956 and in Czechoslovakia in 1968, opened the door to the overthrow of the Eastern European Communist governments. (See The End of Communism in Eastern Europe later in the chapter). On October 3, 1990, the reunification of Germany destroyed one of the most prominent and ominous symbols of the cold war era—the Berlin Wall.

The 1991 Gulf War provided the first major opportunity for testing the new relationship between the United States and the Soviet Union in the post-cold war era. In early August 1990, Iraqi military forces, in a surprise attack, invaded and occupied Kuwait in the northeastern corner of the Arabian Peninsula at the head of the Persian Gulf. The Iraqi pretext for the invasion was that Kuwait was pumping oil from under fields inside Iraqi territory, but the deeper, real reason was Iraq's assertion that Kuwait was legally part of its country. The Iraq invasion of Kuwait prompted an international outcry and the creation of an international force led by the United States (the U.S. supplied over 500,000 military personnel) that ultimately liberated Kuwait and destroyed a substantial part of Iraq's armed forces in the early months of 1991. The Gulf War was the first important military conflict of the post-cold war era. Although Mikhail Gorbachev attempted to persuade Iraq to withdraw its forces from Kuwait before the actual bombing of Iraq began, overall the Soviets played a minor role in the crisis and supported the United States' position and action, including the bombing and invasion of Iraq by primarily U.S. forces. By the end of 1991, the Soviet Union had disintegrated, making any resurrection of global rivalry between the two former adversaries highly unlikely. Although the United States emerged as the world's leading military power by 1992, its role in the creation of a "New World Order" that President George W. Bush, Sr. advocated at the time has yet to be realized.

REFORM AND CHANGE IN THE SOVIET UNION

Between 1964 and 1982 even the slightest change in the Soviet system appeared unlikely. The man in charge, Leonid Brezhnev (1906-1982), had as his slogan "no experimentation." Brezhnev entered the ranks of party leadership during the Stalinist era and, after the overthrow of Krushchev in 1964, became head of both party and state. He had unequivocal faith and commitment to the Soviet system as it was and believed that reforms of any kind would be perceived by the West as a lack of confidence in communist (Marxist-Leninist) ideology. If party leaders did not show the West a whole-hearted belief in Marxist-Leninist doctrine, Brezhnev was convinced such ambivalence would open the door for the Western powers to challenge the Soviet Union's hegemony in Eastern Europe and elsewhere. The Brezhnev doctrine—the right of the Soviet Union to intervene if socialism was threatened in another "socialist state"—became an article of faith and led to the use of Soviet troops in Czechoslovakia in 1968.

Brezhnev benefited from the more relaxed atmosphere associated with détente. The Soviets had reached a rough parity with the United States in nuclear arms and felt secure enough to relax authoritarian rule. The regime permitted more access to Western culture—music, dress, and art—although political dissenters were still punished. Andrei Sakharov, for example, who had played a vital role in the development of the Soviet hydrogen bomb, was placed under house arrest for his defense of human rights, which the Brezhnev regime violated with brutal regularity. In his economic policies, Brezhnev continued to believe (like Stalin) that the Soviet Union lagged behind the West in capital goods production and placed great emphasis on heavy industry. Overall, Soviet industrial growth declined relative to the West, although Soviet production of iron, steel, coal, and cement surpassed that of the United States. Despite such impressive numbers in certain production areas, two problems still bedeviled the Soviet economy. First, the government's insistence on rigid central planning policies led to the creation of a huge, complex, unwieldy, and entrenched bureaucracy that discouraged efficiency, reduced productivity, and, most debilitating, created a byzantine network of corruption, nepotism, and administrative ineptness. Second, equally undermining of production and efficiency was the Soviet system's philosophy of guaranteed employment. This engendered a lack of incentives, while breeding apathy, complacency, absenteeism, and drunkenness.

Joseph Stalin chose the Ukraine as the site of his first kolkhozes, or collective farms.

Agricultural problems compounded Soviet economic woes. Since the 1930s all land was worked "collectively." The state owned all farm land and dictated production and types of crops grown. By the Brezhnev era, Soviet agricultural workers—one cannot use the word farmer—were fed up with collectivization and consequently another Soviet system suffered from lack of worker initiative and incentives. By the 1970s most Soviet agricultural workers preferred working their own small private plots to laboring in the collective in large work gangs. To these modern Russians, to work in such a capacity on the collectives was no different than being a serf—a painful reminder of the type of forced labor their ancestors had done for centuries. To make matters worse, bad harvests in the mid-1970s, caused by a series of droughts, heavy rains, and early frosts, forced the Soviet government to purchase grain from the West, particularly from the United States. To their chagrin, the Soviets were increasingly dependent on capitalist countries to sustain their system.

By the 1970s the Soviet Union had developed a ruling system dependent upon patronage as a means of advancement through party ranks and for the securing of jobs in an increasingly bloated, corrupt, and ineffective bureaucracy that administered the country politically and economically. Ambitious, though incompetent, party hacks and bureaucrats needed the support of successful party leaders. At the same time, party and state leaders—as well as high ranking army officers and the secret police (KGB)—received all matter of "perks" and material privileges the majority of the Russian people would never have. Brezhnev was as responsible for this byzantine network of deceit, corruption, and inefficiency as those at the lower levels who perpetrated it because he refused to reform it. Increasingly, the lack of vigorous leadership in the Soviet Union was becoming all too apparent and difficult to rectify.

By 1980, the Soviet system was on the verge of collapse. A declining economy, a rise in infant mortality rates, a dramatic surge in alcoholism, and a deterioration in working conditions were warning signals that the system was seriously ailing and in desperate need of reform. Within the party a small group of reformers emerged who understood the gravity of the situation. One member of the group was Yuri Andropov (1914-1985), head of the KGB and Brezhnev's successor after the latter's death in November 1982. But Andropov was already old and in poor health when he assumed power, and he was unable to make any significant changes. His most important move may have been his support for a young reformer—Mikhail Gorbachev—who was fast ascending the party hierarchy. After a brief interlude under another sickly member of the old guard, a new era began when party leaders chose Gorbachev to succeed Chernenko in March 1985.

The Gorbachev Era

Born into a peasant family in 1931, Mikhail Gorbachev combined farm work with school and received the Order of the Red Banner for his efforts in helping to increase agricultural productivity on farms in southern Russia. This award coupled with an excellent academic record allowed Gorbachev to go to a university. After graduating from the University of Moscow in 1955 with a law degree, Gorbachev returned home to southern Russia where he eventually became first secretary of the Communist Party in the city of Stavropol (He had joined the party in 1952.) and then first secretary of the regional party committee. After proving himself a loyal party member while implementing some badly needed local reforms without alienating other party members or upsetting the status quo too dramatically, Gorbachev was rewarded by being appointed a member of the party's Central Committee in Moscow in 1978. Two years later, thanks to the patronage of Brezhnev, he became a full member of the ruling Politburo and secretary of the Central Committee. In March 1985 party leaders elected him general secretary of the party, and he became the new leader of the Soviet Union.

No sooner was Gorbachev in power than he quickly renewed some of the earlier attacks on Stalinist rigidity and doctrine while "purging" the party of hardliners, old guard hacks, and other sinecures. He conveyed a new and more Western style of "politicking" and diplomacy, dressing in fashionable clothes (and accompanied by his wife, who was also very personable and charming and equally coiffed), holding open press conferences, and even allowing the Soviet media to engage in active debate and report on problems as well as successes within the system, as well as on events abroad. Gorbachev was determined to pursue détente to the extent of ending the arms race with the United States and ultimately the cold war. Equally important, as far as Soviet foreign policy was concerned, he realized the quagmire of arrogance and futility the invasion of Afghanistan proved to be, and taking a history lesson from the United States ended that conflict before it turned into a Vietnam for his nation.

Educated during the Khrushchev reform years, Gorbachev wanted to take those earlier reforms to their logical conclusions. By the 1980s Soviet economic problems were manifold and obvious. Rigid, centralized planning had led to mismanagement and stifled innovation. Although still in the vanguard of space exploration, the Soviets fell significantly behind the West in high technology, especially in the development and production of computers for private and public use. Of greater visibility and frustration to the Soviet people was the painful reality of their declining standard of living compared to the West. In February 1986 at the Twenty-Seventh Congress of the Communist Party, Gorbachev made clear the need for changes in Soviet society: "The practical actions of the Party and state agencies lag behind the demands of the times and of life itself. . . . Problems grow faster than they are solved. Sluggishness, ossification in the forms and methods of management decrease the dynamism of work. . . . Stagnation begins to show up in the life of society." Thus, from the start of his leadership, Gorbachev advocated broad-sweeping reforms.

The cornerstone of Gorbachev's reform agenda was *perestroika*, or economic restructuring, which the Soviet leader translated into laying the foundations for the gradual evolution toward a market economy with limited free enterprise. In other words, it meant greater leeway for private ownership and, most important, decentralized control of industry and agriculture. For example, farmers were give the opportunity to lease land for fifty years with rights of inheritance. Industrial enterprises were allowed to buy from either private or state operations. Foreign investment was also encouraged, as well as a reduction in Soviet military expenditures, which over the decades of the cold war consumed the lion's share of state revenue. Through agreements with the United States on troop reduction and limitations on nuclear weaponry, Gorbachev was able to free money and resources to help stimulate the creation of and growth of consumer goods industries. Though theoretically and on paper Gorbachev's economic reforms seemed impressive, they proved difficult to implement. Radicals demanded decisive, accelerated transition to capitalism and were impatient with Gorbachev's caution; conservative hardliners feared rapid change would be too painful and lead to upheaval because of capitalism's inherent "flaw" of self-interest and the fostering of rising expectations.

Gorbachev was also perspicacious enough to realize that in the Soviet system, the economic sphere was inextricably linked to the social and political realms. Economic reformation without concomitant meaningful social and political changes would doom the whole experiment to failure. One of the most important aspects of *perestroika* was *glasnost* or "openness." Soviet citizens and officials were encouraged to discuss freely and without fear of reprisals the strengths and weaknesses of the Soviet Union. This policy could be seen in *Pravda,* the official newspaper of the Communist Party, which gave increased coverage to such disasters as the nuclear accident at Chernobyl in 1986 and collisions of ships in the Black Sea. Soon the paper included reports of government corruption, sloppy, hazardous factory work, and protests against official policy. The arts also benefited from glasnost, as previously banned works were now published, and motion pictures began to show negative aspects of Soviet life. Music based on Western styles, such as jazz and rock and roll, began to be performed openly. The discipline of history also benefited greatly from glasnost, as previously closed, secret historical records were now open to not only Russian scholars but foreign ones as well. As a result, within a few years a whole "revisionist" history of the 1917 Russian Revolution, its leaders, and their policies, many of which resulted in mass executions and exile, were revealed for the first time to the world community. Even the once revered Lenin was exposed as a fanatical, almost maniacal, revolutionary ideologue, who, for the sake of the revolution and party, as well as for his own aggrandizement, perpetrated on his people mass arrests and executions, exile to labor camps, secret police, food shortages, mass starvation and epidemics, and bloody civil war. Ironically, such revelations by both Russian and foreign scholars portrayed Lenin and his followers to be just as ruthless and merciless in their policies as the czarist regime they overthrew.

Gorbachev's political reforms were equally profound. In June 1987, the principle of two-candidate elections was introduced; previously voters had been presented with only one candidate, that of the official party designee. Most dissidents, including Andrei Sakharov, who had spent years in internal exile, were released and welcomed back into Soviet/Russian society. At the Communist Party conference in 1988, Gorbachev called for the creation of a new Soviet parliament, the Congress of People's Deputies, whose members were to be chosen in open, free, competitive elections. The Congress convened for the first time in 1989, the first such meeting in Russia since the dissolution of the Duma in 1918. Because of its size, the Congress chose a Supreme Soviet of 450 members to deal with the daily activities and routine of governing the country. The revolutionary nature of Gorbachev's political reforms was evident in Sakharov's rise from dissident to an elected member of the Congress of People's Deputies. As a leader of the dissident faction in the Congress, Sakharov called for the end of the Communist monopoly of power and on the day he died, December 11, 1989, urged the creation of a new non-Communist Party. Early in 1990, Gorbachev legally sanctioned the formation of other political parties and removed Article 6, which had guaranteed the "leading role" of the Communist Party, from the Soviet constitution. At the same time, Gorbachev attempted to consolidate his power by creating a new state presidency. The new position was the result of the separation of the state from the party. Prior to the Gorbachev era, the position of first party secretary was analogous to the head of the Soviet state. As the Communist Party became less closely associated with the state, the powers of this title diminished correspondingly. In March 1990, Gorbachev became the Soviet Union's first president.

Despite all the monumental reforms of the Soviet system, Gorbachev still faced many serious problems, one of which stemmed from the character of the Soviet Union. The U.S.S.R. was a truly multiethnic country, containing 92 na-

tionalities and 112 recognized languages. Previously the iron hand of the Communist Party, headquartered in Moscow, repressed quickly and often ruthlessly any outbursts of ethnic tensions that were endemic in many regions. Gorbachev believed, because of glasnost, that these tensions would not resurface. He was quickly proven wrong. Ethnic groups took advantage of the new openness to protest what they perceived to be ethnically motivated prejudice and slights. As violence erupted, the Soviet army in disarray since Afghanistan had difficulty controlling the situation. In some areas, independence movements and ethnic causes were symbiotic, as in Azerbaijan, where the National Front became the spokesgroup for the Muslim Azerbaijanis in their struggle with the Christian Armenians. The years 1988-1990 also witnessed the emergence of nationalist movements throughout the republics of the Soviet Union. Many were motivated by ethnic concerns with demands for sovereignty of the republics and independence from Russian hegemony centered in Moscow. These movements arose first in Georgia in late 1988 and later in Latvia, Estonia, Moldavia, Uzbekistan, Azerbaijan, and, most dramatically, in Lithuania.

In December 1989, the Lithuanian Communist Party declared itself independent of the Communist Party of the Soviet Union. A leading force in this independence movement was the nationalist Lithuanian Restructuring Movement or Popular Front for Perestroika, commonly known as Sajudis, led by Vytautas Landsbergis. Sajudis also favored independence from the Soviet Union. Gorbachev was willing to grant Lithuania a large degree of autonomy and self-determination but not secession. Despite such concessions, on March 11, 1990, the Lithuanian Supreme Council unilaterally declared Lithuania independent. Its new name was now the Lithuanian Republic; the adjectives Soviet and Socialist had been dropped. On March 15, the Soviet Congress of People's Deputies, though recognizing a general right to secede from the U.S.S.R., declared the Lithuanian promulgation null and void; the Congress stated that proper procedures must be established and followed before secession would be sanctioned.

THE END OF THE SOVIET UNION

During 1990 and 1991, Gorbachev struggled with the Lithuanian crisis and other issues unleashed by his reforms. On the one hand, he tried to placate conservatives who complained about the growing disorder within the Soviet Union by using military force to crush the separatist movements in the nation's Muslim regions. On the other hand, he tried to accommodate liberals, especially those in the Russian republics, who increasingly favored a new kind of decentralized Soviet federation. In particular, Gorbachev labored to cooperate more closely with Boris Yeltsin, who had been elected president of the Russian Republic in June 1991.

By 1991 the conservative elements of traditional Soviet institutions—the government, army, KGB, and military industries—had grown wary of Gorbachev's reforms and general agenda, fearing that the dissolution of the Soviet Union would not only engender worse instability and uncertainty but would impact as well on their own status and fortunes. On August 19, 1991, a group of these alienated rightists arrested Gorbachev and attempted to seize power. Gorbachev refused to capitulate to their demands—a restoration, in effect, of the old order and ways—and largely as a result of Yeltsin's leadership and his ability to rally thousands of Muscovites to Gorbache's rescue, the attempted coup disintegrated. It was obvious from the outpouring of popular support for both Gorbachev and Yeltsin that the Russian people had grown accustomed to their new liberties. Ironically, the attempted coup and its conspirators served to accelerate the very process they had hoped to stop—the disintegration of the Soviet Union.

Despite Gorbachev's desperate pleas, the Soviet Republics soon moved for complete independence. Ukraine voted for independence on December 1, 1991, and a week later the leaders of Russia, Ukraine, and Belarus announced that the Soviet Union no longer existed and would be replaced by a Commonwealth of Independent States. Gorbachev resigned on December 25, 1991 and turned over his responsibilities as commander-in-chief to Boris Yeltsin, the president of Russia. The Soviet flag—the hammer and sickle that had symbolized the nation that for forty years had kept half of Europe in thrall—was lowered for the last time over the Kremlin. By the end of 1991, one of the largest empires in world history had come to an end, and a new era had begun in its lands.

Within Russia, a new power struggle soon emerged. Yeltsin was committed to introducing a free market economy as quickly as possible. In December 1991 he had been granted temporary power to rule by decree by the Congress of People's Deputies. Dominated by the Communists and their allies, who opposed many of Yeltsin's economic measures, the Congress tried to limit his power. Food shortages worsened during the winter of 1992. The value of the ruble plummeted. The republics could not agree on common military policies or resolve difficult and dangerous questions concerning the control of nuclear weapons. Yeltsin's pleas for Western economic assistance brought massive infusions of private and public capital, which unfortunately failed to ameliorate economic hardship and dislocation. The almost forced transition to free enterprise brought unemployment and encouraged profiteering and crime. Yeltsin, however, was determined to forge ahead with his economic agenda. After winning a vote of confidence, both in himself and in his economic reforms on April 25, 1993, Yeltsin continued with plans for a new constitution for Russia that would abolish the Congress of People's Deputies, create a two-chamber parliament, and establish a strong presidency. Despite considerable personal popularity, Yeltsin continued to struggle to gain a political base. No sooner were his political reforms instituted than he found himself pitted against the new parliament, composed mainly of former communists. In the fall of 1993 an armed clash occurred with communist dissidents from which Yeltsin and the army emerged victorious. The ensuing elections produced yet another constitution designed to stabilize democracy, but a divided parliament resulted. The resurgent communists captured the largest block of parliamentary seats, roughly one third. Yeltsin's party, though second in terms of representation, could claim no more than 10 percent.   Perhaps more worrisome for Yeltsin was the emergence of a hard right nationalist block who, led by Vladimir Zhirinovsky, a xenophobe who played on the anxieties of a populace increasingly willing to blame the West for the country's problems. Zhirinovsky and his followers urged militarism and expansionism as a means of restoring Russia to its former greatness. In this muddy situation, Yeltsin slowed economic reforms, generating a set of policies that combined some initiative toward private enterprise with protection for state-run operations. On the diplomatic front, Yeltsin continued collaboration with the West in such trouble spots as the Balkans, although he faced pressures from the nationalists to pursue a more independent Russian policy. Cultural creativity remained high, with greater freedom

to publish, although funding problems paralyzed scientific and technological research.

Meanwhile, ethnic and religious conflict plagued the republics. In the first years following the dissolution of the Soviet Union, warfare flared in Georgia, Armenia, and Azerbaijan. The most serious and bloody conflict erupted in the predominantly Muslim area of Chechyna, bordering Georgia and the Caucasus, which had declared its independence from Russia in late 1991. Three years later the Russian government, weary of this continuing challenge to its authority, launched a military invasion of the area to crush resistance once and for all. The Chechen rebels, however, repulsed the Russian army, demonstrating Russia's military vulnerability in a conflict that led to atrocities on both sides. A truce signed on July 30, 1995, was short lived. The Chechen war dragged on into the new century, a repeat of the Afghanistan conflict for the Russian government.

The Russian economy remained very weak in the late 1990s. Production levels, especially in consumer goods industries, continued a downward spiral and unemployment became a serious problem. In 1998, the economy came near collapse as the value of the ruble plummeted. This jeopardized market reforms and political stability alike as former communists urged new government controls. Only massive loans and investments from the United States stabilized the situation. Many Russians remained convinced that a return to communism was not the answer but were unclear what the alternatives were.

Compounding the political and economic problems was the emergence of organized crime that became widespread and a very lucrative "new" enterprise. Especially profitable was the drug trade, as growing numbers of Russians, especially younger ones, found the use of heroine and other hard drugs to be a way to momentarily escape the uncertainty, frustrations, and disillusionment of the new Russia. Rampant profiteering also became a serious problem, creating a much-resented wealthy class, complete with fancy cars and new nightclubs. There was no clear precedent for this sort of crisis in world history, short of defeat in war, and predictions for the future were uncertain at best. Election of a new president in 2000, Vladimir Putin, did not initially clarify Russia's political or economic directions.

EASTERN EUROPE

From Soviet Satellites to Independent Nations

Inspired by the events in the Soviet Union, the countries of Eastern Europe began to agitate for independence from Moscow. Gorbachev's call for *glasnost* not only applied to his own country but to Eastern Europe as well. He revoked the Brezhnev Doctrine's insistence on single-party socialist governments and made frequent and encouraging trips to the capitals of neighboring satellites. Poland was the first of the satellites in which glasnost rekindled the flame of opposition.

Poland

Under Wladyslaw Gomulka, Poland had achieved a certain stability in the 1960s but economic problems led to Gomulka's ouster in 1971. His replacement, Edward Gierek, attempted to solve Poland's economic crises by borrowing heavily from the West, but in 1980, when he announced huge increases in food prices in an effort to pay off part of the Western debt, workers protested with mass demonstrations and strikes. Unlike the worker unrest of 1956, this time the workers' revolutionary demands led di-

Wladyslaw Gomulka became the Polish Communist Party chief in 1954.

rectly to the rise of the independent labor movement called Solidarity. Led by Lech Walesa, Solidarity represented 10 million of Poland's 35 million people. Almost instantaneously Solidarity became a juggernaut for change and thus a threat to the government's monopoly of power. The movement centered on the vast Lenin shipyard in Gdansk, formerly the German Danzig. Demanding, above all, the right to form their own independent trade unions, seventy thousand workers took over the shipyards. With massive worker support, as well as that of intellectuals and other professionals and, most importantly, that of the Polish Catholic Church, Solidarity was able to win a series of concessions from the ruling Communist Party. Because it had retained some tradition of labor militancy, Poland offered

POPE JOHN PAUL II

the greatest hope for change but an extra ingredient from an unexpected quarter also affected the Polish situation, perhaps in a decisive way. In 1978 the College of Cardinals of the Roman Catholic Church departed from long tradition and for the first time since 1522, elected a non-Italian as Pope. But even more startling was the fact that the new Pope was from Poland, behind the Iron Curtain. This Cardinal, Karol Wojtyla, the archbishop of Cracow, took the name John Paul II. In Poland the Catholic Church had managed to extract a compromise with the communist regime, in contrast to Hungary and Croatia where resistance had led to violent repression. Thus the Polish church remained the most tangible institutional alternative to communism and the focus of Polish national self-consciousness in the face of Soviet domination.

The government seemed powerless to stop the flow of concessions until December 1981, when out of desperation, it arrested Walesa and other Solidarity leaders, outlawed the union, and imposed military rule under General Wojciech Jaruzelski. Martial law, however, did not solve Poland's economic crises. Though Solidarity had been outlawed, the Polish people went "underground" with their support, and when the time was right, the party reemerged, stronger, more popular, and more resolved to overthrow military rule and drive communism out of Poland. The year 1988 proved to be the year of decision. In that year, the union launched a new series of strikes and mass demonstrations. No matter how repressive the government's response, the union was determined to prevail. After much maneuvering and negotiating with Solidarity, the government finally consented to free parliamentary elections—the first free elections in Eastern Europe in forty years—that enhanced Solidarity's strength even further. Accepting the inevitable, Jaruzelski's regime allowed the Solidarity-led coalition in the lower house of the new legislature to elect Tadeus Mazowiecki, one of Solidarity's key leaders, as prime minister. The Communist monopoly of power in Poland had come to an end after forty-five years. In April 1990, it was decided that a new president would be freely elected by the people by the end of the year. In December of that year, Lech Walesa was overwhelmingly chosen as the new Polish president.

The chain of events in Poland culminated in one of the monumental events of modern history—the negotiated end of communist rule. That a communist government might give up power voluntarily was never considered in the realm of even the remotest possibility. Largely because of Gorbachev's desire to reform the Soviet Union, it became clear to the Poles that the likelihood of Soviet military intervention was something they no longer had to fear. Another important factor was the Polish Catholic Church, which acted as mediator, hosting meetings, reminding both sides of their shared responsibilities in the difficult situation facing their country. Even General Jaruzelski, who seemed for most of the 1980s to be just another military strongman, willing to do the Soviet's bidding, proved to be a national hero for his grace, perhaps even ingenuity, in yielding power to the opposition. But most important was the courage, the perseverance, and the vision of Solidarity itself.

Poland's new path has not been an easy one. The presence of more than one hundred political parties has fragmented the political process and created the danger of parliamentary stalemate, while rapid free market reforms have led to severe unemployment and popular discontent. At the same time, the effort of the powerful Catholic Church to secure abortion law reform and religious education in the schools has raised new issues that have divided the Polish people.

Hungary

In Hungary the liberation movement from Communist rule began before 1989. Remaining in power for over thirty years, the government of Janos Kadar enacted the most far-reaching economic reforms in Eastern Europe. In the early 1980s, Kadar legalized small private enterprises, such as retail stores, restaurants, and small craft and artisans shops. His economic agenda was termed "Communism with a capitalist facelift." Most important, Kadar cut not only his country's economic ties to the Soviet Union but political ties as well. He made it clear that he would tolerate no Soviet military intervention in his country and that Hungarian communism was precisely that—uniquely Hungarian. Kadar even established friendly relations with the West. To demonstrate his political independence from Soviet communism, Kadar allowed for multicandidate elections with at least two candidates for each office for the first time on June 8, 1985. As the 1980s progressed, however, the economy sagged, and Kadar fell from power in 1988.

By 1989, the government was aware of the growing dissatisfaction and began to undertake further reforms. New political parties had emerged, and the most dominant ones united to form an opposition Round Table whose negotiations with the Communists led to an agreement that Hungary would become a democratic republic. The government also opened the Hungarian border with Austria and permitted free travel between the two nations, opening the first breach in the Iron Curtain. One immediate result was the movement of thousands of East Germans into Austria through Hungary. From Austria, they proceeded into West Germany. The Hungarian Communist Party changed its name to the Hungarian Socialist Party to have a greater chance of success in the new elections scheduled for March 25, 1990. The party came in fourth, however, winning only 8.5 percent of the popular vote, a clear repudiation of communism despite the party's concessions and reforms. The Democratic Forum, a right of center, highly nationalistic party, won the election and formed a new coalition government that committed Hungary to democratic government and the institution of a free market economy.

Czechoslovakia

Communist regimes in Poland and Hungary had attempted to make some political and economic reforms in the 1970s and 1980s, but this was not the case in Czechoslovakia. After Soviet troops crushed the 1968 reform movement, hardliners under Gustav Husak purged the Czech communist party and pursued a policy of massive repression to maintain their power. Only writers and other intellectuals challenged the regime's often brutal totalitarianism. In January 1977 these dissidents formed Charter 77, an underground organization that protested the government's human rights violations. By the 1980s Charter 77 members became more public in their protestations and not only continued to expose the regime's brutality but also openly criticized its economic policies and political subservience to the Soviet Union. Needless to say, the government responded harshly to such denunciations, rounding up as many movement members as possible and imprisoning them. Despite the government's harsh reprisals, dissident movements continued to grow in the 1980s. Government attempts to suppress mass demonstrations in Prague and other Czechoslovakian cities only led to more and larger protests. By November 1989, crowds as large as 500,000, which included many students, were assembling in Prague. A new opposition group, the Civic Forum, emerged and was officially recognized on November 17. The Czechoslovakian Federal Assembly now voted to delete the constitutional articles giving the Communists the monopoly on state power. In December 1989, as demonstrations escalated, the Communist government, lacking any real support, collapsed. President Husak resigned and at the end of December was replaced by Vaclav Havel, a dissident playwright who had been a leading figure in Charter 77 and who had played an important role in overthrowing the Communist government. In January 1990, Havel declared amnesty for some thirty thousand political prisoners. He also set out on a goodwill tour to various Western countries in which he proved to be an eloquent spokesman for Czech democracy and a new order in Europe.

Within Czechoslovakia, the shift to non-Communist rule was complicated by old problems, especially ethnic issues. Czechs and Slovaks disagreed over the makeup of the new state but were able to agree to a peaceful division of the country. On January 1, 1993, Czechoslovakia split into the Czech Republic and Slovakia. Vaclav Havel, who had resigned as president of Czechoslovakia in July 1992 to protest the planned division of the country, was elected the first president of the new Czech Republic and took office on February 2, 1993.

Romania

In 1948, the Soviets, with the use of military force, helped to establish a Moscow-aligned Communist People's Democratic Front to power in Romania. In 1965, leadership of the Communist government passed into the hands of Nicolae Ceaucescu (1918-1989), who along with his wife and a small coterie of loyal hacks and henchmen, established one of the most brutal and repressive regimes behind the Iron Curtain. Ceausescu ruled Romania with an iron fist, crushing with severe regularity any dissent with his secret police force, the Securitate. His name and regime became synonymous with the worse features of communist totalitarianism. Despite his ferocious determination to crush all opposition to his power (Ceaucescu ruled Romania as a despot, not really accountable to either the Romanian Communist Party or to Moscow) anti-government forces began to gather, as elsewhere behind the Iron Curtain, in the late 1980s. Ceausescu rejected the reforms in Eastern Europe promoted by Gorbachev. Ceausescu's regime had for years stood aloof from the Soviet

Nicolae Ceausescu was repressive and cruel. His secret police ensured the brutal dictator's complete control over Romanian citizens.

Union, especially in foreign policy. In addition, Ceausescu's extreme measures to reduce Romania's external debt led to economic crises. Although he was successful in reducing foreign debt, the dramatic decline in living standards that resulted from the austerity measures generated anger and resentment among many Romanians. Despite food shortages and the rationing of bread, flour, and sugar, Ceausescu insisted that the country continue to export such commodities! Throughout the rest of the Iron Curtain indigenous communist leaders and their respective parties were reforming their systems, albeit reluctantly. They realized, unlike Ceausescu, that Gorbachev's *glasnost* would not allow Soviet intervention to rescue unpopular, fledgling regimes. Thus to forestall or prevent more radical changes, Ceausescu's communist cohorts realized that if they hoped to retain even a modicum of their power, reforms were imperative. Indeed, as already seen in Poland, Hungary, and Czecho-

slovakia, reforms and the ultimate transfer of power from the communist leadership to an opposition group occurred with such minimal violence and upheaval that the transitions in those countries have been dubbed the "Velvet Revolutions." Such was especially the case in Czechoslovakia.

Ceausescu, however, was determined to maintain his hardline, Stalinistic approach. He further alienated Romanians with his plan for rapid urbanization, especially a rural systemization program that called for the bulldozing of entire villages and other rural enclaves. A small incident became the spark that ignited decades of suppressed flames of discontent. The ruthless crushing of a demonstration in Timisoara in December 1989 led to other mass demonstrations. After the dictator was booed at a mass rally on December 21, the army refused to support any further repression. Ceausescu and his wife were captured on December 22 and tried for "crimes against the Romanian people" and executed on Christmas Day 1989. A rather fitting end to one of the most brutal communist regimes in Eastern Europe.

Leadership now passed into the hands of a hastily formed National Salvation Front led by Ion Iliescu, a former Communist who had studied in Moscow with Gorbachev and worked with Ceausescu until they had a falling out. Although the National Salvation Front was the solid victor in spring elections of 1990, questions remained about the new government's commitment to democracy, especially since antigovernment demonstrations were met with Ceausescu-like repression.

Bulgaria and Albania

In Bulgaria Soviet power helped the local Communist Party to assume control of the country. In 1954, Todor Zhivkov became leader of the Bulgarian Communist Party and hence the leader of the nation. Not until the late 1980s did a number of small opposition groups emerge. In October 1989, anti government demonstrations erupted in the capital city of Sofia. On November 10, 1989, Zhivkov was unexpectedly removed by party members from his position as general secretary of the Communist Party, a position he had held for thirty-five years. He was replaced by the minister of foreign affairs, Peter Mladenov, who immediately pledged political and economic reforms. Thus, even in a relatively isolated state like Bulgaria, communist leaders realized how imperative changes were to the old system and how the forces of democratization had to be accommodated if any degree of power was to be retained. In December the central committee struck from the constitution those articles giving the Communist Party a monopoly on power in the government. Free elections were

ENVER HOXHA

slated for the second half of 1990. On February 23,1990, the Bulgarian Communist Party voted to change its name to the Bulgarian Socialist Party; in the first free elections held in June 1990, it managed to retain control of the government. Despite its victory, the Socialists faced increased opposition, especially in urban areas. New elections in November 1991 saw the Socialists vote decline to 34 percent, making it possible for a new government coalition, led by the United Democratic Front, to assume power. Nevertheless, the Socialist Party remains a potent force in Bulgarian politics.

Albania was, and is, Eastern Europe's poorest and smallest country. Isolated from its neighbors, Albania maintained its hardline Stalinist political system well into the 1980s. The oppressive regime of Enver Hoxha (1908-1985), ruled the country from 1944 to 1985, when Hoxha's hand picked successor, Ramiz Alia, assumed power. Throughout the eighties, Albania remained a closed society; it had little contact with the outside world, even with its Balkan neighbors. Thus, Albania, its people, culture, and politics remained a mystery to the rest of the world. Despite its isolation, the revolutions of 1989 impacted the country. Antigovernment demonstrations broke out in Tirana, the Albanian capital in 1990, forcing Alia's regime to promise reforms. New political parties were legalized, and Albania's first free election was held in March 1991, which brought to power, as in Bulgaria, a "reformed" Socialist (Communist) Party, which still rules the country.

East and West Germany

The most significant political change in Eastern Europe during the late 1980s was the collapse of communism in East Germany and the unification of East and West Germany. The ruling Communist government in East Germany, led by Walter Ulbricht, consolidated its power in the early 1950s and became the Soviet Union's staunchest and most important satellite. As noted in the previous chapter, after the 1961 construction of the Berlin Wall, the "brain drain" exodus of East Germans to West Germany via West Berlin virtually ended. As a result of "The Wall," and its containment of skilled and educated East Germans, the East German economy became the strongest among the Soviet satellites. In 1971, Ulbricht was succeeded by Erich Honecker, a party hardliner who was deeply committed to the ideological battle against détente. Propaganda increased and the use of the Stasi, the secret police, became a hallmark of Honecker's brutal dictatorship, which lasted for the next eighteen years.

After infamous Berlin Wall in 1961, which became the most dramatic and ominous physical symbol of the cold war, went up, flight or escape from East Germany virtually ended. The East German economy became the strongest among the Soviet satellites. In 1971, Walter Ulbricht was succeeded by Erich Honecker, a party hardliner who was deeply committed to the ideological battle against détente. Propaganda increased and the use of the Stasi, the secret police, became a hallmark of Honecker's brutal dictatorship, which lasted for the next eighteen years.

As elsewhere in the Soviet empire, beginning in 1988, popular unrest, partly fueled by the continual economic slump of the 1980s (which affected most of Eastern Europe) as well as Honecker's relentless oppression, caused another mass exodus of East German refugees, primarily through the borders shared with Poland and Czechoslovakia . Honecker's refusal to implement reforms only increased East Germans' flight, as well as fueling mass demonstrations against his regime in the summer and fall of 1989. By the beginning of November 1989, the Communist government was in complete disarray as evidence of widespread official corruption finally forced Honecker's resignation. His successor, Egon Krenz, promised reforms, but it was too late to stave off the inevitable: the collapse of communism all together in East Germany. Krenz was faced with continuing mass protests and illegal mass emigration, both of which he could not contain. On November 4, 1989, the government, in a move that acknowledged its powerlessness to hold its citizens captive, opened its borders with Czechoslovakia. This move effectively freed East Germans to travel to the West. In a matter of days, the Berlin Wall—embodiment of the cold war, the Iron Curtain, and the division of East from West—was demolished by groups of ordinary citizens. Jubilant throngs from both sides walked through the gaping holes that now permitted men, women, and children to take the few steps that symbolized the return to freedom and a chance for national unity. Free elections were held throughout Germany in March 1990, resulting in a victory for the Alliance for Germany, a coalition allied with West German chancellor Helmut Kohl's Christian Democratic Union. With heavy emigration continuing, reunification talks quickly culminated in the formal proclamation of a united Germany on October 3, 1990. What had seemed almost impossible at the beginning of 1989 had become reality by the end of 1990—the country of East Germany had ceased to exist.

POST REVOLUTIONARY TROUBLES

Eastern Europe After 1989

The "Velvet Revolutions" of Central and Eastern Europe created great expectations for the region's future. Citizens of the respective nations hoped that an end of authoritarian government would produce economic prosperity and the widespread acceptance of democratic principles and social pluralism. Western Europeans believed that in a few years, if that long, these countries would join them as capitalist partners in an expanded European community. Reality, however, proved otherwise. Within a few years the optimism of 1989 gave way to disappointment, frustration, and even violent bloodshed and unspeakable atrocities. One of the most important of these failed expectations, and one with continuing implications for the continent, has been German reunification. The initial euphoria of a united Germany masked the uncertainty even among Germans themselves about reuniting a country that had been divided for so long and for the purpose of preventing another European

conflagration. Practical and cultural difficulties have only compounded the emotional insecurity. Despite legal unity after 1990, the financial price for rescuing a moribund East German economy has been high. Former West Germans have come to resent their eastern brethren not only because they have become a heavy economic burden but also because they perceive the Easterners to be culturally, educationally, and experientially backward. What the writer Gunter Grass has described as the "Wall in the mind" has long divided the countries. Though there has been great progress in integrating elections and the bureaucracies of the two German states, economic, social, and cultural unity has been much more difficult to achieve.

Adapting to change has always been a difficult process for Eastern Europeans. Attempts to create free-market economies in countries with limited natural resources and no established industrial or only a light manufacturing base has been virtually impossible and has brought inflation, unemployment, food and other shortages, and in their wake anticapitalist demonstrations. Inefficient management and allocation of resources, a tradition-bound work force resistant to change, lack of modern technology and venture capital and sufficient foreign investment, and a severely polluted and despoiled environment have combined to handicap progress and dash hopes. Uprisings in Bulgarian and Albania in 1997 were primarily caused by the inability of those governments to resolve basic social and economic problems. Compounding these countries economic woes are the bitter and virulent racial and ethnic conflicts that led to the Great War (World War I), and that have plagued Eastern Europe for centuries. Since 1989, various minority groups in the region have waged campaigns for autonomous rights or outright secession, and many of these movements have descended into violence. Czechoslovakia's "velvet revolution" collapsed into a "velvet divorce" as Slovakia declared itself independent from the Czechs, forcing Havel's resignation and the slowing down of the promised cultural and economic reforms begun in 1989. Poland enjoyed an economic upturn during the 1990s, after many years of economic struggle and uncertainty, but most of the rest of Eastern Europe continues to find the transformation fraught with disappointment, despair, and hard times. Economic frustration has been compounded by revived ethnic tensions suppressed by centralized communist governments. For example, there has been discrimination and violence against gypsies (Romani) in the Czech Republic and Hungary, and in Romania against ethnic Hungarians.

No where, however, was this problem more explosive and violent than in the former state of Yugoslavia. From its beginning in 1919, Yugoslavia had been an artificial creation. After World War II, Tito had served as a cohesive force for the six republics and two autonomous provinces that constituted the country. In the 1970s, Tito had become concerned that his decentralization policies had gone too far in dispersing power to local authorities and in the process had encouraged regionalism. Consequently, in the late 1970s he purged thousands of local Communist leaders whom he believed were undermining nationalism, such as it was. Despite his often ruthless methods, Tito was the glue that had held Yugoslavia together since the end of World War II. After Tito's death in 1980, the federalist ethnic patchwork he had held together began to come undone. Economic growth during the 1960s and 1970s was uneven, benefiting the capital Belgrade and the provinces of Croatia and Slovenia the most, while heavy industrial areas in Serbia, Bosnia-Hercegovina, and the tiny district of Kosovo began to fall further behind.

After Tito's death, no strong leader or successor emerged, and Tito's dictatorial powers were transferred to a collective state presidency and presidium of the League of Communists of Yugoslavia. At the end of the 1980s, despite attempts to keep reform ideas out, Yugoslavian communists saw the handwriting on the wall, and on January 20, 1990, the League of Communists declared the end of authoritarian socialism and allowed for the creation of a pluralistic political system with freedom of speech and other civil liberties, free elections, an independent judiciary, and a mixed economy with equal status for private property. But divisions between Slovenes who wanted a loose federation and Serbians who wanted to retain the centralized system caused the collapse of the party congress and the Communist Party. New parties quickly emerged. In multiparty elections held in the republics of Slovenia and Croatia in April-May 1990, the Communists fared poorly.

The Yugoslavian political scene was further complicated by the development of separatist movements that brought the disintegration of Yugoslavia in the 1990s. A number of Serb politicians, most notably Slobodan Milosevic, began to channel Serbian frustration with economic hard times toward subjects of national pride and sovereignty. Milosevic, who had become leader of the Serbian Communist Party in 1987, had managed to stay in power by exploiting Serbian nationalism, which included an intense ethnocentrism. Milosevic's nationalism catapulted him to several positions of authority, alienating representatives from the non-Serb republics in the process. Inspired by the events of 1989, representatives of the small province of Slovenia declared that the Serbs denied them adequate representation and economic support inside the republic. In 1991, on a tide of nationalism and reform, the Slovenes and

Bosnian Muslim girls walk on a street in eastern Mostar in September 1998. More conservative Muslim women still wear headscarves and long skirts or traditional baggy trousers. Many urban Bosnian Muslim women, however, have adopted modern Western dress.

Croatians, who cited injustices by Serb officials in the Yugoslav government, seceded from Yugoslavia. Milosevic's government sent the Yugoslavian army, which it controlled, into Slovenia but without much success. In September 1991, it began a full assault against Croatia. Croatia had a well-armed militia, and the Yugoslav army was fast becoming the Serbian army, while Serbian irregular forces played a growing role in military operations. The conflict finally ended in arbitration by the United Nations. The religious nature of the conflict—between Catholic Croats and Orthodox Serbs—and the legacies of fighting in the Second World War produced brutality on both sides. Towns and villages where Serbs and Croats had lived together since the 1940s were torn apart, as each ethnic group rounded up and massacred members of the other.

The recognition of Slovenia, Croatia, and Bosnia-Hercegovina by many European states and the United States in early 1992 did not deter the Serbs from pursuing their goal of conquest and subjugation of these areas. The next conflict came in the same place that in 1914 had sparked a much larger war: the province of Bosnia-Hercegovina. Bosnia was the most ethnically diverse republic in Yugoslavia. Its capital, Sarajevo, was home to several major ethnic groups and had often been praised as an example of peaceful coexistence. When Bosnia joined the round of secessions from Yugoslavia in 1992, ethnic coexistence came apart. Bosnia began the war against the Serbs with no formal army; armed bands equipped by the governments of Serbian Yugoslavia, Croatia, and Bosnia battled each other throughout the new country. The Serbs and Croats, both of whom had reason to dislike

Serbian President Slobodan Milosevic (left), Croatian President Franjo Tudjman (center), and Bosnian President Alija Izetbegovic sign the Dayton Agreement on December 14, 1995. The agreement ended what many regard as Europe's worst conflict since World War II.

the Muslim Bosnians, were especially well-armed and organized. Their artillery rained shells on towns and villages; they burned houses with families inside; rounded up Muslim men in detention camps where they starved to death; and they raped thousands of Bosnian women. All sides committed atrocities. The Serbs, however, were guilty of the worse barbarities. These included what came to be called "ethnic cleansing." This involved the sending of partisan bands on campaigns of genocide and terror through Muslim and Croat territories to encourage much larger populations to flee the area. In the first eighteen months of fighting over 100,000 people were killed, of which 80,000 were innocent civilians, mostly Bosnian Muslims. Although the barbarity and slaughter appalled Western governments, they virtually did nothing to ameliorate, let alone resolve the crisis. The Western powers considered the conflict to be a civil war more complex than that in Spain during the 1930s and wrung their hands that intervention

would result in a Vietnam or Afghanistan-like scenario for them, with no clear resolution of the horrific ethnic killing itself. Outside forces were eventually sent, mostly European troops in United Nations "blue helmets," who offered humanitarian relief, separated combatants, and created "safe areas" for persecuted ethnic populations from all sides.

The crisis reached a climax in the autumn of 1995. Sarajevo had been under siege for three years but a series of mortar attacks on public marketplaces that killed scores of innocent civilians prompted fresh Western outrage, especially from the most important power, the United States. Already Croat forces and the Bosnian army had turned the ground war against the Serb militias, and now they were supported by waves of United States air strikes. The United States bombing, combined with a Croat-Bosnian offensive, forced the Bosnian Serbs to negotiate. French Special Forces augmented by British artillery broke the siege of Sarajevo. Peace talks were held in Dayton, Ohio. The final agreement divided Bosnia, with the majority of land in the hands of Muslims and Croats, and a small autonomous "Serb republic" in areas that had been previously "ethnically cleansed." Stability was restored but three years of war had killed over two hundred thousand people.

The Bosnian legacy created conflict again over Kosovo, the medieval homeland of the Orthodox Serbs, now occupied by mainly Albanian and Muslim populations. Milosevic, smarting from the Dayton peace settlement, was determined not to lose any more "Serbian" territory, and thus accused the Albanians of fomenting secession and persecuting Serbs. In the name of "greater Serbia," Serb soldiers fought Albanian guerrillas rallying under the banner of "greater Albania." Western nations worried that the conflict might spread to the strategic, ethnically divided country of Macedonia and ignite a general Balkan conflict. Talks between Milosevic's government and the Albanian rebels dissolved in early 1999, followed by a fresh and overwhelming wave of American-led bombing against Serbia itself, as well as against Serbian forces in Kosovo. Another "ethnic cleansing" occurred, as Serb forces drove hundreds of thousands of Albanians from their homes. The United States and its European allies, unwilling to become involved in a land war in the mountainous, unforgiving terrain of the southern Balkans, decided that they would use only air power and strategically bombed bridges, power plants, factories, and Serbian military bases. The Russian government, irritated by this unilateral attack on fellow Slavs, nonetheless played an important part in brokering a cease-fire. Milosevic was forced to withdraw from Kosovo, leaving it in the hands of another force of armed NATO peacekeepers.

Meanwhile, Serb-dominated Yugoslavia, torn asunder by ten years of war and economic

United States President Bill Clinton accompanied by General William Nash, commander of U. S. ground forces in Bosnia, walks through the ranks at Tuzla air base on January 13, 1996.

sanctions, turned against Milosevic's regime. War and corruption had destroyed his credibility as a nationalist and populist. After he attempted to reject the results of a democratic election in 2000, his government fell under the duress of popular protests and mass demonstrations. Presently he is being tried for war crimes and other atrocities his regime committed during the Yugoslavian Wars.

As we gain perspective on the twentieth century, it is clear that the Yugoslavian wars of the 1990s were not isolated events, just more rounds of typical, traditional Balkan violence. The issues are Western. The Balkans form one of the West's borderlands; where cultures influenced by Roman Catholicism, Eastern Orthodoxy, and Islam meet, commingle, and contend for political domination and influence. Since the nineteenth century, this region of great religious, cultural, and ethnic diversity has struggled with the dynamics of nationalism. We have seen how conflicts regarding new nation states and ethnic minorities were worked out in central Europe, with many episodes of tragic violence. In many facets, the Yugoslavian wars reflected the same historical patterns.

The 1989 Eastern European revolutions and collapse of the Soviet Union were a revolutionary turning point in European history. Like the 1789 French Revolution, they brought down not only a regime but an empire as well. Like the French Revolution, they gave way to violence; the events are far too recent for historians to predict what new forces and states will emerge. Like the French upheaval, they had profound international ramifications. These revolutions and the fall of the Soviet Union marked the end of the cold war, which had dictated international politics and affected the everyday lives of millions of people since the end of World War II.

WESTERN EUROPE

After two decades of prodigious economic growth, Europe experienced severe economic recessions in the mid-1970s and early 1980s (specifically 1973-1974 and 1979-1983). Like the United States during the same time frame, Europe too suffered from stagflation—inflation and unemployment. No doubt, the substantial increase in oil prices after the 1973 Arab-Israeli conflict was a major factor in the first downturn. Other factors, however, also contributed to the problem. A worldwide recession had led to a decline in demand for European goods. In Europe the reconstruction of many cities after their devastation in World War II had been completed, ending many jobs for thousands of people. The economies of the Western European states recovered in the course of the 1980s, although problems persisted. Unemployment remained high, even after almost a decade of growth. France had a 10.6 unemployment rate in 1993; Spain's had reached 17 percent by then. Despite their economic woes, Western Europeans kept abreast of the period's technological growth and were able to compete with the Americans and Japanese in this area. Perhaps most important, during the eighties and nineties, Europeans continued to further integrate their economies. Even earlier such momentum manifested itself when in 1973 the European Economic Community expanded to include Great Britain, Ireland, and Denmark. By 1986 three additional members—Spain, Portugal, and Greece joined what its members now called the European Community or the EC. This new era of economic cooperation led to further coalescence in international and political affairs as well. The foreign ministers of the twelve members consult frequently and provide a common front for negotiation on important issues.

The European Community remained primarily an economic union, not a political one. By 1992 the EC comprised 344 million people and constituted the world's largest single trading entity, transacting almost one-fourth of the world's commerce. In the 1980s and 1990s, the EC moved toward even greater economic integration. A Treaty on European Union (also called the Maastricht Treaty after the city in the Netherlands where the agreement was promulgated) represented an attempt to create a true economic and monetary union of all EC members. The treaty would not go into effect until all members agreed; ten did so in 1992. The acceptance of the Maastricht Treaty by Denmark and Great Britain in 1993 finally made its implementation possible.

Politically, democracy became embraced by all the nations. Even Spain and Portugal, which endured prewar dictatorships until the mid-1970s, established democratic systems by the late 1970s. Western European Communist Parties declined dramatically in popular support and power. During the mid-1970s, a new variety of communism called Eurocommunism briefly emerged as Communist Parties tried to work within the democratic/parliamentary system as mass movements committed to better government. But by the 1980s, internal political developments in Western Europe and events within the Communist world itself combined to undermine the Eurocommunist experiment.

From West Germany to Germany

After the Adenauer era, German voters moved politically from the acceptance of the center-right ideology of the Christian Democrats to embracing the center-left agenda of the Social Democrats, who became the leading party in 1969. By forming a coalition government with the small Free Democratic Party (FDP), the Social Democrats remained in power until 1982. The first Social Democratic chancellor was Willy Brandt, who was especially successful with his program of "opening toward the east." For his policy of Ostpolitik, Brandt won the Nobel Peace Prize in 1972. Taking advantage of the recent Soviet-U.S. détente, Brandt sought to improve relations with East Germany in a variety of areas, laying a foundation for what he hoped would occur in the not too distant future: German reunification. On March 19, 1971, Brandt met with East German leader Walter Ulbricht and together the two leaders worked out the details of what became known as the Basic Treaty that was signed and went into effect in 1972. Though the agreement did not establish full diplomatic relations

The first Social Democrat to become chancellor, Brandt won the Nobel Peace Prize in 1972 for his efforts to improve Western relations with the Soviets and the East Germans.

between the two countries (something the Soviet Union was not going to sanction at this juncture in the cold war, despite its détente with the United States), it did call for "good neighborly relations" that resulted in greater cultural, personal, and economic contacts and exchanges for a brief period between the two countries. Unfortunately this rapprochement ended abruptly in 1974 when an East German spy was discovered within the Brandt administration. This affair led to Brandt's resignation that same year.

Brandt's successor, Helmut Schmidt, was more of a technocrat than a reform-minded socialist. Instead of trying to repair East-West relations after the spy scandal, or furthering his party's social agenda, Schmidt concentrated primarily on trying to resolve West German economic problems brought about mainly by the high oil prices between 1973 and 1975. Schmidt was successful in eliminating a deficit of 10 billion marks in three years. In 1982, when the coalition of Schmidt's Social Democrats with the Free Democrats disintegrated over the reduction of social welfare expenditures, the Free Democrats joined with the Christian Democratic Union of Helmut Kohl to form a new government. Kohl was perhaps the most political of all post-World War II West German chancellors. Kohl was a moderate centrist who benefited greatly from his country's economic boom of the mid-1980s. Gradually, however, disenchantment set in with German voters with the Christian Democrats lack of an agenda and do-nothing policies, and by 1988, the party's future political prospects seemed bleak. But, unexpectedly, the 1989 revolution in East Germany portended well for both Kohl and the party. Kohl seemed to be in the right place at the right time to exploit the euphoria over German reunification, which he and the Christian Democrats took full credit for. In the first all-German federal election in 1991, the Christian Democrats won 44 percent of the popular vote, while their coalition partner, the Free Democrats, received 11 percent.

The excitement for reunification soon gave way to discontent and myriad, unforeseen problems. All too soon, the realization set in, especially among former West Germans, that integration and revitalization of East Germany would cost much more than anyone originally thought. Consequently, Kohl's government was forced with the unsavory task of having to implement new taxation policies that especially burdened the more affluent West Germans to pay for East German economic integration and resuscitation. The virtual collapse of the East German economy had led to extremely high levels of unemployment in that part of Germany and naturally increased discontent. Perhaps most important were the social ramifications of East German eco-

nomic dislocation and integration. Thousands of East Germans and foreigners emigrated to West Germany because of East Germany's crises. These emigres were unwelcomed in the West partly because they represented the threat of cheap labor but largely because they were considered "foreigners." Even supposedly fellow Germans were met with hostility. Especially persecuted were the Turks, who had come to Germany for job opportunities, as well as other Middle Eastern peoples, like Iranians and Iraqis, and Slavs, primarily from war-torn Yugoslavia, who not only sought employment opportunities but asylum as well from the ravages of war. For years Germany's liberal immigration laws had allowed illegal immigrants a haven. But now, because of reunification and the strains that process put on the German economy, foreigners especially became the targets of an increased xenophobia amongst many former West Germans. Neo-Nazi and other extreme right-wing organizations, which had been underground for years, suddenly appeared and were largely responsible for the violence and terror visited upon the "non-Aryan" immigrants. In the 1990s, these right-wing extremists killed scores of people in Germany. Many of these groups are still active today and continue to terrorize the immigrant communities in Germany.

Northern Ireland

Between 1964 and 1979, Conservatives and Labour alternated in power. Both parties had to face seemingly intractable problems, especially economic ones. While separatist movements in Scotland and Wales were overcome, the conflict between Catholics and Protestants in Northern Ireland was not so easily settled and still rages today. Violence seemed endemic in Northern Ireland, especially in the 1970s, as the Irish Republican Army (IRA) staged a series of dramatic terrorist acts in response to the suspension of Northern Ireland's parliament in 1972 and establishment of direct rule by London. Only in the last two years has a modicum of peace been seen in Northern Ireland as current Prime Minister Tony Blair has worked assiduously to bring both sides to the peace table to try to negotiate an end to close to forty years of incessant violence and terror. So far, it appears that Blair's efforts have resulted in a cease-fire of sorts and an end to the killing, but a genuine political settlement satisfactory to both sides has yet to be hammered out.

Great Britain

Neither party in the seventies was able to deal with Britain's ailing economy. Failure to modernize made British industry less and less competitive. Britain was also hampered by frequent labor strikes, many of them caused by conflicts between rival labor unions. In 1979, after Britain's economic problems had seemed to reach a crisis point under five years of Labour government, the Conservatives returned to power under Margaret Thatcher. She became the first woman to serve as prime minister in British history. Thatcher pledged to lower taxes, reduce government bureaucracy, limit social welfare (especially in the areas of education, national health and public housing), de-nationalize key industries (such as Rolls Royce and British Airways, both of which were privatized), restrict union power, and end inflation. The "Iron Lady," as she was called, did break the power of the labor unions. Thatcher oversaw the implementation of several new laws that curtailed trade-union power, and she refused to consult with union leaders as her predecessors had done since the war. A showdown was reached with the year-long

coal miner's strike of 1984 and 1985, one of the most bitter and violent strikes of the century in Europe. The strike's failure in the face of government intransigence further discredited the labor movement and enhanced Thatcher's prestige. Still the violent encounters between police and picketing strikers, carried nationwide on television, indicated the cracks in the relative social harmony that Britain had long enjoyed. In addition, riots by unemployed young people, mainly young males from working class backgrounds, erupted in several major industrial cities in 1981 and again in 1985. On one issue, however, the Thatcher government managed a meeting of the minds with discontented city dwellers. Even before Thatcher took office increasing immigration from Britain's former colonies was being blamed for a variety of social ills from unemployment to urban crime. In the 1979 electoral campaign, Thatcher's conservatives took a hard line on the immigration issue, sponsoring the Nationality Act of 1982 that restricted nonwhite immigration from the former British colonies.

While she did not eliminate the basic components of the welfare state, she did use austerity measures to control inflation. "Thatcherism," as her economic policy was called, improved the British economic outlook but at a price. Much like United States' President Ronald Reagan's "Reaganomics," which Thatcher said had inspired her, the "fix" seemed short-term rather than long term and in the end caused some serious future socioeconomic setbacks. The south of England, for example, prospered, but the old industrial heartland of the Midlands and northern England further declined and witnessed high unemployment, poverty, and outbursts of violence as a result. Cutbacks in education seriously undermined the quality of British education, especially in the academic areas and related institutions of

Thatcher and former U. S. President Ronald Reagan

secondary and higher learning. For centuries Englishmen had prided themselves on having one of the finest education systems in the world, particularly at the university level, and on being the most literate people in the world. Now, such pride withered in embarrassment as the "Iron Lady" wielded her sharp knife, slicing education budgets across the board, leaving institutions bereft of essential funding. Much of the same occurred simultaneously in the United States during the Reagan years. It seemed that the conservative backlash affecting both nations had produced kindred spirits in Reagan and Thatcher, especially when it came to eliminating what both leaders perceived to be "wasteful" expenditures of the taxpayers money.

In the area of foreign policy, Thatcher, like Reagan, took a hard-line approach against communism. She oversaw a large military buildup aimed at replacing older technology and reestablishing Great Britain as a world policeman and respected power. In 1982, when Argentina attempted to wrest the Falkland Islands (one of England's few remaining colonial outposts of little value, strategically or economically) 300 miles off its coast, the British successfully rebuked the Argentines (with United States naval assistance), although at great economic costs and the loss of 255 lives. The Falklands War, however, generated much popular patriotic support for Thatcher as many Britons hoped the " Iron Lady" was going to resurrect the halcyon days of British imperialism and Pax Britanica.

Margaret Thatcher dominated British politics in the 1980s. The Labour Party, beset by divisions between its moderate and radical wings, offered little effective opposition. With Labour increasingly isolated, identified with decaying inner cities and old industrial regions, Thatcher easily won reelection in 1983 and 1987. Only in 1990 did Labour's fortunes seem to revive when Thatcher's government attempted to replace local property taxes with a flat-rate tax payable by every adult to his or her local authority. Though Thatcher maintained that this would make local government more responsive to its electors, many argued that this was nothing more than a poll tax that would enable the rich to pay the same rate as the poor. In 1990 after antitax riots broke out, Thatcher's once remarkable popularity fell to an all-time low. At the end of November, a revolt within her own party caused the Iron Lady to resign as prime minister. By the time of her departure she was the longest running prime minister of the century. She was replaced by John Major, whose Conservative Party won a narrow victory in the general elections in April 1992. But the Conservatives days were numbered as the once united party, behind the leadership of Margaret Thatcher, began to divide over a variety of issues but most were related to whether one was a "Thatcherite" or anti-Thatcherite. Finally in 1999 a reformed Labour Party returned to power led by the relatively young moderate Tony Blair, who did not campaign on a hard or traditional Labour platform but rather promised to pretty much keep the course and policies established by his Conservative predecessors, most of which were implemented during the Thatcher years.

Controversy over the significance of the Thatcher years intensified after her departure. On the positive side, her efforts helped boost the competitiveness of British industry; productivity grew at an average annual rate of 4.5 percent in Britain from 1979 to 1988, 50 percent above the average of other industrial democracies. The impressive improvement resulted partly from the Thatcher government's anti-union attitude and policies. Prior to Thatcher, the powerful trade unions had impeded productivity growth by protecting redundant labor. Even critics admitted that Thatcher's policies, especially her willingness to directly curtail union power, produced a significant change in British attitudes in favor of enterprise and competition. Privatization became more extensive than had

been expected when Thatcher took office in 1979, while the number of new businesses reflected a revival of entrepreneurship—apparently the basis for better economic performance over the longer term.

Despite the economic upturn of the 1980s the British economy was again in relative decline by the 1990s, weakened by inflation. Whatever the gains during the Thatcher years, the gap between the rich and poor widened, and the old industrial regions of the north were increasingly left behind. Perhaps the most interesting observation about the affect of Thatcherism is not found in statistics but rather in the feeling many Britons presently have that the civility and sense of community that others had long admired in the British seemed to disappear, a notable casualty of the Thatcher revolution. Thatcher apologists insist that Britons respect for order and stability had dissolved by the late 1970s and that Thatcher offered the only way of reversing the economic decline that was destroying the British social fabric.

France

France's prolonged economic decline in the 1970s brought a shift to the left politically by the early 1980s. Unlike Great Britain and the United States, which moved to the right during that decade, French voters opted to go the other direction, giving the Socialists a chance to try to solve their economic woes. In 1981, after gaining the majority in the National Assembly, the Socialists' dominance of France became complete with the election of Francois Mitterrand in 1981. Mitterrand's election and the Socialists' control of the National Assembly was greeted with great enthusiasm among the French people. The Socialists had built up support during the 1970s by claiming the mantle of the "new left" and promising to promote a more participatory democracy at all levels. The French Communist Party, meanwhile, seemed increasingly out of touch and irrelevant to the sociopolitical needs of the French people. By the early 1980s, the Communists could garner only 10 to 12 percent of the vote, about half the support the Socialists enjoyed.

Assuming the presidency in 1981, Mitterrand proclaimed that he was not seeking to merely prove that French Socialists could govern responsibly; rather, he offered a major reform agenda intended to create the first genuinely democratic socialism. In 1982 Mitterrand froze prices and wages in the hope of reducing France's economic difficulties. He also passed a number of liberal measures to aid workers: an increased minimum wage, expanded social benefits, a mandatory fifth week of paid vacation for salaried workers, a thirty-nine hour work week, and higher taxes for the rich. By simultaneously freezing wages and prices and raising the minimum wage, Mitterand hoped to increase the purchasing power of those individuals at the bottom of the French wage scale—unskilled laborers as well as workers in unprotected (non-union) service industries. Though Mitterand strengthened individual rights and gave greater power to local governments, reforms with a definite socialist orientation proved problematic. Mitterrand's more traditional socialist policies increased the government's ownership of French industry from 15 to 35 percent. Key industries, such as banking, steel, aluminum, petrochemical, electronics, and insurance companies, were nationalized. The more radical reforms such as nationalization, however, failed to recover France's ailing economy. Within three years a decline in support for the party caused the Mitterrand government to pursue what it called "modernization," essentially a return of some of

the economy to private enterprise and a narrowing of bureaucratic powers. Some economic improvement allowed Mitterrand to win another seven-year term in the 1988 presidential elections. France's economic decline, however, continued. Although France was still one of postwar Europe's greatest economic success stories, unemployment remained stubbornly high, reaching 10.6 in 1993. When legislative elections were held that year, the ruling Socialists were so unpopular that they were humiliatingly defeated by a conservative backlash. The Socialists won only 28 percent of the vote and less than 10 percent of the seats in the National Assembly. A coalition of conservative parties won 80 percent of the seats, and Edouard Balladur, a member of the neo-Gaullist Rally for the Republic, became France's new premier. In the 1993 presidential elections, the Conservative mayor of Paris, Jacques Chirac, won easily over a splintered Socialist-Leftist coalition. Chirac was re-elected in the spring of 2002 in a runoff election against the far-right, anti-Semitic candidate, Jean LePen. Though LePen had forced a runoff, in a second vote, which saw the highest turn out ever of French voters, Chirac won over 80 percent of the popular vote. Though French voters have apparently turned to the right in the 1990s and early years of the twenty-first century, they are unwilling to embrace the far-right ideology of extremists like LePen.

Italy

In the 1970s, Italy suffered from a severe economic recession. The Italian economy, which depended on imported oil as its chief source of energy, was especially vulnerable to the 1973 Arab oil embargo. Compounding the nation's economic distress were a host of social and political problems: student unrest, mass strikes, and terrorist attacks. Italy had the misfortune to be home to one of the most effective European terrorist organizations, the Red Brigades. In 1978, a former prime minister, Aldo Moro, was kidnapped and executed by the Red Brigades. There was (and still is) the all-pervasive violence and corruptive influence of the Mafia, which had always been an important factor in southern Italy but spread to northern Italy as well in the 1980s.

Italy survived the crises of the 1970s and in the decade of the 1980s began to experience remarkable economic growth. Indeed, the "second economic miracle" (the first was Italy's rapid recovery after World War II) made the nation the world's fifth largest economy by most measures. Politically, during the 1970s and through the mid-1980s, Italy continued to practice the politics of coalition that had characterized much of its history. The Christian Democrats emerged out of World War II as the most dominant party, and they led the coalition governments. In the 1980s, even the Communists had been included briefly in the government. The Italian Communists, like their French counterparts, advocated Eurocommunism, as they attempted to broaden communism's appeal by softening its hard Marxist ideology and rhetoric. Although its vote declined in the 1980s, even in 1987 the Communist Party still garnered 26 percent of the vote. The Communists also won a number of local elections and took control of municipal governments in several large Italian cities, most notably Rome and Naples for a brief time. By the early 1980s, however, both the Christian Democrats and the Communists were losing electoral strength. The Christian Democrats' message seemed increasingly anachronistic as Italy became a more secular society. Moreover, as the Italian Communists declined, and especially as communism in the Soviet bloc weakened by the end of the decade, support for Christian Democracy as

a bulwark against communism seemed no longer imperative. During the early eighties, the Communists moved toward greater democracy within the party and became more vitriolic in their criticisms of the Soviet system. Italian Communists had always prided themselves on their independence from Moscow and now, to revitalize the party and attract voter support, such an unaffiliated stance was especially crucial. Italian denunciations got the desired affect: an open break with the Soviet Union was achieved by the early eighties. Finally, as communism collapsed in the Soviet block at the end of the decade, the party renamed itself the "Democratic Party of the Left," dropping the term communist altogether. With their role and even their political identity uncertain, the Communists' share of the vote in national parliamentary elections steadily declined.

It seemed at first that in Italy, much as in France, a revitalized Socialist Party would not only supplant the Communists but offer a viable alternative to the reigning government party. During the mid-eighties, a Socialist served as Italy's prime minister for the first time, though still within a coalition dominated by the Christian Democrats. By the early 1990s, however, Socialist hopes of winning outright control of the national government, such as occurred in Mitterrand's France, dissipated. Not only did the party have little distinctive to offer, but it was heavily involved in a nationwide scandal that began convulsing the country in 1992. The scandal spread to implicate major figures from other parties, including the Christian Democrats, in a network of public contract kickbacks to finance the political parties. Some leaders were accused of ties to organized crime, which, given the powerful influence of the Mafia in Italian politics for decades, surprised no one. To many Italians, the political system had not only been ineffective but rotten as well. Disgust among Italians grew, threatening the Italian state itself.

One manifestation of this disdain for traditional Italian politics was the growing prominence of regionalist leagues, especially in the north, which protested the exploitative nature of the national government and the continuing economic burden southern Italy imposed on the nation. In reality it was northern Italy that felt aggrieved at having to pay for the south. Northern Italian resentment of the south was not new; it merely intensified in the eighties. The most important of these leagues formed on the north-south issues was the Lombard League, which commanded almost 25 percent of the vote in the prosperous region of Lombardy, centered in the industrial city of Milan.

In the wake of scandal and disillusionment, Italians began a wholesale political housecleaning on the national level. In the nineties, some were speaking of a "revolution of the judges" as members of Italy's relatively independent judiciary took it upon themselves to clean up and hopefully reform and save the Italian body politic. It was the judiciary that spearheaded the corruption investigations that brought the politicians to justice. Those politicians who had sought reform, such as the Christian Democrat Mario Segni, gained a wide audience, and referenda changed the electoral system to weaken the parties and make the politicians more responsive to the public. The system of trasformismo alluded to earlier of regional party bosses seemed to be ending at last in Italian politics. But what new form of democracy will replace it remains unclear.

Further enlargement of the European Community by the entry of Greece, Portugal, and Spain would not have been possible in the 1960s because at that time all three countries were under the repressive rule of authoritarian dictator-

ships. In Greece, a cabal of colonels had seized power in 1967; in Portugal, Antonio de Oliveira Salazar had ruled since the 1930s; and in Spain, the fascist, General Francisco Franco, was entrenched as head of state, a position he had held since his triumph in 1939 at the end of the Spanish civil war. By 1975, however, all three countries had established democratic regimes. In Greece a republican government returned to power in 1973 and brought that nation into the EC in 1981. In Spain and Portugal, the deaths of Franco and Salazar opened the door to membership later in the 1980s.

Spain experienced perhaps the most dramatic turn-around. A moderately large country of over 40 million (in 1990), Spain had not played a major role in European affairs for three centuries. During the 1950s, however, and largely due to cajoling and brow-beating from the United States, Franco decided it was time for Spain to move away from its detachment from Western European affairs and his attempted economic autarky, and slowly bring his country back into the European economic fold. By the time of his death, Spain had undergone an economic transformation similar to those that had occurred in other Western European nations. By the late 1970s, Spain was no longer an isolated, primarily rural and agrarian economy. Millions of former landless peasants had left the countryside and moved to cities where they became part of a growing industrial working class. Simultaneously, the Spanish middle class of professionals also expanded as witnessed by the prodigious growth of Spanish urban centers, where increasing numbers of urban Spaniards had automobiles and televisions. The Spanish birthrate also dropped, and the gross national product had taken off.

King Juan Carlos I, chosen by Franco himself from the deposed Bourbon dynasty, provided the continuity and sage leadership that smoothed the political transition after Franco's death. At the same time, the Socialist Worker's Party, like all the postwar European socialist parties, jettisoned its Marxist baggage and presented itself as a moderate democratic entity. When the first democratic elections in Spain since the Civil War were held in 1977, the big winners were a democratic centrist party and the reformed Socialist Worker's Party. The extremes of both left and right were soundly defeated. When the Socialists won a majority of seats in the next election in 1982, a moderate Socialist, Felipe Suarez, became the new prime minister. The transition suggested that Spain had quickly found its way to an effective two-party system. Meanwhile the new 1978 constitution dismantled what was left of the Franco years so that, for example, Catholicism was no longer recognized as the official religion of the Spanish state. Today, Spain, while still not reaching quite the level of the wealthiest members of the EC, has for the first time in its modern history prospered. It is now a respected and vital member of the international community.

EUROPE AND THE WEST IN THE AFTERMATH OF THE COLD WAR

As noted earlier, the dissolution of the Soviet system and empire signified the end of the cold war, which had defined European history and that of the world since the end of World War II. Though it could claim to have won the cold war, the United States had also declined in relative strength from the unprecedented preeminence it had enjoyed after World War II. Thus, the end of the cold war meant not unchallenged United States hegemony but a new universe of possibilities and uncertainties. For Western Europe, in particular, the end of bipolarism created opportunities to become a superpower in its own right. In the 1990s, the push for greater European integration intensified. Obstacles remained, especially those that were perceived to undermine national sovereignty. At the same time, different forms of multinational organization, from a revitalized United Nations to a grouping of the world's seven leading industrial democracies, offered a different approach to reconfiguring power relationships.

As the power, thus threat, from the Soviet Union waned, the United States lost some of its leverage in Europe because American support no longer seemed essential for European security. Despite a vigorous military buildup in the 1980s, the United States, by the early 1990s, lost its status as the world's preeminent power. The role of superpower had taken its toll on the United States, just as it had on the Soviet Union. Both countries emerged from World War II the big winners, but the subsequent arms race strained their budgets, while the war's major losers, Germany, Japan, and Italy, pulled back from any great power role to prosper (thanks to United States assistance) as never before. In terms of productivity and living standards, the United States was in relative decline compared to Japan and much of Western Europe by the 1990s. Suffering from mounting budget deficits and shifting from net creditor to net borrower in its international accounts, it lost some of its economic edge and thus some of its capacity to lead.

The ambiguities of this new international scene came to the fore during the Persian Gulf War, the first real test of relations in the post-cold war environment. The war was largely a United States led effort against Iraq for its invasion of Kuwait. With superpower rivalry no longer an issue, the United States assembled a broad coalition of other nations, which in a very short ground war (after several months of intense aerial bombing of Iraqi cities) drove the Iraqi army out of Kuwait and restored the Persian Gulf status quo. Though the United States led the coalition to victory, it had to pass the hat among its prosperous allies to pay for the war. Those called on to contribute seemed unlikely to settle for such an arrangement again. This was especially true for Japan and Germany, both of whom had been limited to a circumscribed sphere of action within the international dynamics of the cold war era. Now with the restraints off, both countries were inevitably going to pursue their own self-interest when it came to world affairs. Among the Japanese, this rethinking sometimes assumed a strongly nationalist orientation. Japan might translate its economic power into a more independent military-strategic role, perhaps leading an East Asia bloc encompassing other increasingly prosperous regional associates. Or, Japan might be content to work closely with the United States, its fellow Pacific power, or simply to work within multinational organizations. Currently, much still depends on how others deal with Japan, especially in light of the resentment—and the protectionist sentiment—that Japan's success in international trade produces in both Europe and the United States.

On the European side, much depended, and still does, on Germany, whose economic prospects initially seemed dramatically enhanced with the end of the cold war. Most immediately, the collapse of communism in east-central Europe made possible German reunification in 1990. Despite some nervousness, the four postwar occupying powers gave their blessing as the leaders of the two countries negotiated the incorporation of the East into the Federal Republic. The division of Germany was the central issue of the postwar settlement between the West and the U.S.S.R.; the speed with which Germany has overcome its partition has astonished the world. Reunification also caused some disquiet about the economic role the new Germany might seek to play in Europe and the world. Because 30 percent of the territory of present-day Poland had been taken from Germany after World War II, the Poles were especially concerned. Germany, however, remained cautious and eager to prove its good intentions by continuing to support the movement toward European integration.

TOWARD GREATER EUROPEAN INTEGRATION AND GLOBAL ISSUES

By the 1980s, the issue of European integration surged to the top of practically every Western European nation's agenda for the future. The end of the cold war added urgency to the process. Most immediately, the role of the Common Market in coordinating aid to the former communist countries of Eastern Europe suggested that it needed its own foreign policy to match its growing responsibilities. From the beginning, advocates of European integration had hoped that the Common Market could promote greater uniformity in areas like tax policy and business law, in which national differences prevented full-scale economic integration. Although a full customs union had technically been achieved by the late 1960s, national policies continued to negate the open market concept, especially by catering to certain indigenous companies to give them a competitive advantage. For domestic political reasons, governments too often bought exclusively from national firms or granted subsidies to domestic producers, which allowed them to offer artificially lower prices to compete with foreign enterprises. Despite lingering economic chauvinism, movement toward full-scale integration continued. After another oil crisis in 1979, and amid the growing concern about "Eurosclerosis"—the fear among many Western Europeans that they were no longer competitive in the world market place because they had fallen behind the United States and Japan in the crucial areas of innovation and modernization—the EEC's twelve members committed themselves in 1985 to doing all that was essential to create a true single market with genuinely free competition by the end of 1992. Not only were goods, services, and money to circulate freely, but there would be uniform product standards, as well as equal competition for the government contracts of each country.

It was only natural that the thrust toward economic integration would become politicized. A European Parliament had developed from the assembly of the European Coal and Steel Community in 1962, though it had little initial importance. The provision for direct election to this body, which had formerly comprised delegations from the national parliaments, greatly increased its stature when the first such elections were held in 1979. After the merger of the governing institutions of the several European supranational organizations in 1967, the term "European Community," or EC, replaced "Common Market," indicating the institutional web that had emerged since the inception of the European Coal and Steel Community in 1951. By the late eighties the European Community included a network of interconnected institutions, headquartered in Brussels, Strasbourg, and Luxembourg. Among them the European Parliament and the European Court of Justice assumed increasingly important, powerful roles. Meeting at Maastrict, in the Netherlands in December 1991, the EC members augmented the powers of the European Parliament by agreeing to move toward a common policy of workers' rights and to create a common currency and central banking structure by 1999. But the Maastrict agenda

required the approval of all EC members, and unfortunately, once the proposals hit the debate floor the respective parliaments and assemblies, the idea of such integration proved more divisive than proponents had expected. Many were nervous about the implications of German reunification for the operations of the EC. West Germany had been the strongest economic power in cold war Western Europe, and now many feared that reunification would only strengthen Germany's economic clout and allow Germany to use the EC to dominate the continent. Moreover, the creation of an internal customs union, benign though it seemed, did not commit the EC to freer trade with nonmember countries like the United States and Japan. French farmers, especially, relied on a system of government supports that protected them from U.S. competition. Conversely, high EC agricultural subsidies under cut the chance for Americans to sell their agricultural products in Europe. In 1992 the possibility that the French government would lower those supports, partly in response to U.S. pressure, precipitated massive farmer protest in France.

Despite these fits and starts, the EC seems poised to play an expanding role in the post-cold war world. During the 1990s, the entry of three new countries—Austria, Finland, and Sweden—brought EC membership to fifteen. On January 1, 1993, the EC alliance changed its name to the European Union, or EU, and at the same time put forth the most surprising and potentially significant measure of the decade when it was decided that a new currency would be created, called the euro, which would become the official currency of all the members. Strongly supported by German chancellor Helmut Kohl, the euro came into being in 1999 and became the sole currency in eleven European countries in January 2002. In addition, there were other

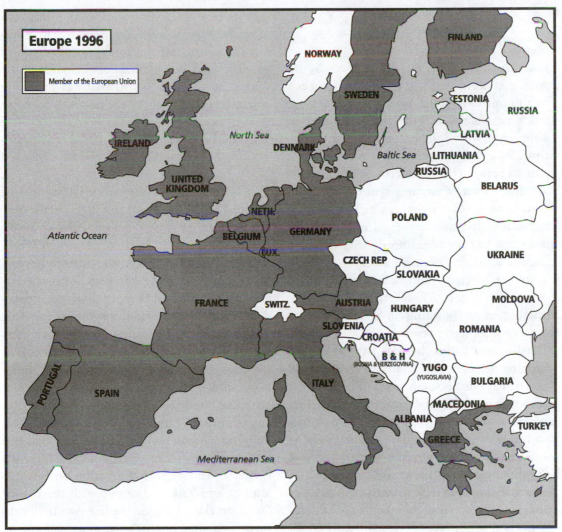

supranational alignments that might prove even more important. The leaders of the seven major industrial democracies—the United States, Japan, Germany, France, Italy, Britain, and Canada—began meeting regularly in 1975, first to deal with effects of the OPEC oil price shock. Their meetings grew steadily in importance, and by the nineties, this "Group of 7" (G7) had become, in a sense, the world's "executive committee," whose decisions and policies greatly determined the functioning and well-being of the world's economy. Needless to say, many non-Western countries, as well as many within continental Europe, greatly resent the incredible economic power of the G7, and at their last several meetings, massive demonstrations took place, some of which resulted in violence and bloodshed across the globe. The end of the cold war seemed to portend not the unipolar hegemony of the United States but a concert of the industrial democracies, with four Western European nation's among the major players.

Global environment

International cooperation took on greater urgency, especially in the last decade, because of a growing concern with the global environment. Such problems as global warming, the destruction of rain forests, and the deterioration of the ozone layer were inherently supranational in scope. Yet environmental concerns complicated relations between the industrialized nations, concentrated in the West, and much of the non-Western world. Countries seeking to industrialize encountered environmental issues and obstacles that had not been impediments or caused concern when the West industrialized, primarily in the nineteenth century. Presently, the challenge for the West is to foster environmental protection without imposing on the non-Western world limitations on economic growth that the West had not had to accept. Simultaneously, changing demographic and economic patterns suggest that North-South tensions between the prosperous countries of the northern hemisphere and the poorer countries in the Third World, most of which lie below the equator, could replace the East-West tensions of the cold war. World population is presently about 6 billion, more than doubling in forty years. This has been the fastest rate of world population growth ever. By the end of the last century, virtually all the growth was in the Third World. During the nineties, Europe's population grew at only 0.2 percent per year, and in several countries the population actually declined. Demographic pressure in the less-developed countries contributed to the increasing immigration to Western Europe that made Africans selling hats, figurines, and sunglasses familiar sights in European cities in the nineties and presently. As Europeans face problems of their own, immigration from Third World countries has become a divisive political issue, often erupting into virulent confrontations in many Western European nations. The problem of how to respond to the needs of poorer countries with burgeoning populations is clearly central to the new world that has gradually emerged with the end of the cold war.

EUROPE AND THE CHALLENGE OF THE UNITED STATES

The vital center of Western civilization had changed before, gradually shifting from the eastern Mediterranean to the north Atlantic by the seventeenth century. In the aftermath of World War II, however, the shift was much shorter and uncertain. Having weakened itself disastrously in two wars, Western Europe found itself dependent on the United States, first for its economic recovery, then for its defense. For over forty years Europe seemed to have little choice but to allow the United States to dictate its economic, diplomatic, and, often, its political agenda. Such subservience rankled many proud Europeans who chafed at the fact and reality that a one time colonial appendage had become, in less than two centuries after securing its independence, the richest and most powerful nation on earth. A kind of love-hate relationship with the United States developed during the late twentieth century. Even after Europe's postwar economic recovery, the United States continued to set the pace, especially in the production of consumer goods and in high technology industries, prompting fears among many Europeans that they would become the economic vassals of the United States, much the same way Eastern Europeans had become for the Soviet Union. To reclaim its distinctiveness over the long term, it apparently had to become, in the short term, more like the United States. The French essayist and social critic, Jean-Jacques Servan-Schreiber, made this case in his widely acclaimed work, *The American Challenge,* first published in France in 1967. Servan-Schreiber's book became the definitive statement of postwar Europe's ambivalent attitude toward Americanization. Haunted by the decline of earlier civilizations, he warned that if Europeans failed to diversity and cooperate, and forged ahead with their own initiatives and ideas, then they not only would be unable to compete with the United States, but indeed would become that colossus's lackey. If Europeans did not soon find their way back to their own identities and uniqueness, then they too, like all the once great civilizations of the world, would gradually sink into decadence and without ever understanding how or why it happened.

Fortunately Servan-Schreiber's alarming treatise was the clarion call Western Europeans needed. By the 1980s much of Western Europe had caught up with the United States in standard of living, and the Western Europeans set the pace in confronting some of the new problems that resulted from continual socioeconomic change. Confined to a small, fragile continent, Europeans pioneered the environmental movement, and they often took the initiative in responding to new social challenges, as with the French daycare system, which was and is recognized still as the best in the industrial world for working families. The end of the cold war freed Europe from its dependence on the United States and perhaps opened still greater scope for leadership.

There is still concern among many Europeans about Americanization. By the late 1990s, consumerism had engulfed especially Western Europe on an unprecedented scale, and the widening impact of American popular culture—from blue jeans and American TV to shopping malls and theme parks—suggested a growing homogenization in the capitalist democracies. Perhaps the best example or symbol of this insidious Americanization was the construction of a Euro-Disneyland, an American "Versailles," in the heart of France. Tangible reminders of Europe's distinctive past remain, but the growing "heritage industry" in Britain and elsewhere suggest that they are merely commodities to be packaged like any other.

The Fragile European Environment

With the disintegration of the Soviet bloc, it became clear that years of Stalinist "five year plans" —forced industrialization—had produced environmental degradation on an appalling scale. It was now left to those who survived communism to clean up the despoliation as best they could.

Germany's autobahn, or expressway system, is intended predominantly for speed. The first stretch was opened in 1935 between Frankfurt and Darmstadt.

In Western Europe, as well, the impact of rapid economic growth on the European landscape and urban ecology had provoked concern since the late 1960s. For urban Europeans especially, the proliferation of automobile use has probably contributed most to cityscape desecration. The number of automobiles in Western Europe increased from 6 million in 1939 to 16 million by 1959 to 42 million by 1969, and to close to 80 million by the late 1990s. Almost overnight, traffic and air pollution fundamentally changed the face of Europe's old cities. Nitrogen oxide and sulfur dioxide emissions from cars, trucks, power plants, and industrial factories was causing respiratory illnesses and having corrosive effects on buildings and monuments. Many of Europe's once pristine historic natural settings had also become ecological nightmares. By the early 1980s, many of its major rivers (the Rhine, for example), lakes, and seas (the Mediterranean) had become so polluted that they posed serious health risks. Acid rain had damaged one-third of the forests of West Germany, including the famous Black Forest of southwest. During much of the seventies and eighties, environmental concerns focused on the difficult question of nuclear power, which solved certain ecological problems while creating potentially more serious ones. By 1990, the West's greatest proponent of nuclear power was France, which was getting 70 percent of its electricity from nuclear power plants and was projecting a goal of 100 percent by the end of the decade. The French could boast that they had experienced no major safety problems and that by using nuclear power they were overcoming the problems of fossil fuels. In much of Europe, however, there was a decisive movement away from nuclear power, even before the Soviet nuclear accident at Chernobyl in 1986. Growing ecological awareness also gave rise to the Green movements, and Green Parties emerged throughout Europe in the 1970s. These movements' origins were by no means uniform. Some sprang from the antinuclear movement; others arose out of such causes as women's liberation and concerns for foreign workers. Most started as grass-roots organizations and then gradually expanded to include activities at the national level, where they coalesced into formalized political parties. Most visible and prominent was the Green Party in Germany, which was officially organized in 1979 and by 1987, had elected forty-two delegates to the West German parliament. Green Parties also competed successfully for office in Sweden, Austria, and Switzerland. In Austria, the Green Party not only had electoral success but in 1978 was instrumental in helping a referendum pass that banned nuclear power altogether.

Although the Green movements and parties have played an important role in making people aware of ecological problems, they have by no means replaced the traditional political parties, as some pundits had forecast in the 1980s. For one thing, the coalitions that made up the Greens found it difficult to agree on all issues and tended to splinter into different cliques. Many of these movements' founders who often expressed a willingness to work with the traditional parties were ousted from leadership positions by the more hardcore true believers unwilling to compromise their principles for the sake of electoral success or co-optation. Finally, traditional political parties have co-opted the Greens' environmental issues. By the 1990s, increasing numbers of European governments were sponsoring projects to safeguard the environment and clean up the worse sources of pollution.

Other environmental issues commanding attention include the continued destruction of global rain forests, with the threatened extinction of plant and animal species, and the problem of global warming due to the depletion of the ozone layer of the atmosphere. In May 1990 a panel of thirty-nine nations concluded that if the warming trend is not checked, rising sea levels will inundate Bangladesh, the Netherlands, and countless other coastal areas and islands. This slow but detectable climatic change is directly linked to the accumulation of carbon dioxide gas. Some 5.6 billion tons of CO_2 are discharged into the atmosphere every year as a result of the burning of fossil fuels and of the annual destruction of the more than 40 million acres of tropical forest. A parallel hazard lies in the depletion of the ozone layer through chemical reaction with chlorofluocarbons (CFCs) used in aerosol sprays and refrigerants. Destruction of the ozone layer would expose living creatures to damaging radiation from the sun's ultraviolet rays. Environmentally induced changes in wind patterns have also produced catastrophic effects. New transatlantic stratospheric currents annually dump millions of tons of rich West African topsoil in Brazil. This uncontrollable phenomenon is enlarging the desert area of West Africa. Despite international conferences on such issues, international response to these issues continues to be tentative and conservative.

THE FEMINIST MOVEMENT

The Search for Liberation

Women's participation in World War I and World War II helped them achieve one of their major aims of the nineteenth century: the right to vote. After World War I, many governments acknowledged the contributions women had made to the war effort by granting them the right to vote. Sweden, Great Britain, Germany, Poland, Hungary, Austria, and Czechoslovakia did so in 1918, followed by the United States in 1920. French and Italian women did not obtain the right to vote until 1945. After World War II, European women tended to retreat back to the traditional roles expected of them, primarily as homemakers. Little was heard of feminist issues until the 1960s when "the rights revolution" provided the entree for women to once again assert their rights—civil, social, and cultural— and speak as feminists. Their grievances against the "patriarchal establishment" of European society were manifold, but at the core of the newly named women's liberation movement was the issue of true equality with men. Though they had attained political and legal equality by the 1960s, there still existed many inequities between the sexes.

Of great importance to the emergence of the postwar women's liberation movement was the work of Simone de Beavoir (1908-1986). Born into a Catholic middle-class family and educated at the Sorbonne in Paris, she supported herself as a teacher and later as a novelist and writer. She maintained a life-long relationship (but not marriage) with the existentialist philosopher Jean-Paul Sarte. Her involvement in the existentialist movement—the leading intellectual impulse of its time—led to her participation in political causes. De Beauvoir believed she lived a liberated life for a twentieth-century European woman, but for all her freedom, she still maintained that as a woman she was limited by artificial patriarchal norms and mores that prevented her from realizing her fullest potential as a human being. There existed a double-standard for men and women, with men enjoying by far the greater freedoms and liberties in their thoughts and actions. De Beavoir was convinced that if she felt such constraint, then the vast majority of woman endured lives of even greater repression. In 1949, she published *The Second Sex,* in which she argued that as a result of male-dominated societies, women had been defined by their difference from men and consequently received second-class status. De Beauvoir became one of the leaders of the French women's movement of the 1970s, and her book was a major influence on both the American and European's women's movements.

Feminists did not blame everything on men for their personal and collective plight. Quite the contrary. Inspired by de Beavoir's assertion that woman were free and autonomous beings like all human creatures, feminists were proactive, calling upon their sisters to take their lives into their own hands and transform the fundamental conditions in which they lived. They did so in a variety of ways. First, in the 1960s and 1970s, women formed numerous "consciousness-raising" groups not only to further each other's awareness of issues but to provide each other with moral support as they battled to break down the bastions of male supremacy and chauvinism. Women also sought and gained a measure of control over their own bodies by seeking to overturn the illegality of both contraception and abortion. In the 1960s and 1970s, hundreds of thousands of European women worked to repeal the laws that outlawed contraception and abortion and began to meet with success. A French law in 1968 permitted the sale of contraception devices. In 1979, another French law legalized abortion. Even in Catholic countries, where the Church remained strongly opposed to abortion, legislation allowing contraception and abortion was passed in the 1970s and 1980s. In the 1980s and 1990s, the women's liberation movement concentrated on developing new cultural attitudes through the new academic field of women's studies and affecting the political and natural environment by allying with the antinuclear and ecological movements.

TERRORISM

Acts of terror by those opposed to governments or Western ideology and values in general have become a frightening aspect of modern Western society. During the late 1970s and early 1980s, in particular, concern about terrorism was often at the top (and presently is for the United States and Israel) of foreign policy agendas of many Western nations. Small bands of terrorists used assassination, indiscriminate killing of civilians, especially by bombing, the taking of hostages, and the hijacking of airplanes and even luxury liners to draw attention to their demands or to destabilize governments in the hope of achieving either their political demands or to further pursue their holy war against their alleged exploitation and oppression by corrupt and decadent Western nations. Terrorist acts garnered (and still do) considerable media attention. When Palestinian terrorists kidnapped and killed eleven Israeli athletes at the Munich Olympic games in 1972, hundreds of millions of people watched the drama unfold on television. More recently, even more people watched New York City's twin towers of the World Trade Center collapse into piles of rubble, killing thousands of innocent civilians, as a result of the most devastating terrorist attack in the history of modern terrorism. Many observers believe that media exposure has been an important catalyst for some terrorist groups.

Motivations for terrorist acts varied considerably. Left-and right-wing terrorist groups flourished in the late 1970s and early 1980s. Left-wing groups, such as the Baader-Menhof gang (also known as the Red Army Faction) in Germany and the Red Brigades in Italy, consisted chiefly of affluent middle-class young people, ideologues, who denounced the injustices of capitalism and supported acts of revolutionary violence in the name of the oppressed peoples of the world to bring down the system. Right-wing terrorist groups, such as the New Order in Italy and the Charles Martel Club in France, used bombings to foment disorder and bring about authoritarian, fascist regimes. Fortunately, these groups aroused little to no public sympathy, and authorities were able to crush them fairly quickly.

Terrorist acts also stemmed from militant nationalists who wished to create separatist states. Because they received considerable support (financial as well as emotional) from local populations, these terrorist groups could sustain their activities over a long period of time. Most legendary of these types of terrorist organizations was the Irish Republican Army, or the IRA, whose goal was (and still is) to liberate Northern Ireland not only from British protection and rule but to annex the state and make it part of greater Ireland. The IRA resorted to vicious attacks against the ruling Protestant/British government and innocent civilians. Over a period of thirty years, IRA terrorists were responsible for the death of over two thousand people in Northern Ireland; three-fourths of the victims were civilians.

Although left-and right-wing terrorist activities declined in Europe by the late 1980s, international terrorism unfortunately intensified and escalated world-wide in the 1990s, climaxing with the September 11, 2001 passenger jet suicide bombings of the World Trade Center. The source and beginnings of international terrorism can be traced back to the late 1960s and early 1970s. Angered over the loss of their territory to Israel in 1967, some militant Palestinians responded with a policy of terrorist attacks against Israel and its supporters, most notably the United States. Palestinian terrorists operated throughout Europe where they gained easy residency because of many Western European countries' liberal immigration laws. Creating "cells" throughout Western Europe by the early 1980s, these terrorists began attacking Europeans and American tourists; it was Palestinian terrorists who massacred vacationers at airports in Rome and Vienna in 1985. As such terrorist networks proliferated, it was discovered by Western intelligence operations that many, if not all of these organizations, were state-sponsored. State-sponsorship added a whole new dimension to international terrorism, strengthening considerably not just the resolve of the various organizations but their ability to carry on their acts in a much more sophisticated and deadlier manner because of the significant financial backing they now had. Militant Islamic governments, most notably those of Iran, Iraq, Syria, and Libya, have become the most readily associated with state-sponsored terrorism. Long before Osama bin Laden and his Al-Qaeda organization became household words, especially in the United States, the above countries were already deeply involved in state-sponsored terrorist acts. Perhaps, the most deadly, until the New York City tragedy, was the bombing of Pan American flight 103 from Frankfurt to New York on December 21, 1988. On that date, the jetliner carrying 259 passengers and crew exploded over Lockerbie, Scotland, killing everyone on board. A massive investigation finally revealed that the bomb responsible for the explosion had been planted by two Libyan terrorists who were connected to terrorist groups based in both Iran and Syria.

Governments fought back by creating special antiterrorist units that became very effective in responding to terrorist acts. The German special antiterrorist unit known as GSG, for example, in 1977 rescued ninety-one hostages from a Lufthansa airplane that had been hijacked to Mogadishu, Somalia. Counterterrorism, or a calculated policy of direct retaliation against ter-

Historians will certainly view the destruction of the World Trade Center in New York City, on September 11, 2001, as a turning point in American foreign, as well as domestic, policy.©Danny C. Sze Photography

rorists, also made states that sponsored terrorism more cautious, at least for awhile in the late 1980s. In 1986, for example, the Reagan administration responded to the terrorist bombing of a West German disco club popular with American soldiers by an air attack on Libya, long suspected as a major sponsor of terrorist organizations. Some observers attributed the overall decline in terrorist attacks in the late 1980s to the American action.

Unfortunately, only momentarily did Western resolve to retaliate against terrorist attacks deter the perpetrators. By the mid-1990s, international terrorism reemerged, more fanatical, more focused, and more violent than previously. Though Israel continued to live in constant fear of Arab terrorist attacks, the United States soon joined Israel as an equally despised nation and a target for terrorist reprisals. Attacks against the property and persons of the United States abroad, both military and civilian, escalated during the 1990s. The first direct attack on United States soil occurred in January 1993 when a car bomb rocked the World Trade Center in New York City, killing six people and injuring over one thousand. Investigators arrested four Muslims with ties to Osama Bin Laden's Al-Qaeda organization, which had emerged by the nineties as the most well-funded, determined, and most dangerous terrorist group in the world. In the 1990s Al-Qaeda publicly proclaimed *jihad* against the United States. The September 11, 2001 attack on the World Trade Center, the Pentagon, and other suspected targets was the well-conceived handiwork of Osama bin Laden and his Al-Qaeda network. So far it has proved to be the most deadly terrorist attack on any country in the history of international terrorism and has awakened the United States to the fact that it is just as susceptible and vulnerable to such devastation and terror as any other country. Long gone are Americans' feelings of security and invincibility that for decades allowed them to project an air of confidence and accomplishment to the rest of the world. Now, in the aftermath of September 11, that perceived "cockiness" has all but disappeared from the American demeanor. Many Americans now face feelings of trepidation and a sense of foreboding that such attacks could occur again in the near future. It is perhaps the wondering, the uncertainty of possible terrorist attacks, that makes terrorism so psychologically and emotionally unnerving.

September 11 came at a time when the national and world economy had entered a period of decline, and the sudden destruction of the proud symbols of triumphant American capitalism and internationalist involvement forced the country to confront aggressive enemies who threatened not only human life and material goods but also the structures that knit together economic, political, and social life. The result was an outpouring of patriotic commitment, of nationalism, the likes of which the United States had not seen since World War II. This transformation of national mood and purpose also altered United States global strategies. Like his two immediate predecessors, Bill Clinton and the elder Bush, George W. Bush immediately scrapped his unilateral foreign policy and moved to strengthen alliances with nations around the world, including some he had earlier labeled as competitors on the global stage. Although the White House had initially spoken about canceling U.S. participation in the ABM missile ban treaty agreement of 1970, and thereby had provoked criticism from Western European allies as well as Russia and China, the global war against terrorism prompted Russian leaders to seek cooperation with the United States, including acceptance of new nuclear defense arrangements. Dozens of other countries shared intelligence information and offered assistance in the war against terrorism. In this capacity, no country has been more helpful and directly involved than Great Britain, the United States' closest ally in a variety of key foreign policy and diplomatic areas since World War II. With the emergence of domestic consensus, international differences about environmentalism, globalization, and nuclear disarmament have been put on the back burner while a shocked and troubled world tries to eliminate a terrorist foe that threatens biological, chemical, and even nuclear catastrophe.

Cultural and Spiritual Life

Just as it is impossible to comprehend the ramifications of environmental issues, so it is equally difficult to assess the present state of Western cultural and spiritual life. It would be fairly easy and customary to list the writers, philosophers, artists, and religious leaders who have been in the forefront in the half-century since the end of World War II. To offer capsule comments on their contributions would also be tedious and boring for the reader. It would be better to ponder where Western civilization has come in our time and what future direction it might take. Singling out creative individuals and labeling them or their work as "seminal" or epoch-making," is a judgment that can only be made with considerable hindsight or from the long perspective of Western history in general. How many great minds or creative geniuses from antiquity, the Middle Ages, the Renaissance, the Enlightenment, or the Romantic era truly speak to us today? On a note of greater inquiry, how many of the "greats" from the past would contemporary Americans or Europeans recognize? It is likely that future generations will do a similar winnowing of the cultural history of our times, and they may well reach conclusions that would bewilder us.

The most recent major turning point in Western cultural and spiritual life seems to have been the outburst of creativity associated with modernism. (See chapter 19) The middle third of the twentieth century, from the 1930s to the 1960s, saw the crescendo of modernism carried forward by the impulses set in motion earlier by Nietzsche, Freud, Weber, Einstein, Picasso, Mahler, and Schoenberg, between about 1880 and 1914. We do have the perspective now to consider whether the generation of creators who are now active—those who matured during and after the 1960s—represent a true refinement of modernism, or the advocates of something new, or simply the hangers-on of a cultural era whose inner spark has dimmed.

The triumph of pluralism at the end of the twentieth century has meant a decline of Western ideological arrogance as well as a questioning of what seemed to be immutable cultural standards. Modernism, much of which springs from Nietzsche's call to reevaluate all values, has in our time prompted a somewhat new school of thought called post-modernism. This rather prevalent academic and critical movement denies that any text (whether it be a work of art or a historical source) has intrinsic meaning and insists that meaning and value are imparted by the reader of that text. Are the post-modernists saying that nothing has inherent value and that anything can "mean" anything we want it too? Are the post-modernists simply relativist run amuck? Debate over this question and related issues became particularly intense and divisive in North America, where it plunged the academic world into the imbroglio that became known as the "culture wars." Both right and left wing protagonists hardened their positions into visions of "political correctness," each claiming to be more pluralist than the other. Although post modernism seems to be losing some of its intel-

lectual strength, exactly what cultural legacy it might leave, or what backlash it might precipitate, remains uncertain.

Religion offers another related example of the West's late twentieth-century embrace of pluralism. Among mainstream Protestants, debates inherited from the Reformation over free will and grace have vanished; ever since the Vatican II church council (1962-1965), Roman Catholicism has lost some of the rigidity that the Counter Reformation spawned and has advocated ecumenism and tolerance; religion has demonstrated remarkable recuperative power in the former Soviet Union and other areas once ruled by Marxist-Leninist atheist regimes; Jews and Christians regard one another with more understanding and forbearance than at any other time since the first century A.D.; all the West's religious traditions now engage the world's other great faiths in constant dialogue. The consensus that Western Europeans and Americans have reached about the value of religious toleration intensifies the shock and disbelief with which they responded to the virulent religious hatreds manifest in the conflict in Ulster and the Wars of Yugoslav Succession. Yet this openness and tolerance come at a time when religious affiliation in most Western European countries (not the United States) has fallen to historically low levels, and when the papacy regards much of Europe as irreligious mission territory and seems to be reorienting Catholicism toward the Third World. Since religion historically has been one of the fundamental determinants of cultural identity, future historians may well consider these religious shifts as deeply significant.

The general stress of everyday life will certainly leave its mark on the West's ever-transforming culture. Western society attacks or ameliorates its local problems of demography, unemployment, ethnic politics, and cultural pluralism. The old ethos provided by the cold war has disappeared. Entirely new problems sweeping across all boundaries will set the future agenda. In a sense, the year 2000 marked the beginning of a new age in Western history and in human history. The growing pains engendered by the Dual Revolution (French and Industrial) are over, at least in the developed world. The Industrial Revolution has passed beyond the manufacturing stage of individually owned factories to an era of huge multinational corporations operating in every part of the world through electronic information networks. The provision of services and the transmittal of information are more vital to the world economy than the production of goods. World trade draws almost every country into contact and competition with almost every other country. Monolithic trading blocks in North America, Europe, and, possibly, even Asia are rearranging traditional economic relations. Politically, the disappearance of fascist and communist states has left the politics of accommodation as the most vigorous survivor of Enlightenment optimism. Whether pluralism will survive the vagaries that lie ahead is uncertain. But history is not over. Religious fundamentalism, nationalism, racism, degradation of the global biosphere, population explosion, genetic engineering, and the abject poverty of a majority of the world's inhabitants, not to mention the human predilection for violence, will provide more than enough grist for the spirit of history's mill in the years to come.

Suggestions for Further Reading

Dennis L. Bark and David R. Gress, *A History of West Germany* (1993).

Michael Beschloss and Strobe Talbott, *At The Highest Levels: The Inside Story of the End of the Cold War* (1993).

Coit D. Blacker, *Reluctant Warriors: The United States, the Soviet Union and Arms Control* (1987).

Zbigniew Brezinski, *The Soviet Bloc: Unity and Conflict* (1961).

David Canute, *The Year of the Barricades: A Journey Through 1968* (1988).

Nicholas Colchester and David Buchan, *Europower: the Essential Guide to Europe's Economic Transformation in 1992* (1990).

Desmond Dinan, *Ever Closer Union? An Introduction to the European Community,* (1994).

Timothy Ash Garton, *The Magic Lantern: The Revolution of '89 Witnessed in Warsaw, Budapest and Prague* (1990).

Paul Ginsborg, *A History of Contemporary Italy: Society and Politics, 1943-1988* (1990).

Geoffrey Hosking, *The Awakening of the Soviet Union* (1990).

Misha Glenny, *The Balkans: 1804-1999: Nationalism War, and the Great Powers* (1999).

Stuart H. Hughes, *Sophisticated Rebels: The Political Culture of European Dissent, 1968-1987* (1990).

Werner Huldsberg, *The German Greens: A Social and Political Profile* (1988).

Konrad H. Jarusch, *The Rush to German Unity* (1994).

Tim Judah, *The Serbs: History, Myth, and the Destruction of Yugoslavia* (1997).

Robert G. Kaiser, *Why Gorbachev Happened: His Triumphs and His Failure* (1991).

Bennett Kovrig, *Of Walls and Bridges: The United States and Eastern Europe* (1991).

Richard F. Kuisel, *Capitalism and the State in Modern France* (1981).

Moshe Lewin, *The Gorbachev Phenomenon* (1991).

Kenneth Maxwell and Steven Spiegel, *The New Spain: From Isolation to Influence* (1994).

Index

M